C000301618

A COMPLETE RECORD

A COMPLETE RECORD

IAN ROSS & GORDON SMAILES

The Breedon Books
Publishing Company
Derby

First published in Great Britain by
The Breedon Books Publishing Company Limited
44 Friar Gate, Derby DE1 1DA
1993

© Ian Ross and Gordon Smailes

All Rights Reserved. No part of this publication may be reproduced, stored in a retrieval system, or transmitted in any form, or by any means, electronic, mechanical, photocopying, recording or otherwise without the prior permission in writing of the Copyright holders, nor be otherwise circulated in any form or binding or cover other than in which it is published and without a similar condition including this condition being imposed on the subsequent publisher.

ISBN 1 873626 43 6

Printed and bound by Butler and Tanner Ltd, Frome and London.
Jacket printed by BDC Printing Services Ltd of Derby.

Contents

Acknowledgments

The authors wish to thanks Everton Football Club, the Football League and Colin Hunt of the Liverpool Post & Echo for their assistance in compiling this book.

Photographs supplied by Liverpool Post & Echo, Colorsport, EMPICS and Steve Hale.

Introduction

EVERTON FOOTBALL CLUB was one of the first big names in soccer. Founded like several of today's Football League clubs, as a humble church team, Everton grew quickly and were natural founder-members of the Football League in 1888. Their Goodison Park ground was the first major football stadium in England, and in the 1890s, Everton were one of the richest clubs in the country.

Over the century, Everton FC has maintained its position as one of the big clubs. Even when playing fortunes have been at a low ebb, the name of Everton has still ranked alongside the best clubs in the game.

In 1985, Everton again proved themselves a big name in every way. On the field they won the Canon League Championship and the European Cup-winner's Cup, as well as the FA Charity Shield; twelve months earlier they had lifted the FA Cup at Wembley, and only the incredible pressures of trying to attain such a feat ultimately denied them a much-vaunted treble when they fell at the final hurdle at Wembley in May 1985. In 1986-7 Everton were League Champions again as the Goodison revival continued and there can be no more appropriate time to re-examine the history of this great club.

The statistics have been collected over a number of years, a task which has involved long hours poring over dusty, crumbling Victorian and Edwardian newspapers, and visiting the Football League headquarters at Lytham.

Football facts and figures can be a minefield of errors for the unwary, and in the compilation of this book, mistakes have been uncovered which have been perpetuated down the years, repeated in books and newspaper articles. Indeed, it will be surprising if this book is without a single error, for the primary sources of information have been those ancient newspaper reports which often failed to give teams and scorers in precise detail.

However, we believe that diligent research has produced a more complete and accurate record of Everton's competitive games than anything else previously published. It updates and corrects the first two editions of this book which was first published in 1985.

Ian Ross
Gordon Smailes
Liverpool, May 1993

The Everton Story

WHEN Liverpool's Stanley Park was officially opened to the public in the summer of 1870, football was taking its first faltering steps towards the game we know today. The Football Association, which had been formed in 1863, was still concerned with unifying the various sets of rules which held sway in different regions, but clubs like Notts County, Nottingham Forest, Sheffield Wednesday, Stoke and Chesterfield were already in existence. And the FA Cup competition, and the first official England-Scotland international, were only two years away.

As the game grew, so working-class sides would eventually take over from the public school, university and army teams as the dominant force. And the young Scotsmen who were drifting south in search of employment would have much to do with that change. They were to prove adept players and dedicated administrators.

Many of the early football clubs were associated with churches and chapels, and were named after them. Cricket clubs in the summer, they turned to football as the days grew shorter. One such organisation can claim the distinction of having been the cradle of Everton Football Club.

The youngsters connected with St Domingo's Church formed a cricket club and in 1878 they added a football section to the rapidly-expanding organisation. The origins of Everton FC can be traced back to that day.

St Domingo's Football Club soon attracted members from outside the Church and in November 1879, at a meeting in the Queen's Head Hotel, Village Street, it was decided to adopt the name of the district of Everton.

The first pitch was situated at the south-east corner of Stanley Park, opposite Stanley House, the home of John Houlding JP, a brewer who was later to become Lord Mayor of Liverpool, and a man who was to become one of the new club's most influential patrons.

From the Park Lodge in Mill Lane, the first Everton players carried the goalposts, fixed them into hand-crafted sockets and marked out the lines. There was no admission charge and, indeed, those few who gathered to watch the forerunners of some of the game's élite were at the mercy of the notoriously inclement North-West weather. Dressing-room facilities were simply non-existent.

For the first few seasons only a handful of dedicated spectators watched them, the Stanley CC cricketers being a conspicuous group among the meagre gathering. Football at that time relied heavily on the art of dribbling. The passing game was something that they would learn from the Scots.

Everton's first-ever match was played in Stanley Park on 20 December 1879, against St Peter's. Everton had the happiest possible start, celebrating their inaugural game with a 6-0 victory. The local newspapers reported the score only — no teams or scorers — so the names of the men who played in that historic match are lost forever.

On 24 January 1880, Everton met St Peter's again, this time winning 4-0. Again, no scorers were mentioned but we do know that the men named for Everton's second match were: W.Jones, T.Evans, J.Douglas, C.Chiles, S.Chalk, R.W.Morris, A.White, F.Brettle, A.Wade, Smith, W.Williams.

Everton's success meant that they were attracting players from rival clubs and in 1880-81 Everton were admitted as members of the newly-formed Lancashire Football Association, an early recognition of merit within the county.

In the draw for the Lancashire Cup, Everton were paired with Great Lever, a side from the Bolton area and one of the better teams in the North of England. It was the first time Everton had travelled to a fixture by train and they returned in great spirits after holding Great Lever to a 1-1 draw. In the replay at Stanley Park, however, the Merseysiders were unceremoniously crushed 8-1.

Notwithstanding this embarrassing reversal, Everton's general play in this period was highly encouraging. Victories over Birkenhead (7-0) and Liverpool (5-0) were important contributions to the club's growing stature in Lancashire, although the Liverpool club was no relation to the one we know today.

Everton's team was greatly strengthened by the arrival of Jack McGill, a former Glasgow Rangers player who proved to be a brilliant footballer and tireless coach. He was elected captain and the quality of his play was such that he added Lancashire representative honours to those he had won with his native Ayrshire.

Everton's colours have seen several changes down the years. Originally they were blue and white stripes, although new players often wore the shirts belonging to their former clubs. This led to a cry for uniformity which was made more pressing when Everton became affiliated to the Lancashire FA.

Short of money themselves, and worried about embarrassing the less affluent playing members, Everton officials decided to dye all the shirts black, a two-inch wide scarlet sash being added as an afterthought to brighten up the morbid strip. The shirts led to the club's first nickname, 'the Black Watch'.

Later, Everton adopted salmon shirts with blue shorts, and later still, ruby shirts with blue trimmings and dark blue shorts. The famous royal blue was introduced much later.

The 1881-2 season opened in quite disastrous fashion, Bolton Wanderers burying Everton under an avalanche of class and style to win 13-1. Yet fortunes improved quickly and by the end of that season Everton had won 15 of their 22 matches. There were big wins over Burscough (8-0) and Halliwell (6-0), and on 22 October, a hat-trick from W.Gibson and two goals from McGill earned 'the Moonlight Dribblers', as they had become known, a 5-0 win in the Lancashire Cup. Everton went out 3-1 at Turton in the next round, but by the end of the season one local newspaper declared them 'the premier Association club in South-West Lancashire'.

But financial problems were an inescapable fact. In March 1882, at a meeting at John Houlding's Sandon Hotel, Everton officials agreed that they had to find a private ground where they could charge for admission. At some of the more important matches at Stanley Park, attendances of 2,000 were not uncommon; there had to be some way of tapping this interest.

After much discussion it was decided to accept the offer of a Mr J.Cruitt of Coney Green, who offered the club use of a field off Priory Road.

The 1882-3 season was Everton's fourth and last at Stanley Park. They reached the semi-final of the Liverpool Cup before losing 3-1 to Bootle who went on to become the first winners.

At Priory Road, Everton built primitive dressing-rooms and a sort of stand for officials, but the opening game, between Liverpool & District and Walsall & District, did not live up to expectations. Only 14 shillings (70p) was taken at the gate and officials set about raising money by other means. Some £20 was raised by a concert given by Sam Crosbie's Teachers' Choral Society at the Hand-in-Hand Club, Foley Street.

On the field, Everton's fortunes soared and in 1883-4 they won their first-ever trophy — the Liverpool Cup. They beat Bootle 5-2 in the semi-final, then won a dramatic Final, again at Bootle, when they emerged 1-0 victors over Earlestown.

On 29 March 1884 their new president, John Houlding, already known as 'King John of Everton', held the Cup aloft.

But Everton's joy was shortlived and within weeks they were homeless. Mr Cruitt, tired of the club's vociferous and often over-exuberant supporters, withdrew his support and told them to find another ground. They did, moving to a field in Anfield Road, a site which was to become one of the most famous football grounds in the world.

John Houlding assumed the tenancy — his Sandon Hotel was now the club's headquarters — and club members set to work. The field was one of two pastures owned by the Orrell Brothers, well-known local brewers. It was hired out on the following conditions. 'That we, the Everton Football Club, keep the existing walls in good repair, pay the taxes, do not cause ourselves to be a nuisance to Mr Orrell and other tenants adjoining, and also pay a small sum of rent or subscribe a donation each year to the Stanley Hospital in the name of Mr Orrell'.

Having readily agreed, Everton's officials and players — helped by supporters — took up spades, hammers and nails, and barrows. They set about turning the Anfield Road field into a football ground and Everton's first match there was played on 27 September 1884 when Earlestown provided the opposition.

Everton won 5-0, fielding the following players: Joliffe, McGill, Pickering, Preston, Parry, Berry, W.Richards, Whittle, Finlay, Higgins, Gibson.

Earlestown were also the opponents in the Liverpool Cup Final when Everton were controversially beaten 1-0. They claimed that they had scored a goal, but the referee, who in those days was on the touchline and only intervened when there was an appeal against the umpires' decision, ruled that the ball had drifted past the wrong side of the post. It was one of the many such arguments that eventually led to the introduction of goal-nets.

For six seasons Everton players had been, in name at least, amateurs, but by 1885 the leading English clubs favoured open professionalism. They knew that success meant bigger attendances and greater income. Players who could devote their time solely to training and playing, without the often tiring distractions of a job in trade or industry, would have the best chances to succeed.

Everton were not slow at falling into line with this thinking. George Dobson, a full-back from Bolton Wanderers, and George Farmer, a forward from Oswestry, became Everton's first official professionals for the 1885-6 season. Alec Dick, a daring, often reckless full-back from Kilmarnock, followed. Dick's wild play was to earn him a two-month suspension.

Everton lifted the Liverpool Cup in 1886, beating their fierce rivals, Bootle, 2-1; and the following season they won the Cup again, this time defeating Oakfield 5-0.

Such successes encouraged the club to enter the FA Cup for the first time. In 1886-7 they were drawn against Glasgow Rangers, but on the eve of the game at Anfield, Everton found that they could not hope to beat the Scots unless they fielded players who were ineligible for the competition. They decided to play their strongest team — they lost 1-0 — but scratched from the competition. So the match that was eventually played on 30 October 1886 was only a prestigious friendly.

The following season Everton tried again. They played no less than four FA Cup-ties against Bolton Wanderers. After losing the first game Everton raised a successful objection to the eligibility of a Bolton player. There followed two drawn matches before Everton won the fourth, whereupon Bolton claimed that seven Everton 'amateurs' had been offered money to play. Everton lost 6-0 to Preston in the next round before they were told that the FA had eliminated them anyway.

Bolton met Preston in a rearranged match — and lost 9-0 — and the 'Everton-seven' were declared professionals and the whole club suspended for a month from 5 December 1887. The Liverpool FA decided that they too would act, and they confiscated the Liverpool Cup which had, for two seasons, stood proudly in the Sandon Hotel. The experience chastened Everton, who did not appear in the 1888-9 FA Cup competition.

By then, however, the club had a new competition to consider. Everton's fixture list had been improving all the time, with matches against teams like Aston Villa, Wolves, Notts County and Derby County. It was obvious, however, that friendly matches did not offer the same attraction — and therefore did not bring in as much cash — as the cup competitions. In 1888, some of the leading clubs in the North and Midlands founded the Football League.

Everton were one of the 12 original members and in September of that year they played their first League match, against Accrington at Anfield. Their record in that first season was disappointing — eighth place with nine wins in 22 matches. But the following year saw a marked improvement and at the end of the season Everton were only two points adrift of Preston North End, who won the League Championship for the second time.

Everton now had some of the best footballers in the land including three players who would all win England caps, half-back Johnny Holt and forwards Edgar Chadwick and Alf Milward.

In 1890-91 Everton overcame the challenge of Preston to become the second club to win the League title. They won 14 matches and took a particular liking to Derby County, who the previous season they had beaten 11-2 in the FA Cup. In League games, Everton scored 13 goals against Derby. Burnley were hit for seven at Anfield and although Preston took all the points off Everton, it was the Merseysiders who stood two points clear at the end of the season.

In Everton's first ten years in the League they scored 324 goals, a figure topped only by Aston Villa (326). But off the field a crisis was looming, a smouldering fire which burst into flames after being fanned by committee-room discontent. At the centre of the row was John Houlding, one of the club's early benefactors.

Houlding, once the tenant of Anfield, was now its owner and therefore Everton's landlord. The row had festered for some time because there were Everton committee members who disliked their club's HQ and dressing-rooms being on licensed premises, namely the Houlding-owned Sandon Hotel.

Houlding responded by telling Everton Football Club that, as their success brought more money through the turnstiles, so he would expect to raise the club's rent. And between 1887-8 and 1888-9 the rent was indeed raised, by 150 per cent.

On 25 January 1892, at a special general meeting, George Mahon, organist at St Domingo's and one of Liverpool's leading accountants, told disenchanted members that he had 'a new ground in his pocket'.

Mahon, at one-time a self-confessed hater of football, had been converted after watching a particularly entertaining match between Everton and Preston, and he was now one of the Anfield club's greatest supporters.

Now he had an option on Mere Green Field. It was situated on the north side of Stanley Park, near Goodison Park, and was later described as having 'degenerated from a nursery into a howling desert'. Some members expressed a view that it might be better to live with Houlding at Anfield than to gamble everything on another move, but Mahon and his supporters were adamant.

It was agreed that: 'The club be formed into a limited company under the name of *The Everton Football Club Limited*, with a capital of £500 in £1 shares, each member to be allowed one share, ten shillings to be called up in monthly instalments of two shillings and sixpence. Such shares as are not taken up to be allotted as the directors may determine'.

For a time it appeared that there would be two Everton Football Clubs, when Houlding insisted that he would keep the name alive at Anfield. But it was ruled

Above and below: *The fiasco of the 1893 FA Cup Final when Everton met Wolves at Fallowfield, Manchester, and many of the crowd could not see the game. The inadequate facilities almost led to the game being abandoned.*

that the name belonged to the majority of members — who were now installed by the Goodison Road — and so Houlding called his club 'Liverpool FC'. Thus began one of football's greatest local rivalries, although even then, Liverpool RFC objected to Houlding's new club name. Eventually 'Liverpool AFC' was agreed.

Meanwhile, Everton's first season at Goodison ended on a high note. The team fought back from a poor start to finish third in the League — now the First Division after members of the Football Alliance had formed a second section — and there was a record Goodison attendance of 30,000 for the visit of Preston. Gate receipts for the season topped £8,000 — a far cry from the Priory Road days when £45 was taken in the first season there.

By 1895 Everton's stature was such that no fewer than 12 players had been capped by their respective countries. That year Everton finished runners-up behind Sunderland, and the following season they were third behind Aston Villa and Derby County.

These were eventful days, both on and off the field. At the 1895 annual meeting, after reporting a profit in excess of £6,000 over the previous three years, chairman George Mahon and four of his fellow directors resigned 'owing to acute administrative difficulties'. Of six new directors elected, one was Wilf Cuff, a man who was to serve them for over 50 years and who was to become one of the most influential figures in Everton's history.

The reasons behind the board-room upheaval have never been made clear, but it must have been a clash over the way the club was being run financially. Ground improvements — a new stand and new covered accommodation — were not unanimously agreed; and there was even a police investigation concerning gatekeepers. It led to improved turnstiles being installed at Goodison.

On the playing side, Everton continued to prosper, reaching the FA Cup Final in 1893 and again four years later. In 1893 they met Wolves at Fallowfield, Manchester, and the game will be best remembered for the totally inadequate facilities which almost led to the match being abandoned. Wolves won when their centre-half, Allen, put in a high ball and Everton's goalkeeper, Williams, was blinded by the sun. The ball found the net and Everton were on their way to defeat.

In 1897 there was the prospect of an all-Merseyside Cup Final, but Liverpool could not overcome Aston Villa in the semi-final. Nor could Everton in the Final at the Crystal Palace. It was a classic match, Villa triumphing 3-2 with all five

There were better arrangements for the 1897 FA Cup Final between Everton and Aston Villa at the Crystal Palace, although again it seems that many spectators had a poor view of the action.

Everton goalkeeper Billy Muir and the rest of his defence look on anxiously as Aston Villa mount an attack during the match at Villa Park in September 1901. Everton were happy with the eventual 1-1 draw.

goals coming in the first-half, although Everton's John Bell was voted the outstanding player.

Everton 'celebrated' their 21st birthday by slumping to 11th position in 1899-1900, their lowest League placing at that time. Yet there were to be two important personnel changes. 'Sandy' Young made his debut at centre-forward and, to the delight of Everton's fans, John Bell returned to play outside-left. Everton finished runners-up in 1901-02, but the inconsistency which had become a hallmark of their play, returned and next season they were 12th in a First Division of 18 clubs.

Everton infuriated their supporters during the ensuing years with a confusing mixture of fine performances and downright disappointing displays. In some seasons they were dazzlingly successful; in others frustratingly mediocre. But always there were magnificent players to watch, and spectacular incidents to be recounted.

Sheffield Wednesday were League Champions in successive seasons, 1902-03 and 1903-04, as Everton finished 11th and then third, one point behind runners-up Manchester City and four points adrift of Wednesday.

The following season Everton signed the eccentric Welsh intellectual and international goalkeeper, Dr Leigh Richmond Roose. They had thoughts of doing the League and Cup double that year — First Division runners-up and FA Cup semi-finalists — and Roose's sometimes outrageous antics between the posts made a lasting impression on those who saw him.

Everton were at the summit of the First Division when they defeated Liverpool in the FA Cup first round in 1904-05. A Harry Makepeace penalty ensured a draw at Anfield, and the replay was won 2-1 with the decisive goal coming five minutes from time.

Everton cantered to a 4-0 win over Stoke in the second round, and Southampton fell by the same score before Everton met Aston Villa in the semi-final.

Some 35,000 people at Stoke's Victoria Ground saw a close-fought 1-1 draw. But Villa were easily the better side in the Nottingham replay, winning 2-1 before going on to defeat Newcastle United 2-0 in the Final.

Everton's title hopes were not helped when a game against Woolwich Arsenal, which they were winning 3-1, was abandoned because of bad weather. When the match was replayed — as the penultimate game of the season — Everton lost 2-1. They found themselves agonizing over the outcome of Newcastle's final match, against Middlesbrough. The Magpies won 3-0 — and with 48 points lifted the title one point ahead of Everton.

The following season quite literally belonged to Merseyside. Everton at last won the FA Cup, while Liverpool took the League Championship.

Everton's path to the Crystal Palace saw them beat West Brom, Chesterfield,

Everton on the attack at Plumstead in the penultimate game of 1904-05. The Toffees lost 2-1 to Woolwich Arsenal after the first game had been abandoned with them leading 3-1.

Action from the 1905 FA Cup semi-final replay at the City Ground. Above: *Everton on the attack.* Below: *Villa's Joe Bache bursts through.*

Bradford City and the formidable Sheffield Wednesday — and Liverpool. A goal by Abbott — whose shot was diverted over the line by Dunlop — and a moment of sheer inspiration by Hardman were more than enough to end Liverpool's dream of the double. The Final against Newcastle United was settled by a solitary goal from Young.

The 1906-07 season saw Everton swoop to another FA Cup Final and mount a sustained challenge for the title. To reinforce the team they signed Stevenson from Accrington; Settle, a local boy; and three skilful Scots, the Wilson brothers and Graham from Third Lanark.

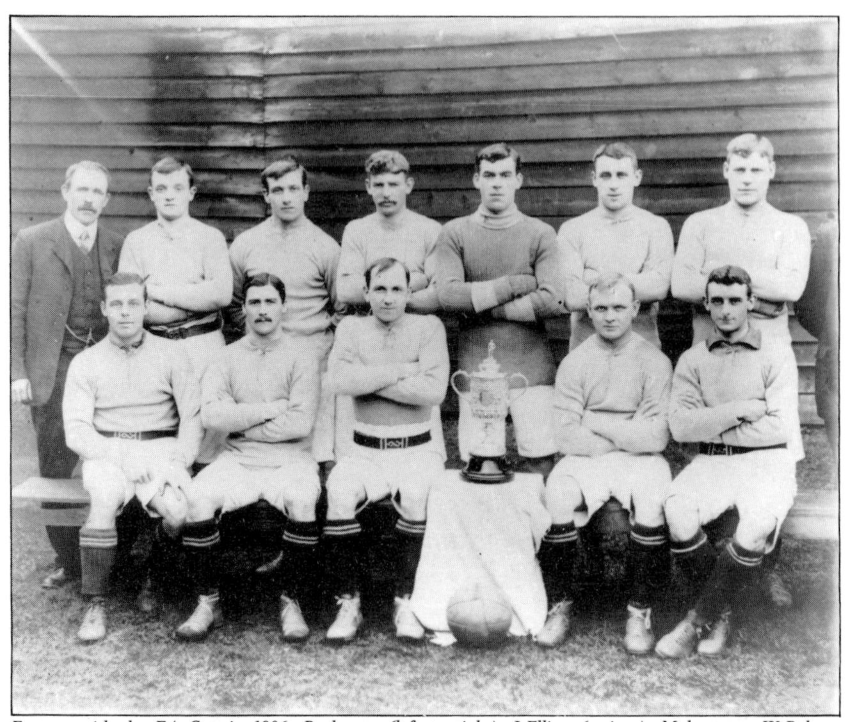

Everton with the FA Cup in 1906. Back row (left to right): J.Elliott (trainer), Makepeace, W.Balmer, Taylor, Scott, Crelley, Abbott. Front row: Sharp, Bolton, Young, Settle, Hardman. Note the former trophy which was replaced in 1911.

By the end of November, Everton were top of the table before losing ground and finishing third behind Newcastle and Bristol City. Sheffield Wednesday, who had enjoyed good fortune to overcome Liverpool in the fourth round, stood between Everton and a second successive FA Cup Final. But there was no glory and the Merseysiders lost 2-1 in one of the poorest Finals for years.

It took a full season for Everton to readjust. Full-backs Walter Balmer and Jack Crelley, and Settle who went to Stockport, were phased out; in came players like full-back Maconnachie of Hibs and half-back Adamson of Lochgelly. Morale was low and results disappointing as Everton finished 1907-08 in 11th place.

The arrival of forwards Bertie Freeman and Tim Coleman from Woolwich Arsenal added a new dimension to Everton's goalscoring potential and in 1908-09 the club finished runners-up again.

That close season Everton helped the development of football in South America by playing two exhibition games against Tottenham Hotspur in Buenos Aires. They also tested the local strength with victories over a club side, Alumini, and representative teams of the Argentinian League and Uruguayan League.

Everton's second League Championship success, which came 24 years after the first, was the last to be achieved before the First Division was extended from 20 to 22 clubs. Their success came in football's twilight season of 1914-15, when many people felt that it was immoral — even treasonable — to continue professional

Everton in 1914-15, League Champions. Back row (left to right): Fleetwood, Grenyer, Thompson, Galt, Fern, Maconnachie, Makepeace. Front row: Chedgzoy, Kersopp, Parker, Clennell, Roberts.

football while the flower of England's youth was preparing to die on the Western Front.

The title was won with several new signings, men like Bobby Parker who solved a goalscoring problem, Tom Fern, who had replaced the seemingly indestructible Billy Scott in goal, and Jimmy Galt, a centre-half from Glasgow Rangers who skippered the side. Outside-right Sam Chedgzoy had his best season, laying on many of Parker's 36 goals.

After several seasons of wartime regional football, Everton, like almost every other club, were forced to make 'perpetual changes' and dropped to 16th place in 1919-20. Their fortunes took a turn for the better in 1920-21, although Liverpool won both derby games within the space of seven days. They triumphed 1-0 at Anfield and 3-0 at Goodison, watched by an aggregate attendance of 100,000 spectators. It unsettled Everton's hitherto consistent form that season and title hopes were forgotten.

It was Liverpool who won the Championship the following season as Everton narrowly avoided the drop to Division Two. The title was again bound for Anfield in 1922-3, while the Goodison club survived the embarrassment of having four goals shot past them in five minutes by McIntyre of Blackburn Rovers, at Ewood Park in September. Everton went on to finish fifth, and made the important signings of Alec Troup, Jack Cock and Neil McBain.

Everton, pictured early in the 1926-7 season. Back row (left to right): Broad, J.Elliott (trainer), McDonald, Harland, Reid, W.Brown, McBain. Front row: Chedgzoy, O'Donnell, Irvine, Hart, Kennedy, Troup.

The quality of Everton's play in the early 1920s, while widely acknowledged by the game's critics, was not always reflected in results. The influential *Athletic News* was adamant that 'no team in the country has served up more delightful football'.

But, well aware that the club's supporters would never settle for second-best, new chairman Wilf Cuff, knew that in spite of such flattery, Everton needed something special to underline their superiority.

The time was right for a hero to emerge, and emerge he did. His name was Billy 'Dixie' Dean, a man who was to become one of the most potent forces that football has ever known, although it is most unlikely that even Cuff could have realised just what sort of a player he was signing when he completed the transfer of Dean from Tranmere Rovers on 16 March 1925, for £3,000.

In personal terms Dean made an immediate impact, scoring 33 League and Cup goals in his first season, but collectively Everton still struggled to find the blend and rhythm which would transform individual talents into a successful team.

The cohesion was not far away, however. In 1927-8, with a new double-decker stand bursting at the seams, Everton won the title for the third time and on occasions it seemed that Dean was taking them to it almost single-handed.

New signings, winger Ted Critchley and full-back Warney Cresswell, were key figures, of course, but it was Dean who captured all the headlines. In 39 League games the muscular scoring-machine hammered home 60 goals — 31 in 15 away games, 29 in 14 at home; 40 shots and 20 headers. It was an astonishing feat, and should have paved the way to seasons of glory at Goodison. That it did not is a mystery which puzzles Evertonians to this day.

The Everton team which lost 5-2 at Villa Park in October 1929. Back row (left to right): Kennedy (12th man), Robson, Cresswell, Davies, White, Griffiths, H.Cooke (trainer). Front row: Critchley, Wheldon, Wilkinson, Martin, Stein, O'Donnell.

An alarming slump in 1928-9 resulted in Everton — Dean and all — finishing fifth from bottom of Division One. The following season Everton finished rock-bottom and were relegated for the first time in their history.

Unmoved by wholesale criticism, the Goodison board refused to implement drastic 'panic' measures and their attitude paid huge dividends. There followed an amazing transformation in both attitudes and results as Everton swept to the Second Division Championship, the League title and the FA Cup in successive seasons. The 1931-2 season saw the emergence of goalkeeper Ted Sagar who was to clock up a record 463 League appearances for Everton.

The club's overall fortunes took a dip in the mid-1930s when Arsenal's great side, under Herbert Chapman, held centre-stage whilst the highest Everton could manage between 1934 and 1938 was eighth in 1935.

But they were re-fashioning their side around the skills of young players like Joe Mercer and the 17-year-old Tommy Lawton who had been bought from Burnley for the princely sum of £6,500 in 1936. The forward line was further strengthened by the signing of Bobby Bell from Tranmere Rovers.

Supervised by Dean, young Lawton became the focal point of an attack which led Everton to a fifth title in 1939.

Everton were one of the last major English clubs to appoint a manager. Their first such appointment was made in 1939 when they gave the job to club secretary Theo Kelly. Although a hard-working and efficient administrator who had superb organising ability, Kelly was never particularly popular with the players.

Despite the flying boots of fellow striker Tommy Johnson and West Brom goalkeeper Harold Pearson, Dixie Dean dives bravely at the ball during the 1931 FA Cup semi-final at Old Trafford.

Everton with the FA Cup in 1933. Back row (left to right): H.Cooke (trainer), Britton, Cresswell, Sagar, Cook, White, Thomson. Front row: Geldard, Dunn, Dean, Johnson, Stein, Critchley.

Dixie Dean holds aloft the FA Cup outside Wembley's front door in 1933.

Cup holders Everton were routed 3-0 by Tottenham Hotspur in the third round of the 1933-4 competition. Here, Ted Sagar fails to stop Spurs' first goal scored by George Hunt.

Alex Stevenson takes Tommy Lawton's pass to put Everton ahead in the 14th minute at Highbury in September 1938. The Blues went on to win 2-1.

Everton's League Championship side of 1938-9. Back row (left to right): Lawton, Jones, Sagar, H.Cooke (trainer), Mercer, Greenhalgh. Front row: Cook, Gillick, Bentham, Thomson, Stevenson, Boyes. The mascot is Billy Shannon.

World War Two erupted shortly after Kelly had taken office and for seven years, Britain's soccer fans were sustained by a diet of regional league and cup football. International matches, although not counting towards official caps, provided some magnificent football and England had one of her strongest-ever teams during this spell. At wing-half in many of them were the Everton pair, Cliff Britton and Joe Mercer.

Attendances boomed when sanity was restored to a grateful world, but for Everton it meant a nose-dive in playing fortunes. Champions for seven years, they surrendered the title to Liverpool in 1946-7, and by the following season they were 14th in Division One. Mercer and Lawton had long since departed for London clubs.

Action was needed and in 1948, Cliff Britton returned as manager. Britton had steered Burnley into Division One and to the FA Cup Final; and he was widely respected by the Everton club, players, officials and supporters alike. Kelly stayed on as secretary, but one face was sadly missing. In 1949, Wilf Cuff, the man who had guided them through triumphs and ills, died.

Britton, meanwhile, went on the look-out for players. He brought centre-forward Dave Hickson from Ellesmere Port and, at the other end of the scale, paid an Everton club record fee of £20,000 for Burnley inside-forward Harry Potts.

Hickson, in particular, played well for Britton. But the widely-predicted revival failed to materialise and, after finishing 18th in successive seasons, Everton were relegated for only the second time in the club's history.

Two undistinguished seasons of Second Division football were highlighted only by a run to the FA Cup semi-finals in 1953, before promotion was gained in 1953-4. There was the inevitable job of returning to the big time, yet the spark

Everton in 1954. Back row (left to right): Donovan, Buckle, Lindsay, O'Neill, Lello, Parker, Jones. Front row: Wainwright, Fielding, Cliff Britton (manager), Hickson, Eglington.

was still missing and during the second half of the 1950s, Everton hovered in the lower reaches of Division One with remarkable consistency.

The monotony was somewhat relieved by an exciting FA Cup run in 1956, before Manchester City ended Everton's gallop in the quarter-final. Everton's board gave Britton the broadest hint when they announced that they would like to appoint a caretaker manager while he was abroad with the team. Inevitably, he left and Everton's playing affairs were run by a three-man committee until the appointment of former Scottish amateur international, Ian Buchan, as team coach.

Britton's successor as manager was not appointed until October 1958 when Johnny Carey arrived to breathe new life into the club. Carey found Bobby Collins already on the pay-roll and he added players like Derek Temple, Albert Dunlop, Brian Labone and Mick Meagan.

Towards the end of the 1950s, there emerged a man who was to steady the club's erratic course. John Moores, millionaire football fanatic, former amateur player, and a member of the family which founded the massive Littlewoods football pools and mail-order organisation, became chief benefactor of a club he had supported from childhood.

With additional cash at his disposal, Carey signed up some fine players with Alex Young, Roy Vernon and Jimmy Gabriel topping the list.

In 1960-61, Carey's team took Everton to fifth place in the First Division, their highest post-war placing. Yet the manager was not allowed to finish the job he had started and chairman Moores decided that a new face was needed.

In came Harry Catterick, a quietly-spoken disciplinarian who had played centre-forward for Everton in the immediate post-war era. In 1961-2 they finished fourth, while across Stanley Park, Liverpool under Shankly were winning the Second Division title.

The following season was one of the worst in terms of weather — the season was extended after hundreds of games had been postponed — but for Everton it was a glorious campaign. They swept to the title, remained unbeaten at home, and set a new club record points total.

Having taken their first steps into European competition (losing a Fairs Cup match on aggregate to Dunfermline) Everton prepared for the European Cup.

They were drawn against Inter-Milan, experts at the art of a two-legged tie, and went out to a solitary goal in Italy after a goalless stalemate at Goodison. Everton's consolation was the performance of debutant Colin Harvey, who survived a baptism of fire to launch his illustrious career.

Having bought Tony Kay to add steel to an already impressive midfield department, Catterick was badly shaken when Kay, along with others was sent to prison and banned from the game for life after being found guilty of accepting bribes to affect the results of matches during his days as a Sheffield Wednesday player.

In 1966, Everton went back to Wembley and one of the most memorable Finals of modern times. From 2-0 down to Sheffield Wednesday, they hauled themselves back from the brink with two goals from unsung Mike Trebilcock, and won a sensational victory with a Temple goal.

In August 1966, Catterick won the race to sign Alan Ball; seven months later he secured the services of Howard Kendall, and another title-winning side was in the making. In 1968, Everton reached another FA Cup Final, this time losing to West Brom in extra-time at Wembley, and a year later they were losing semi-finalists.

But the 1969-70 season capped anything that had gone before. Driven on by the midfield trio of Harvey, Kendall and Ball, a seventh title was secured with a new record points tally (for Everton) of 66. The power and the passion of Everton's play set them well apart from their contemporaries and Catterick's blend of precocious young talent and great experience looked like giving Everton the stage for seasons to come.

Sheffield Wednesday goalkeeper Ron Springett is beaten by Mike Trebilcock's equaliser in the 1966 FA Cup Final.

Everton skipper Alan Ball with the FA Charity Shield after the Blues' victory over Chelsea in 1970.

Only months later they were struggling to beat even an average First Division side. The Goodison faithful looked on in disbelief as a slide of epic proportions left Everton in 14th place. A brave European Cup bid ended when the Greek side, Panathinaikos, went through on the away goals rule.

Catterick's men returned from Athens to face Liverpool in an FA Cup semi-final and saw the last avenue of success that season closed down by a 2-1 defeat.

Catterick, baffled as to why his side had fallen apart, spent the best part of two seasons 'remoulding', but with four years of his contract still to run, and suffering from illness, he was moved into an executive position in April 1973.

Another former Everton player, Billy Bingham, was given the job of steering Everton back on course, his job made even more difficult by the astonishing success that Liverpool were experiencing under the forceful management of Bill Shankly.

Everton finished a respectable, if unspectacular seventh in Bingham's first season in charge, after he had tried to solve the scoring problem by smashing the British transfer record, paying £350,000 for Bob Latchford. The big striker repaid Bingham's faith with goals in plenty.

But still there was no trophy and in January 1977, with Everton drifting in mid-table, Bingham was fired and Gordon Lee appointed. That year, Lee led the side out at Wembley, for the League Cup Final against Aston Villa. It took three games before Villa emerged victorious to break Evertonian hearts.

That was also the year of the FA Cup semi-final against Liverpool, when Welsh referee Clive Thomas disallowed what looked like a perfectly good goal by Bryan Hamilton. It had looked as though Everton had secured a famous victory. Thomas felt otherwise and Liverpool won the replay 3-0.

The 1977-8 season saw Everton finish third with 76 goals to become the First Division's leading scorers. The future looked bright and Lee had built a side which combined flair with commitment. But in 1979-80, things turned sour and after losing an FA Cup semi-final replay to West Ham, the Merseysiders finished 19th, only

Everton 1982-3. Back row (left to right): Ratcliffe, Wright, Walsh, Southall, Arnold, Higgins, Ferguson, Mountfield. Middle row: Harvey, Johnson, Irvine, Richardson, Sharp, Borrows, King, Stevens, Heaton, Clinkard. Front row: Sheedy, McMahon, Heath, Howard Kendall (manager), Ross, Bailey, Ainscow.

four points clear of relegation. After a month of speculation, Lee was sacked on 6 May 1981, after Everton had improved marginally to finish 15th.

The new manager was a familiar face — Howard Kendall, one of the stars of the great 1970 Championship-winning side. In his first season as manager, Kendall guided Everton to eighth place. Twelve months later, despite a catastrophic 5-0 Goodison drubbing by Liverpool, Everton finished seventh.

But the real turning point came in the New Year of 1984. After surviving calls for his dismissal, Kendall saw the team he had moulded begin to climb. On the way to seventh place in the League they met Liverpool in the Milk Cup Final — the first-ever Merseyside Wembley Final — and fought their way to an FA Cup Final meeting with Watford.

The Milk Cup turned sour in a Maine Road replay but, after a 14-year wait, Everton landed a trophy when they beat Watford to lift the FA Cup.

A Charity Shield victory over Liverpool in August 1984 raised the curtain on a magnificent season. The Canon League Championship was lifted in tremendous style; the European Cup-winners' Cup came to Goodison after the destruction of Rapid Vienna in the Final in Rotterdam; and there was honour in defeat when Manchester United, playing bravely with ten men, ended Everton's hopes of what would have been an astonishing treble by winning the 1985 FA Cup Final.

Howard Kendall was named Manager of the Year; Neville Southall was the Football Writers' Association Footballer of the Year; Peter Reid was honoured by his fellow professionals as the PFA's Player of the Year.

Reid, Trevor Steven, Gary Stevens, Paul Bracewell, Graeme Sharp and Pat Van den Hauwe all won their first international caps to underline the coming of age of arguably Everton's greatest-ever side.

Graeme Sharp, one of several Everton stars to gain international recognition in the mid-1980s, bursts through the opposing defence.

The Everton squad display the 1986-7 League Championship and 'Today' trophy at Goodison Park.

Kendall made Gary Lineker the club's most expensive-ever purchase during the summer of 1985 when he paid Leicester City £800,000 for his services. But even Lineker's 40-goal haul during the 1985-6 season could not prevent Liverpool marching to a League and FA Cup double.

Ironically, that historic feat was very much at the expense of Everton who finished runners-up in the League and were beaten by their Merseyside rivals at Wembley in May 1986.

Liverpool knocked Everton out of the Littlewoods Cup in a quarter-final tie at Goodison Park the following season but, despite injuries to several key players, Everton swept to a second League title success in only three years.

The dream of a record-breaking fourth consecutive FA Cup Final appearance perished at Plough Lane when unfashionable Wimbledon won a fifth round tie 3-1 after Adrian Heath had given Everton the lead.

Having become the most successful manager in the club's history, Howard Kendall surprisingly resigned in June 1987 to take over at Spanish club, Athletic Bilbao. He was succeeded by his long-time friend, Colin Harvey, who was very much the people's choice.

Alas, Harvey was unable to bring further success to Goodison in his first season. Although he succeeded in keeping together his predecessor's Championship-winning squad, the 1987-8 season proved to be an immense disappointment.

The uncharacteristically shoddy form of several key players was instrumental in destroying the rhythm of an Everton side which had, in the previous four seasons, proved to be the personification of consistency.

The League title was all but surrendered by Christmas as Kenny Dalglish's new-look Liverpool swept all before them and dreams of a fourth FA Cup Final appearance in just five years were shattered by the old enemy when a late Ray Houghton goal proved decisive in a fifth-round tie at Goodison Park.

The last chance of lending a silver lining to a relatively lacklustre campaign disappeared in the semi-final of the Littlewoods Cup when Arsenal exposed Everton's season-long weaknesses to comfortably win 4-1 on aggregate.

Although the 1988-9 season brought precious little improvement on the League front, Harvey's side swept into the Finals of both the FA Cup and the Simod Cup.

After losing to Nottingham Forest in the Simod Final, Everton were beaten in the FA Cup, 3-2 by Liverpool after extra-time which was, perhaps, fitting in the year of the Hillsborough tragedy.

After three seasons at the helm, Colin Harvey paid a predictable price for his failure to match a past which, ironically, he himself had helped to fashion. On 31 October 1990, Harvey was dismissed after a League Cup defeat at Sheffield United but just six days later he returned to the club as assistant manager following the sensational, totally unexpected, appointment of Howard Kendall who resigned as the manager of Manchester City to 'come home'.

After acknowledging that he had, perhaps, two years in which to turn around the club and awake a sleeping giant, Kendall began to restructure the club's senior squad, selling old heroes and replacing them with fresh talent.

This almost unprecedented revolution met with only minimal success and by the mid-point of the 1991-2 campaign, Everton's season of much promise was almost at an end following an FA Cup fourth-round defeat by Chelsea at Stamford Bridge.

Everton fall behind to a John Aldridge goal in the 1989 FA Cup Final.

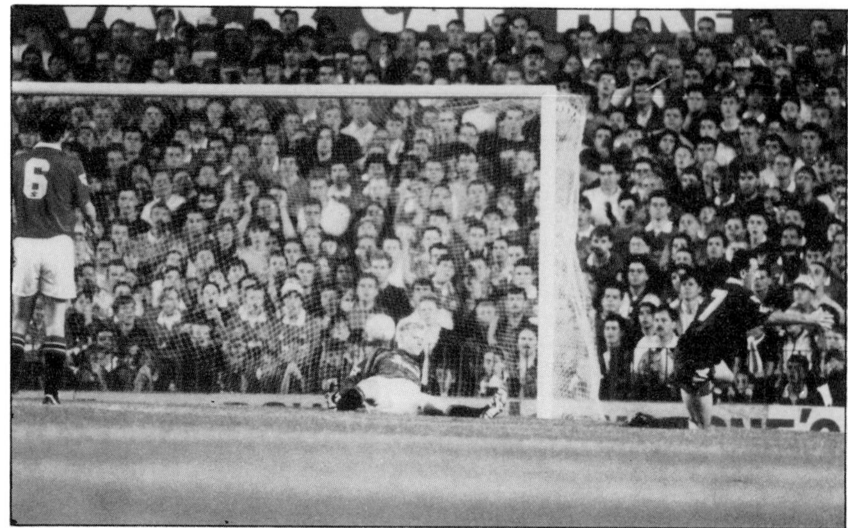

Robert Warzycha (7), Everton's Polish international, scores against Manchester United at Old Trafford in August 1992. The United players are Gary Pallister (6) and Peter Schmeichel.

Rather sadly, those who had been anticipating an upturn in the club's fortunes during 1992-3 were to be disappointed. With Kendall forced to operate within a highly restrictive financial framework, Everton struggled to find any real consistency and all hope of making a genuine impression during the FA Premier League's inaugural season had gone before the turn of the year.

The Coca-Cola League Cup trail ran cold in mid-December with defeat by Chelsea in a fourth-round replay at Stamford Bridge and the FA Cup campaign ended before it had begun in earnest, Wimbledon triumphing in a third-round replay at Goodison Park.

Everton's League form — particularly at home — was so patchy that the prospects of ignominious relegation to the new First Division loomed large on the horizon until the last few days of a season which few at the club will remember with any affection.

The Goodison Park Story

GOODISON Park was the first truly major football stadium in England, yet the magnificent soccer ground which the sporting world knows today would almost certainly not exist, had it not been for one man's dramatic change of heart, back in 1887.

It was then that George Mahon was converted to football. Mahon had professed a hatred for the game until he was enthralled by a match between Everton and Preston North End. Thereafter, he became an avid supporter and in 1892, when a furious row broke out within Everton's ranks, it was Mahon who guided the club towards a field on the north side of Stanley Park, near Goodison Road.

The disaffected Everton members left Anfield, which had staged an England-Ireland international in March that year, and turned their attentions to the job of transforming their new home into a ground good enough to stage League soccer.

The first tasks were to level the land, provide adequate drainage, build dressing-rooms and stands in the close season of 1892 — and all before a penny in gate-money could be taken. There was a massive cash crisis before one club member, Dr James Clement Baxter, loaned an interest-free sum of £1,000.

Mere Green Field cost £8,090 and the total outlay of transforming overgrown wastelands into Goodison Park for 1892-3, and additions in the lease period, was £4,000.

The task of clearing the debris and laying drains was handed to a Mr Barton who charged the princely sum of fourpence-halfpenny for each of the 29,471 square yards.

Walton-based building firm, Kelly Brothers, erected two uncovered stands, each accommodating 4,000, and a covered stand for another 3,000, at a cost of £1,640. They also constructed outside enclosing hoardings for £150 and gates and sheds for £132 10s. Twelve turnstiles cost £7 15s each.

Goodison Park — the ground was renamed immediately — was officially opened by FA officials, Lord Kinnaird and Frederick Wall, on 24 August 1892, 12,000 people turning up to watch members of the Everton side compete in a variety of sports.

Goodison Park in 1905, looking north-west.

Goodison Park pictured in 1905, showing the old grandstand on the Bullens Road side.

The first game played there was on 2 September when Everton beat Bolton Wanderers 4-2. One report stated: '. . .it appears to be one of the finest and most complete grounds in the kingdom . . .'. Indeed, the authorities thought so highly of Everton's new home that the 1894 FA Cup Final between Notts County and Bolton was staged there.

There were more rapid improvements. In 1895 a new Bullens Road Stand was built at a cost of £3,407, and a further £403 was spent on covering the Goodison Road side.

Everton invariably prospered in their new surroundings and further improvements were undertaken after a profit of £3,718 5s 7d was made following the FA Cup success of 1906.

Some £13,000 was spent on building the Park End double-decker stand on the south side of Goodison Park, and in 1909 the club added the Main Stand, which also housed a suite of offices and players' quarters. It rose on the Goodison Road side at a cost of £28,000. This stand survived until 1971. At the same time, Everton spent £12,000 on concreting the terraces and resurfacing the old cinder running-track. A 1909 edition of the *Athletic News* commented: 'Visitors to Goodison Park will be astonished at the immensity of the new double-decker stand'. The following year's FA Cup Final replay between Newcastle and Barnsley was staged at Goodison.

In 1913, Goodison Park became the first Football League ground to be visited by a reigning monarch when King George V and Queen Mary met Liverpool schoolchildren there.

During World War One, Goodison Park saw regular football as Everton played in the regional wartime league. The ground was also used for Army drill, and there was even a baseball match between Chicago Giants and New York Whitesox.

In 1926, a double-decker stand was built by the Bullens Road at a cost of £30,000, and in the '30s Goodison Park saw probably the first trainers' 'dug-outs' in England. It was an idea copied from Aberdeen, whom Everton had visited for a friendly match.

In 1938 work was completed on the new £50,000 Gwladys Street stand, which now made Goodison Park the only British soccer ground to have four double-decker stands. Goodison Park inevitably suffered during German air raids on the city in World War Two. The club received £5,000 from the War Damage Commission for essential repair work. In 1948 the ground was sufficiently safe to hold a record attendance of 78,299 for the visit of Liverpool in a First Division match.

In 1971 came Goodison's latest and most spectacular improvement. The old Main

Aerial picture of Goodison Park in October 1968.

Stand, a wonder in its day, was demolished and the present three-decker Main Stand was completed at a cost of £1 million. It provided seating for 10,000, modern dressing rooms, a treatment room, gymnasium, laundry and restaurant facilities.

The Goodison Park floodlighting system, which had been switched on for a game against Liverpool to mark the 75th anniversary of the Liverpool County FA on 9 October 1957, was also changed at this stage. The pylons were replaced by rows of ultra-powerful lights on the roof of the stands, the Bullens Road stand being re-roofed in the process.

The under-soil heating, which is now one of the finest in the country, has had its problems over the years. Electrical wiring was installed under the pitch in May 1958 at a cost of £16,000, but ultimately it was discovered that the drains could not cope with the melted ice and snow. The pitch was dug up and new drains laid. Further attempts at undersoil heating were tried and abandoned before the present system was introduced.

Everton received a shock when the local authority, acting under the 1975 Safety of Sports Grounds Act, announced that the official capacity of Goodison Park would have to be reduced from 56,000 to a mere 35,000. Work costing in excess of £250,000 was immediately carried out, pushing the limit back up to 52,800. The 1985 capacity was given as 53,091 with some 25,000 seated; by 1992 new safety legislation had reduced this to 38,500 but with 35,235 seats.

This was due largely to a major redevelopment at the ground. At the end of the 1990-91 season, the famous Gwladys Street terracing, where successive generations of the club's supporters had gathered to fete their sporting heroes, was seated as Everton sought to comply with the recommendations of Lord Justice Taylor's report into the 1989 Hillsborough tragedy.

Goodison Park, a great nineteenth-century football stadium, has carried on that tradition. Graced by the likes of Pelé and Eusebio during the 1966 World Cup, today it is one of the finest footballing theatres in Europe.

Everton Managers

Theo Kelly
1939-1948

THEO Kelly was Everton's first-ever manager. He was appointed at the end of the 1938-9 season, shortly after the club had secured the League title for the fifth time.

Everton were one of the last of the big name clubs to appoint a manager. Before Kelly took over the reins, team selection was a matter for senior coaches, prominent board-room executives and specially-appointed committees.

Kelly had been Everton club secretary for many years when it was decided to offer him the newly-created post. A superb organiser with a fine business brain, he was not particularly popular with the players, many finding it difficult to communicate with him.

But Harry Catterick, who played under Kelly, said of him: "He was the best public relations man I have ever known and any shortcomings he might have had with the players were compensated by his ability to open doors that were closed to other people."

His first seven years as manager found him in charge of a team playing in wartime regional football after the Football League had been suspended for the duration of hostilities. As peacetime soccer dawned, he angered many of Everton's loyal followers by selling Tommy Lawton to Chelsea in 1945, but in fairness to Kelly it has to be said that the free-scoring centre-forward had been restless for some time.

Joe Mercer, too, found it difficult to play for Kelly and the manager found himself selling another pre-war star to a London club, this time Arsenal.

Kelly rarely dipped into the transfer market during his time in charge, firmly believing that a manager should make do with what he has, unless an exceptional talent becomes available. Perhaps it was a philosophy which arose from the fact that, as secretary, he had spent so much time studying the administrative and financial problems of football.

The one big deal that he did line up turned sour on him. Constantly on the look-out for a forward to fill the gaping void left by Dixie Dean and Lawton, he pinned his hopes on Newcastle United's Albert Stubbins. But Liverpool chairman, Bill McConnell, got in first and even an increased offer of £12,500 was not good enough to bring Stubbins to Goodison.

In 1948, with Everton hovering just above the relegation zone, Kelly reverted to his old job of secretary when Cliff Britton returned to the club as manager.

Cliff Britton
1948-1956

WHEN Cliff Britton took charge of Everton in September 1948, he was, in effect, coming home.

As a wing-half of great style and polish he had enjoyed a memorable career with the club, culminating in an FA Cup winners' medal in 1933. For three years before rejoining Everton as manager he had been in charge of team matters at Burnley, enjoying great success. He took them from the Second Division to third place in the First, and to the FA Cup Final at Wembley. At Goodison he was handed the daunting task of restoring pride to a club which was struggling to regain the peak it had reached in the immediate pre-war days.

A fair-minded, easy-going man, he was well-liked by fans and players alike and managed to introduce some stability to a side which, although competent and confident, was never really good enough to live with the leading sides of the day.

He took Everton to an FA Cup semi-final with Liverpool at Maine Road in March 1950, but it was the old enemy from across Stanley Park who graced Wembley that season after a comfortable 2-0 win.

Britton paid £20,000 for Burnley's inside-forward, Harry Potts, who later returned to Turf Moor as manager; and in the fateful season of 1950-51 he spent a further £8,000 on Glasgow Rangers full-back, Jack Lindsay.

Things went dramatically wrong for Britton as the campaign reached its climax at the beginning of May. On the fifth day of that month, Everton found themselves with 32 points, with only Chelsea and Sheffield Wednesday, both on 30 points, below them in the table.

Everton, with a goal-average which was inferior to their fellow strugglers, needed one more point to guarantee First Division survival, but in the final matches Chelsea beat Bolton 4-0 — and Everton crashed 6-0 to Sheffield Wednesday.

Britton was naturally distraught, but the Everton board gave him a badly-needed vote of confidence and he diligently set about the task of winning back the club's First Division status. Everton finished seventh and 16th before he brought them back, as Division Two runners-up, in 1953-4.

But past glories still seemed a long way off and in 1956 Britton parted company with the club. It followed a dispute over Everton wanting to appoint an acting manager while Britton was abroad with the team.

He left, saying: "I want all managers to have the freedom to do the job for which they were appointed, which is to manage their clubs."

Ian Buchan
1956-1958

THE appointment of Ian Buchan as team coach in succession to Cliff Britton was an ill-judged move on the part of the Everton board. Buchan, a former Scottish amateur international, was a courteous and intensely loyal man, but his position at Goodison was invidious and he never enjoyed the full trappings of manager.

His main influence during his time at the club was in the area of the players' fitness, and at a time when a few dozen laps of the pitch were all that was considered necessary, Buchan turned Everton into the fittest side in the First Division.

Unfortunately, he did not have players of sufficient quality to capitalize on that. He once said that his side, with its fast, first-time football, was a winning combination in the early months of the season when pitches were well-grassed, but that he yearned for players who could adapt to the mud and ice of an English winter.

He was a deep thinker and his commitment to Everton was unquestioned, but the club needed a big-name manager and Buchan was anything but that. He died in a motor accident in Glasgow in 1965, aged 45.

Johnny Carey
1958-1961

JOHNNY Carey was appointed Everton manager in October 1958, more than two years after Britton had departed. He took over from Ian Buchan, the club coach who never had the title of manager and who failed to drag Everton out of their ever-deepening depression.

Carey, perhaps the best of Matt Busby's players during Manchester United's immediate post-war glory days, arrived not long after chairman Dick Seale had snapped up Celtic star Bobby Collins.

Carey had been a calm, assured footballer and he brought those qualities to the manager's chair when he took over at Blackburn Rovers. He was at Ewood

Park for five years and it was from there that he joined Everton.

At Goodison he inherited a promising squad. Apart from Collins, he had players of the calibre of Derek Temple, Mick Meagan, Brian Labone and Albert Dunlop.

He was also fortunate to arrive at the very moment that millionaire football fanatic and lifelong Everton supporter, John Moores, moved in to become the club's benefactor. With Moores' massive financial backing, Carey went into the transfer market to secure some of the most talented players ever seen at Goodison Park.

The job of transforming Everton into a team with a future as well as a past was handed to men like Roy Vernon, Billy Bingham, Alex Young and Jimmy Gabriel.

After two largely disappointing seasons, Carey took Everton to their highest position since the war when they finished fifth in 1960-61.

But, with the removal of the maximum players' wage, a new football age was dawning and club directors — and supporters — would soon be demanding championships and cups, and viewing anything less as failure.

At the end of the season Carey joined Moores, by now club chairman, at a Football League meeting in London. Rumours of Carey's impending dismissal were rife and the two men were besieged by journalists when they emerged from the meeting.

In the back of a taxi, Moores told Carey that he felt a change of manager was necessary and offered him a golden handshake. It was typical of Carey that, although stunned and saddened, he made no fuss, accepting the decision with great dignity.

Carey later took Leyton Orient to the First Division and spent five successful years as manager of Nottingham Forest.

Harry Catterick
1961-1973

HARRY Catterick was the man who transformed Everton into a great side once more, capable of living with the best. Indeed, he built two Championship-winning teams.

A tough taskmaster and strict disciplinarian, he ruled with a rod of iron while still managing to get the best from his players. He was appointed in 1961 to succeed Johnny Carey and was given a simple brief by Moores: to get Everton back to the very top by means of good, entertaining football.

Never afraid to back his own judgement and put his reputation on the line, Catterick proved adept when wheeling and dealing in the transfer market. He brought a succession of top-quality players to

Goodison, including Gordon West, John Morrissey, Tony Kay, Fred Pickering and Ray Wilson.

When he was appointed manager, he was no stranger to Everton. Older fans remembered the centre-forward who scored 24 League and Cup goals for the club in 71 matches in the late 1940s and early '50s.

In his first season in charge he guided Everton to fourth place in Division One as Liverpool reclaimed their top-flight status by taking the Second Division title.

Twelve months later, the revival, which he had single-handedly sparked, reached its climax as a sixth Championship was taken with some stylish football.

Catterick's belief in the true values of sportsmanship were shattered in January 1965 when Kay was sent to prison and banned from football for life after being found guilty of fixing matches during his time with Sheffield Wednesday.

For a man who always believed that football was primarily a sport, not a business, it was a bitter pill to swallow. But, even without the influence of Kay at wing-half, Everton managed to walk hand in hand with success.

In 1966 they reached Wembley and Catterick's biggest gamble — the inclusion of unknown Mike Trebilcock — paid off. The little Cornishman scored twice in one of the most exciting post-war FA Cup Finals.

Catterick signed Alan Ball from Blackpool at the same time as his youth policy began to pay dividends, Jimmy Husband, Joe Royle and John Hurst all fought their way through the ranks as a new side began to take shape.

In March 1967, Catterick signed Howard Kendall and took Everton back to Wembley in 1968, only to see West Brom snatch the Cup in extra-time.

More glory beckoned, but Manchester City ended dreams of a third Final in four years when they beat Everton in the semi-final. In the League, Everton finished third.

By the start of 1969-70, Catterick had built one of the finest sides of post-war English football. With Harvey, Kendall and Ball running the engine-room, and Royle hitting the target regularly. Everton swept to the title in glorious style.

But Catterick was unable to explain why his famous side then ran out of confidence and ideas and in only 12 months slumped to 14th place.

In January 1972, while driving home from Sheffield, Harry Catterick had a heart attack. In April 1973, with four years of his ten-year contract still to run, he was moved sideways into a senior executive role.

The man who restored pride to a famous club collapsed and died at Goodison Park after an FA Cup quarter-final match against Ipswich Town on 9 March 1985.

Billy Bingham
1973-1977

WHEN Billy Bingham took over in May 1973, he inherited a team badly in need of major reconstruction. A public who, just three years earlier, had grown used to watching superior football week after week, were fast becoming disillusioned as a slide in fortunes continued unchecked.

After playing in the club's 1963 Championship triumph, Bingham had set about learning the arts of management with such diverse teams as Southport and the Greek national side.

He took the job at Goodison with no illusions. The pressures were intense as Bill Shankly's Liverpool cast a giant shadow across Stanley Park.

A likeable man with a keen sense of humour, Bingham pushed the club to seventh spot in Division One in his first season, but he was the first to admit that it was not good enough. He bought Bob Latchford from Birmingham (Kendall moving to St Andrew's as part of the deal); Martin Dobson from Burnley and Jim Pearson from St Johnstone; and said farewell to men like Colin Harvey and Joe Royle.

The 1974-5 season proved to be the closest he would come to triumph during his four years at Goodison.

For long periods it seemed as if the League Championship would return to Everton. But, unable to sustain their form, they slipped to a disappointing fourth.

Convinced that the introduction of new faces would help the club turn the corner, Bingham bought Andy King, the enigmatic Duncan McKenzie and Bruce Rioch.

McKenzie and Rioch had played in only five matches for their new manager — two defeats, two draws and a win — before Bingham was sacked on 10 January 1977, as Everton slumped to 13th place.

With typical honesty and realism he said: "If you're with a top club, you expect to be shot down."

Three months later, he accepted a job in Greece as manager of PAOK Salonika. Bingham, who played for Northern Ireland in the 1958 World Cup Finals, managed the national team when they reached the World Finals, in 1982 and 1986.

Gordon Lee
1977-1981

GORDON Lee arrived in January 1977 with a hard-earned reputation as a soccer troubleshooter.

Clubs in a mess often turned to Lee and he would sort them out, usually sooner rather than later. He had spent 11 years as a defender with Aston Villa before becoming player-coach of Shrewsbury Town.

He took Port Vale up to the Third Division in his first managerial job and won promotion to Division Two for Blackburn Rovers during their centenary year of 1974-5. He steered Newcastle United to the League Cup and into Europe.

When he took charge at Goodison he found the club at a crossroads. Although they were hovering perilously close to the relegation zone, they had battled through to the League Cup semi-finals, while the FA Cup campaign had got underway.

During the last four months of 1976-7, Lee proved a motivator of men. Everton lost only two of their remaining 18 League games to finish an encouraging ninth; and they won through to the League Cup Final and the FA Cup semi-finals.

His dreams of marking his first season with a trophy were shattered by Aston Villa after two replays, while it was Liverpool who won through to the FA Cup Final with two hotly-disputed goals.

Nevertheless, Lee built a side of considerable ability and, perhaps more importantly, one worth watching. In his first full season, Everton finished third and were the First Division's highest scorers with 76 goals.

The following season had an explosive start — 19 games without defeat and a rare victory over Liverpool. Midway through the campaign Lee was charged with bringing the game into disrepute after he criticised a referee for allowing a game to go ahead on a treacherous pitch at Southampton. He was later cleared by an FA disciplinary committee.

Everton went on to finish a disappointing fourth and storm clouds began to gather. Lee swooped into the transfer market on deadline day, in a bid to improve his side's fire-power. He signed Brian Kidd and Peter Eastoe, but they failed to revive the flagging fortunes.

As the 1979-80 season got underway, he spent money in a forlorn bid to buy success. Stanley, Hartford, Gidman and Megson were drafted in, but it was too late and confidence continued to sink, along with attendances.

On 11 April 1981, after an embarrassing 2-0 home defeat by Norwich, chairman Philip Carter gave the first indication that Lee's days as Everton manager were numbered.

Within an hour of the final whistle, Carter issued a statement saying that the positions of the manager and his staff were under review. After nearly a month of speculation, Lee was sacked on 6 May.

Gordon Lee was a dedicated hard-working man whose best was simply not good enough for a club which has always demanded success.

Howard Kendall
1981-1987 and 1990-

"HOWARD was our first choice. He is one of the finest players ever to come out of the club and we know he has always been an Everton man at heart," declared chairman Philip Carter on 8 May 1981, as one of Goodison's favourite sons returned to the scene of his greatest triumphs.

After two poor seasons (the club had finished 19th in 1979-80, avoiding relegation by only four points) a disgruntled Everton public, tired of being force-fed a diet of broken promises, badly needed a lift and who better to provide it than Kendall, a man idolised during his illustrious playing career with the club.

He had served his apprenticeship as a manager, having taken Blackburn Rovers from Division Three to the brink of Division One, and was ready for the big-time. Businesslike and ruthless when the occasion demanded, he immediately brought a feeling of stability and hope to the club, even though he was quick to discover that footballing miracles do not happen overnight.

Although he led the side to eighth place in Division One in his first season in charge, he struggled initially to come to grips with the enormity of the job, spending money on players who were simply not suited to football at the highest level.

Alan Biley, Mick Ferguson, Alan Ainscow and Mike Walsh came and went after making little or no impact. On the plus side, however, were the early buys of Neville Southall and Adrian Heath, two men who were destined to play leading roles in the well-documented revival.

Only days after his arrival, Kendall made his objectives perfectly clear, he wanted to win a trophy, something the club had failed to do since he was a key member of the 1970 Championship-winning side.

But, despite a significant and undeniable improvement in Everton's fortunes, the club's trophy cabinet was still bare two years later. In the 1982-3 season, the momentum had been maintained with seventh place and an FA Cup run ended by a late Manchester United goal in the quarter-finals.

The next season was make or break. Despite having the nucleus of a potentially superb side things went from bad to worse. On 26 October 1983, only 8,067 people turned up to watch a Milk Cup-tie against Chesterfield. A fortnight later the figure was 9,080 for the visit of Coventry City in the same competition.

After a draw at Stoke on 14 January 1984 — Everton had beaten the Potters in the FA Cup third round a week earlier — the club plummeted to 18th place and the knives were out.

A small section of the crowd had made their feelings clear in the days leading up to that black Christmas, circulating leaflets which demanded the dismissal of both Kendall and his chairman.

And then it happened. A Milk Cup quarter-final match at Oxford was drifting away when Heath latched on to a dreadful

back-pass to snatch a late equaliser. Everton cantered to an easy win in the replay and were off and running.

A rejuvenated side strung together a series of impressive League results to climb to seventh place, won through to the first-ever all-Mersey Wembley meeting when they met Liverpool in the Milk Cup Final, and swept to the FA Cup Final against Watford.

With Philip Carter's backing, invaluable assistance from coaches Mick Heaton and Colin Harvey, and belief in his own ability to do the job, Kendall had dragged Everton back on to the glory trail.

The Milk Cup was lost after a replay, but the FA Cup came back to Goodison after an 18-year absence.

The 1984-5 season was simply glorious. A first League title in 15 years, a first European trophy in the shape of the Cup-winners' Cup, and glorious failure in the FA Cup Final against Manchester United.

Just 18 months after supporters had called for his resignation, Howard Kendall, proudly accepted the Manager of the Year award. However, the 1985-6 season was tinged with bitter disappointment for Kendall who saw his side finish as runners-up to neighbours Liverpool in both the Championship and the FA Cup.

But, despite having to negotiate a frightening catalogue of injury problems during the course of the 1986-7 campaign, Kendall's astute leadership guaranteed that the coveted title returned to Goodison Park for the second time in three seasons.

Kendall returned from a club tour of New Zealand and Australia in the summer of 1987 to find an offer he simply could not refuse lying on his table.

After twice turning down the opportunity to succeed Terry Venables at mighty Barcelona, Kendall shocked the footballing world by announcing, on 19 June 1987, that he had agreed to take over at Atheltic Bilbao.

'It has been a difficult decision to make but I feel that it is the right one. I have had six tremendous years at the club', he said after his announcement.

Kendall left for the sunshine of Spain's Basque region safe in the knowledge that he would go down in history as Everton's most successful ever manager.

Kendall spent two happy, and successful, years in Spain before leaving by mutual consent at the end of his second season in charge. Although he returned to England insisting that he wished to enjoy a period of rest before contemplating his future, he was immediately courted by several leading clubs and on 6 December 1989, he was appointed manager of struggling Manchester City following the dismissal of Mel Machin.

Kendall's policy of buying former Everton players to help strengthen a side which was in grave danger of being relegated to the Second Division infuriated a section of the Maine Road public but it proved to be highly successful and the club's top-flight status was preserved.

Kendall had been in charge at City for less than 12 months when he sensationally resigned on 6 November 1990 to return to Everton following the sacking of his closest friend, Colin Harvey. His decision was condemned in some quarters and greeted with astonishment in others but he attempted to silence his critics by using the now-famous phrase: "With Manchester City it was a love affair — with Everton it is a marriage."

Kendall ensured that the threat of relegation was swiftly banished in the remaining six months of the season but the 1991-2 campaign was littered with disappointments as an expensively-restructured team struggled to make any discernible impact.

In attempting to lead Everton forward into a new, brighter, era, Kendall began to sever his links with the recent past, selling such stalwarts as Kevin Sheedy and Graeme Sharp.

Rumours that Kendall was preparing to sever his ties with Goodison Park for a second — and presumably final — time abounded throughout the hugely disappointing 1992-3 season but he remained at the helm, insisting that it was possibly only a lack of cash that was preventing him from building a side capable of living with the very best in the FA Premier League.

Colin Harvey
1987-1990

ON 18 June 1987, Colin Harvey was enjoying a family holiday on a North Wales caravan site when he received a message which was to change his entire life.

He was asked to urgently contact club chairman, Philip Carter, and at the conclusion of a brief telephone conversation he found himself accepting the position of manager in succession to his former teammate and long-time friend Howard Kendall who had surprisingly decided to sever his Goodison Park ties and move to Spain to take charge of Athletic Bilbao.

Twenty-four hours later the relative anonymity he had always craved was a thing of the past as he was thrust into the spotlight and officially handed the unenviable task of keeping Everton at the very summit of English football.

"I don't really want the job under these circumstances, I honestly didn't think that Howard would leave. It is a hard act to follow because Howard is undoubtedly the best manager in England. My job is to make sure that the club stays at the top", he said with typical modesty.

After serving the club for more than 25 years as player, youth-team coach, reserve-team coach and first-team coach, the amiable Harvey had finally been given the top job.

"He has been an integral part of the coaching staff for the past five years and I am sure that he will bring his own brand of management to the club", said Carter.

Within days of succeeding Kendall, Harvey had appointed Peter Reid as player-coach, Terry Darracott as his assistant and Mike Lyons as reserve-team coach.

He enjoyed a dream start to his new career as Everton began the 1987-8 season by winning the FA Charity Shield at Wembley, a solitary goal by Wayne Clarke defeating FA Cup holders Coventry City.

But his attempts to lead the club to a third League title in four seasons floundered as his side were bedevilled by injuries and inconsistency.

The League title was surrendered to Liverpool and, with the age-old enemy inflicting defeat in the fifth round of the FA Cup and Arsenal comfortably winning a two-legged Littlewoods Cup semi-final, there was sadly to be no silver lining to his first season at the helm.

But Harvey's joy at being promoted to the post he had always dreamed of filling was tempered to a degree by the numerous problems he had to contend with, both on and off the field, during the course of his first season at the helm.

Despite exerting a calm authority over a squad of players which had almost begun to take success for granted, inconsistency was ultimately to fuel discontent and at the end of a blank season Harvey had to face up to a mini-rebellion.

In a bold attempt to restore Everton to its position as English football's premier club side, Harvey launched an unprecedented close-season spending spree, parting with in excess of £4 million for Tony Cottee, Pat Nevin, Stuart McCall and Neil McDonald.

This costly rebuilding programme paved the way for the departure of terrace-favourites including Derek Mountfield, who joined Aston Villa, and Alan Harper, who crossed the Pennines to sign for Sheffield Wednesday, while Gary Stevens left for Graeme Souness's 'Anglo army' at Ibrox when he joined Rangers for £1.25 million.

Sadly, a change of personnel did not precipitate a change of fortune and despite several more forays into the transfer market, Harvey struggled to instil a sense of self-belief into a team which was blessed with individuals of great skill but which rarely achieved a satisfactory level of consistency.

Although Everton's interest in the destiny of the League Championship had all but been ended by the mid-way point of the 1988-9 season, an ability to perform with clinical efficiency in knock-out football promised much.

As the campaign neared its climax, Harvey's men had fought their way through to the Finals of both the FA Cup and the Simod Cup. Expectations were high but disappointment was to follow.

Having been beaten by Nottingham Forest, 4-3, in a thrilling Simod Final, Everton went down to Liverpool in the FA Cup, 3-2 in extra-time. The fact that the game was immediately hailed as one of the finest ever played beneath Wembley's twin towers was little consolation to Harvey as he sought to unearth a winning formula.

The 1989-90 season was another indistinguished affair with Everton finishing a disappointing sixth in Division One.

Harvey continued to sell and buy at regular intervals but after ten weeks of the 1990-91 season, Everton were in serious trouble near the foot of the table. The final

straw for a board which had displayed great patience and loyalty came on 30 October when the club's interest in the League Cup was ended by lowly Sheffield United at Bramall Lane. Less than 24 hours later, Harvey was summoned to Goodison

Playing days: Colin Harvey and teammate John Morrissey have a word with the referee.

Park and told that he was to be dismissed.

Six days after being sacked, Harvey was to return to the club as assistant manager following the appointment of Howard Kendall.

Everton Stars A-Z

Walter Abbott joined Everton in the close season of 1899 because club officials were impressed with the form he had shown as an inside-left with Small Heath where his hard-hitting had brought him 33 goals in 1898-9. But it was as an equally hard-shooting left-half that Abbott flourished at Goodison Park and where he made the bulk of his 250-plus League appearances before moving to Burnley in the summer of 1908. Abbott had abundant stamina and he seemed to cover every inch of the pitch, urging on colleagues. Strangely, Abbott's one England cap came at centre-half, a position he never played in the League. He was drafted into the team against Wales at Wrexham in 1902, at a time when England were constantly changing their pivot. He played well enough in the goalless draw but was never invited to represent his country again. He played in Everton's Cup Finals of 1906 and 1907 and also represented the Football League. After Burnley he returned briefly to Small Heath, a club by now renamed Birmingham, and retired through injury in 1910. Later he worked in the early motor industry in Birmingham.

	LEAGUE		*FA CUP*		*TOTAL*	
	App	*Gls*	*App*	*Gls*	*App*	*Gls*
1899-1900	25	1	1	0	26	1
1900-01	34	5	2	0	36	5
1901-02	31	4	2	0	33	4
1902-03	33	4	3	2	36	6
1903-04	32	4	1	0	33	4
1904-05	28	4	6	0	34	4
1905-06	27	5	5	1	32	6
1906-07	26	4	7	1	33	5
1907-08	21	1	7	1	28	2
	257	32	34	5	291	37

WALTER ABBOTT

The unusually-named Smart Arridge started his football career with the Welsh club, Bangor, and after they had converted him to full-back he began to attract the attentions of leading clubs of the day. It was Second Division Bootle who landed his signature but inevitably a First Division club, Everton, soon lured him away. Yet, having signed for the Goodison club in 1893, he had to wait until the 1895-6 season before he could establish a place at left-back in the League side. He had two full seasons in the Everton team but his run did not extend to the 1897 Cup Final side. After appearing in the first three rounds he missed the semi-final and Final. Disappointed and not a little bitter, he wanted to get away and in the close season signed for New Brighton Tower. A full-back who could play on either flank, Arridge was renowned for his fearsome shoulder-charges 'which are events to be thought over long after the person has been the recipient of such a favour'. Although born in Sunderland, his Welsh boyhood meant that, when he was good enough, he was selected for Wales and won eight full caps.

	LEAGUE		*FA CUP*		*TOTAL*	
	App	*Gls*	*App*	*Gls*	*App*	*Gls*
1893-94	2	0	0	0	2	0
1894-95	3	0	0	0	3	0
1895-96	23	0	2	0	25	0
1896-97	23	0	3	0	26	0
	51	0	5	0	56	0

SMART ARRIDGE

Although he lost his regular full-back berth in October 1984, following the arrival of Pat Van den Hauwe from Birmingham City, John Bailey was still very much the joker in Everton's pack. A local lad with a typically cutting Scouse sense of humour, Bailey was an invaluable member of Howard Kendall's squad, more than capable of lifting spirits and morale when things were not going quite right. He was signed from Blackburn Rovers in July 1979 for £300,000, and within 12 months had forced his way on to the international scene by being called up for England 'B'. A clever defender who loved to push forward, Bailey remained a firm favourite with the Goodison crowd. The crowning moment of his career came at Wembley in May 1984, when he helped Everton to their first FA Cup success in 18 years, but just months later he found himself out of the picture. After a clear-the-air meeting with manager Howard Kendall in March 1985, Bailey was placed on the transfer list but changed his mind a month later and signed a new one-year contract. He finally severed his Everton ties in October 1985 when he joined Newcastle United in an £80,000 deal. He joined Bristol City on a free transfer in 1988 before returning to Everton as 'B' team coach in 1992. He was dismissed in May 1993.

JOHN BAILEY

	LEAGUE		FA CUP		FL CUP		EUROPE		TOTAL	
	App	Gls	App	Gls	App	Gls	App	Gls	App	Gls
1979-80	42	2	6	0	5	0	2	0	55	2
1980-81	31	0	4	0	1/1	0	-	-	36/1	0
1981-82	12	0	0	0	3	0	-	-	15	0
1982-83	37	0	5	0	2	0	-	-	44	0
1983-84	33	0	7	0	7	0	-	-	47	0
1984-85	15	1	0	0	1	0	4	0	20	1
1985-86	1	0	-	-	1	0	-	-	2	0
	171	3	22	0	20/1	0	6	0	219/1	3

Alan Ball was one of the greatest players ever to pull on an Everton — and England — shirt. The flame-haired fire-brand who inspired his country to World Cup triumph in 1966, and who played a major role in Everton's Championship success in 1970, was never out of the spotlight. Constantly at odds with authority, Ball insisted on playing the game his way and although his hell-for-leather approach won him few friends on the field, he was immensely popular with supporters. His greatest asset was his extraordinary appetite for work. The ultimate competitor, he refused to accept defeat and that approach rubbed off on those around him. Ball's workrate more than made up for his temperamental outbursts and he will forever be remembered for his grim determination and defence-splitting passes. Ball was born in Farnworth, Lancashire, and was on the books of nearby Bolton Wanderers but signed professional for Blackpool. He joined Everton in August 1966 for a then British record fee of £110,000. He clocked up more than 200 League games in five years at Goodison. With Howard Kendall and Colin Harvey, he was part of the celebrated midfield trio which swept Everton to the title in 1969-70. For no apparent reason, that side broke up within two years and Harry Catterick sensationally transferred Ball to Arsenal in 1971 for another record fee, £220,000. After a successful career at Highbury, Ball moved to Southampton for £60,000 in 1976, then to Blackpool as manager in 1980. He resigned in March 1981 and returned to Southampton, playing his last game in the top flight in October 1982, against Everton. He joined former England colleague Bobby Moore in Hong Kong for a short spell, then resumed his colourful playing career with Bristol Rovers in January 1983. One of the game's great characters went on to manage Portsmouth and took them into Division One in 1987. After leaving Portsmouth in 1989 he went on to manage Stoke City, spending two years at the Victoria Ground before being dismissed following a string of poor results. He was placed in charge of Exeter City in the summer of 1991 and in February 1992, Graham Taylor invited him to help the England national squad prepare for the European Championship finals in Sweden.

ALAN BALL

	LEAGUE		FA CUP		FL CUP		EUROPE		TOTAL	
	App	Gls	App	Gls	App	Gls	App	Gls	App	Gls
1966-67	41	15	6	2	-	-	4	1	51	18
1967-68	34	20	4	0	2	0	-	-	40	20
1968-69	40	16	5	0	4	2	-	-	49	18
1969-70	37	10	1	1	3	1	-	-	41	12
1970-71	39	2	5	2	1	0	6	3	51	7
1971-72	17	3	0	0	0	0	-	-	17	3
	208	66	21	5	10	3	10	4	249	78

ROBERT BALMER

The younger brother of Walter Balmer, by four years, Robert was an extremely effective full-back who partnered his brother in the 1907 FA Cup Final against Sheffield Wednesday at the Crystal Palace. Born in Liverpool, he was of much slighter build than Walter, standing 5ft 7in and weighing 10st 2lb. He made his League debut in the 3-0 win over Middlesbrough at Goodison Park on 3 January 1903 and he became a regular member of the side in 1905-06. After his brother's departure, Robert formed another good partnership with the stylish Scottish full-back, John Maconnachie. While Maconnachie liked to play his way out of trouble, Robert Balmer's technique was more traditional — the big clearance to relieve pressure — but their contrasting styles combined effectively and they had a good understanding with goalkeeper Billy Scott.

	LEAGUE		*FA CUP*		*TOTAL*	
	App	*Gls*	*App*	*Gls*	*App*	*Gls*
1902-03	1	0	0	0	1	0
1903-04	3	0	0	0	3	0
1904-05	11	0	3	0	14	0
1905-06	20	0	2	0	22	0
1906-07	25	0	8	0	33	0
1907-08	26	0	7	0	33	0
1908-09	35	0	2	0	37	0
1909-10	20	0	0	0	20	0
1910-11	23	0	1	0	24	0
1911-12	1	0	0	0	1	0
	165	0	23	0	188	0

Liverpool-born Walter Balmer served Everton well for more than a decade. A thick-set full-back, he signed as a 20-year-old in 1897 and played over 250 League games for the club as well as appearing in two FA Cup Finals and winning an England cap. Balmer made his League debut against West Bromwich Albion at The Hawthorns in November 1897 and played his last game at home to Sunderland in April 1908. He had the major attributes of a full-back of the day, a crunching tackle and a hefty clearance which sent the ball way out of the danger area. He could play on either flank and formed a good partnership with Jack Crelley, another locally-born defender who found his way to Goodison via Millwall. For some time he also partnered his younger brother, Robert, in Everton's rearguard. Balmer played in consecutive Cup Finals, collecting a winners' medal in 1906. He made his England appearance against Ireland in 1905, playing right-back in the 1-1 draw at Middlesbrough. He also represented the Football League before moving to Croydon Common, then a Southern League side. After World War One he was appointed Huddersfield Town coach. His nephew, Jack Balmer, made his name with Liverpool either side of World War Two.

WALTER BALMER

	LEAGUE		*FA CUP*		*TOTAL*	
	App	*Gls*	*App*	*Gls*	*App*	*Gls*
1897-98	12	0	5	0	17	0
1898-99	23	0	2	0	25	0
1899-1900	32	1	1	0	33	1
1900-01	31	0	2	0	33	0
1901-02	28	0	2	0	30	0
1902-03	28	0	3	0	31	0
1903-04	32	0	1	0	33	0
1904-05	30	0	3	0	33	0
1905-06	18	0	5	0	23	0
1906-07	33	0	8	0	41	0
1907-08	26	0	6	0	32	0
	293	1	38	0	331	1

One of the most gifted footballers of his generation, Peter Beardsley astonished the sporting world in the summer of 1991 by making the short journey across Stanley Park from Anfield to Goodison Park. Ironically, it was Howard Kendall's failure to persuade Dean Saunders to join Everton which hastened Beardsley's departure from Liverpool for once the Welsh striker had chosen red — and not blue — a parting of the ways was an inevitability. Having sanctioned the sale of Graeme Sharp to Oldham Athletic, Kendall needed a replacement of proven ability and did not hesitate to meet an asking price of £1 million. After failing to score in his opening six games, Beardsley rediscovered his golden touch, finding the target eight times in his next six outings. A player whose speed of thought matches his speed of limb, Beardsley went on to become the mainstay of the Everton side during the disappointing 1991-2 and 1992-3 seasons.

PETER BEARDSLEY

	LEAGUE		*FA CUP*		*FL CUP*		*EUROPE*		*TOTAL*	
	App	*Gls*	*App*	*Gls*	*App*	*Gls*	*App*	*Gls*	*App*	*Gls*
1991-92	42	15	2	1	4	3	-	-	48	19
1992-93	39	10	2	0	4	2	-	-	45	12
	81	25	4	1	8	5	-	-	93	31

The sight of John Bell wriggling his way down the right flank was a familiar one around the turn of the century. A masterful dribbler who played as though he had the ball glued to the inside of his right foot at times, he was a member of Dumbarton's 1891-2 Scottish League championship side before signing for Everton in 1892. Regarded as one of the most inventive forwards of his day, Bell was an undoubted sporting craftsman who spent the best part of a decade thrilling audiences at Goodison Park. He played in the 1897 FA Cup Final, and although Everton were beaten 3-2 by Aston Villa, it was Bell who won the plaudits, universally praised for an heroic performance which nearly swung the game the Merseysiders' way. He left Everton to serve Spurs and Glasgow Celtic before returning to Goodison via New Brighton Tower FC, and later played for Preston where he became player-coach. He was chairman of the first attempt at a players' union. In one First Division match he is alleged to have saved the life of a fellow player when he re-positioned his dislocated neck with one firm wrench of his massive hands. Bell made ten appearances for Scotland between 1890 and 1900.

JOHN BELL

	LEAGUE		*FA CUP*		*TOTAL*	
	App	*Gls*	*App*	*Gls*	*App*	*Gls*
1892-93	3	0	0	0	3	0
1893-94	24	9	1	0	25	9
1894-95	27	15	3	3	30	18
1895-96	27	9	3	1	30	10
1896-97	27	15	5	2	32	17
1897-98	22	4	5	0	27	4
1901-02	24	5	2	0	26	5
1902-03	23	5	3	2	26	7
	177	62	22	8	199	70

Stan Bentham spent the best years of his life at Everton, first as a player and then as a key member of the backroom staff. Born in Leigh, he played most of his early football with a church team, Lowton St Mary's, before attracting the attention of Bolton Wanderers with whom he had a series of trials. In December 1933 he turned professional with Wigan Athletic and within a matter of months found himself the target of several top clubs. In February 1934 he threw in his lot with Everton, along with Springfield Park teammate Terry Kavanagh. Bentham made a dream League debut in November 1935. Everton claimed their first away success of the season with a superb 4-0 win at Grimsby and Bentham netted twice. He was an honest, hard-working inside-right and a pioneer of the roving midfield role which is so popular today. In 1938-9, when Everton won the Championship, Bentham missed only one match. He left Goodison in 1962 to take up a coaching post with Luton Town.

	LEAGUE		*FA CUP*		*TOTAL*	
	App	*Gls*	*App*	*Gls*	*App*	*Gls*
1935-36	7	4	1	0	8	4
1936-37	2	0	0	0	2	0
1938-39	41	9	5	0	46	9
1945-46	-	-	2	0	2	0
1946-47	37	3	2	0	39	3
1947-48	10	0	5	0	15	0
1948-49	13	1	0	0	13	1
	110	17	15	0	125	17

STANLEY BENTHAM

Mike Bernard was a solid and reliable defender who was rather unfortunate not to make a bigger name for himself during his time with Everton. Highly competitive and a superb ball-winner, he reached his own footballing peak when the Blues were hardly enjoying the best of fortunes. He began his career with Stoke City. Sir Alf Ramsey gave him the first of his England Under-23 caps in 1970, and he was a member of the Stoke side which ended a 108-year wait for success when, in March 1972, they lifted the League Cup by defeating Chelsea. Harry Catterick signed Bernard for Everton in May of that year for £140,000. He arrived as a midfielder but was later converted into a defender where he made the vast majority of his appearances. After losing his place in early 1977, Bernard was linked with a return to Stoke, but eventually settled for a move to Oldham Athletic. He took over a pub in the Dee Valley after he was forced to quit the game because of injury in early 1979.

	LEAGUE		*FA CUP*		*FL CUP*		*EUROPE*		*TOTAL*	
	App	*Gls*	*App*	*Gls*	*App*	*Gls*	*App*	*Gls*	*App*	*Gls*
1972-73	30/2	1	2	0	1	0	-	-	33/2	1
1973-74	35/2	4	3	0	2	0	-	-	40/2	4
1974-75	31/2	0	2/1	0	2	0	-	-	35/3	0
1975-76	29/1	2	1	0	2/1	0	2	0	34/2	2
1976-77	14/1	1	1	0	4	0	-	-	19/1	1
	139/8	8	9/1	0	11/1	0	2	0	161/10	8

MIKE BERNARD

BILLY BINGHAM

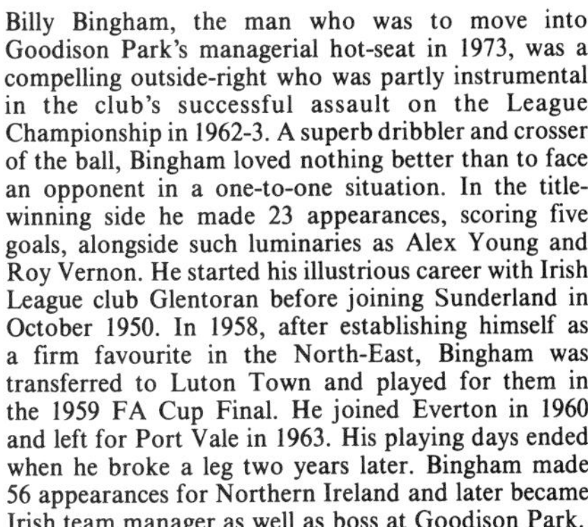

Billy Bingham, the man who was to move into Goodison Park's managerial hot-seat in 1973, was a compelling outside-right who was partly instrumental in the club's successful assault on the League Championship in 1962-3. A superb dribbler and crosser of the ball, Bingham loved nothing better than to face an opponent in a one-to-one situation. In the title-winning side he made 23 appearances, scoring five goals, alongside such luminaries as Alex Young and Roy Vernon. He started his illustrious career with Irish League club Glentoran before joining Sunderland in October 1950. In 1958, after establishing himself as a firm favourite in the North-East, Bingham was transferred to Luton Town and played for them in the 1959 FA Cup Final. He joined Everton in 1960 and left for Port Vale in 1963. His playing days ended when he broke a leg two years later. Bingham made 56 appearances for Northern Ireland and later became Irish team manager as well as boss at Goodison Park.

	LEAGUE		*FA CUP*		*FL CUP*		*EUROPE*		*TOTAL*	
	App	*Gls*	*App*	*Gls*	*App*	*Gls*	*App*	*Gls*	*App*	*Gls*
1960-61	26	9	1	0	3	1	-	-	30	10
1961-62	37	9	3	1	-	-	-	-	40	10
1962-63	23	5	3	1	-	-	2	0	28	6
	86	23	7	2	3	1	2	0	98	26

TOM BOOTH

Tom Booth was unlucky to miss Everton's 1906 FA Cup Final, and to be disappointed when the club reached the Final again a year later. Injury in the days leading up to the 1906 semi-final ruled him out and there was no room for him 12 months later. Born in Manchester, Booth played for the Rest of Lancashire against Nelson in 1896 and his form as a strong half-back alerted Blackburn Rovers officials who claimed his signature. He moved from right-half to centre-half, the position in which he was first capped, against Wales in 1898. He joined Everton in April 1900, because Blackburn needed the cash, and went on to captain a side that challenged for the League title in the early days of this century. Although he continued to live in Manchester, no one could doubt his commitment to Merseyside and when Everton met Manchester City in a vital end-of-the-season clash in 1905, Booth and his City namesake, Frank, were both cautioned in what became an infamous off-the-ball incident. He left Everton in 1908, for Preston, but was soon on his way to Carlisle United without playing a League game at Deepdale. He retired in 1909.

	LEAGUE		*FA CUP*		*TOTAL*	
	App	*Gls*	*App*	*Gls*	*App*	*Gls*
1900-01	31	0	2	0	33	0
1901-02	34	1	2	0	36	1
1902-03	29	2	3	1	32	3
1903-04	34	4	1	0	35	4
1904-05	8	0	0	0	8	0
1905-06	17	0	2	1	19	1
1906-07	14	1	0	0	14	1
1907-08	8	1	0	0	8	1
	175	9	10	2	185	11

WALLY BOYES

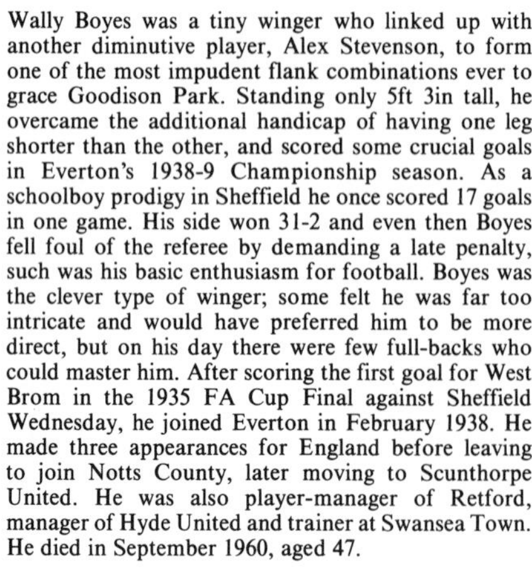

Wally Boyes was a tiny winger who linked up with another diminutive player, Alex Stevenson, to form one of the most impudent flank combinations ever to grace Goodison Park. Standing only 5ft 3in tall, he overcame the additional handicap of having one leg shorter than the other, and scored some crucial goals in Everton's 1938-9 Championship season. As a schoolboy prodigy in Sheffield he once scored 17 goals in one game. His side won 31-2 and even then Boyes fell foul of the referee by demanding a late penalty, such was his basic enthusiasm for football. Boyes was the clever type of winger; some felt he was far too intricate and would have preferred him to be more direct, but on his day there were few full-backs who could master him. After scoring the first goal for West Brom in the 1935 FA Cup Final against Sheffield Wednesday, he joined Everton in February 1938. He made three appearances for England before leaving to join Notts County, later moving to Scunthorpe United. He was also player-manager of Retford, manager of Hyde United and trainer at Swansea Town. He died in September 1960, aged 47.

	LEAGUE		*FA CUP*		*TOTAL*	
	App	*Gls*	*App*	*Gls*	*App*	*Gls*
1937-38	13	3	0	0	13	3
1938-39	36	4	5	4	41	8
1945-46	-	-	2	0	2	0
1946-47	9	3	0	0	9	3
1947-48	4	1	0	0	4	1
1948-49	4	0	0	0	4	0
	66	11	7	4	73	15

RICHARD BOYLE

Another of Everton's famous Scottish imports, Richard Boyle came to Goodison Park in 1890 after spells with Dumbarton Episcopalians, Dumbarton Union and Dumbarton. He made an immediate impact on the English game and within four years he was appointed club captain. He was a sturdy half-back who led by example. Strong in the tackle and renowned for his ability to deliver a pin-point pass over any distance, Boyle was the kingpin in a side which, at the time, was built for stability rather than mobility. There was said to be no more stirring sight than Boyle robbing a forward and then proceeding to canter half the length of the field before releasing one of his own front men with a simple, yet incisive pass. In the days when the centre-half was no mere stopper, he often took it upon himself to push forward in search of goals and he scored many, particularly from free-kicks.

	LEAGUE		*FA CUP*		*TOTAL*	
	App	*Gls*	*App*	*Gls*	*App*	*Gls*
1892-93	25	0	7	0	32	0
1893-94	21	1	0	0	21	1
1894-95	30	2	4	0	34	2
1895-96	30	3	3	0	33	3
1896-97	29	0	5	1	34	1
1897-98	22	0	0	0	22	0
1898-99	34	1	2	0	36	1
1899-1900	29	0	0	0	29	0
1900-01	2	0	0	0	2	0
	222	7	21	1	243	8

Paul Bracewell holds the rare distinction of making his Everton debut at Wembley Stadium. After signing from Sunderland for £250,000 at the end of 1983-4, the talented midfielder was thrown in at the deep end in the Charity Shield showpiece against Liverpool three months later. It was perhaps the ultimate baptism of fire, but the Heswall-born youngster came through with flying colours as Howard Kendall's men tuned up for what was to be their Championship-winning season with a deserved 1-0 win. Bracewell had been high on Kendall's wanted list for two years. Indeed, he nearly moved to Goodison Park in 1983 while at Stoke City, but eventually decided to try his luck in the North-East. Things did not really work out for him at Roker Park and he jumped at the chance to return south. Whilst not the quickest of players, he is a superb passer of the ball and formed a telling partnership at the heart of the midfield alongside Peter Reid. He played a major part in Everton's success during 1984-5 and won his first full England cap when he came on as substitute for Bryan Robson against West Germany on the summer tour to Mexico. Bracewell suffered a serious ankle injury at Newcastle on New Year's Day 1986 and although he saw out the season. he was then sidelined for more than 20 months, undergoing five operations. He returned to the senior side towards the end of 1987-8 but after only two full appearances was forced to undergo yet more surgery on his right ankle. After proving his fitness but losing his first-team place, he rejoined Sunderland in a £250,000 transfer in 1989. He played for the Wearsiders in the 1992 FA Cup Final and later made a contribution to Newcastle's promotion to the FA Premier League.

	LEAGUE		*FA CUP*		*FL CUP*		*EUROPE*		*TOTAL*	
	App	*Gls*	*App*	*Gls*	*App*	*Gls*	*App*	*Gls*	*App*	*Gls*
1984-85	37	2	7	0	4	1	8	1	56	4
1985-86	38	3	6	0	5	1	-	-	49	4
1987-88	0	0	0/2	0	1	0	-	-	1/2	0
1988-89	20	2	6	0	1	0	0	0	27	2
	95	7	19/2	0	11	2	8	1	133/2	10

PAUL BRACEWELL

George Brewster was a tall, influential centre-half whose form while he was at Goodison led to him being capped for Scotland. Yet he could never be certain of a regular place in the Everton first team. He was born at Culsalmond, near Aberdeen, and played Scottish junior soccer with Mugiemoss before signing for Aberdeen in 1913. During World War One he guested for Falkirk before returning to Aberdeen. Everton heard of the 6ft centre-half who was playing a commanding role with the Dons and they brought him to England in January 1920 for £1,500. He played a handful of games in the second half of that season and the following campaign saw him as a regular, although he played all his games when Tom Fleetwood was switched to right-half. He caught the eye of the Scottish selectors and was capped in the 3-0 win over England in April that season. The following season he again covered for Fleetwood in the Everton team when that player was required to switch roles. But Brewster was unhappy at not being the first-choice centre-half. In November 1922, after playing in the first five games of the season before being dropped, he signed for Wolverhampton Wanderers. From there he moved to Lovells' Athletic and Wallasey United, coached Brooklands Athletic in New York, then became player-manager of Inverness.

	LEAGUE		*FA CUP*		*TOTAL*	
	App	*Gls*	*App*	*Gls*	*App*	*Gls*
1919-20	5	0	0	0	5	0
1920-21	29	0	4	0	33	0
1921-22	25	3	0	0	25	3
1922-23	5	1	0	0	5	1
	64	4	4	0	68	4

GEORGE BREWSTER

Cliff Britton was a footballing genius who was later to turn his considerable talents to the even more demanding task of management. Extraordinarily gifted, he was a cultured wing-half whose passing ability was second to none. He began his lengthy and hugely successful career in local football in his native Bristol. He signed professional forms for Bristol Rovers in 1926 and was transferred to Everton four years later. On his arrival at Goodison Park he was considered too lightweight to deal with the rough and tumble of a central position and was played at outside-right in the Central League side. Once he made the breakthrough into League football he never looked back and he was in the side in 1933 when the FA Cup was lifted at the expense of Manchester City. He made his England debut in 1934, against Wales, and went on to win nine full caps. He appeared only once in the 1938-9 title-winning side but was a player, and something of an advisor, to the reserve squad. During World War Two his career enjoyed a revival and he won 12 wartime caps, forming a fine England half-back line with Joe Mercer and Stan Cullis.

	LEAGUE		*FA CUP*		*TOTAL*	
	App	*Gls*	*App*	*Gls*	*App*	*Gls*
1930-31	10	0	0	0	10	0
1932-33	36	0	6	0	42	0
1933-34	42	0	1	0	43	0
1934-35	36	0	5	0	41	0
1935-36	25	2	1	0	26	2
1936-37	40	0	4	1	44	1
1937-38	31	0	2	0	33	0
1938-39	1	0	0	0	1	0
	221	2	19	1	240	3

CLIFF BRITTON

Alex 'Sandy' Brown was brought to Goodison in the wake of the 1963 Championship win. He had impressed Harry Catterick with a series of sterling displays for Partick Thistle and the Everton boss was quick to snap him up for £38,000 when the opportunity arose in September of that year. He was a real utility man, a defender who could move forward to stamp his authority on midfield. He could even play in goal and his versatility led to him being named substitute in no less than 33 League games. During the opening minutes of a bad-tempered encounter with Leeds United at Goodison in the mid-1960s, he was sent off and the referee was later forced to lead both teams from the field for a cooling-down period. Brown played in four ties in Everton's FA Cup-winning year of 1966 but missed the Final itself. He made 36 appearances (five as substitute) as a full-back in the Championship season, 1969-70. After joining Shrewsbury in 1971 he moved to Southport and played in their 1972-3 Fourth Division championship side. In the summer of 1973 he signed for Northern Premier League club Fleetwood.

	LEAGUE		*FACUP*		*FLCUP*		*EUROPE*		*TOTAL*	
	App	*Gls*	*App*	*Gls*	*App*	*Gls*	*App*	*Gls*	*App*	*Gls*
1963-64	30	0	5	0	-	-	0	0	35	0
1964-65	28	5	1	0	-	-	4	0	33	5
1965-66	14/2	0	4	0	-	-	1	0	19/2	0
1966-67	15/5	1	1/3	0	-	-	1	1	17/8	2
1967-68	12/13	1	0/2	0	2	1	-	-	14/15	2
1968-69	40	1	5	0	4	0	-	-	49	1
1969-70	31/5	0	0/1	0	4	0	-	-	35/6	0
1970-71	6/8	1	0/2	0	0	0	0/2	0	6/12	1
	176/33	9	16/8	0	10	1	6/2	1	208/43	11

SANDY BROWN

WILLIAM BROWN

William Brown was a product of a famous Scottish nursery, Cambuslang. He was a member of Everton's classic half-back line of the early 1920s and won national recognition for his cultured, patient displays. By trade he was an engineer's fitter but he had always dreamt of a career in football and did not hesitate to sign when offered a contract in 1913. He was only 17 when he made his First Division debut against Manchester City in December the following year. He was transferred to Nottingham Forest for what was diplomatically described as a 'nominal fee' in May 1928. Even in his later years he proved to be a useful wing-half with a flair for goalscoring. In August 1930 he was appointed player-coach of Liverpool Cables FC.

	LEAGUE		*FA CUP*		*TOTAL*	
	App	*Gls*	*App*	*Gls*	*App*	*Gls*
1914-15	4	0	0	0	4	0
1919-20	20	0	1	0	21	0
1920-21	10	0	0	0	10	0
1921-22	16	0	1	0	17	0
1922-23	8	0	2	0	10	0
1923-24	37	0	2	0	39	0
1924-25	20	0	3	0	23	0
1925-26	28	0	0	0	28	0
1926-27	25	0	0	0	25	0
1927-28	2	0	0	0	2	0
	170	0	9	0	179	0

TED BUCKLE

Ted Buckle was a Londoner who joined Everton from Manchester United in November 1949. A brash, bold winger with a lightning turn of speed, he quickly developed into a player of real class and quality. Less than 18 hours after completing his move from Old Trafford he made his debut — against United. His compelling flank play was one of the main reasons for Everton's remarkable FA Cup run in 1953. Inspired by his greyhound-like pace, the side reached the semi-finals only to be beaten, rather unfortunately, 4-3 by Bolton Wanderers at Maine Road. He was transferred to Exeter City in June 1955 after 107 League and Cup games. In the 1960s, at the age of 35, he took over as player-manager at Welsh League club Prestatyn. He was forced to resign less than 12 months later due to business commitments.

	LEAGUE		*FA CUP*		*TOTAL*	
	App	*Gls*	*App*	*Gls*	*App*	*Gls*
1949-50	26	6	5	2	31	8
1950-51	22	5	0	0	22	5
1951-52	15	12	1	0	16	12
1952-53	14	5	4	0	18	5
1953-54	19	3	0	0	19	3
1954-55	1	0	0	0	1	0
	97	31	10	2	107	33

Mick Buckley had the football world very much at his feet during the early days of his career. A schoolboy star in his home town of Manchester, he received offers from both City and United but surprised everyone by opting for Everton. His small frame belied his naturally aggressive instincts and he developed into a terrier-like midfielder, respected throughout the game for his totally professional attitude. Buckley fought his way through the ranks to claim a first-team spot in 1971-2 at the age of 18. He made two appearances for England Under-23s and was a member of the England Youth side that carried off the 'Little World Cup' in Spain in 1972. He lost his Everton place to Trevor Ross in 1977 after injury and was loaned to Queen's Park Rangers for a month, along with full-back Neil Robinson, at the start of the following season. He was transferred to Sunderland in 1978 but, despite his 100 per cent efforts, the going was far from smooth in the North-East. He recovered from a bad start at Roker Park to rescue the Wearsiders from relegation when he scored a vital goal against Manchester City on 15 May 1982. Shortly afterwards he left Sunderland and joined Carlisle.

MICK BUCKLEY

	LEAGUE		*FA CUP*		*FL CUP*		*EUROPE*		*TOTAL*	
	App	*Gls*	*App*	*Gls*	*App*	*Gls*	*App*	*Gls*	*App*	*Gls*
1971-72	6	1	0	0	0	0	-	-	6	1
1972-73	9	1	2	1	0	0	-	-	11	2
1973-74	33	3	3	0	2	1	-	-	38	4
1974-75	31/2	2	0	0	2	0	-	-	33/2	2
1975-76	30/1	1	0	0	5	0	2	0	37/1	1
1976-77	7/4	0	2	0	0	0	-	-	9/4	0
1977-78	12	2	0	0	3	0	-	-	15	2
	128/7	10	7	1	12	1	2	0	149/7	12

A native of Blackburn, Edgar Chadwick was one of the great names of football in the 1890s. His first senior club was Blackburn Olympic and he had one season with Blackburn Rovers before signing for Everton in the summer of 1888, in time for the Football League's inaugural season. An inside-left of enormous talent, he was quick and cunning and he passed the ball accurately and shot hard and often. His left-wing partnership with Alf Milward was probably the best in the League, with both men able to read the other's game with uncanny accuracy. Chadwick was a lightweight — he stood 5ft 6in and weighed 10st 7lb — but that never stopped him from being in the thick of the action. He won seven England caps, scoring after 30 seconds against Scotland in 1892. He won a League Championship medal with Everton, and a Southern League Championship medal with Southampton, but played on the losing side in three FA Cup Finals (with Everton in 1893 and 1897, and Southampton in 1902). He played for the Football League against the Scottish League and the Football Alliance and was reputed to be the first Englishman to coach abroad when he worked with teams in Holland and Germany before pursuing his trade as a baker in Blackburn. His cousin, Arthur Chadwick, lived in his shadow at Goodison and managed only five League games in five years before moving to Portsmouth where his career finally blossomed and he was capped for England. Edgar Chadwick died in Blackburn in February 1942, aged 73.

EDGAR CHADWICK

	LEAGUE		*FA CUP*		*TOTAL*	
	App	*Gls*	*App*	*Gls*	*App*	*Gls*
1888-89	22	6	0	0	22	6
1889-90	22	9	2	0	24	9
1890-91	22	10	1	0	23	10
1891-92	25	10	1	1	26	11
1892-93	27	10	7	3	34	13
1893-94	24	13	0	0	24	13
1894-95	28	11	4	3	32	14
1895-96	28	11	3	1	31	12
1896-97	28	7	5	2	33	9
1897-98	22	8	5	2	27	10
1898-99	22	2	2	1	24	3
	270	97	30	13	300	110

Sam Chedgzoy was the man directly responsible for a major change in the game's laws. An intelligent man who was never scared to challenge authority, he discovered a glaring loophole in the laws and proceeded to exploit it during a match at White Hart Lane in 1924. A new rule had been introduced so that a goal could be scored direct from a corner. Chedgzoy took a corner by dribbling along the by-line as members of both sides looked on in astonishment. They saw Chedgzoy hammer the ball into the net and score a goal which led to a rule change. Twelve months later football's embarrassed hierarchy introduced a rule whereby the taker of a corner could only play the ball once before a second player had touched it. Chedgzoy was born in Ellesmere Port in 1890 and initially played for Burnell's Ironworks alongside Joe Mercer's father. His lengthy career as an industrious outside-right saw him win a League Championship medal in 1914-15. On retirement, he went to Canada where he died in 1967. He made eight appearances for England between 1920 and 1925 and he had a son, also called Sam, who also joined Everton.

	LEAGUE		*FA CUP*		*TOTAL*	
	App	*Gls*	*App*	*Gls*	*App*	*Gls*
1910-11	3	0	0	0	3	0
1912-13	1	0	0	0	1	0
1913-14	7	1	0	0	7	1
1914-15	30	2	5	1	35	3
1919-20	18	3	1	0	19	3
1920-21	35	5	5	0	40	5
1921-22	35	5	1	0	36	5
1922-23	36	3	2	1	38	4
1923-24	38	5	2	1	40	6
1924-25	38	2	3	0	41	2
1925-26	38	7	2	0	40	7
	279	33	21	3	300	36

SAM CHEDGZOY

Dave Clements was one of Everton's most intelligent and erudite footballers. He became Billy Bingham's first signing when he joined from Sheffield Wednesday for £60,000 in September 1973. He won the great majority of his Northern Ireland caps as a midfield player, although he began as a winger in Wolves' reserve team. He moved to Coventry City for £1,000 in 1964 in what proved to be Stan Cullis' last deal, and it was while at Highfield Road that he was developed into a half-back of some consequence. He played 227 League games for Coventry, scoring 26 goals, before moving to Hillsborough in August 1971 in a £100,000 deal involving Brian Joicey. The Yorkshire side moved him to the full-back berth, but it was at Goodison that he matured into an influential midfielder with a game based on accurate passing. On 18 March 1975, while playing for Everton at Middlesbrough, he learned that he had been appointed manager of Northern Ireland. While still in charge of the national side he joined the star-studded New York Cosmos in January 1976 and went on to play with the legendary Pelé. His decision to play in America cost him his job as manager of his country.

	LEAGUE		*FA CUP*		*FL CUP*		*EUROPE*		*TOTAL*	
	App	*Gls*	*App*	*Gls*	*App*	*Gls*	*App*	*Gls*	*App*	*Gls*
1973-74	31	3	2	1	2	0	-	-	35	4
1974-75	39/1	1	4	1	2	0	-	-	45/1	2
1975-76	11/1	2	0	0	4	0	0/1	0	15/2	2
	81/2	6	6	2	8	0	0/1	0	95/3	8

DAVE CLEMENTS

When Everton signed Joe Clennell from Blackburn Rovers in January 1914 they found the balance that had for some time been lacking in their attack. He scored on his debut, against Aston Villa, and showed supporters enough skill to help them understand why he had been bought. Thereafter he was a regular fixture in the League side and on the opening day of the following season he netted a hat-trick as Everton began with a 3-1 win at White Hart Lane. It was the signal for a successful assault on the League Championship and Clennell continued to play a full part. He was one of several new signings which were to help Everton to their first title success for 24 years and, with Sam Chedgzoy and George Harrison, he threatened to run riot as Everton headed towards a possible League and Cup double. They failed in the Cup semi-final but Clennell could still be well pleased with his efforts. In wartime football he really excelled, scoring 114 goals in only 104 games. When the League resumed in 1919 he continued to score regularly until he was injured. The following season he played only once before moving to Cardiff City in October 1921. Clennell played for the Football League in 1920.

	LEAGUE		*FA CUP*		*TOTAL*	
	App	*Gls*	*App*	*Gls*	*App*	*Gls*
1913-14	12	4	0	0	12	4
1914-15	36	14	5	3	41	17
1919-20	18	12	1	0	19	12
1920-21	1	0	0	0	1	0
1921-22	1	0	0	0	1	0
	68	30	6	3	74	33

JOE CLENNELL

Thomas Clinton was the man who signed for Everton under perhaps the most unusual circumstances in the club's history. The young Irishman had been recommended by a local scout, and secretary Theo Kelly travelled to Ireland to discuss terms. As they chatted on the platform at Dundalk station, Clinton's train began to move out and he actually put pen to paper while hanging out of a lowered carriage window. He was the rugged type of full-back when he eventually landed at Goodison Park and Central League wingers soon found that they bred them tough in Eire. He made his League debut against Burnley on 26 February 1949, staying for a further seven years. He missed a penalty in the 1953 FA Cup semi-final against Bolton at Maine Road. In 1955 he was transferred to Blackburn.

	LEAGUE		*FA CUP*		*TOTAL*	
	App	*Gls*	*App*	*Gls*	*App*	*Gls*
1948-49	4	0	0	0	4	0
1950-51	15	0	0	0	15	0
1951-52	26	4	2	0	28	4
1952-53	22	0	5	1	27	1
1953-54	6	0	0	0	6	0
	73	4	7	1	80	5

THOMAS CLINTON

JACK COCK

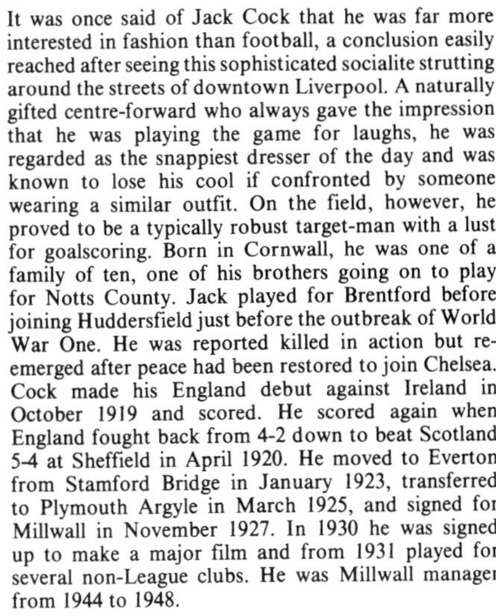

It was once said of Jack Cock that he was far more interested in fashion than football, a conclusion easily reached after seeing this sophisticated socialite strutting around the streets of downtown Liverpool. A naturally gifted centre-forward who always gave the impression that he was playing the game for laughs, he was regarded as the snappiest dresser of the day and was known to lose his cool if confronted by someone wearing a similar outfit. On the field, however, he proved to be a typically robust target-man with a lust for goalscoring. Born in Cornwall, he was one of a family of ten, one of his brothers going on to play for Notts County. Jack played for Brentford before joining Huddersfield just before the outbreak of World War One. He was reported killed in action but re-emerged after peace had been restored to join Chelsea. Cock made his England debut against Ireland in October 1919 and scored. He scored again when England fought back from 4-2 down to beat Scotland 5-4 at Sheffield in April 1920. He moved to Everton from Stamford Bridge in January 1923, transferred to Plymouth Argyle in March 1925, and signed for Millwall in November 1927. In 1930 he was signed up to make a major film and from 1931 played for several non-League clubs. He was Millwall manager from 1944 to 1948.

	LEAGUE		*FA CUP*		*TOTAL*	
	App	*Gls*	*App*	*Gls*	*App*	*Gls*
1922-23	15	9	0	0	15	9
1923-24	35	15	2	2	37	17
1924-25	19	5	1	0	20	5
	69	29	3	2	72	31

BILLY COGGINS

Billy Coggins joined Everton from Bristol City in 1930 and made his debut in the crushing defeat by Grimsby Town, a reversal which condemned the Goodison side to Second Division football. When he arrived at the club, the only other goalkeeper on the books was Ted Sagar, then nothing more than another teenage hopeful. Coggins played in every game as Everton swept majestically to the Second Division title in 1931 but the following season Sagar stepped out of the shadows to launch his famous career. After sitting disconsolately on the sidelines for the best part of 12 months, Coggins left to play for Queen's Park Rangers and Bath City before retiring to his native Bristol. He died, aged 56, at West Town, Somerset, in July 1958.

	LEAGUE		*FA CUP*		*TOTAL*	
	App	*Gls*	*App*	*Gls*	*App*	*Gls*
1929-30	6	0	0	0	6	0
1930-31	42	0	5	0	47	0
1931-32	1	0	0	0	1	0
1933-34	2	0	0	0	2	0
	51	0	5	0	56	0

Without any doubt Bobby Collins was one of the finest inside-forwards of the last 50 years. This diminutive man — he stood only 5ft 4in and weighed 10st 3lb — was the heartbeat of every side he played for, fully justifying his nickname 'the Little General'. He joined Everton straight from Scottish junior soccer during the reign of Theo Kelly, but returned north to sign for Celtic after confessing that he was desperately homesick. In 1951 he made his international debut against Wales and seven years later he rejoined Everton, for £39,000. He made his debut only hours after signing, scoring a goal in the 3-1 win at Maine Road. He scored seven League goals in his first season and in the next he was top marksman with 14 in 42 games and continued to find the net throughout his time with Everton. Many experts thought his career had taken a nosedive when he surprisingly signed for Leeds United for £30,000, but in many respects it was only the beginning. He helped steer a side which seemed destined to drop into Division Three back on to the straight and narrow, and by 1965 the Yorkshire club had won promotion and dramatically missed out on a League and Cup double. Collins won a recall to the Scotland side but broke a thigh bone in a bruising Fairs Cup match in Turin. It was typical of the man that he fought back to play first-team football again. He left Elland Road to join Bury on a free transfer in 1967 and from there moved to Morton. He travelled the world as a coach, taking up appointments in Australia and South Africa. In October 1972, at the age of 41, he joined Oldham Athletic as player-coach. He went on to manage Hull City before moving to Blackpool as coach in 1978. Collins also managed Huddersfield Town and Barnsley. He left Oakwell in 1985.

BOBBY COLLINS

	LEAGUE		*FA CUP*		*FL CUP*		*TOTAL*	
	App	*Gls*	*App*	*Gls*	*App*	*Gls*	*App*	*Gls*
1958-59	32	7	4	3	-	-	36	10
1959-60	42	14	1	0	-	-	43	14
1960-61	40	16	1	0	5	1	46	17
1961-62	19	5	3	2	-	-	22	7
	133	42	9	5	5	1	147	48

A talented if inconsistent winger, John Connolly twice fought his way back from the heartbreak of a broken leg. He cost Everton £75,000 when Harry Catterick raised himself from his sickbed to complete a hastily-arranged deal with St Johnstone in March 1972. Connolly was a direct sort of player, more than willing to take on a full-back. He never really hit it off with Catterick's successor, Billy Bingham, and was placed on the transfer list at his own request before the start of the 1976-7 season. He finally won his battle to leave Goodison in September 1976 when he joined up with former teammates Howard Kendall and Gary Jones at Birmingham City in a £90,000 deal. He did not last long at St Andrew's and was transferred to Newcastle United. In September 1980 he moved to Hibernian.

JOHN CONNOLLY

	LEAGUE		*FA CUP*		*FL CUP*		*TOTAL*	
	App	*Gls*	*App*	*Gls*	*App*	*Gls*	*App*	*Gls*
1971-72	2	0	0	0	0	0	2	0
1972-73	41	7	2	0	1	0	44	7
1973-74	26	5	0	0	1	0	27	5
1974-75	22/2	3	1	0	2	0	25/2	3
1975-76	14/1	1	0/1	0	0	0	14/2	1
	105/3	16	3/1	0	4	0	112/4	16

Billy Cook is one of the élite band of players to have won both a Scottish Cup winners' medal (with Celtic in 1931) and an FA Cup winners' medal (Everton 1933). An Irish international right-back, he joined Everton from Celtic for £3,000 in December 1932. In a Goodison career which spanned eight years he played nearly 250 senior games and was described at the time as a 'grand and whole-hearted' player. He joined Wrexham in October 1945, and after inconclusive talks with Ellesmere Port moved to Rhyl as player-manager 12 months later. In February 1948 he was appointed Sunderland coach and four years later moved to, of all places, Peru after being appointed coach to the Peruvian FA in Lima. He spent a considerable amount of time coaching in Norway before being appointed Wigan Athletic manager in succession to Ron Suart in late 1966. By the turn of the decade he was at Norwich as player-coach.

BILLY COOK

	LEAGUE		*FA CUP*		*TOTAL*	
	App	*Gls*	*App*	*Gls*	*App*	*Gls*
1932-33	20	0	6	0	26	0
1933-34	35	0	1	0	36	0
1934-35	29	0	5	0	34	0
1935-36	25	0	1	0	26	0
1936-37	41	0	4	0	45	0
1937-38	35	0	2	0	37	0
1938-39	40	5	5	1	45	6
	225	5	24	1	249	6

Colin Harvey's prolonged search for a forward capable of combining skill and a natural predatory instinct ended in the summer of 1988 when he beat off the challenge of Arsenal to sign Tony Cottee from West Ham United for £2.2 million — a British transfer record fee at the time. Cottee quickly settled into a talented, if inconsistent, side and marked his debut with a magnificent hat-trick against Newcastle United on the opening day of the season. Although his new teammates were often guilty of not playing to his particular strengths, Cottee confounded his critics by emerging as Everton's leading marksman in each of his first three seasons at Goodison Park. Despite his fine scoring record, Cottee constantly found himself at odds with his manager and in August of 1989 he was fined £5,000 after refusing to play in a reserve team fixture against Coventry City at Highland Road. An old-fashioned 'poacher' in the Bob Latchford mould, he played in both the 1989 FA and Simod Cup finals.

TONY COTTEE

	LEAGUE		*FA CUP*		*FL CUP*		*EUROPE*		*TOTAL*	
	App	*Gls*	*App*	*Gls*	*App*	*Gls*	*App*	*Gls*	*App*	*Gls*
1988-89	35/1	13	8	0	5	2	-	-	48/1	15
1989-90	25/2	13	3/2	2	1/2	0	-	-	29/6	15
1990-91	20/9	10	1/3	2	3	4	-	-	24/12	16
1991-92	17/7	8	1/1	0	3/1	1	-	-	21/9	9
1992-93	25/1	12	0	0	2/1	1	-	-	27/2	13
	122/20	56	13/6	4	14/4	8	-	-	149/30	68

Jackie Coulter was a winger of undoubted craft and skill, a born footballer. He was completely unorthodox when in possession and used to enjoy toying with opposition full-backs before speeding past them on his way to the by-line. He was far more adventurous than the vast majority of wingers of the day and amassed a very respectable goal tally. He was born and raised in Belfast, learning his football with Cliftonville before joining the highly-rated Belfast Celtic. From there he joined Everton in 1934 for £3,000. He became established immediately, along with players like Dixie Dean and Billy Cook, and proved a crowd-pleaser. He was a first-team regular until he broke a leg playing for Northern Ireland against Wales at Wrexham. He never fully recovered and was transferred to Grimsby Town late in 1937. Coulter went on to play for Swansea and non-League Chelmsford before retiring. He died in Belfast in January 1981.

	LEAGUE		*FA CUP*		*TOTAL*	
	App	*Gls*	*App*	*Gls*	*App*	*Gls*
1933-34	3	0	0	0	3	0
1934-35	24	11	5	6	29	17
1936-37	21	5	3	2	24	7
1937-38	2	0	0	0	2	0
	50	16	8	8	58	24

JACKIE COULTER

Though a Liverpool man, Jack Crelley was signed from Millwall Athletic in 1899, one of many young North-West footballers recruited by Southern League clubs. Crelley was a sturdy defender and he formed a fine full-back partnership with Walter Balmer. He played left-back in the successful 1906 FA Cup Final team, but missed out a year later when Robert Balmer was selected to partner his elder brother in another Final. Even then, Crelley might have played because there were doubts about Walter Balmer until just before the game at the Crystal Palace. Crelley was a strong-tackling full-back who stood 5ft 9in and weighed 12st. His stay at Millwall was a short one and he played his best football at Everton. He made 127 first-team appearances before moving to Exeter City in 1907.

	LEAGUE		*FA CUP*		*TOTAL*	
	App	*Gls*	*App*	*Gls*	*App*	*Gls*
1899-1900	1	0	0	0	1	0
1900-01	1	0	0	0	1	0
1902-03	18	0	1	0	19	0
1903-04	29	0	1	0	30	0
1904-05	26	0	6	0	32	0
1905-06	23	0	3	0	26	0
1906-07	15	0	0	0	15	0
1907-08	3	0	0	0	3	0
	116	0	11	0	127	0

JACK CRELLEY

WARNEY CRESSWELL

Warney Cresswell was one of the classiest defenders ever to pull on a pair of football boots. He was the forerunner of the modern style of full-back with a superb sense of both position and timing. He was a fast mover and thinker who could quickly marshall the men in front of him. When he kicked the ball forward, it usually landed exactly where he wanted it. He had the gift of anticipation, constantly astounding forwards by turning up in crucial positions even before the ball had been delivered. Defensively he was not for the full-blooded tackle but preferred to jockey his opponents into impossible positions. His move from South Shields to Sunderland in 1922 for £5,500 was a British record. Strangely, he played for England only seven times in a career which spanned nine years and three clubs. He joined Everton in February 1927, staying with them until 1936. In all, he made more than 500 appearances for South Shields, Sunderland and Everton. After his playing days were over, he moved into management with Port Vale and Northampton. He died in his native North-East in 1973.

	LEAGUE		*FA CUP*		*TOTAL*	
	App	*Gls*	*App*	*Gls*	*App*	*Gls*
1926-27	15	0	0	0	15	0
1927-28	36	0	2	0	38	0
1928-29	32	1	1	0	33	1
1929-30	30	0	0	0	30	0
1930-31	42	0	5	0	47	0
1931-32	40	0	0	0	40	0
1932-33	41	0	6	0	47	0
1933-34	25	0	1	0	26	0
1934-35	25	0	1	0	26	0
1935-36	4	0	0	0	4	0
	290	1	16	0	306	1

Ted Critchley was the flamboyant outside-right who provided much of the ammunition for Dixie Dean. He was discovered playing in junior football in his native Stockport and transferred to Everton from Stockport County for a nominal fee in 1926. He succeeded Sam Chedgzoy wide on the right and proved to be an admirable replacement with his deft control and quick turn of speed. He was a key member of the 1927-8 Championship-winning side and was instrumental in helping Dean set his unsurpassable record of 60 League goals in one season. In an Everton career which spanned eight years, he had two quite remarkable FA Cup experiences. He was ruled out of the 1931 semi-final against West Brom through injury and, when the club reached the last four two years later, he had been dropped in favour of Albert Geldard. At the last minute Geldard was forced to drop out and in stepped Critchley. With just minutes remaining and the game deadlocked at 1-1, he forced West Ham defender Jim Barnett into conceding an own-goal to set up a Wembley showdown with Manchester City. Geldard was fit for the Final, which Everton won 3-0, so Critchley missed out. One year later he signed for Preston.

TED CRITCHLEY

	LEAGUE		*FA CUP*		*TOTAL*	
	App	*Gls*	*App*	*Gls*	*App*	*Gls*
1926-27	15	0	0	0	15	0
1927-28	40	6	2	0	42	6
1928-29	25	1	0	0	25	1
1929-30	30	4	2	2	32	6
1930-31	37	13	4	2	41	15
1931-32	37	8	1	0	38	8
1932-33	17	2	2	1	19	3
1933-34	16	3	1	0	17	3
	217	37	12	5	229	42

CHARLIE CROSSLEY

Signed from Sunderland in 1920, Charlie Crossley had only one full season in the Everton first-team, but he made his mark by being leading scorer with 15 League goals and forming, with George Harrison, a dynamic left-wing pairing. Crossley, who was born in Walsall, had an unusually 'top-heavy' build with broad shoulders but generally of small stature. A foraging inside-left, his star waned after that first season and in 1921-2 he was in and out of the team. In June 1922, Everton sold him to West Ham United and he played 14 times in their side which won promotion to Division One in 1922-3. But he could not find a place in the Hammers team which reached the first Wembley FA Cup Final that same season.

	LEAGUE		*FA CUP*		*TOTAL*	
	App	*Gls*	*App*	*Gls*	*App*	*Gls*
1920-21	35	15	5	3	40	18
1921-22	15	3	0	0	15	3
	50	18	5	3	55	21

JIMMY CUNLIFFE

James 'Nat' Cunliffe will forever be remembered as the man who played alongside the legendary Dixie Dean. But for the great Dean and his all-encompassing brilliance, the youngster from Blackrod, Lancashire, would almost certainly have made an even bigger impact in the famous Everton side of the early 1930s. He arrived at Goodison from Adlington FC in 1930 after quitting his job as an apprentice plater. After three years in the 'A' and Central League sides he finally got his big break in 1933 when he played two senior games, against Aston Villa (scoring on his debut) and Middlesbrough. His chance to stake a regular first-team spot came in his second season when he stood in at centre-forward for the injured Dean. When the fearsome striker returned to the side Cunliffe kept his place, being moved to inside-right. An exceptional ball-player with two good feet, he proved to be extremely versatile and filled every forward position except outside-right. He twice scored four goals in a game, against Stoke and West Brom. His most memorable contribution to the Everton cause was in 1935 when he snatched a dramatic equaliser in a Cup tie at Roker Park. Everton went on to win the replay against Sunderland 6-4 with Cunliffe producing a virtuoso performance which went a long way to him winning his solitary England cap against Belgium.

	LEAGUE		*FA CUP*		*TOTAL*	
	App	*Gls*	*App*	*Gls*	*App*	*Gls*
1932-33	2	1	0	0	2	1
1933-34	27	9	1	0	28	9
1934-35	39	15	5	2	44	17
1935-36	37	23	1	0	38	23
1936-37	28	9	4	1	32	10
1937-38	34	13	2	0	36	13
1938-39	7	3	0	0	7	3
	174	73	13	3	187	76

Terry Darracott is one of the most genuine and well-loved characters Merseyside football has ever produced. Although he never really hit the heights as a player, he was worth his presence for the sheer impact of his personality on the players around him. A local lad, he first experienced Division One life against Arsenal in April 1968 while still an apprentice. After struggling to hold down a regular place, he was offered the post of youth team coach by Gordon Lee in 1979 but turned it down and moved to NASL club Tulsa Roughnecks. From there he signed for Wrexham and then went to Prescot as player-coach in February 1984. His overwhelming desire to return to the big time was rewarded when he was appointed reserve team coach at Everton three months later. In November 1985 he became assistant to his former Everton teammate Mike Lyons at Grimsby but eight months later resigned to rejoin the Goodison coaching staff. Following Colin Harvey's appointment, Darracott was promoted to managerial assistant. He was sacked following the return of Howard Kendall to Goodison Park in November 1990 but linked up with another Everton old-boy, Peter Reid, at Manchester City just three months later.

	LEAGUE		*FA CUP*		*FL CUP*		*EUROPE*		*TOTAL*	
	App	*Gls*	*App*	*Gls*	*App*	*Gls*	*App*	*Gls*	*App*	*Gls*
1967-68	1	0	0	0	0	0	-	-	1	0
1968-69	1	0	0	0	0	0	-	-	1	0
1970-71	2	0	0	0	0	0	0	0	2	0
1971-72	16/1	0	2	0	1	0	-	-	19/1	0
1972-73	11/5	0	0	0	0	0	-	-	11/5	0
1973-74	36	0	3	0	2	0	-	-	41	0
1974-75	5	0	0	0	0	0	-	-	5	0
1975-76	20	0	1	0	1	0	0	0	22	0
1976-77	20/3	0	4	0	5	0	-	-	29/3	0
1977-78	19/1	0	1	0	2	0	-	-	22/1	0
1978-79	7	0	1	0	1	0	4	0	13	0
	138/10	0	12	0	12	0	4	0	166/10	0

TERRY DARRACOTT

Dai Davies was a natural successor to Gordon West when he signed from Swansea City in a deal worth £20,000 in late December 1970. The only thing the genial six-footer valued more than his ability to thwart opposing forwards was his Welsh heritage. He had never played on the losing side as a professional before his move to Merseyside (he made nine appearances for Swansea) but, despite his near-perfect goalkeeping physique and his undoubted talent, he found the going tough. After spending four years in the shadow of West and his understudy David Lawson, during which time he made only two first-team appearances, Davies went back to Swansea on loan. The deal would almost certainly have been made permanent had the Welsh club been able to meet Everton's asking price. Davies eventually returned to Goodison and went on to make 94 first-team appearances before signing for Wrexham in September 1977 for £8,000. In his first season at The Racecourse, Wrexham suffered the lowest number of defeats in their history. In the 1978-9 Second Division campaign, Davies helped establish the club's best-ever League defensive record of only 42 goals conceded. He again returned to Swansea before joining Tranmere Rovers in June 1983. He played 52 times for Wales, breaking Jack Kelsey's long-standing record of 41 Welsh goalkeeping caps in May 1981 when he appeared in a British Championship match against Scotland.

	LEAGUE		*FA CUP*		*FL CUP*		*EUROPE*		*TOTAL*	
	App	*Gls*	*App*	*Gls*	*App*	*Gls*	*App*	*Gls*	*App*	*Gls*
1970-71	2	0	0	0	0	0	0	0	2	0
1974-75	35	0	4	0	0	0	-	-	39	0
1975-76	19	0	1	0	2	0	1	0	23	0
1976-77	26	0	0	0	4	0	-	-	30	0
	82	0	5	0	6	0	1	0	94	0

DAI DAVIES

DIXIE DEAN

Dixie Dean was arguably the greatest goalscoring machine that football has ever known. A larger than life, 'Roy of the Rovers' character, Dean carved for himself a very special niche in Merseyside sporting folklore. A positive giant of a man in both physique and application, Dean was years ahead of his time and, in many respects, the complete footballer. Typifying the robust, single-minded centre-forward of the day, he struck sheer terror into the hearts of defenders who were handed the unenviable task of stopping the man with the no-nonsense, never-say-die attitude. Arguably the most lethal header of a ball in the history of the game, Dean could achieve absolutely anything in the air when provided with the right service. After making his League debut for Tranmere Rovers in January 1924, he notched up 27 goals in 27 games for the Prenton Park club the following season before being lured across the River Mersey to Goodison Park. His scoring feats while wearing the royal blue of Everton are legendary. In his first full season he scored 32 goals in 38 appearances, but the pinnacle of his career was reached in 1927-8 when he logged the unsurpassable total of 60 League goals in only 39 games. A measure of his indomitable spirit was his recovery from a bad road accident in 1926. In June that year he fractured his skull and jaw in a motorcycle crash, yet on 23 October he returned to score at Leeds and help Everton to only their second win of the season. He severed his ties with Everton in 1938 when he moved to Notts County where he played only nine games, scoring three goals. He signed for Irish club Sligo Rovers in 1939 and, between January and May, played in 11 matches and scored 11 goals, thus maintaining the consistency he applied to goalscoring throughout his illustrious career in whatever standard of football he played. When he was demobbed after the war, Dean took over a pub in Chester called the Dublin Packet. Here he quite literally hung up his boots, together with his many trophies, and stayed for 15 years. Christened William Ralph, he disliked the nickname 'Dixie'. He became a popular after-dinner speaker, filling halls and clubs wherever he appeared. Dean, who scored 349 goals for Everton and won 16 England caps, had his right leg amputated in 1976 after a long illness. It was somewhat fitting that he died at his beloved Goodison Park in March 1980, minutes after the final whistle of an Everton-Liverpool derby match.

	LEAGUE		*FA CUP*		*TOTAL*	
	App	*Gls*	*App*	*Gls*	*App*	*Gls*
1924-25	7	2	0	0	7	2
1925-26	38	32	2	1	40	33
1926-27	27	21	4	3	31	24
1927-28	39	60	2	3	41	63
1928-29	29	26	1	0	30	26
1929-30	25	23	2	2	27	25
1930-31	37	39	5	9	42	48
1931-32	38	45	1	1	39	46
1932-33	39	24	6	5	45	29
1933-34	12	9	0	0	12	9
1934-35	38	26	5	1	43	27
1935-36	29	17	0	0	29	17
1936-37	36	24	4	3	40	27
1937-38	5	1	0	0	5	1
	399	349	32	28	431	377

When he moved to Goodison Park in August 1974 for £300,000, Martin Dobson set a new British transfer record. After making 200 appearances for Burnley and picking up three England caps, he opted for a move into the big time, choosing Everton from a whole pack of would-be buyers. It took him a considerable length of time to settle into his new role — one of the major reasons being the enormous price tag which weighed heavily around his shoulders. He started his career as a centre-forward and went to Bolton as a professional but was eventually handed a free transfer. He considered giving up the game but was persuaded to continue by his father. He joined Burnley as a front runner but eventually switched to midfield where he won massive acclaim and continued international recognition. Hugely skilful and with the ability to drift forward to create openings and goals out of next-to-nothing, he was an integral part of the Everton set-up between 1974 and 1979. He surprised the football world after five years at Goodison by returning to Burnley for £100,000. Tired of the pressures which inevitably envelope every top-flight club, he yearned for the more tranquil surroundings of Turf Moor. After failing to halt Burnley's slide towards lower division obscurity, Dobson took over as Bury's player-manager in 1984. He later served brief spells as manager of Northwich Victoria and Bristol Rovers.

	LEAGUE		*FA CUP*		*FL CUP*		*EUROPE*		*TOTAL*	
	App	*Gls*	*App*	*Gls*	*App*	*Gls*	*App*	*Gls*	*App*	*Gls*
1974-75	30	5	3	0	2	0	-	-	35	5
1975-76	42	5	1	0	5	1	2	0	50	6
1976-77	40	8	6	1	8	2	-	-	54	11
1977-78	38	7	2	0	4	1	0	0	44	8
1978-79	40	4	1	1	3	4	3	1	47	10
	190	29	13	2	22	8	5	1	230	40

MARTIN DOBSON

Ephraim Dodds, known to everyone as simply 'Jock', was an enormous, no-nonsense centre-forward who led the line with his own distinctive brand of robust football. It was said that he was so good in the air that centre-halves used to dread being handed the task of marking him. His career covered the pre-World War Two and post-war periods and although he was never to win a full Scottish cap he did play eight times for his country in wartime internationals. He was born at Grangemouth in 1915 and played junior football in Lanarkshire and Durham before joining the staff at Huddersfield Town at the age of 15. He joined Sheffield United on a free transfer two years later and topped the scoring list in four seasons with the Blades. He played in the 1936 FA Cup Final against Arsenal and was transferred to Blackpool for £10,000 in March 1939. Everton, with no Dean or Lawton, nor 'Bunny' Bell, struggled to find a centre-forward immediately after the war and they signed Dodds in November 1946. He served them with 36 goals in 56 League games before moving to Lincoln City in October 1948. By the time he retired he had scored well over 200 League goals.

	LEAGUE		*FA CUP*		*TOTAL*	
	App	*Gls*	*App*	*Gls*	*App*	*Gls*
1946-47	21	17	2	0	23	17
1947-48	27	13	1	1	28	14
1948-49	7	6	0	0	7	6
	55	36	3	1	58	37

EPHRAIM DODDS

One of an élite band of players who enjoyed two spells at Goodison Park, Joe Donnachie was a tricky winger with a deceptive turn of speed and widely acknowledged in his heyday as the finest far-post crosser of the ball in the English game. Quick into the tackle and difficult to dispossess, he was famous for his jinking runs down the flanks. A versatile player with a flair for the unusual, he played at both outside-left and outside-right for Scotland in three internationals between 1913 and 1915. Before World War One he played with Newcastle United, Everton and Oldham, but returned to Glasgow Rangers after the hostilities. He rejoined Everton and moved on to Blackpool before ending his playing days with Chester. He became a publican after retirement from football, running the Mariners' Arms Inn near Sealand Road. His son, Joe, was on Liverpool's books before he was killed in a World War Two flying accident.

	LEAGUE		*FA CUP*		*TOTAL*	
	App	*Gls*	*App*	*Gls*	*App*	*Gls*
1905-06	8	0	0	0	8	0
1906-07	13	0	2	0	15	0
1907-08	16	0	0	0	16	0
1908-09	3	0	0	0	3	0
1919-20	16	0	0	0	16	0
	56	0	2	0	58	0

JOE DONNACHIE

One of Everton's famous Irish 'colony' during the early 1950s, Don Donovan was discovered purely by chance during the summer of 1949 when the club were enjoying a close-season tour of Eire. Manager Cliff Britton and a small band of directors took an evening stroll in Cork and ended up watching a local amateur Cup tie. Donovan, whose first name, Donal, was shortened to Don by his Goodison Park team-mates, was playing at inside-right for Maymount Rovers and did enough to impress the watching English contingent. Britton immediately contacted the youngster's family and invited their talented son to join Everton's junior school. He began as an inside-forward with the 'B' team but developed at such pace that he soon graduated to the senior side. He was tried at wing-half and took to the new position like a natural. Exceptionally good in the air and commanding on the ground, he helped Everton gain promotion in 1953-4. He scored a quite spectacular goal from 35 yards when Everton, fighting against relegation in 1956, defeated Manchester United 5-2 at Old Trafford and so halted United's astonishing run of 26 League games without defeat. He was a full Republic of Ireland international and succeeded fellow countryman Peter Farrell as captain of Everton.

	LEAGUE		*FA CUP*		*TOTAL*	
	App	*Gls*	*App*	*Gls*	*App*	*Gls*
1951-52	22	0	2	0	24	0
1952-53	7	0	0	0	7	0
1953-54	42	0	2	0	44	0
1954-55	35	0	0	0	35	0
1955-56	8	1	0	0	8	1
1956-57	36	1	3	0	39	1
1957-58	29	0	1	0	30	0
	179	2	8	0	187	2

DON DONOVAN

DICKY DOWNS

Because of his ability at overhead kicks and other acrobatic feats, Dicky Downs was known as the 'India Rubber Man' during his three years with Everton. A very small man, he developed into one of the most influential full-backs of his day. He joined the club from Barnsley with whom he played in the 1910 and 1912 FA Cup Finals. In 1912, West Brom were firm favourites but the first game, at the Crystal Palace, ended in a goalless draw. Against all the odds, the Second Division side from South Yorkshire won the replay 1-0 after extra-time. Downs was one of the Barnsley stars but it was not until March 1920 that Everton secured his signature, for £3,000. He made the transition into a big-time player look remarkably easy, holding down a first-team spot until his departure for Brighton in 1923. Injury forced his retirement in 1924 and he later coached in Germany and Holland. He made one international appearance for England, against Ireland in 1920. Some claim that he was the inventor of the sliding tackle. His real name was John Thomas Downs, although he was always known as 'Dicky'.

	LEAGUE		*FA CUP*		*TOTAL*	
	App	*Gls*	*App*	*Gls*	*App*	*Gls*
1919-20	12	0	0	0	12	0
1920-21	40	0	5	0	45	0
1921-22	28	0	0	0	28	0
1922-23	9	0	0	0	9	0
1923-24	3	0	0	0	3	0
	92	0	5	0	97	0

GORDON DUGDALE

One of the unluckiest men ever to play professional football at the highest level, Gordon Dugdale was a brilliant left-back who seemingly had the world at his feet as his career reached its climax in the late 1940s. A superb ball-winner and distributor, he looked a certainty for England's 1950 World Cup team when he was compelled to give up the game he loved. A heart complaint, which had developed during his service in the Far East as a pilot in the Fleet Air Arm, suddenly recurred. Dugdale was deceptively fast and, at a time when full-backs were supposed to stay back, he constantly defied tradition by making sudden forays into attack. He joined Everton in 1947 on his demob from the Royal Navy. He was described at the time as looking 'more like a solicitor's clerk than a sportsman' because of his light build. He had played with Linacre School, Bootle Schoolboys and Lancashire Schoolboys. He once incurred the wrath of the legendary Ted Sagar when, in a game against Middlesbrough, he tried to chip the ball back but only succeeded in scoring an own-goal. In three seasons he managed only 58 League games. In 1952 he became a director of South Liverpool FC and 18 months later he stood as the Conservative candidate for the Low Hill ward but failed to unseat the Labour member. A genial man, he remained passionately interested in Everton's fortunes until the day he died at his Anfield home in May 1986, aged 62.

	LEAGUE		*FA CUP*		*TOTAL*	
	App	*Gls*	*App*	*Gls*	*App*	*Gls*
1947-48	19	0	4	0	23	0
1948-49	19	0	1	0	20	0
1949-50	20	0	0	0	20	0
	58	0	5	0	63	0

ALBERT DUNLOP

A dependable and reliable goalkeeper who never really managed to fulfil his rich potential, Dunlop joined Everton in 1949 at the age of 17 but had to wait seven years for his League debut. Then he endured a baptism of fire when he was thrust into the club's desperate fight to avoid relegation. He made his debut in front of more than 50,000 people at Old Trafford when Everton claimed the shock result of the season by ending Manchester United's unbeaten run of 26 League games with a conclusive 5-2 victory. His main attributes were a safe pair of hands and good vision. He managed to instil confidence into his defenders in much the same way Neville Southall does. While prone to the occasional error as a direct result of lack of concentration, he was an effective last line of defence and a larger-than-life character off the pitch. His personal life became something of a disaster after he quit the game in the late 1960s. In 1979 he was put on probation for two years after being found guilty of three charges of deception.

	LEAGUE		*FA CUP*		*FL CUP*		*TOTAL*	
	App	*Gls*	*App*	*Gls*	*App*	*Gls*	*App*	*Gls*
1956-57	29	0	3	0	-	-	32	0
1957-58	36	0	3	0	-	-	39	0
1958-59	33	0	4	0	-	-	37	0
1959-60	37	0	1	0	-	-	38	0
1960-61	42	0	1	0	5	0	48	0
1961-62	30	0	3	0	-	-	33	0
1962-63	4	0	0	0	-	-	4	0
	211	0	15	0	5	0	231	0

JIMMY DUNN

Watching Jimmy Dunn play football was said to be an emotional experience. He was a hugely gifted inside-forward with the passion and pace to leave experienced defenders rooted to the spot. He joined Everton from Hibernian in 1928, along with his right-wing partner Harry Ritchie, both players making their debut at Bolton in the opening game of the 1928-9 season. He won a Second Division championship medal, League Championship medal and FA Cup winners' medal in successive seasons. He scored the third goal in the 1933 FA Cup Final triumph over fancied Manchester City. Dunn remained at Goodison Park until 1935 when he was transferred to Exeter City. He later joined Cheshire County League side, Runcorn. He had three footballing sons, the most famous of which was Jimmy Dunn junior, who was an England and Liverpool schoolboy player and who also won an FA Cup winners' medal with Wolves against Leicester in 1949. Dunn senior made six appearances for Scotland and played in the famous 'Wembley Wizards' team of 1928 when Scotland trounced England 5-1.

	LEAGUE		*FA CUP*		*TOTAL*	
	App	*Gls*	*App*	*Gls*	*App*	*Gls*
1928-29	24	4	1	0	25	4
1929-30	12	0	1	0	13	0
1930-31	28	14	5	3	33	17
1931-32	22	10	0	0	22	10
1932-33	25	10	6	4	31	14
1933-34	23	4	1	0	24	4
1934-35	6	0	0	0	6	0
	140	42	14	7	154	49

As a youngster Peter Eastoe looked set for great things. Born in Tamworth, he was given an apprenticeship by Wolverhampton Wanderers and did so well that he won a string of England youth caps. But Wolves were well off for strikers with Derek Dougan, John Richards and Alan Sunderland all in the squad. That left little room for Eastoe and after only four League games he was allowed to join Swindon Town for £80,000. He realised his rich potential there, scoring an impressive 43 goals in 91 matches, before he was transferred to Queen's Park Rangers for £100,000 in March 1976. He was a member of the QPR side which went agonisingly close to taking the League Championship, but frequently found himself to be the odd man out. When he moved to Everton in an exchange deal involving Mick Walsh in 1979, he had managed only 56 League appearances in three years at Loftus Road. He was Everton's leading scorer in 1980-81 but moved to West Bromwich in a straight swop for Andy King in August 1982.

	LEAGUE		*FA CUP*		*FL CUP*		*EUROPE*		*TOTAL*	
	App	*Gls*	*App*	*Gls*	*App*	*Gls*	*App*	*Gls*	*App*	*Gls*
1978-79	7/1	0	0	0	0	0	0	0	7/1	0
1979-80	23/3	6	5	2	3	0	2	0	33/3	8
1980-81	41/1	15	6	3	3	1	-	-	50/1	19
1981-82	17/2	5	1	1	0	0	-	-	18/2	6
	88/7	26	12	6	6	1	2	0	108/7	33

PETER EASTOE

Tommy Eglington was one of Everton's greatest-ever servants, making more than 400 appearances in a Goodison career which spanned 11 years. He signed along with Peter Farrell from Shamrock Rovers in 1946 for a joint fee of £10,000, the deal proving to be one of the finest strokes of business Everton ever pulled off. He was widely recognised as the greatest match-winning left-winger in the British game and was seen by many as the natural successor to Billy Liddell in terms of poise and grace. The very mention of his name sent shivers of apprehension down the spines of right-backs the country over and he repaid the Everton board for putting their faith in him with an illustrious and golden career. He guaranteed himself a place in the pages of Everton history when, on 27 September 1952, he single-handedly demolished Doncaster Rovers at Goodison Park with five goals in a 7-1 win. He offset his devastating speed with intricate close control and stunning shooting power. He appeared alongside Farrell in the historic game at Goodison Park in 1949 when the Republic of Ireland defeated mighty England 2-0 to become the first 'overseas' nation to win on English soil. He gained his first international recognition the year he joined Everton and went on to win 24 Eire caps and make six appearances for Northern Ireland when that country could select Republic-born players for the Home International Championship. He was transferred to Tranmere Rovers in 1957 and now runs a butcher's shop in his native Dublin.

	LEAGUE		*FA CUP*		*TOTAL*	
	App	*Gls*	*App*	*Gls*	*App*	*Gls*
1946-47	34	5	2	0	36	5
1947-48	29	3	5	1	34	4
1948-49	34	7	2	0	36	7
1949-50	34	1	5	0	39	1
1950-51	39	8	1	0	40	8
1951-52	38	8	2	0	40	8
1952-53	39	14	5	2	44	16
1953-54	41	11	3	1	44	12
1954-55	41	9	2	0	43	9
1955-56	38	8	4	2	42	10
1956-57	27	2	3	0	30	2
	394	76	34	6	428	82

TOMMY EGLINGTON

Peter Farrell helped to make history when he scored one of the goals for the Republic of Ireland team that defeated the star-studded and seemingly invincible England side in 1949. Fittingly, the venue for an Irish triumph which sent shock waves spinning around the football world was Goodison Park, a ground which Farrell graced for more than a decade. Strangely, the man who built an enviable reputation as a sturdy wing-half was forced to play out of position that day, figuring at inside-right. He joined Everton from Shamrock Rovers in 1946 along with his long-time friend Tommy Eglington. The package deal cost the Goodison board just £10,000, making it arguably the best double signing the club ever made. A resilient player who never shirked a tackle, Farrell was popular on the field and something of a hero off it, mixing freely with supporters in his down-to-earth manner. He captained the side for many years before, in October 1957 at the age of 33, he agreed to join Tranmere Rovers as player-manager for a fee of £2,500. He was later to become manager until leaving in December 1960. The following season he took over as player-boss of Welsh League club Holyhead Town but eventually returned to Ireland to continue in management. He played 28 times for Eire and represented Northern Ireland seven times when they could select players born in the Republic for the Home International Championship.

	LEAGUE		*FA CUP*		*TOTAL*	
	App	*Gls*	*App*	*Gls*	*App*	*Gls*
1946-47	27	0	2	0	29	0
1947-48	38	2	3	1	41	3
1948-49	38	0	2	0	40	0
1949-50	41	2	5	0	46	2
1950-51	42	3	1	0	43	3
1951-52	40	0	2	0	42	0
1952-53	38	1	5	1	43	2
1953-54	39	1	3	0	42	1
1954-55	41	0	2	0	43	0
1955-56	42	1	4	1	46	2
1956-57	36	3	2	1	38	4
	422	13	31	4	453	17

PETER FARRELL

Measham-born Tom Fern was the man who succeeded where others had failed, filling the gap left by the departure of goalkeeper Billy Scott. Fern was signed from Lincoln City in 1913 and his goalkeeping was a vital ingredient of revitalised Everton's 1914-15 League Championship success. That same season Everton reached the FA Cup semi-final but Fern missed the game against Chelsea at Villa Park because of injury. Indeed, injury was never far away — not suprising for a goalkeeper who was always in the thick of the action — and in the infamous 6-0 thrashing by Crystal Palace in the 1921-2 FA Cup, Fern kept goal with a damaged hand while his opposite number, Palace goalkeeper Jack Alderson, was eating oranges at the other end. Fern's career spanned World War One, but for which he would have added to his 219 League appearances for Everton. Fern who moved to Port Vale in June 1924.

	LEAGUE		*FA CUP*		*TOTAL*	
	App	*Gls*	*App*	*Gls*	*App*	*Gls*
1913-14	21	0	1	0	22	0
1914-15	36	0	4	0	40	0
1919-20	34	0	1	0	35	0
1920-21	40	0	5	0	45	0
1921-22	38	0	1	0	39	0
1922-23	25	0	0	0	25	0
1923-24	25	0	0	0	25	0
	219	0	12	0	231	0

TOM FERN

Alfred Walter Fielding was the little Londoner who travelled north to find sporting fame with Everton. He was at the centre of a row when he signed professional forms at Goodison in 1945. Before joining the army he was on Charlton's books as an amateur.

WALLY FIELDING

He went to the Middle East where his form as an inside-forward was good enough to get him into army representative sides. When Fielding returned to England he was immediately offered terms by Charlton who naturally assumed they had first refusal. But despite the attentions of numerous other leading clubs of the day, he opted for Everton and started a furious debate which lasted many months. He was a brilliant ball player and strategist who ran the Everton engine-room with cool authority. Although he proved to be lethal when within striking distance of goal, he was regarded as a supplier rather than a striker. Despite his all-round ability he made only one appearance in the white shirt of England, the Bolton Disaster Fund match against Scotland at Manchester in 1946, a game that did not count as an official full cap.

	LEAGUE		*FA CUP*		*TOTAL*	
	App	*Gls*	*App*	*Gls*	*App*	*Gls*
1945-46	-	-	2	0	2	0
1946-47	31	4	2	1	33	5
1947-48	33	8	5	2	38	10
1948-49	36	1	2	0	38	1
1949-50	14	0	3	0	17	0
1950-51	34	3	1	0	35	3
1951-52	37	4	2	0	39	4
1952-53	26	5	1	1	27	6
1953-54	39	5	3	0	42	5
1954-55	33	4	2	1	35	5
1955-56	29	3	4	0	33	3
1956-57	34	6	3	0	37	6
1957-58	24	4	0	0	24	4
1958-59	10	2	0	0	10	2
	380	49	30	5	410	54

Tom Fleetwood had a disappointing finale to an Everton career that eventually realised well over 200 senior appearances in a 12-year span interrupted by World War One. When he was awarded a benefit match, against Sheffield United in 1921-2, Everton were playing badly. They narrowly missed relegation and were humiliated 6-0 in the Cup by Second Division Crystal Palace. The result for Fleetwood was that the attendance was far less than might have been hoped for by a player who had given the club such splendid service as a versatile half-back. He could perform equally well at left-half, or in the centre, and he had even tried his luck at centre-forward when emergency measures were needed. Indeed, he had joined Everton as a forward from Rochdale. Some of his best football was played in the Lancashire Section which prevailed between 1915 and 1919 and he was rewarded with two appearances for England in Victory internationals. Both games were against Scotland, one draw and a 4-3 victory when he did the bulk of the defensive work while his right-half colleague Arthur Grimsdell of Spurs found time to go forward and score twice. Fleetwood, who was born in Liverpool but joined Everton from Rochdale, signed for Oldham Athletic in August 1923.

TOM FLEETWOOD

	LEAGUE		*FA CUP*		*TOTAL*	
	App	*Gls*	*App*	*Gls*	*App*	*Gls*
1910-11	8	1	0	0	8	1
1911-12	34	1	5	0	39	1
1912-13	28	1	2	1	30	2
1913-14	27	1	1	0	28	1
1914-15	35	2	5	0	40	2
1919-20	37	1	1	0	38	1
1920-21	39	1	4	0	43	1
1921-22	33	1	1	0	34	1
1922-23	23	0	2	0	25	0
	264	9	21	1	285	10

BERTIE FREEMAN

Bertie Freeman was a man who always scored goals regardless of what level of football he was involved in. After playing with Aston Villa and Arsenal he came to Everton and replaced Sandy Young — a feat in itself. A tenacious front-runner with good aerial ability and a lethal shot, he created a First Division record in 1908-09 when he scored 36 goals. After three impressive seasons with the club, he was transferred to Burnley and played at centre-forward against Liverpool in the 1914 FA Cup Final, scoring the winning goal. He played in the North v South England trial at Fulham in 1909, with Jack Sharp, and scored four goals for the Football League against the Irish League in the same year.

	LEAGUE		*FA CUP*		*TOTAL*	
	App	*Gls*	*App*	*Gls*	*App*	*Gls*
1907-08	4	1	0	0	4	1
1908-09	37	38	1	0	38	38
1909-10	34	22	7	4	41	26
1910-11	11	2	0	0	11	2
	86	63	8	4	94	67

A powerhouse of a right-half, Jimmy Gabriel became one of the most expensive teenagers in British football when he arrived from Dundee for £30,000 in March 1960. He made his Everton debut against West Ham United only 72 hours after putting pen to paper and went on to make eight senior appearances in his first full season at Goodison. He was capped by Scotland at Youth, Under-23 and full international levels, making his first senior appearance against Wales in October 1960. In his youth days he played alongside Denis Law. While Gabriel was struggling to find his feet in English football, in only his third game for Everton he came up against big Derek Kevan, the West Brom 'bomber', on an afternoon he will never forget. Kevan hammered five goals, but Gabriel shrugged off the experience and went on to build a fine career. His strong, forceful style, particularly effective in defence, made him the near-perfect foil for the more adventurous wanderings of Brian Harris on the opposite flank. He played a major part in the title success of 1962-3 and was a member of the 1966 FA Cup-winning side. The date 18 March 1967 marked the beginning of the end of his Everton career. On that day he was sent to Blackpool with the reserves while a newcomer, Howard Kendall, was making his League debut against Southampton. After more than 300 senior appearances Gabriel moved to The Dell and after a spell with another south coast club, Bournemouth, he moved to North America where he played for Seattle Sounders. He was appointed to Everton's managerial team during the reign of Colin Harvey, a position he retained following the return of Howard Kendall in November 1990.

JIMMY GABRIEL

	LEAGUE		*FA CUP*		*FL CUP*		*EUROPE*		*TOTAL*	
	App	*Gls*	*App*	*Gls*	*App*	*Gls*	*App*	*Gls*	*App*	*Gls*
1959-60	8	0	0	0	-	-	-	-	8	0
1960-61	40	1	1	0	5	0	-	-	46	1
1961-62	42	6	3	0	-	-	-	-	45	6
1962-63	40	5	3	1	-	-	2	0	45	6
1963-64	33	5	5	1	-	-	1	0	39	6
1964-65	37	4	4	0	-	-	5	0	46	4
1965-66	24	6	6	0	-	-	3	1	33	7
1966-67	31/1	6	3	0	-	-	4	0	38/1	6
	255/1	33	25	2	5	0	15	1	300/1	36

Jimmy Galt, who captained Everton when they won the League Championship and reached the FA Cup semi-finals in 1914-15, was a classic example of a footballer whose career was ruined by war. After only one season with Everton he found that the road to more triumphs had been barred by events in Europe. It was the end of his Everton days, before they had barely started. Born in Ayrshire in 1885, Galt started as a left-half but moved into the centre of the half-back line with equal success. He signed for Rangers in January 1906 and won Scottish League Championship medals at Ibrox (1911-13 inclusive) and a Scottish Cup runners-up medal (1909). He won two Scottish caps in 1908 and played four times in the prestigious Glasgow versus Sheffield fixture. He joined Everton in the 1914 close season and looked set to lead the club to great heights when war was declared. He was officially transferred to Third Lanark in October 1920, although he rarely played for Everton after 1915. After retirement from football he became a motor engineer. He died in November 1935.

	LEAGUE		*FA CUP*		*TOTAL*	
	App	*Gls*	*App*	*Gls*	*App*	*Gls*
1914-15	32	2	4	2	36	4
	32	2	4	2	36	4

JIMMY GALT

It would be fair to say that Fred Geary was the Dixie Dean of his day, leading the Everton forward line with his own particular and distinctive brand of robust front-running. Born in Nottingham, and once with Notts County, he was brought to Everton's attention while playing for Notts Rangers. He went to Grimsby and was eventually signed by Everton in 1889, quickly establishing himself as an indispensable member of a side which firmly believed attack was the best form of defence. He scored twice on his League debut for the club. He was capped for England against Ireland in 1890 (scoring a hat-trick in Belfast) and against Scotland the following year. He picked up one of the first gold medals struck in recognition of international service when he played in the inter-League fixture against Scotland three years later. At that time the payment to professionals in such representative games was two guineas and the side expressed a desire to have a more tangible souvenir to commemorate the occasion. Famed for his penetrating runs, he once said that he was lucky to have played alongside Chadwick and Milward in the Everton team. He signed for Liverpool in 1894 and ended his playing days at Anfield. His last six seasons of League soccer saw him make only 56 appearances due to injury and loss of form.

	LEAGUE		*FA CUP*		*TOTAL*	
	App	*Gls*	*App*	*Gls*	*App*	*Gls*
1889-90	18	21	2	4	20	25
1890-91	22	20	1	0	23	20
1891-92	10	6	0	0	10	6
1892-93	24	19	3	4	27	23
1893-94	9	8	0	0	9	8
1894-95	8	4	1	0	9	4
	91	78	7	8	98	86

FRED GEARY

When Charlie Gee was called up to play for England against Wales at Anfield on 18 November 1931, he completed an astonishing rise to international stardom. Less than 12 months previously he had still been waiting to make his First Division debut for Everton. Born in Stockport, he began with Reddish Gren Wesleyans and signed for Stockport County in 1928. Everton bought him in July 1930 and he began his big-time apprenticeship in the reserve team. When Tommy Griffiths was injured, Gee stepped in for his League debut on New Year's Day 1931 and never looked back, helping Everton to promotion that year as well as the FA Cup semi-final. Then came his England call-up when, ironically, he found that his opposite number on the Welsh side was Griffiths, the man he had displaced from the Everton side. Gee was an uncomplicated centre-half who was always striving for something better than his best. A deep thinker with an ambitious vein, he gave his all and was consequently loved by the Goodison crowd. His progress was halted by a cartilage operation in 1932, and although he reclaimed his place, he was never quite the same player. His last appearance for Everton was at Fulham in May 1940, in the fourth round of the War League Cup, after which he retired.

	LEAGUE		*FA CUP*		*TOTAL*	
	App	*Gls*	*App*	*Gls*	*App*	*Gls*
1930-31	20	2	5	0	25	2
1931-32	38	0	1	0	39	0
1932-33	7	0	0	0	7	0
1933-34	29	0	0	0	29	0
1934-35	37	0	5	0	42	0
1935-36	9	0	0	0	9	0
1936-37	40	0	4	0	44	0
1937-38	14	0	0	0	14	0
1938-39	2	0	0	0	2	0
	196	2	15	0	211	2

CHARLIE GEE

Albert Geldard was the youngest footballer ever to play in a peacetime League match. At the tender age of 15 years 156 days he turned out for Bradford at Millwall in September 1929. Regarded as a schoolboy prodigy — he once scored 22 goals in a match — Geldard signed for Everton as an 18-year-old in November 1932. He made his debut against Middlesbrough the same month, scoring once in a 2-0 win. He was discovered by another famous outside-right, Jack Sharp, who was correct when he forecast an international future for the youngster labelled by Tommy Lawton as 'The fastest thing on two legs over ten yards'. Geldard won four England caps while at Goodison and he laid on the pass which enabled Jimmy Dunn to score the third goal in the 1933 FA Cup Final win over Manchester City. He was exceptionally fast, controlled the ball well and was not slow to cut inside and deliver a telling shot. His chief hobby outside football was conjuring and he was a member of the Magic Circle. In 1938 he joined Bolton for £4,500 and ended his career with them in 1946-7.

	LEAGUE		*FA CUP*		*TOTAL*	
	App	*Gls*	*App*	*Gls*	*App*	*Gls*
1932-33	26	5	4	0	30	5
1933-34	24	5	0	0	24	5
1934-35	31	5	5	5	36	10
1935-36	39	7	1	1	40	8
1936-37	13	3	1	0	14	3
1937-38	34	6	1	0	35	6
	167	31	12	6	179	37

ALBERT GELDARD

JOHN GIDMAN

An attacking full-back famous for his fearsome tackles, John Gidman has sustained and overcome a series of injuries which would have forced lesser men into premature retirement. A Garston lad, he was with Liverpool as an apprentice but joined Aston Villa after the Anfield club discarded him. He enjoyed ten years in the Midlands, winning an England cap, before being brought back to Merseyside when Everton paid a then club record fee of £650,000 in October 1979. He spent less than two years at the club. In July 1981, while lying on a Spanish beach, he discovered that Manchester United had made a substantial bid for him. He became Ron Atkinson's first signing in a deal which brought Welsh winger Mickey Thomas to Goodison. After four injury-plagued years at Old Trafford, he established himself as a first-team regular and was in the side which denied Everton their glorious treble by winning the 1985 FA Cup Final. During a Milk Cup tie at Old Trafford in October 1984, he scored a sensational own-goal two minutes from time to send his old club Everton through to the fourth round. In March 1986 United announced that Gidman had been given a free transfer but then recalled him to the side for vital League games. Eventually he moved across to Maine Road and in January 1988 appeared for Manchester City at Goodison in the Littlewoods Cup quarter-final. He signed for Stoke City in August 1988. He was forced to retire because of injury in 1990.

	LEAGUE		*FA CUP*		*FL CUP*		*TOTAL*	
	App	*Gls*	*App*	*Gls*	*App*	*Gls*	*App*	*Gls*
1979-80	29	1	6	0	0	0	35	1
1980-81	35	1	5	0	3	1	43	2
	64	2	11	0	3	1	78	3

TORRY GILLICK

Torrance Gillick was a man who helped to maintain the tradition of top-class Scottish players at Everton. A stockily-built winger and natural entertainer, he was an exhilarating sight when in full flight down the flanks. His major problem was his attitude to the game. Far too often he played it strictly for laughs, so annoying the more studious members of the side. Sometimes he was brilliant, sometimes woefully ineffective, but no matter what the circumstances, he was always entertaining. Sadly, the Merseyside public never really saw the best of him for, like so many others, his peak years came and went during the course of World War Two. He joined Everton from Rangers in December 1935 in an £8,000 deal. He played on either wing, and very occasionally at inside-right, and won five Scotland caps. He rejoined Rangers in November 1945. He died in 1971.

	LEAGUE		*FA CUP*		*TOTAL*	
	App	*Gls*	*App*	*Gls*	*App*	*Gls*
1935-36	23	9	1	0	24	9
1936-37	42	14	4	2	46	16
1937-38	16	3	2	0	18	3
1938-39	40	14	5	2	45	16
	121	40	12	4	133	44

RONNIE GOODLASS

Ronnie Goodlass achieved a life's ambition when he joined the club in 1968. He was born just down the road from Goodison Park and despite attracting the attentions of several leading sides after his impressive displays for England Schoolboys, he was always determined to play for Everton. He was a winger in the old-fashioned sense, always willing to take on defenders and wend his way to the by-line. He was a firm favourite with the Gwladys Street fans but his tendency to drift in and out of the game led to him being dropped several times. He was a key man in the 1976-7 side which reached the League Cup Final and the FA Cup semi-finals. His chances were limited after the arrival of Dave Thomas from QPR and he was transferred to Dutch club, Breda, for £75,000 in October 1977. Two years later he moved to Den Haag for £80,000 but became homesick and signed for Fulham. From there he drifted to Scunthorpe, Hong Kong, and came back to Merseyside to join Tranmere Rovers in 1983. In the 1984 close season he signed for Barrow.

	LEAGUE		*FA CUP*		*FL CUP*		*TOTAL*	
	App	*Gls*	*App*	*Gls*	*App*	*Gls*	*App*	*Gls*
1975-76	2/1	0	0	0	0	0	2/1	0
1976-77	29/2	2	7	0	9	0	45/2	2
1977-78	0/1	0	0	0	0	0	0/1	0
	31/4	2	7	0	9	0	47/4	2

JACKIE GRANT

Jackie Grant was signed in December 1942 and although he was a first-team regular for just one season, in 1950-51 when he played in all 42 League games, he was a popular player who possessed great flair. Small, yet highly competitive, he played in no fewer than seven different positions in his Everton career. When Joe Mercer left for the army, Grant took his place in wartime soccer. He was the star man in the club's 3-2 FA Cup fourth round replay win over Wolves at Goodison in 1947-8. After failing to hold down a regular place he became an integral part of Everton's Central League side, captaining them to numerous successes. He severed his ties with Everton, after 133 senior appearances, in June 1956 when he was signed by the then Rochdale manager, Harry Catterick. He made over 100 appearances for Rochdale before ending his League career with Southport.

	LEAGUE		*FA CUP*		*TOTAL*	
	App	*Gls*	*App*	*Gls*	*App*	*Gls*
1946-47	5	1	0	0	5	1
1947-48	18	4	5	1	23	5
1948-49	7	0	1	0	8	0
1949-50	23	3	5	0	28	3
1950-51	42	2	1	0	43	2
1951-52	5	0	0	0	5	0
1952-53	17	0	0	0	17	0
1953-54	3	0	0	0	3	0
1954-55	1	0	0	0	1	0
	121	10	12	1	133	11

Andy Gray would be the first to admit that he was his own worst enemy, going in where it hurts, pushing himself through the pain barrier, and then suffering the consequences. Arguably the bravest striker of his generation, his determination to win the ball at all costs is near-legendary. For a man who is not particularly tall, his heading ability was quite outstanding at his peak. Allied to his brilliant aerial skills were deft and incisive flicks on the ground which so often transformed half-chances into goals, if not for Gray himself, then for one of his colleagues. A total professional both on and off the field, he breathed new life into a club which appeared to be going nowhere when he completed a hurriedly arranged £250,000 transfer from ailing Wolves in November 1983. Using his vast experience in the dressing-room and on the pitch he lifted the youngsters around him and was largely instrumental in steering Everton back on to the trophy trail. He joined Aston Villa from Dundee United for £100,000 in 1975 and four years later moved to Wolves for a British record fee of £1.5 million. He scored the second goal in Everton's 1984 FA Cup Final win and the first in the 1985 European Cup-winners' Cup triumph. His remarkable resurrection as a quality striker was capped when he was dramatically recalled into the Scotland side at the end of 1984-5, when he was 29. In July 1985 he rejoined Aston Villa for £150,000. After a loan spell with Notts County he signed for West Brom in 1987. He retired from football shortly afterwards but was lured back to the game in the summer of 1991 when Ron Atkinson persuaded him to accept the post of assistant manager at Aston Villa. He resigned in 1992 to pursue a career in television.

ANDY GRAY

	LEAGUE		*FA CUP*		*FL CUP*		*EUROPE*		*TOTAL*	
	App	*Gls*	*App*	*Gls*	*App*	*Gls*	*App*	*Gls*	*App*	*Gls*
1983-84	23	5	7/1	3	0	0	-	-	30/1	8
1984-85	21/5	9	7	0	0/1	0	3	5	31/6	14
	44/5	14	14/1	3	0/1	0	3	5	61/7	22

Like so many others, Norman Greenhalgh had to move away from his home town to find fame. A Bolton lad, he graduated in the hard school of Division Three North where, apart from knocking football sense into the minds of young hopefuls, they also instilled a measure of toughness into the physical frame. In 1935 New Brighton, desperate to secure a rugged half-back, persuaded Bolton Wanderers to let them sign Greenhalgh. After a while he dropped to full-back before appendix trouble ruled him out for several months. After his return he had a spell up front before reverting to his more familiar duties and began to interest several leading clubs. He chose Everton and made his League debut for them in 1937-8, forming a formidable partnership with the equally ferocious Willie Cook. Stanley Matthews once said that Greenhalgh was the opponent he least enjoyed playing against. He made over 100 senior appearances and was an ever-present when Everton won the League Championship in 1938-9. He also represented the Football League. Greenhalgh had a good season in the first post-war campaign but then quickly lost his place. His last appearance for Everton was in the 6-0 hammering at Stamford Bridge in September 1948. He was given a free transfer and moved to Bangor City. After retiring he became a licensee.

	LEAGUE		*FA CUP*		*TOTAL*	
	App	*Gls*	*App*	*Gls*	*App*	*Gls*
1937-38	12	0	0	0	12	0
1938-39	42	1	5	0	47	1
1945-46	-	-	2	0	2	0
1946-47	38	0	2	0	40	0
1947-48	12	0	0	0	12	0
1948-49	2	0	0	0	2	0
	106	1	9	0	115	1

NORMAN GREENHALGH

Alan Grenyer had to wait for two seasons after joining Everton before he could stake a first-team place. Everton bought him from his home town club, South Shields, in 1910, but in his first two years at Goodison Park he managed only four appearances because Harry Makepeace had made the left-half position his own. Slowly he began to establish a place on the fringes of selection, and in the Championship-winning season of 1914-15, he managed 14 games and one goal. It was an important goal too, helping Everton to a 2-1 win at Bradford's Park Avenue ground. There were only two League games to play after that and the success helped Everton to the top of the table for the first time that season. Like so many players, Grenyer played his best football in wartime soccer. It earned him a place in the England side for a Victory international against Wales but that was an unhappy experience. It was December 1919 and Grenyer allowed the great Billy Meredith to escape him. Meredith's shot-cum-centre slid through the hands of England goalkeeper Williamson to give Wales a 2-1 win. In January 1922 Grenyer selected the Aston Villa game for his benefit match — Everton won 3-2 with a hat-trick from Irvine — and in November 1924 he went back home and signed for North Shields.

	LEAGUE		*FA CUP*		*TOTAL*	
	App	*Gls*	*App*	*Gls*	*App*	*Gls*
1910-11	1	0	0	0	1	0
1911-12	3	0	0	0	3	0
1912-13	26	0	4	0	30	0
1913-14	22	0	0	0	22	0
1914-15	14	1	0	0	14	1
1919-20	33	5	1	0	34	5
1920-21	23	1	1	0	24	1
1921-22	13	1	0	0	13	1
1922-23	7	1	0	0	7	1
	142	9	6	0	148	9

ALAN GRENYER

Tom Griffiths' footballing philosophy was basic. A tall, rangy centre-half, he was of the opinion that all defenders should relieve themselves of the ball as quickly as possible. He based his strategy on the simplistic premise that if you do not have the ball at your feet, then you cannot be dispossessed — and against all odds it proved remarkably successful. He began his career with Wrexham and succeeded the immortal Fred Keenor as the regular Welsh centre-half until he in turn was succeeded by another Everton star, T.G.Jones. In 1929-30 he was a regular member of the side that suffered the indignity of being relegated for the first time in the club's history. He played for the first half of the following season before losing his place, through injury, to Charlie Gee. He was transferred to Bolton Wanderers, moving to Middlesbrough shortly afterwards. In 1935 he joined Aston Villa for £5,000 but despite his heroic efforts, the Midlands club was still relegated. He became a publican in Wrexham and died on Christmas Day 1981.

	LEAGUE		*FA CUP*		*TOTAL*	
	App	*Gls*	*App*	*Gls*	*App*	*Gls*
1926-27	1	0	0	0	1	0
1928-29	26	2	1	0	27	2
1929-30	26	4	1	0	27	4
1930-31	23	3	0	0	23	3
	76	9	2	0	78	9

TOM GRIFFITHS

BRYAN HAMILTON

Bryan Hamilton will always be remembered for scoring 'the goal that never was'. In an evenly-balanced FA Cup semi-final against the old enemy Liverpool at Maine Road in 1977, the teams were deadlocked at 2-2 and the minutes ticking away when Hamilton hammered the ball beyond the outstretched fingers of Ray Clemence to apparently clinch a place at Wembley. For no obvious reason, controversial referee Clive Thomas ruled out the effort and Liverpool went on to win the replay 3-0. A terrier-like midfielder, Hamilton spent two years with Everton after signing for £40,000 from Ipswich Town in 1975. He had made nearly 200 first-team appearances for the East Anglian club after moving there from Linfield. He played for Everton in the 1977 League Cup Final against Aston Villa before moving to Millwall, then Swindon. Capped 50 times for Northern Ireland, he became player-manager of Tranmere Rovers in October 1980 but was sacked in February 1985. Hamilton led Wigan Athletic to Wembley glory in the Freight/Rover Trophy Final at the end of 1984-5. Appointed Leicester manager in June 1986, he was sacked 18 months later and in March 1988 returned to Wigan as chief executive.

	LEAGUE		*FA CUP*		*FL CUP*		*TOTAL*	
	App	*Gls*	*App*	*Gls*	*App*	*Gls*	*App*	*Gls*
1975-76	22/1	5	1	0	0	0	23/1	5
1976-77	16/2	0	1/2	0	7/2	0	24/6	0
	38/3	5	2/2	0	7/2	0	47/7	5

HAROLD HARDMAN

A pint-sized winger of great flair, and one of the leading amateur footballers of his day, Harold Hardman went on to become one of the game's great adminstrators when he retired from playing. He was a stylish forward who played for Everton, Manchester United and Northern Nomads. He appeared in FA Cup Finals in consecutive years, in 1906 when Everton defeated Newcastle United, and 12 months later when they lost to Sheffield Wednesday. The 1906 success meant that he was one of only three amateurs this century to take an FA Cup winners' medal, joining Manchester City's S.B.Ashworth (1904) and Wolves' Rev K.R.G.Hunt (1908). Manchester-born Hardman joined Everton from Blackpool in 1903 and left for United in 1908, the year he won an Olympic Games soccer gold medal with Great Britain. He had already won four full England caps with Everton. A solicitor with offices in the centre of Manchester, he was a Manchester United director for 50 years, and chairman from 1951 until his death in June 1965. He was also an FA councillor and president of the Lancashire FA.

	LEAGUE		*FA CUP*		*TOTAL*	
	App	*Gls*	*App*	*Gls*	*App*	*Gls*
1903-04	26	5	0	0	26	5
1904-05	32	8	6	1	38	9
1905-06	31	6	6	2	37	8
1906-07	19	3	7	1	26	4
1907-08	22	3	7	0	29	3
	130	25	26	4	156	29

Alan Harper is widely acknowledged as a 'player's player' — a model professional who will approach any task with enthusiasm and commitment. Born in Liverpool, he began his career at Anfield, joining the club as an apprentice in 1978. After five frustrating years of Central League football, he joined Everton for £100,000 in June 1983 and, while he had to learn to live with the tag of 'utility player', he quickly became an integral part of Howard Kendall's rapidly-maturing squad. Harper was on the substitutes' bench in 1984 when Everton defeated Watford to lay claim to the FA Cup for the first time in 18 years and he won League Championship honours in both 1985 and 1987. After slipping back into the Goodison shadows following Colin Harvey's appointment as manager, Harper was sold to Sheffield Wednesday for £275,000 in 1988 but endured a traumatic 17 months at Hillsborough before Kendall rescued his career in December 1989 by taking him to Manchester City. Although he swiftly established himself as a firm favourite at Maine Road he had no hesitation in following Kendall back to Merseyside in the summer of 1991 as part of a £1.3 million package deal which also included another former Evertonian, Mark Ward. At the end of 1992-3 he was put on the transfer list.

ALAN HARPER

	LEAGUE		*FA CUP*		*FL CUP*		*EUROPE*		*TOTAL*	
	App	*Gls*	*App*	*Gls*	*App*	*Gls*	*App*	*Gls*	*App*	*Gls*
1983-84	26/3	1	1/1	0	6/1	0	-	-	33/5	1
1984-85	10/2	0	101	0	1	0	3/1	0	15/4	0
1985-86	17/4	0	4/2	1	4	0	-	-	25/6	1
1986-87	29/7	3	1/1	0	4	0	-	-	34/8	3
1987-88	21/7	0	3/3	0	2/1	0	-	-	26/11	0
1991-92	29/4	0	1	0	1/1	0	-	-	31/5	0
1992-93	16/2	0	1/1	0	4	0	-	-	21/3	0
	148/29	4	12/9	1	22/3	0	3/1	0	185/42	5

Joe Harper was hailed as one of the new breed of strikers when he joined Everton in December 1972. His gift was sharpness in and around the penalty area, the quick eye and lightning reaction needed to take full advantage of split-second situations. At 5ft 6in he did not have the build to bustle around in the old-style centre-forward way. He relied on positional sense and timing. He came to Goodison at a time of crisis when it was learned that Joe Royle had been ruled out for the season which still had five months to run. Harry Catterick paid Aberdeen £180,000 for him — a Scottish League club record incoming fee — and his early form was encouraging. Although he missed a penalty on his League debut against Spurs, his potential was clear for all to see. However, after only 14 months with Everton he was homesick and signed for Hibernian for £120,000. He hit the headlines in 1975 when he was one of five Scotland stars banned from international football after an incident in Copenhagen. He moved back to Aberdeen for £50,000 in April 1976. His return to Pittodrie was successful and he won a League Cup winners' medal and was leading scorer for three successive seasons before an injury in 1979 effectively ended his career. Later he was player-manager of Peterhead.

JOE HARPER

	LEAGUE		*FA CUP*		*FL CUP*		*TOTAL*	
	App	*Gls*	*App*	*Gls*	*App*	*Gls*	*App*	*Gls*
1972-73	20	7	2	1	0	0	22	8
1973-74	20/3	5	2	1	2	0	24/3	6
	40/3	12	4	2	2	0	46/3	14

Bebington-born Brian Harris was a winger when he joined Everton from Port Sunlight in January 1954, but his classy play and subtle skills could adapt to almost every position. Indeed, in the 11 years after making his League debut in August 1955, he played in every position except goal for the first team. And in the 1960s, when Everton could afford to compete at the top of the transfer market, Harris could still hold his place. Although he cost only a £10 signing-on fee, he ranked alongside expensive purchases and only once lost his place, briefly to Tony Kay. Perhaps best remembered as a defensive wing-half, he played 24 times in the 1962-3 Championship-winning team (before losing his number-six shirt to Kay) and he was a star of the 1966 FA Cup Final win over Sheffield Wednesday. In the October following the Cup Final victory he went to Cardiff City for £15,000. No stranger to European soccer (he played in Everton's early European Cup and Fairs' Cup games), Harris appeared in all nine of Cardiff's European Cup-winners' Cup matches in 1967-8 when they narrowly missed the Final. Later he played for, and managed, Newport County. His League career totalled 541 games (plus three as a substitute).

	LEAGUE		*FA CUP*		*FL CUP*		*EUROPE*		*TOTAL*	
	App	*Gls*	*App*	*Gls*	*App*	*Gls*	*App*	*Gls*	*App*	*Gls*
1955-56	20	2	4	1	-	-	-	-	24	3
1956-57	3	0	0	0	-	-	-	-	3	0
1957-58	30	6	3	0	-	-	-	-	33	6
1958-59	35	1	4	0	-	-	-	-	39	1
1959-60	32	1	1	0	-	-	-	-	33	1
1960-61	30	3	1	0	5	0	-	-	36	3
1961-62	33	1	3	0	-	-	-	-	36	1
1962-63	24	1	1	1	-	-	2	0	27	2
1963-64	28	3	5	2	-	-	2	0	35	5
1964-65	31	3	1	0	-	-	4	0	36	3
1965-66	40	2	8	0	-	-	4	2	52	4
1966-67	4	0	0	0	-	-	0	0	4	0
	310	23	31	4	5	0	12	2	358	29

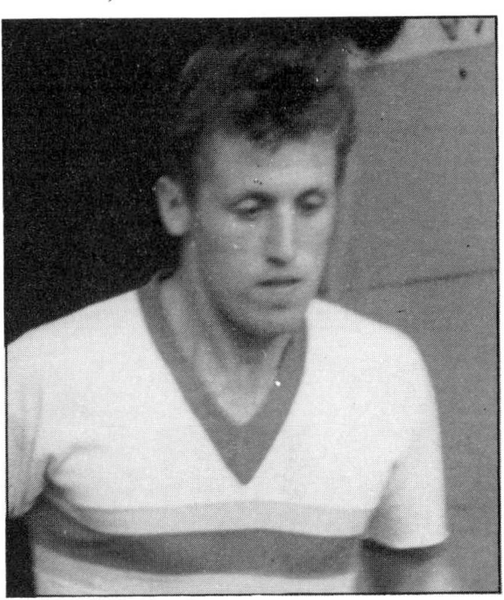

BRIAN HARRIS

Jimmy Harris was a pacey centre-forward whose greatest asset was his appetite for sheer hard work. Birkenhead-born and a member of the district's successful schoolboy side, he joined Everton as an amateur before making the transition to full-time professional. He made his debut at Burnley on 27 August 1955, replacing local hero Dave Hickson, and was to succeed the great man on a permanent basis when Hickson was transferred to Aston Villa a month later. Once established in the side, his form was a revelation. Within five months he had forced his way into the England Under-23 side for an international against Scotland at Hillsborough. When Hickson returned to Goodison Park in the 1957 close season, Harris switched to outside-right where his speed and power-shooting made him one of the finest and most dangerous wingers in the First Division. He holds the rare distinction of scoring a hat-trick and still finishing up on the losing side. It happened in October 1958 when Tottenham defeated Everton 10-4 at White Hart Lane. He moved to Birmingham City in December 1960 for a 'substantial' fee. He also represented the Football League.

	LEAGUE		*FA CUP*		*FL CUP*		*TOTAL*	
	App	*Gls*	*App*	*Gls*	*App*	*Gls*	*App*	*Gls*
1955-56	40	19	4	2	-	-	44	21
1956-57	13	4	2	1	-	-	15	5
1957-58	41	14	3	1	-	-	44	15
1958-59	42	14	4	1	-	-	46	15
1959-60	36	9	1	0	-	-	37	9
1960-61	19	5	0	0	2	2	21	7
	191	65	14	5	2	2	207	72

JIMMY HARRIS

Everton signed Dublin-born Valentine Harris from Shelbourne in 1907 and the Irishman proved to be one of their most consistent and effective players over the next six years. Harris was already an Irish international when he went to Goodison, winning his first cap at centre-forward. Thereafter he played at inside-forward, wing-half and centre-half for his country. He was wonderfully light on his feet and during his time at Everton he managed to steer clear of injuries, clocking up 214 senior appearances. Although Ireland made more use of his versatility than did Everton, Harris still turned out in six different positions for the Goodison club, although the vast majority of his appearances were at right-half. In 1914 he completed his 20th international appearance, playing in two of the three matches which gave Ireland their first outright Home International Championship title. He returned to Shelbourne the same year.

VAL HARRIS

	LEAGUE		*FA CUP*		*TOTAL*	
	App	*Gls*	*App*	*Gls*	*App*	*Gls*
1907-08	3	0	1	0	4	0
1908-09	36	0	2	0	38	0
1909-10	31	0	7	0	38	0
1910-11	32	0	3	0	35	0
1911-12	34	0	5	0	39	0
1912-13	28	1	5	1	33	2
1913-14	26	0	1	0	27	0
	190	1	24	1	214	2

George Harrison was a stocky player for a conventional winger. He weighed nearly 13st and that made him a difficult man to shake off the ball in the days when the shoulder-charge was a full-back's chief weapon. He was born in Church Gresley, Derbyshire, in 1891 and began his senior career with Leicester Fosse who signed him in the close season of 1910. Three years later he joined Everton and was their regular outside-left the following season. He had one of the hardest shots in football, and was a notable penalty-taker, although his strike-rate at Everton — 17 goals in 190 League and Cup games — suggests that he was not all that successful in the role of out-and-out scorer. Yet he made plenty of goals for other people, notably for Bobby Parker when Everton won the Championship in 1914-15. He played wartime football with Everton and was a regular when the League resumed. His form in the immediate post-war era led to him winning two England caps. Midway through 1923-4 he signed for Preston North End, joined Blackpool in 1931, and retired the following year to become a licensee in Preston.

GEORGE HARRISON

	LEAGUE		*FA CUP*		*TOTAL*	
	App	*Gls*	*App*	*Gls*	*App*	*Gls*
1913-14	35	1	1	0	36	1
1914-15	26	4	4	0	30	4
1919-20	25	0	1	0	26	0
1920-21	38	8	5	0	43	8
1921-22	40	2	1	0	41	2
1922-23	2	2	1	0	13	2
1923-24	1	0	0	0	1	0
	177	17	13	0	190	17

HUNTER HART

Glasgow-born Hunter Hart was signed by Everton from Airdrie for £4,000 in 1922 and arrived in time to make his debut against Bolton Wanderers that month. Everton lost 1-0 at Burnden Park but Hart, who had signed professional forms for Airdrie when the war ended, impressed and retained his place. He made most of his appearances at left-half, although towards the middle and end of his career at Goodison he switched to centre-half. He was a member of the team which helped Dixie Dean to his record-breaking 60 League goals in 1927-8, and for a time he skippered Everton. Sadly, the latter part of his career coincided with Everton's fall from grace. When he arrived at Goodison Park, the club were struggling to avoid relegation and they needed his strength in defence. When he played his final few games, in 1929-30, the club were again in trouble and this time his powers were waning and he could not help them. As the side plunged into Division Two for the first time, so the powerful half-back of earlier days was unable to hold his place. Just after Christmas he played his last game in Everton's first team and retired shortly afterwards.

	LEAGUE		*FA CUP*		*TOTAL*	
	App	*Gls*	*App*	*Gls*	*App*	*Gls*
1921-22	17	0	0	0	17	0
1922-23	40	1	2	0	42	1
1923-24	42	2	1	0	43	2
1924-25	24	0	0	0	24	0
1925-26	26	0	0	0	26	0
1926-27	39	1	3	0	42	1
1927-28	41	1	2	0	43	1
1928-29	40	0	1	0	41	0
1929-30	20	0	2	0	22	0
	289	5	11	0	300	5

ASA HARTFORD

Asa Hartford was a midfield purist in the mould of Colin Harvey and Howard Kendall. A tough-tackling pocket dynamo who won 50 Scottish caps, in the late 1970s he was involved in two transfer deals worth a total of £1 million in the space of 63 turbulent days midway through his chequered career. He made his name with West Brom before Don Revie lured him to Leeds in November 1971. The £170,000 deal was sensationally called off 24 hours later after a routine medical revealed that Hartford had a heart condition. He underwent exhaustive tests and was quickly given the go-ahead to resume his career. He moved to Manchester City for £250,000 in August 1974. After five years at Maine Road he chose Nottingham Forest in preference to Everton, but he never took to Brian Clough and two months and three games later he was on his way to Goodison in another £500,000 deal. He quickly became the hub of Everton's vastly improved midfield and was voted Player of the Year by supporters. His stay lasted two years and he moved back to Maine Road in October 1981 for £350,000. He went on to Norwich City and picked up a Milk Cup winners' medal at Wembley in 1985. In July 1985 he joined Bolton Wanderers and then became player-manager of Stockport County in June 1987.

	LEAGUE		*FA CUP*		*FL CUP*		*TOTAL*	
	App	*Gls*	*App*	*Gls*	*App*	*Gls*	*App*	*Gls*
1979-80	35	1	5	1	3	0	43	2
1980-81	39	5	6	0	3	0	48	5
1981-82	7	0	0	0	0	0	7	0
	81	6	11	1	6	0	98	7

Colin Harvey was a classical type of midfield player. At his best he managed to pack into his tiny frame every attribute needed for the testing role. Liverpool-born, he made a dramatic first-team debut for Everton as an 18-year-old when he was thrown into a European Cup clash with mighty Inter-Milan in the famous San Siro stadium in 1963. It took time for the ultra-critical scrutineers of Goodison to accept him, but they ultimately realised that he was a player of genuine quality and style. He showed class in everything he did, linking it with colossal workrate, skill on the ball, excellent positional play and passing ability. Many would argue that he trained and performed with such vigour that he pushed his body beyond its limits, so cutting perhaps one or two years from what was an extraordinarily successful career. When he hit his peak he was a treat to watch, delighting football purists with his uncanny passing ability. He made only one England appearance, against Malta in 1971. With Howard Kendall and Alan Ball he formed the famous midfield triangle which steered Everton to the League Championship in 1970. After a superb Goodison career covering more than 380 first-team games, he was transferred to Sheffield Wednesday in 1974. His career was brought to an untimely end by a niggling hip injury. He returned to Everton in 1976 to work behind the scenes with the club's youngsters. His promotion to first-team coach in 1983 helped spark Everton's much vaunted revival and after Kendall's departure he was appointed manager. After three disappointing seasons at the helm, he was sacked in October 1990 following a League Cup defeat by struggling Sheffield United at Bramall Lane. Six days later, following the appointment of Howard Kendall, he returned to Everton as assistant manager.

COLIN HARVEY

	LEAGUE		*FA CUP*		*FL CUP*		*EUROPE*		*TOTAL*	
	App	*Gls*	*App*	*Gls*	*App*	*Gls*	*App*	*Gls*	*App*	*Gls*
1963-64	2	0	0	0	-	-	1	0	3	0
1964-65	32	2	4	1	-	-	4	2	40	5
1965-66	40	1	8	1	-	-	4	0	52	2
1966-67	42	1	6	0	-	-	4	0	52	1
1967-68	34	0	4	0	2	0	-	-	40	0
1968-69	36	4	4	0	4	0	-	-	44	4
1969-70	35	3	0	0	3	0	-	-	38	3
1970-71	36	2	5	1	0	0	6	0	47	3
1971-72	17	3	3	1	0	0	-	-	20	4
1972-73	24/2	0	0	0	1	0	-	-	25/2	0
1973-74	15/1	1	0	0	0/1	0	-	-	15/2	1
1974-75	4	1	0	0	0	0	-	-	4	1
	317/3	18	34	4	10/1	0	19	2	380/4	24

Adrian Heath became Everton's record signing when Howard Kendall paid struggling Stoke City £700,000 for his services in January 1982, just four days before Heath's 21st birthday. He arrived with a reputation as a powerhouse midfielder, capable of playing up front when required. Something of a pocket dynamo, he was talked about as a natural successor to two diminutive stars of the past, Alan Ball and Bobby Collins. A natural ball-player with a superb turn of speed, he had an aggressive streak which belied his frail frame. He struggled in his early days at Goodison, often trying too hard to justify the enormous price tag. He alternated between two or three different roles and despite flashes of brilliance rarely suggested that he was on the verge of becoming an inspirational driving-force behind the long overdue Everton revival. In 1983-4, four minutes from the end of a Milk Cup match at Oxford, he scored the goal which many people regard as the turning point in the club's fortunes. Everton went on to a first-ever Wembley showdown with neighbours Liverpool. Heath scored the FA Cup semi-final winner against Southampton in the same season. He hit peak form at the start of 1984-5 before being ruled out for the remainder of the season after severely damaging knee ligaments during a game against Sheffield Wednesday. Heath recovered to help Everton finish runners-up in both League and FA Cup in 1986; and he was a key figure when the League Championship was won 12 months later. No longer able to command a regular, first-team place, he joined Spanish club, Espanol, in a £650,000 deal in 1988 before joining Aston Villa for £550,000 in August 1989. In February 1990, he again linked up with Howard Kendall when he moved to Manchester City in a £300,000 deal. After a brief return to Stoke he joined Burnley in 1992.

ADRIAN HEATH

	LEAGUE		*FA CUP*		*FL CUP*		*EUROPE*		*TOTAL*	
	App	*Gls*	*App*	*Gls*	*App*	*Gls*	*App*	*Gls*	*App*	*Gls*
1981-82	22	6	0	0	0	0	-	-	22	6
1982-83	37	10	5	1	4	0	-	-	46	11
1983-84	36	12	7	2	11	4	-	-	54	18
1984-85	17	11	0	0	4	1	4	1	25	13
1985-86	24/12	10	2/4	2	3	1	-	-	29/16	13
1986-87	41	11	3	0	4	3	-	-	48	14
1987-88	23/6	9	7/1	1	5/2	2	-	-	35/9	12
1988-89	6/1	2	0	0	2	0	0	0	8/1	2
	206/19	71	24/5	6	33/2	11	4	1	267/26	89

Dave Hickson will always be remembered on Merseyside as a talented and forceful centre-forward with tremendous heading ability. Off the field he was a quiet, retiring man who craved privacy, but as soon as he pulled on a football strip he was transformed into an aggressive, robust player who often fell foul of referees. He was initially with his local club Ellesmere Port before signing professional forms for Everton in May 1948 as an 18-year-old. After losing his place to Jimmy Harris in September 1955 he was transferred to Aston Villa for £17,500. He moved to Huddersfield Town for £16,000 only two months later, and back to Everton in a deal worth £7,500 in July 1957. Sadly, little went right for him after his return. In November 1959 Liverpool took him across Stanley Park for £12,000. Weeks later, Bill Shankly, who had been Hickson's boss at Huddersfield, joined Liverpool. In January 1960 Hickson was sent off for the third time in his stormy career during a game against Sheffield United. A bitter war of words followed which ended with Hickson found 'guilty of misconduct during the match'. The FA report continued: 'However the commission is not satisfied that Hickson was guilty of deliberate violent conduct'. Twelve months later he left Anfield and went into non-League football with Cambridge United. He later joined Tranmere Rovers and spent two years as player-manager of Irish League club Ballymena United.

	LEAGUE		*FA CUP*		*TOTAL*	
	App	*Gls*	*App*	*Gls*	*App*	*Gls*
1951-52	31	14	2	0	33	14
1952-53	27	12	5	4	32	16
1953-54	40	25	3	3	43	28
1954-55	39	12	2	1	41	13
1955-56	2	0	0	0	2	0
1957-58	35	9	2	3	37	12
1958-59	39	17	4	5	43	22
1959-60	12	6	0	0	12	6
	225	95	18	16	243	111

DAVE HICKSON

Mark Higgins, who won a record 19 England Schoolboy caps, took over the mantle of 'Mr Everton' when Mike Lyons left Goodison to pursue a career with Sheffield Wednesday. An Evertonian through and through, Higgins was on the verge of a call-up to the full England squad when his career was threatened by a potentially crippling pelvic injury when he was still only 26. Born in Buxton, he quickly followed in the footsteps of his father, John, who was a giant centre-back with Bolton Wanderers. He joined Everton straight from school, registered as an apprentice in April 1975 and made his senior debut 18 months later in the 2-2 draw against Manchester City at Goodison Park. Exceptionally good in the air, he matured at an astonishing rate under the careful guidance of Lyons. He was a strong, brave centre-back who quickly showed he had great qualities of leadership. After partnering Billy Wright at the heart of Howard Kendall's defence he teamed up with Kevin Ratcliffe and was appointed captain. His injury problems began in December 1983 after a Milk Cup replay against West Ham. What was initially diagnosed as a simple groin injury turned out to be a serious pelvic disorder. Despite being told that he would never play professional football again, Higgins joined Manchester United on Central League forms, 18 months after announcing his retirement. After proving his fitness he signed a two-year contract in January 1986, with United handing over £60,000 insurance compensation. He made eight senior appearances for United before enjoying brief spells at both Bury and Stoke City.

	LEAGUE		*FA CUP*		*FL CUP*		*EUROPE*		*TOTAL*	
	App	*Gls*	*App*	*Gls*	*App*	*Gls*	*App*	*Gls*	*App*	*Gls*
1976-77	2	0	0	0	0	0	-	-	2	0
1977-78	25/1	1	1	0	5	0	-	-	31/1	1
1978-79	20	1	0	0	0	0	0/2	0	20/2	1
1979-80	19	0	0	0	5	0	2	0	26	0
1980-81	2	0	0	0	0	0	-	-	2	0
1981-82	29	3	1	0	2	0	-	-	32	3
1982-83	39	1	5	0	2	0	-	-	46	1
1983-84	14	0	0	0	5	0	-	-	19	0
	150/1	6	7	0	19	0	2/2	0	178/3	6

MARK HIGGINS

Johnny Holt was a fine centre-half nicknamed the 'Little Everton Devil' by supporters who worshipped him. Enormously powerful in the air, he was one of the best one-to-one markers in the game, relying on his muscular physique to subdue rival centre-forwards. He was an expert at last-ditch tackles and made a habit of appearing from nowhere to scoop the ball to safety. He played ten times for England but his finest moment came against Scotland at Ibrox in 1892. He was part of the side dubbed 'the Old Crocks' because Old Etonian Arthur Dunn, who had been centre-forward in 1884, was recalled as captain and full-back. Scottish journalists had a positive field-day in the weeks leading up to the international, predicting that their star man, Sandy McMahon, would lead Holt a merry dance. In fact the Everton defender marked him out of the game. The official history of the club tells how Holt was 'an artist in the perpetuation of clever minor fouls. When they were appealed for, his shocked look of innocence was side-splitting'. He joined Everton from Bootle in 1888, in time for the League's first season, and played regularly for ten years before moving to Reading.

	LEAGUE		*FA CUP*		*TOTAL*	
	App	*Gls*	*App*	*Gls*	*App*	*Gls*
1888-89	17	0	0	0	17	0
1889-90	21	1	2	0	23	1
1890-91	21	1	1	0	22	1
1891-92	21	0	1	0	22	0
1892-93	26	0	7	0	33	0
1893-94	26	0	1	0	27	0
1894-95	27	0	3	0	30	0
1895-96	14	0	2	0	16	0
1896-97	25	1	5	1	30	2
1897-98	27	0	5	0	32	0
	225	3	27	1	252	4

JOHNNY HOLT

John Hurst was the sort of player every manager dreams of having in his side. A dedicated club man, he arrived at Everton in a blaze of publicity as a 14-year-old England Schoolboy international in May 1962. Blackpool-born, he was a product of Everton's hugely successful youth policy. After learning his trade in the Central League, he forced his way into the senior squad in August 1965 when he was named, alongside such greats as Brian Labone and Fred Pickering, for a game against newly-promoted Northampton. However, he had to wait for a substitute appearance against Stoke for his debut. He was originally a striker but Harry Catterick transformed him into one of the finest wing-halves in the country. A solid tackler with an eye for an opening, he quickly established himself and began a career which spanned 11 years. In 1968 he confounded medical experts who told him that he would not play again that season after contracting hepatitis on the eve of the FA Cup semi-final against Leeds United. Against the odds he recovered to play in the Final against West Brom. He won England Under-23 honours, and an FA Youth Cup winners' medal in 1965.

	LEAGUE		*FA CUP*		*FL CUP*		*EUROPE*		*TOTAL*	
	App	*Gls*	*App*	*Gls*	*App*	*Gls*	*App*	*Gls*	*App*	*Gls*
1965-66	19/2	2	0	0	-	-	0	0	19/2	2
1966-67	23/2	2	6	0	-	-	0	0	29/2	2
1967-68	40	5	5	0	2	1	-	-	47	6
1968-69	42	7	5	2	4	0	-	-	51	9
1969-70	42	5	1	0	3	0	-	-	46	5
1970-71	40	3	5	0	0	0	6	0	51	3
1971-72	28/1	0	1/2	1	1	0	-	-	30/3	1
1972-73	28/1	1	2	0	0	0	-	-	30/1	1
1973-74	39	3	3	1	2	0	-	-	44	4
1974-75	29/2	1	1	0	0	0	-	-	30/2	1
1975-76	6/3	0	1	0	1	0	0/1	0	8/4	0
	336/11	29	30/2	4	13	1	6/1	0	385/14	34

JOHN HURST

JIMMY HUSBAND

Jimmy Husband was a likeable and talented Geordie, nicknamed 'Skippy' by supporters because of his distinctive running style. He was signed from North-East side Shields in July 1963 and became one of the most exciting strikers in the country. Unorthodox and totally unpredictable, he was capable of moments of genuine brilliance. He was fast, skilful on the ball, with a superb swerve and dribble and was deadly when presented with a half-chance. He became a full-time professional in October 1964 and made his debut towards the end of that season. He won a Fairs Cup place against the Hungarian side Ujpest Dozsa as a 17-year-old in 1965-6. He was a regular member of Everton's title-winning side of 1970 and also picked up an FA Cup runners-up medal in 1968. He won England Under-23 honours but, despite being on the fringes for a couple of seasons, never gained a full international cap. In 1984 he was tempted out of retirement to play for a Bedfordshire village side. Perhaps their name appealed to him. It was Everton.

	LEAGUE		*FA CUP*		*FL CUP*		*EUROPE*		*TOTAL*	
	App	*Gls*	*App*	*Gls*	*App*	*Gls*	*App*	*Gls*	*App*	*Gls*
1964-65	1	0	0	0	-	-	0	0	1	0
1965-66	4	0	0	0	-	-	1	0	5	0
1966-67	19	6	6	4	-	-	1	0	26	10
1967-68	19/1	5	6	3	0	0	-	-	25/1	8
1968-69	36	19	5	0	2	1	-	-	43	20
1969-70	30	6	0	0	2	0	-	-	32	6
1970-71	15	6	4	3	0	0	2/1	0	21/1	9
1971-72	25/2	1	1	0	0	0	-	-	26/2	1
1972-73	8/1	0	0	0	0	0	-	-	8/1	0
1973-74	1/3	1	0	0	1	0	-	-	2/3	1
	158/7	44	22	10	5	1	4/1	0	189/8	55

ALAN IRVINE

Alan Irvine, was an 'old-fashioned' winger who arrived at Everton at a time when such players were not in vogue. A natural crowd-pleaser with superb close control and tremendous dribbling ability, he was signed as an amateur from Queen's Park in May 1981 after helping them to the Scottish Second Division title. Howard Kendall made several attempts to introduce him into a struggling side but Irvine was never able to hold down a regular senior place. Nevertheless, he did play in the historic Milk Cup Final and subsequent replay against Liverpool. Frustrated at playing Central League football, he asked for a transfer in September 1983 and eventually moved to Steve Coppell's Crystal Palace for £50,000. After a spell with Dundee he was transferred to Blackburn Rovers for a fee of £25,000 in 1989.

	LEAGUE		*FA CUP*		*FL CUP*		*TOTAL*	
	App	*Gls*	*App*	*Gls*	*App*	*Gls*	*App*	*Gls*
1981-82	25	3	0	0	0	0	25	3
1982-83	7/7	1	2	0	0/1	0	9/8	1
1983-84	19/2	0	7	2	10	0	36/2	2
	51/9	4	9	2	10/1	0	70/10	6

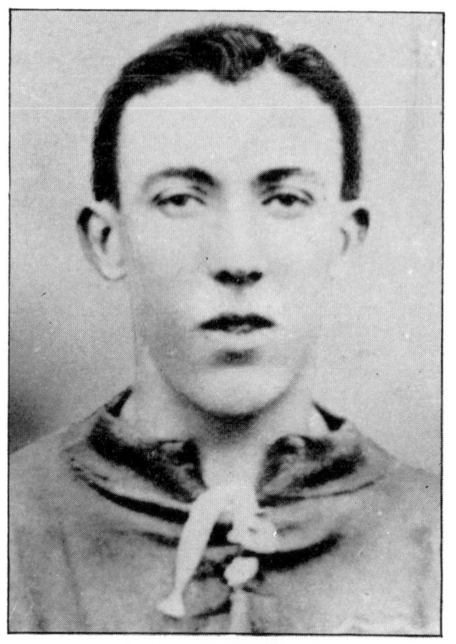

BOBBY IRVINE

Lisburn-born Bobby Irvine played at both centre-forward and inside-right. He was a magical dribbler, a brave forward who thrilled the crowd with his foraging runs. He won his first Ireland cap, against Scotland, in March 1922 and as an Everton player he collected 11 altogether. He played twice in teams that beat England (1923 and 1927) and he scored in the 3-3 draw with England at Liverpool in 1926. He joined Everton from Dunmurry in September 1921 and was transferred to Portsmouth in March 1928, one short of 200 League appearances for Everton. He made only nine appearances in the 1927-8 Championship season before signing for Pompey. On his departure from Goodison it was written of him: 'There is no man who takes harder knocks and squeals less than Irvine'. But injury robbed him of a place in the 1929 FA Cup Final after he had played in the earlier rounds. In two years Irvine made only 35 League appearances for Portsmouth. He went to Connah's Quay, then Derry City, where he won the last of his 15 caps, almost ten years after his first.

	LEAGUE		*FA CUP*		*TOTAL*	
	App	*Gls*	*App*	*Gls*	*App*	*Gls*
1921-22	25	11	1	0	26	11
1922-23	32	8	1	0	33	8
1923-24	40	9	2	0	42	9
1924-25	28	4	3	1	31	5
1925-26	31	8	2	0	33	8
1926-27	34	11	4	1	38	12
1927-28	9	3	2	1	11	4
	199	54	15	3	214	57

GEORGE JACKSON

George 'Stonewall' Jackson was a full-back who served Everton well in the inter-war years. Born within a stone's throw of Goodison Park, he began his football apprenticeship with Arnott Street School which turned out many notable players shortly before World War Two. He was spotted by Everton while playing for Walton Parish Church and while working his way through the ranks he was loaned to Crosby side, Marine. He played with the Mariners through their memorable FA Amateur Cup bid when they met Dulwich Hamlet in the Final at Upton Park. Tough in the tackle and with a fine turn of speed, he made his senior debut against Wolverhampton Wanderers in February 1935. In seven seasons he totalled 75 League appearances before transferring to Caernarvon Town in 1949.

	LEAGUE		*FA CUP*		*TOTAL*	
	App	*Gls*	*App*	*Gls*	*App*	*Gls*
1934-35	8	0	1	0	9	0
1935-36	18	0	0	0	18	0
1936-37	26	0	0	0	26	0
1937-38	4	0	0	0	4	0
1938-39	2	0	0	0	2	0
1945-46	0	0	2	0	2	0
1946-47	15	0	1	0	16	0
1947-48	2	0	0	0	2	0
	75	0	4	0	79	0

Frank Jefferis was a first-rate tactician and the driving force behind the Everton forward line in the years leading up to World War One. He was born in Hampshire in 1887 and joined Southampton, his local Southern League club, in the close season of 1905. After 171 appearances for the Saints he moved to Goodison in March 1911 and won a Championship medal in 1914-15, although injury ruled him out of the latter part of the season. At Goodison he created goals for players like Browell and Bradshaw. He was capped twice for England shortly after arriving on the First Division scene, playing as a scheming inside-forward against Wales and Scotland in 1912. After wartime football with Everton he managed half a season when League soccer resumed. He moved to Preston in January 1920 and two years later was a member of their beaten FA Cup Final side. In 1923 he was appointed Southport player-coach and retired in the close season of 1925. In 1927 he was forced back into action and played two League games when Southport were short of players. In 1936 he became trainer at Millwall and remained there until his death two years later.

	LEAGUE		*FA CUP*		*TOTAL*	
	App	*Gls*	*App*	*Gls*	*App*	*Gls*
1910-11	5	2	0	0	5	2
1911-12	36	7	5	1	41	8
1912-13	27	5	5	2	32	7
1913-14	27	3	1	0	28	3
1914-15	18	4	0	0	18	4
1919-20	12	1	1	0	13	1
	125	22	12	3	137	25

FRANK JEFFERIS

Striker David Johnson's colourful career came full-circle when he signed for Everton in August 1982. Howard Kendall's surprise decision to bolster his shot-shy forward line with the 30-year-old former England international came ten years after he had left Goodison Park for Ipswich Town. Johnson, who was nothing like as skilful as many of his contemporaries, was nevertheless a natural goalscorer who could amble through a game seemingly uninterested before switching up a gear to carve out the decisive opening. He joined Everton in 1969 but despite his success was transferred to Ipswich three years later. In 1976 Bob Paisley took him to Anfield as a replacement for John Toshack and during a distinguished Anfield career he scored 78 goals and won eight full England caps. He missed the European Cup triumphs in Rome and at Wembley but was a key member of the side which won the trophy for the third time in Paris in 1981. His second spell with Everton was little short of a disaster, the goal touch which had at one time made him one of the most feared strikers in Europe was sadly missing. He spent a month on loan to Barnsley in February 1984 before moving to Manchester City. He then had a brief spell with Tulsa Roughnecks in the NASL before being transferred to Preston North End.

	LEAGUE		*FA CUP*		*FL CUP*		*EUROPE*		*TOTAL*	
	App	*Gls*	*App*	*Gls*	*App*	*Gls*	*App*	*Gls*	*App*	*Gls*
1970-71	10/1	1	1	1	0	0	0/2	1	11/3	3
1971-72	27	9	4	1	1	1	-	-	32	11
1972-73	10/1	1	0	0	1	0	-	-	11/1	1
1982-83	25/6	3	0	0	4	1	-	-	29/6	4
1983-84	7/2	1	0	0	1	0	-	-	8/2	1
	79/10	15	5	2	7	2	0/2	1	91/12	20

DAVID JOHNSON

TOMMY JOHNSON

Tommy Johnson was a member of the famous Everton side that raced away with the Second Division championship in 1930-31 when they clinched a return to the top-flight immediately after being relegated for the first time in the club's history. He was a tricky inside-left who could turn a game on its head with one flash of brilliance. Technically superb, he was the perfect foil to the stunning power of Dixie Dean. Born near Barrow, he was playing for his local team, Dalton Casuals, when Manchester City discovered him and gave him his chance in wartime football. He played for City in the 1926 FA Cup Final against Bolton and signed for Everton in March 1930, the season after he had helped the Maine Road side destroy Everton 6-2 at Goodison Park. That season Johnson scored 38 League goals for City and when he left for Everton he had netted 158 altogether, both records which still stand. He went back to Wembley with Everton in 1933 and helped them to a 3-0 victory — ironically over City. He joined Liverpool shortly afterwards and finished his career with a total of 222 League goals.

	LEAGUE		*FA CUP*		*TOTAL*	
	App	*Gls*	*App*	*Gls*	*App*	*Gls*
1929-30	10	4	0	0	10	4
1930-31	36	14	5	4	41	18
1931-32	41	22	1	0	42	22
1932-33	40	13	6	4	46	17
1933-34	19	3	1	0	20	3
	146	56	13	8	159	64

GARY JONES

Gary Jones was one of the most talented yet controversial players to wear an Everton shirt during the mid-1970s. On his day he was a mercurial forward, the sort of player who could change the course of a game with one devastating piece of skill. Huyton-born, he was robbed of a dramatic debut as a 19-year-old when illness prevented him from playing in a European Cup-tie against Keflavick in 1970. He then had to endure a seven-month wait on the sidelines before his League debut at Coventry. Although he made 90 appearances for Everton, he never quite fulfilled his rich potential and controversy dogged the final days of what should have been a long and illustrious Goodison career. Following a defeat at Manchester City in February 1976, he submitted a transfer request which was turned down by a board all too aware of his immense popularity on the terraces. A month later he was suspended for a fortnight and fined two weeks' wages by manager Billy Bingham for making a gesture to the bench when substituted during a match against Leeds United, and for subsequently airing his grievances in public. At the end of that season he moved to Birmingham City for £110,000 and made 33 appearances there before joining Fort Lauderdale in America. He is now a publican on Merseyside.

	LEAGUE		*FA CUP*		*FL CUP*		*EUROPE*		*TOTAL*	
	App	*Gls*	*App*	*Gls*	*App*	*Gls*	*App*	*Gls*	*App*	*Gls*
1970-71	1	0	0	0	0	0	0	0	1	0
1971-72	5	0	1	0	0	0	-	-	6	0
1972-73	11/1	0	0	0	0	0	-	-	11/1	0
1973-74	10/3	0	2/1	0	0	0	-	-	12/4	0
1974-75	25/1	6	3	0	0	0	-	-	28/1	6
1975-76	24/1	6	1	1	5	1	2	0	32/1	8
	76/6	12	7/1	1	5	1	2	0	90/7	14

Through sheer hard work Jack Jones developed into one of the most astute and reliable full-backs of his day. After playing for Bebington in numerous boys' representative games he enjoyed a spell with Bromborough Pool before switching his allegiance to Ellesmere Port Town. Jones was with Town at the same time as Joe Mercer. He was snapped up by Everton in 1933 and was an automatic choice during 1935-6. Like so many other defenders he started his career as a centre-forward before deciding that it was a far simpler task to stop goals than to score them. His first reserve-team appearance at Goodison came quite by chance. In early 1933 he had been selected to play for the third team at Whiston and was on his way to the match when he literally bumped into second-team manager Bill Gibbins who found himself one man short for a fixture at Stockport. Jones filled the vacancy and was so impressive that he held his place. His one moment of controversy came in 1937 when he was sent off during the final match of Everton's tour of Denmark. Eventually he moved to Sunderland.

	LEAGUE		*FA CUP*		*TOTAL*	
	App	*Gls*	*App*	*Gls*	*App*	*Gls*
1933-34	5	0	0	0	5	0
1934-35	10	0	3	0	13	0
1935-36	34	0	1	0	35	0
1936-37	16	0	4	0	20	0
1937-38	33	0	2	0	35	0
	98	0	10	0	108	0

JACK JONES

Liverpool-born Tommy E.Jones was Everton's first-choice centre-half through the 1950s. Although for many years regarded exclusively as a stopper, he was originally a full-back. He signed professional forms in January 1948 after successfully captaining the England and Liverpool County FA youth teams. It was manager Cliff Britton who recognised his potential as a pivot and guided him into a new career. He made his senior debut against Arsenal at Highbury on 6 September 1950. Cool, unruffled and a most gentlemanly player, his consistency spoke for itself down the years. Although full international honours surprisingly passed him by, he played for an England XI against the British Army at Maine Road, and was captain of the FA side that toured Ghana and Nigeria in the summer of 1958. A smashed knee-cap sustained in a Central League game at Barnsley ended his career and he left Britain to coach Italian club Montreal.

	LEAGUE		*FA CUP*		*FL CUP*		*TOTAL*	
	App	*Gls*	*App*	*Gls*	*App*	*Gls*	*App*	*Gls*
1950-51	30	0	1	0	-	-	31	0
1951-52	37	0	0	0	-	-	37	0
1952-53	42	0	5	0	-	-	47	0
1953-54	37	1	3	0	-	-	40	1
1954-55	41	4	2	0	-	-	43	4
1955-56	39	2	4	0	-	-	43	2
1956-57	39	3	1	0	-	-	40	3
1957-58	31	0	3	0	-	-	34	0
1958-59	38	4	4	0	-	-	42	4
1959-60	35	0	1	0	-	-	36	0
1960-61	13	0	1	0	3	0	17	0
1961-62	1	0	0	0	-	-	1	0
	383	14	25	0	3	0	411	14

TOMMY E.JONES

Tommy G.Jones was always regarded as one of the footballing 'scientists' of his day. He was never the battering-ram stopper of centre-forwards, but a thoughtful, neat player who read his opponents' intentions superbly before stepping in with great nonchalance to sweep the ball away and use it to good advantage. He signed for Everton from Wrexham in March 1936 for £3,000 and picked up the first of his 17 Welsh caps two years later. He was appointed club captain in August 1949, succeeding Peter Farrell. In 1948 he might have become a trailblazer to Europe when Italian giants Roma made desperate and prolonged attempts to sign him. Everton initially accepted a considerable fee but the deal fell through after a row over the currency transaction. Towards the end of his career he upset the Everton board by publicly expressing his concern at the way the club was being run. He eventually moved to Pwllheli where he was appointed player-manager.

	LEAGUE		*FA CUP*		*TOTAL*	
	App	*Gls*	*App*	*Gls*	*App*	*Gls*
1936-37	1	0	0	0	1	0
1937-38	28	0	2	0	30	0
1938-39	39	0	5	0	44	0
1946-47	22	3	1	1	23	4
1947-48	24	1	0	0	24	1
1948-49	37	0	2	0	39	0
1949-50	14	0	0	0	14	0
	165	4	10	1	175	5

TOMMY G.JONES

Tony Kay was at the centre of football's greatest-ever scandal when, in 1965, he was banned for life — and imprisoned — after the infamous soccer bribes trial. It was a sad end to the career of a man who was one of the most talented wing-halves of his day. A small, flame-haired tiger of a footballer, he was hard-tackling and a superb passer of the ball who cost Everton £55,000 — then a British record for a wing-half — when he signed from Sheffield Wednesday in late December 1962. He had spent nine years at Hillsborough and was on the verge of a call-up to the full England squad when he arrived at Goodison. He was appointed captain during Harry Catterick's reign and was to play a leading role in the Championship success of 1962-3. Despite his qualities as a leader and his considerable skill, he won only one full cap, against Switzerland in 1963.

	LEAGUE		*FA CUP*		*EUROPE*		*TOTAL*	
	App	*Gls*	*App*	*Gls*	*App*	*Gls*	*App*	*Gls*
1962-63	19	1	2	0	0	0	21	1
1963-64	31	3	3	0	2	0	36	3
	50	4	5	0	2	0	57	4

TONY KAY

BOB KELSO

Bob Kelso came from the famous Scottish football breeding-ground of the 1880s and he first made his name with Renton when they were a prominent force in football north of the border. He moved to Newcastle West End in the close season of 1888. Kelso made one appearance for Everton in the League's first season of 1888-9, at right-half against Preston North End, and the following season was a member of the Preston side which won the League again. Eventually he threw in his lot with Everton and they persuaded him to convert to full-back with good effect. Strong-tackling and hard-kicking, he was in the Everton team which lost the 1893 FA Cup Final to Wolves at Fallowfield, and also played in the side which came second in the First Division two seasons later. In the 1896 close season Kelso moved to Dundee where he won another Scottish cap. In those days the Scots did not select players with English clubs and ten years had elapsed between Kelso's last two international appearances.

	LEAGUE		*FA CUP*		*TOTAL*	
	App	*Gls*	*App*	*Gls*	*App*	*Gls*
1888-89	1	0	0	0	1	0
1891-92	23	2	1	0	24	2
1892-93	14	1	7	0	21	1
1893-94	26	1	1	0	27	1
1894-95	19	1	4	0	23	1
1895-96	6	0	1	0	7	0
	89	5	14	0	103	5

Few people with a basic knowledge of the modern game would argue with the sentiment that Howard Kendall was the finest player never to win full international honours. The stylish, competitive midfielder who restored pride to a great club after moving into the Goodison managerial hot-seat, was a positive inspiration during his seven-year playing career with the club. He became the youngest player ever to appear in an FA Cup Final when he played at left-half for Preston North End against West Ham United in 1964 — just 20 days before his 18th birthday. After 104 appearances for Preston he was signed for £80,000 in March 1967 and went on to be part of the most influential midfield combination Everton has ever known. Along with Colin Harvey and Alan Ball, he ran the side's engine-room as Everton swept to an emphatic Championship success in 1969-70. It is one of football's great unsolved mysteries as to why that superb team faltered so badly in following seasons. After playing over 250 games for the club, Kendall departed to Birmingham City in February 1974 as part of a complicated £350,000 deal which brought striker Bob Latchford to Goodison. In August 1977 he was transferred to Stoke City for a mere £40,000 and despite being tempted by an offer from North American side, Minnesota Kicks, he became club coach under Alan Durban in 1978.

HOWARD KENDALL

	LEAGUE		*FA CUP*		*FL CUP*		*EUROPE*		*TOTAL*	
	App	*Gls*	*App*	*Gls*	*App*	*Gls*	*App*	*Gls*	*App*	*Gls*
1966-67	4	0	0	0	-	-	0	0	4	0
1967-68	38	6	6	1	2	2	-	-	46	9
1968-69	28/1	1	3	0	4	0	-	-	35/1	1
1969-70	36	4	1	0	4	1	-	-	41	5
1970-71	40	2	5	2	0	0	6	2	51	6
1971-72	34/1	4	4	0	0	0	-	-	38/1	4
1972-73	40	4	2	0	1	0	-	-	43	4
1973-74	7	0	1	0	0	0	-	-	8	0
1981-82	4	0	1	0	1	0	-	-	6	0
	231/2	21	23	3	12	3	6	2	272/2	29

ROGER KENYON

Roger Kenyon was a reliable and consistent centre-half who was handed the unenviable task of following Brian Labone into the heart of Everton's defence. He was substitute, but did not play, in the 1968 FA Cup Final against West Bromwich Albion and was called into the side to help clinch the League Championship two years later. Seen as the natural successor to Labone, he earned a long series of glowing write-ups in the closing weeks of the 1970 title campaign. Mystifyingly that famous team went into decline, Kenyon's progress being badly interrupted by a car accident in 1974. He was dogged by a series of niggling injuries but, every time he fought his way back to full fitness, he proved conclusively that he had lost none of his speed or superb timing. He was an England substitute for the European Championship games against West Germany, Cyprus and Wales at Wembley in 1975. He stayed with Everton for around 15 years before moving to the west coast of Canada to join Vancouver Whitecaps. In 1979 he helped steer them to the North American Soccer League title.

	LEAGUE		*FA CUP*		*FL CUP*		*EUROPE*		*TOTAL*	
	App	*Gls*	*App*	*Gls*	*App*	*Gls*	*App*	*Gls*	*App*	*Gls*
1967-68	12/4	0	2	0	0	0	-	-	14/4	0
1968-69	4/3	0	0/1	0	0/2	0	-	-	4/6	0
1969-70	8/1	0	0	0	0/1	0	-	-	8/2	0
1970-71	28/1	0	2	0	0	0	4	0	34/1	0
1971-72	34/2	0	3	1	1	0	-	-	38/2	1
1972-73	40	2	2	0	1	0	-	-	43	2
1973-74	36	2	1	0	2	0	-	-	39	2
1974-75	40	0	2	1	2	0	-	-	44	1
1975-76	28/2	1	1	0	4	1	2	0	35/2	2
1976-77	14	1	1	0	3	0	-	-	18	1
1977-78	7	0	1	0	0	0	-	-	8	0
1978-79	3	0	0	0	0	0	1	0	4	0
	254/13	6	15/1	2	13/3	1	7	0	289/17	9

Oxford-born Martin Keown began his career with Arsenal in the early eighties but despite amassing a total of 27 senior appearances for the North London club he was unable to command a regular first-team place and joined Aston Villa for £200,000 in 1986 after enjoying a brief loan period at Brighton and Hove Albion. During his three-year spell at Villa Park, Keown established himself as a more than competent central defender, one capable of combining natural aggression and sound distribution. Colin Harvey brought Keown to Goodison Park in August 1989, paying £750,000 for a man he initially regarded as little more than a useful, if experienced, squad player. After struggling to come to terms with life at one of British football's biggest clubs, he began to settle in but not until the 1991-2 season could he fully regard himself as a regular on the team sheet. Keown's rapid development into a top-class defender was finally recognised by England manager Graham Taylor in February 1992 when he was selected for the friendly international against France at Wembley. Keown was a model of consistency on his international debut, subduing totally the talented and dangerous Eric Cantona. He joined Arsenal in a £2 million deal in 1993.

MARTIN KEOWN

	LEAGUE		*FA CUP*		*FL CUP*		*EUROPE*		*TOTAL*	
	App	*Gls*	*App*	*Gls*	*App*	*Gls*	*App*	*Gls*	*App*	*Gls*
1989-90	19/1	0	4	0	2	0	-	-	25/1	0
1990-91	21/3	0	4/1	0	1	0	-	-	26/4	0
1991-92	39	0	2	0	4	0	-	-	45	0
1992-93	13	0	2	0	4	0	-	-	19	0
	92/4	0	12/1	0	11	0	-	-	115/5	0

When Everton signed Brian Kidd they acquired not only a man with a proven goalscoring record, but also someone who cherished the traditional values of football. In Kidd's book, qualities like loyalty, hard work and respect had a high rating. An exhilarating forward when playing to the peak of his form, he hit the heights of his career when it had barely started. On his 19th birthday in 1968 he lined up alongside such greats as Bobby Charlton and George Best to score a goal in Manchester United's famous European Cup Final victory over Portuguese aces Benfica at Wembley. He arrived at Everton 11 years later, for £150,000 in March 1979. By that point he had picked up England caps at Schoolboy, Youth, Under-23 and full international levels. He started at Old Trafford, breaking into the League side after a tour of Australia in 1967. After playing more than 200 games for United he moved to Arsenal for £110,000 and was top scorer for the Gunners in each of his two seasons at Highbury. But he was anxious to return north and in June 1976 he jumped at the chance of joining Manchester City for £100,000. He finished his first season at Maine Road as top scorer with 21 goals and topped the charts 12 months later with 16. Although his time at Goodison was a happy one he never really recaptured the stunning form which made him a household name in the 1970s and was transferred to Bolton for £150,000 in May 1980. He was appointed assistant manager of Manchester United in 1991.

BRIAN KIDD

	LEAGUE		*FA CUP*		*FL CUP*		*EUROPE*		*TOTAL*	
	App	*Gls*	*App*	*Gls*	*App*	*Gls*	*App*	*Gls*	*App*	*Gls*
1978-79	9	2	0	0	0	0	0	0	9	2
1979-80	31	10	4	4	5	4	2	0	42	18
	40	12	4	4	5	4	2	0	51	20

Andy King was the man who simply could not live without Everton. A hugely gifted yet erratic and inconsistent player, he enjoyed two spells at Goodison Park and would almost certainly have gone on to full England honours had he been capable of matching his undoubted skill with a degree of self-discipline. A thoughtful midfield general who could score goals, he was a magnificent ball-player on his day. Sadly he was unable to maintain his best form when it really mattered and far too often found himself the odd man out. He was originally signed by Billy Bingham from Luton Town for £35,000 in 1976. He was idolised by the fans who appreciated his flair for the unusual. He joined Tommy Docherty's QPR in a £450,000 deal in September 1980, but was unhappy at Loftus Road and moved to West Brom for a similar fee only 12 months later. He encountered problems both on and off the field and was on the verge of ending up on football's scrapheap when Howard Kendall rescued his career in July 1982. At the age of 25 he was brought back to Everton in a straight swop which took Peter Eastoe to The Hawthorns. At the time Kendall described him as a 'technically superb player and finisher' but he failed to realise his full potential and after around 50 senior games he was allowed to leave and went to Holland. He finished his playing career at Aldershot and is now pursuing a career in journalism.

	LEAGUE		*FA CUP*		*FL CUP*		*EUROPE*		*TOTAL*	
	App	*Gls*	*App*	*Gls*	*App*	*Gls*	*App*	*Gls*	*App*	*Gls*
1975-76	3	2	0	0	0	0	0	0	3	2
1976-77	36/1	7	4/1	0	9	5	-	-	49/2	12
1977-78	42	8	2	1	5	2	-	-	49	11
1978-79	40	12	1	0	3	0	3	4	47	16
1979-80	29	9	4	1	4	1	2	0	39	11
1982-83	24	9	4	2	4	2	-	-	32	13
1983-84	19/1	2	1	0	4/1	1	-	-	24/2	3
	193/2	49	16/1	4	29/1	11	5	4	243/4	68

ANDY KING

One of the greatest players to wear the royal blue of Everton, Brian Labone was the model professional for both club and country. An exemplary character in the mould of Tom Finney and Bobby Charlton, he was booked only twice in a career which spanned 14 years. He started with Everton in 1957, several years before the maximum wage was abolished, and played the game as much for the love of it as for the money he took home. From being a schoolboy fan on the terraces Labone went on to captain the club he idolised and led them out at Wembley. He was a cultured and effective defender who made full use of his height. Unlike so many of his centre-back contemporaries, Labone had little interest in straying upfield in search of goals. He was a stopper pure and simple, and managed to find the net only twice in his lengthy career. Altogether he made 533 first-team appearances and his League tally — 451 — was only 12 short of the record held by Ted Sagar whose career was nine years longer than Labone's. He won two League Championship medals and FA Cup winners' and runners-up medals. He was a key member of England's 1970 World Cup squad and altogether won 26 full caps. He injured an Achilles tendon in a reserve game in September 1971 and was forced to quit the following year.

	LEAGUE		*FA CUP*		*FL CUP*		*EUROPE*		*TOTAL*	
	App	*Gls*	*App*	*Gls*	*App*	*Gls*	*App*	*Gls*	*App*	*Gls*
1957-58	4	0	0	0	-	-	-	-	4	0
1958-59	4	0	0	0	-	-	-	-	4	0
1959-60	31	0	1	0	-	-	-	-	32	0
1960-61	42	0	1	0	4	0	-	-	47	0
1961-62	41	0	3	0	-	-	-	-	44	0
1962-63	40	0	3	0	-	-	2	0	45	0
1963-64	34	0	4	0	-	-	2	0	40	0
1964-65	42	0	4	0	-	-	6	0	52	0
1965-66	37	2	8	0	-	-	3	0	48	2
1966-67	40	0	6	0	-	-	4	0	50	0
1967-68	40	0	6	0	2	0	-	-	48	0
1968-69	42	0	5	0	4	0	-	-	51	0
1969-70	34	0	1	0	4	0	-	-	39	0
1970-71	16	0	3	0	0	0	2	0	21	0
1971-72	4	0	0	0	1	0	-	-	5	0
	451	2	45	0	15	0	19	0	530	2

BRIAN LABONE

A big, bustling centre-forward in the traditional mould, Bob Latchford was one of the finest goal-getters ever to play for Everton. He made his name with Birmingham City before joining Everton for £350,000 in 1974. Initial doubts about whether he had the speed to match his instinctive ability in front of goal were soon dispelled as he made the transition from raw material to finished product within the space of two seasons. His greatest asset was his uncanny knack of turning half-chances into goals. He was devastating in the penalty area, firing home literally dozens of goals from seemingly impossible angles. Although not a particularly tall man, he was dangerous in the air. Latchford was top League scorer in his first four full seasons with the club, reaching his peak in 1977-8 when he became the first Division One player for six years to reach the 30 goals mark. He entered the final game of that season, against Chelsea at home, needing two to claim a national newspaper prize of £10,000, and a double blast in a comprehensive victory was enough to snatch the money and carve for himself a place in Merseyside football folklore. After a glittering career in which he picked up 12 full England caps, he was transferred to Swansea City for £125,000 in July 1981. He left as Everton's highest post-war League goalscorer with 106 from 235 games. He enjoyed mixed fortunes at Vetch Field but still managed 32 goals in 1982-3. He was given a free transfer in January 1984 and joined Dutch club, Breda. Five months later he returned to England, signing for Coventry City. In July 1985 he signed for Lincoln City and then drifted into non-League football.

BOB LATCHFORD

	LEAGUE		*FA CUP*		*FL CUP*		*EUROPE*		*TOTAL*	
	App	*Gls*	*App*	*Gls*	*App*	*Gls*	*App*	*Gls*	*App*	*Gls*
1973-74	13	7	0	0	0	0	-	-	13	7
1974-75	36	17	3	1	2	1	-	-	41	19
1975-76	31	12	1	0	4	1	2	0	38	13
1976-77	36	17	5	3	9	5	-	-	50	25
1977-78	39	30	2	1	5	1	-	-	46	32
1978-79	36	11	1	0	3	6	4	3	44	20
1979-80	26	6	5/1	5	2	2	0/1	0	33/2	13
1980-81	18/1	6	0	0	3	3	-	-	21/1	9
	235/1	106	17/1	10	28	19	6/1	3	286/3	138

Alex Latta was Everton's regular outside-right during their early days in the Football League, forming a much-feared partnership with inside-forward Alex Brady. Latta was born in Dumbarton in 1867 and played for Dumbarton Athletic before joining Everton in 1889. He made his debut against Blackburn Rovers on 7 September 1889. Latta, who was tall for a winger, won two Scotland caps, against England and Wales, and played for Everton in the 1893 FA Cup Final. Two years earlier he had been a member of the Championship-winning team. A teetotaller, Latta left for Liverpool in 1896 and when he retired from football began a yacht-making business. Later he worked for 20 years as manager of a boat-building yard. He died in August 1928.

ALEX LATTA

	LEAGUE		*FA CUP*		*TOTAL*	
	App	*Gls*	*App*	*Gls*	*App*	*Gls*
1889-90	19	9	2	0	21	9
1890-91	10	4	1	0	11	4
1891-92	25	17	1	0	26	17
1892-93	28	18	7	1	35	19
1893-94	29	9	1	0	30	9
1894-95	20	11	0	0	20	11
1895-96	5	1	0	0	5	1
	136	69	12	1	148	70

David Lawson became Britain's most expensive goalkeeper when he joined Everton from Huddersfield Town for £80,000 in June 1972. A quietly-spoken Geordie, he had a rather topsy-turvy career which saw him both as a disillusioned reserve rooted at the bottom of the Fourth Division, and a player tasting the big-time with the Goodison club. When he arrived at Everton he was involved in a straight dog-fight with Dai Davies for the goalkeeping jersey. His career got off to a stuttering start when he joined Newcastle United as an apprentice. He was allowed to leave and joined now extinct Bradford, but even at Park Avenue he could not be guaranteed a place. He had a spell with Shrewsbury and trials with various other clubs, including Liverpool, before ending up at Huddersfield in 1969. It was not until regular-choice Terry Poole broke a leg that he was given an extended first-team run. He made his Everton debut on the opening day of 1972-3 at Norwich. He played in every game the following season, but after seven matches in 1974-5 he lost his place through injury. He was a fine, brave last line of defence with a very safe pair of hands and good positional sense. He was transferred to Luton Town for £15,000 in October 1978.

DAVID LAWSON

	LEAGUE		*FA CUP*		*FL CUP*		*EUROPE*		*TOTAL*	
	App	*Gls*	*App*	*Gls*	*App*	*Gls*	*App*	*Gls*	*App*	*Gls*
1972-73	38	0	2	0	1	0	-	-	41	0
1973-74	42	0	3	0	2	0	-	-	47	0
1974-75	7	0	0	0	2	0	-	-	9	0
1975-76	22	0	0	0	3	0	1	0	26	0
1976-77	15	0	7	0	5	0	-	-	27	0
	124	0	12	0	13	0	1	0	150	0

Many critics would argue that Tommy Lawton was a better footballer than the legendary Dixie Dean, if not a better goalscorer. Certainly the youngster who went on to international fame with England was a superlative athlete who stood head and shoulders above his contemporaries in terms of skill and determination to succeed. When he was in full flow he was simply too hot to handle and in the days when sides played with only one central defender, Lawton often found himself shadowed by a posse of attendants, desperately anxious to cut short his famous surging runs before he reached the edge of the penalty area. Despite his flat feet (he was forced to wear arch-supports in his boots) he was brilliant on the ground, spraying passes around with astonishing ease. His heading ability was second to none; they used to say that if the ball was in the air he would inevitably connect with it. He was born in Bolton and in three seasons of schoolboy football scored a staggering total of 570 goals. Burnley snapped him up and he played his first League game for them just four days after his 17th birthday. It was a prophetic debut, for the youngster scored a hat-trick. He cost Everton £6,500 in March 1937 and repaid them with 65 goals in 87 games. He topped the Football League scorers list in 1937-8 with 28 (jointly with Roberts of Port Vale) and again in 1938-9 (with Mickey Fenton of Middlesbrough). In November 1945, he joined Chelsea for £11,500, then Notts County (who paid a British record £20,000 for him), Brentford and Arsenal before becoming manager of Notts County, ending a career in which he had scored 231 goals in 390 League games, and 22 goals in 23 full England matches. Taking his wartime and Victory internationals into account, his England figures were 46 goals in 45 games. On one memorable day in 1940 he played in two matches for different clubs within the space of a few hours. In 1972 a testimonial game which raised £6,300 was held for him at Goodison Park between Everton and Great Britain XI. Lawton was a true giant of the game and Dean once said of him, "He was a 100 per cent club man."

TOMMY LAWTON

	LEAGUE		*FA CUP*		*TOTAL*	
	App	*Gls*	*App*	*Gls*	*App*	*Gls*
1936-37	10	3	1	1	11	4
1937-38	39	28	2	0	41	28
1938-39	38	34	5	4	43	38
	87	65	8	5	95	70

Signed from Shrewsbury Town in September 1947, Cyril Lello stayed with Everton for over nine years, serving them as a hard-working right-half, although he began his Goodison career as an inside-forward. A native of Shropshire, Lello played wartime football with Lincoln City — in December 1943 he scored seven goals in a League North match against Notts County — before joining the Shrews. When Everton were relegated from Division One in 1950-51, Lello was injured and did not play a single game. But he was an ever-present when Everton won promotion in 1953-4, and again during their first season back in the First Division. In 1953 he was a member of the side which reached the semi-final of the FA Cup before losing to Bolton Wanderers. In November 1956, Harry Catterick, who had played with Lello in the immediate post-war era, signed him for Rochdale but he made only 11 League appearances there before ending his first-class career.

	LEAGUE		*FA CUP*		*TOTAL*	
	App	*Gls*	*App*	*Gls*	*App*	*Gls*
1947-48	9	2	0	0	9	2
1948-49	20	0	1	0	21	0
1949-50	35	0	2	0	37	0
1951-52	21	1	0	0	21	1
1952-53	26	0	5	0	31	0
1953-54	42	2	3	0	45	2
1954-55	42	2	2	0	44	2
1955-56	37	2	4	0	41	2
1956-57	5	0	0	0	5	0
	237	9	17	0	254	9

CYRIL LELLO

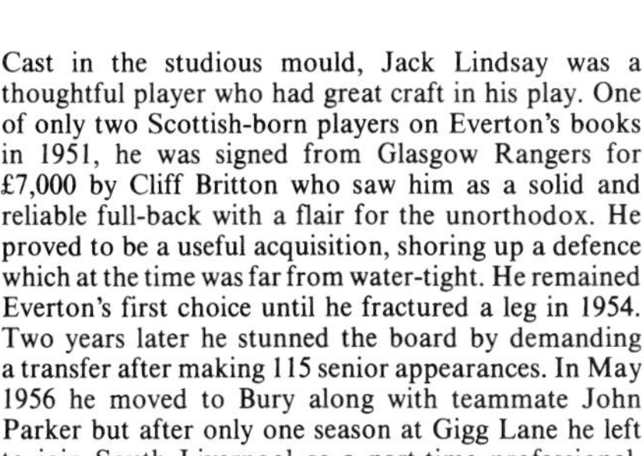

Cast in the studious mould, Jack Lindsay was a thoughtful player who had great craft in his play. One of only two Scottish-born players on Everton's books in 1951, he was signed from Glasgow Rangers for £7,000 by Cliff Britton who saw him as a solid and reliable full-back with a flair for the unorthodox. He proved to be a useful acquisition, shoring up a defence which at the time was far from water-tight. He remained Everton's first choice until he fractured a leg in 1954. Two years later he stunned the board by demanding a transfer after making 115 senior appearances. In May 1956 he moved to Bury along with teammate John Parker but after only one season at Gigg Lane he left to join South Liverpool as a part-time professional.

	LEAGUE		*FA CUP*		*TOTAL*	
	App	*Gls*	*App*	*Gls*	*App*	*Gls*
1950-51	4	0	0	0	4	0
1951-52	40	0	2	0	42	0
1952-53	30	0	5	0	35	0
1953-54	31	2	3	0	34	2
	105	2	10	0	115	2

JACK LINDSAY

Although Gary Lineker spent only 13 months with Everton, his goalscoring exploits were enough to earn him a place in Merseyside's 'Hall of Fame'. He arrived at Goodison Park in June 1985 after protracted negotiations between Howard Kendall and Leicester City had threatened to break down on numerous occasions. Everton valued Lineker at £400,000 whilst City demanded £1.25 million — the fee ultimately being set at £800,000 by an independent tribunal. Lineker's arrival was followed, one month later, by the departure of Andy Gray who returned to Aston Villa, leaving Everton supporters without a hero upon whom to lavish praise and adoration. It was a role well-suited to the articulate youngster with the temperament of a chess player and his one season at Goodison was an unmitigated success as he struck up a superb attacking partnership with Graeme Sharp. Lineker tormented defences the length and breadth of the League and finished with 30 goals, a feat which saw him voted Player of the Year by both the PFA and the Football Writers' Association. Alas, his efforts were unrewarded in terms of tangible success as Everton finished runners-up in the League and FA Cup, although Lineker did score the opening goal of the historic all-Merseyside FA Cup Final. Along with teammates Peter Reid, Trevor Steven and Gary Stevens, he was a key figure in England's 1986 World Cup campaign and ended it as the leading scorer in the Finals with six goals. He travelled back from Mexico amidst mounting speculation that he was to be sold to the highest bidder and after four weeks of intense negotiations he pledged his future to Spanish giants Barcelona in a massive £2.5 million deal. After a hugely successful spell in Spain, he returned to English football in 1989 when he joined Tottenham Hotspur for £1.2 million. He later skippered England and in 1993 joined the new Japanese club, Grampus 8.

GARY LINEKER

	LEAGUE		*FA CUP*		*FL CUP*		*TOTAL*	
	App	*Gls*	*App*	*Gls*	*App*	*Gls*	*App*	*Gls*
1985-86	41	30	6	5	5	3	52	38
	41	30	6	5	5	3	52	38

Regarded as a model professional, Duggie Livingstone was said to have a 'schoolgirl complexion' when he joined Everton from his native Scotland in 1921. A former Celtic player, he earned great praise in his formative years for his cool and calculated play at full-back although many felt him too slow to play the game at the highest level. He became totally disillusioned with the Goodison heirarchy towards the end of 1925 and eventually opted for a move, joining Plymouth Argyle in February 1926. Within four years he was back on Merseyside with Tranmere Rovers, with whom he stayed until 1935. After ending his playing career at Prenton Park, he was appointed trainer at Exeter City before he moved on to fill a similar post at Sheffield United. After spending the best part of a decade learning the ropes, he moved into management with Sheffield Wednesday. Eventually he left Hillsborough to try his luck on the continent where he coached Sparta of Holland before offering his services to the Belgian national side. On New Year's Day 1955 he moved into the hot-seat at St James' Park, Newcastle, and looked on in horror as United conceded four goals in only seven minutes against his old club, Sheffield United. But by the end of the season Newcastle had won the FA Cup. Livingstone left the North-East after a furious row with the United board who took away his powers of team selection early in 1956.

	LEAGUE		*FA CUP*		*TOTAL*	
	App	*Gls*	*App*	*Gls*	*App*	*Gls*
1921-22	24	0	1	0	25	0
1922-23	8	0	2	0	10	0
1923-24	38	0	2	0	40	0
1924-25	20	0	0	0	20	0
1925-26	5	0	0	0	5	0
	95	0	5	0	100	0

DUGGIE LIVINGSTONE

To many supporters the world over, Mick Lyons will always be 'Mr Everton'. He was a player who once admitted that he would readily run through a brick wall to further the Everton cause, but for the most part he contented himself with halting opposition forwards. He was born in Croxteth and joined the club as a striker, playing in the forward role in both youth and Central League teams. He was demoted to the 'A' team when David Johnson emerged from the shadows and it was during this period that Tommy Casey switched him to centre-back. He made his first-team debut in 1970-71 and went on to build a brilliant career. He lost his regular place at the age of 30, early in 1982 when Billy Wright was brought into Howard Kendall's constantly-changing side to partner Mark Higgins. After waiting patiently for a recall which was never to come, he severed his ties with the club in August 1982, joining Sheffield Wednesday whom he helped to steer into the First Division. Sadly, Lyons, who dedicated the best years of his life to a club he dearly loved, won nothing during his time at Goodison Park. In November 1985 he became Grimsby Town player-coach but was sacked in June 1987 after they were relegated to Division Three. In July 1987 he rejoined Everton as reserve-team coach. "I'm coming home" he said. He was dismissed following the return of Howard Kendall in November, 1990 and was later appointed first-team coach at Wigan Athletic.

MICK LYONS

	LEAGUE		*FA CUP*		*FL CUP*		*EUROPE*		*TOTAL*	
	App	*Gls*	*App*	*Gls*	*App*	*Gls*	*App*	*Gls*	*App*	*Gls*
1970-71	1/1	1	0	0	0	0	0	0	1/1	1
1971-72	20/4	3	4	0	0	0	-	-	24/4	3
1972-73	19/6	2	0	0	1	0	-	-	20/6	2
1973-74	37/4	9	3	0	1	0	-	-	41/4	9
1974-75	36/2	8	4	3	2	0	-	-	42/2	11
1975-76	42	5	1	0	5	1	2	0	50	6
1976-77	39/1	4	7	1	9	2	-	-	55/1	7
1977-78	42	5	2	1	5	2	-	-	49	8
1978-79	37	6	1	0	2	0	3	0	43	6
1979-80	35/3	0	6	0	5	0	2	0	48/3	0
1980-81	30/3	2	0/1	1	0	0	-	-	30/4	3
1981-82	26/1	3	1	0	4	0	-	-	31/1	3
	364/25	48	29/1	6	34	5	7	0	434/26	59

Neil McBain is the oldest player ever to appear in a Football League match. In March 1947, when he was manager of New Brighton, he found himself one player short — a goalkeeper — for a Third Division North match at Hartlepool. At the age of 52 years and four months he boldly placed himself between the posts and, for the record, Hartlepools won 3-0. He signed for Everton in early 1923 from Manchester United, a transfer which caused uproar at Old Trafford. When the deal was announced, more than a thousand supporters packed into a local hall to protest about his impending departure. McBain was a useful wing-half whose greatest strength was his heading ability. He was an elegant player, perhaps too elegant for his own good at times. He often foresook his defensive duties in favour of an over-adventurous approach. In a long and varied career he also played for Liverpool, St Johnstone and Watford. After hanging up his boots he turned to management with Watford, New Brighton, Luton and Leyton Orient. He was a full Scottish international, making three appearances between 1922 and 1924. After becoming disenchanted with the English game, he went to South America to coach the Argentinian club, Estudiantes de la Plata. He died, aged 78, in May 1974.

NEIL McBAIN

	LEAGUE		*FA CUP*		*TOTAL*	
	App	*Gls*	*App*	*Gls*	*App*	*Gls*
1922-23	15	0	0	0	15	0
1923-24	37	0	2	0	39	0
1924-25	35	0	4	0	39	0
1925-26	10	1	0	0	10	1
	97	1	6	0	103	1

JOHN McDONALD

Everton signed full-back John McDonald from Airdrie in 1920 and he went straight into the League side for the start of 1920-21, making his debut in the 3-3 draw at Bradford Park Avenue on 28 August. McDonald missed only three games that season and in August 1921 he was appointed club captain. His inspiration was vital that season as Everton struggled against relegation, and although he missed some games through injury, he was a telling influence in the dressing-room. A native of Dykehead, McDonald had appeared in Scottish representative football during World War One, but his move to Everton did not coincide with one of the more successful periods in the club's history. By the time the League Championship next came to Goodison Park (1927-8), McDonald was playing Third Division North football with New Brighton, for whom he signed in August 1927. He went on to give them several years valuable service.

	LEAGUE		*FA CUP*		*TOTAL*	
	App	*Gls*	*App*	*Gls*	*App*	*Gls*
1920-21	39	0	5	0	44	0
1921-22	26	0	1	0	27	0
1922-23	29	0	0	0	29	0
1923-24	24	0	2	0	26	0
1924-25	29	0	4	0	33	0
1925-26	37	0	2	0	39	0
1926-27	24	0	2	0	26	0
	208	0	16	0	224	0

DUNCAN McKENZIE

Duncan McKenzie was one of football's great enigmas. A player of unquestionable brilliance, he turned into a sporting nomad, constantly moving from club to club in a forlorn bid to find the right stage for his stunning skills. A tremendous showman, at one stage he seemed to spend more time amusing supporters by jumping over cars than actually playing football. A slight, wiry man, he was one of the game's most dazzling dribblers, the sort of player who could comfortably glide around four opponents in the space of ten yards. He started his career with Nottingham Forest and was loaned to Mansfield before moving to Leeds United where he witnessed first hand the sensational coming and going of Brian Clough. After a turbulent period at Elland Road he quit English football for the Continent, joining Anderlecht. After only 30 games, and 16 goals, for the Belgian side, he was signed by Goodison boss Billy Bingham in December 1976. Shortly after his £200,000 signing, Bingham was sacked and replaced by Gordon Lee. McKenzie and Lee never got on and eventually the player left. He later played with Chelsea and Blackburn, and with Tulsa Roughnecks and Chicago Sting in the NASL. He returned to live on Merseyside and is presently working as a journalist.

	LEAGUE		*FA CUP*		*FL CUP*		*TOTAL*	
	App	*Gls*	*App*	*Gls*	*App*	*Gls*	*App*	*Gls*
1976-77	20	5	6	4	4	1	30	10
1977-78	28	9	1/1	1	2	1	31/1	11
	48	14	7/1	5	6	2	61/1	21

Steve McMahon's burning desire to win trophies forced him to quit Goodison Park just months before Howard Kendall steered Everton back on the glory trail. A former Goodison ball-boy, he joined Everton as an apprentice in December 1977. He made his first-team debut at Sunderland in August 1980, and the following season was voted Player of the Year by supporters who appreciated his honest endeavour and total commitment. A bright future seemed assured when he was picked to play for the England Under-21 side against the Republic of Ireland. He continued to perform at a consistently high level even though he was not playing in a particularly good side. Eventually he came to the conclusion that the only way to further his career was to move away from the club he had always supported. His contract expired at the end of 1982-3 and he refused to sign another, even though manager Howard Kendall was adamant that he wanted McMahon to stay. Liverpool made a firm offer for him, but after discussions with his family he opted for a move to Aston Villa for £250,000 in May 1983. Ironically, less than 12 months later, Everton defeated Villa to reach the Milk Cup Final. In September 1985, however, he became Kenny Dalglish's first major signing when he moved to Anfield for £375,000. He won his first full England cap in a match against Israel in Tel Aviv in February 1988. He joined Manchester City in a £900,000 deal on Boxing Day, 1991.

	LEAGUE		*FA CUP*		*FL CUP*		*TOTAL*	
	App	*Gls*	*App*	*Gls*	*App*	*Gls*	*App*	*Gls*
1980-81	34	5	5	0	3	0	42	5
1981-82	31/1	2	0	0	4	2	35/1	4
1982-83	34	4	4	0	4	1	42	5
	99/1	11	9	0	11	3	119/1	14

STEVE McMAHON

A tall, blond centre-half, Ken McNaught joined Everton as a 16-year-old apprentice before signing full professional forms in 1972. His greatest asset was his powerful heading which proved immensely valuable in both defence and up front. A tough, rugged Scot, he had set his heart on making the grade as a striker before the timely intervention of his father, Willie, a former Scottish international who played with Raith Rovers. He was persuaded to drop back and he made an immediate impression, being selected for the Scotland amateur youth side. The scouts were soon showing interest and McNaught decided to move to Goodison only after completing his school studies which yielded seven GCE 'O' levels. He moved out of the 'A' team and into the reserves at the end of his first season in 1971 and made his big breakthrough in 1975. In 1976-7 he was Everton's only ever-present, appearing in all 58 League and Cup games, but less than three months later he was on his way to Aston Villa for £200,000. McNaught won League Championship and European Cup winners' medals with Villa in a six-year career before joining West Brom for £125,000. Later he went on loan to Manchester City before being transferred to Sheffield United in June 1985. A year later he was forced to retire through injury In 1988 he was coach to Dunfermline.

	LEAGUE		*FA CUP*		*FL CUP*		*TOTAL*	
	App	*Gls*	*App*	*Gls*	*App*	*Gls*	*App*	*Gls*
1974-75	4	0	3	0	0	0	7	0
1975-76	18/2	0	0	0	1	0	19/2	0
1976-77	42	3	7	0	9	0	58	3
	64/2	3	10	0	10	0	84/2	3

KEN McNAUGHT

John Smith Maconnachie was a Scottish left-back, cool and polished, who joined Everton in April 1907 from Hibernian. Aberdeen-born Maconnachie made his Everton debut at centre-half, playing in the third game of 1907-08 against Preston North End at Goodison Park. Slowly he established himself in the side, settling down at left-back for the last few games of that season. The following year, as Everton pushed for the League Championship before settling for runners-up spot, Maconnachie was an ever-present and he played regularly until the outbreak of war eventually ended League soccer for the duration. Everton fans appreciated his cool, authoritative approach to the game and he seldom seemed ruffled, often playing his way out of tight situations in his own penalty area. In 1919-20 he completed 270 League and Cup appearances for Everton and then signed for Swindon Town at the start of the following season. He was one of the more skilful defenders to wear Everton's colours in an era when a full-back's main function was to punt the ball downfield as far as possible with little regard for its eventual destination. Maconnachie of Everton was too much of a footballer to settle for that.

	LEAGUE		*FA CUP*		*TOTAL*	
	App	*Gls*	*App*	*Gls*	*App*	*Gls*
1907-08	21	0	0	0	21	0
1908-09	38	0	2	0	40	0
1909-10	31	0	7	0	38	0
1910-11	22	0	2	0	24	0
1911-12	31	0	5	1	36	1
1912-13	23	4	5	0	28	4
1913-14	35	0	1	0	36	0
1914-15	28	0	3	0	31	0
1919-20	16	2	0	0	16	2
	245	6	25	1	270	7

JOHN MACONNACHIE

Harry Makepeace represented England at both football and cricket — a distinction he shared with his Everton and Lancashire colleague, Jack Sharp. Although practically all his sporting life was spent west of the Pennines, he was born in Middlesbrough, moving to Liverpool when he was ten. He signed for Everton in 1902 and made his debut in an FA Cup tie against Manchester United in February 1903. He began life as a forward but was quickly switched to the half-back line where his fearsome tackling and excellent distribution were better employed. He was a regular member of the side between 1904 and 1914 and played in the FA Cup-winning team of 1906 and again in the 1907 Final. He was chosen as England's left-half against Scotland on three occasions (1906, 1910 and 1912) and against Wales (1912). He also played for the Football League in 1910. His connection with Everton resumed after World War One when he was appointed coach. An opening batsman, he played in four Tests, all of them abroad, and scored 117 in the 1920-21 Melbourne Test. He died, aged 70, at Bebington in December 1952.

	LEAGUE		*FA CUP*		*TOTAL*	
	App	*Gls*	*App*	*Gls*	*App*	*Gls*
1902-03	3	0	1	0	4	0
1904-05	19	5	6	2	25	7
1905-06	27	2	6	2	33	4
1906-07	23	0	8	0	31	0
1907-08	31	2	7	0	38	2
1908-09	33	0	2	0	35	0
1909-10	32	4	7	2	39	6
1910-11	33	1	3	0	36	1
1911-12	34	1	5	1	39	2
1912-13	10	0	1	0	11	0
1913-14	16	0	1	0	17	0
1914-15	23	1	5	0	28	1
	284	16	52	7	336	23

HARRY MAKEPEACE

GEORGE MARTIN

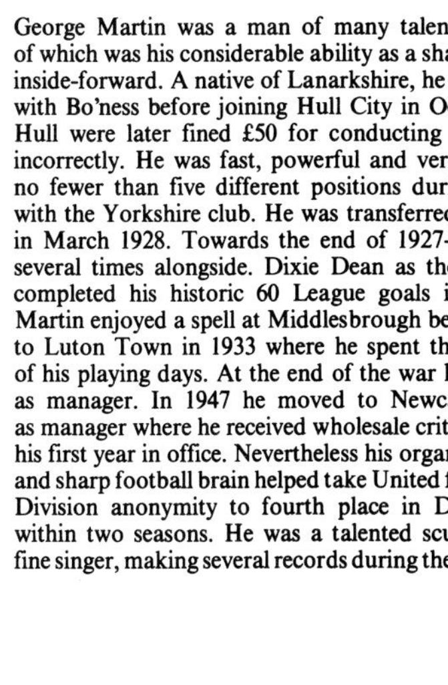

George Martin was a man of many talents, not least of which was his considerable ability as a sharp-shooting inside-forward. A native of Lanarkshire, he spent a time with Bo'ness before joining Hull City in October 1922. Hull were later fined £50 for conducting the transfer incorrectly. He was fast, powerful and versatile, filling no fewer than five different positions during his time with the Yorkshire club. He was transferred to Everton in March 1928. Towards the end of 1927-8 he played several times alongside. Dixie Dean as the great man completed his historic 60 League goals in a season. Martin enjoyed a spell at Middlesbrough before moving to Luton Town in 1933 where he spent the remainder of his playing days. At the end of the war he took over as manager. In 1947 he moved to Newcastle United as manager where he received wholesale criticism during his first year in office. Nevertheless his organising ability and sharp football brain helped take United from Second Division anonymity to fourth place in Division One within two seasons. He was a talented sculptor and a fine singer, making several records during the early 1940s.

	LEAGUE		*FA CUP*		*TOTAL*	
	App	*Gls*	*App*	*Gls*	*App*	*Gls*
1927-28	10	3	0	0	10	3
1928-29	18	6	0	0	18	6
1929-30	40	15	1	1	41	16
1930-31	15	7	0	0	15	7
1931-32	2	0	0	0	2	0
	85	31	1	1	86	32

MICK MEAGAN

Born in Dublin on 19 May 1934, Mick 'Chick' Meagan began his career with Eire junior clubs, Rathfarnhan and Johnville. A versatile competitor who firmly believed that no game was won or lost until the final whistle, he signed for Everton in September 1952. He turned full-time professional 18 months later and his League debut came in August 1957 against Wolves at Goodison. He went on to make 175 appearances for the club before he was effectively used as bait to lure Ray Wilson to Merseyside. The deal was struck in July 1964 with Meagan joining Huddersfield Town and Wilson coming in the other direction with a cash adjustment. He continued to play for the Republic of Ireland and was made captain of Huddersfield. He was transferred to Halifax Town in 1968, given a three-year contract and made skipper at The Shay.

	LEAGUE		*FA CUP*		*FL CUP*		*EUROPE*		*TOTAL*	
	App	*Gls*	*App*	*Gls*	*App*	*Gls*	*App*	*Gls*	*App*	*Gls*
1957-58	38	1	3	0	-	-	-	-	41	1
1958-59	21	0	0	0	-	-	-	-	21	0
1959-60	19	0	0	0	-	-	-	-	19	0
1960-61	11	0	0	0	0	0	-	-	11	0
1961-62	18	0	0	0	-	-	-	-	18	0
1962-63	32	0	3	0	-	-	1	0	36	0
1963-64	26	0	4	0	-	-	0	0	30	0
	165	1	10	0	0	0	1	0	176	1

One of the European game's all-time greats, Joe Mercer had a superb tactical brain and outstanding ability. He started as a junior with Everton in September 1932 and forced himself into the first team on a regular basis in 1935 when he took over in the half-back line from Jock Thomson. Devloping quickly, he became England's left-half. The war came and went and Sergeant Major Mercer, captain of his country and his appetite whetted by recent events, returned to Goodison, having won 26 wartime caps. But Everton had both a captain and a manager and Mercer became disconsolate. It was the low-point of his career. For a fortnight after returning he rarely left his house. Mighty Arsenal heard about his disenchantment and had his signature on a transfer form within 24 hours, for £7,000. He captained the Gunners from his second season at Highbury onwards and won a League Championship medal in 1948 and an FA Cup winners' medal in 1950. Arsenal narrowly missed the double, in 1952, and then topped the League once more in 1953. During this time he continued to live on Merseyside, training at Anfield. That he was captain of the side that beat Liverpool at Wembley in 1950 was rather embarrassing; that he should sustain the double fracture of a leg (which ended his playing days) against them four years later was tragic. He stepped into management, serving a brief apprenticeship at money-conscious Sheffield United before moving to Villa Park as manager, coach, chief scout and money-raiser. Villa won the Second Division championship, reached the FA Cup semi-finals twice, won the League Cup, built a £120,000 stand and finished halfway up the First Division before Mercer's health gave way. In 1965 he came out of what many had assumed was permanent retirement to take charge of Manchester City. Together with a bright young man called Malcolm Allison he restored pride to a great club. In 1977 he took temporary charge of the England team after the resignation of Don Revie. He became a director of Coventry City but resigned in 1981 after nine years. One of Everton's most beloved sons died on his 76th birthday in August 1990.

JOE MERCER OBE

	LEAGUE		*FA CUP*		*TOTAL*	
	App	*Gls*	*App*	*Gls*	*App*	*Gls*
1932-33	1	0	0	0	1	0
1934-35	8	0	0	0	8	0
1935-36	33	1	1	0	34	1
1936-37	39	0	4	0	43	0
1937-38	36	0	2	0	38	0
1938-39	41	0	5	0	46	0
1945-46	-	-	2	1	2	1
1946-47	12	0	0	0	12	0
	170	1	14	1	184	2

WILLIE MILLER

Everton had high hopes of landing a major find when they brought Willie Miller from Partick Thistle in 1935. Miller had made 38 appearances for Partick in the Scottish League the previous season and he went straight into the Everton team for the opening day of the 1935-6 campaign and helped his new club to score a resounding 4-0 success over Derby County. But Miller's personal fortunes at Goodison were not so happy. It was surprising that he never settled there, because he was an exciting inside-right who had plenty of dash and good close control. His spirited runs straight at the heart of a defence had been a feature of the Scottish game. In 1935 he played for the Scottish League against the Football league, and that summer went to the USA and Canada with the Scotland team. He played in six of the 12 games on that tour, but none of them counted as full internationals and he was never capped. He managed one goal for Everton, in the 5-1 thrashing of Chelsea in October 1935, then lost his place. After one game the following season he signed for Burnley in October 1936. He was a potentially brilliant player whose star flashed all too briefly across the Goodison sky.

	LEAGUE		*FA CUP*		*TOTAL*	
	App	*Gls*	*App*	*Gls*	*App*	*Gls*
1935-36	15	1	1	0	16	1
1936-37	1	1	0	0	1	1
	16	2	1	0	17	2

Alfred Milward was one of five Everton players to line up for England against Scotland at Blackburn in 1891. He was a hard-working outside-left with a superior technical brain and tremendous vision. Although his angled crossfield passes were an integral part of his game, he was at his very best when rampaging down the flanks, leaving confused defenders trailing in his wake. Born at Great Marlow, he joined Everton in 1888 from Old Borlasians, and Marlow, and quickly established himself as a first-team regular. Perhaps his greatest attribute was that he never surrendered. Indeed, he lost his temper on more than one occasion with teammates who had opted to accept defeat long before the final whistle. He performed with great consistency for Everton between 1888 and 1897 and was rewarded with four full England caps. Both he and Edgar Chadwick were great players, but together they were devastating and it was their left-wing partnership for Everton that shattered many a defence. Milward joined New Brighton Tower in the close season of 1897, moved to Southampton (with whom he won a Southern League Championship medal and appeared in an FA Cup Final) two years later and finished his career with New Brompton (later Gillingham) before retiring in 1903. He died in June 1941, aged 70.

	LEAGUE		*FA CUP*		*TOTAL*	
	App	*Gls*	*App*	*Gls*	*App*	*Gls*
1888-89	6	2	0	0	6	2
1889-90	22	10	2	4	24	14
1890-91	22	12	1	0	23	12
1891-92	26	6	1	0	27	6
1892-93	27	11	7	2	34	13
1893-94	24	8	1	0	25	8
1894-95	18	10	3	0	21	10
1895-96	29	17	3	2	32	19
1896-97	27	9	5	3	32	12
	201	85	23	11	224	96

ALFRED MILWARD

A product of Haydock, Eric Moore had his fair share of ups and downs during his eight years at Goodison Park. After a solid start in the Central League side, in which he figured at both centre-forward and right-half, he was transformed into a full-back, signing professional forms in February 1949. He made his first-team debut in December that year at right-back. From that point he was a regular for the best part of 18 months but a troublesome knee injury sidelined him for long spells during the following two seasons. When he was fully fit again he missed only one game in two seasons, but in December 1956, unhappy at making only one First Division appearance that season, he asked for a transfer. He moved to Chesterfield in a deal worth £10,000 in January 1957, after nearly 200 outings for Everton. In July 1957 he was signed by Tranmere Rovers. Later he became a publican in Atherton.

	LEAGUE		*FA CUP*		*TOTAL*	
	App	*Gls*	*App*	*Gls*	*App*	*Gls*
1949-50	22	0	5	0	27	0
1950-51	37	0	1	0	38	0
1951-52	5	0	0	0	5	0
1952-53	14	0	0	0	14	0
1953-54	9	0	1	0	10	0
1954-55	41	0	2	0	43	0
1955-56	42	0	4	0	46	0
1956-57	1	0	0	0	1	0
	171	0	13	0	184	0

ERIC MOORE

Johnny Morrissey was the man who guaranteed Everton's place in the 1968 FA Cup Final with a dramatic penalty winner against high-fliers Leeds United at Old Trafford. The tenacious and gutsy winger hammered the spot-kick beyond Gary Sprake to set up a Wembley showdown with West Bromwich Albion, a match Everton were to lose 1-0. Regarded as the 'Pocket Hercules' of a side which won national acclaim for its cultured football, Morrissey arrived at Goodison from neighbours Liverpool for the bargain fee of £10,000 in 1962. His competitive style and fearsome shooting quickly saw him rise through the oft-crowded ranks and claim a regular first-team spot. He was instrumental in Everton's League Championship triumph in 1970 but shortly afterwards found his place threatened. He was transferred to Oldham Athletic in the summer of 1972 but was forced to retire from the game six months later because of injury.

	LEAGUE		*FA CUP*		*FL CUP*		*EUROPE*		*TOTAL*	
	App	*Gls*	*App*	*Gls*	*App*	*Gls*	*App*	*Gls*	*App*	*Gls*
1962-63	28	7	3	1	-	-	2	0	33	8
1963-64	7	1	0	0	-	-	0	0	7	1
1964-65	25	5	4	0	-	-	4	1	33	6
1965-66	10/1	2	1	0	-	-	3	0	14/1	2
1966-67	31	6	6	0	-	-	3	1	40	7
1967-68	26	3	5	2	1	0	-	-	32	5
1968-69	40	4	5	0	4	1	-	-	49	5
1969-70	41	9	1	0	3	0	-	-	45	9
1970-71	34	6	4	0	0	0	6	1	44	7
1971-72	15/1	0	0	0	0	0	-	-	15/1	0
	257/2	43	29	3	8	1	18	3	312/2	50

JOHN MORRISSEY

A Merseyside-grown talent, Derek Mountfield arrived at Goodison Park from Fourth Division Tranmere Rovers for £30,000 in June 1982. As a schoolboy he used to stand on the Goodison terraces and dream of emulating his sporting heroes by one day playing for the club he has always supported. A fine athlete with good pace and vision, his greatest asset is his considerable heading ability which frustrated quality strikers the length and breadth of the country after he made the number-five shirt his own. He made his League debut against Birmingham City at St Andrew's on 23 April 1983 and was given an unexpected chance to press for a regular place when centre-back Mark Higgins suffered the first of a series of cruel injuries. Mountfield grabbed his golden opportunity with both hands and proved to be mature beyond his years as the Everton revival got underway. An added bonus during the magnificent 1984-5 season were the goals, he scored 14, including the last-gasp equaliser against Ipswich Town in the FA Cup quarter-final tie at Goodison Park and the dramatic extra-time winner against Luton Town in the semi-final. The following Setpember, however, he was badly injured and underwent a cartilage operation. He lost his place following the arrival of Dave Watson from Norwich and handed in a transfer request towards the end of 1986-7, eventually moving to Aston Villa in the close season of 1988. He joined Wolverhampton Wanderers for £250,000 in January 1992.

	LEAGUE		*FA CUP*		*FL CUP*		*EUROPE*		*TOTAL*	
	App	*Gls*	*App*	*Gls*	*App*	*Gls*	*App*	*Gls*	*App*	*Gls*
1982-83	1	0	0	0	0	0	-	-	1	0
1983-84	31	3	8	0	8	0	-	-	47	3
1984-85	37	10	7	2	4	2	9	0	57	14
1985-86	15	3	2	0	0	0	-	-	17	3
1986-87	12/1	3	0	0	4	1	-	-	16/1	4
1987-88	4/5	0	0	0	0	0	-	-	4/5	0
	100/6	19	17	2	16	3	9	0	142/6	24

DEREK MOUNTFIELD

PAT NEVIN

Few players of modern times could justifiably claim to have the natural balance and grace of movement enjoyed by Pat Nevin. Unorthodox both on and off the field of play, Nevin joined Everton from Chelsea in the summer of 1988. With the two clubs unable to agree on the size of the transfer fee, the matter was laid before an independent tribunal which fixed the price at £925,000 — much to the chagrin of Colin Harvey who had valued one of English football's great enigmas at around £500,000. Although Nevin's ability to leave defenders trailing in his wake ensured that he was swiftly accepted by the discerning Goodison audience, he lacked consistency and an inability to fulfil a rich potential resulted in him being dropped from the first team on numerous occasions. His finest moment in an Everton shirt came in 1989 when he scored the goal which defeated Norwich City in the semi-final of the FA Cup. Sadly, Nevin's joy was totally overshadowed by the tragic events which had unfolded at Hillsborough on the same afternoon. The return of Howard Kendall to the club in 1990 failed to bring about a change of fortune and he was placed on the transfer list, at his own request, during the 1991-2 season and later joined Tranmere Rovers.

	LEAGUE		*FA CUP*		*FL CUP*		*EUROPE*		*TOTAL*	
	App	*Gls*	*App*	*Gls*	*App*	*Gls*	*App*	*Gls*	*App*	*Gls*
1988-89	20/5	2	5/1	2	1	0	-	-	26/6	4
1989-90	23/7	4	1/3	0	4	1	-	-	28/10	5
1990-91	31/6	8	5/1	0	2/1	1	-	-	38/8	9
1991-92	7/10	2	1/1	0	3	0	-	-	11/11	2
	81/28	16	12/6	2	10/1	2	-	-	103/35	20

Henry Newton arrived at Goodison Park in October 1970 after doing what few players of the day had the courage to do — turn down the ever-persuasive Brian Clough. As skipper of Nottingham Forest, Newton had been pursued for the best part of 18 months by then Derby County manager Clough. When he finally decided to quit the City Ground, Newton surprisingly accepted the terms offered by Harry Catterick, although it should be said that after selling Alan Hinton and Terry Hennessey to Derby, Forest were reluctant to let Newton make the same journey. Everton paid £150,000, plus Irish international Tommy Jackson, for his services, looking at Newton as a long-term investment. Sadly, after making his debut in the nightmare 4-0 defeat at Highbury, his career was handicapped by a series of long-term injuries. In three years with the club he played only 83 League and Cup games, and would be the first to admit that he never settled on Merseyside. Despite his problems he proved an effective defender (he started as a midfielder but switched to left-back when Keith Newton was injured) when playing at his peak. In September 1973, Clough at last got his man when Newton jumped at the chance to return to the Midlands for £110,000. It was Clough's last major signing for Derby before he sensationally quit but Newton and the rest recovered to win the League Championship in 1975. Newton struggled to overcome injuries and ended his career at Walsall whom he joined in May 1977. An arthritic hip was replaced and today Newton runs a sub-Post Office in Derby.

HENRY NEWTON

	LEAGUE		*FA CUP*		*FL CUP*		*TOTAL*	
	App	*Gls*	*App*	*Gls*	*App*	*Gls*	*App*	*Gls*
1970-71	23	3	4	1	0	0	27	4
1971-72	24	1	2	0	0	0	26	1
1972-73	23	1	0	0	1	0	24	1
1973-74	6	0	0	0	0	0	6	0
	76	5	6	1	1	0	83	6

KEITH NEWTON

Although Keith Newton was to spend only two and a half years at Everton, he will always be remembered as a fine, attacking full-back. He arrived at Goodison Park in December 1969 from Blackburn Rovers in a deal worth £80,000. After laying the foundations for what everyone presumed would be a lengthy and illustrious career, he was selected to play for England in the 1970 World Cup finals in Mexico, along with teammate Tommy Wright. On his return, his career took a down-turn and he lost his place in the Everton team after 14 games of 1971-2, after a series of uncharacteristically poor performances. In June 1972 he was transferred to Burnley where he played a leading role in the Turf Moor club's promotion from the Second Division in 1972-3. After his departure, he attacked Harry Catterick in the Press, claiming that his creative style and determination to play his way out of trouble led to friction. Newton made 27 appearances in the full England side.

	LEAGUE		*FA CUP*		*FL CUP*		*EUROPE*		*TOTAL*	
	App	*Gls*	*App*	*Gls*	*App*	*Gls*	*App*	*Gls*	*App*	*Gls*
1969-70	12	0	1	0	0	0	-	-	13	0
1970-71	21/1	1	1	0	0	0	6	0	28/1	1
1971-72	15	0	0	0	1	0	-	-	16	0
	48/1	1	2	0	1	0	6	0	57/1	1

GEOFF NULTY

In March 1980 Geoff Nulty was stretchered away from a derby match against Liverpool at Goodison Park and out of football for good. A tackle by Jimmy Case caused extensive damage to the polished defender's left knee and he was told immediately that he would never play again. It was a shattering blow to a player who had worked so hard to prove his worth after a £40,000 move from Newcastle less than two years earlier. While he could never be described as world-beater, Nulty was a dedicated professional with a no-nonsense approach to the defensive arts. He was firm in the tackle and more than capable of delivering a telling pass when given the space. He made less than 40 appearances for Everton, and was approaching the 250-mark in his career when tragedy struck. As the holder of an Open University degree in social sciences he was better prepared than most players to face a life without football. In fact he stayed in the game and took a coaching job at Goodison under Gordon Lee, later following Lee to Preston.

	LEAGUE		*FA CUP*		*FL CUP*		*EUROPE*		*TOTAL*	
	App	*Gls*	*App*	*Gls*	*App*	*Gls*	*App*	*Gls*	*App*	*Gls*
1978-79	13/4	1	0	0	2	0	2/1	0	17/5	1
1979-80	9/1	1	0	0	4	0	2	0	15/1	1
	22/5	2	0	0	6	0	4/1	0	32/6	2

Goalkeeper Jimmy O'Neill's father was a leading golf professional in the 1930s. Born in Dublin, Jimmy was spotted by an Everton scout while playing in local junior circles and invited to Goodison Park for a trial period. He was taken on at the end of 1948-9 and offered full professional terms. He made his debut in the Central League on 24 August 1949, and 364 days later made his full debut in a defeat at Middlesbrough. He enjoyed a successful career, becoming one of Britain's outstanding goalkeepers, forcing his way into the Republic of Ireland side to win 17 caps. He was exceptionally safe when handling crosses and he utilised his speed well. Indeed, he was often seen halting opposing forwards in their tracks on the edge of the penalty area. He eventually lost his Everton place to Albert Dunlop. He was transferred to Stoke City for £5,000 in July 1960, before joining Darlington in March 1965. Later he played with Port Vale.

	LEAGUE		*FA CUP*		*TOTAL*	
	App	*Gls*	*App*	*Gls*	*App*	*Gls*
1950-51	10	0	0	0	10	0
1951-52	20	0	0	0	20	0
1952-53	35	0	5	0	40	0
1953-54	28	0	3	0	31	0
1954-55	41	0	2	0	43	0
1955-56	34	0	2	0	36	0
1956-57	13	0	0	0	13	0
1957-58	6	0	0	0	6	0
1958-59	9	0	0	0	9	0
1959-60	5	0	0	0	5	0
	201	0	12	0	213	0

JIMMY O'NEILL

Alex Parker was a full-back in the classic mould. Fast, adventurous and very strong in the tackle, he became the latest in a long line of superb Everton defenders when he joined the club from Falkirk in 1958. Born in Irvine, Ayrshire, he began his career as a centre-forward but was switched to wing-half after joining Scottish junior club Kelso Rovers. Shortly after completing his move to Goodison he was posted to Cyprus with the Royal Scots Fusiliers, delaying his Everton debut until 8 November 1958. He won the first of 15 full international caps against Portugal in May 1955. He left Everton in September 1965 to join Southport where he finished his playing career. In 1968 he was released by the Haig Avenue club to become player-manager of Irish League side, Ballymena United. He returned to Southport in May 1970 to take over as manager.

	LEAGUE		*FA CUP*		*FL CUP*		*EUROPE*		*TOTAL*	
	App	*Gls*	*App*	*Gls*	*App*	*Gls*	*App*	*Gls*	*App*	*Gls*
1958-59	26	1	4	0	-	-	-	-	30	1
1959-60	38	2	1	0	-	-	-	-	39	2
1960-61	41	0	1	0	5	0	-	-	47	0
1961-62	31	0	3	0	-	-	-	-	34	0
1962-63	33	2	3	0	-	-	2	0	38	2
1963-64	17	0	0	0	-	-	2	0	19	0
1964-65	12	0	0	0	-	-	0	0	12	0
	198	5	12	0	5	0	4	0	219	5

ALEX PARKER

John Willie Parker spent more than four years in the shadows before establishing himself in the Everton side in the early 1950s. He was a tall, stylish inside-forward with two good feet and the ability to score as well as make goals. He arrived as an amateur in 1947, from St Lawrence CYMS, and quickly graduated through the junior sides, signing professional forms in December 1948. Within 18 months he was a regular in the Cetnral League side but he did not make his full debut until 24 March 1951 when he filled the outside-left berth against Blackpool at Goodison. He was a very deceptive player who was often criticised for being too casual in his approach to the game. He had his faults but was widely regarded as one of the more cultured performers of the day. He appeared in 176 League and Cup matches, scoring a highly creditable 89 goals before signing for Bury in May 1956. Parker died in August 1988.

JOHN WILLIE PARKER

	LEAGUE		*FA CUP*		*TOTAL*	
	App	*Gls*	*App*	*Gls*	*App*	*Gls*
1950-51	7	0	0	0	7	0
1951-52	36	15	2	1	38	16
1952-53	32	13	4	4	36	17
1953-54	38	31	3	2	41	33
1954-55	34	19	0	0	34	19
1955-56	20	4	0	0	20	4
	167	82	9	7	176	89

When Bobby Parker signed from Glasgow Rangers in November 1913, he immediately solved the Everton goal-scoring problem, hammering 17 goals in 24 League games after Everton had sold Tommy Browell to Manchester City for £1,450. The next season Parker did even better. Equalling Freeman's Everton record of six years earlier, his 36 goals in 35 games established him as the First Division's leading scorer and, more importantly, helped Everton to take the League Championship. His goals were scored out of an Everton total of 76 for that season, and, like Freeman's they came under the old offside law which was more restrictive, needing three players goalside of the attacker rather than two. It was said of Parker that he was 'a dandy of a player who likes to score them in twos and threes'. He moved to Nottingham Forest in May 1921.

BOBBY PARKER

	LEAGUE		*FA CUP*		*TOTAL*	
	App	*Gls*	*App*	*Gls*	*App*	*Gls*
1913-14	24	17	1	0	25	17
1914-15	35	36	5	2	40	38
1919-20	8	4	0	0	8	4
1920-21	17	11	2	1	19	12
	84	68	8	3	92	71

CHARLIE PARRY

Welsh international Charlie Parry started his Everton career as a wing-half and finished it as a full-back. He signed from Welsh junior football in 1889 and made his debut on the opening day of the League's second season, scoring in Everton's home 3-2 win over Blackburn Rovers. Parry was a regular that season, but his appearances dwindled until he forced his way back into the League side at left-back. He was competent in all the defender's arts, having a sure kick with either foot, a fair turn of speed, a bone-crunching tackle and the ability to get high above the heads of opposing forwards when the ball came over from the wing. His positional sense was sound and one contemporary writer praised his ability to be up with his forwards one minute, and back helping out in defence the next. He made his Welsh international debut in 1891, at left-half against England and won six caps while with Everton, and another seven after he left. He gained particular praise in the 1894 game against England at the Queen's Club in London. The Welsh managed a 1-1 draw and Parry kept the English star forwards, Smith and Gosling, at bay with a sterling performance.

	LEAGUE		*FA CUP*		*TOTAL*	
	App	*Gls*	*App*	*Gls*	*App*	*Gls*
1889-90	22	4	2	0	24	4
1890-91	13	0	1	0	14	0
1891-92	1	0	0	0	1	0
1892-93	10	0	0	0	10	0
1893-94	11	0	1	0	12	0
1894-95	27	1	4	0	31	1
1895-96	2	0	0	0	2	0
	86	5	8	0	94	5

JOE PEACOCK

Born in Wigan in 1900, Joe Peacock joined Everton from Atherton in the close season of 1919 and proved an important part of the club's plans as they rebuilt after the war. After a couple of outings at right-half he was given the centre-forward berth and in his second match in that role, he scored a goal which helped Everton beat Sheffield United — their first home victory for two months. Peacock also played at inside-forward, but it was as a wing-half that he settled down and found international honours. They came after he had moved to Middlesbrough in 1927. He played in 'Boro's Second Division championship side of 1928-9. In the summer of 1929 Peacock joined the England team which toured the Continent. The former Everton man won his three caps against France, Belgium and Spain. later he played with Sheffield Wednesday and Clapton Orient. From March 1933 he coached in Sweden and in July 1939 was appointed Wrexham trainer.

	LEAGUE		*FA CUP*		*TOTAL*	
	App	*Gls*	*App*	*Gls*	*App*	*Gls*
1919-20	9	2	0	0	9	2
1920-21	28	3	2	0	30	3
1921-22	29	1	1	0	30	1
1922-23	39	4	2	0	41	4
1923-24	8	1	1	0	9	1
1924-25	17	0	1	0	18	0
1925-26	18	1	2	0	20	1
1926-27	3	0	1	0	4	0
	151	12	10	0	161	12

JIM PEARSON

Jim Pearson was a highly-talented striker who never really settled at Goodison Park. Capable of moments of genuine brilliance he too often allowed his fiery Scottish temperament to disrupt both his form and his concentration. He arrived from St Johnstone in a £100,000 deal in July 1974 after scoring 39 goals in 96 League appearances north of the border. A Scottish Youth and Schoolboy international, he played for the Under-23 side against Wales and England in 1973-4 and was substitute for the Scottish League against the Football League the same season. He was brought to Goodison to score goals but they dried up whenever he was given an extended run in the first team, and just three years after his arrival he was on the transfer list. Gordon Lee sold him to Newcastle United in August 1978 for £70,000. Pearson, who played in 93 League games for Everton, scoring 15 goals, made an immediate impact at St James' Park before losing his place through injury.

	LEAGUE		*FA CUP*		*FL CUP*		*EUROPE*		*TOTAL*	
	App	*Gls*	*App*	*Gls*	*App*	*Gls*	*App*	*Gls*	*App*	*Gls*
1974-75	17/9	3	4	1	0/1	0	-	-	21/10	4
1975-76	26/3	5	1	0	5	0	2	0	34/3	5
1976-77	12/4	4	3	1	1/1	0	-	-	16/5	5
1977-78	21/1	3	1	0	4	2	-	-	26/1	5
	76/17	15	9	2	10/2	2	2	0	97/19	19

MIKE PEJIC

Mike Pejic was regarded as the last piece in Gordon Lee's jigsaw as he fought to stave off relegation. Pejic joined Everton in February 1977 for £150,000 and took to Goodison arguably the fiercest tackle ever seen there. Pejic won a host of admirers with his rugged style and adventurous forward thrusts. Like so many of his contemporaries he was dogged by injury and was eventually forced to quit the game after losing a prolonged battle to overcome a severe pelvic disorder. The tragedy that ended in premature retirement in March 1981, started in December 1978 when he was very much in his prime and rightly rated as the finest English left-back in the game. He broke down in agony during a match at Leeds and never played for Everton in a League match again. Even though he returned to full match fitness and successfully completed a close-season tour of Egypt, the Goodison picture was changing. John Bailey had forced his way on to the scene and Pejic was on his way to Aston Villa for £250,000.

	LEAGUE		*FA CUP*		*FL CUP*		*EUROPE*		*TOTAL*	
	App	*Gls*	*App*	*Gls*	*App*	*Gls*	*App*	*Gls*	*App*	*Gls*
1976-77	17	1	4	0	0	0	-	-	21	1
1977-78	40	1	2	0	4	0	-	-	46	1
1978-79	19	0	0	0	3	0	4	0	26	0
	76	2	6	0	7	0	4	0	93	2

Fred Pickering was one of Everton's finest post-war strikers. After beginning his turbulent career as a full-back with Blackburn Rovers he made the transition to front-runner in the early 1960s before joining Everton for £85,000 in 1964. He soon demonstrated his immense power and pace. Quickly blooded in the first team, he went on to fulfil his rich promise with 56 goals in only 97 League games. He had a memorable international debut when he lined up against the USA in New York in 1964 and scored a hat-trick in the 10-0 win. He picked up two more caps, against Northern Ireland and Belgium, the same year. In 1966 many considered him unlucky to miss the FA Cup Final meeting with Sheffield Wednesday. He was transferred to Birmingham City for £50,000 in August 1967 and moved to Blackpool two years later for £45,000. In March 1971 he returned to his old hunting ground, Ewood Park, but left the club 11 months later after a series of rows with manager Ken Furphy.

FRED PICKERING

	LEAGUE		*FA CUP*		*EUROPE*		*TOTAL*	
	App	*Gls*	*App*	*Gls*	*App*	*Gls*	*App*	*Gls*
1963-64	9	9	0	0	0	0	9	9
1964-65	41	27	4	4	6	6	51	37
1965-66	39	18	5	4	3	0	47	22
1966-67	8	2	0	0	0	0	8	2
	97	56	9	8	9	6	115	70

After 15 years with Manchester City, Paul Power had entered the twilight of his career, and it looked as though he had missed out on major honours. At the age of 32 he was skipper of one of the most ineffectual City sides in living memory and was fully expecting to play out the last 12 months of his contract at Maine Road before accepting the almost inevitable free transfer. But, to the astonishment of both himself and a high percentage of the Everton public, he was signed by Howard Kendall on 27 June 1986, for £65,000. At the time Kendall was adamant that it was money well-invested and his prediction that Power would prove to be a 'useful buy' was amply underlined as something akin to a modern-day sporting fairytale began to unfold. As a result of a crippling injury crisis Power was thrown in at the deep end, making his senior Everton debut in the Charity Shield game against Liverpool. His versatility and vast experience proved invaluable as Everton wiped away the bitter memories of the previous season's failures and went on to win the Championship for the second time in three years. Power played in all 42 League games that season and after more than a decade and a half in football he finally won a major honour. He was a key member of the Everton backroom staff during Colin Harvey's time as manager but lost his job in November 1990 when Howard Kendall returned to the club.

PAUL POWER

	LEAGUE		*FA CUP*		*FL CUP*		*TOTAL*	
	App	*Gls*	*App*	*Gls*	*App*	*Gls*	*App*	*Gls*
1986-87	40	4	3	0	5	0	48	4
1987-88	12	2	2	0	1	0	15	2
	52	6	5	0	6	0	63	6

Dundee discovered full-back David Raitt playing Army football during World War One. Born at Buckhaven, Fife, he was not quite the build one expected in a full-back during an era when the ability to knock an opponent off the ball was as important as tackling ability and positional sense. Raitt stood barely 5ft 9in tall and weighed around 11st. He played Scottish League football with Dundee from 1919 until he signed for Everton in May 1922. Raitt came to Goodison at a particularly dismal time for the club who had struggled all season to avoid relegation while, across Stanley Park, Liverpool were celebrating their League Championship success. Raitt won an immediate place in a shaky Everton defence and his presence helped the club's rapid improvement to fifth place in his first season. Then Duggie Livingstone won a regular place at left-back, with McDonald switching flanks, so Raitt's chances were restricted. He fought to win back his place, only to find that Warney Cresswell had arrived at Goodison. It was clear that Cresswell was going to be a First Division star. Raitt managed only six games in the Championship season of 1927-8 and before the start of the next campaign he was a Blackburn Rovers player.

	LEAGUE		*FA CUP*		*TOTAL*	
	App	*Gls*	*App*	*Gls*	*App*	*Gls*
1922-23	36	0	2	0	38	0
1923-24	19	0	0	0	19	0
1924-25	20	0	4	0	24	0
1925-26	30	0	2	0	32	0
1926-27	11	0	1	0	12	0
1927-28	6	0	0	0	6	0
	122	0	9	0	131	0

DAVID RAITT

Andy Rankin was a technically superb goalkeeper who was sadly plagued by misfortune and injury at crucial times during his ten years with Everton. He was on the verge of quitting football for the police force when Harry Catterick took over at Goodison Park. After being gently persuaded to continue he was rewarded with his first-team chance at Nottingham Forest on 16 November 1963 when Gordon West was dropped. Despite his obvious talent he was never able to lay claim to a regular place and spent much of his time as West's understudy. He was out in the cold when Everton won the FA Cup in 1966, and again in 1968 when they lost to West Brom at Wembley. In the Championship-winning season of 1969-70 he did not manage a single game. Perhaps he will be best remembered for his performance against Borussia Mönchengladbach in the 1970-71 European Cup. The match went to a penalty shoot-out and Rankin became the unlikely hero of the hour when he put Everton into the third round with a vital save. He was transferred to Watford for £20,000 in November 1971 after making 104 senior appearances.

	LEAGUE		*FA CUP*		*FL CUP*		*EUROPE*		*TOTAL*	
	App	*Gls*	*App*	*Gls*	*App*	*Gls*	*App*	*Gls*	*App*	*Gls*
1963-64	20	0	2	0	-	-	0	0	22	0
1964-65	22	0	0	0	-	-	4	0	26	0
1965-66	9	0	0	0	-	-	2/1	0	11/1	0
1966-67	6	0	1	0	-	-	0	0	7	0
1970-71	28	0	4	0	0	0	5	0	37	0
	85	0	7	0	0	0	11/1	0	103/1	0

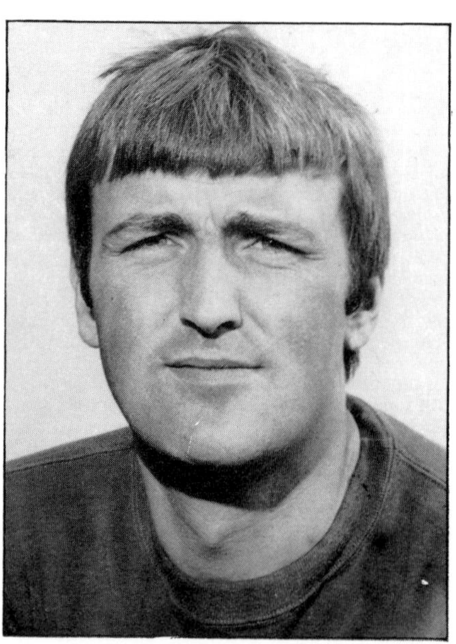

ANDY RANKIN

At the age of 24, Kevin Ratcliffe was already the most successful captain in Everton's history. In the 12 months between May 1984 and May 1985, the quietly-spoken Welshman led his team forward to pick up the FA Cup, the FA Charity Shield, the Canon League Championship and the European Cup-winners' Cup. Thereafter he skippered them to runners-up in the League and FA Cup in 1985-6, and to another League title in 1986-7. He was taken on as an apprentice professional straight from school in June 1977, after picking up schoolboy caps at Under-15 and Under-18 levels. Within 18 months he signed full forms and began a fairytale march through the ranks. After making his debut in the goalless draw at Old Trafford in March 1980 he found himself on the verge of leaving Everton in 1981 when Ipswich Town manager Bobby Robson expressed interest. Unhappy at being asked to play full-back, he struggled to find his true form and asked for a transfer when he was dropped for the home game against Birmingham City in December 1982. Manager Howard Kendall reluctantly agreed to circulate his name, but he was soon recalled in favour of Billy Wright. He formed a brilliant partnership at the heart of a revitalised defence, first alongside Mark Higgins, then Derek Mountfield. In December 1983 he was appointed Everton skipper and three months later captain of his country. He is superb in the air and is rated as the quickest defender in the First Division. Ratcliffe, Everton's most capped player, was acknowledged as one of the best centre-backs in British football. He lost his place to the fast-emerging Martin Keown during 1990-91 and was placed on the transfer list in January 1992, later joining Cardiff City and helping them to promotion to the new Division Two

KEVIN RATCLIFFE

	LEAGUE		*FA CUP*		*FL CUP*		*EUROPE*		*TOTAL*	
	App	*Gls*	*App*	*Gls*	*App*	*Gls*	*App*	*Gls*	*App*	*Gls*
1979-80	2	0	1	0	0	0	0	0	3	0
1980-81	20/1	0	5	0	2	0	-	-	27/1	0
1981-82	25	0	1	0	1	0	-	-	27	0
1982-83	29	1	5	0	4	0	-	-	38	1
1983-84	38	0	8	0	11	0	-	-	57	0
1984-85	40	0	7	0	4	0	9	0	60	0
1985-86	39	1	5	0	5	0	-	-	49	1
1986-87	42	0	3	0	5	0	-	-	50	0
1987-88	24	0	1	0	4	0	-	-	29	0
1988-89	30	0	8	0	4	0	0	0	42	0
1989-90	24	0	7	0	2	0	0	0	33	0
1990-91	35/1	0	6	0	3	0	0	0	44/1	0
	348/2	2	57	0	45	0	9	0	459/2	2

Tenacious Peter Reid became one of the bargain buys of all time when Howard Kendall bought him from Bolton Wanderers for £60,000 in December 1982. That deal was struck just two and a half years after Everton, then managed by Gordon Lee, had agreed to pay ten times that amount for a player who was to overcome a potentially devastating catalogue of injuries on the road to international acclaim. Indeed, Peter Reid has no right to be standing without support, never mind performing near miracles in the heart of Everton's impressive engine-room. In 1978 he broke his left kneecap; in 1979 he tore ligaments in his right leg; in 1980 he underwent a cartilage operation on his left knee; and in 1981 he broke his right leg. He was kept going through those dark days only by his appetite for a battle, and his perseverence was finally rewarded when he established himself in the senior side after a prolonged wait. What Reid lacks in pace he makes up for in sheer enthusiasm. He is a no-holds-barred workaholic with an astonishing will to win. He was a member of the 1984 beaten Milk Cup Final team, but has since picked up an FA Cup winners' medal, Canon League Championship medals and a European Cup-winners' Cup medal as well as playing in two losing FA Cup Final sides. In 1985 he was voted Player of the Year by the PFA, and the same year won his first full England cap during the summer tour to Mexico. Reid overcame further serious injury problems to win a place in the England team which reached the 1986 World Cup quarter-finals. In June 1987, following the departure of Howard Kendall, he was appointed Everton's player-coach. He severed his ties with Everton in February 1989 when he joined Queen's Park Rangers on a free transfer. Following Howard Kendall's appointment as the manager of Manchester City he moved to Maine Road as player-coach in December 1989. He was appointed City's manager in November 1990 following Kendall's return to Goodison Park.

PETER REID

	LEAGUE		*FA CUP*		*FL CUP*		*EUROPE*		*TOTAL*	
	App	*Gls*	*App*	*Gls*	*App*	*Gls*	*App*	*Gls*	*App*	*Gls*
1982-83	7	0	3	0	0	0	-	-	10	0
1983-84	34/1	2	8	1	9/1	1	-	-	51/2	4
1984-85	36	2	7	1	4	0	9	1	56	4
1985-86	15	1	5	0	0	0	-	-	20	1
1986-87	15/1	1	2	0	0	0	-	-	17/1	1
1987-88	32	1	8	1	6	0	-	-	46	2
1988-89	16/2	1	2	0	4/1	0	0	0	22/3	1
	155/4	8	35	3	23/2	1	9	1	222/6	13

KEVIN RICHARDSON

Kevin Richardson is one of only a handful of footballers to have won a League Championship medal with two clubs. Richardson, a versatile utility player with an exceptional passing ability, was a key member of the Everton side which successfully emerged from the shadows in the early eighties to reach the pinnacle of English football. He was a member of the 1985 title-winning side, played in the 1984 FA Cup Final victory over Watford and also the European Cup-winners' Cup triumph 12 months later. Despite winning many plaudits for his healthy contribution to the Everton success story he eventually tired of being the 'odd man out' and in 1986 he was sold to Watford for a mere £250,000. After a largely unproductive spell at Vicarage Road, he joined Arsenal for £350,000 in 1987 and helped the Gunners return the Championship to Highbury in 1989. In 1990 he joined Spanish club, Real Sociedad but returned to England within a matter of months to sign for Aston Villa.

	LEAGUE		*FA CUP*		*FL CUP*		*EUROPE*		*TOTAL*	
	App	*Gls*	*App*	*Gls*	*App*	*Gls*	*App*	*Gls*	*App*	*Gls*
1981-82	15/3	2	1	0	-	-	-	-	16/3	2
1982-83	24/5	3	2	0	1/2	0	-	-	27/7	3
1983-84	25/3	4	5	1	6/1	2	-	-	36/4	7
1984-85	14/1	4	0	0	1	0	2/1	0	17/2	4
1985-86	16/3	3	5	0	2	1	-	-	23/3	4
1986-87	1	0	0	0	0	0	-	-	1	0
	95/15	16	13	1	10/3	3	2/1	0	120/19	20

NICK ROSS

Although he played only one season for Everton — the League's inaugural campaign of 1888-89 — Nick Ross goes down as one of the greatest defenders ever to wear an Everton shirt. In July 1883, Ross, the 20-year-old captain of Hearts, was given work as a slater in Preston and signed for Preston North End. He was the subject of a furious debate over professionalism but, undaunted, Preston made him their captain, converting him from a forward to one of the best backs of any generation. In many ways he was an unlucky footballer. He was on the losing side when Preston were defeated by West Brom in the 1888 FA Cup Final; he missed the famous Preston double-winning season of 1888-89 because he had joined Everton; and he was never capped by Scotland who were ignoring players south of the border. He arrived at Everton on 30 July 1888 and within two weeks was made captain. His wage was reported to be £10 per month, nearly twice that of most players. He stayed one season and then rejoined Preston, at last tasting success when they won the League again in 1889-1990. In April 1891 he played in the first-ever Football League representative side, against the Football Alliance. He died of consumption when only 31. His brother Jimmy, was also one of the League's earliest stars, playing for Preston, Liverpool, Burnley and Manchester City.

	LEAGUE		*FA CUP*		*TOTAL*	
	App	*Gls*	*App*	*Gls*	*App*	*Gls*
1888-89	19	5	-	-	19	5
	19	5	-	-	19	5

Trevor Ross joined Everton for £180,000 from Arsenal in November 1977. He was brought to Goodison to help stabilize a midfield which, at the time, was considered skilful but woefully lacking in bite and aggression. Initially he seemed the perfect solution to a problem which had dogged successive Everton managers, but in the final count it has to be said that he failed to make a major impression during his six years at the club. He was cool when on the ball, and capable of delivering telling passes with great accuracy, but he suffered long periods of inconsistency. He was in and out of the side before being given a free transfer in February 1983. He went to Portsmouth on loan, and to Sheffield United, also on loan, as Everton tried to tempt the Blades to part with Terry Curran. Eventually he was drawn to the leading Greek side AEK Athens. He spent only six months there and after describing the move as 'the worst mistake of my life', he rejoined Sheffield United on a permanent basis.

	LEAGUE		*FA CUP*		*FL CUP*		*EUROPE*		*TOTAL*	
	App	*Gls*	*App*	*Gls*	*App*	*Gls*	*App*	*Gls*	*App*	*Gls*
1977-78	18/2	4	2	1	0	0	-	-	20/2	5
1978-79	26	6	1	0	2/1	0	4	1	33/1	7
1979-80	31/1	3	3	1	4	0	1	0	39/1	4
1980-81	17	2	6	1	0	0	-	-	23	3
1981-82	27	1	1	0	2	0	-	-	30	1
1982-83	1/1	0	0	0	0	0	-	-	1/1	0
	120/4	16	13	3	8/1	0	5	1	146/5	20

TREVOR ROSS

Joe Royle was widely acknowledged as Everton's finest post-war centre-forward. He became the youngest-ever player to wear the famous royal blue when, at the tender age of 16, he was thrown into a First Division match by Harry Catterick, against Blackpool in 1966. He enjoyed a rapid rise to stardom, utilising his massive physique to good effect. He was a tremendous header of the ball and capable of clinical finishing when presented with a scoring chance inside the penalty area. He won his first England cap against Malta in 1971 and went on to pick up five more, the last being against Luxembourg at Wembley in 1977. His power up front and his crucial goals made him a key member of the 1970 Championship-winning side. After more than 15 years in League football he was forced to retire in April 1982, the result of a painful knee injury sustained in a game four months earlier. At the time he was with Norwich City, and it proved to be the last of his 473 League games in a career which included spells at Manchester City and Bristol City. He was appointed manager of Second Division Oldham Athletic in July 1982. In 1991 he steered Oldham back into the First Division after an absence of more than 50 years.

	LEAGUE		*FA CUP*		*FL CUP*		*EUROPE*		*TOTAL*	
	App	*Gls*	*App*	*Gls*	*App*	*Gls*	*App*	*Gls*	*App*	*Gls*
1965-66	2	0	0	0	-	-	0	0	2	0
1966-67	4	3	0	0	-	-	0	0	4	3
1967-68	33/1	16	6	3	1	1	-	-	40/1	20
1968-69	42	22	5	4	4	3	-	-	51	29
1969-70	42	23	1	0	4	0	-	-	47	23
1970-71	40	17	5	2	0	0	6	4	51	23
1971-72	26/2	9	3	0	1	0	-	-	30/2	9
1972-73	14	7	0	0	1	0	-	-	15	7
1973-74	18	2	3	0	1	0	-	-	22	2
1974-75	8	3	0	0	2	0	-	-	10	3
	229/3	102	23	9	14	4	6	4	272/3	119

JOE ROYLE

An Everton legend, Ted Sagar was one of the finest goalkeepers of all time, combining sheer ahtleticism with bravery and tremendous vision. His handling, particularly of crosses, was exemplary. He spent an astonishing 24 years and one month with the club between 1929 and 1953 — the longest spell any player has ever had professionally with one Football League club. He played in a record number of League games for Everton with 463 appearances (some record books give the erroneous figure of 465). Yet, but for a lack of foresight on the part of Hull City, Sagar would never have found his way to Goodison Park. As a lad he was playing with Thorne Colliery in the Doncaster Senior League when he was spotted by a Tigers' scout. He was given a trial, but the Yorkshire club were slow to offer him a contract, so allowing Everton to nip in and sign him from under their noses. He won his first England cap against Northern Ireland in October 1935 and was honoured on three further occasions in 1936, against Scotland, Austria and Belgium. He won two League Championship medals and an FA Cup winners' medal with Everton. Slim and perhaps underweight for a goalkeeper in the days when it was legitimate for centre-forwards to bounce both 'keeper and ball into the back of the net, Sagar survived by skill alone. He had the uncanny ability to judge the high flight of a ball from the wings and he was completely without nerves. He was famous for launching himself headlong at the ball, regardless of the number of players blocking his path. He died on 16 October 1986.

	LEAGUE		*FA CUP*		*TOTAL*	
	App	*Gls*	*App*	*Gls*	*App*	*Gls*
1929-30	8	0	1	0	9	0
1931-32	41	0	1	0	42	0
1932-33	42	0	6	0	48	0
1933-34	40	0	1	0	41	0
1934-35	35	0	4	0	39	0
1935-36	37	0	0	0	37	0
1936-37	29	0	4	0	33	0
1937-38	26	0	0	0	26	0
1938-39	41	0	5	0	46	0
1946-47	29	0	2	0	31	0
1947-48	42	0	5	0	47	0
1948-49	40	0	2	0	42	0
1949-50	18	0	0	0	18	0
1950-51	24	0	1	0	25	0
1951-52	10	0	0	0	10	0
1952-53	1	0	0	0	1	0
	463	0	32	0	495	0

TED SAGAR

George Saunders was a product of Merseyside junior football, recommended to Everton by Dixie Dean. Although he was never to reach the same heights as his sponsor — few did — Saunders was a reliable, consistent defender, well respected both on the terraces and in the Goodison dressing-room. His motto was 'safety first' and he adamantly refused to embroider his play with fancy touches. He was a firm believer that it was the first duty of any full-back to clear his lines as quickly and as clinically as possible. He was an expert in killing stone-dead an awkward, bouncing ball and he was very useful in the air, often outjumping taller opponents. He signed as a professional in February 1939, but before that had played for two seasons with the 'A' team. His debut was in wartime football, against Liverpool at Anfield on 2 December 1939. His first peacetime League match was against Arsenal at Goodison on 11 September 1946. He was also a fine golfer, and cousin of Ron Saunders who spent five years at Everton in the early 1950s.

	LEAGUE		*FA CUP*		*TOTAL*	
	App	*Gls*	*App*	*Gls*	*App*	*Gls*
1946-47	23	0	1	0	24	0
1947-48	37	0	5	0	42	0
1948-49	36	0	1	0	37	0
1949-50	24	0	0	0	24	0
1950-51	10	0	0	0	10	0
1951-52	3	0	0	0	3	0
	133	0	7	0	140	0

GEORGE SAUNDERS

ALEX SCOTT

Alex Scott pledged his immediate future to Everton in February 1963, only after one of the fiercest transfer battles of the decade. Already established as a Scotland regular while with Glasgow Rangers, he was pursued by a number of leading English clubs when it became known that he was keen to move south of the border. Everton and Tottenham Hotspur led the way with a long series of bids, offers and pledges. Ultimately it was a £40,000 bid by Harry Catterick which won the day, and the flamboyant outside-right was on his way to Merseyside. By the end of the season he had picked up a Championship medal, and was an integral part of the set-up. In 1966 he won an FA Cup winners' medal to add to his winners' medals from a Scottish League Championship, two Scottish League Cup Finals and a Scottish Cup Final. Never a man to shirk responsibilty, Scott, known as 'Chico' to the fans, enjoyed a thoroughly successful career with Everton before being transferred to Hibernian for £15,000 in September 1967.

	LEAGUE		*FA CUP*		*EUROPE*		*TOTAL*	
	App	*Gls*	*App*	*Gls*	*App*	*Gls*	*App*	*Gls*
1962-63	17	4	0	0	0	0	17	4
1963-64	40	7	5	2	2	0	47	9
1964-65	36	6	4	0	4	1	44	7
1965-66	35	5	8	0	2	0	45	5
1966-67	21	1	0	0	2	0	23	1
	149	23	17	2	10	1	176	26

BILLY SCOTT

Goalkeeper Billy Scott succeeded Dick Roose at Everton — and then recommended his younger brother, Elisha, to Liverpool. Billy was born in Belfast and joined Everton from Irish League club Linfield in 1904. He was already an Irish international with six caps to his credit and he continued his run in the Ireland team after arriving at Goodison. Indeed, there always seemed to be a Scott in the Ireland goal. Even after he left Everton, for Leeds City in 1912, Billy continued to win caps, taking his overall tally to 25 in an international career which lasted from 1903 to 1913. Elisha kept goal 30 times between 1920 and 1936. Billy was Everton's goalkeeper in their 1906 and 1907 FA Cup Finals and he won three League Championship runners-up medals with the club (1904-05, 1908-09 and 1911-12). His departure for Yorkshire caused Everton some concern and until the emergence of Tom Fern, Billy Scott proved a difficult man to replace, so well had he guarded Everton's net in his eight years at Goodison.

	LEAGUE		*FA CUP*		*TOTAL*	
	App	*Gls*	*App*	*Gls*	*App*	*Gls*
1904-05	16	0	0	0	16	0
1905-06	35	0	6	0	41	0
1906-07	35	0	8	0	43	0
1907-08	34	0	7	0	41	0
1908-09	36	0	2	0	38	0
1909-10	27	0	7	0	34	0
1910-11	31	0	3	0	34	0
1911-12	37	0	5	0	42	0
	251	0	38	0	289	0

JIMMY SETTLE

Jimmy Settle was one of the English game's most instinctive finishers at the turn of the century. Although strictly an inside-forward, he was always on hand to help out up front and his goals, usually poached from inside the penalty area, were as vital to Everton as his classy, defence-splitting passes. Below average height, he was uncommonly fast and it was said that he would have made a first-class sprinter had he chosen athletics instead of football. He started with Bolton Wanderers before joining Bury, but it was while at Goodison that he hit peak form. It was written of him: 'Few are more dangerous near goal, often scores when the goalkeeper isn't looking. This diminutive marvel has won the highest honours and deserves them all.' Settle won six full England caps between 1899 and 1903 and he also played for the Football League. He played in the 1906 and 1907 FA Cup Finals before moving to Stockport County in the summer of 1908. He retired a year later.

	LEAGUE		*FA CUP*		*TOTAL*	
	App	*Gls*	*App*	*Gls*	*App*	*Gls*
1898-99	1	0	0	0	1	0
1899-1900	26	10	1	0	27	10
1900-01	30	10	2	1	32	11
1901-02	29	18	0	0	29	18
1902-03	20	5	2	0	22	5
1903-04	29	8	1	0	30	8
1904-05	32	9	6	4	38	13
1905-06	28	11	5	1	33	12
1906-07	21	6	8	4	29	10
1907-08	21	7	7	3	28	10
	237	84	32	13	269	97

Graeme Sharp was a virtually unknown striker when Gordon Lee splashed out £120,000 to bring him to Goodison Park from Dumbarton in April 1980. A powerful header of the ball with an eye for an opening, he was bought as an investment for the future. He made his League debut as a substitute in a goalless draw at Brighton a month after his arrival and, although he took time to settle down, he won a host of admirers with a series of spectacular goals. After partnering numerous strikers, he hit form following the arrival of fellow Scot Andy Gray in November 1983. Under the veteran striker's influence he matured at an astonishing rate to become a key member of Howard Kendall's new-look side. He scored the first goal in the 1984 FA Cup Final success over Watford and found the back of the net 30 times in 1984-5. His meteoric rise to stardom was capped when Jock Stein gave him his first full Scottish outing in the World Cup qualifier against Iceland in May 1985. His value increased enormously and he was high on the wanted lists of several leading Italian clubs. Sharp formed a good partnership with Gary Lineker when Everton were runners-up in both League and FA Cup in 1985-6 but injury restricted his appearances towards the end of the Championship-winning season of 1986-7. After 11, glorious years at Everton he left to join Oldham Athletic in a £500,000 deal in the summer of 1991.

GRAEME SHARP

	LEAGUE		*FA CUP*		*FL CUP*		*EUROPE*		*TOTAL*	
	App	*Gls*	*App*	*Gls*	*App*	*Gls*	*App*	*Gls*	*App*	*Gls*
1979-80	1/1	0	0	0	0	0	0	0	1/1	0
1980-81	2/2	0	0	0	0	0	-	-	2/2	0
1981-82	27/2	15	1	0	1	0	-	-	29/2	15
1982-83	39/2	15	5	2	4	0	-	-	48/2	17
1983-84	27/1	7	5/2	1	11	3	-	-	43/3	11
1984-85	36	21	6	2	4	3	8	4	54	30
1985-86	35/2	19	7	1	5	1	-	-	47/2	21
1986-87	27	5	1	2	5	2	-	-	33	9
1987-88	32	13	8	6	6/1	1	-	-	46/1	20
1988-89	26	7	6	3	4	2	0	0	36	12
1989-90	30/3	6	7	1	3/1	0	0	0	40/4	7
1990-91	24/3	3	6	2	3	3	0	0	33/3	8
	306/16	111	52/2	20	46/2	15	8	4	412/20	150

Double-international Jack Sharp was Everton's regular outside-right for 11 seasons after signing from Aston Villa in 1899. Born in Hereford, he started out with Hereford Thistle before Villa signed him in 1897. Sharp could not fit in at Villa Park and made only 23 League appearances. But Everton had no reservations about signing him and he repaid them with a career which saw him play 300 League games before retiring in 1910. He was an ideal wingman, possessing a telling burst of speed and an accurate centre. He liked to cut inside his full-back too, and that brought him his fair share of goals. He was a short, stocky man and one writer described him as a 'Pocket Hercules'. He played in Everton's two FA Cup Finals of 1906 and 1907 and won two England caps as well as representing the Football League. J.T.Howcroft, 30 years a referee, nominated Sharp the best outside-right he had ever seen, better even than Meredith or Matthews. His brother, Bert, played as a full-back with him at Villa and Everton. Jack Sharp was also a fine cricketer, good enough to win three Test caps and score 105 against Australia at The Oval in 1909. He played for Lancashire from 1899 to 1925, captaining them for a time, and his first-class career brought him 22,715 runs (38 centuries). A fast-medium bowler, he took 440 wickets and held 223 catches. He was a particularly brilliant cover-point. He ran a thriving sports outfitters in Liverpool and both he and his son were Everton directors. He died in January 1938, aged 59.

	LEAGUE		*FA CUP*		*TOTAL*	
	App	*Gls*	*App*	*Gls*	*App*	*Gls*
1899-1900	29	5	1	0	30	5
1900-01	25	7	2	0	27	7
1901-02	32	6	2	1	34	7
1902-03	27	6	2	1	29	7
1903-04	31	6	1	0	32	6
1904-05	21	8	6	2	27	10
1905-06	29	9	6	2	35	11
1906-07	27	7	6	3	33	10
1907-08	23	4	7	0	30	4
1908-09	31	6	2	1	33	7
1909-10	25	4	7	2	32	6
	300	68	42	12	342	80

JACK SHARP

An unwritten agreement stretching back nearly 20 years was broken when Kevin Sheedy joined Everton from Liverpool in June 1982. The young Irish midfield star, tired of waiting in the Anfield shadows, decided to throw in his lot with Everton, so breaking the barrier which had prevented players moving between the two clubs for almost two decades. He signed for Liverpool for £70,000 from Hereford United in June 1978, but despite his outstanding Central League form, he was restricted to only two League outings in four years. Bob Paisley, who recognised his immense potential, was reluctant to release him, and the deal went to a tribunal before the fee of £100,000 was fixed. Sheedy is undoubtedly one of the finest left-sided midfield players that Everton have ever had, combining accurate passing with deadly shooting. He is a free-kick expert, capable of flighting a shot in to the top corner from anywhere up to 30 yards away. Although he has struggled with injuries since establishing himself, he is a consistent performer. He scored the third goal in the 1985 European Cup-winners' Cup Final victory over Rapid Vienna and won a regular place in the Republic of Ireland side. Sheedy was one of several key players injured during the 1986-7 Championship-winning season. Although the passing of the years did little to diminish Sheedy's subtle skills, he lost his first-team place following the return of Howard Kendall in 1990 and joined Newcastle United on a free transfer in February 1992.

	LEAGUE		*FACUP*		*FLCUP*		*EUROPE*		*TOTAL*	
	App	*Gls*	*App*	*Gls*	*App*	*Gls*	*App*	*Gls*	*App*	*Gls*
1982-83	40	11	5	2	3	0	-	-	48	13
1983-84	28	4	6	2	10	4	-	-	44	10
1984-85	29	11	6	4	2	0	5	2	42	17
1985-86	31	5	3	0	4	2	-	-	38	7
1986-87	28	13	1	0	4	1	-	-	33	14
1987-88	14/3	1	0	0	1	0	-	-	15/3	1
1988-89	24/2	8	8	4	1/1	0	0	0	33/3	12
1989-90	33/4	9	6	2	4	2	0	0	43/4	13
1990-91	20/2	4	3	1	1	0	0	0	24/2	5
1991-92	16/1	0	0	0	2	0	0	0	18/1	0
	263/12	66	38	15	32/2	9	5	2	338/13	92

KEVIN SHEEDY

Ian Snodin is an almost unique figure in modern football insomuch as he declined an invitation which few receive and virtually no one declines when he turned down the chance to join Liverpool in January 1987. Having established himself as an aggressive, yet thoughtful, midfielder in a struggling Leeds United side during the mid-eighties, Snodin was pursued by several leading clubs but only two — Everton and Liverpool — were willing to meet an asking price of £840,000. Having agreed personal terms with Kenny Dalglish, Snodin was expected to move to Anfield but an eleventh-hour intervention by Howard Kendall proved to be decisive and within a matter of hours he had pledged his future to Everton. Although his never-say-die attitude was warmly received by the Goodison public it was not until Snodin was pressed into service as an emergency right-back that he truly began to flourish. His transformation from midfielder to defender was accomplished with such speed and in such style that he was called up into the full England squad for a friendly international in Greece in February 1989. Unfortunately, Snodin was forced to withdraw because of injury and his problems were compounded a matter of only a few weeks later when he was carried off during a game against Sheffield Wednesday with a serious hamstring problem. Despite lengthy periods of rest and several operations, Snodin struggled to regain his fitness and spent the whole of the 1991-2 season convalescing.

IAN SNODIN

	LEAGUE		*FA CUP*		*FL CUP*		*EUROPE*		*TOTAL*	
	App	*Gls*	*App*	*Gls*	*App*	*Gls*	*App*	*Gls*	*App*	*Gls*
1986-87	15/1	0	2	1	0/1	0	-	-	17/2	1
1987-88	29/2	2	8	1	7	1	-	-	44/2	4
1988-89	23	0	5	0	5	0	-	-	33	0
1989-90	25	0	7	0	3	0	-	-	35	0
1990-91	1	0	0	0	0	0	-	-	1	0
1991-92	-	-	-	-	-	-	-	-	-	-
1992-93	19/1	1	2	0	2	0	-	-	23/1	1
	112/4	3	24	2	17/1	1	-	-	153/5	6

Neville Southall is a goalkeeper of outstanding ability who is now rated alongside Peter Shilton. It was in July 1981 that he completed the remarkable two-year transformation from Llandudno hod-carrier to First Division footballer. He turned his back on the building site after an eventful career in Welsh non-League football. He was a centre-back in his teens and had unsuccessful trials with several clubs including Crewe and Bolton. He moved between the posts after joining Llandudno Swifts, then had short spells with Conway United and Bangor City before moving to Cheshire League side Winsford. Bury bought him for £6,000 in 1980, and then Howard Kendall moved in with a £150,000 bid. After claiming a first-team place, he was dropped in favour of Jim Arnold and in 1982-3 he was one of ten Everton players loaned out when he went to Port Vale. He returned to win back his place and proved so consistently brilliant that Kendall felt able to compare him with Gordon Banks. Southall is magnificent in the air and has the sort of cat-like reflexes that leave opposing forwards pounding the turf in disbelief. He is firmly established as first-choice for Wales and in 1985 he was voted Footballer of the Year by the Football Writers' Association. A serious injury kept him out of the Everton side from March 1986 until October and although he missed the 1986 FA Cup Final he went on to collect another Championship medal in 1987.

	LEAGUE		*FA CUP*		*FL CUP*		*EUROPE*		*TOTAL*	
	App	*Gls*	*App*	*Gls*	*App*	*Gls*	*App*	*Gls*	*App*	*Gls*
1981-82	26	0	1	0	0	0	-	-	27	0
1982-83	17	0	0	0	2	0	-	-	19	0
1983-84	35	0	8	0	11	0	-	-	54	0
1984-85	42	0	7	0	4	0	9	0	62	0
1985-86	32	0	5	0	5	0	-	-	42	0
1986-87	31	0	3	0	3	0	-	-	37	0
1987-88	32	0	8	0	7	0	-	-	47	0
1988-89	38	0	8	0	5	0	0	0	51	0
1989-90	38	0	7	0	4	0	0	0	49	0
1990-91	38	0	6	0	3	0	0	0	47	0
1991-92	42	0	2	0	4	0	0	0	48	0
1992-93	40	0	1	0	6	0	0	0	47	0
	411	0	56	0	54	0	9	0	530	0

NEVILLE SOUTHALL

JACK SOUTHWORTH

Although illness and injury meant that he served Everton for only one full season, the impression Jack Southworth made at Goodison Park lasted long after his enforced retirement. He began with Blackburn Olympic, for whom he once scored six goals in a match against Leigh when he was 16, and moved to Blackburn Rovers where he won FA Cup winners' medals in 1890 and 1891. They thought so much of him at Blackburn that in 1892 Rovers arranged a floodlit testimonial match — white ball and all — for him against Darwen. Everton paid £400 for his signature in August 1893 and after a slow start he began to pile in the goals, scoring four against Sheffield Wednesday and six against West Brom in successive matches. By the end of the season he had rattled in 27 goals in 22 games. Nine goals in his first nine games the following season indicated that he would carry on this incredible scoring rate, but then injury forced him into premature retirement. Southworth had scored one goal for each of his 139 League appearances with the two clubs, yet he made only three appearances for England (inevitably scoring three goals). This talented centre-forward had the misfortune to play at the same time as other great English goalscorers like Lindley, Goodall, Bloomer and G.O.Smith. He became a professional violinist, good enough to play with the Halle Orchestra.

	LEAGUE		*FA CUP*		*TOTAL*	
	App	*Gls*	*App*	*Gls*	*App*	*Gls*
1893-94	22	27	1	0	23	27
1894-95	9	9	0	0	9	9
	31	36	1	0	32	36

JIMMY STEIN

Everton have had some exciting Scottish players on their books over the years, but they never had a better servant than Jimmy Stein. In eight years with the club he was a model professional, never once complaining or grumbling when he was left out of the side in favour of younger, less experienced players. He was a quiet man, but was anything but friendly to the opposition. His long stride ate up space and he was a winger who liked to adopt the now standard ploy of cutting inside to deliver telling shots. His link-up with his inside partners was near perfect. A native of Coatbridge, he helped Dunfermline to gain promotion in 1925-6 before joining Everton in 1928. He was part of the side which won the Second Division title, the League Championship and the FA Cup in successive seasons between 1930 and 1933. He scored the first goal in the Wembley triumph over Manchester City in 1933. He moved to Burnley in October 1936 before returning to Merseyside to help New Brighton.

	LEAGUE		*FA CUP*		*TOTAL*	
	App	*Gls*	*App*	*Gls*	*App*	*Gls*
1928-29	4	0	1	0	5	0
1929-30	29	10	2	0	31	10
1930-31	28	10	5	3	33	13
1931-32	37	9	1	0	38	9
1932-33	40	16	6	5	46	21
1933-34	42	8	1	0	43	8
1934-35	19	4	0	0	19	4
	199	57	16	8	215	65

TREVOR STEVEN

Howard Kendall took on the role of marathon man in his dogged chase to land Burnley's brilliant young midfielder Trevor Steven. The Goodison boss was so sure of Steven's ability to shine in the big time that he carefully followed the progress of the Burnley starlet for two years before the Turf Moor club finally relented and agreed to a £300,000 deal in July 1983. One of the finest natural talents that Everton have ever had on their books, Steven established a regular place in the England side and was favourably compared to Steve Coppell. A brilliant dribbler with superb close control, he complemented the more aggressive style of Peter Reid in the Everton midfield. Although regarded as a supplier rather than a finisher, he scored 16 goals in 1984-5 as the club came within one match of landing an unprecedented treble. He supplied the cross for Andy Gray's decisive goal in the 1984 FA Cup Final triumph over Watford and won his first England cap, against Northern Ireland, on 27 February 1985. His consistency was a telling factor in Everton's 1986-7 Championship success, following his appearances in the 1986 World Cup Finals. He refused to sign a new contract at Everton in the summer of 1989 and joined Glasgow Rangers for a fee of £1.5 million shortly afterwards. His tranformation into a player of world standing was emphasised in 1991 when he joined Marseille for £4.5 million. He later rejoined Rangers.

	LEAGUE		*FA CUP*		*FL CUP*		*EUROPE*		*TOTAL*	
	App	*Gls*	*App*	*Gls*	*App*	*Gls*	*App*	*Gls*	*App*	*Gls*
1983-84	23/4	1	2	0	3	1	-	-	28/4	2
1984-85	40	12	7	2	4	0	9	2	60	16
1985-86	41	9	6	0	5	0	-	-	52	9
1986-87	41	14	3	0	5	1	-	-	49	15
1987-88	36	6	8	2	6	0	-	-	50	8
1988-89	29	6	7	0	4	2	0	0	40	8
	210/4	48	33	4	27	4	9	2	279/4	58

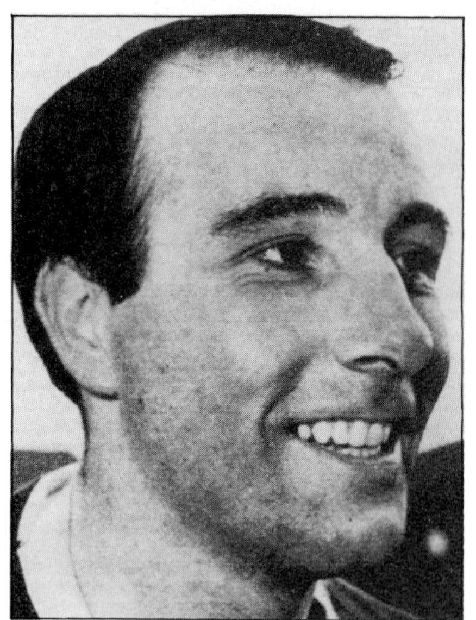

DENNIS STEVENS

When Everton strode so majestically to the First Division title in 1963, it was players like Alex Young and Roy Vernon who captured so many of the headlines. They commanded — and at times demanded — attention because they had abundant skill. But strength, courage and determination are also needed in a team with title aspirations and it was Dennis Stevens who provided these qualities in that famous Everton line-up, with his quiet yet effective midfield play. He came from Bolton Wanderers (for whom he had played outside-right in the 1958 FA Cup Final) in March 1962, just days before Bobby Collins left for Leeds United. He was a tireless worker who switched to wing-half in 1964. With the arrival of youngsters like Colin Harvey and John Hurst, he found it increasingly difficult to retain his place and was eventually transferred to Oldham Athletic for £20,000 in December 1965. Two years later, at the age of 32, he joined Tranmere Rovers on a free transfer. His last game for Tranmere was, ironically, against Everton.

	LEAGUE		*FA CUP*		*EUROPE*		*TOTAL*	
	App	*Gls*	*App*	*Gls*	*App*	*Gls*	*App*	*Gls*
1961-62	12	4	0	0	0	0	12	4
1962-63	42	7	3	1	2	1	47	9
1963-64	42	9	5	0	2	0	49	9
1964-65	18	0	2	0	6	0	26	0
1965-66	6	0	0	0	2	0	8	0
	120	20	10	1	12	1	142	22

In just over two years Gary Stevens developed into one of the finest defenders in Britain. Born in Barrow-in-Furness, he joined Everton straight from school, signing as an apprentice in July 1979. He made an impact in the Central League and was given his first-team debut in the 1-1 draw at West Ham on 10 October 1981. Content to bide his time, he returned to the reserves before taking over from Brian Borrows in November 1982. After a short period of acclimatization, his form was a revelation. His natural sprinting ability and great composure when in possession led to him being called into Bobby Robson's England squad for the World Cup qualifier against Northern Ireland in February 1985. He made his full international debut in Mexico later that year, against World Cup holders Italy. By the time he was 22 he had already made more than 150 senior appearances for Everton. He was one of an Everton quartet — Lineker, Reid and Steven were the others — in England's team which reached the 1986 World Cup quarter-finals but missed the first half of Everton's Championship-winning season through injury. He moved to Glasgow Rangers in the 1988 close season for £1.25 million.

	LEAGUE		*FA CUP*		*FL CUP*		*EUROPE*		*TOTAL*	
	App	*Gls*	*App*	*Gls*	*App*	*Gls*	*App*	*Gls*	*App*	*Gls*
1981-82	19	1	1	0	4	0	-	-	24	1
1982-83	28	0	5	0	2	1	-	-	35	1
1983-84	26	1	8	0	8	0	-	-	42	1
1984-85	37	3	7	1	4	0	9	0	57	4
1985-86	41	1	6	1	5	0	-	-	52	2
1986-87	25	2	3	0	1	0	-	-	29	2
1987-88	31	0	8	0	6	1	-	-	45	1
	207	8	38	2	30	2	9	0	284	12

GARY STEVENS

Alex Stevenson was one of the finest ball-players of his generation. His control was near perfect, his stocky body able to withstand the sometimes ruthless tackling of his contemporaries. But it was his brain that made him a truly great player and he graced the Everton team either side of World War Two. Although born in Dublin — he won his first Republic of Ireland caps while with the Dolphin club — he rose to stardom in Scotland with Glasgow Rangers. His love for Rangers was such that it took a good deal of coaxing before Everton persuaded him to leave Ibrox in 1934. He went on to score 90 goals in 271 games for the club — respectable figures for a man not employed primarily as a scorer. His partnership with fellow Irishman Jackie Coulter was a feature of the First Division before the war. The impish pair tore many defences to shreds with their speedy interplay and remarkable understanding of each other's intentions. Stevenson was capped 17 times for Northern Ireland and seven times for Eire, his last cap for the Republic coming in 1949, 17 years after the first.

	LEAGUE		*FA CUP*		*TOTAL*	
	App	*Gls*	*App*	*Gls*	*App*	*Gls*
1933-34	12	1	0	0	12	1
1934-35	36	15	5	3	41	18
1935-36	29	10	0	0	29	10
1936-37	41	19	3	2	44	21
1937-38	35	13	2	1	37	14
1938-39	36	11	5	2	41	13
1946-47	30	8	0	0	30	8
1947-48	17	3	0	0	17	3
1948-49	19	2	1	0	20	2
	255	82	16	8	271	90

ALEX STEVENSON

Born in Arbroath, Billy Stewart first made his reputation playing with the Black Watch team which won the Army Cup. Whilst stationed with the Royal Scots Greys in Ireland, he helped Belfast Distillery win the Irish Cup. Preston North End bought him out of the army and he played for them for several years before joining Everton in 1893. One of the key features of his play was his exceptionally long throw-in, although his running and jumping technique was eventually outlawed. He formed part of a famous Everton half-back line with Holt and Campbell and he played left-half in the 1897 FA Cup Final. Once, when the Everton team were training at Hoylake, he was the victim of a typical footballers' practical joke. As he slept, string was attached to every piece of bedroom furniture; then out in the hotel corridor the rest of the team pulled on the strings as hard as they could. Stewart woke up with the biggest fright of his life. He signed for Bristol City in 1897 and was appointed captain as they established themselves as a professional club.

	LEAGUE		*FA CUP*		*TOTAL*	
	App	*Gls*	*App*	*Gls*	*App*	*Gls*
1893-94	29	1	1	0	30	1
1894-95	27	2	3	0	30	2
1895-96	28	0	3	0	31	0
1896-97	29	3	4	0	33	3
1897-98	9	0	4	0	13	0
	122	6	15	0	137	6

BILLY STEWART

One of the stars of his day, Jack Taylor was a versatile player who could be relied upon to give a good account of himself in almost any position. An inspirational footballer, he coaxed the very best out of those around him. He played on the right wing in the 1897 FA Cup Final and was the sole playing survivor from that side when Everton returned to the Crystal Palace in 1906 and 1907, turning out at centre-half. He played first for Dumbarton Athletic, moved to St Mirren and then joined Everton in 1896. A freak accident in the 1910 FA Cup semi-final effectively brought his career to an end. Against Barnsley at Manchester, he was struck in the throat by a fierce shot and sustained severe damage to the larynx, an injury from which he never fully recovered. After 400 League games for Everton, he went into non-League football for the first time in his career, with South Liverpool. He was 77 when he died, in West Kirby in 1949, after a motoring accident.

	LEAGUE		*FA CUP*		*TOTAL*	
	App	*Gls*	*App*	*Gls*	*App*	*Gls*
1896-97	30	13	5	2	35	15
1897-98	30	3	5	3	35	6
1898-99	34	3	2	1	36	4
1899-1900	32	7	1	0	33	7
1900-01	25	11	2	1	27	12
1901-02	26	8	2	0	28	8
1902-03	33	3	3	1	36	4
1903-04	22	6	1	1	23	7
1904-05	34	4	6	0	40	4
1905-06	36	4	6	2	42	6
1906-07	34	1	8	2	42	3
1907-08	23	2	7	0	30	2
1908-09	27	1	1	0	28	1
1909-10	14	0	7	1	21	1
	400	66	56	14	456	80

JACK TAYLOR

GEORGE TELFER

George Telfer was a speedy winger who scored some spectacular goals during his time with Everton. After making his debut in 1973 his form was so impressive that he was talked about as a future England international. An aggressive, robust striker with tremendous sprinting ability, he was lethal when presented with time and space in the penalty area. Things appeared to be going well for him until the arrival of Duncan McKenzie cost him his first-team place. His belief in his own ability was such that he decided to stay at Goodison and fight for a recall despite offers from other clubs. In November 1980 he turned down a move to Chester who were willing to pay £30,000 for him, to replace Ian Rush. Eventually Telfer tired of Central League football however, and signed for NASL club San Diego. He returned to England to play for Scunthorpe United — where England cricket star Ian Botham cleaned his boots — and Preston. After spells in non-League football, with Runcorn and Barrow, he was appointed Football Development Officer for Merseyside Youth Association in October 1984.

	LEAGUE		*FA CUP*		*FL CUP*		*EUROPE*		*TOTAL*	
	App	*Gls*	*App*	*Gls*	*App*	*Gls*	*App*	*Gls*	*App*	*Gls*
1973-74	15	3	1/1	0	0	0	-	-	16/1	3
1974-75	11/4	2	2/2	0	0	0	-	-	13/6	2
1975-76	20/4	8	0	0	2/1	0	1	0	23/5	8
1976-77	17/2	4	0/1	0	3	0	-	-	20/3	4
1977-78	7/3	1	1	1	0/1	1	-	-	8/4	3
1978-79	10/2	2	0	0	0	0	0	0	10/2	2
1980-81	1/1	0	0	0	0	0	-	-	1/1	0
	81/16	20	4/4	1	5/2	1	1	0	91/22	22

DEREK TEMPLE

Derek Temple's place in Everton's 'Hall of Fame' was guaranteed when he scored the winning goal in the 1966 FA Cup Final against Sheffield Wednesday and so completed one of the great Wembley fightbacks. Not very tall, but powerfully built, Temple was a utility man who could fill a variety of roles. Born in Liverpool, he played for Lancashire and England Schoolboys during 1953-4 before joining Everton shortly after leaving school. His form with the Colts was astonishing. In one season alone he scored 70 goals, sometimes claiming five or six in a match. He made his senior debut against Newcastle at Goodison in March 1957 and went on to make 231 League appearances. After 11 seasons with Everton he was transferred to Preston for £35,000 in September 1967. Three years later he joined Wigan Athletic. Temple won one England cap, against West Germany in Nuremberg in 1965.

	LEAGUE		*FA CUP*		*FL CUP*		*EUROPE*		*TOTAL*	
	App	*Gls*	*App*	*Gls*	*App*	*Gls*	*App*	*Gls*	*App*	*Gls*
1956-57	7	3	0	0	0	0	0	0	7	3
1957-58	28	8	1	0	0	0	0	0	29	8
1958-59	4	2	0	0	0	0	0	0	4	2
1960-61	20	4	0	0	3	0	0	0	23	4
1961-62	17	10	0	0	0	0	0	0	17	10
1962-63	5	1	0	0	0	0	0	0	5	1
1963-64	41	12	5	0	0	0	2	0	48	12
1964-65	39	11	4	1	0	0	6	2	49	14
1965-66	38	9	8	6	0	0	4	0	50	15
1966-67	27/1	12	3	1	0	0	4	0	34/1	13
1967-68	5	0	0	0	1	0	0	0	6	0
	231/1	72	21	8	4	0	16	2	272/1	82

DAVE THOMAS

Dave Thomas had speed and the ability to cross the ball with unerring accuracy and that made him a key man in Gordon Lee's side. After making his name with Burnley, where he won England Under-23 honours, he surprisingly turned down the likes of Manchester United, Leeds and Everton for Second Division QPR. The London club paid £165,000 for his signature in October 1972 and provided him with an excellent stage on which to display his silky skills. He enjoyed five very successful years at Loftus Road, winning eight full international caps, before he decided to seek a move back north. Everton, desperately searching for a provider of ammunition for their shot-shy front line, headed a lengthy queue and completed his transfer, for £200,000, in August 1977. He performed with restrained brilliance during his days at Goodison before being sold to Wolves in October 1979, as part of a wholesale clear-out. He never settled at Molineux and jumped at the chance to join NASL side Vancouver Whitecaps, then managed by Johnny Giles. But the motivation was not there and after only ten matches he returned to sign for Middlesbrough. He made 13 appearances before joining Portsmouth, where he became youth-team coach.

	LEAGUE		*FA CUP*		*FL CUP*		*EUROPE*		*TOTAL*	
	App	*Gls*	*App*	*Gls*	*App*	*Gls*	*App*	*Gls*	*App*	*Gls*
1977-78	38	2	1	0	5	1	0	0	44	3
1978-79	33	2	1	0	2	0	4	1	40	3
	71	4	2	0	7	1	4	1	84	6

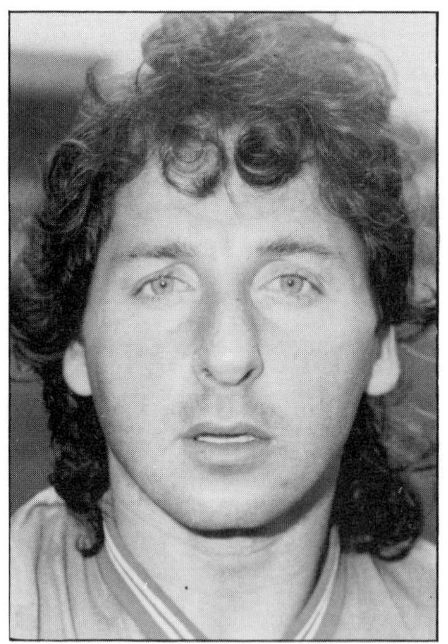

MICKEY THOMAS

Gifted Mickey Thomas had a brief and stormy stay with Everton. It was an unhappy relationship that began with smiles in July 1981, and ended in bitter recriminations a little over three months later. After sparkling with Wrexham, the club he joined as a boy, Thomas attracted several top clubs before Manchester United, under the managership of Dave Sexton, emerged from the pack to sign him in November 1978. The price paid by the Old Trafford club was £330,000, a huge fee for a youngster who had never played First Division football. Flamboyant and fiery, Thomas was an instant success with the fans, but not with the United management. He could take on and beat an opponent with apparent ease, but his skills were often overlooked as he tried to keep his temper in check. In the summer of 1981 he was transferred to Everton in the deal which saw John Gidman move to Old Trafford. After recovering from injury in November that year, Thomas refused to play in a Central League game at Newcastle, claiming that he should have been selected for the First Division game against Manchester City. After only 11 senior games, Thomas was placed on the transfer list. Brighton bought him for £400,000 and he has since served Stoke, Chelsea, West Brom, Derby (loan), Wichita Wings and, more recently, Shrewsbury Town, Leeds United and Wrexham.

	LEAGUE		*FA CUP*		*TOTAL*	
	App	*Gls*	*App*	*Gls*	*App*	*Gls*
1981-82	10	0	1	0	11	0
	10	0	1	0	11	0

John Ross Thomson played for Everton in two League Championship sides, an FA Cup-winning team, and a Second Division title-winning side. Born in Thornton, Fifeshire, in 1906, he went from Scottish junior football to Dundee in 1925, and to Everton in March 1930 where he found himself in a side destined for relegation to the Second Division. Twelve months later Everton were back in the First as Thomson missed only one game, playing a key role in the promotion drive with his forceful play at left-half. One year on, Everton were League Champions, and a year after that they won the FA Cup. So, in a little over 36 months, Thomson had known the agony of relegation, the joy of promotion, the elation of a Championship and the ultimate ecstacy of Wembley triumph. In October 1932 he won his solitary Scotland cap, against Wales at Tynecastle, but by the late 1930s he found his Everton place hard to come by after the emergence of the young Joe Mercer. There was one last triumph however. In the 1938-9 Championship year he played 26 times when Cliff Britton ended his career and Mercer switched to right-half. Thomson retired in 1939 and from 1947 to 1950 was Manchester City manager. Until his retirement in 1974 he ran a pub in Carnoustie. He died in 1979.

	LEAGUE		*FA CUP*		*TOTAL*	
	App	*Gls*	*App*	*Gls*	*App*	*Gls*
1929-30	9	0	0	0	9	0
1930-31	41	0	5	0	46	0
1931-32	39	0	1	0	40	0
1932-33	41	3	6	0	47	3
1933-34	38	0	1	0	39	0
1934-35	42	1	5	0	47	1
1935-36	25	0	0	0	25	0
1936-37	2	0	0	0	2	0
1937-38	9	1	0	0	9	1
1938-39	26	0	4	0	30	0
	272	5	22	0	294	5

JOCK THOMSON

Colin Todd was that rare footballer — a defender who could excite spectators. As a sweeper, his ability to send a crossfield pass perhaps 60 yards to the feet of a colleague was breathtaking and he was undoubtedly one of the classiest defenders English football has ever produced. Todd, who also proved a resilient full-back — he played there for England as well as at sweeper — arrived at Goodison in the twilight of an illustrious career which yielded 27 full England caps. He was the England Under-23 skipper when Brian Clough astonished football by paying £170,000 for a defender, taking Todd to Derby in February 1971. He spent seven years at the Baseball Ground, winning two League Championship medals and being named PFA Player of the Year in 1975. Everton beat off Southampton and signed the 29-year-old football perfectionist for £300,000 in September 1978. Todd brought a calm assurance to an inconsistent side before losing his place after being laid low with a mystery stomach complaint. After falling out with Gordon Lee he was transferred to Birmingham City for £275,000, exactly one year and three days after moving to Goodison. In December 1982 he linked up with Clough again, at Nottingham Forest, and then signed for Oxford United. He also appeared in the NASL with Vancouver Whitecaps and in 1988 was assistant manager of Middlesbrough. He was briefly in charge of first-team affairs at Ayresome Park following the departure of Bruce Rioch in 1990.

	LEAGUE		*FA CUP*		*EUROPE*		*TOTAL*	
	App	*Gls*	*App*	*Gls*	*App*	*Gls*	*App*	*Gls*
1978-79	29	1	1	0	2	0	32	1
1979-80	3	0	0	0	0	0	3	0
	32	1	1	0	2	0	35	1

COLIN TODD

Mike Trebilcock is the little Cornishman who won a permanent place in the hearts of all Evertonians when he took centre-stage in one of the most famous of all FA Cup Finals. It was only his second Cup match for the club but he brought about one of the greatest of all Wembley recovery stories. The player who never established himself at Goodison nevertheless left an indelible entry in the club's history. Virtually unknown, he signed from Plymouth Argyle for £20,000 on the last day of 1965. Less than four months later he was dramatically drafted into the FA Cup semi-final against Manchester United, replacing Fred Pickering. Surprisingly, he kept his place for the Final against Sheffield Wednesday. Although his name was not even on the Wembley programme, his moment of destiny came that afternoon, with Everton trailing 2-0 after 57 minutes. Within two minutes Trebilcock pulled a goal back. Soon afterwards he equalised, leaving Derek Temple to complete one of the great Cup Final fight-backs. It was Trebilcock's last Cup game for Everton. After two years on Merseyside — and only 11 League games — he joined Portsmouth before ending his career with Torquay. He now works as a storeman in Newcastle, Australia.

	LEAGUE		*FA CUP*		*FL CUP*		*EUROPE*		*TOTAL*	
	App	*Gls*	*App*	*Gls*	*App*	*Gls*	*App*	*Gls*	*App*	*Gls*
1965-66	7	2	2	2	-	-	0	0	9	4
1966-67	2	0	0	0	-	-	1	0	3	0
1967-68	2	1	0	0	0	0	0	0	2	1
	11	3	2	2	0	0	1	0	14	5

MIKE TREBILCOCK

After Dixie Dean had completed his magnificent 60-goal haul in 1927-8, he said that the achievement would not have been possible but for the assistance of Alec Troup. The tiny Scottish winger — he stood 5ft 5in — with the fantastic ball control was the man who supplied many of the pin-point crosses which Dean so regularly dispatched into the net. Troup seemed able to make the ball 'hang' in the air while Dean found a suitable launching-pad. It was such a cross, in the final League game of that season, which enabled Dean to reach the 60-goal mark. Troup was born in Forfar in 1895 and played for Forfar Athletic and Dundee before joining Everton in January 1923. He made light of a weak collarbone which had to be heavily strapped before every game. He won five full Scotland caps — the presence of the great Alan Morton denied him more — and rejoined Dundee in February 1930. He retired in 1933 to run a clothiers in Forfar. Troup died in 1951.

	LEAGUE		*FA CUP*		*TOTAL*	
	App	*Gls*	*App*	*Gls*	*App*	*Gls*
1922-23	17	2	0	0	17	2
1923-24	41	1	2	0	43	1
1924-25	32	2	0	0	32	2
1925-26	38	6	2	0	40	6
1926-27	37	5	4	2	41	7
1927-28	42	10	2	1	44	11
1928-29	38	5	0	0	38	5
1929-30	4	1	0	0	4	1
	249	32	10	3	259	35

ALEC TROUP

Pat Van den Hauwe is a ferocious tackler who plays the game in the old-fashioned way, believing that a defender's first priority is to win the ball and then release it as quickly as possible. After a relatively low-key career with Birmingham City, he was signed from the recently-relegated Midlanders in late September 1984 when Howard Kendall paid £100,000 for his services. He immediately replaced John Bailey at left-back and retained his place for the rest of what was to become a famous season. Born in Belgium, he moved to London at an early age. After becoming an important link in Everton's defensive chain, he appeared to be on the verge of a call-up to the Belgian national side when manager Guy Thees flew to Old Trafford to watch him in March 1985. After being pencilled in as an over-age player for the Under-21 match against Spain, he discovered that he had unwittingly signed away his birthright by opting out of National Service. That led to much Press speculation as to which of the British nations would pursue him. Eventually he joined Goodison colleagues Kevin Ratcliffe and Neville Southall in the Welsh team, making his debut in the splendid World Cup victory over Spain at Wrexham in April 1985. His appearances were restricted when Everton regained the League Championship in 1986-7. He joined Tottenham Hotspur for £575,000 in 1989 and was a member of their FA Cup-winning side in 1991.

PAT VAN DEN HAUWE

	LEAGUE		*FA CUP*		*FL CUP*		*EUROPE*		*TOTAL*	
	App	*Gls*	*App*	*Gls*	*App*	*Gls*	*App*	*Gls*	*App*	*Gls*
1984-85	31	0	7	0	3	0	5	0	46	0
1985-86	40	1	7	1	5	0	-	-	52	2
1986-87	11	1	2	0	0	0	-	-	13	1
1987-88	28	0	8	0	7	0	-	-	43	0
1988-89	24/1	0	6	0	5	0	0	0	35/1	0
	134/1	2	30	1	20	0	5	0	189/1	3

Imre Varadi was one of the game's most exciting new faces when he joined Everton early in 1979 after a handful of games for Sheffield United. A fast, tricky forward, he was an acknowledged goalscorer, despite having been 'sacked' by a non-League club in his formative days. London-born of Hungarian parents, his career appeared to be in tatters in 1978 when, while working as an asphalter, he was asked to leave Letchworth Town. Sheffield United spotted him in Sunday football and manager Harry Haslam offered him terms. He had played only ten League games for the Bramall Lane club when Gordon Lee paid £80,000 for him. Although, erratic, he proved a gifted front-runner with an exciting turn of speed and an explosive shot. He scored seven goals in 28 appearances in 1980-81, the highspot of his Goodison career coming when he netted the club's second goal in their 2-1 FA Cup win over Liverpool. After losing his place he looked set to join mighty Portuguese side, Benfica, in May 1981, but the deal fell through at the last moment. After becoming a free agent in 1981 he moved to Newcastle United for £125,000, and later Sheffield Wednesday and West Brom. In October 1986, Varadi moved to Manchester City in a straight exchange deal which took Robert Hopkins to The Hawthorns. He later played for Sheffield Wednesday and Leeds United.

IMRE VARADI

	LEAGUE		*FA CUP*		*FL CUP*		*EUROPE*		*TOTAL*	
	App	*Gls*	*App*	*Gls*	*App*	*Gls*	*App*	*Gls*	*App*	*Gls*
1979-80	2/2	0	0/1	0	0	0	0/1	0	2/4	0
1980-81	20/2	6	6	1	0	0	-	-	26/2	7
	22/4	6	6/1	1	0	0	0/1	0	28/6	7

ROY VERNON

Roy Vernon was an inside-forward, mature beyond his years, who revelled in producing the unexpected. He made his League debut for Blackburn Rovers as an 18-year-old in September 1955. On that day he played on the right wing against Liverpool and in direct opposition was his fellow countryman, Roy Lambert. Four days before his 20th birthday, Vernon won the first of 32 caps for Wales, against Northern Ireland. In February 1960, Johnny Carey, his former manager at Blackburn, lured him to Goodison Park in a £27,000 deal which took Eddie Thomas to Ewood Park in part-exchange. Yet Everton might have had him for nothing. He was once offered a trial but opted for a place on Blackburn's groundstaff. Three months after he eventually signed for Everton, Blackburn were at Wembley for the FA Cup Final. Vernon shook off that disappointment and went on to captain Everton. He scored 24 League goals when Everton won the Championship in 1962-3. An expert penalty-taker, he was regarded as one of the finest strikers of a dead ball. He moved to Stoke for £40,000 in March 1965 and in 1970 spent a short time playing in South Africa. In September that year he joined his former Blackburn colleagues Bryan Douglas and Ronnie Clayton at Great Harwood.

	LEAGUE		*FA CUP*		*FL CUP*		*EUROPE*		*TOTAL*	
	App	*Gls*	*App*	*Gls*	*App*	*Gls*	*App*	*Gls*	*App*	*Gls*
1959-60	12	9	0	0	-	-	-	-	12	9
1960-61	39	21	1	0	4	1	-	-	44	22
1961-62	37	26	3	2	-	-	-	-	40	28
1962-63	41	24	3	3	-	-	2	0	46	27
1963-64	31	18	5	2	-	-	2	0	38	20
1964-65	16	3	0	0	-	-	3	1	19	4
	176	101	12	7	4	1	7	1	199	110

ALBERT VIRR

Six-feet tall, long-legged Albert Virr was a local boy who succeeded in two vocations. After training as an engineer, he became a full-time footballer in the early 1920s and was a vital member of Everton's Championship-winning side of 1927-8. He was a colourful character, a half-back who liked to play the simple but effective way. Although there was probably no firmer tackler in the League, he was a scrupulously fair player. His career was wrecked by a serious knee injury sustained during an FA Cup match against Chelsea in January 1929. The damage was diagnosed as severe cartilage trouble and although he did attempt a comeback the following season, he was eventually forced into retirement. He became a schoolteacher, survived a major lung operation in 1954, but died, aged 57, in Sefton General Hospital in July 1959.

	LEAGUE		*FA CUP*		*TOTAL*	
	App	*Gls*	*App*	*Gls*	*App*	*Gls*
1924-25	1	0	1	0	2	0
1925-26	16	0	2	0	18	0
1926-27	32	1	4	1	36	2
1927-28	39	1	1	0	40	1
1928-29	24	0	1	0	25	0
1929-30	5	0	0	0	5	0
	117	2	9	1	126	3

Eddie Wainwright was one of Southport's major gifts to football. He started with High Park in the resort's amateur league before being spotted by Everton and signing amateur forms in 1939. In his early days he was 'farmed out' to Fleetwood to aid his development. He improved rapidly during the early years of the war and played a great deal of army representative football where he came under the eye of Arthur Rowe, later to manage Spurs' famous 'push and run' side. His goalscoring feats rekindled Everton's interest and in September 1943 they gave him his first-team debut, in a League North game against Manchester United when the youngster played alongside pre-war internationals like Tommy Lawton and Joe Mercer. An intelligent ball-player with a fierce shot, Wainwright played a major role in Everton's 1949-50 FA Cup run which was ended in the semi-final by Liverpool. The same year he toured the USA and Canada with an FA party. He also played for the Football League against the Irish League. The latter stages of his career were ruined by injuries. In December 1950, a tackle by Derby's Chick Musson broke his leg but he fought back and eventually ran up 228 appearances and 76 goals.

	LEAGUE		*FA CUP*		*TOTAL*	
	App	*Gls*	*App*	*Gls*	*App*	*Gls*
1946-47	27	13	2	2	29	15
1947-48	30	9	4	2	34	11
1948-49	17	10	1	0	18	10
1949-50	37	11	5	2	42	13
1950-51	11	1	0	0	11	1
1952-53	7	4	0	0	7	4
1953-54	23	8	3	0	26	8
1954-55	24	4	2	0	26	4
1955-56	31	8	4	2	35	10
	207	68	21	8	228	76

EDDIE WAINWRIGHT

In August 1986 while Everton were preparing for the new season with a series of friendly games in Holland, manager Howard Kendall was informed that centre-back Derek Mountfield would be out of action for several weeks through injury. Determined to start the campaign with a fully-fit complement of senior players Kendall contacted his Norwich City counterpart, Ken Brown, to ask about the availability of Dave Watson, and in doing so started a ten-day tug-of-war. Kendall's initial advances were spurned by Norwich but on 21 August, having raised his bid from £700,000 to £900,000, Kendall got his man and Watson booked a return ticket to his native Merseyside. Ironically Watson began his career with Liverpool but during a prolonged stay at Anfield he managed only four reserve-team games before moving to Carrow Road in November 1980 — City paying an initial fee of £50,000, a similar sum after he had made 25 senior appearances and a further £100,000 after he had collected his first full England cap. A solid and competitive defender renowned for his aerial prowess, Watson struggled to make his mark immediately after his transfer. He failed to recapture his best form and constantly found himself at odds with supporters who idolised Mountfield, the man he had replaced. But as the 1986-7 Championship-winning season began to unfold, Watson won a place in the hearts of the Everton faithful with his raw courage and never-say-die attitude. He was appointed club captain in January 1992, succeeding Kevin Ratcliffe.

	LEAGUE		*FA CUP*		*FL CUP*		*TOTAL*	
	App	*Gls*	*App*	*Gls*	*App*	*Gls*	*App*	*Gls*
1986-87	35	4	3	0	2	0	40	4
1987-88	37	4	8	1	7	1	52	6
1988-89	32	3	7	0	4	1	43	4
1989-90	28/1	1	4	0	3	0	35/1	1
1990-91	32	2	6	2	3	0	41	4
1991-92	35	3	2	0	4	0	41	3
1992-93	40	1	2	1	6	0	48	2
	239/1	18	32	4	29	2	300/1	24

DAVE WATSON

Tommy Watson, who prefers to be known as 'Gordon', arrived at Goodison Park in January 1933 and went on to become one of Everton's greatest servants. He had been playing with Blyth Spartans in his native North-East and quickly impressed with his close control and fierce tackling. He made his League debut in 1937 and appeared in 27 pre-war League games. He was 12th man on so many occasions during the 1938-9 Championship season that his teammates clubbed together to buy him a special cushion so that he would have a comfortable seat on the trainer's bench. He had an impish sense of humour and took it all in good spirit, never once bemoaning the fact that he was not in the team. After the war he was appointed first-team trainer and in 1968 joined the club's promotions department. By 1985 he had celebrated 52 years with Everton and is now a part-time barman in the '300 Club'.

	LEAGUE		*FA CUP*		*TOTAL*	
	App	*Gls*	*App*	*Gls*	*App*	*Gls*
1936-37	2	0	0	0	2	0
1937-38	9	1	0	0	9	1
1938-39	16	0	1	0	17	0
1946-47	12	0	0	0	12	0
1947-48	18	0	4	0	22	0
1948-49	4	0	0	0	4	0
	61	1	5	0	66	1

TOMMY (GORDON) WATSON

When he joined Everton from Blackpool in March 1962 for a then record fee for a goalkeeper of £27,000, Gordon West became the first signing made by new manager Harry Catterick. A superb athlete with a theatrical dash about him, West was a technically brilliant last line of defence. He immediately took over from Albert Dunlop and in just over 12 months won a Championship medal. His consistency brought him to the attention of Sir Alf Ramsey, but West staggered the football world when he refused to join the party for the 1970 World Cup Finals in Mexico, preferring to remain at home with his family. He was a regular choice at Goodison for four years before being dropped in favour of Andy Rankin in 1970-71. Typically, this exuberant character fought back and in 1971-2 he was ever-present. In June 1972, however, David Lawson arrived from Huddersfield and West made only four more League appearances and retired after nearly 400 appearances for Everton and three England caps. In 1975 he began a brief comeback with Tranmere.

	LEAGUE		*FA CUP*		*FL CUP*		*EUROPE*		*TOTAL*	
	App	*Gls*	*App*	*Gls*	*App*	*Gls*	*App*	*Gls*	*App*	*Gls*
1961-62	12	0	0	0	-	-	-	-	12	0
1962-63	38	0	3	0	-	-	2	0	43	0
1963-64	22	0	3	0	-	-	2	0	27	0
1964-65	20	0	4	0	-	-	2	0	26	0
1965-66	24	0	8	0	-	-	2	0	34	0
1966-67	36	0	5	0	-	-	4	0	45	0
1967-68	41	0	6	0	2	0	-	-	49	0
1968-69	42	0	5	0	4	0	-	-	51	0
1969-70	42	0	1	0	4	0	-	-	47	0
1970-71	12	0	1	0	0	0	1	0	14	0
1971-72	42	0	4	0	1	0	-	-	47	0
1972-73	4	0	0	0	0	0	-	-	4	0
	335	0	40	0	11	0	13	0	399	0

GORDON WEST

TOMMY WHITE

When Everton signed Tommy White from Southport in 1927 they bought a player of exceptional versatility. White could play almost anywhere and was guaranteed to give a good account of himself in whatever position he was asked to perform. As a schoolboy he was a centre-half, but he joined Everton as a goalscorer who could play anywhere in the forward line. His aggressive style won him many admirers and on occasions he stood in for Dixie Dean, which in itself was quite a daunting task. Towards the end of his Everton career he reverted to centre-half and he was a tower of strength in the 1935-6 season as Everton battled to avoid relegation. White made 193 League appearances for Everton, scoring 66 goals. He played centre-half for England against Italy in Rome in 1933. In October 1937 he signed for Northampton Town.

	LEAGUE		*FA CUP*		*TOTAL*	
	App	*Gls*	*App*	*Gls*	*App*	*Gls*
1927-28	1	2	0	0	1	2
1928-29	21	6	0	0	21	6
1929-30	35	11	0	0	35	11
1930-31	10	10	0	0	10	10
1931-32	23	18	1	0	24	18
1932-33	34	2	6	0	40	2
1933-34	28	14	1	0	29	14
1934-35	5	0	0	0	5	0
1935-36	35	3	1	0	36	3
1936-37	1	0	0	0	1	0
	193	66	9	0	202	66

ALAN WHITTLE

Harry Catterick described Alan Whittle as "the greatest Everton discovery of all time." Sadly, however, the gritty forward with a flair for goalscoring failed to live up to expectations. He was hailed as a 'new Denis Law' when, as a precocious 18-year-old, he helped Everton shatter West Brom 6-2 on his debut in March 1968, and he went on to win a League Championship medal in 1970. But, while nobody could dispute his commitment and determination, he was largely inconsistent and found himself out of the side on numerous occasions. After such a blistering start to his career, things did not work out and in December 1972 he was transferred to Crystal Palace for £100,000. The same day, Catterick paid Aberdeen £180,000 for Joe Harper. Whittle looked set to join Wrexham in 1975 but eventually found his way to Sheffield United on a free-transfer in July 1976. He went on to play for Bournemouth before trying his luck in Australia.

	LEAGUE		*FA CUP*		*FL CUP*		*EUROPE*		*TOTAL*	
	App	*Gls*	*App*	*Gls*	*App*	*Gls*	*App*	*Gls*	*App*	*Gls*
1967-68	6	0	0	0	0	0	-	-	6	0
1968-69	4	0	0	0	1	2	-	-	5	2
1969-70	15	11	1	0	2	0	-	-	18	11
1970-71	24	7	1	0	0	0	4/1	1	29/1	8
1971-72	18/1	0	4	2	1	0	-	-	23/1	2
1972-73	5/1	3	0	0	0	0	-	-	5/1	3
	72/2	21	6	2	4	2	4/1	1	86/3	26

BEN WILLIAMS

Ben Williams was a strong full-back who captained Everton when the club marched back to the First Division in 1930-31. He was born in Penhriwceiber, South Wales, a fact which led to him being called 'Khyber' by his teammates. As a schoolboy he was a good boxer and seriously considered a career in the ring before Swansea Town convinced him that his future lay in soccer. He signed for the Swans in 1923 and played 97 games for them before Everton took him to Goodison Park in December 1929. He formed a brilliant partnership with Warney Cresswell and won international recognition, playing ten times for Wales. In January 1933 his career received a serious blow when he underwent a cartilage operation. He never fully recovered and was transferred to Newport County in 1936. Twelve months later he was appointed club coach. He retired from football to pursue a business career.

	LEAGUE		*FA CUP*		*TOTAL*	
	App	*Gls*	*App*	*Gls*	*App*	*Gls*
1929-30	9	0	2	0	11	0
1930-31	36	0	5	0	41	0
1931-32	33	0	1	0	34	0
1932-33	20	0	0	0	20	0
1933-34	18	0	0	0	18	0
1934-35	12	0	0	0	12	0
1935-36	3	0	0	0	3	0
	131	0	8	0	139	0

RAY WILSON

Ramon Wilson was one of the most cultured full-backs ever to play on Merseyside. Born near Mansfield, he joined Huddersfield Town from local amateur circles in 1951. He stayed at Leeds Road for 13 years before signing for Everton in July 1964. A tough tackler with superb tactical knowledge, he was widely regarded as the finest full-back in European football when he won a World Cup winners' medal with England in 1966. His career in the top flight ended in July 1968 when a knee injury sustained in training required surgery. He fought back, but although the finesse which had been the hallmark of his play was still evident, he had lost some of his old speed and confidence and he was given a free transfer. The experience of 18 years in the game, and 63 England appearances, made him an attractive proposition for several clubs. He joined Oldham Athletic in 1969 before moving to Bradford City as player-coach. He quit football in 1971 and is now an undertaker.

	LEAGUE		*FA CUP*		*FL CUP*		*EUROPE*		*TOTAL*	
	App	*Gls*	*App*	*Gls*	*App*	*Gls*	*App*	*Gls*	*App*	*Gls*
1964-65	17	0	4	0	-	-	2	0	23	0
1965-66	35	0	8	0	-	-	4	0	47	0
1966-67	30	0	6	0	-	-	4	0	40	0
1967-68	28	0	6	0	0	0	-	-	34	0
1968-69	4/2	0	2	0	0/1	0	-	-	6/3	0
	114/2	0	26	0	0/1	0	10	0	150/3	0

Sam Wolstenholme was still a current international when Everton surprisingly let him go to Blackburn Rovers in 1904. It may have been that they thought he was past his best — certainly his prematurely balding pate and bandy legs gave the impression that he was nearing the end of his career — but he was only 25 and enjoyed several more seasons at the top. Born at Little Lever, he joined Everton in late 1897 and made one appearance that season. Thereafter he soon forced his way into the side as a wing-half whose anticipation made up for any shortcomings he might have had in the tackle. In 1900-01 he was an ever-present. In April 1904 he made his England debut, against Scotland. By the time he played in the next two games, against Ireland and Wales, he was a Blackburn player. In 1908 he went to Croydon Common and helped them into the Southern League before moving to another Southern League club, Norwich City, and then retiring in 1913. He was coaching in Germany when war was declared and was interned along with fellow England internationals Steve Bloomer and Fred Spikesley. Together they persuaded their camp commandant to allow them to organise a football league for prisoners' teams.

	LEAGUE		*FA CUP*		*TOTAL*	
	App	*Gls*	*App*	*Gls*	*App*	*Gls*
1897-98	1	0	0	0	1	0
1898-99	15	0	2	0	17	0
1899-1900	29	0	1	0	30	0
1900-01	34	2	2	0	36	2
1901-02	27	1	2	0	29	1
1902-03	22	1	2	0	24	1
1903-04	32	4	1	0	33	4
	160	8	10	0	170	8

SAM WOLSTENHOLME

Gordon Lee had been searching for a goalkeeper for nearly six months before he landed George Wood in August 1977. Standing 6ft 3in and weighing around 14st, Wood was surprisingly agile for such a big man. He proved capable of acts of great athleticism between the Everton posts. He was signed from Blackpool for £150,000, at the same time that Dave Thomas came from QPR for £200,000. Born at Douglas, Wood joined Blackpool in 1971-2 from East Stirling and in his last season at Bloomfield Road he played in every League match for the Seasiders. In his first two seasons at Goodison Park he was also an ever-present, his displays winning him three full Scotland caps. But the inconsistency which had dogged his early days gradually returned and he lost his place to newcomer Martin Hodge. Wood made 103 League appearances for Everton before signing for Arsenal in August 1980 for £150,000 and after three seasons at Highbury he moved to Crystal Palace.

	LEAGUE		*FA CUP*		*FL CUP*		*EUROPE*		*TOTAL*	
	App	*Gls*	*App*	*Gls*	*App*	*Gls*	*App*	*Gls*	*App*	*Gls*
1977-78	42	0	2	0	5	0	0	0	49	0
1978-79	42	0	1	0	3	0	4	0	50	0
1979-80	19	0	1	0	5	0	2	0	27	0
	103	0	4	0	13	0	6	0	126	0

GEORGE WOOD

Tommy Wright was the classic case of local boy made good. He joined Everton straight from school as a talented inside-forward, but was converted to wing-half, then right-back. A former England Schoolboy international, he made his first-team debut in 1964, aged 19. He took over from Scottish international Alex Parker and in 1966 won an FA Cup winners' medal against Sheffield Wednesday. He added Under-23 honours to his caps before his first full appearance, against Russia in the 1968 European Championships third-place play-off. One of the most constructive back-four men in British football, he played in the 1970 World Cup Finals in Mexico. He was a solid defender who liked to force his way down the flanks when the opportunity arose. One of Everton's 1970 Championship side, Tommy Wright will be remembered as one of football's natural gentlemen.

TOMMY WRIGHT

	LEAGUE		*FA CUP*		*FL CUP*		*EUROPE*		*TOTAL*	
	App	*Gls*	*App*	*Gls*	*App*	*Gls*	*App*	*Gls*	*App*	*Gls*
1964-65	22	0	3	0	-	-	3	0	28	0
1965-66	35/1	0	6	0	-	-	4	0	45/1	0
1966-67	42	0	6	0	-	-	4	0	52	0
1967-68	38	0	6	0	2	0	-	-	46	0
1968-69	41	1	5	0	4	0	-	-	50	1
1969-70	42	1	1	0	4	0	-	-	47	1
1970-71	40	2	5	0	0	0	6	0	51	2
1971-72	17	0	1	0	0	0	-	-	18	0
1972-73	30	0	2	0	1	0	-	-	33	0
	307/1	4	35	0	11	0	17	0	370/1	4

Billy Wright will be remembered as the towering centre-back who lost his Everton place because he was overweight. Only hours before a League game at Ipswich on 11 December 1982, manager Howard Kendall told his club captain that he was being left out as a disciplinary measure for weighing 8lb more than the club decreed. Wright, a life-long Everton supporter, never recovered fom the blow to his confidence and never played for Everton again. Within six months he was on his way to Birmingham City. A hard-working defender, Wright had proved a pillar of strength in Everton's back-four. He made 164 League appearances and was the club's longest-serving professional at the time he left Goodison. As he fought to trim down his frame, the makeshift central defensive partnership of Kevin Ratcliffe and Mark Higgins came good. That left Wright little alternative but to accept the free transfer in June 1983. He joined a Birmingham side destined for relegation, but in 1984-5 he helped them back to Division One. Later he went on loan to Chester. He is a nephew of Tommy Wright.

BILLY WRIGHT

	LEAGUE		*FA CUP*		*FL CUP*		*EUROPE*		*TOTAL*	
	App	*Gls*	*App*	*Gls*	*App*	*Gls*	*App*	*Gls*	*App*	*Gls*
1977-78	3/1	1	0	0	0	0	0	0	3/1	1
1978-79	39	2	1	0	3	0	4	0	47	2
1979-80	40/1	0	6	0	3	0	2	0	51/1	0
1980-81	41	2	6	0	3	0	0	0	50	2
1981-82	24	2	0	0	0	0	0	0	24	2
1982-83	17	3	0	0	4	0	0	0	21	3
	164/2	10	13	0	13	0	6	0	196/2	10

Alex 'Sandy' Young — no ancestor of Everton's star of the 1960s — was the man who scored the 75th-minute goal which won the 1906 FA Cup Final for the club when he converted a centre from Jack Sharp to sink Newcastle United. The reception which greeted Young's effort was likened by one newspaper to the San Francisco earthquake which had happened a week earlier. Born in Slamannan, Stirlingshire, in June 1880, Young's career took him to St Mirren and Falkirk before he joined Everton in the summer of 1901. A centre-forward who occasionally turned out at outside-left, he made his Everton debut at Villa Park on 28 November 1901, but it took him until the first week in December to score his first goal for the club, against Sheffield Wednesday at Goodison. In subsequent seasons Young showed Everton fans just why he had been bought. He scored 110 goals in 275 League games and topped the scoring charts in 1906-07 when his 28 goals included four against Manchester City as Everton romped home 9-1. In the close season of 1911 he moved to Tottenham Hotspur but was not at White Hart Lane long. A year later he began to wind down his career with Burslem Port Vale. He won two Scottish caps whilst at Everton, against England and Wales.

ALEX YOUNG

	LEAGUE		*FA CUP*		*TOTAL*	
	App	*Gls*	*App*	*Gls*	*App*	*Gls*
1901-02	30	6	2	1	32	7
1902-03	19	5	1	0	20	5
1903-04	22	10	0	0	22	10
1904-05	31	14	6	0	37	14
1905-06	30	12	5	2	35	14
1906-07	33	28	8	1	41	29
1907-08	33	16	6	5	39	21
1908-09	23	9	1	0	24	9
1909-10	24	2	7	3	31	5
1910-11	30	8	3	3	33	11
	275	110	39	15	314	125

Alex Young was one of the most talked-about players of his generation. His instinctive, flowing style combined with the on-field arrogance of a great performer made him a sporting hero on Merseyside. The adulation which rolled down from the Goodison terraces when he touched the ball verged on unashamed hero-worship. In the eyes of a public which searched desperately for a focal point for their affection, the young Scotsman with the magic boots could do no wrong. In many respects he was an infuriating player, capable of seemingly impossible feats one minute, unable or unwilling to complete a far simpler task the next. Critics said that he 'disappeared' for lengthy periods when the going got tough. Certainly he was not built for a fight. He was a graceful, compact player who could turn a match with one flick of a spidery leg. He was so revered that he inspired a television play centred around Everton and entitled *The Golden Vision*, the nickname Young carries to this day. He arrived at Goodison in November 1960, along with Hearts colleague George Thomson. Within two years of establishing his place, he helped Everton to the Championship with a series of stunning solo displays. He played in the 1966 FA Cup-winning side, leaving Goodison in 1968 to become player-manager of Irish League club Glentoran. He stayed only a matter of weeks. He joined Stockport County but was forced to retire in August 1969 because of a knee injury.

ALEX YOUNG

	LEAGUE		*FA CUP*		*FL CUP*		*EUROPE*		*TOTAL*	
	App	*Gls*	*App*	*Gls*	*App*	*Gls*	*App*	*Gls*	*App*	*Gls*
1960-61	13	6	0	0	1	1	-	-	14	7
1961-62	40	14	3	0	-	-	-	-	43	14
1962-63	42	22	3	0	-	-	2	0	47	22
1963-64	27	12	3	0	-	-	2	0	32	12
1964-65	20	3	1	0	-	-	3	3	24	6
1965-66	26	7	8	2	-	-	2	0	36	9
1966-67	35	8	5	2	-	-	4	0	44	10
1967-68	24/1	5	2/2	0	2	2	-	-	28/3	7
	227/1	77	25/2	4	3	3	13	3	268/3	87

Matches to Remember

Match to Remember 1 — 8 September 1888

Everton 2 Accrington 1

MORE than 10,000 people, twice as many as had been expected, turned up to witness Everton's first match in the newly-formed Football League.

Cloudless skies brought even the most fickle Evertonians to Anfield despite the fact that seven days earlier Everton had been beaten by fierce local rivals, Bootle.

The match kicked off 20 minutes late, Accrington having lost their way to the ground. The visitors won the toss and surprisingly opted to kick into the sun.

The early pressure came from Everton. A fierce drive from Farmer brought the best out of Accrington goalkeeper, Horne, who gratefully conceded a corner.

The closest Accrington came to snatching a goal against the run of play was midway through the first-half when a huge clearance by Horne was headed against the Everton crossbar by Holden.

Lewis and Dobson both went close for the Merseysiders before the luckless Chadwick was guilty of the most glaring miss, two minutes before the interval. Fleming worked his way down the right before delivering an inch-perfect cross which the normally reliable inside-forward blasted high over the bar.

With the sun at their backs, Accrington were a different proposition. They pushed forward in great numbers and were unfortunate not to break the deadlock when Holden fired narrowly wide.

After 60 minutes Everton grabbed the lead after Horne conceded a corner on the left. Ross worked the ball to Waugh who neatly fed Farmer on the touchline. His cross was met perfectly by Fleming who headed firmly into the bottom corner from ten yards. The *Liverpool Daily Post* reported that the goal was greeted 'with tremendous cheering and waving of hats'.

Accrington came within a whisker of levelling affairs straight from the restart when Lewis cleared a Kirkham shot off the line with goalkeeper Smalley well beaten.

An incident 15 minutes from time virtually guaranteed an Everton victory. As Chadwick rose to meet a Waugh cross, Horne rushed off his goal-line and collided with the big forward before falling to the turf clutching his chest.

He had fractured a rib and was carried off in agony as McLennan took over in goal. Within two minutes Everton had made the most of their advantage, Fleming sweeping home a Farmer cross.

Accrington launched a furious late assault and Holden scored from close range after striking the crossbar with a header. In the last minute, Smalley came to Everton's rescue as he clawed away a dipping Holden volley.

Everton: Smalley, Dick, Ross, Holt, Jones, Dobson, Fleming, Waugh, Lewis, E.Chadwick, Farmer.
Accrington: Horne, Stevenson, McLennan, Haworth, Wilkinson, Pemberton, Lofthouse, Benar, Kirkham, Holden, Chippendale.

Referee: J.J.Bentley (Bolton) *Attendance: 10,000*

Everton, First Division champions 1890-91. Back row (players only, left to right): Hannah, Smalley, Doyle. Middle row: Brady, Kirkwood, Holt, Parry, Chadwick. Front row: Latta, Geary, Millward.

Match to Remember 2 — 30 December 1893

Everton 7 West Bromwich Albion 1

JACK Southworth was one of the great goalscorers of nineteenth-century football. For one full season Everton enjoyed his services and he left a telling impression at Goodison Park. In one match alone he scored six goals for the club, a record which still stands in 1992.

Despite foggy weather, there was a crowd of some 25,000 people for the visit of West Brom to Goodison in the closing hours of 1893. Their interest was repaid when Jack Southworth achieved the biggest single scoring feat in the club's history.

Within a minute of the kick-off Everton were ahead through John Bell, and although Smart Arridge had to react quickly to prevent a rapid equaliser, it was the Merseysiders who went on to put the result beyond doubt — and Southworth was the hero of the hour.

Latta and Bell combined to give Southworth his first goal. His second came when Reader, the Albion goalkeeper, failed to hold a shot from Bell, and his hat-trick goal was a brilliant solo effort. From the halfway line the former Blackburn Rovers player dribbled through the Albion defence before shooting home.

Albion reached half-time trailing 4-0, and reflecting that it could have been more, had Chadwick not fired over the bar.

The second half was not many minutes old when Bell laid on a fourth goal for Southworth, but the Midlanders battled on gamely and Williams was forced to make two fine saves. England star Billy Bassett was in particularly fine form, trying hard to salvage some pride for his team.

A mistake by Stewart allowed Norman through and at last West Brom opened their account. But any wild dreams of a sensational fightback were soon dashed. Bell beat three men to lay on Southworth's fifth, and then Latta wriggled his way through to give Southworth the chance of a sixth goal. The Everton man gratefully accepted it and wrote himself into the record book.

Everton: Williams, Parry, Arridge, Kelso, Holt, Stewart, Latta, Bell, Southworth, Chadwick, Milward.
West Bromwich Albion: Reader, Nicholson, Crone, Taggart, C.Perry, T.Perry, Bassett, Norman, McLeod, Williams, Pearson.

Attendance: 25,000

Match to Remember 3 — 31 March 1906

Everton 2 Liverpool 0

MERSEYSIDE took over Villa Park for the day when Everton met Liverpool in the semi-final of the FA Cup. Long before midday, the centre of Birmingham was a sea of red, white and blue as thousands of supporters arrived for the big game.

The teams enjoyed a more leisurely journey, Liverpool staying overnight in Tamworth, while Everton, after a morning train journey from Merseyside, arrived in time for lunch at the Grand Hotel.

It was the game everyone wanted to see and there were 50,000 people present when Parkinson kicked off for Liverpool. It was Everton who had the first attempt at goal, through Settle, but it was Liverpool who applied early pressure with Scott making some fine saves in the Everton goal.

Abbott stopped an attack by Dunlop and Bradley, then Hewitt rounded Walter Balmer and put in a dangerous cross which Scott did well to fist away.

Parkinson went close for Liverpool but the flustered Everton defence held on and towards the end of an absorbing first-half, it was the Goodison men who might have taken the lead and were denied only by a last-ditch clearance from Parry.

As the second-half progressed, Everton asserted themselves, although not before Jack Crelley had been momentarily knocked-out during a fierce Liverpool raid.

Eventually the deadlock was broken when Abbott found the back of the Liverpool net with a rasping drive from just inside the penalty area.

A second goal, from Harold Hardman, made the match safe for Everton and took them through to their third FA Cup Final appearance. The following month Liverpool were crowned League Champions while Everton went to the Crystal Palace to meet Newcastle United. These were good times for Merseyside football followers.

Everton: Scott, R.Balmer, Crelley, Makepeace, Taylor, Abbott, Sharp, Bolton, Young, Settle, Hardman.
Liverpool: Hardy, West, Dunlop, Parry, Raisbeck, Bradley, Goddard, Robinson, Parkinson, Carlin, Hewitt.

Attendance: 50,000

Everton in 1905-06. Back row (left to right): J.Elliott (trainer), McDermott, Booth, R.Balmer, Abbott, Taylor, Young, Crelley. Front row: Sharp, Makepeace, Settle, Scott, W.Balmer, Hardman.

Match to Remember 4 — 21 April 1906

Everton 1 Newcastle United 0

MIGHTY Newcastle United were firm favourites to lift the FA Cup in 1906, having been surprisingly beaten 2-0 by Aston Villa 12 months earlier to be denied a League and Cup double.

Yet Everton were quietly confident that, after the disappointment of seeing the trophy snatched from their grasp in 1893 and again four years later, it would be a case of third time lucky.

Seventy-five thousand people filled the Crystal Palace stadium on a bright, breezy April afternoon, many of them having made the long journey south from Merseyside and Tyneside.

Both clubs were so determined to name full-strength line-ups that they were each fined for fielding weakened teams in games the week before the Final.

The first-half was a dull affair. Chances were created, then subsequently squandered at both ends as over-wary forwards met firm, unrelenting resistance from well-drilled defenders.

The game certainly failed to live up to the expectations of tens of thousands of fans. Everton and Newcastle effectively cancelled each other out as they battled for midfield supremacy.

In the days leading up to the match, United's much-vaunted half-back line had promised to make mincemeat out of the Goodison forwards but, while clear-cut openings were few, Everton supporters pinned their hopes on players of the calibre of Sandy Young and Jimmy Settle.

Action in front of Newcastle's goal during the 1906 FA Cup Final at the Crystal Palace.

Settle saw a fierce header well saved by Lawrence after 15 minutes, but generally the penetration which had hallmarked Everton's route to the Crystal Palace was sadly missing.

United were restricted to two chances in the goalless first-half, Gosnell and Rutherford both firing wide.

Eight minutes after the restart, with Everton in total command, the deadlock appeared to have been broken when Lawrence failed to hold Sharp's cross. Settle passed across goal and Young turned the ball home — only to be ruled offside.

Frustrated at the prospect of a second successive Cup Final defeat, Newcastle cut up rough and the referee stopped the game to warn the Magpies about their ungentlemanly conduct.

With 13 minutes remaining, Taylor, sole playing survivor of Everton's last Cup Final appearance, found Sharp who evaded the lunging tackles of two United defenders before sending a low centre to Young. This time there was no waving linesman's flag as Young fired beyond Lawrence to give Everton the FA Cup for the first time.

Everton: Scott, W.Balmer, Crelley, Makepeace, Taylor, Abbott, Sharp, Bolton, Young, Settle, Hardman.
Newcastle United: Lawrence, McCombie, Carr, Gardner, Aitken, McWilliam, Rutherford, Howie, Veitch, Orr, Gosnell

Referee: F.Kirkham (Preston) *Attendance: 75,000*

Match to Remember 5 — 5 May 1928

Everton 3 Arsenal 3

EVERTON had already clinched the League Championship when they faced Arsenal on the final Saturday of the season.

Sixty thousand people crowded into Goodison Park, not so much to pay homage to the newly-crowned kings of the English game, as to witness one man's attempt

Everton, First Division champions 1927-28. Back row (left to right, players only): O'Donnell, Brown, Hardy, Hart, McDonald. Front row: Millington, Irvine, Dean, Dominy, Troup, Virr.

to rewrite the record book. That man was Dixie Dean who stood on the threshold of a unique and quite astonishing personal triumph.

In the space of 90 minutes he needed three more goals to become the first player ever to notch 60 League goals in one season. It was a daunting task, particularly against a side which had already signalled their intentions to spoil the party.

Arsenal, a methodical side, held the early advantage and after only two minutes they went ahead when Everton goalkeeper Davies made the first of several mistakes by failing to hold a hopeful drive by Shaw.

Exactly 60 seconds later Everton were level and the scorer, almost inevitably, was Dean. Critchley swung over one of his famous drifting corners and the powerful centre-forward bundled the ball over the line with Gunners' goalkeeper Patterson well beaten.

Three minutes later, as Everton began to get into their stride, Dean was upended in the penalty area by Butler. It was Dean who ambled forward to drive the penalty low into the bottom corner, leaving himself one goal short of the magical figure.

Everton's overwhelming desire to give Dean the ball every time they ventured forward, allowed Arsenal time and space, and they equalised ten minutes from the interval when O'Donnell, under pressure from four opponents, mis-cued to send the ball spinning past his goalkeeper.

The second-half was played at a frantic pace as the massive crowd, sensing that time was running out for their hero, tranformed Goodison into a seething cauldron.

With only eight minutes to play, Patterson palmed a fierce Martin drive for a corner. Troup, the man who had served as Dean's main provider throughout the

Dixie Dean's record-breaking effort against Arsenal, his 60th League goal of the season.

season, took the flag-kick. Dean rose magnificently to outjump his markers and head powerfully home for his 60th goal of the season.

Joy was mixed with relief as 60,000 people stood to acknowledge a great player's finest hour. Even a late equaliser by Shaw could not dampen the enthusiasm as Arsenal players took advantage of stoppages to shake Dean's hand.

Everton: Davies, Cresswell, O'Donnell, Kelly, Hart, Virr, Critchley, Martin, Dean, Weldon, Troup.
Arsenal: Patterson, Parker, John, Baker, Butler, Blythe, Hulme, Buchan, Shaw, Brain, Peel.

Attendance: 60,000

Match to Remember 6 — 12 October 1932

Newcastle United 3 Everton 5

EVERTON travelled to St James' Park as First Divison Champions, determined to land a piece of early-season silverware by lifting the Charity Shield at the expense of FA Cup-holders Newcastle.

Everton, urged on by a small but vociferous travelling army of fans in the 10,000 crowd, began well, carving out several excellent early openings. Dixie Dean went close before Ted Critchley hit the crossbar to underline the visitors' growing superiority.

Against the run of play, United snatched the opening goal when McMenemy broke free to comfortably beat Ted Sagar from ten yards.

Undaunted, Everton continued to sweep forward and they were rewarded when Dean rose unchallenged to head home. The goal deflated Newcastle and what followed was a display of vintage football from the League Champions.

With the irrepressible Dean acting as a human battering ram, and Cliff Britton and his defensive colleagues mopping up with great precision at the back, Everton took the North-Easterners apart.

Everton, First Division champions, 1931-32. Back row (players only, left to right): Thomson, Clark, Gee, Sagar, Williams, Cresswell, Bocking. Front row: Critchley, Dunn, Dean, Johnson, Stein, White.

Tommy Johnson added a second just before half-time and Dean headed another to give Everton a 3-1 interval lead.

Their advantage would have been halved had Sagar not brilliantly saved a 44th-minute penalty from Weaver, controversially awarded when Britton was adjudged to have upended Richardson.

Two minutes into the second half, Dean put the game beyond Newcastle's reach by completing his hat-trick from close range after an inspired piece of midfield play by the industrious Britton.

Dazed but defiant, United, fearing that they were now on the verge of a humiliating drubbing, hit back with a near goal from Boyd. But it was the remarkable Dean who was to have the last say.

With two minutes remaining he turned sharply in the penalty area and smashed home his fourth goal, and Everton's fifth. McMenemy scored Newcastle's third.

Newcastle United: Burns, Nelson, Fairhurst, Bell, Higson, Weaver, Boyd, Richardson, Allen, McMenemy, Lang.
Everton: Sagar, Williams, Cresswell, Britton, White, Thomson, Critchley, McGourty, Dean, Johnson, Stein. *Attendance: 10,000*

Match to Remember 7 — 29 April 1933

Everton 3 Manchester City 0

THE clash between royal blue and sky blue in the 1933 FA Cup Final meant that

Players numbered 1-22 in action during the 1933 FA Cup Final between Everton and Manchester City.

neutral strips had to be found. Everton and Manchester City were given the choice of red or white shirts. City preferred red.

The game's place in football history was assured, even before the kick-off, because it was the first time that players in a Final had been numbered. It was decided to employ a strict sequence, so Everton wore 1-11 and City were numbered through to 22, which meant that Eric Brook was the first man to wear number 12 in a Wembley Cup Final.

Many Everton supporters were dismayed at the decision to play Albert Geldard on the right wing in preference to Ted Critchley who, despite losing his regular place seven months earlier, had been brought back to score the winning goal in the semi-final defeat of West Ham.

Everton had no proper manager so the decision to omit Critchley from the Wembley team was almost certainly taken after lengthy consultations with skipper Dixie Dean, a man whom few questioned and no one argued with.

City had their problems too. Centre-forward Freddie Tilson was ruled out and Marshall came in at inside-right with Herd moving to centre-forward. Veteran Jimmy McMullan played inside-left in his last game before retirement.

City took only 15 seconds to get into their stride, Toseland flinging over a high, searching far-post cross which Sagar did well to hold. Although hardly overworked, Sagar's calm assurance when he handled the ball had a noticeable effect on his teammates.

His confidence spread through the ranks and within 20 minutes Everton were in complete control, forcing City to defend furiously.

With Dean in tremendous form it was only a matter of time before City's defence crumbled and in the 41st minute the floodgates were opened when Langford, under

Dixie Dean gets the ball into the net for Everton's second goal after City's Langford (22) fumbled a cross from Cliff Britton.

Dean and his Everton colleagues with the FA Cup after their Wembley victory over Manchester City.

a fierce challenge from Dean, dropped a Britton cross which winger Stein side-footed home from close range.

The hapless Langford was guilty of another dreadful error seven minutes into the second half when he failed to hold another Britton cross and Dean headed powerfully home.

Ten minutes from time Everton took advantage of City's dejection, Jimmy Dunn heading a third goal from Geldard's looping centre.

Sheffield referee Mr E.Wood ended the first-ever FA Cup meeting between Everton and Manchester City. Everton climbed the steps to the royal box and collected the trophy.

Everton Sagar, Cook, Cresswell, Britton, White, Thomson, Geldard, Dunn, Dean, Johnson, Stein.
Manchester City: Langford, Cann, Dale, Busby, Cowan, Bray, Toseland, Marshall, Herd, McMullan, Brook.
Referee: E.Wood (Sheffield) *Attendance: 92,950*

Everton 6 Sunderland 4

AFTER a 1-1 draw at Roker Park, two of English football's finest sides met again four days later to continue their fight for a place in the fifth round of the FA Cup.

Nearly 60,000 people crammed inside Goodison Park for a match which was later described as 'the game of a lifetime'. Unlike the first encounter which had been reported as an over-cautious affair, it was a full-blooded cup-tie with enough excitement and passion to fill a dozen lesser games.

Even so, it was far from the frantic hammer-and-tongs clash which the goal-laden scoreline suggests. Both sides performed with efficiency and flair; the football was, for the most part, quite breathtaking.

Left-winger Jackie Coulter opened the scoring after 14 minutes when he cut inside to unleash a powerful drive which Thorpe in the Sunderland goal was unable to hold. After half an hour he doubled Everton's lead to climax a spell of sustained pressure by the home side.

Sunderland were not a team to surrender easily and they hit back four minutes before the interval when Davis drove home from close range. As the Wearsiders searched for an equaliser, Everton slipped into their familiar defensive role, never looking likely to loosen their stranglehold.

Everton's Gee gets in a tackle on Sunderland's Gurney during the action-packed Cup tie at Goodison.

Victory seemed assured when Stevenson broke through the middle to restore Everton's two-goal advantage.

The goal served only to spur on Sunderland who threw caution to the wind, attacking down both flanks and firing in shots from all angles. Their reward came when Connor picked up a back pass and shot beneath Sagar's diving body.

The drama was not over. This extraordinary game had more twists. Gurney scored a memorable goal with only seconds remaining, and the tie went into extra-time.

Within two minutes of the extra period, Coulter completed his hat-trick to put his side back in front. Back came Sunderland, equalising with a well-taken goal by Connor.

With a second replay looking increasingly likely, Everton winger Albert Geldard took matters into his own hands. He raced upfield to smash home a stunning goal with nine minutes to play. Eight minutes later he collected another as leg-weary Sunderland accepted defeat.

Everton: Sagar, Cook, Jones, Britton, Gee, Thomson, Geldard, Cunliffe, Dean, Stevenson, Coulter.
Sunderland: Thorpe, Murray, Hall, Thompson, Johnston, Hastings, Davis, Carter, Gurney, Gallacher, Connor.

Referee: Mr Pinkeston (Birmingham) *Attendance: 59,213*

Match to Remember 9 — 21 March 1953

Everton 3 Bolton Wanderers 4

EVERTON had travelled to Manchester to contest an FA Cup semi-final on three previous occasions — and each time had returned home with the bitter taste of defeat in their mouths.

In 1953, however, they were expected to dispose comfortably of a Bolton side which, although workmanlike, was not brimming with talent. The one exception was centre-forward Nat Lofthouse who, ten months earlier, had been dubbed 'Lion of Vienna' after his two goals in Austria had won England a famous victory.

It was to be Everton's misfortune that they would encounter this exceptional footballer on a day when he would again be in quite irresistible form.

Yet if the final glory was to be Bolton's, then the medals for courage and commitment were Everton's. They launched one of the most memorable fightbacks in the history of the FA Cup to come within a whisker of earning a replay.

The prospect of the Merseysiders winning a reprieve was unthinkable as they trooped off dejectedly at half-time, 4-0 down. Bolton deserved their impressive lead, not simply because they took their chances, but because they were so far ahead of Everton individually and tactically.

Everton had collapsed in the face of a furious onslaught. It took Bolton only seven minutes to break open a defence which had been creaking from the first whistle. Hassall, Langton and Lofthouse combined superbly to set up Doug Holden who scored from ten yards.

Ten minutes later Willie Moir took a long throw from Hassall, raced clear and struck the ball beyond the reach of the stranded O'Neill. Worse was to follow for Everton as Lofthouse scored from Moir's pass and then blasted home a brilliant solo effort.

Everton's cause had not been helped by the loss of Dave Hickson, with a head injury, for 15 minutes midway through the first-half.

And right on half-time, Clinton missed a penalty after Hartle had handled Parker's shot. The Everton right-back fired wide from the spot.

Two minutes into the second half, Everton pulled a goal back when Parker headed home Buckle's corner. It was the signal for Everton to launch their revival and they poured forward.

They had to wait until the 76th minute for another goal, when Peter Farrell drove home a twice-taken free-kick. With less than a quarter of an hour remaining, Everton saw a glimmer of hope.

Hope turned to belief that they could snatch a replay when, with six minutes left, Hickson rose at the far post to knock the ball back across the face of the goal and Parker headed their third.

But, although they threw everything at Bolton in the closing stages, Everton could not complete what would have been an epic recovery.

Everton: O'Neill, Clinton, Lindsay, Farrell, Jones, Lello, Buckle, Cummins, Hickson, Parker, Eglington.
Bolton Wanderers: Hanson, Hartle, Higgins, Wheeler, Barrass, Bell, Holden, Moir, Lofthouse, Hassell, Langton.

Attendance: 72,213

Match to Remember 10 — 14 May 1966

Everton 3 Sheffield Wednesday 2

MANAGER Harry Catterick dropped a pre-match bombshell when he announced that Goodison favourite Fred Pickering was being left out of the side for the 1966 FA Cup Final.

His replacement was a young Cornishman, Mike Trebilcock, a relatively unknown striker signed for £20,000 from Plymouth Argyle the previous New Year's Eve.

Trebilcock had played only one previous FA Cup match for Everton — the semi-final against Manchester United — and only seven League games.

'Fred was popular and could score goals,' said Catterick later, 'but he'd been injured and had gone off the boil a bit. Trebilcock was a first-rate goal-poacher. I always felt his sharpness would show.'

Catterick, astute as ever, was right. Trebilcock emerged as the unlikely hero of a day which will never be forgotten by those who saw one of the best of all FA Cup Finals, with its superior football and heart-stopping climax.

Wednesday opened in sensational style, taking the lead after only four minutes when a shot by Jim McCalliog took a wicked deflection off Ray Wilson and flew into the net past the helpless Gordon West.

The Owls dominated the game for the best part of an hour. Everton, meanwhile, toiled manfully in midfield, but the service to the strikers was virtually non-existent.

Everton felt they should have had a penalty when Ron Springett appeared to bring down Alex Young, but it was Wednesday who edged further in front when David Ford drove powerfully home in the 57th minute, after West had parried Fantham's shot.

Brian Labone and Brian Harris parade the FA Cup after Everton's win over Sheffield Wednesday.

What followed was one of the greatest Cup Final fightbacks of them all, as Everton dragged themselves off the floor and set about snatching an improbable victory.

Two minutes after Ford had struck, Trebilcock ran into a purple patch. Shaking off his markers he tore into the Owls' defence and threw his side a lifeline when he drove past Springett after Temple's header had been blocked.

Five minutes later Everton were level. Alex Scott's free-kick was headed hesitatingly down by Sam Ellis and Trebilcock fired home, low and hard.

Now in command for the first time, Everton mounted pressure and with ten minutes to play, Gerry Young failed to control a bouncing ball and Temple collected and was off upfield. He drew Springett from his goal before scoring the goal which gave Everton perhaps their most famous victory.

Everton: West, Wright, Wilson, Gabriel, Labone, Harris, Scott, Trebilcock, A.Young, Harvey, Temple.

Sheffield Wednesday: Springett, Smith, Megson, Eustace, Ellis, G.Young, Pugh, Fantham, McCalliog, Ford, Quinn.

Referee: J.F.Taylor (Wolverhampton) *Attendance: 100,000*

Everton with the FA Cup in 1966. Back row (left to right): Harris, Labone, West, Gabriel, Wright, Tommy Eggleston (trainer). Front row: Scott, Trebilcock, Young, Harry Catterick (manager), Harvey, Temple, Wilson.

Match to Remember 11 — 30 August 1969

Everton 3 Leeds United 2

WHEN League Champions Leeds United visited Goodison Park in the early stages of 1969-70, they could have had no idea that they were being entertained by the heirs-apparent to their throne.

Mighty Leeds arrived at Goodison with an unbeaten run of 34 League games behind them, but with designs of making up some of the ground they had lost because of a series of drawn matches in the first weeks of the new season.

Don Revie's ultra-professional side were always difficult opponents but Everton performed marvellously. It was the afternoon on which winger Johnny Morrissey turned in perhaps his finest performance in an Everton shirt.

Morrissey ran riot against the normally reliable Paul Reaney to provide numerous chances for the game's other outstanding player, big Joe Royle.

Twenty-year-old Royle gave Jack Charlton an afternoon which the England centre-half would soon want to forget, constantly beating him in the air and leaving him behind on the ground, thanks to sheer pace. But for the sterling work of Billy

Bremner and Norman Hunter, Leeds would have found themselves on the end of a rare drubbing.

Leeds' otherwise rigid defensive pattern was at its most vulnerable early in the game and, after Jimmy Husband squandered a good chance in the opening minute, Everton went ahead three minutes later when Brown rolled a free-kick to Husband who let fly from just outside the penalty area. The ball cannoned off the defensive wall and this time Husband found his spot perfectly.

With Brian Labone and John Hurst snuffing out Leeds' dual strikers, Allan Clarke and Mick Jones, Everton held the upper hand and increased their lead after 21 minutes.

Morrissey floated over a cross from the left and Royle rose magnificently to send a fierce header thumping against the bar. As the ball bounced back, Royle was the quickest to react, darting forward again to head home.

Leeds, run ragged by this point, went further behind four minutes after half-time when Hurst and Husband linked to set up Royle who fired in from 20 yards.

Typically, Leeds refused to surrender and in the 62nd minute Bremner nipped between Brown and Jackson to chest home an inswinging corner from Giles.

West pawed to safety an overhead kick from Bremner, before that magnificent poacher of goals, Allan Clarke, struck with 15 minutes remaining. Cooper's cross from the right was missed by substitute Lorimer, but Clarke was on hand, swooping to force the ball over the line.

Leeds had fought back to set up a thrilling finale, but Everton held on to pick up two points. They were on their way to the title.

Everton: West, Wright, Brown, Jackson, Labone, Harvey, Husband, Ball, Royle, Hurst, Morrissey.
Leeds United: Sprake, Reaney, Cooper, Bremner, Charlton, Hunter, Madeley, Giles, Jones, Clarke, Gray (Lorimer).

Referee: G.Hill (Leicester) *Attendance: 51,797*

Match to Remember 12 4 November 1970

Everton 1 Borussia Mönchengladbach 1

AFTER sweeping majestically to the League Championship seven months earlier, Everton entered their European Cup second round match against West German champions, Borussia Mönchengladbach, with a huge question-mark hanging over their heads.

Since the start of the new season, Everton had failed miserably to recapture the form which had seen them hailed as the potential 'team of the '70s'. They were now desperate to prove, on the European stage, that their problems were short-term and not terminal.

They secured a commendable 1-1 draw in the first-leg of their match with the Germans, giving a fine display of defensive football after Kendall had scored a vital goal. Now Harry Catterick's team were confident of moving into the last eight of the great club competition.

Despite pouring rain more than 42,000 fans were present. They were rewarded with a match of nail-biting intensity and high drama.

Everton felt that they needed an early goal and they found it, though perhaps

Andy Rankin celebrates after saving from Müller in the penalty shoot-out.

even they were astonished at the speed of its arrival. Only 23 seconds had elapsed when Morrissey flighted over a cross which appeared to pose no threat as the German goalkeeper, Wolfgang Kleff, rose unchallenged to meet it.

Unbelievably Kleff, who was to go on to give a brilliant display, allowed the greasy ball to slip through his fingers. It skidded off the wet turf and over the line to give Everton a sensational lead.

A second Everton goal would surely prove decisive, yet although the Merseysiders mounted an onslaught on Borussia's goal, Kleff redeemed himself with a series of world-class saves.

At the other end, Andy Rankin had been little more than a spectator. But in the 34th minute, he could only parry a shot by Laumen and the German picked himself up to net the rebound.

In the dying stages, Everton unleashed a furious barrage but Kleff defiantly stood his ground and the game went into extra-time.

Koppel hit the woodwork in the first period but the unwelcome prospect of a cruel penalty shoot-out became a harsh reality as legs tired and heads dropped.

The tension was almost unbearable as Joe Royle stepped forward to take the first kick. It was saved and the pendulum swung back in the German's favour.

Sielhoff and Ball both found the back of the net before Laumen missed. Morrissey was on target to nose Everton in front at 2-1. Heynckes levelled matters, then Kendall restored Everton's lead.

Koppel and Brown each converted their kicks leaving Everton 4-3 in front with one kick remaining.

Rankin's moment had arrived. Muller struck the kick hard and to Rankin's right. It was a well-taken penalty but the Everton goalkeeper dived to make a brilliant save and Everton were through.

Everton: Rankin, Wright, K.Newton(Brown), Kendall, Kenyon, Harvey, Whittle(Husband), Ball, Royle, Hurst, Morrissey.
Borusia Mönchengladbach: Kleff, Vogts, Wittmann, Muller, Sielhoff, Deitrich, Le Fevre, Laumen, Koppel, Netzer, Heynckes.

Referee: A.Sbardella (Italy) *Attendance: 42,744*

Match to Remember 13 — 24 March 1984

Liverpool 0 Everton 0

FOR so many years it had been the impossible dream — a Wembley Cup Final between the great Merseyside rivals.

In the weeks leading up to the Milk Cup Final, it had been suggested by people outside Liverpool that the famous stadium would be home to a less than capacity attendance. The sceptics, who still fail to grasp the enormous passions aroused by Merseyside Derby matches, could see no way that a city racked by unemployment and economic gloom could dispose of their full quotas of expensive Wembley tickets.

How wrong they were. It was estimated that some 25,000 people were disappointed and had to join tens of thousands of other Merseysiders who watched the game on television.

The occasion itself in many ways overshadowed the match. Both sets of supporters behaved impeccably, and the releived — and somewhat startled — Metropolitan Police labelled it the 'Friendly Final'.

While no classic, the match was an intriguing encounter between a side which had dominated English soccer for nearly two decades, and a team which was emerging dramatically from the shadows to challenge for that crown.

Everton shrugged off their lack of Wembley experience, tearing into Liverpool's rearguard. It was during this early period that the game's one controversial incident occurred.

After six minutes John Bailey pumped a high ball forward; Graeme Sharp outjumped his marker to flick it on, leaving Adrian Heath in the clear. Inevitably, Bruce Grobbelaar raced off his line, but too late to prevent Heath's drive.

The shot hit Alan Hansen's knee before he appeared to scoop the ball away

Adrian Heath just fails to get to the ball as Alan Kennedy and Bruce Grobbelaar scramble it clear at Wembley.

with his left hand. Referee Robinson waved play on, but the arguments about the 'penalty that never was' will rage for years.

The first half belonged almost exclusively to Everton; the second period was Liverpool's. Shaken by the ferocity of their closest rivals, the Reds took some time to settle down before launching a series of telling raids.

Kennedy, Dalglish and Johnston all went close, but the best chances fell to ace marksman Ian Rush. Three times the normally lethal Welshman squandered great opportunities, thus guaranteeing extra-time.

One could almost sense that both teams were ready to settle for a replay as the sun took its toll on bodies that had already endured a hard season.

Both sides had the chance to snatch a late victory, but a draw was the perfect end to a remarkable day. As the players trooped off, blue mingled with red and the chant, 'Merseyside, Merseyside, Merseyside,' echoed around Wembley.

Four days later at Maine Road, a Graeme Souness volley from 25 yards was enough to give Liverpool the trophy for the fourth consecutive year.

Everton: Southall, Stevens, Bailey, Ratcliffe, Mountfield, Reid, Irvine, Heath, Sharp, Richardson, Sheedy(Harper).
Liverpool: Grobbelaar, Neal, Kennedy, Lawrenson, Whelan, Hansen, Dalglish, Lee, Rush, Johnston(Robinson), Souness.

Referee: A.Robinson (Portsmouth) *Attendance: 100,000*

Match to Remember 14 19 May 1984

Everton 2 Watford 0

AFTER the bitter disappointment of going so close to ending neighbours Liverpool's astonishing Milk Cup monopoly, Howard Kendall's Everton had a second Wembley appointment, this time with Graham Taylor's Watford.

Andy Gray celebrates his goal against Watford in the 1984 FA Cup Final.

Everton desperately needed victory and if ever there was an instance of the result being of far greater importance than the manner in which it was achieved, then it was here. Everton's maxim down the years has been that the performance is more important than the spoils themselves. But now everyone at Goodison Park needed tangible proof that a revival had begun.

The outcome was highly satisfactory to Goodison. Both the purists and the success-starved Everton supporters were well pleased. Everton duly won the FA Cup, and won it in some style.

It was a memorable day not just on the field, but on the terraces also, where northerner and southerner applauded their teams and gave no hint of trouble.

Taylor's enthusiastic but largely inexperienced side were comprehensively beaten by an Everton side on the threshold of a new golden age for the club.

Watford were outplayed for long spells, yet never once did they give the impression of capitulating in the face of a near-ceaseless barrage. They had their chances and, despite their inability to match the tireless midfield play of Peter Reid and Adrian Heath, they might have gone to the dressing-room to contemplate a half-time lead.

As early as the second minute George Reilly flicked on Lee Sinnott's massive throw, only for John Barnes to mis-cue his shot with only Neville Southall blocking his route.

Les Taylor saw a 25-yard drive deflected just wide of an upright by John Bailey's outstretched leg, and Mo Johnston went close with a header but it was Everton who held the greater initiative.

Graeme Sharp headed Trevor Steven's raking cross fractionally wide and Kevin Richardson hit the side-netting before Watford's defence was made to pay for a moment of slackness.

Richardson hooked a vague cross in from the left and as the Watford's defenders

Everton with the FA Cup in 1984. Back row (left to right): Mountfield, Bailey, Reid, Harper, Gray. Front row: Steven, Richardson, Southall, Ratcliffe, Sharp, Heath, Stevens.

looked on, thinking that there was no danger, Gary Stevens fired in low and hard. Sharp stopped the ball dead before turning to lash a drive into the bottom corner via a post.

One goal would probably have been enough but Everton wanted a more comfortable margin. Six minutes after the interval, Andy Gray rose superbly to head home Steven's deep cross. Television slow-motion replays showed that the fearless Scot had made contact with the back of goalkeeper Sherwood's hands before heading the ball home, but referee Hunting's decision to let the goal stand found no one at Goodison arguing.

Everton: Southall, Stevens, Bailey, Ratcliffe, Mountfield, Reid, Steven, Heath, Sharp, Gray, Richardson, Sub: Harper.
Watford: Sherwood, Bardsley, Price(Atkinson), Taylor, Perry, Sinnott, Callaghan, Johnston, Reilly, Jackett, Barnes.

Referee: Mr J Hunting (Leicester) *Attendance: 100,000*

Match to Remember 15 27 October 1984

Everton 5 Manchester United 0

RON Atkinson's multi-million pound side arrived at Goodison Park as favourites to succeed Liverpool as League Champions. They had been beaten only once that

Graham Sharp's fifth goal in the hammering of Manchester United.

season and saw this as the perfect opportunity to halt the Everton revival in its infancy.

In many respects, however, this was the day that Howard Kendall's team came of age; the day when the Goodison men proved conclusively that Everton was once again a name to rank with the best in British football.

With a staggering virtuoso performance which personified everything that is best about modern football, Kevin Ratcliffe and his colleagues put United to flight.

From the first whistle, Everton never once looked like relinquishing their stranglehold. Someone remarked that, if this had been a boxing match, it would have been stopped after ten minutes, so groggy were United at that point.

Kendall's blue-shirted terriers destroyed United in a manner which reminded many of the halcyon days of the 1969-70 Championship season; others felt it was the best single performance of the last two decades.

Joe Mercer, watching from the stand, went further. He said it was the best performance he had ever seen by an Everton side.

The pattern was set in the opening two minutes as Derek Mountfield fired just over Bailey's crossbar. Three minutes later there was no such escape for United. Kevin Sheedy, not famed for his aerial prowess, outjumped Moran to glide home a beautiful header. The young Everton star needed stitches to a head wound but bravely carried on.

After 23 minutes Sheedy made it 2-0 when Heath had put him clear. Everton's dazed hero hammered the ball into the bottom corner from 12 yards.

Unable to halt the swirling blue tide, United found themselves 3-0 down after 34 minutes when Heath rammed the ball home from close range.

Everton were hungry for more goals and they surged forward again in the second half. Albiston cleared Heath's header off the line before Stevens almost casually moved into position to lash a fierce drive into the United net via a post.

United's humiliation was complete with four minutes left when Sharp marked his own magnificent performance with the fifth goal of the afternoon.

Everton: Southall, Stevens, Van den Hauwe, Ratcliffe, Mountfield, Reid, Steven, Heath, Sharp, Bracewell, Sheedy(Gray).
Manchester United: Bailey, McQueen, Albiston, Moses(Stapleton), Moran, Hogg, Robson, Strachan, Hughes, Brazil, Olsen.

Referee: G. Tyson (Sunderland) *Attendance: 40,769*

Match to Remember 16 — 15 May 1985

Everton 3 Rapid Vienna 1

EVERTON arrived in Rotterdam for the European Cup-winners' Cup Final at the end of a long, hard season. There were many who feared that this might be the night they were made to pay for their relentless pursuit of a much-vaunted 'treble'.

Having already clinched their first League Championship for 15 years, they had to face the tough-tackling Austrians, controversial conquerors of Celtic in an earlier round. Four days later, they had to walk out at Wembley in a bid to retain the FA Cup.

Manager Howard Kendall had watched Rapid Vienna in action the previous week. He knew that if Everton could maintain the form they had shown week after week

Andy Gray (9) scores for Everton in the Cup-winners' Cup Final.

Gray celebrates his strike which set Everton on the road to European glory.

Kevin Sheedy scores Everton's second goal against Rapid Vienna.

in the League, they would be more than capable of taking their first-ever European title.

Vienna's pre-match declaration that they would attack Everton from the start proved to be nonsense as they sat back and tamely soaked up the mounting pressure.

Aware that Rapid had publicly expressed reservations about their ability to cope with the aerial power of Scotsmen Andy Gray and Graeme Sharp, Everton pumped in high crosses from all angles.

Rapid were unsettled by this, but somehow they managed to hold firm. Everton thought that their long-overdue breakthrough had arrived in the 39th minute when a superbly-worked free-kick was climaxed by Gray.

Sheedy swung the ball over, Mountfield headed it down, and there was Gray to sweep it home. But Mountfield was adjudged to have been offside although millions back home saw television replays appear to prove that he was not.

It was not until the 57th minute that Everton eventually broke the deadlock. Graeme Sharp easily beat goalkeeper Konsel to an under-hit backpass. Sharp had time to turn and look up before chipping deftly across goal where Gray raced in to force the ball home, unchallenged, from eight yards.

Everton's victory was sealed in the 72nd minute when Trevor Steven found himself on the end of a Sheedy corner which had eluded the lunging boots of three defenders. Steven thumped the ball home at the far post before turning to begin the celebrations.

Astonishingly, Rapid managed to claw their way back into the game when veteran Hans Krankl beat Neville Southall from close range.

It was a minor and very temporary setback. Straight from the restart Sheedy hammered home a third goal, brilliantly from 25 yards.

Krankl summed up the game: 'Everton were just too good for us. It's been a long time since we played against anyone of their class. They are possibly the best side in the whole of Europe.'

Everton: Southall, Stevens, Van den Hauwe, Ratcliffe, Mountfield, Reid, Steven, Sharp, Gray, Bracewell, Sheedy.
Rapid Vienna: Konsel, Lainer, Brauneder, Weber, Garger, Kranjcar, Kienast, Hrstick, Pacuit(Gross), Krankl, Winhofer(Panenka).

Referee: Paolo Casarin (Italy) *Attendance: 45,000*

Match to Remember 17 — 10 May 1986

Everton 1 Liverpool 3

HAVING already surrendered their League title to Kenny Dalglish's Liverpool, Everton were determined to deny their rivals the 'double' when they walked out at Wembley to contest the first-ever all-Merseyside FA Cup Final.

Everton began at a furious pace and launched a series of inspired assaults which were repelled only by a mixture of sound defence and a little good fortune.

After 18 minutes Everton had a penalty appeal turned down when Steve Nicol appeared to hold back Graeme Sharp as he attempted to connect with a Gary Stevens cross. But Everton were not to be denied ten minutes later when Peter Reid split the Liverpool defence with a long, raking pass and Gary Lineker set off in pursuit, leaving Alan Hansen trailing in his wake. After seeing his first shot blocked by Bruce Grobbelaar the England striker coolly steered the ball home for his 40th goal of the season.

Having gained the upper hand Everton went forward in search of a second, killer goal, but Liverpool held firm.

Kevin Sheedy went closest to finding the target when, shortly after half-time, he fired narrowly wide with a right foot shot.

As the game edged towards the hour mark Liverpool began to find their cohesion and rhythm, breaking swiftly from the back and utilising the pace of Craig Johnston and Ronnie Whelan to good advantage. Even so, they seemed unlikely to conjure

Bruce Grobbelaar outjumps Graeme Sharp in the 1986 FA Cup Final.

up an equaliser until one tragic mistake by Stevens turned the game completely on its head.

As he attempted to clear, Stevens drove the ball straight to the feet of Whelan who picked out Molby. The big Dane delivered the sweetest of passes to Ian Rush and, despite a suspicion of offside, the world-class striker did the rest, rounding the unprotected Bobby Mimms before firing into an empty net.

Five minutes later Liverpool edged in front as Everton began to visibly tire. Molby and Rush linked up well leaving Johnston with the simplest of chances at the far post.

With just six minutes remaining the final blow for Everton came when Rush lashed home a glorious third goal after the Everton defence had failed to intercept Whelan's chipped cross.

Everton: Mimms; Stevens(Heath), Van den Hauwe, Ratcliffe, Mountfield, Reid, Steven, Lineker, Sharp, Bracewell, Sheedy.
Liverpool: Grobbelaar; Nicol, Beglin, Lawrenson, Whelan, Hansen, Dalglish, Johnston, Rush, Molby, MacDonald.

Referee: A.Robinson (Portsmouth) *Attendance: 100,000*

Match to Remember 18 27 January 1988

Sheffield Wednesday 0 Everton 5

EVERTON travelled to Hillsborough on a wet and windy night desperate to bring the curtain down on an FA Cup third round marathon.

The three previous games had all ended in deadlock and with the Yorkshiremen enjoying home advantage they were the clear favourites to progress through into the next round and a home tie against Second Division Middlesbrough.

Shortly before the kick-off Wednesday learned that they would be without the injured Lawrie Madden who had performed so heroically at the heart of defence in the first three games. His absence was to prove crucial as Colin Harvey's men produced their finest performance of a season which had been plagued by uncharacteristic inconsistency.

Having survived a first minute scare when Colin West squandered a gilt-edged opportunity to put his side in front, Everton took complete control and with Peter Reid and Trevor Steven in compelling form they took a stranglehold on the midfield.

The game was barely five minutes old when Everton's immense pressure was rewarded. Gary Stevens' long pass from deep within his own half drifted over the head of centre-back Larry May and Graeme Sharp had plenty of time to pick his spot before firing past goalkeeper Martin Hodge.

Nine minutes later victory was all but assured when an Ian Snodin pass released Adrian Heath who deftly rounded Hodge before firing into an empty net.

With Wednesday reeling helplessly on the ropes Everton, never a side to show mercy, rammed home their advantage and scored a third goal after 39 minutes when Sharp chipped home spectacularly from just inside the penalty area after Heath had stolen the ball off the toe of Nigel Pearson.

As the home supporters began to jeer their team, Everton continued to pour forward in search of more goals.

After 43 minutes Sharp completed a memorable hat-trick when he headed home a Steven cross from the left and on the stroke of half-time Snodin grabbed the fifth after collecting a pass from Heath.

Everton's perfect night was completed in the second half when Paul Bracewell came on for his first senior appearance since the 1986 FA Cup Final defeat against Liverpool.

Sheffield Wednesday: Hodge; Sterland, Worthington, May, Pearson, Proctor, Marwood, Megson, Chapman(Owen), West, Chamberlain.
Everton: Southall; Stevens, Pointon, Van den Hauwe, Watson, Reid, Steven, Heath, Sharp(Clarke), Snodin(Bracewell), Harper.

Referee: L.Shapter (Torquay) *Attendance: 38,956*

Match to Remember 19 20 February 1991

Everton 4 Liverpool 4

UNBEKNOWN to the players and supporters, this FA Cup, fifth-round replay was to signal the end of Kenny Dalglish's managerial career with Liverpool for less than 48 hours after arguably the greatest Merseyside derby game of all time had been confined to the pages of history, he announced his retirement from professional football for personal reasons.

In many respects it was a fitting way for Dalglish to close a memorable chapter in his career for this classic confrontation will be forever remembered, not only by those fortunate enough to be in attendance but also by the millions around the world who saw the game on television. Having held Liverpool to a draw at

Steve Nicol cannot prevent Graeme Sharp scoring Everton's second goal in the Blues' hammering of Merseyside rivals, Liverpool.

Anfield in the tie's first game a few days earlier, Everton were confident of moving forward into the quarter-finals of the competition but, after a closely-contested opening period had yielded no goals, it was the visitors who moved in front on the night when Peter Beardsley stabbed home a low drive in the 32nd minute after Andy Hinchcliffe had cleared an Ian Rush shot off the line. The goal did not, however, lessen Everton's sense of purpose and two minutes after the interval they were back on level terms when Graeme Sharp headed in a Hinchcliffe cross.

Beardsley's second goal, a magnificent solo effort in the 70th minute, gave every indication of deciding the issue but just three minutes later, Bruce Grobbelaar and Steve Nicol collided as they attempted to clear the ball and Sharp stepped in to score a simple equaliser. As a game of high drama and limitless passion began to drift towards its climax, Rush put Liverpool back in front with a rare header. Most sides would have accepted the inevitable and folded but Everton were not to be denied. With just 90 seconds remaining, Tony Cottee, an 85th minute substitute for Pat Nevin, punished some uncharacteristic defensive hesitancy to push the game into a period of extra-time.

For a fourth time, Liverpool moved in front when John Barnes bent a spectacular shot from 25 yards beyond Neville Southall and just inside a post.

An extraordinary evening was to have one final twist. With three minutes left on the clock, Cottee burst through a static defence to drag his side back on to level terms.

Everton: Southall; Atteveld(McCall), Hinchcliffe, Ratcliffe, Watson, Keown, Nevin(Cottee), McDonald, Sharp, Newell, Ebbrell.
Liverpool: Grobbelaar; Hysen, Burrows, Nicol, Molby, Ablett, Beardsley, Staunton, Rush, Barnes, Venison.

Referee: Neil Midgley (Bolton) *Attendance: 37,766*

EVERTON'S
League Record
1888-89 to 1992-93

SEASON	P	HOME W	D	L	F	A	AWAY W	D	L	F	A	Pts	Pos
						FOOTBALL LEAGUE							
1888-89	22	8	0	3	23	14	1	2	8	12	32	20	8th
1889-90	22	8	2	1	40	15	6	1	4	25	25	31	2nd
1890-91	22	9	0	2	39	12	5	1	5	24	17	29	1st
1891-92	26	8	2	3	32	22	4	2	7	17	27	28	5th
						DIVISION ONE							
1892-93	30	9	3	3	44	17	7	1	7	30	34	36	3rd
1893-94	30	11	1	3	63	23	4	2	9	27	34	33	6th
1894-95	30	12	2	1	47	18	6	4	5	35	32	42	2nd
1895-96	30	10	4	1	40	17	6	3	6	26	26	39	3rd
1896-97	30	8	1	6	42	29	6	2	7	20	28	31	7th
1897-98	30	11	3	1	33	12	2	6	7	15	27	35	4th
1898-99	34	10	2	5	25	13	5	6	6	23	28	38	4th
1899-1900	34	11	1	5	30	15	2	6	9	17	34	33	11th
1900-01	34	10	4	3	37	17	6	1	10	18	25	37	7th
1901-02	34	11	2	4	31	11	6	5	6	22	24	41	2nd
1902-03	34	10	2	5	28	18	3	4	10	17	29	32	12th
1903-04	34	13	0	4	36	12	6	5	6	23	20	43	3rd
1904-05	34	14	2	1	36	11	7	3	7	27	25	47	2nd
1905-06	38	12	1	6	44	30	3	6	10	26	36	37	11th
1906-07	38	16	2	1	50	10	4	3	12	20	36	45	3rd
1907-08	38	11	4	4	34	24	4	2	13	24	40	36	11th
1908-09	38	11	3	5	51	28	7	7	5	31	29	46	2nd
1909-10	38	8	6	5	30	28	8	2	9	21	28	40	10th
1910-11	38	12	3	4	34	17	7	4	8	16	19	45	4th
1911-12	38	13	5	1	29	12	7	1	11	17	30	46	2nd
1912-13	38	8	2	9	28	31	7	5	7	20	23	37	11th
1913-14	38	8	7	4	32	18	4	4	11	14	37	35	15th
1914-15	38	8	5	6	44	29	11	3	5	32	18	46	1st
1919-20	42	8	6	7	42	29	4	8	9	27	39	38	16th
1920-21	42	9	8	4	40	26	8	5	8	26	29	47	7th
1921-22	42	10	7	4	42	22	2	5	14	15	33	36	20th
1922-23	42	14	4	3	41	20	6	3	12	22	39	47	5th
1923-24	42	13	7	1	43	18	5	6	10	19	35	49	7th
1924-25	42	11	4	6	25	20	1	7	13	15	40	35	17th
1925-26	42	9	9	3	42	26	3	9	9	30	44	42	11th
1926-27	42	10	6	5	35	30	2	4	15	29	60	34	20th
1927-28	42	11	8	2	60	28	9	5	7	42	38	53	1st
1928-29	42	11	2	8	38	31	6	2	13	25	44	38	18th
1929-30	42	6	7	8	48	46	6	4	11	32	46	35	22nd
						DIVISION TWO							
1930-31	42	18	1	2	76	31	10	4	7	45	35	61	1st
						DIVISION ONE							
1931-32	42	18	0	3	84	30	8	4	9	32	34	56	1st
1932-33	42	13	6	2	54	24	3	3	15	27	50	41	11th
1933-34	42	9	7	5	38	27	3	9	9	24	36	40	14th
1934-35	42	14	5	2	64	32	2	7	12	25	56	44	8th
1935-36	42	12	5	4	61	31	1	8	12	28	58	39	16th
1936-37	42	12	7	2	56	23	2	2	17	25	55	37	17th

SEASON	P	HOME W	D	L	F	A	AWAY W	D	L	F	A	Pts	Pos
					DIVISION ONE								
1937-38	42	11	5	5	54	34	5	2	14	25	41	39	14th
1938-39	42	17	3	1	60	18	10	2	9	28	34	59	1st
1946-47	42	13	5	3	40	24	4	4	13	22	43	43	10th
1947-48	42	10	2	9	30	26	7	4	10	22	40	40	14th
1948-49	42	12	5	4	33	25	1	6	14	8	38	37	18th
1949-50	42	6	8	7	24	20	4	6	11	18	46	34	18th
1950-51	42	7	5	9	26	35	5	3	13	22	51	32	22nd
					DIVISION TWO								
1951-52	42	12	5	4	42	25	5	5	11	22	33	44	7th
1952-53	42	9	8	4	38	23	3	6	12	33	52	38	16th
1953-54	42	13	6	2	55	27	7	10	4	37	31	56	2nd
					DIVISION ONE								
1954-55	42	9	6	6	32	24	7	4	10	30	44	42	11th
1955-56	42	11	5	5	37	29	4	5	12	18	40	40	15th
1956-57	42	10	5	6	34	28	4	5	12	27	51	38	15th
1957-58	42	5	9	7	34	35	8	2	11	31	40	37	16th
1958-59	42	11	3	7	39	38	6	1	14	32	49	38	16th
1959-60	42	13	3	5	50	20	0	8	13	23	58	37	16th
1960-61	42	13	4	4	47	23	9	2	10	40	46	50	5th
1961-62	42	17	2	2	64	21	3	9	9	24	33	51	4th
1962-63	42	14	7	0	48	17	11	4	6	36	25	61	1st
1963-64	42	14	4	3	53	26	7	6	8	31	38	52	3rd
1964-65	42	9	10	2	37	22	8	5	8	32	38	49	4th
1965-66	42	12	6	3	39	19	3	5	13	17	43	41	11th
1966-67	42	11	4	6	39	22	8	6	7	26	24	48	6th
1967-68	42	18	1	2	43	13	5	5	11	24	27	52	5th
1968-69	42	14	5	2	43	10	7	10	4	34	26	57	3rd
1969-70	42	17	3	1	46	19	12	5	4	26	15	66	1st
1970-71	42	10	7	4	32	16	2	6	13	22	44	37	14th
1971-72	42	8	9	4	28	17	1	9	11	9	31	36	15th
1972-73	42	9	5	7	27	21	4	6	11	14	28	37	17th
1973-74	42	12	7	2	29	14	4	5	12	21	34	44	7th
1974-75	42	10	9	2	33	19	6	9	6	23	23	50	4th
1975-76	42	10	7	4	37	24	5	5	11	23	42	42	11th
1976-77	42	9	7	5	35	24	5	7	9	27	40	42	9th
1977-78	42	14	4	3	47	22	8	7	6	29	23	55	3rd
1978-79	42	12	7	2	32	17	5	10	6	20	23	51	4th
1979-80	42	7	7	7	28	25	2	1	9	15	26	35	19th
1980-81	42	8	6	7	32	25	5	4	12	23	33	36	15th
1981-82	42	11	7	3	33	21	6	6	9	23	29	64	8th
1982-83	42	13	6	2	43	19	5	4	12	23	29	64	7th
1983-84	42	9	9	3	21	12	7	5	9	23	30	62	7th
1984-85	42	16	3	2	58	17	12	3	6	30	26	90	1st
1985-86	42	16	3	2	54	18	10	5	6	33	23	86	2nd
1986-87	42	16	4	1	49	11	10	4	7	27	20	86	1st
1987-88	40	14	4	2	34	11	5	9	6	19	16	70	4th
1988-89	38	10	7	2	33	18	4	5	10	17	27	54	8th
1989-90	38	14	3	2	40	16	3	5	11	17	30	59	6th
1990-91	38	9	5	5	26	15	4	7	8	24	31	51	9th
1991-92	42	8	8	5	28	19	5	6	10	24	32	53	12th
					FA PREMIER LEAGUE								
1992-93	42	7	6	8	26	27	8	2	11	27	28	53	13th

1880-81

1	Oct	9	(a)	Liverpool	W 3-1	McGill, Morris, Unknown
2		30	(h)	Darwen	L 1-2	Provan
3	Nov	13	(h)	Birkenhead	D 0-0	
4		20	(h)	St Mary's	W 7-0	McGill 2, Provan, Turner 2, W.Williams, Unknown
5	Dec	4	(h)	Earlestown	W 5-0	McGill 2, Dixon, Provan, Richards
6		27	(h)	Birkenhead	W 3-1	McGill 2, Provan
7	Jan	8	(h)	St Mary's	W 3-1	Unknown 3
8		22	(a)	Burscough	W 5-1	Jackson 2, Smith 2, W.Williams
9		29	(h)	Liverpool	W 5-0	Provan 2, W.Williams 2, Brettle
10	Feb	12	(a)	Haydock	W 3-2	Knightly 2, Provan
11		19	(a)	Garswood Park	W 1-0	McGill
12		26	(h)	Haydock	W 2-0	Asbury, Morris
13	Mar	5	(h)	Bootle	W 1-0	Knightly
14		12	(a)	Birkenhead	W 7-0	Asbury, Knightly, Jackson, McGill, Richards
15		19	(h)	Halliwell Jub	W 4-0	McGill 2, Provan 2
16		26	(h)	Garswood Park	W 2-0	Hiles, Morris
17	Apr	2	(a)	Earlestown	W 1-0	W.Williams

Appearances
Goals

Lancashire Cup

18	Nov	6	(a)	Great Lever	D 1-1	Unknown
19		27	(h)	Great Lever	L 1-8	Unknown

Appearances
Goals

1881-82

1	Sep	24	(h)	Chester R	W 3-0	McGill 2, W.Williams
2	Oct	1	(h)	Burscough	W 8-0	McGill 4, Morris 2, Provan 2
3		15	(a)	Northwich V	W 2-0	Provan 2
4		29	(h)	Halliwell Jub	W 4-0	D.Williams 2, W.Gibson, McGill 1
5	Nov	5	(a)	Chester R	D 1-1	Provan
6		12	(h)	Liverpool	W 1-0	McGill
7		19	(h)	Over Wanderers	W 1-0	J.Richards
8		26	(a)	Earlestown	W 1-0	W.Williams
9	Dec	3	(h)	St Peter's	W 1-0	Richards
10		26	(a)	Northwich V	L 2-6	McGill, Provan
11	Jan	7	(h)	St Peter's	W 4-0	Provan 2, J.Richards, W.Williams
12		14	(a)	Bootle	W 4-1	McGill 4
13	Feb	4	(h)	Haydock	W 5-1	W.Gibson 2, Brettle, McGill, Morris
14		11	(a)	Over Wanderers	W 4-0	McGill 4
15		25	(a)	Haydock	W 3-1	Provan 2, Morris
16	Mar	4	(a)	Oswestry	L 0-1	
17		11	(h)	Chester College	D 1-1	Provan
18		18	(h)	Bootle Mr Sloan	W 7-4	McGill 3, Williams 2, Evans, Morris
19		25	(h)	Oswestry	D 2-2	McGill, Opp own-goal
20	Apr	1	(a)	Halliwell Jub	W 6-1	Provan 3, Evans 2, McGill

Appearances
Goals

Lancashire Cup

21	Oct	22	(h)	Middleton	W 5-0	W.Gibson 3, McGill 2
22	Dec	10	(a)	Turton	L 1-3	Unknown

Appearances
Goals

Astbury J	Aston	Bargery GR	Blackie	Bourne	Brettle F	Brown	Clarke	Dixon	Douglas J	Evans T	Ferguson	Gibson W	Glover H	Higgins M	Hiles CH	Jackson	Jones W	Knightly	Leach H	McGill J	McGregor JF	Marriott T	Morris RW	Parry WH	Provan A	Richards	Sharp	Smith	Turner	Walker	White	Williams J	Williams T	Williams W	
																																			1
		1								2				4	5					8			6		11	9				3	10	7			2
																																			3
		5			8			3		2				4	1					7					9				6			11		10	4
																																			5
					9		1	4	11	5					3					6		2			7	8								10	6
																																			7
									11		4	9				8	10				1	2		5				6				3		7	8
					6				11			10		5	2				3			4			8							9	1	7	9
																																			10
	8			3	11		1								5					6		2	9		7	10	4								11
9					11	5	1			2					4					6		3	8		7	10									12
		1			9			4		2			5					7		6		3	10		11	8									13
10		1			9					2			5			11		7		6		3	4			8									14
11		1			9					2			5							6		3	10	4	7									8	15
		5											4	8	7					11		2	9	3	10			6					1		16
		4	10		7					2										9	1	3	5		8			6						11	17
3	1	7	1	1	9	1	3	3	3	8	1	2	4	4	7	2	1	2	1	10	2	10	8	3	10	6	1	3	1	1	1	4	2	6	
3					1			1							1	3		5		11			3		9	2		2	2					5	

5 goals unknown

No team line-ups have been traced for matches 1, 3, 5, 7 and 10.

No line-ups traced for the Lancashire Cup matches and scorers are unknown.

Armstrong RB	Asbury J	Ashley	Bargery GR	Bentley R	Brettle F	Brownlie	Clarke	Dale F	Dixon	Earl C	Evans T	Fletcher	Gibson F	Gibson W	Glover	Heaton FG	Higgins M	Hiles CH	Houlgrave J	Jones	McGill J	McGregor JF	Marriott T	Morris RW	Parry WH	Provan A	Richards	Richards H	Richards J	Richards T	Richardson	Roberts W	Sharp	Smith J	Walters	Williams DH	Williams J	Williams W	
		1			8		10		4												9		2	3	5	11	6											7	1
							3							6	1			4		10	8			9		11		2									5		2
	9		1											11				5			6		2	3	4	7	10											8	3
			1										5	11							8		2	3	4	7			10							6		9	4
														5							6		1	2	3	7	4												* 5
			1								4										8		2	3	5	10	6					7				11		9	6
			1								2										8		3	4	5	10			6			7				11		9	7
					11						2										8	1	4	3	5	6			10							7		9	8
			1		7				5												8		2	3	4	10	6									11		9	9
											2					4	7				6		3	5	11	8	10				1					9			10
					3														1		6	5		2	4	8			11			10				9		7	11
			1								2										9		3	4	5	8			6			7				11		10	12
					9	1					2			11							8		3	4	5	7						10						6	13
								7		8	2	5									10		3	11	4	9						6				1			14
														8									2	6	3	9			10	5			1		11		4	7	15
				2							3							1					4	9	5				11			10		8		6		7	16
				2														4			8		1	3	5	9			7			6				10		11	17
3			1								2										8		5	7	4	9			6							10		11	18
2	10										3										8		1	4	5	9			7			6						11	19
3											11										8		2	5	4	9		1	10							6		7	20
3	2	1	7	2	5	1	2	1	2	1	11	1	1	6	1	1	1	4	1	1	18	2	18	20	19	19	6	2	11	1	1	9	1	1	1	13	2	16	
					1						3			3							23			5		14	1		2							2		3	

1 own-goal

Armstrong RB	Asbury J	Ashley	Bargery GR	Bentley R	Brettle F	Brownlie	Clarke	Dale F	Dixon	Earl C	Evans T	Fletcher	Gibson F	Gibson W	Glover	Heaton FG	Higgins M	Hiles CH	Houlgrave J	Jones	McGill J	McGregor JF	Marriott T	Morris RW	Parry WH	Provan A	Richards	Richards H	Richards J	Richards T	Richardson	Roberts W	Sharp	Smith J	Walters	Williams DH	Williams J	Williams W	
			1						5					9							6		2	3	4	7	10									11		8	21
			1		9						2			11							8		3	4	5		6		10										22
			2		1				1		1			2							2		2	2	2	1	2		1							1		1	
														3							2																		

1 goal unknown

* In Match 5 only seven players have been traced.
T.Williams played number 7 in Match 2; Williams played number 7 in Match 22.
The identity of the Williams who scored two goals in Match 18 is unknown.

1882-83

1	Sep	30	(h)	Burscough	W 3-0	McGill 2, D.Williams
2	Oct	14	(a)	Wirral	W 5-0	Unknown 5
3		21	(h)	Crewe	D 2-2	Provan 2
4	Nov	11	(a)	Wrexham	L 3-7	Morris, J.Richards, D.Williams
5		18	(h)	Eagley	W 4-0	Higgins 2, Pickering 2
6		25	(a)	Birkenhead	W 5-2	Edwards 2, Higgins, Mellor, D.Williams
7	Dec	2	(a)	Bootle	L 0-2	
8		9	(a)	Crewe	L 1-2	Westland
9		23	(a)	Southport	D 2-2	W.Evans, Parry
10	Jan	20	(h)	Bootle	L 0-1	
11	Feb	10	(a)	Turton	L 0-7	
12	Mar	3	(h)	Bolton	L 2-8	McGill, D.Williams
13		10	(h)	Oswestry	L 0-2	
14		24	(h)	Oswestry	L 2-5	Unknown 2
15	Apr	7	(h)	Wirral	W 8-0	Williams 3, Gibson 2, McGill 2, Richards
16		14	(h)	Turton	D 1-1	McGill

Appearances
Goals

Lancashire Cup

17	Oct	2	(a)	Blackburn R	L 0-8	

Appearances
Goals

Liverpool Cup

18	Jan	13	(a)	Liverpool	W 8-0	Richards 3, McGill 2, Parry, Pickering, Opp own-goal
19	Feb	17	(h)	Liverpool R	W 6-0	Higgins 2, D.Williams 2, Brettle, McGill
20	Mar	31	(a)	Bootle	L 1-3	Cartwright

Appearances
Goals

1883-84

1	Sep	15	(h)	Southport	W 3-0	McGill, Pickering, J.Richards
2	Oct	6	(a)	Eagley	W 4-3	C.Jones 2, Bell, McGill
3		13	(a)	Crewe A	D 1-1	D.Williams
4		20	(a)	Earlestown	W 2-1	McGill 2
5	Nov	3	(h)	Hartford St John	W 3-1	McGill 2, D.Williams
6		17	(h)	Burslem PV	L 0-1	
7		24	(h)	Croston	W 8-0	Unknown 8
8	Dec	1	(h)	Everton 2nd Team	D 1-1	Unknown
9		8	(a)	Burslem PV	D 2-2	C.Jones, McGill
10	Jan	12	(h)	Crewe	D 1-1	McGill
11	Feb	9	(h)	Ormskirk	W 2-1	Gibson, D.Williams
12		23	(h)	Eagley	L 3-5	W.Williams 2, Gibson
13	Mar	1	(h)	Earlestown	W 9-0	McGill 3, Higgins 2, Gibson, Morris, J.Richards, D.Williams
14		15	(a)	Southport	D 2-2	Brown, Gibson
15	Apr	5	(h)	Burscough	W 8-1	Berry, McGill, Unknown 6
16	May	3	(a)	Birkenhead & Dis	W 4-0	J.Richards 2, McGill, D.Williams

Appearances
Goals

Liverpool Cup

17	Nov	10	(h)	St Peter's	W 10-0	McGill 3, Brown 2, Berry, Higgins, Welsh, D.Williams, Opp own-goal
18	Dec	22	(a)	Liverpool Ramble	W 4-1	Gibson, Higgins, McGill, D.Williams
19	Jan	26	(a)	Bootle	W 5-2	Gibson 2, Higgins, McGill, D.Williams
20	Mar	29	(a*)	Earlestown	W 1-0	Parry

*Final

Appearances
Goals

Astbury J	Bargery GR	Brettle F	Cartwright J	Edwards G	Evans T	Evans W	Finlay W	Flood	Gibson	Hayhurst J	Higgins M	Jackson	Lindsay C	McGill J	Marriott T	Mellor	Morris RW	Parry WH	Pickering JW	Provan D	Richards	Richards EH	Richards J	Richards W	Sinnot	Walsh	Walsh AE	Walsh J	Westland	Wilkinson	Williams DH	Williams J	Williams W	
		1		7			5				6			8	2			3			9					4					10		11	1
																																		2
	1						11				8				3		2	4		10			9					5			6		7	3
		1									7		9		2		8	5	3				6			4					11		10	4
				10							9				2		3	4	11				8				5				7	1	6	5
				8					5		11				3	7	2	4					10						9	1	6			6
		1		10							9				3		2	5	11				8				4				6		7	7
		7	6				8				11	1					3	4					10	2	5				9					8
11			5		3	9		1	7						2			4					6								10		8	9
7		1									9			10	3		2	4	11				8			5					6			10
10		8									7			9	3		2		4			1	6			5					11			11
		10	4								9		1	11	3	7	2						8					5			6			12
7			5								10			9	1		2		3				11				4				6		8	13
																																		14
																																		15
			6							11	8		1	9	2		3		5				7	10			4							16
4	1	7	5	4	1	1	3	1	2	1	12	1	3	6	12	2	11	9	7	1	1	1	12	2	1	4	4	2	2	1	11	1	7	
				2		1			2		3			6		1	1	1	2	2	1		1						1		4			

5 goals unknown

Astbury J	Bargery GR	Brettle F	Cartwright J	Edwards G	Evans T	Evans W	Finlay W	Flood	Gibson	Hayhurst J	Higgins M	Jackson	Lindsay C	McGill J	Marriott T	Mellor	Morris RW	Parry WH	Pickering JW	Provan D	Richards	Richards EH	Richards J	Richards W	Sinnot	Walsh	Walsh AE	Walsh J	Westland	Wilkinson	Williams DH	Williams J	Williams W	
		1		10							11			8	3		2	5						9			4				6		7	17
		1		1							1			1	1		1	1						1			1				1		1	

Astbury J	Bargery GR	Brettle F	Cartwright J	Edwards G	Evans T	Evans W	Finlay W	Flood	Gibson	Hayhurst J	Higgins M	Jackson	Lindsay C	McGill J	Marriott T	Mellor	Morris RW	Parry WH	Pickering JW	Provan D	Richards	Richards EH	Richards J	Richards W	Sinnot	Walsh	Walsh AE	Walsh J	Westland	Wilkinson	Williams DH	Williams J	Williams W	
11		1									7			9	3		2	5	6				8				4		10					18
		9	4								10			8			2	6	3								5				7	1	11	19
7		1	4								11			9			2		3				10					5			6		8	20
2		3	2								3			3	1		3	2	3				2				2	1	1		2	1	2	
		1	1								2			3				1	1				3								1		1	

No team line-ups have been traced for Matches 2, 14 and 15.
The identity of the Williams who scored three goals in Match 15 is unknown.

1 own-goal

Bell G	Berry E	Brown W	Cartwright J	Finlay W	Gibson W	Higgins M	Joliffe C	Jones C	Jones M	Lindsay C	McGill J	McGregor	Marriott T	Morris RW	Munroe J	Parry WH	Pickering J	Preston	Richards EH	Richards J	Sinnot J	Twemlow C	Walsh AE	Watson W	Williams DH	Williams W	
	11		5			9				1	6		3	2		4	7			8						10	1
11	6							9			10		3	2		5	4			8	1				7		2
	6					9				1	10		3	2		5	4			8					7	11	3
	6					9					10		3	2		4	5			8		1			7	11	4
	7									1	9		3	2		4	6	5		11					8	10	5
	8	11							10	1	9		3	2		5	4	6							7		6
		8				10				1	7		3	2		6	5	4		11					9		7
																											8
	7				10			11		1	9		3	2		6	5	4		8							9
	10			8	6	7					9		2			4	1	5	3						11		10
				8	7	6	1						3	2		4		5						11	10	9	11
	10			9	7	6					8		3	2	1	5	4									11	12
					8	7				1	9		3	2		6	4	5		11					10		13
	7	9			11	10				1		5	2			4	6		3						8		14
	7	9			10	11					8		3	1		5	4		2						6		15
					10	9				1	11		3			4	5	6	2	7					8		16
1	11	4	1	3	8	11	1	2	1	9	13	1	15	12	1	15	14	8	4	9	1	1		1	12	6	
1	1	2			4	2		3			13			1			1			4					4	3	

15 goals unknown

Bell G	Berry E	Brown W	Cartwright J	Finlay W	Gibson W	Higgins M	Joliffe C	Jones C	Jones M	Lindsay C	McGill J	McGregor	Marriott T	Morris RW	Munroe J	Parry WH	Pickering J	Preston	Richards EH	Richards J	Sinnot J	Twemlow C	Walsh AE	Watson W	Williams DH	Williams W	
	11	7				8				1	9		3	2		5	4						6		10		17
	8				10	11				1	7		3	2		5	4	6							9		18
	10				7	8				1	9		3	2		6	4	5							11		19
	7				10	11				1	9		3	2		5	4	6								8	20
	4	1			3	4				4	4		4	4		4	4	3					1		3	1	
	1	2			3	3					5					1							1		3		

No team line-ups have been traced for match 8.

1 own-goal

1884-85

1	Sep	13	(a)	Burslem PV	L 0-7	
2		20	(a)	Wallasey & Dist	W 5-1	McGill 2, Berry, Richards, D.Williams
3		27	(h)	Earlestown	W 5-0	Whittle 2, Gibson, Higgins, Richards
4	Oct	4	(a)	Crewe	L 2-8	Richards, Opp own-goal
5		11	(h)	Bolton A	W 6-0	McGill 3, Whittle 2, Higgins
6	Nov	1	(a)	Bootle	W 2-1	McGill 2
7		8	(h)	Davenham	W 5-4	Gibson 3, McGill, Richards
8		15	(a)	Davenham	W 2-1	Gibson, McGill
9		22	(h)	Bolton W	D 2-2	Brown 2
10		29	(a)	Liverpool Ramble	W 5-1	Gibson 2, McGill 2, Whittle
11	Dec	13	(a)	Stanley	W 2-1	Gibson, Richards
12		27	(h)	Blackburn R	W 2-1	Gibson, McGill
13	Jan	3	(h)	Birkenhead	W 2-0	Jones 2
14		5	(h)	Dumbarton	L 0-5	
15		10	(h)	Stanley	W 4-1	Gibson 2, McGill 2
16		17	(h)	Darwen Old Wdrs	D 1-1	Pickering
17		24	(h)	Liverpool Cambrian	L 3-4	Finlay, Jones, Unknown
18	Feb	14	(a)	Birkenhead	L 0-2	
19	Mar	7	(h)	Bootle	W 3-1	Pollock, Richards, Whittle
20		14	(h)	Blackburn R	L 1-2	Higgins
21		21	(h)	Liverpool Ramble	L 1-4	McGill
22		28	(a)	Darwen Old Wdrs	L 0-7	
23	Apr	3	(h)	Blackburn R	W 1-0	Higgins
24		4	(h)	Witton	L 0-1	
25		6	(h)	Blackburn O	L 0-3	
26		11	(h)	Crewe	W 3-0	Gibson, Higgins, Pickering
27		18	(a)	Haydock	W 8-2	Farmer 3, Gibson 2, Jefferson 2, McGill
28		25	(h)	Preston Zingari	W 6-0	Gibson 2, Farmer, Unknown 3
29	May	9	(a)	Blackburn R	W 2-1	Farmer, Gibson
30		16	(h)	Earlestown W	W 3-0	Farmer, Gibson, McGill
31		23	(h)	Liverpool Select	W 5-3	Farmer 2, Pickering 2, Douglas
32		25	(h)	Bolton W	L 1-2	McGill
						Appearances
						Goals

Liverpool Cup

33	Oct	25	(a)	Toxteth	W 7-0	Gibson 3, Richards 2, Higgins, Pickering
34	Dec	20	(a)	Southport	W 2-1	Higgins 2
35	Jan	31	(h)	Bootle	W 2-1	Parry, Whittle
36	Feb	21	(h)	Golbourne	W 9-0	McGill 4, Richards 2, Finlay, Gibson, Whittle
37		28	(a*)	Earlestown	L 0-1	
						Appearances
						Goals

*Final

Arlow J	Berry E	Brown W	Cartwright J	Chambers G	Derham	Dobson G	Douglas	Edwards	Evans T	Fairhurst	Farmer G	Fecitt	Finlay W	Gibson W	Grant J	Gurley R	Higgins M	James W	Jefferson	Joliffe C	Jones C	Lindsay C	McGill J	Marriott T	Morris RW	Mowbray	Owen D	Parkinson J	Pickering J	Pollock	Powell W	Preston J	Richards W	Scott T	Walsh AE	Whittle J	Williams DH	Williams W	
														11	5		8					1	9	2				3				4	6	7		10			1
	9													6			7					1	10	2	3			4				5	8				11		2
	6												11	8			10			1			3					5	2			4	7			9			3
																																							4
														11			10					1	9	3	2			5	4			6	8			7			5
														8			10					1	9	2	3			5	4			6	7	11					6
													11	9			10					1	8	2	3		4	6				5	7						7
														11			10						9	3	5		2	4	1				7						8
		8												11			10					1	9	3	2			6	4			5	7						9
														11			10					1	9	3	2			6	4			5	7			8			10
														11			10					1	9	3	2			6	4			5	7			8			11
														11			4				10	1	9	2				6	3			5	7			8			12
		10						1						8			11				7		9	2				3	4			6			5				13
		9											11				10					1		2		3		5	4			6	7			8			14
									2					6		7	8					1	9	3				5	4		10		11						15
																	6	10				1	11	3	2			5	4		7					9		8	16
									6				9	10		8					7			3	2			4	1			5				11			17
			5										9	10							11	1		2	3			6	4				7			8			18
5				1													4						7	3					6	8			11			10			19
6				1	5									9			7						8	2					4				11			10			20
	11			1									5	6			9				7		8	2	3				4				10						21
																																							22
						2							4	8			6		11			1	3						5		10		7			9			23
								3						10		9	6					1	2						4		8	5	7			11			24
				1		2										8	9						3						6		7		11		5	10			25
						6					11		5	10			9		8			1	3	2					4				7						26
											11		5	10			9		7			1	3	2	6				4							8			27
											11		5	10			9					1	3	2					4			6		8		7			28
				1		3				10	9		5	11			8							2					4						6	7			29
		3									11		4	9			5			1			10	2					6				8	7					30
						6	7				10	9		11			5					1		2					4							8			31
						3					10			6		11	5					1	9	2					4				7			8			32
2	3	4	1	5	1	6	1	2	2	1	7	1	12	26	1	5	25	1	3	2	5	20	25	26	13	1	2	17	27	1	5	15	23	4	3	20	1	1	
	1	2					1				8		1	18			5		2		3		18						4	1			6			6	1		

1 own-goal; 4 goals unknown

Arlow J	Berry E	Brown W	Cartwright J	Chambers G	Derham	Dobson G	Douglas	Edwards	Evans T	Fairhurst	Farmer G	Fecitt	Finlay W	Gibson W	Grant J	Gurley R	Higgins M	James W	Jefferson	Joliffe C	Jones C	Lindsay C	McGill J	Marriott T	Morris RW	Mowbray	Owen D	Parkinson J	Pickering J	Pollock	Powell W	Preston J	Richards W	Scott T	Walsh AE	Whittle J	Williams DH	Williams W	
														11			10					1	9	3	2			5	4			6	7					8	33
														11			10					1	9	3	2			6	4			5	7						34
													11	10			5					1	9	3	2			4	6				7						35
													5	10			4				11	1	9	2	3				6				7						36
													5	11			10					1	9	2	3				4			6	7						37
													3	5			5				1	5	5	5	5			3	5			3	5					1	
													1	4			3						4					1	1				4						

No team line-ups traced for matches 4 and 22.
J.Parkinson played number 2 in Match 19; H.Richards played number 8 in Match 8; J.Scowcroft played number 9 in Match 19; Smith played number 6 in Match 8; E.Stewart-Brown played number 3 in Match 20; Sutton played number 4 in Match 25.

1885-86

1	Aug	15	(h)	Burnley	L 2-4	Farmer, Higgins
2		22	(h)	Darwen	D 1-1	W.Richards
3		29	(h)	Great Lever	L 0-1	
4	Sep	2	(h)	Bootle	W 2-0	Farmer, Gurley
5		5	(h)	Blackburn R	L 0-4	
6		12	(h)	Blackburn O	L 2-3	Farmer 2
7		19	(h)	Accrington	L 2-3	Fleming, W.Richards
8	Oct	3	(a)	Oswestrey	W 2-1	Farmer, Fryer
9		10	(a)	Stanley	W 2-0	Dobson, Wilding
10		17	(h)	Bolton W	L 1-4	Farmer
11		31	(h)	Bootle	D 2-2	Farmer, Fraser
12	Nov	7	(h)	Southport	W 3-0	Fraser, Wilding, Unknown
13		14	(a)	Druids	L 0-4	
14		21	(h)	Clitheroe	W 1-0	Fraser
15	Dec	19	(h)	Liverpool Ramble	W 5-0	Wilding 2, Farmer, Finlay, Fleming
16		25	(h)	Stanley	W 1-0	Wilding
17		26	(h)	Ulster	D 2-2	W.Parry
18	Jan	1	(h)	Partick T	L 0-3	
19		2	(h)	Limauady	L 0-1	
20		9	(h)	Wrexham O	W 9-1	George 3, Higgins 2, Wilding 2, Farmer, Finlay
21		16	(a)	Witton	L 2-4	Wilding 2
22		23	(a)	Bootle	W 1-0	Wilding
23		30	(h)	Fishwick Ramble	W 4-2	Farmer 2, McGill, W.Richards
24	Feb	2	(a)	Liverpool Ramble	W 5-0	Farmer 2, Finlay 2, George
25		13	(h)	Bury	W 5-0	W.Richards, Farmer, Fayer, Wilding
26		20	(h)	Druids	W 1-0	Farmer
27	Mar	6	(h)	Stanley	W 2-1	Finlay, Gibson
28		13	(h)	Oswestry	W 2-0	Farmer, Fleming
29		20	(h)	Southport	W 8-2	Wilding 3, Farmer 2, Findlay, W.Richards, Opp own-goal
30	Apr	3	(h)	Fishwick Ramble	D 1-1	Higgins
31		23	(h)	NE Counties	W 9-0	Farmer 4, Finlay 2, Fleming 2, Wilding
32		24	(h)	Davenham	W 3-2	George 2, Fleming
33		26	(h)	Sheffield W	W 3-1	Fleming 2, Farmer
34	May	1	(h)	Rossendale	W 3-2	Farmer, Opp own-goal, Unknown
35		8	(h)	Blackburn O	L 1-4	W.Parry
36		10	(h)	Preston	L 1-2	Dewhurst
37		22	(a*)	Bootle Wdrs	W 2-0	Fleming 2
38		29	(a†)	Stanley	W 2-0	Fayer, Wilding
39		31	(a‡)	Bootle	W 2-1	Farmer, Wilding

*Athletic Sheild, †Semi-final, ‡Final.

Appearances
Goals

Lancs Junior Cup

40	Sep	26	(h)	Adlington	W 8-1	Gurley 2, Jones 2, W.Richards, Finlay, Higgins

Appearances
Goals

Liverpool Cup

41	Oct	24	(h)	Southport W	W 3-1	Dobson, Farmer, Gurley
42	Dec	12	(h)	New Ferry	W 14-0	Fraser 8, Finaly 2, Wilding 2, McGoldrick, Marriott
43	Feb	27	(a)	High Park	W 2-1	W.Richardson, Opp own-goal
44	Mar	27	(a)	Stanley	W 3-0	Wilding 2, Finlay
45	Apr	10	(a*)	Bootle	W 1-0	Wilding

* Final

Appearances
Goals

Brown W	Chambers	Corey E	Dewhurst	Dobson G	Duckworth	Farme G	Fayer T	Finlay W	Fleming G	Fraser	George W	Gibson W	Groves J	Gurley	Hamilton	Heyes	Higgins M	Jefferson	Joliffe C	Jones C	Lindsay C	McGill J	McGoldrick	Marriott T	Morris RW	Parry F	Parry WH	Pickering J	Powell W	Preston J	Richards J	Richards W	Roche	Scowcroft	Sutton	Veitch T	Walsh AE	Wilding J	
11				2		8		5									9		1			7		3				4				10			6				1
		6		2		7		5	10					8										3	4			1				11						9	2
		4		2		11		5				6		10			7											1				8				3		9	3
		3		2		8	5	4	10					7														1				11					6	9	4
		4		2		8		5	10								7					3						1				11					6	9	5
		6		2	3	11		5	7								4											1				8		9				10	6
		6		2		8	4		10					7							1			3								11		9			5		7
	1	4		2		9	7						8			5								3						6				11				10	8
		6		3		7	10		9							5	4		1					2								11						8	9
		4		2		9	6		10							5	7		1					3								11						8	10
		6		2		7				11	1					5	4	8						3								10						9	11
10		4		3		7				9						5	6		1					2								11						8	12
				2		4				9	10					5	6		1				11					3					7					8	13
		6		2		7				10						5	4		1			9		3								11						8	14
5		4		2		11		10	7						8		6		1					3														9	15
6				2			5	7				11					8		1					3				4				10						9	16
				2		11		10									8		1					3		5	4	6			7							9	17
							4	7						8			5		1				9	2				3	11			10					6		18
				2		10	4	11									6		1				9	3		5			8			7							19
		6		2		8	5	7			11						4		1					3								10						9	20
		4		2		10	5	11			8						6		1					3								7						9	21
		4		2		10	5	11			8						6		1					3								7						9	22
				2		7	5	8			10						4		1			9		3			6					11							23
		6		2		10	4	11			8						7		1					3			5											9	24
6		4		2		11	5				8						10		1					3								7						9	25
		4		2		11	5		8								10		1					3			6					7						9	26
		6		2			5	4	10			7					8		1					3								11						9	27
		4		2		10	5		7			11					6		1					3								8						9	28
		4		2		10	5	11	7								6		1					3								8						9	29
3		5		2		10		11				6					4		1				7									8						9	30
		4		2		11	5	10	8		7						6		1					3														9	31
		4				11	5	10	8		7	2					6		1					3														9	32
		4		2		8	5	7	11		10						6		1					3														9	33
		4		2		10		11	7		8								1					3		5	5											9	34
		6		2		8		7	11		10						4		1					3			5											9	35
		6	10	2		8			11								4		1					3			5											9	36
		6		2		8	4		11		7						10		1					3			5											9	37
		8		2		6	3		9		5								1					7			4					11						10	38
		6		2		10	5		7		8						11		1					3			4											9	39
6	1	32	1	37	1	36	24	24	21	4	16	6	1	5	1	9	33	1	31		1	4	4	33	1	3	10	10	2	1	1	26	1	3	1	1	4	34	
			1	1		25	3	8	10	3	6	1		1			4					1					3					6						17	

2 own-goals; 2 goals unknown

Brown W	Chambers	Corey E	Dewhurst	Dobson G	Duckworth	Farme G	Fayer T	Finlay W	Fleming G	Fraser	George W	Gibson W	Groves J	Gurley	Hamilton	Heyes	Higgins M	Jefferson	Joliffe C	Jones C	Lindsay C	McGill J	McGoldrick	Marriott T	Morris RW	Parry F	Parry WH	Pickering J	Powell W	Preston J	Richards J	Richards W	Roche	Scowcroft	Sutton	Veitch T	Walsh AE	Wilding J	
		4		2			5	8						7			9			11				3			1	6				10							40
		1		1			1	1						1			1			1				1			1	1				1							
								1						2			1			2												2							

Brown W	Chambers	Corey E	Dewhurst	Dobson G	Duckworth	Farme G	Fayer T	Finlay W	Fleming G	Fraser	George W	Gibson W	Groves J	Gurley	Hamilton	Heyes	Higgins M	Jefferson	Joliffe C	Jones C	Lindsay C	McGill J	McGoldrick	Marriott T	Morris RW	Parry F	Parry WH	Pickering J	Powell W	Preston J	Richards J	Richards W	Roche	Scowcroft	Sutton	Veitch T	Walsh AE	Wilding J	
		6		2		7								8			4		1				11	3				5				10						9	41
		4		2		6		7									5		1				9	3								10						8	42
		4		2		11	5	9	8								10		1					3				6				7							43
		4		2		10	5	11	7			6							1					3								8						9	44
		6		2		11	5	10	8			7					4		1					3														9	45
		5		5		5	3	4	3			2		1			3		5				2	5				2				4						4	
				1		9		3						1									1	1								1						5	

1 own-goal

Yates played number 7 in Match 36.

1886-87

1	Aug	7	(h)	Rawtenstall	L 3-4	Briscoe, Farmer, Fleming
2		14	(h)	Bolton W	L 1-3	Shaw
3		21	(h)	Darwen	W 1-0	Pearson
4		28	(h)	Accrington	W 2-1	Briscoe 2
5	Sep	4	(h)	Astley Bridge	W 4-0	Costley 2, Gibson, Higgins
6		11	(h)	Derby C	W 4-1	Farmer 2, Costley, Unknown
7		18	(h)	Rossendale	W 3-0	Briscoe, Fleming, Wilding
8		25	(h)	South Shore	W 5-0	Briscoe, Farmer, Fleming
9	Oct	9	(h)	Bury	W 4-1	Farmer 2, Higgins, Stevenson
10		16	(a)	Hurst	D 2-2	Dobson, Unknown
11		30	(h)	Rangers	L 0-1	
12	Nov	13	(a)	Stanley	W 4-0	Briscoe, Fleming, Gibson, Higgins
13		20	(h)	Police Ath	W 4-0	Farmer, Fleming, Gibson, Higgins
14		27	(a)	Halliwell	W 1-0	Richards
15	Dec	11	(a)	Astley Bridge	W 2-1	Briscoe 2
16		18	(h)	Corinthians	L 2-4	Briscoe, Richards
17		25	(h)	Ulster	W 4-0	Richards 3, Costley
18		27	(h)	Northwich V	W 2-0	Richards 2
19	Jan	1	(h)	Partick T	D 1-1	Briscoe
20		15	(a)	Blackburn R	D 0-0	
21		22	(h)	Rawtenstall	W 7-0	Fleming 3, Farmer 2, Briscoe, Corey
22		29	(a)	Burnley	L 0-5	
23	Feb	5	(h)	Halliwell	D 0-0	
24		12	(h)	Blackburn R	D 1-1	Briscoe
25		26	(h)	Bury	L 1-4	Gurley
26	Mar	7	(a)	Ulster	W 2-1	Unknown 2
27		12	(a)	Church	L 3-5	Unknown 3
28		26	(h)	Church	W 4-1	Farmer 2, Costley, Richards
29	Apr	8	(h)	Padiham	W 4-1	Dobson 2, George, Whittle
30		9	(h)	Hurst	W 5-2	Whittle 2, Dobson, Farmer, Gibson
31		11	(h)	Burnley	L 0-3	
32		16	(h)	Aston Villa	D 2-2	Fleming, Whittle
33		18	(h)	Halliwell	D 1-1	Fleming
34		23	(a)	Rossendale	W 3-0	Cartwright, Finlay, Gibson
35		25	(h)	Blackburn O	W 2-0	Goodall, Richards
36		30	(h)	Church	W 5-1	Farmer 2, Costley, Goodall, Whittle
37	May	2	(h)	Stanley	L 1-3	Briscoe
38		7	(a)	South Shore	L 2-7	
39		11	(h)	Lancs Nomads	W 4-0	Farmer 2, Briscoe, McGoodall
40		14	(h)	Padiham	D 1-1	Briscoe
41		21	(h)	Bolton W	W 5-0	Fleming 2, Gibson, Goodall, McPherson
42		23	(h)	Stanley D	W 1-0	Whittle
43		28	(h)	Preston	L 0-5	
44		30	(h)	Accrington	L 2-4	Fleming, Goodall

Appearances
Goals

Lancashire Junior Cup

45	Oct	2	(h)	Fleetwood Zingari	W 9-0	Crosbie 3, Gurley 2, Briscoe, Costley, Higgins, Richards
46	Nov	6	(h)	Bells Temperance	L 2-3	Higgins 2

Appearances
Goals

Liverpool Cup

47		23	(a)	Bootle	W 2-0	Briscoe, Richards
48	Dec	4	(h)	Haydock	W 5-0	Fleming 2, Richards 2, Gibson
49	Feb	19	(h)	Linacre	W 13-1	Farmers, Briscoe 3, Gibson 2, Richards 2, Costley
50		19	(h)	Tranmere R	W 9-1	Richards 3, Costley 2, Farmer 2, Briscoe, George
51	Apr	2	(a*)	Oakfield R	W 5-0	Fleming 2, Costley, Dick, Gibson

*Final

Appearances
Goals

Briscoe W	Brown W	Cartwright J	Corey E	Costley JT	Crosbie	Dick A	Dobson G	Farmer G	Finlay W	Fleming G	George W	Gibson A	Gilder	Goodall A	Griffiths	Gurley	Higgins M	Johnston	Joliffe C	Jones W	McGill J	McGoldrick	McPherson J	Marriott T	Mee	Parry F	Parry WH	Pearson	Richards W	Robson	Roche	Savage	Shaw	Sourbutts	Stevenson G	Townley	Whittle J	Wilding J	
10	3		5				2	7		11							4		1							6							8					9	1
8			4				2	7			10	5					6		1								3						11					9	2
8			4				2	7			3	5					6		1									10									11	9	3
8			5				2	7		11	3	6					4		1																		9	10	4
11			6	8			2	7			3	9					4		1	5										10									5
10			4	8		3	2	7		11		5					6		1																			9	6
8			4	10		3		11		7	2	5					6		1																			9	7
8			4	10		3	2	11		7		5					6		1																			9	8
7			5	11		3	4	10			8						9		1					2											6				9
																																							10
8			4	11		3	2	10		7		5					6		1										9										11
10			4	8		2	3	7		11		9					5		1																6				12
10			4	7		3	2	8		11		5					9		1																6				13
9			4	7		3	2	11		8		5							1										10						6				14
8				11		3	2	10				5		9					1	4												7			6				15
8			4			3	2	9		7		5							1										11						6	10			16
8				11		2	3	10		7		5					4		1										9						6				17
8				11		2	3	10		7		5					4		1										9						6				18
8				11		2	3	10	7			5					6		1										9						4				19
8				11		2	3	10	7			5					4		1										9						6				20
8			4	11		2	3	10		7		5					6		1										9										21
8			4	11		2	3	10				5					7		1										9						6				22
8				11		3	2	10		7		5					4		1										9						6				23
8				11		3	2	10		7		5					4		1										9						6				24
10			6						7	11	2					8	5		1					3			4		9										25
10				8		2	3	7		11		5					6		1															9	4				26
																																							27
10			4	8			2	7			9	5					6		1	3									11										28
			6	11		2	3	10		7	8	4							1					5													9		29
			6	7		2	3	8		11	10	4							1					5													9		30
			6	11		3	5	10		7	8	4							1					2							9								31
				7		2	3			11		5		8					1				6						9						4		10		32
			6			2	3	10		7		5		11					1				4						8								9		33
		7		11		2	3	10	8			5		9			4		1				6																34
				11		2	3	10				5		9			4		1				6						8								7		35
				7		2	3	8				5		9			6		1				4						11								10		36
8				11		2	3	10					7							6			4		1				9						5				37
																																							38
10				7		2	3	8		11		5							1	6		9	4																39
8				11		2	3	10		7		5		4					1				6														9		40
				7		2	3	8		11		5		9			6		1				4						10										41
8				11		2	3	10		7							5		1	4			6														9		42
10						3		11		7		4		9			6		1				5						8										43
8				11		2		10		7				5	3		4		1				6						9										44
32	1	1	22	33		34	37	39	4	28	11	35	1	10	1	1	30		40	6		1	12	5	1	1	2	1	19	1	1	1	2	1	16	1	10	7	
16		1	1	6			4	16	1	13	1	6		4		1	4					1	1					1	9				1		1		6	2	

7 goals unknown

Briscoe W	Brown W	Cartwright J	Corey E	Costley JT	Crosbie	Dick A	Dobson G	Farmer G	Finlay W	Fleming G	George W	Gibson A	Gilder	Goodall A	Griffiths	Gurley	Higgins M	Johnston	Joliffe C	Jones W	McGill J	McGoldrick	McPherson J	Marriott T	Mee	Parry F	Parry WH	Pearson	Richards W	Robson	Roche	Savage	Shaw	Sourbutts	Stevenson G	Townley	Whittle J	Wilding J	
7			4	11	10						2					9	5		1					3		6			8										45
10			4	7							11						5	8	1		3			2		6			9										46
2			2	2	1						2					1	2	1	2		1			2		2			2										
1				1	3											2	3												1										

Briscoe W	Brown W	Cartwright J	Corey E	Costley JT	Crosbie	Dick A	Dobson G	Farmer G	Finlay W	Fleming G	George W	Gibson A	Gilder	Goodall A	Griffiths	Gurley	Higgins M	Johnston	Joliffe C	Jones W	McGill J	McGoldrick	McPherson J	Marriott T	Mee	Parry F	Parry WH	Pearson	Richards W	Robson	Roche	Savage	Shaw	Sourbutts	Stevenson G	Townley	Whittle J	Wilding J	
8			4	11			2	10		7	3	5					6		1										9										47
8			4	11		3	2	10		7		5							1								6		9										48
8			4	10		2	3	11		7		5					6		1										9										49
10			4	8			2	7			11	5					6		1					3					9										50
8			4	11		2	3	10		7		5					6		1										9										51
5			5	5		3	5	5		4	2	5					4		5					1			1		7										
5				4		1		7		4	1	4																	8										

No team line-ups have been traced for Matches 10, 27 and 38.
T.Veitch played number 2 in Match 43.

1887-88

1	Aug	13	(a)	Chester St Oswalds	L 3-4	Unknown 3
2		20	(h)	South Shore	L 1-2	Watson
3		27	(h)	Witton	L 3-5	Cassidy, Dobson, Watson
4	Sep	3	(h)	Bury	W 9-0	Fleming 2, Goudie 2, Watson 2, Cassidy, Gibson, Higgins
5		10	(h)	Darwen	W 1-0	Farmer
6		17	(a)	Church	D 2-2	Gibson, Watson
7	Oct	8	(a)	Notts C	D 1-1	Farmer
8	Nov	5	(h)	Haydock St James	W 8-0	Watson 3, Izatt 2, Farmer, Gibson, Higgins
9	Jan	7	(h)	Notts R	L 1-3	Gibson
10		14	(h)	Witton	W 2-0	Farmer, Lea-Jones
11		21	(a)	Stanley	L 0-3	
12		28	(a)	Darwen	L 2-5	Farmer, Roach
13	Feb	4	(h)	Port Vale	W 3-1	Farmer, Fleming, Roach
14		11	(h)	Padiham	W 2-0	Roach 2
15		25	(h)	Church	W 4-0	Costley, Eyton-Jones, Farmer, Fleming
16	Mar	3	(h)	Burnley	W 2-1	Eyton-Jones, Fleming
17		10	(h)	Notts C	W 3-1	Costley, Farmer, Fleming
18		17	(h)	Derby C	D 1-1	Fleming
19		24	(h)	Aston Villa	L 1-2	Fleming
20		30	(h)	Padiham	W 2-1	Costley, Fleming
21		31	(h)	Halliwell	W 2-0	Costley, Fleming
22	Apr	2	(h)	Bolton W	L 1-2	Smalley
23		4	(h)	Corinthians	L 1-3	Falls
24		7	(h)	West Brom A	L 0-1	
25		14	(a)	North Ulster	L 2-3	Farmer, Fleming
26		16	(a)	Cliftonville	W 10-1	Fleming 6, Sourbutts 2, Costley, Gibson
27		21	(h)	Burnley	W 2-0	Sourbutts 2
28		28	(a)	South Shore	D 2-2	Halliwell, Langley
29	May	2	(h)	Bolton W	W 4-0	Briscoe 2, Farmer, Fleming
30		5	(h)	Blackburn O	W 3-1	Briscoe, Costley, Waugh
31		12	(h)	Accrington	L 0-2	
32		19	(h)	Darwen	W 3-0	Costley, Farmer, R.Jones
33		21	(h)	Wolverhampton	D 0-0	
34		24	(h)	Halliwell	W 2-1	Gibson, McGoudrick
35		29	(h)	Stanley	D 1-1	R.Jones
						Appearances
						Goals

FA Cup

1	Oct	15	(a)	Bolton W*	L 0-1	
R		29	(h)	Bolton W	D 2-2	Farmer, Watson
2R	Nov	12	(a)	Bolton W	D 1-1	Farmer
3R		19	(h)	Bolton W†	W 2-1	Goudie, Watson
2		26	(a)	Preston NE	L 0-6	
						Appearances
						Goals

Lancashire Cup

1	Oct	1	(h)	Witton	L 1-4	Farmer
						Appearances
						Goals

Liverpool Cup

1	Sep	24	(h)	St John's	W 12-0	Dick 4, Higgins 4, Costley 2, Richards 2
2	Dec	3	(h)	Bootle	W 2-0	Farmer, Gibson
						Appearances
						Goals

* Everton lodged an appeal that Bolton centre-forward, Struthers, was ineligible. The appeal was upheld.
† Bolton lodged an appeal that seven Everton players were ineligible. Everton were suspended for one month and Bolton met Preston.

Briscoe W	Cartwright J	Cassidy	Charteris	Costley JT	Currier	Dick A	Dobson G	Eyton-Jones JA	Falls	Farmer G	Fayer	Fleming G	Gibson A	Gilder	Goodall A	Goudie	Halliwell	Higgins M	Houldsworth	Izatt	Joliffe C	Jones R	Jones W	Langley	McGoldrick	McPherson J	Murray	Nidd	Pollock	Richards	Roche	Smalley RE	Smalley W	Sourbutts	Watson R	Waugh D	Weir J	Whittle J	
9				11	8		2			10		7	5					6			1		4																1
		7				2	5			8		11						6									4			9					10				2
10		7				3	2			8		11	5					6			1						4								9				3
		7				3	2			8		11	5			9		6			1						4								10				4
		7				3	2			8			5			9		6			1					11	4								10				5
		7				3	2			8			5			9		6			1					11	4								10				6
8			11			2	3			7			5			9		4									6					1			10				7
		7				2	3			8			5			9		4		11	1														10		6		8
	6						2			7	3		8									4										1							9
	10						2	7		8			6	11				4	3			5										1						9	10
			11			9	2	7		8				10				4	3			5	6									1							11
						2		7		8	3	11			9			6					4					5			10	1							12
				10		2	3	7		8		11						6				4						5			9	1							13
9						2	3	10		8		11						6				4						5			7	1							14
				8		2	3	10		7		11						6				4						5			9	1							15
9				8		2	3	10		7		11	4					6				5										1							16
9				8		2	3	10		7		11	4					6				5										1							17
9				8		2	3	10		7		11	4					6				5										1							18
9				8		2	3	10		7		11	4					6				5										1							19
7				9		2	3	10		8		11						6				5						4				1							20
7				9		2	3	10		8		11						6				5						4				1							21
7						2	3	10		8		11						6				5						4				1	9						22
10				9		2	3		7	8		11	6					4				5										1							23
10						2	3		7	8		11	6					4				5										1						9	24
8				9		2	3			10		7	6					4				5										1		11					25
8				9		2	3			10		7	6					4					5									1		11					26
10				9		2	3			8		11	5					4	6													1		7					27
9						2	3			7		11	6				5							8				4				1							28
10				9			2			7		11	5		3			4										6				1				8			29
8				9		2	3			11		7	5					6										4				1				10			30
10						2	3			8		11	5		9			6										4				1		7					31
10				9		2	3	11		8			5		4							6										1		7					32
11						2	3		7				9					8				10	6					4	5			1							33
10				9		2	3			7			5		8								6		11				4			1							34
8						2	3			10			5			9						6							4			1		11	7				35
24	2	6	2	17	1	31	34	14	3	34	2	24	26	2	5	6	1	30	3	1	6	19	6	1	1	2	6	12	3	1	4	28	1	6	8	2	1	2	
3		2		7			1	2	1	11		18	6			2	1	2		2		2		1	1						4		1	4	8	1		1	

3 goals unknown

Briscoe W	Cartwright J	Cassidy	Charteris	Costley JT	Currier	Dick A	Dobson G	Eyton-Jones JA	Falls	Farmer G	Fayer	Fleming G	Gibson A	Gilder	Goodall A	Goudie	Halliwell	Higgins M	Houldsworth	Izatt	Joliffe C	Jones R	Jones W	Langley	McGoldrick	McPherson J	Murray	Nidd	Pollock	Richards	Roche	Smalley RE	Smalley W	Sourbutts	Watson R	Waugh D	Weir J	Whittle J	
		7				2	3			8			5			9		4		11	1						6								10				1
		7				2	3			8			5			9		4		11	1						6								10				R
						2	3			8		11	5			9		4		7												1			10		6		2R
11						2	3			8			5			9		4		7												1			10		6		3R
						2	3			8			5			9		4		7										11		1			10		6		2
1		2				5	5			5		1	5			5		5		5	2						2			1		3			5		3		
										2						1																			2				

Briscoe W	Cartwright J	Cassidy	Charteris	Costley JT	Currier	Dick A	Dobson G	Eyton-Jones JA	Falls	Farmer G	Fayer	Fleming G	Gibson A	Gilder	Goodall A	Goudie	Halliwell	Higgins M	Houldsworth	Izatt	Joliffe C	Jones R	Jones W	Langley	McGoldrick	McPherson J	Murray	Nidd	Pollock	Richards	Roche	Smalley RE	Smalley W	Sourbutts	Watson R	Waugh D	Weir J	Whittle J	
10				7		2	3			8			5			9		4												11									1
				1		1	1			1			1			1		1												1									
1										1																													

Briscoe W	Cartwright J	Cassidy	Charteris	Costley JT	Currier	Dick A	Dobson G	Eyton-Jones JA	Falls	Farmer G	Fayer	Fleming G	Gibson A	Gilder	Goodall A	Goudie	Halliwell	Higgins M	Houldsworth	Izatt	Joliffe C	Jones R	Jones W	Langley	McGoldrick	McPherson J	Murray	Nidd	Pollock	Richards	Roche	Smalley RE	Smalley W	Sourbutts	Watson R	Waugh D	Weir J	Whittle J	
7						2	5						4					8	3		1		6							10									1
		7		11		9	3			8		11	5			9		4			1														10		6		2
1		1		1		3	2			1		1	2			1		2	1		2		1							1					1		1		
				2		4				1			1					4												2									

Douglas played number 10 in Match 9; Evans played number 9 in Match 9; Hughes played number 3 in Match 1; C.Jones played number 6 in Match 41; Lea-Jones played number 9 in Match 41; W.Lewis played number 3 in match 2; T.Marriott played number 2 in Match 42; Pollard played number 10 in Match 28; Taylor played number 1 in Match 2; Tynsley played number 1 in Match 41; Welsh played number 5 in Match 9.

1888-89

1	Sep	8	(h)	Accrington	W 2-1	Fleming 2
2		15	(h)	Notts C	W 2-1	E.Chadwick, Ross
3		22	(a)	Aston Villa	L 1-2	Watson
4		29	(a)	Bolton W	L 2-6	Lewis, Watson
5	Oct	6	(h)	Aston Villa	W 2-0	Farmer, Waugh
6		13	(a)	Notts C	L 1-3	Ross
7		20	(a)	Derby C	W 4-2	Costley 2, E.Chadwick, McKinnon
8		27	(h)	Derby C	W 6-2	McKinnon 3, Ross 2, Watson
9	Nov	3	(h)	Bolton W	W 2-1	Brown, Ross
10		10	(a)	Blackburn R	L 0-3	
11		17	(a)	Burnley	D 2-2	E.Chadwick, Watson
12		24	(h)	Burnley	W 3-2	E.Chadwick, Costley, Coyne
13	Dec	1	(a)	West Brom A	L 1-4	E.Chadwick
14		15	(a)	Stoke C	D 0-0	
15		22	(a)	Preston NE	L 0-3	
16		29	(a)	Accrington	L 1-3	Brown
17	Jan	12	(h)	Stoke C	W 2-1	Davies, Milward
18		19	(h)	Preston NE	L 0-2	
19		26	(a)	Wolves	L 0-4	
20	Feb	9	(h)	Wolves	L 1-2	E.Chadwick
21		23	(h)	West Brom A	L 0-1	
22	Mar	30	(h)	Blackburn R	W 3-1	Davies, Milward, Waugh

FINAL LEAGUE POSITION: 8th in Football League

Appearances

Goals

Angus J	Briscoe W	Brown W	Chadwick A	Chadwick E	Costley J	Coyne	Davie	Davies J	Dick A	Dobson G	Farmer G	Fleming G	Higgins M	Holt J	Joliffe C	Jones R	Kelso R	Keys	Lewis W	McKinnon A	Milward A	Morris	Parkinson H	Pollock	Roberts	Ross N	Smalley R	Stevenson G	Sugg F	Warmby	Watson R	Waugh D	Weir J	Wilson W	
				10					2	6	11	7		4		5			9							3	1					8			1
				10					2	6	11	7		4					9	5						3	1					8			2
				10					2		11		6					9								3	1			5	7	8	4		3
				9					2	6	10								11					4		3	1				7	8	5		4
				11					2		6			5						7						3	1		9		8	10	4		5
	10			11					2		6			5						7						3	1		9		8		4		6
				10	11					2	6			5	1					7						3			9		8		4		7
				10	11					2	6			5						7						3	1		9		8		4		8
		11		10					2	3	6			5						7						9	1				8		4		9
		11		10						2	7			6							9					3	1		5		8		4		10
		11		10	9					2	6	7		4												3	1		5		8				11
				10	11	8	9				6	7		5												3	1		2				4		12
			3	10	11	8	9	7		2	4																1		6				5		13
				10	11			7		2	6			5								9				3	1				8		4		14
11	8	9		10						2	6			5												3	1				7		4		15
11	7	9		10						2					1								6			3			5		8		4		16
9				10				7		2	6			5	1						11					3					8		4		17
11				10				7		2	6			5	1		4				9					3					8				18
11				10				7		2	6			5							9					3	1	4			8				19
		11	6	10				7	3	2	4										9				5		1				8				20
				10				7	3	2	4			5												9	1				8	11	6		21
				10				7		2	4			5							9						1				8	11	6	3	22
5	3	6	2	22	6	2	2	8	9	18	21	4	1	17	4	1	1	1	3	6	6	1	1	1	1	19	18	1	9	1	18	7	16	1	
		2		6	3	1		2			1	2							1	4	2					5					4	2			

1889-90

1	Sep	7	(h)	Blackburn R	W 3-2	Geary 2, Parry
2		14	(h)	Burnley	W 2-1	Geary, Parry
3		16	(a)	Wolves	L 1-2	Parry
4		21	(a)	Bolton W	W 4-3	Geary 2, Chadwick, Milward
5		28	(h)	Bolton W	W 3-0	Geary 2, Latta
6		30	(h)	Wolves	D 1-1	Chadwick
7	Oct	5	(a)	Derby C	D 2-2	Chadwick, Orr
8		19	(a)	Notts C	L 3-4	Milward 2, Geary
9		26	(h)	Accrington	D 2-2	Chadwick, Geary
10	Nov	2	(h)	Stoke C	W 8-0	Geary 3, Brady 2, Latta 2, Milward
11		9	(a)	Stoke C	W 2-1	Geary, Latta
12		16	(h)	Preston NE	L 1-5	Geary
13		23	(a)	Aston Villa	W 2-1	Geary 2
14	Dec	7	(h)	Notts C	W 5-3	Latta 3, Chadwick, Parry
15		21	(a)	Preston NE	W 2-1	Geary, Milward
16		28	(a)	Blackburn R	W 4-2	Milward 2, Brady, Latta
17	Jan	4	(h)	Aston Villa	W 7-0	Brady 2, Chadwick 2, Geary 2, Latta
18	Feb	8	(a)	Burnley	W 1-0	Chadwick
19		22	(a)	Accrington	L 3-5	Brady 2, Geary
20	Mar	8	(h)	West Brom A	W 5-1	Milward 2, Brady, Chadwick, Holt
21		15	(h)	Derby C	W 3-0	Milward, Opp own goals 2
22		22	(a)	West Brom A	L 1-4	Geary

FINAL LEAGUE POSITION: 2nd in Football League

Appearances
Goals

FA Cup

1	Jan	18	(h)	Derby C	W 11-2	Brady 3, Geary 3, Milward 3, Doyle, Kirkwood
2	Feb	3	(a)	Stoke C	L 2-4	Geary, Milward

Appearances
Goals

Brady A	Cain R	Chadwick E	Cox W	Doyle D	Farmer G	Geary F	Hammond H	Hannah A	Holt J	Jamieson R	Joliffe C	Jones R	Kirkwood D	Latta A	Milward A	Orr	Parry C	Smalley R	Sugg F	Weir J	
		10		3	4	9		2	5					7	11		8	1		6	1
		10		3	4	9		2	5					7	11		8	1		6	2
		10		3	4	9		2	5					7	11		8	1		6	3
		10		3	6	9		2	5		1	8		7	11		4				4
		10		3	6	9		2	5				8	7	11		4	1			5
		10		3	6	9		2	5				8	7	11		4	1			6
		10		3	6			2	5				8	7	11	9	4	1			7
		10		3	6	9		2	5				8	7	11		4	1			8
		10		3	6	9		2	5				8	7	11		4	1			9
8	6	10		3		9		2	5					7	11		4	1			10
8	6	10		3		9		2	5					7	11		4	1			11
8		10		3	6	9		2	5					7	11		4	1			12
8	6	10		3		9		2	5					7	11		4	1			13
8	4	10		3		9		2	5					7	11		6	1			14
8	4	10		3		9		2	5					7	11		6	1			15
8	4	10		3				2	5				6	7	11		9	1			16
8		10		3		9		2	5				4	7	11		6	1			17
8		10		3		9		2	5				4	7	11		6	1			18
8	4	10	1	3		9		2	5					7	11		6				19
8	4	10	1	9			3	2	5				7		11		6				20
8	4	10	1	3				2		9			7		11		6		5		21
8	4	10	1	3		9		2	5				7		11		6				22
13	10	22	4	22	10	18	1	22	21	1	1	1	11	19	22	1	22	17	1	3	
8		9				21			1					9	10	1	4				

2 own-goals

Brady A	Cain R	Chadwick E	Cox W	Doyle D	Farmer G	Geary F	Hammond H	Hannah A	Holt J	Jamieson R	Joliffe C	Jones R	Kirkwood D	Latta A	Milward A	Orr	Parry C	Smalley R	Sugg F	Weir J	
8		10		3		9		2	5				4	7	11		6	1			1
8		10		3		9		2	5				4	7	11		6	1			2
2		2		2		2		2	2				2	2	2		2	2			
3				1		4							1		4						

1890-91

1	Sep	6	(a)	West Brom A	W 4-1	Geary 2, Brady, Campbell
2		13	(h)	Wolves	W 5-0	Geary 2, Milward 2, Chadwick
3		20	(a)	Bolton W	W 5-0	Geary 2, Milward 2, Latta
4		27	(a)	Accrington	W 2-1	Geary, Milward
5	Oct	4	(h)	Derby C	W 7-0	Geary 2, Milward 2, Brady, Chadwick, Kirkwood
6		11	(a)	Aston Villa	D 2-2	Geary 2
7		18	(h)	Bolton W	W 2-0	Brady 2
8		25	(h)	West Brom A	L 2-3	Holt, Latta
9	Nov	1	(a)	Notts C	L 1-3	Geary
10		8	(a)	Blackburn R	L 1-2	Chadwick
11		15	(h)	Sunderland	W 1-0	Robertson
12		22	(a)	Preston NE	L 0-2	
13		29	(h)	Blackburn R	W 3-1	Geary 2, Brady
14	Dec	6	(a)	Wolves	W 1-0	Geary
15		13	(a)	Derby C	W 6-2	Wylie 4, Brady, Geary
16		20	(a)	Sunderland	L 0-1	
17		26	(h)	Accrington	W 3-2	Milward 2, Chadwick
18		27	(h)	Burnley	W 7-3	Chadwick 3, Latta 2, Brady, Milward
19	Jan	1	(h)	Aston Villa	W 5-0	Brady 2, Chadwick, Geary, Milward
20		3	(h)	Notts C	W 4-2	Chadwick 2, Geary, Milward
21		10	(h)	Preston NE	L 0-1	
22	Mar	14	(a)	Burnley	L 2-3	Geary 2

FINAL LEAGUE POSITION: 1st in Football League

Appearances
Goals

FA Cup

1	Jan	17	(a)	Sunderland	L 0-1	

Appearances
Goals

Angus J	Brady A	Campbell W	Chadwick E	Doyle D	Elliott J	Geary F	Gordon P	Hannah A	Holt J	Jardine D	Kirkwood D	Latta A	Lochhead A	McLean D	Milward A	Parry C	Robertson H	Smalley R	Wylie T	
1	8	6	10	3		9		2	5		4	7			11					1
1	8	6	10	3		9		2	5		4	7			11					2
1	8	6	10	3		9		2	5		4	7			11					3
1	8	6	10	3		9		2	5		4	7			11					4
1	8	6	10	3		9		2	5		7				11	4				5
1	8	6	10	3		9		2	5		7				11	4				6
1	8		10	3		9	7	2	5		6				11	4				7
1	8	2	10	3		9			5		6	7			11	4				8
1	8	5	10	3	7	9		2						4	11	6				9
	8		10	3		9		2	5					6	11	4	7	1		10
1	8	6	10	3		7		2	5		4				11		9			11
1	8	4	10	3		9	7	2	5		6				11					12
	8	6	10	3		9	7	2	5	1	4				11					13
	8		10			9		2	5	1	4			3	11	6			7	14
	8	6	10			9		2	5	1	4			3	11				7	15
	8	6	10	3		9		2	5	1	4				11				7	16
	8		10	3		9		2	5	1	4				11	6			7	17
	8		10	3		9		2	5	1	4	7			11	6				18
	8		10	3		9		2	5	1	4	7			11	6				19
			10	3		9		2	5	1	4	7			11	6	8			20
	8		10	3		9		2	5	1	4	7			11	6				21
	8		10	3		9			5	1		7	4	2	11	6				22
11	21	13	22	20	1	22	3	20	21	10	19	10	1	5	22	13	3	1	4	
	9	1	10			20			1		1	4			12		1		4	

Angus J	Brady A	Campbell W	Chadwick E	Doyle D	Elliott J	Geary F	Gordon P	Hannah A	Holt J	Jardine D	Kirkwood D	Latta A	Lochhead A	McLean D	Milward A	Parry C	Robertson H	Smalley R	Wylie T	
1			10	3		8			5		4	7		2	11	6	9			1
1			1	1		1			1		1	1		1	1	1	1			

1891-92

1	Sep	5	(a)	West Brom A	L 0-4	
2		7	(h)	Darwen	W 5-3	Geary 2, Milward 2, Latta
3		19	(h)	Blackburn R	W 3-1	Geary, Kelso, Latta
4		26	(a)	Accrington	D 1-1	Gordon
5	Oct	3	(a)	Sunderland	L 1-2	Geary
6		10	(h)	Preston NE	D 1-1	Thomson
7		17	(a)	Bolton W	L 0-1	
8		24	(a)	Derby C	W 3-0	Latta 2, Chadwick
9		31	(a)	Preston NE	L 0-4	
10	Nov	7	(h)	West Brom A	W 4-3	Latta 3, Milward
11		14	(a)	Darwen	L 1-3	Latta
12		21	(a)	Wolves	L 1-5	Latta
13		28	(h)	Aston Villa	W 5-1	Chadwick 2, Latta, Maxwell, Wylie
14	Dec	5	(a)	Blackburn R	D 2-2	Latta, Opp own-goal
15		12	(h)	Wolves	W 2-1	Chadwick, Latta
16		25	(h)	Sunderland	L 0-4	
17		28	(a)	Aston Villa	W 4-3	Chadwick 2, Maxwell 2
18	Jan	2	(h)	Burnley	D 1-1	Milward
19		9	(a)	Notts C	W 3-1	Latta, Maxwell, Milward
20	Feb	13	(a)	Burnley	L 0-1	
21	Mar	5	(h)	Stoke C	W 1-0	Chadwick
22		12	(a)	Stoke C	W 1-0	Chadwick
23		19	(h)	Accrington	W 3-0	Chadwick 2, Latta
24	Apr	15	(h)	Derby C	L 1-2	Kelso
25		16	(h)	Notts C	W 4-0	Latta 3, Geary
26		18	(h)	Bolton W	L 2-5	Geary, Milward

FINAL LEAGUE POSITION: 5th in Football League

Appearances
Goals

FA Cup

1	Jan	16	(h)	Burnley	L 2-4	Chadwick, Robertson

Appearances
Goals

Campbell W	Chadwick E	Collins J	Earp F	Elliott J	Geary F	Gordon P	Holt J	Howarth R	Jardine D	Jones R	Kelso R	Kent J	Kirkwood D	Latta A	Lochhead A	McLean D	Marsden J	Maxwell A	Milward A	Murray J	Parry C	Robertson H	Thomson S	Williams R	Wylie T	
5	10				8				1		4			7		3	2		11		6		9			1
5	10	2			8				1		4			7	6	3			11				9			2
	10	3			9	8	5		1		4			7	6	2			11							3
	10	3			9	8	5		1		4				6	2			11						7	4
3	10				9	8	5		1		4			7	6	2			11							5
3	10					8	5		1		4			7		2			11			6	9			6
	10			9			5		1		2		4	7		3			11	8		6				7
	10						5				2		4	9		3			11	8		6		1	7	8
	10						5		1		2		4	9		3		8	11			6			7	9
	10						5				2		4	9		3			11	8		6		1	7	10
	10		2				5		1		4	3		9					11	8		6			7	11
	10		2				5		1				4	7	6	3		9	11						8	12
	10	3	2				5							7		6		9	11			4		1	8	13
	10		2				5	3						7		6		9	11			4		1	8	14
	10		2				5	3			4			7				9	11			6		1	8	15
	10						5	3			4			7		2		9	11			6		1	8	16
	10		2				5	3			4			7				9	11			6		1	8	17
	10		2				5	3			4			7				9	11			6		1	8	18
	10		2				5	3			4			7				9	11			6		1	8	19
	10						5	2	1		4			7		3		9	11			6			8	20
	10		3					2	1	5	4			7				9	11			6			8	21
	10				8			3	1	5	4			7		2		9	11			6				22
	10				8			3	1	5	4			7		2		9	11			6				23
					8		5	3	1		4			7		2		9	11			6			10	24
	10	3			8		5		1		4			7		2		9	11			6				25
	10	3			8		5		1		4			7		2		9	11			6				26
4	25	6	9	1	10	4	21	11	17	3	23	1	5	25	5	20	1	16	26	4	1	20	3	9	16	
	10				6	1					2			17				4	6				1		1	

1 own-goal

Campbell W	Chadwick E	Collins J	Earp F	Elliott J	Geary F	Gordon P	Holt J	Howarth R	Jardine D	Jones R	Kelso R	Kent J	Kirkwood D	Latta A	Lochhead A	McLean D	Marsden J	Maxwell A	Milward A	Murray J	Parry C	Robertson H	Thomson S	Williams R	Wylie T	
	10		3			9	5	2			4			7					11			6		1	8	1
	1		1			1	1	1			1			1					1			1		1	1	
	1																					1				

1892-93

1	Sep	3	(h)	Nottingham F	D	2-2	Geary, Milward
2		10	(a)	Aston Villa	L	1-4	Geary
3		17	(a)	Blackburn R	D	2-2	Latta, Maxwell
4		24	(h)	Newton Heath	W	6-0	E.Chadwick 2, Geary 2, Maxwell, Milward
5	Oct	1	(h)	Aston Villa	W	1-0	Maxwell
6		8	(h)	Sunderland	L	1-4	Latta
7		15	(a)	West Brom A	L	0-3	
8		19	(a)	Newton Heath	W	4-3	Latta 4
9		22	(h)	Accrington	D	1-1	Milward
10		29	(a)	Bolton W	L	1-4	Latta
11	Nov	5	(a)	Derby C	W	6-1	Geary 3, Latta 3
12		12	(h)	Stoke C	D	2-2	Geary, Milward
13		26	(h)	Sheffield W	L	3-5	E.Chadwick 2, Milward
14	Dec	3	(a)	Preston NE	L	0-5	
15		10	(h)	Wolves	W	3-2	E.Chadwick, Geary, Gordon
16		17	(a)	Notts C	W	2-1	Geary, Latta
17		24	(h)	Burnley	L	0-1	
18	Jan	3	(a)	Sunderland	L	3-4	Milward 2, Latta
19		7	(h)	Notts C	W	6-0	Geary 2, E.Chadwick, Latta, Maxwell, Milward
20		12	(a)	Nottingham F	L	1-2	Stewart
21		14	(h)	West Brom A	W	1-0	Geary
22		28	(a)	Stoke C	W	1-0	Milward
23	Feb	11	(h)	Preston NE	W	6-0	Maxwell 2, E.Chadwick, Gordon, Latta, Milward
24		13	(a)	Sheffield W	W	2-0	E.Chadwick, Opp own-goal
25		25	(a)	Accrington	W	3-0	E.Chadwick 2, Kelso
26	Mar	18	(a)	Wolves	W	4-2	Geary 2, Elliott, Hartley
27	Apr	1	(h)	Blackburn R	W	4-0	Geary, Jones, McMillan, Maxwell
28		3	(h)	Bolton W	W	3-0	Latta 2, Geary
29		8	(a)	Burnley	L	0-3	
30		15	(h)	Derby C	W	5-0	Geary 2, Latta 2, Milward

FINAL LEAGUE POSITION: 3rd in Division One

Appearances
Goals

FA Cup

1	Jan	21	(h)	West Brom A	W	4-1	Geary 2, Latta, Maxwell
2	Feb	4	(h)	Nottingham F	W	4-2	Milward 2, E.Chadwick, Geary
3		18	(h)	Sheffield W	W	3-0	E.Chadwick, Geary, Maxwell
SF	Mar	4	(n*)	Preston NE	D	2-2	E.Chadwick, Gordon
R		16	(n†)	Preston NE	D	0-0	
2R		20	(n‡)	Preston NE	W	2-1	Gordon, Maxwell
F		25	(n§)	Wolves	L	0-1	

* Played at Bramall Lane. † Played at Ewood Park. ‡ Played at Trent Bridge. § Played at Fallowfield, Manchester.

Appearances
Goals

Bell J	Boyle R	Chadwick A	Chadwick E	Collins J	Dewar J	Elliott J	Geary F	Gordon P	Hartley A	Holt J	Howarth R	Jamieson R	Jardine D	Jones R	Kelso R	Latta A	McMillan J	Maxwell A	Milward A	Murray J	Parry C	Pinnell A	Rennie A	Robertson H	Stewart A	Thomas W	Thompson R	Williams R	
	4		10		3		9			5	2		1			7		8	11					6					1
	4		10	3			9			5	2		1		6	7		8	11										2
	4		10	3			9			5					2	7		8	11			1		6					3
	4		10	3			9			5	2					7		8	11			1		6					4
	4		10	3			9			5	2		1			7		8	11					6					5
	4		10	3			9			5	2					7		8	11			1		6					6
	4		10	3			9			5	2					7		8	11					6		1			7
	4		10	3		5		8			2	6				7		9	11	1									8
	4		10	3			7	8		5	2	6						9	11	1									9
	4			3			7	8		5	2	6				9		10	11	1									10
	4	3	10				9			5	2	6				7		8	11									1	11
	4	3	10				9			5	2	6				7		8	11									1	12
	4	3	10					9		5	2	6				7			11	8			1						13
	4		10					8		5	2	6				7		9	11								3	1	14
	4		10				9	8		5	3	6	1		2	7			11										15
			10				9	8		5	3	6	1		2	7			11						4				16
			10				9	8		5	3	6	1		2	7			11						4				17
			10				9			5	2		1		6	7		8	11		3				4				18
			10				9			5	2	6				7		8	11		3		1		4				19
			10				9			5	2	6				7		8	11		3		1		4				20
	5		10				9				2	6				7		8	11		3		1		4				21
	4		10				9			5	3				2	7		8	11						6			1	22
	4		10					8		5	3				2	7		9	11						6			1	23
	4		10					8		5	2	6				7		9	11		3							1	24
	4		10				7	8		5					2			9	11		3				6			1	25
	4					11	9		8				1	5	2	7	10				3				6				26
	6					11	9				3			5	2	8	10	7			4							1	27
7	4		10				9			5	3				2	8			11		6							1	28
8	4		10			11				5					2	7		9			3				6			1	29
8	4		10				9			5	3				2	7			11						6			1	30
3	25	3	27	9	1	4	24	11	1	26	26	14	8	2	14	28	2	23	27	4	10	3	4	6	12	1	1	11	
			10			1	19	2	1					1	1	18	1	7	11						1				

1 own-goal

Bell J	Boyle R	Chadwick A	Chadwick E	Collins J	Dewar J	Elliott J	Geary F	Gordon P	Hartley A	Holt J	Howarth R	Jamieson R	Jardine D	Jones R	Kelso R	Latta A	McMillan J	Maxwell A	Milward A	Murray J	Parry C	Pinnell A	Rennie A	Robertson H	Stewart A	Thomas W	Thompson R	Williams R	
	4		8				9			5	2				3	11		10	7						6			1	1
	4		10				9			5	3				2	7		8	11						6			1	2
	4		10				9			5	3				2	7		8	11						6			1	3
	4		10					8		5	3				2	7		9	11						6			1	SF
	4		10					8		5	3				2	7		9	11						6			1	R
	4		10					8		5	3				2	7		9	11						6			1	2R
	4		10					8		5	3				2	7		9	11						6			1	F
	7		7				3	4		7	7				7	7		7	7						7			7	
			3				4	2								1		3	2										

1893-94

1	Sep	2	(h)	Sheffield U	L 2-3	Latta, Milward
2		4	(h)	Nottingham F	W 4-0	McMillan 2, Boyle, Milward
3		9	(a)	Derby C	L 3-7	Chadwick, Milward, Southworth
4		16	(h)	Aston Villa	W 4-2	Bell, Kelso, McMillan, Walker
5		23	(a)	Aston Villa	L 1-3	Southworth
6		30	(h)	Sunderland	W 7-1	Chadwick 3, Latta 2, Milward, Southworth
7	Oct	7	(a)	Burnley	L 1-2	Stewart
8		14	(h)	Blackburn R	D 2-2	Milward, Southworth
9		21	(h)	Darwen	W 8-1	Latta 2, Maxwell 2, Southworth 2, Bell, Chadwick
10		28	(h)	Preston NE	L 2-3	Southworth 2
11	Nov	4	(a)	Sheffield W	D 1-1	Milward
12		11	(h)	Derby C	L 1-2	Latta
13		25	(h)	Burnley	W 4-3	Bell 2, Chadwick, Geary
14	Dec	2	(a)	Newton Heath	W 3-0	Geary 2, Chadwick
15		4	(a)	Wolves	L 0-2	
16		9	(a)	Sheffield U	W 3-0	Southworth 2, Milward
17		16	(a)	Blackburn R	L 3-4	Bell, Chadwick, Southworth
18		23	(h)	Sheffield W	W 8-1	Southworth 4, Bell 2, Chadwick, Latta
19		30	(h)	West Brom A	W 7-1	Southworth 6, Bell
20	Jan	1	(a)	Darwen	D 3-3	Chadwick, Southworth, Opp own-goal
21		6	(h)	Newton Heath	W 2-0	Chadwick, Southworth
22		13	(a)	Preston NE	W 4-2	Chadwick, Milward, Southworth, Opp own-goal
23		18	(a)	Nottingham F	L 2-3	Geary, Opp own-goal
24	Feb	3	(a)	West Brom A	L 1-3	Bell
25		6	(a)	Sunderland	L 0-1	
26	Mar	3	(a)	Stoke C	L 1-3	Southworth
27		24	(h)	Wolves	W 3-0	Geary 2, Southworth
28		26	(h)	Bolton W	W 3-2	Chadwick, Hartley, Southworth
29	Apr	7	(h)	Stoke C	W 6-2	Geary 2, Latta 2, Hartley, McMillan
30		16	(a)	Bolton W	W 1-0	Reay

FINAL LEAGUE POSITION: 6th in Division One

Appearances
Goals

FA Cup

1	Jan	27	(a)	Stoke C	L 0-1	

Appearances
Goals

Arridge S	Bell J	Boyle R	Chadwick E	Elliott J	Geary F	Hartley A	Holt J	Howarth R	Jardine D	Kelso R	Latta A	Lindsay W	McMillan J	Maxwell A	Milward A	Parry C	Reay H	Southworth J	Stewart W	Storrier D	Walker J	Whitehead J	Williams R	
	8	4	10				5	3		2	7			9	11				6				1	1
	8	4		11			5	3		2	7		10		9				6				1	2
	8	4	10				5	3		2	7				11			9	6				1	3
	8	4		11				3		2	7		10					9	6		5		1	4
	8	4		11				3		2	7		10					9	6		5		1	5
	8	4	10				5	3		2	7				11			9	6				1	6
	8	4	10				5	3		2	7				11			9	6				1	7
	8	4	10				5	3		2	7				11			9	6				1	8
	11	4	10				5	3		2	7			8				9	6				1	9
	11	4	10				5	3		2	7			8				9	6				1	10
	11	4	10				5	2			7	3		9	8				6				1	11
	8	4	10				5	3		2	7				11			9	6				1	12
	9		10		8		5			2	7	3			11				6		4		1	13
	8	4	10		9		5	2			7	3			11				6				1	14
	8	4	10		9		5	2			7	3			11				6				1	15
	8		10				5	2		4	7	3			11			9	6				1	16
	8		10				5	2		4	7	3			11			9	6				1	17
	8		10				5			4	7	3			11	2		9	6				1	18
3	8		10				5			4	7				11	2		9	6				1	19
3	8		10				5			4	7				11	2		9	6			1		20
	8	4	10				5			6	7	3			11	2		9				1		21
	8	4	10				5			3	7				11	2		9	6				1	22
	8	4	10		7		5			3					11	2		9	6				1	23
	8				10		5	2		4	7				11	3		9	6				1	24
					10	8	5	2		4	7				11	3		9	6				1	25
			10			8				4	7	2			11	3		9	6	5			1	26
		4	10		11	8	5	3	1	2	7							9	6					27
		4	10		11	8	5	3	1	2	7							9	6					28
		5			9	8		2		4	7		10		11	3			6				1	29
		4	10			9	5	2			8				11	3	7		6				1	30
2	24	21	24	3	9	6	26	22	2	26	29	9	4	4	24	11	1	22	29	1	3	2	26	
	9	1	13		8	2				1	9		4	2	8		1	27	1		1			

3 own-goals

Arridge S	Bell J	Boyle R	Chadwick E	Elliott J	Geary F	Hartley A	Holt J	Howarth R	Jardine D	Kelso R	Latta A	Lindsay W	McMillan J	Maxwell A	Milward A	Parry C	Reay H	Southworth J	Stewart W	Storrier D	Walker J	Whitehead J	Williams R	
	8					10	5	2		4	7				11	3		9	6				1	1
	1					1	1	1		1	1				1	1		1	1				1	

1894-95

1	Sep	1	(h)	Sheffield W	W 3-1	Bell, Chadwick, McInnes
2		3	(h)	Small Heath	W 5-0	Southworth 3, Bell 2
3		8	(a)	Stoke C	W 3-1	Chadwick, Latta, McInnes
4		15	(h)	Nottingham F	W 6-1	Southworth 3, Bell, Latta, McInnes
5		22	(a)	Nottingham F	W 3-2	Bell, Chadwick, Southworth
6		29	(h)	West Brom A	W 4-1	Bell, Chadwick, McInnes, Southworth
7	Oct	6	(a)	Bolton W	W 3-1	Bell, Latta, McInnes
8		13	(h)	Liverpool	W 3-0	Bell, Latta, McInnes
9		20	(a)	Blackburn R	L 3-4	Chadwick, Hartley, Southworth
10		27	(h)	Sunderland	D 2-2	Boyle, McInnes
11	Nov	3	(a)	Small Heath	D 4-4	Latta 3, Bell
12		17	(a)	Liverpool	D 2-2	Kelso, Latta
13		24	(h)	Blackburn R	W 2-1	Bell, Milward
14	Dec	1	(a)	West Brom A	W 4-1	Chadwick, Latta, Milward, Stewart
15		8	(h)	Bolton W	W 3-1	Chadwick, Latta, McInnes
16		15	(a)	Preston NE	W 2-1	Hartley, Milward
17	Jan	1	(a)	Sheffield W	L 0-3	
18		5	(a)	Wolves	L 0-1	
19		7	(h)	Stoke C	W 3-0	Chadwick, Geary, W.Williams
20		12	(a)	Derby C	D 2-2	Geary, Parry
21		17	(h)	Aston Villa	W 4-2	Milward 2, Bell, Geary
22		26	(h)	Sheffield U	D 1-1	McInnes
23	Feb	23	(h)	Preston NE	W 4-2	Bell, Chadwick, Hartley, Milward
24		26	(a)	Sheffield U	L 2-4	Hartley, McInnes
25	Mar	16	(a)	Burnley	W 4-2	Bell, Chadwick, Milward, Stewart
26		21	(h)	Burnley	W 3-2	Bell, Latta, Milward
27	Apr	8	(h)	Wolves	W 2-1	Bell, Milward
28		13	(h)	Derby C	L 2-3	Geary, Milward
29		20	(a)	Sunderland	L 1-2	Chadwick
30		24	(a)	Aston Villa	D 2-2	Boyle, Hartley

FINAL LEAGUE POSITION: 2nd in Division One

Appearances
Goals

FA Cup

1	Feb	2	(a)	Southport	W 3-0	Bell 3
2		16	(h)	Blackburn R	D 1-1	Chadwick
R		20	(a)	Blackburn R	W 3-2	Chadwick 2, Hartley
3	Mar	2	(a)	Sheffield W	L 0-2	

Appearances
Goals

Adams J	Arridge S	Bell J	Boyle R	Cain T	Chadwick E	Elliott J	Geary F	Hartley A	Hillman J	Holt J	Kelso R	Latta A	McInnes T	McMillan J	Milward A	Parry C	Reay H	Southworth J	Stewart W	Storrier D	Sutton W	Williams R	Williams W	
2		11	4		10					5		7	8			3		9	6			1		1
2		11	4		10					5		7	8			3		9	6			1		2
2		11	4		10			9		5		7	8			3			6			1		3
2		11	4		10					5		7	8			3		9	6			1		4
2		11	4		10					5		7	8			3		9	6			1		5
2		11	4		10					5		7	8			3		9	6			1		6
		11	4	1	10					5	2	7	8			3		9	6					7
2		11	4	1				10		5		7	8			3		9	6					8
2		11	4	1	10			8		5		7				3		9	6					9
			4	1	10					5	2	7	8		11	3		9	6					10
2		11	4	1	10			9		5		7	8			3			6					11
		11	4	1	10			9		5	2	7	8			3			6					12
		11	4	1	10					5	2	7	8		9	3			6					13
		11	4	1	10					5	2	7	8		9	3			6					14
		11	4	1	10					5	2	7	8		9	3			6					15
			4	1	10			9		5	2	7	8		11	3			6					16
2		11	4	1	10			8		5		7			9	3			6					17
		11	4		10		7			5	2		8		9	3			6			1		18
			4		10		9			5	2		8		11	3			6			1	7	19
		11	4		10		9			5	2		8			3			6		1		7	20
		11	4		10		9			5	2		8		7	3			6			1		21
		11	4		10		9				2		8		7	3			6	5		1		22
2		11	4		10	6		9			5		8		7	3						1		23
	3	11	4			6		9		5	2		8	10	7							1		24
		8	4		10		9		1	5	2	7			11	3			6					25
		9	4		10				1	5	2	7	8		11	3			6					26
		8	4		10		9		1	5	2	7			11	3			6					27
	3	8	5		10	4	9		1		2				11				6				7	28
	3	8	4		10			9	1	5	2				11				6				7	29
2		8	4		10	6		9	1	5					11	3							7	30
12	3	27	30	11	28	4	8	11	6	27	19	20	23	1	18	27		9	27	1	1	12	5	
		15	2		11		4	5			1	11	10		10	1		9	2				1	

Adams J	Arridge S	Bell J	Boyle R	Cain T	Chadwick E	Elliott J	Geary F	Hartley A	Hillman J	Holt J	Kelso R	Latta A	McInnes T	McMillan J	Milward A	Parry C	Reay H	Southworth J	Stewart W	Storrier D	Sutton W	Williams R	Williams W	
		11	4		10			9		5	2		8			3	7		6			1		1
		11	4		10			9		5	2		8		7	3			6			1		2
			4		10		7	9		5	2		8		11	3			6			1		R
		11	4	1	10	6		9			2		8		7	3				5				3
		3	4	1	4	1	1	4		3	4		4		3	4	1		3	1		3		
		3			3			1																

1895-96

1	Sep	2	(h)	Sheffield W	D 2-2	Boyle, Milward
2		7	(h)	Nottingham F	W 6-2	Chadwick 2, Milward 2, Bell, Flewitt
3		9	(h)	Bury	W 3-2	Bell, Chadwick, Milward
4		14	(a)	Bolton W	L 1-3	McInnes
5		21	(h)	Blackburn R	L 0-2	
6		28	(a)	Wolves	W 3-2	McInnes 2, Milward
7		30	(a)	Aston Villa	L 3-4	Bell 3
8	Oct	5	(h)	Sheffield U	W 5-0	Chadwick 3, Latta, Milward
9		12	(a)	Nottingham F	L 1-2	Chadwick
10		19	(h)	West Brom A	D 1-1	Milward
11		26	(a)	Burnley	D 1-1	Hartley
12	Nov	2	(h)	Wolves	W 2-0	Chadwick, Milward
13		9	(a)	Sheffield U	W 2-1	Hartley, Milward
14		16	(h)	Sunderland	W 1-0	Milward
15		23	(a)	West Brom A	W 3-0	Hartley, McInnes, Milward
16		30	(h)	Burnley	W 2-1	Adams, Boyle
17	Dec	7	(a)	Small Heath	W 3-0	Milward 3
18		14	(h)	Stoke C	W 7-2	McInnes 3, Bell 2, Cameron, Milward
19		21	(h)	Aston Villa	W 2-0	Bell, McInnes
20	Jan	1	(a)	Blackburn R	W 3-2	Bell, Chadwick, Opp own-goal
21		11	(a)	Bury	D 1-1	Milward
22		25	(a)	Preston NE	D 1-1	Chadwick
23	Feb	3	(h)	Small Heath	W 3-0	Hartley 2, Goldie
24		18	(a)	Sheffield W	L 1-3	Cameron
25		22	(a)	Sunderland	L 0-3	
26	Mar	7	(h)	Preston NE	W 3-2	Boyle, Hartley, Milward
27	Apr	3	(h)	Derby C	D 2-2	Cameron 2
28		6	(h)	Bolton W	D 1-1	Chadwick
29		7	(a)	Derby C	L 1-2	Williams
30		11	(a)	Stoke C	W 2-1	Hartley, Schofield

FINAL LEAGUE POSITION: 3rd in Division One

Appearances
Goals

FA Cup

1	Feb	1	(a)	Nottingham F	W 2-0	Chadwick, Milward
2		15	(h)	Sheffield U	W 3-0	Bell, Cameron, Milward
3		29	(a)	Sheffield W	L 0-4	

Appearances
Goals

Adams J	Arridge S	Bell J	Boyle R	Briggs H	Cameron J	Chadwick E	Elliott J	Flewitt A	Goldie H	Hartley A	Hillman J	Holt J	Kelso R	Latta A	McInnes T	Milward A	Parry C	Robertson J	Schofield A	Stewart W	Storrier D	Williams W	
	3	8	4			10				9	1		2			11				6	5	7	1
3		8	4			10		9			1	5	2			11				6		7	2
3		8	5			10		9	4		1		2			11				6		7	3
3		8	4			10		9			1	5	2		7	11				6			4
3		8	4			10				9	1	5	2			11				6		7	5
3			4			10				9	1	5			8	11	2			6		7	6
3		9	4			10					1	5			8	11	2			6		7	7
2	3	8	4		9	10					1	5		7		11				6			8
2	3	8	4		9	10					1	5		7		11				6			9
2	3	9	5			10			4		1			7	8	11				6			10
2	3	8	5			10			4	9	1			7		11				6			11
2	3	8	5			10			4	9	1			7		11				6			12
2	3	7	5			10			4	9	1				8	11				6			13
2	3	7	5			10			4	9	1				8	11				6			14
2	3	7	5			10			4	9	1				8	11				6			15
2	3	7	5		9	10			4	8	1					11				6			16
2	3	7	5		9	10			4		1				8	11				6			17
2	3	7	5		9	10			4		1				8	11				6			18
2	3	7	5		9	10			4		1				8	11				6			19
2	3	7	5		9	10	6		4		1				8	11							20
2	3	7	5		9	10			6		1		4		8	11							21
2	3	7	4		9	10					1	5			8	11				6			22
2	3	7	4			10			8	9	1	5				11				6			23
2	3	7	4		10					9	1	5			8	11				6			24
2	3		4			10				9	1	5			8	11				6		7	25
2	3	7	4							10	1	5			8	9			11	6			26
2	3	7	4		9	10					1	5			8	11				6			27
2	3	7	4		9	10					1				8	11		5		6			28
	3		5			10			4	9	1				8	11				6	2	7	29
2		7	4	1	9	10				8		5							11	6	3		30
28	23	27	30	1	13	28	1	3	15	15	29	14	6	5	19	29	2	1	2	28	3	8	
1		9	3		4	11		1	1	7				1	8	17			1			1	

1 own-goal

Adams J	Arridge S	Bell J	Boyle R	Briggs H	Cameron J	Chadwick E	Elliott J	Flewitt A	Goldie H	Hartley A	Hillman J	Holt J	Kelso R	Latta A	McInnes T	Milward A	Parry C	Robertson J	Schofield A	Stewart W	Storrier D	Williams W	
2	3	7	4		8	10				9	1	5				11				6			1
2	3	7	4		9	10					1	5			8	11				6			2
2		7	5		8	10			4		1		3			11				6	9		3
3	2	3	3		3	3			1	1	3	2	1		1	3				3	1		
		1			1	1										2							

1896-97

1	Sep	5	(h)	Sheffield W	W 2-1	Cameron, Taylor
2		12	(a)	Wolves	W 1-0	Opp own-goal
3		19	(h)	Aston Villa	L 2-3	Milward, Taylor
4		26	(a)	Aston Villa	W 2-1	Hartley, Stewart
5	Oct	3	(h)	Liverpool	W 2-1	Hartley, Milward
6		10	(a)	Burnley	L 1-2	Stewart
7		17	(h)	Sheffield U	L 1-2	Opp own-goal
8		24	(a)	Sheffield W	L 1-4	Milward
9		31	(h)	Wolves	D 0-0	
10	Nov	14	(h)	Bolton W	L 2-3	Chadwick, Milward
11		21	(a)	Liverpool	D 0-0	
12		28	(h)	Burnley	W 6-0	Cameron 3, Bell, Chadwick, Milward
13	Dec	7	(a)	Bolton W	L 0-2	
14		12	(a)	Sunderland	D 1-1	Holt
15		19	(h)	Stoke C	W 4-2	Bell 2, Cameron, Taylor
16		26	(h)	Sunderland	W 5-2	Bell 2, Chadwick, Hartley, Milward
17	Jan	1	(a)	Sheffield U	W 2-1	Taylor 2
18		2	(a)	Stoke C	W 3-2	Bell, Hartley, Taylor
19		9	(h)	Nottingham F	W 3-1	Bell 2, Taylor
20		16	(a)	West Brom A	W 4-1	Taylor 3, Bell
21	Feb	6	(h)	Preston NE	L 3-4	Chadwick, Hartley, Taylor
22	Mar	2	(a)	Bury	L 1-3	Milward
23		6	(a)	Blackburn R	L 2-4	Bell, Taylor
24		10	(a)	Nottingham F	L 0-3	
25		13	(h)	Blackburn R	L 0-3	
26	Apr	3	(a)	Preston NE	L 1-4	Campbell
27		16	(h)	Derby C	W 5-2	Chadwick 2, Bell, Hartley, Milward
28		17	(h)	West Brom A	W 6-3	Bell 3, Chadwick, Milward, Taylor
29		20	(a)	Derby C	W 1-0	Stewart
30		24	(h)	Bury	L 1-2	Bell

FINAL LEAGUE POSITION: 7th in Division One

Appearances

Goals

FA Cup

1	Jan	30	(h)	Burton W	W 5-2	Bell, Chadwick, Holt, Milward, Opp own-goal
2	Feb	13	(h)	Bury	W 3-0	Taylor 2, Milward
3		27	(h)	Blackburn R	W 2-0	Hartley 2
SF	Mar	20	(n*)	Derby C	W 3-2	Chadwick, Hartley, Milward
F	Apr	10	(n†)	Aston Villa	L 2-3	Bell, Boyle

* Played at Victoria Ground, Stoke. † Played at the Crystal Palace.

Appearances

Goals

Arridge S	Banks H	Barker G	Bell J	Boyle R	Briggs H	Cameron J	Campbell W	Chadwick E	Goldie H	Hartley A	Holt J	Maley W	Meecham P	Meiklejohn G	Menham R	Milward A	Molyneux G	Palmer J	Patrick J	Robertson J	Schofield A	Stewart W	Storrier D	Taylor J	Williams W	
3			7	4	1	9		10			5					11						6	2	8		1
		3	7	4	1	9		10			5					11						6	2	8		2
		3	7	4	1	9		10			5					11						6	2	8		3
3			7	4	1			10		9	5					11						6	2	8		4
3			7	4	1			10		9	5					11						6	2	8		5
3			7	4	1			10		9	5					11						6	2	8		6
3			7	4	1	9		10			5					11						6	2	8		7
3		2	11	4	1		8	10			5					9						6		7		8
3			7		1	9		10	4		5					11						6	2	8		9
3			8	4	1	9		10			5					11						6	2	7		10
3			8	4		9		10			5				1	11						6	2	7		11
3			8	4		9		10			5					11			1			6	2	7		12
3			8	4		9		10			5				1						11	6	2	7		13
3			8	4		9		10			5				1	11						6	2	7		14
3			8	4		9		10			5				1	11						6	2	7		15
			8	5				10	4	9					1	11	3					6	2	7		16
3				4				10		9	5	8			1	11						6	2	7		17
3			8	4				10		9	5				1	11						6	2	7		18
3		2	8	4				10		9	5				1	11						6		7		19
3			8	4				10		9	5				1	11						6	2	7		20
3			8	4				10		9	5				1	11						6	2	7		21
3				5		8		10	4	9			2		1	11						6		7		22
3			7	4				10		9	5		2			11		1				6		8		23
3			7	4		9		10			5				1	11						6	2	8		24
3			8	4				10							1	11				5		6	2	7	9	25
	11			4		9	10					8	2	5	1					6			3	7		26
			8	4				10		9	5		2		1	11						6	3	7		27
3			8	4				10		9	5		2		1	11						6		7		28
			8	4				10		9	5		2		1	11						6	3	7		29
	11		8	4		9	10						2		1					5		6	3	7		30
23	2	4	27	29	10	15	3	28	3	14	25	2	7	1	18	27	1	1	1	3	1	29	25	30	1	
			15			5	1	7		6	1					9						3		13		

2 own-goals

Arridge S	Banks H	Barker G	Bell J	Boyle R	Briggs H	Cameron J	Campbell W	Chadwick E	Goldie H	Hartley A	Holt J	Maley W	Meecham P	Meiklejohn G	Menham R	Milward A	Molyneux G	Palmer J	Patrick J	Robertson J	Schofield A	Stewart W	Storrier D	Taylor J	Williams W	
3			8	4				10		9	5				1	11				6			2	7		1
3			8	4				10		9	5		2		1	11						6		7		2
3			8	4				10		9	5		2		1	11						6		7		3
			8	4				10		9	5		2		1	11						6	3	7		SF
			8	4				10		9	5		2		1	11						6	3	7		F
3			5	5				5		5	5		4		5	5				1		4	3	5		
			2	1				2		3	1					3								2		

1 own-goal

1897-98

1	Sep	4	(h)	Bolton W	W 2-1	L.Bell 2
2		11	(a)	Derby C	L 1-5	Divers
3		18	(h)	Wolves	W 3-0	Hartley 3
4		25	(a)	Liverpool	L 1-3	Taylor
5	Oct	2	(h)	Blackburn R	D 1-1	Divers
6		9	(a)	Wolves	W 3-2	L.Bell, Cameron, Divers
7		16	(h)	Liverpool	W 3-0	Williams 2, L.Bell
8		23	(a)	Bury	W 1-0	Divers
9		30	(h)	Sheffield U	L 1-4	L.Bell
10	Nov	6	(a)	West Brom A	D 2-2	Divers, Taylor
11		13	(a)	Aston Villa	L 0-3	
12		20	(a)	Preston NE	D 1-1	Taylor
13		27	(h)	West Brom A	W 6-1	Chadwick 2, Divers 2, J.Bell, L.Bell
14	Dec	11	(h)	Notts C	W 1-0	Divers
15		18	(a)	Sunderland	D 0-0	
16		25	(h)	Aston Villa	W 2-1	Chadwick, Robertson
17	Jan	1	(a)	Blackburn R	D 1-1	Chadwick
18		8	(h)	Sheffield W	W 1-0	Chadwick
19		15	(a)	Notts C	L 2-3	J.Bell, Opp own-goal
20		17	(h)	Stoke C	D 1-1	Cameron
21	Feb	5	(a)	Sheffield W	L 1-2	Cameron
22		22	(a)	Sheffield U	D 0-0	
23	Mar	5	(h)	Bury	W 4-2	J.Bell, L.Bell, Chadwick, Divers
24		12	(a)	Nottingham F	D 2-2	L.Bell 2
25		21	(h)	Preston NE	D 1-1	J.Bell
26		26	(a)	Bolton W	L 0-1	
27	Apr	2	(h)	Nottingham F	W 2-0	L.Bell, Divers
28		8	(h)	Derby C	W 3-0	L.Bell 2, Divers
29		9	(a)	Stoke C	L 0-2	
30		11	(h)	Sunderland	W 2-0	Chadwick 2

FINAL LEAGUE POSITION: 4th in Division One

Appearances
Goals

FA Cup

1	Jan	29	(h)	Blackburn R	W 1-0	Williams
2	Feb	12	(a)	Stoke C	D 0-0	
R		17	(h)	Stoke C	W 5-1	L.Bell 2, Cameron, Chadwick, Taylor
3		26	(a)	Burnley	W 3-1	Taylor 2, L.Bell
SF	Mar	19	(n*)	Derby C	L 1-3	Chadwick

* Played at Molineux.

Appearances
Goals

Balmer W	Barker G	Barlow J	Bell J	Bell L	Boyle R	Cameron J	Chadwick E	Divers J	Gee E	Hartley A	Holt J	Keeley S	McFarlane R	Meecham P	Muir W	Robertson J	Stewart W	Storrier D	Taylor J	Williams W	Wolstenholme S	
			11	9	4	8	10				5		1	2			6	3	7			1
				9	4	8	10	11			5		1	2			6	3	7			2
	3				4	8	10	11		9	5		1	2		6			7			3
	3		11		4	8	10			9	5		1	2		6			7			4
				8	4	10		11		9	5		1	2		6		3	7			5
				9	4	10		11			5		1	2		6		3	7	8		6
				9	4	10		11			5		1	2		6		3	7	8		7
				9	4	10		11			5		1	2		6		3	7	8		8
				9	4	10		11			5		1	2		6		3	7	8		9
3	2		9		4	10		11			5				1	6			7	8		10
	2		9		4	10		11			5				1	6		3	7	8		11
2			8	9	4		10	11			5				1	6		3	7			12
			8	9	4		10	11			5			2	1	6		3	7			13
			8	9	4		10	11			5			2	1	6		3	7			14
			8	9	4		10	11			5			2	1	6		3	7			15
			8	9			10	11			5			2	1	6	4	3	7			16
			8	9			10	11			5			2	1	6	4	3	7			17
			8	9			10	11			5			2	1	6	4	3	7			18
			8	9			10	11			5			2	1	6	4	3	7			19
			8			9	10	11			5			2	1		6	3	7		4	20
2			11	9		8	10				5				1	6		3	4	7		21
2			11			9	10	8			5				1	6	4	3	7			22
2	3		11	9	5		10	8							1	6			4	7		23
2	3		11	9	5		10	8							1	6	4		7			24
2			11	9	4		10	8			5				1	6		3	7			25
2		8	11	9	4		10				5				1	6		3	7			26
2		10		9	4			8	11		5				1			3	6	7		27
2			7	9	5		10	8	11						1	6		3	4			28
2			7				10	8	11		5	9			1	6		3	4			29
2			11	9	4		10	8			5				1	6		3	7			30
12	6	2	22	23	22	14	22	26	3	3	27	1	9	17	21	26	9	25	30	9	1	
			4	12		3	8	11		3						1			3	2		

1 own-goal

Balmer W	Barker G	Barlow J	Bell J	Bell L	Boyle R	Cameron J	Chadwick E	Divers J	Gee E	Hartley A	Holt J	Keeley S	McFarlane R	Meecham P	Muir W	Robertson J	Stewart W	Storrier D	Taylor J	Williams W	Wolstenholme S	
2			11	9		8	10				5				1	6		3	4	7		1
2			11	9		8	10				5				1	6	4	3	7			2
2			11	9		8	10				5				1	6	4	3	7			R
2			11	9			10	8			5				1	6	4	3	7			3
2			11	9			10	8			5				1	6	4	3	7			SF
5			5	5		3	5	2			5				5	5	4	5	5	1		
				3		1	2												3	1		

1898-99

1	Sep	1	(h)	Blackburn R	W 2-1	Clarke, Proudfoot
2		3	(a)	Sheffield U	D 1-1	Proudfoot
3		10	(h)	Newcastle U	W 3-0	Clarke, Owen, Opp own-goal
4		17	(a)	Preston NE	D 0-0	
5		24	(h)	Liverpool	L 1-2	Proudfoot
6	Oct	1	(a)	Nottingham F	D 0-0	
7		8	(h)	Bolton W	W 1-0	Oldham
8		15	(a)	Derby C	D 5-5	Oldham 2, Owen 2, Bell
9		22	(h)	West Brom A	W 1-0	Oldham
10		29	(a)	Blackburn R	W 3-1	Bell, Oldham, Proudfoot
11	Nov	5	(h)	Sheffield W	W 2-0	Bell, Kirwan
12		7	(a)	West Brom A	L 0-3	
13		12	(a)	Sunderland	L 1-2	Bell
14		19	(h)	Wolves	W 2-1	Bell, Kirwan
15		26	(h)	Bury	L 0-1	
16	Dec	3	(a)	Notts C	W 1-0	Proudfoot
17		10	(h)	Stoke C	W 2-0	Chadwick, Oldham
18		17	(a)	Aston Villa	L 0-3	
19		24	(h)	Burnley	W 4-0	Proudfoot 2, Kirwan, Oldham
20		31	(h)	Sheffield U	W 1-0	Proudfoot
21	Jan	2	(h)	Nottingham F	L 1-3	Kirwan
22		7	(a)	Newcastle U	D 2-2	Proudfoot 2
23		14	(h)	Preston NE	W 2-0	Crompton, Kirwan
24		21	(a)	Liverpool	L 0-2	
25	Feb	25	(a)	Bolton W	W 4-2	Oldham 2, Proudfoot, Taylor
26	Mar	4	(a)	Sheffield W	W 2-1	Chadwick, Oldham
27		11	(h)	Sunderland	D 0-0	
28		18	(a)	Bury	L 1-3	Taylor
29	Apr	1	(h)	Notts C	L 1-2	Proudfoot
30		3	(h)	Derby C	L 1-2	Taylor
31		8	(a)	Stoke C	L 1-2	Boyle
32		15	(h)	Aston Villa	D 1-1	Oldham
33		22	(a)	Burnley	D 0-0	
34		29	(a)	Wolves	W 2-1	Schofield, Toman

FINAL LEAGUE POSITION: 4th in Division One

Appearances
Goals

FA Cup

1	Jan	28	(h)	Jarrow	W 3-1	Chadwick, Proudfoot, Taylor
2	Feb	11	(h)	Nottingham F	L 0-1	

Appearances
Goals

Balmer W	Barlow J	Bell L	Blythe J	Boyle R	Chadwick E	Clarke H	Crompton T	Divers J	Eccles G	Gee E	Hughes E	Kirwan J	Kitchen G	Molyneux G	Muir W	Oldham W	Owen W	Proudfoot J	Schofield A	Settle J	Taylor J	Toman W	Turner J	Vaughan A	Wolstenholme S	
2				4	10	7		8		11				3	1		5	9			6					1
2				4	10	7		8		11				3	1		5	9			6					2
2	8			4	10	7				11				3	1		5	9			6					3
2				4	10	7				11		8		3	1		5	9			6					4
2		8		4		7				11		10		3	1		5	9			6					5
2		9		4		7		8				10		3	1		5		11		6					6
2		8		4		7		11				10		3	1	9	5				6					7
2		8		4		7						10		3	1	9	5		11		6					8
2		8		4		7						10		3	1	9	5		11		6					9
2		7		5						11		10		3	1	9		8			6				4	10
2		7		5						11		10		3	1	9		8			6				4	11
2	11	9		5		7						10		3	1			8			6				4	12
2		7		5						11		10		3	1	9		8			6				4	13
2		7		5						11		10		3	1	9		8			6				4	14
2		7		5						11		10		3	1	9		8			6				4	15
2		9		4	10					11	6			3	1		5	8			7					16
2				4	10					11	6			3	1	9	5	8			7					17
2		9		4	10					11	6			3	1		5	8			7					18
2		7		4	10						5	11		3	1	9		8			6					19
		7		4	10						5	11		3	1	9		8			6		2			20
2				4	10	7					5	11		3	1	9		8			6					21
2				4	10		9		3		5	11			1			8	7		6					22
2		7		4	10		9					11	1	3				8			6			5		23
2		7		4	10		9				6	11		3	1			8			5					24
			6	5	10				2			11		3	1	9		8			7				4	25
			6	5	10				2			11		3	1	9		8			7				4	26
			6	5	10				2			11		3	1	9		8			7				4	27
			6	5	10				2			11		3	1	9		8			7				4	28
			6	5	10				2			11		3	1	9		8			7				4	29
			6	5	10				2			11		3	1	9		8			7				4	30
		8	6	5		10			2	11				3	1			9			7				4	31
				5	10					11				3	1	9		8	7		6		2		4	32
				5	10				2	11				3	1				7	8	6	9			4	33
			6	5	10				2	11				3	1		4		7		8	9				34
23	2	18	8	34	22	12	3	4	10	17	8	24	1	33	33	19	13	28	7	1	34	2	2	1	15	
		5		1	2	2	1					5				11	3	12	1		3	1				

1 own-goal

Balmer W	Barlow J	Bell L	Blythe J	Boyle R	Chadwick E	Clarke H	Crompton T	Divers J	Eccles G	Gee E	Hughes E	Kirwan J	Kitchen G	Molyneux G	Muir W	Oldham W	Owen W	Proudfoot J	Schofield A	Settle J	Taylor J	Toman W	Turner J	Vaughan A	Wolstenholme S	
2		7		4	10		9					11		3	1			8			5				6	1
2		9		5	10					11		7		3	1			8			6				4	2
2		2		2	2		1			1		2		2	2			2			2				2	
					1													1			1					

1899-1900

1	Sep	2	(h)	Sheffield U	L 1-2	Settle
2		9	(a)	Newcastle U	L 0-2	
3		16	(h)	Aston Villa	L 1-2	Toman
4		23	(a)	Liverpool	W 2-1	Settle, Taylor
5		30	(h)	Burnley	W 2-0	Toman 2
6	Oct	7	(a)	Preston NE	D 1-1	Settle
7		14	(h)	Nottingham F	W 2-1	J.Sharp, Toman
8		21	(a)	Glossop NE	D 1-1	Toman
9		28	(a)	Stoke C	D 1-1	Taylor
10	Nov	4	(a)	Sunderland	L 0-1	
11		11	(h)	West Brom A	L 1-3	J.Sharp
12		25	(a)	Blackburn R	L 1-3	Settle
13	Dec	2	(h)	Derby C	W 3-0	Settle, J.Sharp, Taylor
14		9	(a)	Bury	L 1-4	Toman
15		16	(h)	Notts C	L 0-2	
16		23	(a)	Manchester C	W 2-1	Gray, Settle
17		25	(h)	Stoke C	W 2-0	Settle, Taylor
18		26	(a)	West Brom A	D 0-0	
19		30	(a)	Sheffield U	L 0-5	
20	Jan	1	(h)	Preston NE	W 1-0	Proudfoot
21		6	(h)	Newcastle U	W 3-2	Proudfoot 2, Settle
22		13	(a)	Aston Villa	D 1-1	Taylor
23		20	(h)	Liverpool	W 3-1	Settle 2, Blythe
24	Feb	3	(a)	Burnley	L 1-3	Proudfoot
25		17	(a)	Nottingham F	L 2-4	Balmer, Proudfoot
26	Mar	10	(h)	Sunderland	W 1-0	Toman
27		17	(a)	Wolves	L 1-2	Taylor
28		24	(h)	Wolves	L 0-1	
29		31	(h)	Blackburn R	D 0-0	
30	Apr	7	(a)	Derby C	L 1-2	J.Sharp
31		14	(h)	Bury	W 2-0	Abbott, Proudfoot
32		16	(h)	Glossop NE	W 4-1	McDonald, Proudfoot, J.Sharp, Taylor
33		21	(a)	Notts C	D 2-2	McDonald, Opp own-goal
34		28	(h)	Manchester C	W 4-0	Turner 2, Proudfoot, Toman

FINAL LEAGUE POSITION: 11th in Division One

Appearances
Goals

FA Cup

1	Jan	27	(a)	Southampton	L 0-3	

Appearances
Goals

Abbott W	Balmer W	Blythe J	Boyle R	Crelley J	Eccles G	Gee E	Gray R	Kitchen G	McDonald A	Molyneux G	Muir W	Oldham W	Proudfoot J	Schofield A	Settle J	Sharp B	Sharp J	Taylor J	Toman W	Turner J	Watson J	Wolstenholme S	
10	2		5			11				3	1				8		7	6	9			4	1
10	2		5			11				3	1				8		7	6	9			4	2
10	2		5			11		1		3			8				7	6	9			4	3
	2	6	5							3	1			11	10		8	7	9			4	4
	3	6	5		2						1			11	8		7	10	9			4	5
	3	6	5		2						1			11	8		7	10	9			4	6
	3	6	5		2	11					1				8		7	10	9			4	7
	3	6	5		2	11					1				8		7	10	9			4	8
	3	6	5		2	11					1				8		7	10	9			4	9
	3	6	5		2	11					1				8		7	10	9			4	10
	3	6	5		2	11					1	9					7	10	8			4	11
	3		5		2	11					1	9	8		10		7	6				4	12
6	3		5				11				1				10	2	8	7	9			4	13
6	3		5				11				1				10	2	8	7	9			4	14
6	3		5				11				1				10	2	8	7	9			4	15
6	3		5		2		11				1		9		10		7	8				4	16
6	3	4	5		2		11				1		9		10		7	8					17
6	3	4	5		2		11				1		9		10		7	8					18
6	3		5		2		11				1		9		10		7	8				4	19
6	3	5			2		11				1		9		10		7	8				4	20
6	3	5			2		11				1		9		10		7	8				4	21
6	3	5			2		11				1		9		10		7	8				4	22
6	3	5			2		11				1		9		10		7	8				4	23
6	2	5					11	1		3			9		10			7	8			4	24
6	2		5				11			3	1		9		10			7	8			4	25
6	2	4	5				11			3	1		9		10			7	8				26
6	2	4	5				11			3	1		9		10			7	8				27
6	2	4	5			11				3	1		9		10			7	8				28
6	2		5	3		11			9		1	10					7		8			4	29
10		6	5		2						1		9				7	11	8		3	4	30
6	3		5		2				10		1		9				7	11	8			4	31
6	3		5		2				10		1		9				7	11	8			4	32
6			5		2				10		1		9				7	11	8		3	4	33
6	2		5						10		1		9				7		8	11	3	4	34
25	32	19	29	1	20	11	15	2	5	9	32	3	20	3	26	3	29	32	25	1	3	29	
1	1	1					1		2				8		10		5	7	8	2			

1 own-goal

Abbott W	Balmer W	Blythe J	Boyle R	Crelley J	Eccles G	Gee E	Gray R	Kitchen G	McDonald A	Molyneux G	Muir W	Oldham W	Proudfoot J	Schofield A	Settle J	Sharp B	Sharp J	Taylor J	Toman W	Turner J	Watson J	Wolstenholme S	
6	3	5			2		11				1		9		10		7	8				4	1
1	1	1			1		1				1		1		1		1	1				1	

1900-01

1	Sep	1	(a)	Preston NE	W 2-1	Proudfoot, Sharp
2		8	(h)	Wolves	W 5-1	Turner 2, McDonald, Proudfoot, Settle
3		15	(a)	Aston Villa	W 2-1	Settle, Turner
4		22	(h)	Liverpool	D 1-1	McDonald
5		29	(a)	Newcastle U	L 0-1	
6	Oct	6	(h)	Sheffield U	W 3-1	Abbott, Proudfoot, Turner
7		13	(a)	Manchester C	L 0-1	
8		27	(a)	Nottingham F	L 1-2	Settle
9	Nov	3	(h)	Blackburn R	D 0-0	
10		10	(a)	Stoke C	W 2-0	McDonald, Taylor
11		17	(h)	West Brom A	W 1-0	Taylor
12		24	(h)	Sheffield W	D 1-1	Proudfoot
13	Dec	1	(a)	Sunderland	L 0-2	
14		8	(h)	Derby C	W 2-0	McDonald, Wolstenholme
15		15	(a)	Bolton W	L 0-1	
16		22	(h)	Notts C	L 0-1	
17		25	(a)	Sheffield U	L 1-2	Settle
18		26	(h)	Bury	D 3-3	Abbott, Proudfoot, Turner
19		29	(h)	Preston NE	W 4-1	Sharp 2, Abbott, Taylor
20	Jan	1	(a)	Bury	L 0-3	
21		5	(a)	Wolves	D 1-1	Taylor
22		12	(h)	Aston Villa	W 2-1	Settle, Wolstenholme
23		19	(a)	Liverpool	W 2-1	Taylor 2
24	Feb	16	(h)	Manchester C	W 5-2	Settle 2, Taylor 2, Sharp
25	Mar	2	(h)	Nottingham F	W 4-1	Proudfoot 2, Abbott, Settle
26		9	(a)	Blackburn R	L 1-2	Turner
27		16	(h)	Stoke C	W 3-0	Proudfoot, Settle, Sharp
28		30	(a)	Sheffield W	L 1-3	Taylor
29	Apr	6	(h)	Sunderland	W 1-0	Sharp
30		8	(h)	Newcastle U	L 0-1	
31		9	(a)	Notts C	L 2-3	Proudfoot, Settle
32		13	(a)	Derby C	W 1-0	Proudfoot
33		20	(h)	Bolton W	L 2-3	Sharp, Taylor
34		22	(a)	West Brom A	W 2-1	Abbott, Taylor

FINAL LEAGUE POSITION: 7th in Division One

Appearances
Goals

FA Cup

1	Feb	9	(a)	Southampton	W 3-1	Settle, Taylor, Turner
2		23	(a)	Sheffield U	L 0-2	

Appearances
Goals

Abbott W	Balmer W	Beveridge R	Blythe J	Booth T	Boyle R	Corrin T	Crelley J	Eccles G	Gray R	McDonald A	Muir W	Proudfoot J	Settle J	Sharp J	Taylor J	Turner J	Watson J	Wolstenholme S	
6	2			5						8	1	9	10	7		11	3	4	1
6	2			5						8	1	9	10	7		11	3	4	2
6	2			5						8	1	9	10	7		11	3	4	3
6	2			5						8	1	9	10	7		11	3	4	4
6	2			5						8	1	9	10	7		11	3	4	5
6	2			5						8	1	9	10	7		11	3	4	6
6	2			5						8	1	9	10	7		11	3	4	7
6	2	9		5						8	1		10	7		11	3	4	8
6	2	9		5						8	1		10	7		11	3	4	9
6	2	9		5						8	1		10		7	11	3	4	10
6	2	9		5						8	1		10		7	11	3	4	11
6				5				2		8	1	9	10		7	11	3	4	12
6	2			5		11			10	8	1	9			7		3	4	13
6	2			5		11			10	8	1	9			7		3	4	14
6	2			5					10	8	1	9			7	11	3	4	15
6	2			5					10	9	1		8		7	11	3	4	16
6	2			5							1	9	10	7	8	11	3	4	17
6	2			5							1	9	10	7	8	11	3	4	18
6	2			5							1	9	10	7	8	11	3	4	19
6	2			5							1	9	10	7	8	11	3	4	20
6	2				5					8	1	9	10		7	11	3	4	21
6	2			5							1	9	10	7	8	11	3	4	22
6				5			3	2			1	9	10	7	8	11		4	23
6	2			5		11		3			1	9	10	7	8			4	24
6	2			5				3			1	9	10	7	8	11		4	25
6	2			5				3			1	9	10	7	8	11		4	26
6	2			5							1	9	10	7	8	11	3	4	27
6	2			5				3	10		1	9		7	8	11		4	28
6	2			5				3			1	9	10	7	8	11		4	29
6	2			5				3			1	9	10	7	8	11		4	30
6			5					2			1	9	10	7	8	11	3	4	31
6	2				5			3		8	1	9	10		7	11		4	32
6	2			5				3			1	9	10	7	8	11		4	33
6	2			5				3			1	9	10	7	8	11		4	34
34	31	4	1	31	2	3	1	12	5	18	34	29	30	25	25	31	24	34	
5										4		10	10	7	11	6		2	

Abbott W	Balmer W	Beveridge R	Blythe J	Booth T	Boyle R	Corrin T	Crelley J	Eccles G	Gray R	McDonald A	Muir W	Proudfoot J	Settle J	Sharp J	Taylor J	Turner J	Watson J	Wolstenholme S	
6	2			5				3			1	9	10	7	8	11		4	1
6	2			5				3			1	9	10	7	8	11		4	2
2	2			2				2			2	2	2	2	2	2		2	
													1		1	1			

1901-02

1	Sep	2	(h)	Manchester C	W 3-1	Bell 2, Toman
2		7	(h)	Wolves	W 6-1	Settle 3, Taylor 3
3		14	(a)	Liverpool	D 2-2	Settle, J.Sharp
4		21	(h)	Newcastle U	D 0-0	
5		28	(a)	Aston Villa	D 1-1	Abbott
6	Oct	5	(h)	Sheffield U	W 2-1	Abbott, Settle
7		12	(a)	Nottingham F	L 0-4	
8		19	(h)	Bury	D 1-1	Settle
9		26	(a)	Blackburn R	L 1-3	Paterson
10	Nov	2	(h)	Stoke C	W 1-0	J.Sharp
11		9	(a)	Grimsby T	W 2-0	Settle 2
12		16	(a)	Sunderland	W 4-2	Settle 2, Abbott, J.Sharp
13		23	(h)	Small Heath	W 1-0	Bell
14		30	(a)	Derby C	L 1-3	Settle
15	Dec	7	(h)	Sheffield W	W 5-0	Settle 2, J.Sharp 2, Young
16		14	(a)	Notts C	W 2-0	Settle, Taylor
17		21	(h)	Bolton W	W 1-0	Settle
18		25	(h)	Aston Villa	L 2-3	Taylor 2
19		26	(a)	Wolves	L 1-2	Bell
20	Jan	11	(h)	Liverpool	W 4-0	Settle 2, Bell, Young
21		18	(a)	Newcastle U	D 1-1	Young
22	Feb	1	(a)	Sheffield U	D 0-0	
23		15	(a)	Bury	L 0-1	
24		22	(h)	Blackburn R	L 0-2	
25	Mar	1	(a)	Stoke C	W 2-1	Abbott, Booth
26		8	(h)	Grimsby T	L 0-1	
27		15	(h)	Sunderland	W 2-0	Taylor, Young
28		17	(a)	Manchester C	L 0-2	
29		22	(a)	Small Heath	W 1-0	Taylor
30		29	(h)	Derby C	W 2-0	Settle, Young
31		31	(h)	Nottingham F	W 1-0	J.Sharp
32	Apr	5	(a)	Sheffield W	D 1-1	Bowman
33		12	(h)	Notts C	L 0-1	
34		19	(a)	Bolton W	W 3-1	Wolstenholme, Young, Opp own-goal

FINAL LEAGUE POSITION: 2nd in Division One

Appearances

Goals

FA Cup

1	Jan	25	(a)	Liverpool	D 2-2	J.Sharp, Young
R		30	(h)	Liverpool	L 0-2	

Appearances

Goals

Abbott W	Balmer W	Bell J	Blythe J	Bone J	Booth T	Bowman A	Boyle D	Chadwick T	Clark C	Eccles G	Kitchen G	Muir W	Paterson	Proudfoot J	Rankin G	Roche	Settle J	Sharp B	Sharp J	Singleton B	Taylor J	Toman W	Watson J	Wolstenholme S	Young A	
6	2	11			5		4					1					10		7		8	9	3			1
6	2	11			5		4					1					10		7		8	9	3			2
6	2	11			5		4					1		9			10		7		8		3			3
6	2	11			5		4					1		9			10		7		8		3			4
6	2	11			5							1				7	10				8		3	4	9	5
6	2	11			5							1	8				10				7		3	4	9	6
6	2				5							1	8				10		7		11		3	4	9	7
10	2		6		5						1		8				11		7				3	4	9	8
6	2	11			5						1		8				10		7				3	4	9	9
6	2	11			5				4		1		8				10		7				3		9	10
	2	11	6		5				4	3	1			8			10		7						9	11
6	2	11			5					3	1			8			10		7					4	9	12
6	2	11			5					3	1			8			10		7					4	9	13
6	2	11			5					3	1						10		7		8			4	9	14
6	2	11			5					3	1						10		7		8			4	9	15
6	2	11			5					3	1						10		7		8			4	9	16
6	2	11			5					3	1						10		7		8			4	9	17
6	2	11			5					3	1						10		7		8			4	9	18
6	2	11			5						1						10		7		8		3	4	9	19
6	2	11			5						1						10	3	7		8			4	9	20
	2	11	6		5					3	1						10		7		8			4	9	21
6	2				5						1			10	8			3	7	11				4	9	22
6	2	11			5						1			8			10	3	7					4	9	23
6	2			10	5			11			1							3	7		8			4	9	24
6	2	11			5						1						10	3	7		8			4	9	25
6	2			10	5				4		1							3	7	11	8				9	26
6	2	11			5					3	1						10		7		8			4	9	27
6					5					2	1						10		7	11	8		3	4	9	28
10	2		6		5	11				3	1								7		8			4	9	29
			6		5	11				2	1						10		7		8		3	4	9	30
6					5	11	2				1						10		7		8		3	4	9	31
10			6		5	11	2				1								7		8		3	4	9	32
6		11			5		2				1						10		7		8		3	4	9	33
6		11			5					2	1						10		7		8		3	4	9	34
31	28	24	6	2	34	4	7	1	3	14	27	7	5	7	1	1	29	6	32	3	26	2	17	27	30	
4		5			1	1							1				18		6		8	1		1	6	

1 own-goal

6	2	11			5	10				3	1								7		8			4	9	1
6	2	11			5	10					1							3	7		8			4	9	R
2	2	2			2	2				1	2							1	2		2			2	2	
																			1						1	

1902-03

1	Sep	1	(a)	West Brom A	L 1-2	Young
2		6	(a)	Middlesbrough	L 0-1	
3		13	(h)	Newcastle U	L 0-1	
4		20	(a)	Wolves	D 1-1	Rankin
5		27	(h)	Liverpool	W 3-1	Abbott, Brearley, Young
6	Oct	2	(a)	Nottingham F	D 2-2	Sharp 2
7		4	(a)	Sheffield U	W 2-0	Abbott, Booth
8		11	(h)	Grimsby T	W 4-2	Bowman 2, Abbott, Brearley
9		18	(a)	Aston Villa	L 1-2	Bell
10		25	(h)	Nottingham F	D 1-1	Young
11	Nov	1	(a)	Bolton W	W 3-1	Bell 2, Sharp
12		8	(a)	Blackburn R	L 2-3	Bell, Brearley
13		15	(a)	Sunderland	L 1-2	Young
14		22	(h)	Stoke C	L 0-1	
15		29	(h)	Derby C	W 2-1	Bell, Settle
16	Dec	6	(a)	Sheffield W	L 1-4	Settle
17		13	(h)	West Brom A	W 3-1	Brearley, Settle, Wolstenholme
18		20	(a)	Notts C	L 0-2	
19		25	(a)	Grimsby T	D 0-0	
20		27	(h)	Bolton W	W 3-1	Sheridan 2, Sharp
21	Jan	1	(a)	Bury	L 2-4	Taylor 2
22		3	(h)	Middlesbrough	W 3-0	Brearley 3
23		17	(h)	Wolves	W 2-1	Abbott, Settle
24		31	(h)	Sheffield U	W 1-0	Rankin
25	Feb	14	(h)	Aston Villa	L 0-1	
26		28	(h)	Bury	W 3-0	Sharp 2, Clark
27	Mar	14	(h)	Sunderland	L 0-3	
28		21	(a)	Stoke C	L 0-2	
29		28	(a)	Derby C	W 1-0	Booth
30	Apr	1	(a)	Newcastle U	L 0-3	
31		4	(h)	Sheffield W	D 1-1	Settle
32		10	(a)	Liverpool	D 0-0	
33		13	(h)	Blackburn R	L 0-3	
34		18	(h)	Notts C	W 2-0	Taylor, Young

FINAL LEAGUE POSITION: 12th in Division One

Appearances
Goals

FA Cup

1	Feb	7	(h)	Portsmouth	W 5-0	Bell 2, Abbott, Brearley, Sharp
2		21	(h)	Manchester U	W 3-1	Abbott, Booth, Taylor
3	Mar	7	(a)	Millwall	L 0-1	

Appearances
Goals

Abbott W	Balmer R	Balmer W	Bell J	Booth T	Bowman A	Brearley J	Clark C	Crelley J	Dilly T	Henderson W	Kitchen G	Lee J	Makepeace H	Rankin G	Russell J	Settle J	Sharp J	Sheridan J	Taylor J	Whitley J	Wolstenholme S	Young A	
6		2	11	5		8					1	3				10	7		4			9	1
6		2	11	5		8					1	3				10	7		4			9	2
6		3	11	5		8				2	1					10	7		4			9	3
6			11	5		8		3		2	1			7				10	4			9	4
6		3	11	5		8				2	1						7	10	4			9	5
6		2	11	5		8					1						7	10	4		3	9	6
6		3	11	5		8					1					10	7		4		2	9	7
6		3	11		9	8	5				1						7	10	4		2		8
6		3	11	5	9	8					1						7	10	4		2		9
6		3	11	5		8					1						7	10	4		2	9	10
6		3	11			8		2			1				5		7	10	4			9	11
6		2	11	5		8		3			1						7	10	4			9	12
6		2	10	5		8		3	11		1			7					4			9	13
6		2	11	5		8				3	1			7				10	4			9	14
6		2	11	5		9		3			1					10	7	8	4				15
6		2		5	9			3	11		1					10	7	8	4				16
6		2		5		9		3			1			11		10	7		8		4		17
6		2		5		9		3			1			11		10	7		8		4		18
6				5		9		3		2				11		10	7	8		1	4		19
6				5		9		3						11		10	7	8	4	1	2		20
6		3		5		9				2				11			7	10	8	1	4		21
6	3	2	11	5		9										10	7		8	1	4		22
6		3		5					11	2						9	7	10	8	1	4		23
6		3		5	9					2				11		10	7		8	1	4		24
6		3	11	5	10	9		2						7					8	1	4		25
6		3	11	5			4			2	1		10				7		8			9	26
			11				5	3		2			6			9	7	10	8	1	4		27
6			11	5				3		2	1		9	7		10			8		4		28
6		2		5				3	11		1					10	7		8		4	9	29
6		2						3	11		1			7	5	10			8		4	9	30
6		2							11	3	1			7	5	10			8		4	9	31
6		2	11	5				3			1					10	7		8		4	9	32
6			11	5				3		2	1					10	7		8		4	9	33
6		2	11	5				3			1						7	10	8		4	9	34
33	1	28	23	29	5	22	3	18	6	13	26	2	3	13	3	20	27	17	33	8	22	19	
4			5	2	2	7	1							2		5	6	2	3		1	5	

Abbott W	Balmer R	Balmer W	Bell J	Booth T	Bowman A	Brearley J	Clark C	Crelley J	Dilly T	Henderson W	Kitchen G	Lee J	Makepeace H	Rankin G	Russell J	Settle J	Sharp J	Sheridan J	Taylor J	Whitley J	Wolstenholme S	Young A	
6		3	11	5		9				2						10	7		8	1	4		1
6		2	11	5		9		3					10	7					8	1	4		2
6		3	11	5			4			2						8	7		9	1		10	3
3		3	3	3		2	1	1		2			1	1		2	2		3	3	2	1	
2			2	1		1											1		1				

1903-04

1	Sep	1	(h)	Blackburn R	W 3-1	Hardman, Sharp, Young
2		5	(h)	Notts C	W 3-1	McDermott, Settle, Sharp
3		12	(a)	Sheffield U	L 1-2	Young
4		19	(h)	Newcastle U	W 4-1	Booth, Hardman, Settle, Young
5		26	(a)	Aston Villa	L 1-3	Settle
6	Oct	3	(h)	Middlesbrough	W 2-0	Sharp, Wolstenholme
7		10	(a)	Liverpool	D 2-2	Sheridan 2
8		17	(h)	Bury	W 2-1	McDermott, Wolstenholme
9		24	(a)	Blackburn R	W 2-0	Booth, Wolstenholme
10		31	(h)	Nottingham F	L 0-2	
11	Nov	7	(a)	Sheffield W	L 0-1	
12		14	(h)	Sunderland	L 0-1	
13		21	(a)	West Brom A	D 0-0	
14		28	(h)	Small Heath	W 5-1	Abbott, Booth, Sharp, Taylor, Young
15	Dec	5	(a)	Wolves	D 2-2	McDermott 2
16		12	(a)	Stoke C	W 3-2	Taylor 2, Corrin
17		19	(h)	Derby C	L 0-1	
18		26	(a)	Manchester C	W 3-1	McDermott, Settle, Taylor
19	Jan	2	(a)	Notts C	W 3-0	Booth, McDermott, Sharp
20		9	(h)	Sheffield U	W 2-0	Abbott, Settle
21		16	(a)	Newcastle U	L 0-1	
22		23	(h)	Aston Villa	W 1-0	Settle
23		30	(a)	Middlesbrough	L 0-3	
24	Feb	13	(a)	Bury	D 0-0	
25		27	(a)	Nottingham F	W 4-0	Sharp 2, Rankin, Taylor
26	Mar	12	(a)	Sunderland	L 0-2	
27		26	(a)	Small Heath	D 1-1	McDermott
28	Apr	1	(h)	Liverpool	W 5-2	Young 4, Wolstenholme
29		2	(h)	Wolves	W 2-0	Hardman, Settle
30		4	(h)	Sheffield W	W 2-0	Hardman 2
31		9	(h)	Stoke C	L 0-1	
32		16	(a)	Derby C	W 1-0	Abbott
33		18	(h)	West Brom A	W 4-0	Abbott, Rankin, Settle, Young
34		25	(h)	Manchester C	W 1-0	Taylor

FINAL LEAGUE POSITION: 3rd in Division One

Appearances
Goals

FA Cup

1	Feb	6	(h)	Tottenham H	L 1-2	Taylor

Appearances
Goals

Abbott W	Balmer R	Balmer W	Booth T	Corrin T	Crelley J	Hardman H	Henderson W	Kitchen G	McDermott T	Murray D	Rankin G	Settle J	Sharp J	Sheridan J	Simpson T	Taylor J	Whitley J	Wolstenholme S	Young A	
6		2	5		3	11		1	8			10	7					4	9	1
6		2	5		3	11		1	8			10	7					4	9	2
6		2	5		3	11		1	8			10	7					4	9	3
6		2	5		3	11		1	8			10	7					4	9	4
6		2	5		3	11		1	8			10	7					4	9	5
6			5		3	11	2	1	8			10	7					4	9	6
6			5		3	11	2	1	8					10		7		4	9	7
6		2	5		3	11		1	8			10	7					4	9	8
6		2	5		3	11		1	8			10	7					4	9	9
6		2	5		3	11		1	8			10	7					4	9	10
6		2	5			11		1	8	3		10	7					4	9	11
6		2	5	9		11		1	8	3			7	10				4		12
6		2	5		3	11		1	8			10	7					4	9	13
6		2	5	11	3			1				10	7			8		4	9	14
6		2	5	11	3			1	10			9	7			8		4		15
6		2	5	11	3			1	10			9	7			8		4		16
		2	5	11	3			1	8			9	7	10		6		4		17
6		2	5	11	3			1	10			9	7			8		4		18
6		2	5	11	3			1	10				7			8		4	9	19
6	2	3	5	11				1	10			9	7			8		4		20
6		2	5		3			1	10			9	7		11	8		4		21
6		2	5		3	11		1	10			9	7			8		4		22
6		2	5		3	11		1	10			9	7			8		4		23
6		2	5		3	11		1	10			9	7			8		4		24
6		2	5		3	11		1			10		7			8		4	9	25
6		2	5		3	11		1	8			10	7			4			9	26
6		2	5		3	11		1	10			9	7			8		4		27
6		2	5		3	11		1	10				7			8		4	9	28
6		2	5		3	11		1	10			9	7			8		4		29
	2	3	5			11		1	8			10	7			6		4	9	30
6		2	5		3	11		1	8			10	7			4			9	31
6		2	5		3	11					7	10				8	1	4	9	32
6		2	5		3	11					7	10				8	1	4	9	33
6	2	3	5			11						10	7			8	1	4	9	34
32	3	32	34	8	29	26	2	31	29	2	3	29	31	3	1	22	3	32	22	
4			4	1		5			7		2	8	6	2		6		4	10	

Abbott W	Balmer R	Balmer W	Booth T	Corrin T	Crelley J	Hardman H	Henderson W	Kitchen G	McDermott T	Murray D	Rankin G	Settle J	Sharp J	Sheridan J	Simpson T	Taylor J	Whitley J	Wolstenholme S	Young A	
6		2	5	11	3			1	10			9	7			8		4		1
1		1	1	1	1			1	1			1	1			1		1		

1904-05

1	Sep	3	(a)	Notts C	W 2-1	McDermott, Settle
2		10	(h)	Sheffield U	W 2-0	Hardman, Young
3		12	(a)	Aston Villa	L 0-1	
4		17	(a)	Newcastle U	L 2-3	Hardman, Settle
5		24	(h)	Preston NE	W 1-0	McDermott
6	Oct	1	(a)	Middlesbrough	L 0-1	
7		8	(h)	Wolves	W 2-1	Sharp, Young
8		15	(a)	Bury	W 2-1	McDermott, Young
9		22	(h)	Aston Villa	W 3-2	Abbott, Hardman, McDermott
10		29	(a)	Blackburn R	L 0-1	
11	Nov	5	(h)	Nottingham F	W 5-1	Young 4, Taylor
12		12	(a)	Sheffield W	D 5-5	Settle 2, Abbott, Hardman, Young
13		19	(h)	Sunderland	L 0-1	
14	Dec	3	(h)	Derby C	D 0-0	
15		10	(h)	Stoke C	W 4-1	Sharp 2, Abbott, Young
16		17	(a)	Small Heath	W 2-1	Makepeace, Taylor
17		24	(h)	Manchester C	D 0-0	
18		26	(a)	Wolves	W 3-0	McDermott, Settle, Young
19		27	(a)	Derby C	W 2-1	Hardman, McLaughlin
20		31	(h)	Notts C	W 5-1	Abbott, Hardman, McLaughlin, Sharp, Taylor
21	Jan	7	(a)	Sheffield U	L 0-1	
22		14	(h)	Newcastle U	W 2-1	Rankin, Settle
23		21	(a)	Preston NE	D 1-1	McDermott
24		28	(h)	Middlesbrough	W 1-0	Makespeace
25	Feb	11	(h)	Bury	W 2-0	Hardman, Settle
26		25	(h)	Blackburn R	W 1-0	Sharp
27	Mar	11	(h)	Sheffield W	W 5-2	Young 2, Makepeace, Sharp, Taylor
28		18	(a)	Sunderland	W 3-2	Sharp 2, McDermott
29	Apr	5	(h)	Woolwich Arsenal	W 1-0	Young
30		8	(a)	Stoke C	D 2-2	Hardman, Makepeace
31		15	(h)	Small Heath	W 2-1	Makepeace, Young
32		21	(a)	Manchester C	L 0-2	
33		22	(a)	Woolwich Arsenal	L 1-2	Settle
34		24	(a)	Nottingham F	W 2-0	McLaughlin, Settle

FINAL LEAGUE POSITION: 2nd in Division One

Appearances
Goals

FA Cup

1	Feb	2	(a)	Liverpool	D 1-1	Makepeace
R		8	(h)	Liverpool	W 2-1	Hardman, McDermott
2		18	(a)	Stoke C	W 4-0	McDermott 2, Makepeace, Settle
3	Mar	3	(h)	Southampton	W 4-0	Settle 3, McDermott
SF		25	(n*)	Aston Villa	D 1-1	Sharp
R		29	(n†)	Aston Villa	L 1-2	Sharp

* Played at Victoria Ground, Stoke. † Played at Trent Bridge, Nottingham.

Appearances
Goals

Abbott W	Ashworth S	Balmer R	Balmer W	Booth T	Chadwick T	Crelley J	Dilly T	Hardman H	McDermott T	McLaughlin W	Makepeace H	Rankin G	Roose L	Scott W	Settle J	Sharp J	Taylor J	Wildman W	Young A	
6			2	5		3		11	8					1	10	7	4		9	1
6			2		5	3		11	8					1	10	7	4		9	2
			2		5	3	11		8		6			1	10	7	4		9	3
			2		5	3		11	8		6	7		1	10		4		9	4
			2	5		3		11	8		6	7		1	10		4		9	5
	4		2			3		11	8		6	7		1	10		5		9	6
	4		2			3		11	8		6			1	10	7	5		9	7
6			2			3		11	8		4	7		1	10		5		9	8
6	4		2			3		11	8			7		1	10		5		9	9
	4		2			3		11	8		6	7		1	10		5		9	10
6	4		2			3		11	8					1	10	7	5		9	11
6	4		2			3		11	8					1	10	7	5		9	12
6	4		2			3		11	8				1		10	7	5		9	13
6	4		2			3		11	8				1		10	7	5		9	14
6			2			3		11		8	4		1		10	7	5		9	15
6			2			3		11		8	4		1		10	7	5		9	16
6			2			3		11		8	4			1	10	7	5		9	17
6	4		2			3		11	8				1		10	7	5		9	18
6			2			3		11	8	9	4	7		1	10		5			19
6	4	3	2					11	8	10			1			7	5		9	20
6			2	4		3		11	8			7	1		10		5		9	21
6		3	2	4				11	8			7	1		10		5		9	22
6	4	3	2					11	9			8	1		10	7	5			23
6		3						11	8		4	7	1		10		5	2	9	24
6		3	2					11			4	8	1		10	7	5		9	25
6		2				3		11	8	10	4		1			7	5		9	26
6		2				3			8		4	11	1		10	7	5		9	27
6		2				3		11	8		4		1		10	7	5		9	28
6			2			3		11	8		4	7	1		10		5		9	29
6		3	2					11	8		4	7		1	10		5		9	30
6		3	2	5				11			4	7	1		10		8		9	31
6			2	4		3		11	8				1		10	7	5		9	32
6			2	4		3		11	8				1		10	7	5		9	33
6		3	2	4				11	8	10				1	9	7	5			34
28	11	11	30	8	3	26	1	32	29	7	19	16	18	16	32	21	34	1	31	
4								8	7	3	5	1			9	8	4		14	

Abbott W	Ashworth S	Balmer R	Balmer W	Booth T	Chadwick T	Crelley J	Dilly T	Hardman H	McDermott T	McLaughlin W	Makepeace H	Rankin G	Roose L	Scott W	Settle J	Sharp J	Taylor J	Wildman W	Young A	
6		2				3		11	8		4		1		10	7	5		9	1
6		2				3		11	8		4		1		10	7	5		9	R
6		2				3		11	8		4		1		10	7	5		9	2
6			2			3		11	8		4		1		10	7	5		9	3
6			2			3		11	8		4		1		10	7	5		9	SF
6			2			3		11	8		4		1		10	7	5		9	R
6		3	3			6		6	6		6		6		6	6	6		6	
								1	4		2				4	2				

1905-06

1	Sep	2	(h)	Middlesbrough	W 4-1	Settle 2, Rankin, Young
2		9	(a)	Preston NE	D 1-1	Opp own-goal
3		16	(h)	Newcastle U	L 1-2	Sharp
4		23	(a)	Aston Villa	L 0-4	
5		30	(h)	Liverpool	W 4-2	Abbott, Hardman, Settle, Sharp
6	Oct	7	(a)	Sheffield U	L 2-3	McDermott, Young
7		14	(h)	Notts C	W 6-2	Oliver 3, Abbott, Hardman, Settle
8		21	(a)	Stoke C	D 2-2	Hardman, Oliver
9		28	(h)	Bolton W	W 3-1	Settle 2, Taylor
10	Nov	4	(a)	Woolwich Arsenal	W 2-1	Settle, Young
11		11	(h)	Blackburn R	W 3-2	Abbott, Rankin, Settle
12		18	(a)	Sunderland	L 1-2	Settle
13		25	(h)	Birmingham	L 1-2	Hardman
14	Dec	2	(a)	Wolves	W 5-2	Young 2, Hardman, McLaughlin, Makepeace
15		9	(a)	Derby C	D 0-0	
16		16	(h)	Sheffield W	W 2-0	Settle, Sharp
17		23	(a)	Nottingham F	L 3-4	Abbott, Makepeace, Young
18		25	(a)	Bury	L 2-3	Sharp, Young
19		26	(h)	Bury	L 1-2	McLaughlin
20		30	(a)	Middlesbrough	D 0-0	
21	Jan	1	(a)	Manchester C	L 0-1	
22		6	(h)	Preston NE	W 1-0	Hardman
23		20	(a)	Newcastle U	L 2-4	Dilly 2
24		27	(h)	Aston Villa	W 4-2	Sharp 2, Settle, Taylor
25	Feb	10	(h)	Sheffield U	W 3-2	Sharp 3
26		17	(a)	Notts C	D 0-0	
27	Mar	3	(a)	Bolton W	L 2-3	Cook, Taylor
28		17	(a)	Blackburn R	W 2-1	Bolton, Cook
29		21	(h)	Woolwich Arsenal	L 0-1	
30		24	(h)	Sunderland	W 3-1	Young 2, Abbott
31	Apr	3	(h)	Stoke C	L 0-3	
32		7	(h)	Wolves	D 2-2	Bolton, Young
33		9	(a)	Birmingham	L 0-1	
34		13	(a)	Liverpool	D 1-1	Taylor
35		14	(h)	Derby C	W 2-1	Cook, Jones
36		16	(h)	Manchester C	L 0-3	
37		23	(a)	Sheffield W	L 1-3	Bolton
38		28	(h)	Nottingham F	W 4-1	Bolton 2, Young 2

FINAL LEAGUE POSITION: 11th in Division One

Appearances
Goals

FA Cup

1	Jan	13	(h)	West Brom A	W 3-1	Hardman, Makepeace, Sharp
2	Feb	3	(h*)	Chesterfield	W 3-0	Settle, Taylor, Young
3		24	(h)	Bradford C	W 1-0	Makepeace
4	Mar	10	(h)	Sheffield W	W 4-3	Bolton, Booth, Sharp, Taylor
SF		31	(n‡)	Liverpool	W 2-0	Abbott, Hardman
F	Apr	21	(n†)	Newcastle U	W 1-0	Young

*Chesterfield were drawn at home but agreed to the match being played at Goodison Park.
‡ Played at Villa Park. †Played at Crystal Palace.

Appearances
Goals

Abbott W	Balmer R	Balmer W	Birnie A	Black W	Bolton H	Booth T	Chadwick T	Collins H	Cook H	Crelley J	Dilly T	Donaldson J	Donnachie J	Grundy H	Hannan J	Hardman H	Hill P	Jones T	McDermott T	McLaughlin W	Makepeace H	Oliver F	Rankin G	Scott W	Settle J	Sharp J	Taylor J	Wildman W	Wright R	Young A	
6	2									3						11			8		4		7	1	10		5			9	1
6		2								3						11			8	10	4			1		7	5			9	2
6		2		4						3						11			8					1	10	7	5			9	3
		2		6						3						11					4		8	1	10	7	5			9	4
6	2									3						11			8		4			1	10	7	5			9	5
6	2									3						11			8		4			1	10	7	5			9	6
6	2					4		1		3						11			8			9			10	7	5				7
6	2					5				3						11					4	9		1	10	7	8				8
6	2	3				5										11					4	9		1	10	7	8				9
6	2									3						11				8	4			1	10	7	5			9	10
6	2									3						11				8	4		7	1	10		5			9	11
6		2								3											4	9	11	1	10	7	5			8	12
6	2					5				3						11					4			1	10	7	8			9	13
6	3					5										11	2			10	8			1		7	4			9	14
6	2					5				3						11					8			1	10	7	4			9	15
6	2					5										11					8			1	10	7	4	3		9	16
6	2					5				3						11					8			1	10	7	4			9	17
	2			6		5				3						11					8			1	10	7	4			9	18
9		2	7	6		5									3	11				10				1			4			8	19
	3	2		6		5								11							8			1	10	7	4			9	20
		3		6		5										11	2				8			1	10	7	4			9	21
6		3				5					9					11	2				8			1	10	7	4				22
6		3			8						9			11			2			10	4			1		7	5				23
		3		4	8											11	2				6			1	10	7	5			9	24
		3			8							6				11	2				4			1	10	7	5			9	25
6		2			8					3			7			11					4			1	10		5			9	26
			7		8	4			10	3			11				2				6			1			5		9		27
		2		4	8				10	3						11					6			1		7	5			9	28
	3					4			8				7			11	2				6			1	10		5			9	29
6		2			8	4				3			11											1	10	7	5			9	30
6	2				8	4				3			7			11								1	10		5			9	31
6	3			4	8		5									11	2							1	10	7				9	32
				4			6	1	10	3			11				2			8						7	5			9	33
6	3	2		4	8				10							11								1		7	5			9	34
6				4	8		5		10	3			7			11	2	9						1							35
		3	7				4	1	10			6	11				2	9		8							5				36
6	3			4	8											11	2							1	10	7	5			9	37
6		2			8					3						11					4			1	10	7	5			9	38
27	20	18	3	13	13	17	4	3	7	23	2	2	8	2	1	31	13	2	6	8	27	4	4	35	28	29	36	1	1	30	
5					5				3		2					6		1	1	2	2	4	2		11	9	4			12	

1 own-goal

Abbott W	Balmer R	Balmer W	Birnie A	Black W	Bolton H	Booth T	Chadwick T	Collins H	Cook H	Crelley J	Dilly T	Donaldson J	Donnachie J	Grundy H	Hannan J	Hardman H	Hill P	Jones T	McDermott T	McLaughlin W	Makepeace H	Oliver F	Rankin G	Scott W	Settle J	Sharp J	Taylor J	Wildman W	Wright R	Young A	
6		3				5										11	2				4			1	10	7	8			9	1
6		3							8							11	2				4			1	10	7	5			9	2
6		2			8				10	3						11					4	9		1		7	5				3
	2	3			8	4										11					6			1	10	7	5			9	4
6	2				8					3						11					4			1	10	7	5			9	SF
6		2			8					3						11					4			1	10	7	5			9	F
5	2	5			4	2			2	3						6	2				6	1		6	5	6	6			5	
1					1	1										2					2				1	2	2			2	

1906-07

1	Sep	1	(a)	Middlesbrough	D 2-2	Bolton, Young
2		3	(h)	Manchester C	W 9-1	Young 4, Settle 2, Abbott, Bolton, Taylor
3		8	(h)	Preston NE	W 1-0	Hardman
4		15	(a)	Newcastle U	L 0-1	
5		17	(h)	Notts C	D 2-2	Abbott, Young
6		22	(h)	Aston Villa	L 1-2	Abbott
7		29	(a)	Liverpool	W 2-1	Young 2
8	Oct	6	(h)	Bristol C	W 2-0	Bolton, Sharp
9		13	(a)	Notts C	W 1-0	Young
10		20	(h)	Sheffield U	W 4-2	Young 2, Bolton, G.Wilson
11		27	(a)	Bolton W	W 3-1	Bolton, Sharp, Young
12	Nov	3	(h)	Manchester U	W 3-0	Settle, G.Wilson, Young
13		10	(a)	Stoke C	L 0-2	
14		17	(h)	Blackburn R	W 2-0	Settle, Young
15		24	(a)	Sunderland	L 0-1	
16	Dec	1	(h)	Birmingham	W 3-0	Young 2, Sharp
17		8	(h)	Derby C	W 2-0	Bolton, G.Wilson
18		15	(a)	Woolwich Arsenal	L 1-3	Sharp
19		22	(h)	Sheffield W	W 2-0	Sharp, Young
20		25	(a)	Bury	W 2-1	Sharp, Young
21		26	(a)	Manchester C	L 1-3	Bolton
22		29	(h)	Middlesbrough	W 5-1	Bolton 3, Hardman, Young
23	Jan	1	(h)	Bury	W 1-0	Young
24		5	(a)	Preston NE	D 1-1	Young
25		19	(h)	Newcastle U	W 3-0	Young 2, Sharp
26		26	(a)	Aston Villa	L 1-2	Bolton
27	Feb	9	(a)	Bristol C	L 1-2	Young
28	Mar	2	(h)	Bolton W	W 1-0	Hardman
29		4	(a)	Sheffield U	L 1-4	Rouse
30		16	(h)	Stoke C	W 3-0	Abbott, Bolton, Young
31		29	(h)	Liverpool	D 0-0	
32		30	(h)	Sunderland	W 4-1	Jones 2, Bolton, Settle
33	Apr	6	(a)	Birmingham	L 0-1	
34		8	(a)	Blackburn R	L 1-2	Settle
35		10	(h)	Woolwich Arsenal	W 2-1	Young 2
36		13	(a)	Derby C	L 2-5	Booth, Couper
37		22	(a)	Manchester U	L 0-3	
38		27	(a)	Sheffield W	D 1-1	Young

FINAL LEAGUE POSITION: 3rd in Division One

Appearances
Goals

FA Cup

1	Jan	12	(h)	Sheffield U	W 1-0	Opp own-goal
2	Feb	2	(a)	West Ham U	W 2-1	Settle, Sharp
3		23	(h)	Bolton W	D 0-0	
R		27	(a)	Bolton W	W 3-0	Abbott, Settle, Taylor
4	Mar	9	(a)	Crystal P	D 1-1	Taylor
R		13	(h)	Crystal P	W 4-0	Settle 2, Hardman, Young
SF		25	(n*)	West Brom A	W 2-1	Sharp, G.Wilson
F	Apr	20	(n†)	Sheffield W	L 1-2	Sharp

* Played at Burnden Park. † Played at the Crystal Palace.

Appearances
Goals

Abbott W	Balmer R	Balmer W	Black W	Bolton H	Booth T	Chadwick T	Couper G	Crelley J	Depledge R	Donnachie J	Graham R	Hardman H	Hill P	Jones T	Makepeace H	Rouse F	Scott W	Settle J	Sharp J	Sloan D	Strettle S	Taylor J	Wilson D	Wilson G	Young A	
6		2		8				3				11			4		1	10	7			5			9	1
6		2		8	4			3									1	10	7			5		11	9	2
6		3		8	4					7		11	2				1	10				5			9	3
6		2		8				3							4		1		7			5	10	11	9	4
6		2		8	4			3									1		7			5	10	11	9	5
6		2		8				3							4		1		7			5	10	11	9	6
6		2		8				3				11			4		1		7			5		10	9	7
6		2		8				3				11			4		1		7			5		10	9	8
6		2		8				3		7					4		1					5	10	11	9	9
	3	2		8	4							11			6		1		7			5		10	9	10
6	3	2		8	4												1	10	7			5		11	9	11
6	3	2		8	4												1	10	7			5		11	9	12
6		2		8	4			3				11					1	10	7			5			9	13
6	3	2	4	8								11				7	1	10				5			9	14
6	3	2	4													8	1	10	7			5		11	9	15
6	3	2		8											4		1	10	7			5		11	9	16
6	3	2		8								11			4		1		7			5		10	9	17
6	3	2													4	8	1	10	7			5		11	9	18
6	3	2		8								11			4		1		7			5		10	9	19
6	3	2		8											4		1	10	7			5		11	9	20
	3	2	6	8								11			4		1		7			5		10	9	21
	3	2		8	4	6				7		11					1					5		10	9	22
		2		8	4	6		3		7		11					1					5		10	9	23
	3	2		8	4	6				7							1	10				5		11	9	24
6	3	2		8								11			4		1		7			5		10	9	25
6	3	2		8								11			4		1		7			5		10	9	26
6	3	2	4		5					11						10	1	8	7						9	27
	3					6				7	8	11			4	9	1				2	5		10		28
		3				6				11	8				4	9	1		7		2	5		10		29
6	3	2		8					1	7		11			4			10				5			9	30
6	3	2										11			4		1	8	7			5		10	9	31
	3	2		8	5	6				7				9	4		1	10						11		32
6	2			8				3		11					4		1	10	7			5			9	33
	2			8	5	6	7	3		11				9	4			10		1						34
	2	3	4	8		6	7					11								1		5		10	9	35
6		2	4		5		9	3									1	8	7				11	10		36
	2			8		6		3				11			4		1	10	7			5			9	37
	2		4	8		6		3		11							1	10	7			5			9	38
26	25	33	7	31	14	10	3	15	1	13	2	19	1	2	23	6	35	21	27	2	2	34	5	28	33	
4				13	1		1					3		2		1		6	7			1		3	28	

Abbott W	Balmer R	Balmer W	Black W	Bolton H	Booth T	Chadwick T	Couper G	Crelley J	Depledge R	Donnachie J	Graham R	Hardman H	Hill P	Jones T	Makepeace H	Rouse F	Scott W	Settle J	Sharp J	Sloan D	Strettle S	Taylor J	Wilson D	Wilson G	Young A	
	3	2		8		6				7					4		1	10				5		11	9	1
6	3	2										11			4		1	8	7			5		10	9	2
6	3	2										11			4	10	1	8	7			5			9	3
6	3	2										11			4		1	8	7			5		10	9	R
6	3	2								7		11			4		1	8				5		10	9	4
6	3	2										11			4		1	8	7			5		10	9	R
6	3	2										11			4		1	8	7			5		10	9	SF
6	3	2		8								11			4		1	10	7			5			9	F
7	8	8		2		1				2		7			8	1	8	8	6			8		6	8	
1												1						4	3			2		1	1	

1 own-goal

1907-08

1	Sep	2	(a)	Bristol C	L 2-3	Bolton, Hardman
2		7	(h)	Manchester C	D 3-3	Young 2, Rouse
3		9	(h)	Preston NE	W 2-1	Abbott, Makepeace
4		14	(a)	Preston NE	D 2-2	Bolton, Sharp
5		21	(h)	Bury	W 6-1	Bolton 2, Young 2, Hardman, Taylor
6		28	(a)	Aston Villa	W 2-0	Settle, Sharp
7	Oct	5	(h)	Liverpool	L 2-4	Makepeace, Settle
8		12	(a)	Middlesbrough	W 2-0	Bolton, Young
9		19	(h)	Sheffield U	W 2-1	Young 2
10		26	(a)	Chelsea	L 1-2	Booth
11	Nov	2	(h)	Nottingham F	W 1-0	Mountford
12		9	(a)	Manchester U	L 3-4	Bolton, Hardman, Settle
13		16	(h)	Blackburn R	W 4-1	Settle 2, Bolton, Young
14		23	(a)	Bolton W	L 0-3	
15	Dec	7	(a)	Newcastle U	L 1-2	Settle
16		14	(a)	Sunderland	W 2-1	Jones, Mountford
17		21	(h)	Woolwich Arsenal	D 1-1	Jones
18		25	(a)	Notts C	L 1-2	Young
19		26	(h)	Bristol C	D 0-0	
20		28	(a)	Sheffield W	W 2-1	Bolton, Young
21	Jan	4	(a)	Manchester C	L 2-4	Bolton, Taylor
22		18	(a)	Bury	L 0-3	
23		25	(h)	Aston Villa	W 1-0	Sharp
24	Feb	8	(h)	Middlesbrough	W 2-1	Young 2
25		15	(a)	Sheffield U	L 0-2	
26		29	(a)	Nottingham F	L 2-5	Mountford, Opp own-goal
27	Mar	14	(a)	Blackburn R	L 0-2	
28		18	(h)	Birmingham	W 4-1	Young 2, Coleman, Settle
29		21	(h)	Bolton W	W 2-1	Coleman, Sharp
30		28	(a)	Birmingham	L 1-2	Coleman
31	Apr	1	(h)	Chelsea	L 0-3	
32		4	(h)	Newcastle U	W 2-0	Coleman, Young
33		8	(h)	Manchester U	L 1-3	Young
34		11	(h)	Sunderland	L 0-3	
35		17	(a)	Liverpool	D 0-0	
36		18	(a)	Woolwich Arsenal	L 1-2	Coleman
37		20	(h)	Notts C	W 1-0	Freeman
38		25	(h)	Sheffield W	D 0-0	

FINAL LEAGUE POSITION: 11th in Division One

Appearances
Goals

FA Cup

1	Jan	11	(h)	Tottenham H	W 1-0	Young
2	Feb	1	(a)	Oldham A	D 0-0	
R		5	(h)	Oldham A	W 6-1	Bolton 4, Abbott, Young
3		22	(a)	Bolton W	D 3-3	Settle 2, Bolton
R		26	(h)	Bolton W	W 3-1	Young 2, Settle
4	Mar	7	(h)	Southampton	D 0-0	
R		11	(a)	Southampton	L 2-3	Bolton, Young

Appearances
Goals

Abbott W	Adamson H	Balmer R	Balmer W	Bolton H	Booth T	Borthwick J	Chadwick T	Coleman J	Couper G	Crelley J	Donnachie J	Freeman B	Graham R	Hardman H	Harris V	Jones T	Maconnachie J	Makepeace H	Mountford H	Rafferty D	Rouse F	Scott W	Settle J	Sharp J	Sloan D	Stevenson W	Strettle R	Taylor J	Winterhalder A	Woods L	Young A	
6		2	3	8	4						7			11							10	1						5			9	1
6		2	3	8										11				4			10	1		7				5			9	2
6		2	3	8										11			5	4			10	1		7							9	3
6		2	3	8														4				1	10	7				5	11		9	4
6		2	3	8										11				4				1	10	7				5			9	5
6			3	8						2				11				4				1	10	7				5			9	6
6		3	2	8										11				4				1	10	7				5			9	7
6		3	2	8	5		4							11								1	10	7							9	8
6		3	2	8	5						7			11				4				1	10								9	9
6		3	2	8	5									11				4				1	10	7							9	10
		3	2	8			6							11				4	10			1		7				5			9	11
6		3	2	8										11				4				1	10	7				5			9	12
6		3	2	8														4				1	10	7				5		11	9	13
6		3	2	8										11				4				1	10	7				5			9	14
6				8						3				11		9	5	4				1	10	7		2						15
6		3		8												9	5	4	10			1		7		2				11		16
6	4	3		8												9	5					1	10	7		2				11		17
6	4	3									7					8	5		10			1				2				11	9	18
	4		2	8										11			5	6				1	10	7		3					9	19
				8							7			11			4	6	10						1	2	3	5			9	20
	4	3		8							7							6	10			1				2		5	11		9	21
		3		8			5							11			4	6	10			1		7		2					9	22
6		3	2	8										11				4				1	10	7				5			9	23
6	4	3	2	8							7			11								1	10					5			9	24
6		3	2								11							4	10				8	7	1			5			9	25
6			2		5			8		3	7					9	4		10			1							11			26
	6		2		5			8									3	4		7			10		1				11		9	27
	6		2		5			8			11						3	4		7		1	10								9	28
	6		2	10				8						11			3	4				1		7				5			9	29
	6	2						8			11						3	4				1	10	7				5			9	30
	6	2		10	5			8						11			3	4				1		7							9	31
	6		2	10				8			7			11			3	4				1						5			9	32
	6		2					8			11						3	4		7		1	10					5			9	33
	6		2					8						11			3	4					10	7	1			5			9	34
	6	2						8	7		11	9					3	4				1						5			10	35
	6	2						8			7	9			4		3		11			1						5			10	36
	6	2						8			11	9			7		3	4				1						5			10	37
			2	10		5		8			7	9			4		3	6	11			1										38
21	16	26	26	27	8	1	3	13	1	3	16	4		22	3	5	21	31	10	3	3	34	21	23	4	8	1	23	4	4	33	
1				9	1			5				1		3		2		2	3		1		7	4				2			16	

1 own-goal

Abbott W	Adamson H	Balmer R	Balmer W	Bolton H	Booth T	Borthwick J	Chadwick T	Coleman J	Couper G	Crelley J	Donnachie J	Freeman B	Graham R	Hardman H	Harris V	Jones T	Maconnachie J	Makepeace H	Mountford H	Rafferty D	Rouse F	Scott W	Settle J	Sharp J	Sloan D	Stevenson W	Strettle R	Taylor J	Winterhalder A	Woods L	Young A	
6		3		8										11				4				1	10	7		2		5			9	1
6		3	2										8	11	9			4				1	10	7				5				2
6		3	2	8										11				4				1	10	7				5			9	R
6		3	2	8										11				4				1	10	7				5			9	3
6		3	2	8										11				4				1	10	7				5			9	R
6		3	2	8										11				4				1	10	7				5			9	4
6		3	2	8										11				4				1	10	7				5			9	R
7		7	6	6									1	7	1			7				7	7	7		1		7			6	
1				6																			3								5	

1908-09

1	Sep	2	(a)	Woolwich Arsenal	W 4-0	Coleman 2, Freeman 2
2		5	(a)	Bristol C	W 2-0	Freeman 2
3		7	(h)	Woolwich Arsenal	L 0-3	
4		12	(h)	Preston NE	L 0-1	
5		19	(a)	Middlesbrough	W 3-2	Barlow, Coleman, Freeman
6		26	(h)	Manchester C	W 6-3	Young 3, Freeman, Sharp, Taylor
7	Oct	3	(a)	Liverpool	W 1-0	Barlow
8		10	(h)	Bury	W 4-0	Freeman 2, Coleman, Young
9		17	(a)	Sheffield U	W 5-1	Freeman 3, Coleman, Sharp
10		24	(h)	Aston Villa	W 3-1	Coleman, Freeman, Sharp
11		31	(a)	Nottingham F	W 2-1	Freeman, Young
12	Nov	7	(h)	Sunderland	W 4-0	Freeman 3, Coleman
13		14	(a)	Chelsea	D 3-3	Freeman 2, Coleman
14		21	(h)	Blackburn R	D 4-4	Coleman 2, Freeman, Opp own-goal
15		28	(a)	Bradford C	D 1-1	Freeman
16	Dec	5	(h)	Manchester U	W 3-2	Freeman 2, Barlow
17		12	(h)	Sheffield U	W 1-0	Freeman
18		19	(a)	Leicester C	W 2-0	Sharp, Young
19		25	(h)	Notts C	L 0-1	
20		26	(a)	Notts C	D 0-0	
21	Jan	1	(h)	Newcastle U	L 0-1	
22		2	(h)	Bristol C	W 5-2	Freeman 2, Young 2, White
23		9	(a)	Preston NE	D 3-3	Barlow, Sharp, White
24		23	(h)	Middlesbrough	D 1-1	Young
25		30	(a)	Manchester C	L 0-4	
26	Feb	13	(a)	Bury	D 2-2	Freeman, Sharp
27		20	(h)	Sheffield U	W 5-1	Freeman 3, Coleman 2
28		27	(a)	Aston Villa	L 1-3	Freeman
29	Mar	13	(a)	Sunderland	L 0-2	
30		20	(h)	Chelsea	W 3-2	Freeman 3
31		24	(h)	Nottingham F	D 3-3	Coleman 2, Freeman
32		27	(a)	Blackburn R	D 0-0	
33	Apr	3	(h)	Bradford C	L 0-1	
34		9	(h)	Liverpool	W 5-0	Freeman 2, Coleman, Turner, White
35		10	(a)	Manchester U	D 2-2	Coleman 2
36		12	(a)	Newcastle U	L 0-3	
37		17	(a)	Sheffield W	L 0-2	
38		24	(h)	Leicester C	W 4-2	Coleman 2, Freeman 2

FINAL LEAGUE POSITION: 2nd in Division One

Appearances
Goals

FA Cup

1	Jan	16	(h)	Barnsley	W 3-1	Coleman, Sharp, White
2	Feb	6	(a)	Manchester U	L 0-1	

Appearances
Goals

Adamson H	Balmer R	Barlow G	Berry C	Bolton H	Borthwick J	Buck H	Clifford R	Coleman J	Dawson H	Donnachie J	Freeman B	Harris V	Jones T	Lacey W	Maconnachie J	Makepeace H	Mountford H	Rafferty D	Scott William	Sharp J	Stevenson W	Strettle S	Taylor J	Turner R	White W	Young A	
	2			10				8		11	9	4			3	6			1	7			5				1
	2			10				8		11	9	4			3	6			1	7			5				2
	2			10				8	11	7	9	4			3	6			1				5				3
	2			10				8	11		9	4			3	6			1	7			5				4
	2	11						8			9	4			3	6			1	7			5			10	5
	2	11						8			9	4			3	6			1	7			5			10	6
	2	11						8			9	4			3	6			1	7			5			10	7
6	2	11						8			9	4			3				1	7			5			10	8
	2	11						8			9	4			3	6			1	7			5			10	9
	2							8	11		9	4			3	6			1	7			5			10	10
	2	11						8			9	4			3	6			1	7			5			10	11
	2	11						8			9	4			3	6			1	7			5			10	12
	2	11						8			9	4			3	6			1	7			5			10	13
	2	11						8			9	4			3	6			1	7			5			10	14
	2	11						8			9	4			3	6			1	7			5			10	15
	2	11						8			9	4			3	6			1	7			5			10	16
	2	11					5				9	4			3	6			1	7					8	10	17
	2	11					5	8			9	4			3	6			1	7						10	18
	2	11									9	4			3	6			1	7			5		8	10	19
		11					5				9	4			3	6			1	7	2				8	10	20
		11					5	8			9	4			3	6			1	7	2					10	21
							5		11		9	4	7		3	6			1			2			8	10	22
	2	11					5	8			9	4			3	6			1	7					10		23
	2	11					5				9	4	7		3	6			1						8	10	24
	2	11					5	8			9	4	7		3	6			1						10		25
4	2	11	1					8			9				3	6				7			5			10	26
	2							8			9	4			3	6			1	7			5		11	10	27
6	2							8			9	4			3				1	7			5		11	10	28
	2	11						8			9	4			3	6			1	7			5			10	29
	2	11	1					8			9				3	6		4		7			5		10		30
6	2							8			9	4			3		11		1	7			5		10		31
6	2							8			9	4	7		3		11		1				5		10		32
6	2	11				7		8				4		9	3				1				5		10		33
	2							8			9	4			3	6			1	7			5	11	10		34
	2						5	8			9	4			3	6			1	7				11	10		35
	2							8			9	4			3	6			1	7			5	11	10		36
4	2							8			9	5			3	6			1	7				11	10		37
	2				5			8			9	4	7		3	6			1					11	10		38
7	35	23	2	4	1	1	9	33	4	3	37	36	5	1	38	33	2	1	36	31	2	1	27	5	18	23	
		4						19			38									6			1	1	3	9	

1 own-goal

Adamson H	Balmer R	Barlow G	Berry C	Bolton H	Borthwick J	Buck H	Clifford R	Coleman J	Dawson H	Donnachie J	Freeman B	Harris V	Jones T	Lacey W	Maconnachie J	Makepeace H	Mountford H	Rafferty D	Scott William	Sharp J	Stevenson W	Strettle S	Taylor J	Turner R	White W	Young A	
	2	11					5	8			9	4			3	6			1	7					10		1
	2							8	11			4			3	6			1	7			5		10	9	2
	2	1					1	2	1		1	2			2	2			2	2			1		2	1	
								1												1					1		

1909-10

1	Sep	1	(h)	Sheffield W	D	1-1	White
2		4	(h)	Tottenham H	W	4-2	Freeman 2, White, Young
3		6	(h)	Newcastle U	L	1-4	Freeman
4		11	(a)	Preston NE	W	1-0	Freeman
5		18	(h)	Notts C	W	2-0	Freeman, Sharp
6		20	(a)	Sheffield W	W	3-1	Freeman 3
7		25	(a)	Newcastle U	W	2-1	Freeman, Mountford
8	Oct	2	(h)	Liverpool	L	2-3	Coleman, Freeman
9		9	(a)	Aston Villa	L	1-3	White
10		16	(h)	Sheffield U	L	1-2	Young
11		23	(a)	Woolwich Arsenal	L	0-1	
12		30	(h)	Bolton W	W	3-1	Freeman 3
13	Nov	6	(a)	Chelsea	W	1-0	Sharp
14		13	(h)	Blackburn R	L	0-2	
15		20	(a)	Nottingham F	L	0-1	
16		27	(h)	Sunderland	W	2-1	Coleman 2
17	Dec	4	(a)	Middlesbrough	D	1-1	Coleman
18		18	(h)	Bradford C	D	1-1	Freeman
19		25	(a)	Bristol C	L	1-3	Freeman
20		27	(h)	Bristol C	W	1-0	Sharp
21	Jan	1	(a)	Bury	D	2-2	Freeman 2
22		8	(a)	Tottenham H	L	0-3	
23		22	(h)	Preston NE	W	2-1	Makepeace 2
24	Feb	12	(a)	Liverpool	W	1-0	Freeman
25		26	(a)	Sheffield U	L	0-3	
26	Mar	7	(h)	Woolwich Arsenal	W	1-0	White
27		12	(a)	Bolton W	W	1-0	Freeman
28		14	(h)	Aston Villa	D	0-0	
29		19	(h)	Chelsea	D	2-2	Gourlay, Makepeace
30		28	(h)	Bury	W	3-0	Freeman 2, Gourlay
31	Apr	2	(h)	Nottingham F	L	0-4	
32		6	(a)	Manchester U	L	2-3	Sharp, White
33		9	(a)	Sunderland	W	1-0	Mountford
34		11	(a)	Blackburn R	L	1-2	Weller
35		13	(a)	Notts C	W	3-2	Coleman, Lacey, Makepeace
36		16	(h)	Middlesbrough	D	1-1	Freeman
37		23	(h)	Manchester U	D	3-3	Berry 2, White
38		30	(a)	Bradford C	L	0-2	

FINAL LEAGUE POSITION: 10th in Football League

Appearances
Goals

FA Cup

1	Jan	15	(a)	Middlesbrough	D	1-1	White
R		19	(h)	Middlesbrough	W	5-3	Freeman, Makepeace, Taylor, White, Young
2	Feb	5	(h)	Woolwich Arsenal	W	5-0	Sharp 2, Barlow, Freeman, Young
3		19	(h)	Sunderland	W	2-0	Makepeace, Young
4	Mar	5	(a)	Coventry C	W	2-0	Freeman 2
SF		26	(n*)	Barnsley	D	0-0	
R		31	(n†)	Barnsley	L	0-3	

* Played at Elland Road. † Played at Old Trafford.

Appearances
Goals

Adamson H	Allan J	Balmer R	Bardsley J	Barlow G	Berry A	Borthwick J	Clifford R	Coleman J	Freeman B	Gourlay J	Harris V	Jones T	Lacey W	Maconnachie J	Makepeace H	Michaels W	Mountford H	Pinkney E	Pratt C	Rafferty D	Scott Walter	Scott William	Sharp J	Stevenson W	Taylor J	Turner R	Weller L	White W	Young A	
4		2							9					3	6							1	7		5	11		8	10	1
		2							9		4			3	6		11					1	7		5			8	10	2
		2						8	9		4			3	6		11					1	7		5			10		3
		2						8	9		4			3	6							1	7		5	11			10	4
		2						8	9		4			3	6		11					1	7		5				10	5
		2						8	9		4			3	6		11					1	7		5			10		6
		2						8	9		4			3	6		11					1	7		5				10	7
		2					5	8	9		4			3	6							1	7			11			10	8
		2					5	8			4			3	6							1	7			11		10	9	9
		2						8	9		5			3	6	7				4		1				11			10	10
		2				5		8	9		4			3	6							1	7			11			10	11
						5	2		9		4		8	3	6							1	7			11		10		12
						5	2		9		4		8	3	6							1	7			11		10		13
						5	2		9		4		8	3	6							1	7			11		10		14
						5	2		9		4		8	3	6	7	11					1							10	15
6		3					2	8	9		4											1	7		5	11			10	16
		3				5	2	8	9		4				6							1	7			11			10	17
		3		11		5	2	8	9		4				6							1	7					10		18
				11		5	2	8	9		4			3	6							1	7					10		19
							2	8	9		4				6							1	7	3	5			10	11	20
							2	8	9		4			3	6							1	7		5			10	11	21
							2	8	9		4				6							1	7	3	5	11		10		22
				11		5	2		9		4			3	6	7						1						8	10	23
	4			11			2		9					3	6						1		7		5			8	10	24
				11	7	5	2	8	9		4			3						6		1							10	25
	4				7		2		9					3	6		11					1			5			8	10	26
	6				7	5	2	10	9		4		8	3			11					1								27
				11		5			9		4			3	6						1		7	2				8	10	28
	4	2								9				3	6		11				1		7		5			8	10	29
	6	2				5		8	9	10	4			3				7				1				11				30
	6		3		7	5	2	8		10	4	9									1					11				31
							2		9		4			3	6				5		1		7			11		8	10	32
	4	2				5		8	9					3	6		11	7			1								10	33
		2							9	10				3			11	7	5	4	1						6	8		34
	4				7	5	2	8					10	3	6		9				1					11				35
						5	2	8	9		4			3	6			7			1					11		10		36
		2			7	5			9		4			3	6						1					11		8	10	37
		3				5	2		9		4				6						1		7			11		8	10	38
2	8	20	1	6	6	19	23	23	34	4	31	1	6	31	32	3	12	4	2	3	11	27	25	3	14	19	1	23	24	
					2			5	22	2			1		4		2						4				1	6	2	

Adamson H	Allan J	Balmer R	Bardsley J	Barlow G	Berry A	Borthwick J	Clifford R	Coleman J	Freeman B	Gourlay J	Harris V	Jones T	Lacey W	Maconnachie J	Makepeace H	Michaels W	Mountford H	Pinkney E	Pratt C	Rafferty D	Scott Walter	Scott William	Sharp J	Stevenson W	Taylor J	Turner R	Weller L	White W	Young A	
				11			2		9		4			3	6							1	7		5			8	10	1
				11			2		9		4			3	6							1	7		5			8	10	R
				11			2		9		4			3	6							1	7		5			8	10	2
				11			2		9		4			3	6							1	7		5			8	10	3
				11			2		9		4			3	6							1	7		5			8	10	4
				11			2		9		4			3	6							1	7		5			8	10	SF
				11			2		9		4			3	6							1	7		5			8	10	R
				7			7		7		7			7	7							7	7		7			7	7	
				1					4						2								2		1			2	3	

1910-11

1	Sep	1	(h)	Tottenham H	W 2-0	Freeman 2
2		3	(a)	Middlesbrough	L 0-1	
3		10	(h)	Preston NE	W 2-0	White, A.Young
4		17	(a)	Notts C	D 0-0	
5		24	(h)	Manchester U	L 0-1	
6	Oct	1	(a)	Liverpool	W 2-0	Makepeace, A.Young
7		8	(h)	Bury	W 2-1	Gourlay, R.Young
8		15	(a)	Sheffield U	W 1-0	Barlow
9		22	(h)	Aston Villa	L 0-1	
10		29	(a)	Sunderland	L 0-4	
11	Nov	5	(h)	Woolwich Arsenal	W 2-0	Berry, Lacey
12		12	(a)	Bradford C	L 1-3	A.Young
13		19	(h)	Blackburn R	W 6-1	A.Young 3, Beare 2, Lacey
14		26	(a)	Nottingham F	D 1-1	Gourlay
15	Dec	3	(h)	Manchester C	W 1-0	Gourlay
16		10	(h)	Oldham A	W 1-0	Berry
17		17	(a)	Sheffield W	W 2-0	Gourlay, Lacey
18		24	(h)	Bristol C	W 4-3	Berry 2, Lacey, A.Young
19		26	(a)	Newcastle U	L 0-1	
20		27	(h)	Liverpool	L 0-1	
21		31	(h)	Middlesbrough	W 2-0	Beare, R.Young
22	Jan	2	(h)	Newcastle U	L 1-5	Beare
23		7	(a)	Preston NE	W 2-0	Magner, Pinkney
24		21	(h)	Notts C	W 5-0	Lacey 3, Beare, R.Young
25		28	(a)	Manchester U	D 2-2	Beare, Berry
26	Feb	11	(a)	Bury	D 0-0	
27		18	(h)	Sheffield U	W 1-0	A.Young
28	Mar	4	(h)	Sunderland	D 2-2	Magner, R.Young
29		11	(a)	Woolwich Arsenal	L 0-1	
30		18	(h)	Bradford C	D 0-0	
31		27	(a)	Aston Villa	L 1-2	Lacey
32	Apr	6	(a)	Blackburn R	W 1-0	Beare
33		8	(a)	Manchester C	L 1-2	Jefferis
34		14	(h)	Nottingham F	W 2-1	Gracie, R.Young
35		15	(a)	Oldham A	L 0-2	
36		17	(a)	Tottenham H	W 1-0	Fleetwood
37		22	(h)	Sheffield W	D 1-1	Beare
38		29	(a)	Bristol C	W 1-0	Jefferis

FINAL LEAGUE POSITION: 4th in Football League

Appearances
Goals

FA Cup

1	Jan	14	(a)	Crystal Palace	W 4-0	Gourlay, Magner, A.Young, R.Young
2	Feb	4	(h)	Liverpool	W 2-1	A.Young 2
3		25	(a)	Derby C	L 0-5	

Appearances
Goals

Allan J	Balmer R	Barlow G	Beare G	Berry A	Borthwick J	Chedgzoy S	Clifford R	Fleetwood T	Freeman B	Gourlay J	Gracie T	Grenyer A	Harris V	Jefferis F	Lacey W	Maconnachie J	Magner E	Makepeace H	Meunier J	Mountford H	Pinkney E	Scott Walter	Scott William	Stevenson W	Turner R	Weller L	White W	Young A	Young R	
	2								9				4		8	3		6			7		1		11			10	5	1
	2								9				4		8	3		6			7		1		11			10	5	2
	2								9				4			3		6			7		1		11		8	10	5	3
	2			7					9				4			3		6					1		11		8	10	5	4
	2			7						10			4		8	3		6					1		11			9	5	5
	2			7					9	8			4			3		6					1		11			10	5	6
				7					9	8			4			3		6					1	2	11			10	5	7
	2	11		7					9	8			4			3		6					1					10	5	8
	2	11		7					9	8			4			3		6					1					10	5	9
				7			2		9	10			4		8	3		6		11			1						5	10
	3	11		7			2		9	10			4		8			6					1						5	11
	3		11	7			2			10			4		8			6					1					9	5	12
		11	7				2			10			4		8			6	3				1					9	5	13
		11	7		5					10			4		8			6	3				1	2				9		14
			11	7	5					10			4		8			6	3				1	2				9		15
			11	7			2			10			4		8			6					1	3				9	5	16
6	3		11	7						10			4		8								1	2				9	5	17
6	3		11	7						10			4		8								1	2				9	5	18
	3		11			7				10			4		8			6					1	2				9	5	19
	3		11	7						10			4		8			6					1	2				9	5	20
	3		8	7						10			4					6					1	2	11			9	5	21
	3		8	7						10			4					6					1	2	11			9	5	22
6	3		11			7							4				9				8		1	2				10	5	23
	3		11	7									4		8		9	6					1	2				10	5	24
4			11	7						8						3	9	6				1		2				10	5	25
4			11	7						8						3	9	6				1		2				10	5	26
			11		5					8			4		7	3	9	6					1	2				10		27
	3		11	7						8			4				9	6				1		2				10	5	28
	2		11	7					9	8			4			3		6					1					10	5	29
4	2		7					8		9						3		6				1			11			10	5	30
			7					9		8					11	3		6					1	2		4		10	5	31
			7							8	9		4	10	11	3		6					1	2		5				32
			7					8			9		4	10	11	3		6					1	2		5				33
	2		7					8			9	6	4	10	11	3							1						5	34
4			7		5			8			9			10	11	3							1	2		6				35
						7		8		10	9		4		11			6	3			1		2					5	36
			7					8			9		4		11	3		6				1		2				10	5	37
	2		7					5		10	9			8	11	3		6				1				4				38
7	23	5	26	21	4	3	5	8	11	28	7	1	32	5	24	22	6	33	4	1	4	7	31	22	10	5	2	30	31	
		1	8	5				1	2	4	1			2	8		2	1			1						1	8	5	

Allan J	Balmer R	Barlow G	Beare G	Berry A	Borthwick J	Chedgzoy S	Clifford R	Fleetwood T	Freeman B	Gourlay J	Gracie T	Grenyer A	Harris V	Jefferis F	Lacey W	Maconnachie J	Magner E	Makepeace H	Meunier J	Mountford H	Pinkney E	Scott Walter	Scott William	Stevenson W	Turner R	Weller L	White W	Young A	Young R	
	3		11	7						8			4				9	6					1	2				10	5	1
			11							8			4		7	3	9	6					1	2				10	5	2
			11	7									4		8	3	9	6					1	2				10	5	3
	1		3	2						2			3		2	2	3	3					3	3				3	3	
										1							1											3	1	

1911-12

1	Sep	2	(h)	Tottenham H	D	2-2	Burton, Jefferis
2		6	(a)	Newcastle U	L	0-2	
3		9	(a)	Manchester U	L	1-2	Lacey
4		16	(h)	Liverpool	W	2-1	Beare, Gourlay
5		23	(a)	Aston Villa	L	0-3	
6		30	(h)	Newcastle U	W	2-0	Burton, Davidson
7	Oct	7	(a)	Sheffield U	L	1-2	Young
8		14	(h)	Oldham A	D	1-1	Young
9		21	(a)	Bolton W	W	2-1	Burton, Lacey
10		28	(h)	Bradford C	W	1-0	Davidson
11	Nov	4	(a)	Woolwich Arsenal	W	1-0	Jefferis
12		11	(h)	Manchester C	W	1-0	Burton
13		18	(a)	Preston NE	L	1-2	Bradshaw
14		25	(a)	West Brom A	L	0-1	
15	Dec	2	(h)	Sunderland	W	1-0	Gourlay
16		9	(a)	Blackburn R	L	1-2	Bradshaw
17		16	(h)	Sheffield W	W	1-0	Jefferis
18		23	(a)	Bury	W	2-1	Bradshaw, Jefferis
19		25	(a)	Middlesbrough	D	0-0	
20		26	(h)	Middlesbrough	W	1-0	Bradshaw
21		30	(a)	Tottenham H	W	1-0	Beare
22	Jan	6	(h)	Manchester U	W	4-0	Bradshaw 2, Browell 2
23		20	(a)	Liverpool	W	3-1	Beare, Browell, Jefferis
24		27	(h)	Aston Villa	D	1-1	Bradshaw
25	Feb	10	(h)	Sheffield U	W	3-2	Browell 2, Fleetwood
26		17	(a)	Oldham A	L	0-3	
27		28	(h)	Bolton W	W	1-0	Bradshaw
28	Mar	2	(a)	Bradford C	L	0-1	
29		16	(a)	Manchester C	L	0-4	
30		23	(h)	Preston NE	W	1-0	Browell
31		27	(h)	Woolwich Arsenal	W	1-0	Jefferis
32	Apr	5	(a)	Notts C	W	1-0	Browell
33		6	(a)	Sunderland	L	0-4	
34		8	(h)	Notts C	D	1-1	Browell
35		13	(h)	Blackburn R	L	1-3	Davidson
36		20	(a)	Sheffield W	W	3-1	Browell 2, Jefferis
37		22	(h)	West Brom A	W	3-0	Browell, Makepeace, Uren
38		27	(h)	Bury	D	1-1	Browell

FINAL LEAGUE POSITION: 2nd in Division One

Appearances
Goals

FA Cup

1	Jan	13	(a)	Clapton O	W	2-1	Beare, Browell
2	Feb	3	(h)	Bury	D	1-1	Maconnachie
R		8	(h*)	Bury	W	6-0	Browell 4, Davidson, Jefferis
3		24	(a)	Oldham A	W	2-0	Browell 2
4	Mar	9	(a)	Swindon T	L	1-2	Makepeace

*Everton and Bury agreed to stage the replay at Goodison Park.

Appearances
Goals

Allan J	Balmer R	Beare G	Berry C	Bradshaw F	Browell T	Burton A	Davidson W	Fleetwood T	Gourley J	Gracie T	Grenyer A	Harris V	Holbem W	Jefferis F	Jordan W	Lacey W	Maconnachie J	Makepeace H	Meunier J	Scott William	Smith J	Stevenson W	Uren H	Weller L	Young R	
		7				10	11			9		4		8			3	6		1		2			5	1
		7				10	11			9		4	3	8				6		1		2			5	2
		7						5	10			4		8	9	11		6	3	1		2				3
		7							10			4	3	8	9	11		6		1		2			5	4
		7						5	10	9	6	4		8		11	3			1		2				5
		7				10	11	9				4		8			3	6		1		2			5	6
		7				10	11	9				4		8			3	6		1		2			5	7
		7				10	11	9				4		8			3	6		1		2			5	8
		7				10	11					4		8		9	3	6		1		2			5	9
		7				10	11	5	9			4		8			3	6		1		2				10
4		7				10	11	5	9					8			3	6		1		2				11
4		7		9		10	11	5						8			3	6		1		2				12
		7		9		10	11	5				4		8			3	6		1		2				13
		7		9		10	11	5				4		8			3	6		1		2				14
		7		10			11	5	9			4		8			3	6		1		2				15
		7		10			11	5	9			4		8			3	6		1		2				16
		7		10			11	5	9			4		8			3	6		1		2				17
		7		10			11	5	9			4		8			3	6		1		2				18
		7		10				5		9		4		8		11	3	6		1		2				19
		7		10				5		9		4		8		11	3	6		1		2				20
		7		10			11	5		9		4		8			3	6		1		2				21
		7		10	9		11	5				4		8			3	6		1		2				22
		7		10	9		11	5				4		8			3	6		1		2				23
		7		10	9		11	5				4		8			3	6		1		2				24
4		7	1		9		11	5	10					8			3					2		6		25
		7			9	10	11	5	8		6	4					3			1		2				26
		7		10	9			5				4		8			3	6		1		2	11			27
		7		10	9			5				4		8			3	6		1		2	11			28
				10	9		11	5				4	2	8			3	6		1	7					29
				10	9			5	8		6	4	3							1	7	2	11			30
				10	9		11	5				4	3	8				6		1	7	2				31
				10	9			5				4	3	8				6		1	7	2	11			32
				10	9			5				4	3	8				6		1	7	2	11			33
		7		10	9		11	5				4	3	8			2	6		1						34
	2	7			9		11	5	10			4		8			3	6		1						35
					9			5	10			4	2	8			3	6		1	7		11			36
4					9			5	10				2	8			3	6		1	7		11			37
					9			5	10			4	2	8			3	6		1	7		11			38
4	1	30	1	21	17	12	25	34	16	6	3	34	11	36	2	6	31	34	1	37	8	32	8	1	7	
		3		8	12	4	3	1	2					7		2		1					1		2	

Allan J	Balmer R	Beare G	Berry C	Bradshaw F	Browell T	Burton A	Davidson W	Fleetwood T	Gourley J	Gracie T	Grenyer A	Harris V	Holbem W	Jefferis F	Jordan W	Lacey W	Maconnachie J	Makepeace H	Meunier J	Scott William	Smith J	Stevenson W	Uren H	Weller L	Young R	
		7		10	9		11	5				4		8			3	6		1		2				1
		7		10	9		11	5				4		8			3	6		1		2				2
		7			9		11	5	10			4		8			3	6		1		2				R
		7		10	9			5				4		8		11	3	6		1		2				3
		7		10	9		11	5				4		8			3	6		1		2				4
		5		4	5		4	5	1			5		5		1	5	5		5		5				
		1			7		1							1			1	1								

1912-13

1	Sep	2	(a)	Tottenham H	W 2-0	T.Browell, Maconnachie
2		7	(a)	Middlesbrough	D 0-0	
3		14	(h)	Notts C	W 4-0	T.Browell 2, Bradshaw, Harris
4		18	(a)	Derby C	W 4-1	Maconnachie 2, Beare, Uren
5		21	(a)	Manchester U	L 0-2	
6		28	(h)	Aston Villa	L 0-1	
7	Oct	5	(a)	Liverpool	W 2-0	T.Browell, Gault
8		12	(h)	Bolton W	L 2-3	T.Browell 2
9		19	(a)	Sheffield U	L 1-4	T.Browell
10		26	(h)	Newcastle U	L 0-6	
11	Nov	2	(a)	Oldham A	L 0-2	
12		9	(h)	Chelsea	W 1-0	Bradshaw
13		16	(a)	Woolwich Arsenal	D 0-0	
14		23	(h)	Bradford C	W 2-1	Bradshaw, T.Browell
15		30	(a)	Manchester C	L 0-1	
16	Dec	7	(h)	West Brom A	L 1-3	T.Browell
17		14	(h)	Sunderland	L 0-4	
18		21	(a)	Sheffield W	W 2-1	Fleetwood, Wareing
19		25	(h)	Blackburn R	W 2-1	Beare, Uren
20		26	(a)	Blackburn R	W 2-1	Brannick, Simms
21		28	(h)	Middlesbrough	W 1-0	Maconnachie
22	Jan	1	(h)	Tottenham H	L 1-2	Bradshaw
23		4	(a)	Notts C	W 1-0	Brannick
24		18	(h)	Manchester U	W 4-1	T.Browell 2, Jefferis, Wareing
25		25	(a)	Aston Villa	D 1-1	Beare
26	Feb	8	(h)	Liverpool	L 0-2	
27		15	(a)	Bolton W	D 0-0	
28	Mar	1	(a)	Newcastle U	L 0-2	
29		12	(h)	Sheffield U	L 0-1	
30		15	(a)	Chelsea	W 3-1	Beare, T.Browell, Jefferis
31		21	(h)	Derby C	D 2-2	Bradshaw 2
32		22	(h)	Woolwich Arsenal	W 3-0	Beare 2, Bradshaw
33		29	(a)	Bradford C	L 1-4	Jefferis
34	Apr	2	(h)	Oldham A	L 2-3	Bradshaw 2
35		5	(h)	Manchester C	D 0-0	
36		9	(a)	Sunderland	L 1-3	Bradshaw
37		12	(a)	West Brom A	D 0-0	
38		26	(h)	Sheffield W	W 3-1	Jefferis 2, Beare

FINAL LEAGUE POSITION: 11th in Division One

Appearances
Goals

FA Cup

1	Jan	15	(h)	Stockport C	W 5-1	T.Browell 3, Bradshaw, Wareing
2	Feb	1	(a)	Brighton & HA	D 0-0	
R		5	(h)	Brighton & HA	W 1-0	Jefferis
3		22	(a)	Bristol R	W 4-0	T.Browell, Fleetwood, Harris, Jefferis
4	Mar	8	(h)	Oldham A	L 0-1	

Appearances
Goals

Beare G	Bradshaw F	Brannick J	Bromilow W	Browell A	Browell T	Caldwell J	Chedgzoy S	Davidson W	Fleetwood T	Gault W	Gourlay J	Grenyer A	Harris V	Hodge W	Holbem W	Houston J	Jefferis F	Maconnachie J	Makepeace H	Simms S	Simpson R	Smith J	Stevens T	Stevenson W	Uren H	Wareing W	
7	10				9	1			5				4				8	3	6					2	11		1
7	10				9	1			5				4				8	3	6					2	11		2
7	10				9	1			5				4				8	3	6					2	11		3
7	10				9	1			5	8			4					3	6					2	11		4
7	10				9	1			5	8			4					3	6					2	11		5
7	10				9	1			5				4				8	3	6					2	11		6
7	10				9	1		11	5	8			4		3				6					2			7
7	10				9	1		11	5	8		6	4		3									2			8
7	10				9	1		11	5			6	4		3		8							2			9
7	10				9	1		11	5	8	4				3						2					6	10
11	10				9	1			5		8	6			3							7		2		4	11
11	9					1			5		10	6					8	3				7		2		4	12
7	10				9	1			5			6					8	3						2	11	4	13
7	10				9	1			5			6					8	3						2	11	4	14
7				5	9	1				10		6					8	3						2	11	4	15
7	10				9	1			5			6					8	3						2	11	4	16
7	10					1			5	9			4				8	3	6					2	11		17
7	10					1			9				4				8	3	6					2	11	5	18
7	10					1			9			6	4				8	3						2	11	5	19
7	10	8				1						6	4					3		9				2	11	5	20
7	10					1			9			6	4				8	3						2	11	5	21
7	10					1		11	9			6	4				8	3						2		5	22
	10	8			9	1	7	11				6	4					3						2		5	23
7	10				9	1		11				6	4				8	3						2		5	24
7	10				9	1		11				6	4				8	3						2		5	25
7					10	1		11	5				4		2	9	8	3	6								26
7					9	1			4	10		6					8	3						2	11	5	27
11					10	1			9			6	4			7	8	3						2		5	28
11	10	8			9						4	6	5	1	3	7								2			29
7	9				10			11	5		4	6		1			8				3			2			30
7	9				10	1		11	5		6		4				8				3			2			31
7	9				10	1						6	4				8				3		11	2		5	32
7	9				10	1						6	4				8				3		11	2		5	33
7	10		1									6	4			9	8				3		11	2		5	34
7	10								4			6		1		9	8				3		11	2		5	35
7	10								9			6	4	1		8					3		11	2		5	36
7	10							11				6	4	1		8				9	3			2		5	37
7	10							11	9			6	4	1			8				3			2		5	38
37	34	3	1	1	26	31	1	13	28	8	6	26	28	6	7	7	27	23	10	2	10	2	5	36	16	24	
7	10	2			12				1	1			1				5	4		1					2	2	

Beare G	Bradshaw F	Brannick J	Bromilow W	Browell A	Browell T	Caldwell J	Chedgzoy S	Davidson W	Fleetwood T	Gault W	Gourlay J	Grenyer A	Harris V	Hodge W	Holbem W	Houston J	Jefferis F	Maconnachie J	Makepeace H	Simms S	Simpson R	Smith J	Stevens T	Stevenson W	Uren H	Wareing W	
7	10				9	1		11				6	4				8	3						2		5	1
7	10				9	1		11				6	4				8	3						2		5	2
7					9	1		11			10		4				8	3	6					2		5	R
11					10	1			9			6	4			7	8	3						2		5	3
11	10				9	1			4			6	5			7	8	3						2			4
5	3				5	5		3	2		1	4	5			2	5	5	1					5		4	
	1				4				1				1				2									1	

1913-14

1	Sep	1	(h)	Burnley	D 1-1	Browell
2		6	(h)	Preston NE	W 2-0	Bradshaw, Jefferis
3		13	(a)	Newcastle U	W 1-0	Palmer
4		20	(h)	Liverpool	L 1-2	Wareing
5		27	(a)	Aston Villa	L 1-3	Fleetwood
6	Oct	4	(h)	Middlesbrough	W 2-0	Browell, T.Page
7		11	(a)	Sheffield U	L 1-4	Houston
8		18	(h)	Derby C	W 5-0	Nuttall 2, Houston, T.Page, Wareing
9		25	(a)	Manchester C	D 1-1	Nuttall
10	Nov	1	(h)	Bradford C	D 1-1	Harrison
11		8	(a)	Blackburn R	L 0-6	
12		15	(h)	Sunderland	L 1-5	Nuttall
13		22	(a)	Tottenham H	L 1-4	Johnson
14		29	(a)	West Brom A	D 1-1	Nuttall
15	Dec	6	(h)	Sheffield W	D 1-1	Parker
16		13	(a)	Bolton W	D 0-0	
17		20	(h)	Chelsea	D 0-0	
18		25	(a)	Manchester U	W 1-0	Parker
19		26	(h)	Manchester U	W 5-0	Parker 3, Nuttall 2
20		27	(a)	Preston NE	L 0-1	
21	Jan	1	(a)	Oldham A	L 0-2	
22		3	(h)	Newcastle U	W 2-0	Jefferis, Parker
23		17	(a)	Liverpool	W 2-1	Parker 2
24		24	(h)	Aston Villa	L 1-4	Clennell
25	Feb	7	(a)	Middlesbrough	L 0-2	
26		14	(h)	Sheffield U	W 5-0	Clennell 2, Parker 2, Weller
27		21	(a)	Derby C	L 0-1	
28		28	(h)	Manchester C	W 1-0	Parker
29	Mar	7	(a)	Bradford C	W 1-0	Jefferis
30		14	(h)	Blackburn R	D 0-0	
31		21	(a)	Sunderland	L 2-5	Parker 2
32		28	(h)	Tottenham H	D 1-1	Chedgzoy
33	Apr	4	(h)	West Brom A	W 2-0	Clennell, Parker
34		10	(a)	Burnley	L 0-2	
35		11	(a)	Sheffield W	D 2-2	Parker 2
36		13	(h)	Oldham A	L 0-2	
37		18	(h)	Bolton W	D 1-1	Parker
38		25	(a)	Chelsea	L 0-1	

FINAL LEAGUE POSITION: 15th in Division One

Appearances
Goals

FA Cup

1	Jan	10	(a)	Glossop NE	L 1-2	Bradshaw

Appearances
Goals

Beare G	Bradshaw F	Browell T	Chedgzoy S	Clennell J	Fern T	Fleetwood T	Grenyer A	Harris V	Harrison G	Hodge W	Houston J	Jefferis F	Johnston L	Maconnachie J	Makepeace H	Mitchell F	Nuttall T	Page J	Page T	Palmer W	Parker R	Simpson R	Stevenson W	Thompson R	Wareing W	Weller L	
7	10	9					6	4				8		3		1				11			2		5		1
7	10	9					6	4				8		3		1				11			2		5		2
7		10				9	6	4				8		3		1				11			2		5		3
7	10	9					6	4	11			8		3		1							2		5		4
		10				9		4	11		7	8		3	6	1							2		5		5
	8	10						4	11		7			3	6	1			9					2	5		6
		8						4	11		7		10	3	6	1			9					2	5		7
								4	11		7		10	3	6	1	8		9					2	5		8
								4	11		7		10	3	6	1	8		9					2	5		9
								4	11	1	7		10	3	6		8		9					2	5		10
						9	6	4	11	1	7		10	3			8							2	5		11
							6	4	11	1	7		10	3			8		9				2		5		12
						5	6	4	11		7		10	3		1	8	2	9								13
7	10					5		4	11	1		8		3	6		9							2			14
7	10				1	5		4	11			8		3	6						9			2			15
			7		1	5		4	11			8		3	6		10				9			2			16
7					1	5		4	11			8		3	6		10				9			2			17
7					1	5		4	11			8	10	3	6						9			2			18
7					1	5		4	11			8		3	6		10				9			2			19
7	4				1	5	6		11			8		3			10				9			2			20
					1	5	10	4	11		7	8			6						9	3		2			21
					1	5	10	4	11		7	8		3							9			2	6		22
	10				1	5		4	11			8		3	6					7	9			2			23
				10	1	4			11			8		3	6					7	9			2	5		24
				10	1	5	6		11		7	8		3							9			2	4		25
				10	1	5	6		11		7	8		3							9			2		4	26
				10	1	5	6		11		7	8		3							9			2		4	27
				10	1	5	6		11		7	8		3							9			2		4	28
				10	1	5	6		11		7	8		3							9			2		4	29
7				10	1	5	6		11			8		3							9			2		4	30
				10	1	5		6	11		7	8									9		3	2		4	31
			7	10	1	5	6		11			8									9	3		2		4	32
			7	10	1		6		11			8		3							9			2	5	4	33
	10		7		1		6		11			8		3							9			2	5	4	34
	10					5	6	4	11		7			3		1	8				9			2			35
	10		7			5			11					3	6	1	8				9			2		4	36
			7	10		5	6	4	11			8		3		1					9			2			37
			7	10	1	5	6	4	11					3			8				9		2				38
11	11	7	7	12	21	27	22	26	35	4	18	27	8	35	16	13	14	1	7	5	24	2	8	30	17	10	
	1	2	1	4		1			1		2	3	1				7		2	1	17				2	1	

Beare G	Bradshaw F	Browell T	Chedgzoy S	Clennell J	Fern T	Fleetwood T	Grenyer A	Harris V	Harrison G	Hodge W	Houston J	Jefferis F	Johnston L	Maconnachie J	Makepeace H	Mitchell F	Nuttall T	Page J	Page T	Palmer W	Parker R	Simpson R	Stevenson W	Thompson R	Wareing W	Weller L	
7	10				1	5		4	11			8		3	6						9			2			1
1	1				1	1		1	1			1		1	1						1			1			
	1																										

1914-15

1	Sep	2	(a)	Tottenham H	W 3-1	Clennell 3
2		5	(a)	Newcastle U	W 1-0	Jefferis
3		7	(a)	Burnley	L 0-1	
4		12	(h)	Middlesbrough	L 2-3	Parker 2
5		19	(a)	Sheffield U	L 0-1	
6		26	(h)	Aston Villa	D 0-0	
7	Oct	3	(a)	Liverpool	W 5-0	Parker 3, Clennell 2
8		10	(h)	Bradford	W 4-1	Parker 2, Chedgzoy, Galt
9		17	(a)	Oldham A	D 1-1	Jefferis
10		24	(h)	Manchester U	W 4-2	Parker 2, Makepeace, Palmer
11		31	(a)	Bolton W	D 0-0	
12	Nov	7	(h)	Blackburn R	L 1-3	Parker
13		14	(a)	Notts C	D 0-0	
14		21	(h)	Sunderland	W 7-1	Parker 3, Clennell 2, Harrison, Jefferis
15		28	(a)	Sheffield W	W 4-1	Parker 4
16	Dec	5	(h)	West Brom A	W 2-1	Clennell, Parker
17		12	(h)	Manchester C	W 4-1	Parker 3, Clennell
18		19	(a)	Chelsea	L 0-2	
19		25	(h)	Bradford C	D 1-1	Jefferis
20		26	(a)	Bradford C	W 1-0	Chedgzoy
21	Jan	1	(h)	Tottenham H	D 1-1	Kirsopp
22		2	(h)	Newcastle U	W 3-0	Harrison, Kirsopp, Parker
23		16	(a)	Middlesbrough	L 1-5	Parker
24		23	(h)	Sheffield U	D 0-0	
25	Feb	6	(h)	Liverpool	L 1-3	Clennell
26		10	(a)	Aston Villa	W 5-1	Parker 3, Galt, Kirsopp
27		27	(a)	Manchester U	W 2-1	Harrison, Parker
28	Mar	13	(a)	Blackburn R	L 1-2	Kirsopp
29		17	(h)	Oldham A	L 3-4	Parker 2, Kirsopp
30		20	(h)	Notts C	W 4-0	Kirsopp 2, Clennell, Parker
31		24	(h)	Bolton W	W 5-3	Parker 3, Clennell 2
32	Apr	2	(h)	Burnley	L 0-2	
33		3	(h)	Sheffield W	L 0-1	
34		6	(a)	Sunderland	W 3-0	Parker 2, Kirsopp
35		10	(a)	West Brom A	W 2-1	Fleetwood, Harrison
36		14	(a)	Bradford	W 2-1	Grenyer, Kirsopp
37		17	(a)	Manchester C	W 1-0	Clennell
38		26	(h)	Chelsea	D 2-2	Fleetwood, Parker

FINAL LEAGUE POSITION: 1st in Division One

Appearances
Goals

FA Cup

1	Jan	9	(h)	Barnsley	W 3-0	Galt 2, Parker
2		30	(h)	Bristol C	W 4-0	Clennell, Kirsopp, Parker, Wareing
3	Feb	20	(a*)	Queen's Park R	W 2-1	Clennell, Opp own-goal
4	Mar	6	(a)	Bradford C	W 2-0	Chedgzoy, Clennell
SF		27	(n†)	Chelsea	L 0-2	

* Played at Stamford Bridge. † Played at Villa Park.

Appearances
Goals

Brown W	Chedgzoy S	Clennell J	Fern T	Fleetwood T	Galt J	Grenyer A	Harrison G	Houston J	Howarth H	Jefferis F	Kirsopp W	Macconnachie J	Makepeace H	Mitchell F	Nuttall T	Palmer W	Parker R	Roberts J	Simpson R	Thompson R	Wareing W	Weller L	Wright W	
	7	10	1	4	5	6	11			8		3					9			2				1
	7	10	1	4	5	6	11			8		3					9			2				2
	7	10	1	4	5	6	11			8		3					9			2				3
	7	10	1	4	5	6						3			8	11	9			2				4
	7	10	1	4	5	6						3			8	11	9			2				5
	7	10	1	4	5					8		3	6			11	9			2				6
	7	10	1	4	5					8		3	6			11	9			2				7
	7	10	1	4	5					8		3	6			11	9			2				8
	7	10	1	4	5					8		3	6			11	9		2					9
	7	10	1	4	5					8		3	6			11	9		2					10
	7	10	1	4	5					8		3	6			11	9		2					11
	7	10	1	4	5					8		3	6			11	9		2					12
	7	10	1	4	5		11			8		3	6				9			2				13
	7	10	1	4	5		11			8		3	6				9			2				14
	7	10	1	4	5		11			8		3	6				9			2				15
	7	10	1	4	5		11			8		3	6				9			2				16
4	7	10	1		5		11			8		3					9			2	6			17
	7	10	1	4	5		11			8		3	6				9			2				18
	7	10	1	4	5		11			8		3	6				9			2				19
	7	10	1	4	5		11			8		3	6				9			2				20
	7	10	1	4	5		11				8	3	6				9			2				21
4		10	1		5		11	7			8	3	6				9			2				22
	7	10	1	4	5		11				8	3	6				9			2				23
	7	10	1	4	5								6		8	11			3	2			9	24
	7	10	1	4	5						8	3	6			11	9			2				25
	7	10	1	4	5						8	3	6				9	11		2				26
	7	10	1	4	5		11				8	3	6				9			2				27
	7	10	1	4			11				8	3	6				9			2	5			28
			1	4		6	11				8	3				7	9			2	5		10	29
4		10					11				8		6	1		7	9			2	5	3		30
		10		4		6	11		8					1		7	9		3	2	5			31
	7	10	1	4	5	6	11				8						9		3	2				32
		10	1	4	5	6	11				8					7	9		3	2				33
		10	1	4		6	11				8					7	9			2	5	3		34
4		10	1	9		6	11				8					7			2		5	3		35
	7		1	4	5	10	11				8				9					2	6	3		36
		10	1	4	5	6	11				8				7		9			2		3		37
	7	10	1	4	5	6	11				8						9			2		3		38
4	30	36	36	35	32	14	26	1	1	18	16	28	23	2	5	17	35	1	9	33	8	6	2	
	2	14		2	2	1	4			4	9		1			1	36							

Brown W	Chedgzoy S	Clennell J	Fern T	Fleetwood T	Galt J	Grenyer A	Harrison G	Houston J	Howarth H	Jefferis F	Kirsopp W	Macconnachie J	Makepeace H	Mitchell F	Nuttall T	Palmer W	Parker R	Roberts J	Simpson R	Thompson R	Wareing W	Weller L	Wright W	
	7	10	1	4	5		11				8	3	6				9			2				1
	7	10	1	4							8		6			11	9		3	2	5			2
	7	10	1	4	5		11				8	3	6				9			2				3
	7	10	1	4	5		11				8	3	6				9			2				4
	7	10		4	5		11				8		6	1			9		3	2				SF
	5	5	4	5	4		4				5	3	5	1		1	5		2	5	1			
	1	3			2						1						2				1			

1 own-goal

1915-16

1	Sep	4	(h)	Bury	W 5-0	Clennell 2, Kirsopp 2, Grenyer
2		11	(a)	Manchester U	W 4-2	Nuttall 2, Clennell, Kirsopp
3		18	(h)	Blackpool	W 4-2	Chedgzoy 2, Clennell, Kirsopp
4		25	(a)	Southport	L 1-2	Clennell
5	Oct	2	(h)	Oldham A	L 2-3	Clennell, Jefferis
6		9	(a)	Rochdale	W 2-1	Jefferis, Kirsopp
7		16	(a)	Bolton W	W 4-3	Clennell 2, Grenyer, Kirsopp
8		23	(h)	Manchester C	W 4-2	Parker 3, Chedgzoy
9		30	(a)	Stoke C	L 2-3	Clennell 2
10	Nov	6	(h)	Burnley	L 1-2	Parker
11		13	(a)	Preston NE	W 2-0	Clennell 2
12		20	(h)	Stockport C	L 2-5	Clennell, Kirsopp
13		27	(a)	Liverpool	L 1-4	Clennell
14	Dec	4	(a)	Bury	W 3-0	Parker 2, Kirsopp
15		11	(h)	Manchester U	W 2-0	Clennell, Harrison
16		18	(a)	Blackpool	W 4-1	Clennell 2, Harrison, Wright
17		25	(h)	Southport	W 2-0	Clennell, Galt
18	Jan	8	(h)	Rochdale	W 3-2	Chedgzoy, Harrison, Parker
19		15	(h)	Bolton W	W 2-1	Chedgzoy, Clennell
20		22	(a)	Manchester C	L 1-2	Clennell
21		29	(h)	Stoke C	W 4-1	Kirsopp 2, Chedgzoy, Clennell
22	Feb	5	(a)	Burnley	L 1-2	Clennell
23		12	(h)	Preston NE	W 2-0	Clennell, Kirsopp
24		19	(a)	Stockport C	L 1-3	Clennell
25		26	(h)	Liverpool	L 0-1	

FINAL LEAGUE POSITION: 4th in Lancashire Section Principal Tournament — Appearances
In that competition, the postponed Oldham Athletic v Everton match was not subsequently played. — Goals

26	Mar	4	(a)	Manchester U	W 2-0	Kirsopp, Wareing
27		11	(h)	Stockport C	W 2-0	Williamson 2
28		18	(h)	Manchester C	D 1-1	Williamson
29		25	(a)	Oldham A	W 2-1	Clennell, Harrison
30	Apr	1	(h)	Liverpool	W 1-0	Clennell
31		8	(h)	Manchester U	W 3-1	Clennell 2, Rigsby
32		15	(a)	Stockport C	W 2-1	Clennell, Rigsby
33		21	(a)	Liverpool	L 2-5	Kirsopp 2
34		22	(a)	Manchester C	L 4-5	Clennell 2, Williamson, Opp own-goal
35		29	(h)	Oldham A	L 0-2	

FINAL LEAGUE POSITION: 2nd in Lancashire Section Subsidiary Tournament, Southern Division — Appearances
Goals

Baines	Bromilow W	Brown W	Chedgzoy S	Clennell J	Donnachie J	Fern T	Fleetwood T	Galt J	Grenyer A	Harrison G	Howarth H	Jefferis F	Johnson	Kirsopp W	McNeal	Maconnachie J	Mitchell F	Nuttall T	Parker R	Rigsby H	Roberts J	Simpson R	Smith J	Snoddy	Stewart R	Thompson R	Wareing W	Williamson	Wright W	
			7	10	11	1	4		6					8		3		9								2	5			1
			7	10	11		4		6					8			1	9				3				2	5			2
		6	7	10	11		4							8			1	9				3				2	5			3
			7	10		1	4		6					8		3		9			11					2	5			4
			7	10			4		6			9		8		3	1				11					2	5			5
			7	10		1	4		6			9		8		3					11					2	5			6
			7	10		1	4		6		11	9		8		3										2	5			7
			7	10		1	4		6	11				8		3			9							2	5			8
		4	7	10		1			6	11		9		8											3	2	5			9
			7	10		1	4		6	11				8		3			9							2	5			10
			7	10		1	4		6	11		9		8		3										2	5			11
		6	7	10		1	4			11		8		9		3										2	5			12
			7	10		1	4		6	11				8		3		9								2	5			13
	1	6	7	10			4		11					8		3			9							2	5			14
	1	6	7	10			4			11				8		3										2	5		9	15
			7	10		1	4		6	11		8				3										2	5		9	16
			7	10		1	4	5	11			8							9			3				2	6			17
		5	7	10		1	4			11		8			6	3			9				2							18
		4	7	10		1	5			11		8							9					3		2	6			19
		4	7	10		1	5			11		8			6				9				3			2				20
	1	4	7	10			5			11				8										3		2	6		9	21
		4	7	10		1	5		6	11				8		3										2			9	22
9		4	7	10		1			6	11				8		3						2					5			23
		4	7	10		1	9		6	11				8								3				2	5			24
		4	7				5		10	11		8			6		1					3				2	9			25
1	3	13	25	24	3	18	23	1	18	16	1	12		19	3	16	4	5	7		3	6	2	2	1	23	22		4	
			6	24				1	2	3		2		11				2	7										1	

Baines	Bromilow W	Brown W	Chedgzoy S	Clennell J	Donnachie J	Fern T	Fleetwood T	Galt J	Grenyer A	Harrison G	Howarth H	Jefferis F	Johnson	Kirsopp W	McNeal	Maconnachie J	Mitchell F	Nuttall T	Parker R	Rigsby H	Roberts J	Simpson R	Smith J	Snoddy	Stewart R	Thompson R	Wareing W	Williamson	Wright W	
		4	7			1	5		6	11				8		3				10						2	9			26
	1	4	7				5			11				8	6					10		3				2		9		27
		4	7	10		1	5			11				8	6							3				2		9		28
			7	10		1	5			11			4	8								3				2	6	9		29
		4	7	10		1	5							8							11	3				2	6	9		30
		4	7	10		1	5			11				8		3				9						2	6			31
		4	7	9		1	5			11		8				3				10						2	6			32
	1	4		9			5			11				8		3				10						2	6	7		33
	1	4		10					6	11		7		8		5						3				2		9		34
		4	7	10		1	5			11				8		3						2					6	9		35
	3	9	8	8		7	9		2	9		2	1	9	2	6				5	1	6				9	7	7		
				7						1				3						2							1	4		

1 own-goal

1916-17

1	Sep	2	(a)	Bury	W 3-0	Clennell 3
2		9	(h)	Stoke C	D 1-1	Clennell
3		16	(a)	Southport	L 0-1	
4		23	(h)	Blackburn R	L 2-5	Harrison, Sheldon
5		30	(a)	Manchester C	L 1-4	Clennell
6	Oct	7	(h)	Blackpool	W 3-1	Clennell 2, Kirsopp
7		14	(h)	Rochdale	W 3-0	Clennell, Harrison, Wareing
8		21	(a)	Bolton W	W 3-1	Harrison, Kirsopp, Morris
9		28	(h)	Port Vale	W 3-1	Harrison, Kirsopp, Morris
10	Nov	4	(a)	Oldham A	W 3-2	Kirsopp 2, Lloyd
11		11	(h)	Preston NE	W 3-1	Clennell 2, Harrison
12		18	(a)	Burnley	D 2-2	Clennell 2
13		25	(h)	Manchester U	W 3-2	Clennell 2, Kirsopp
14	Dec	2	(a)	Liverpool	L 1-2	Kirsopp
15		9	(h)	Stockport C	L 0-1	
16		16	(h)	Bury	W 5-0	Blair 2, Clennell 2, Jefferis
17		23	(a)	Stoke C	W 2-0	Clennell 2
18		30	(h)	Southport	D 1-1	Clennell
19	Jan	6	(a)	Blackburn R	W 5-1	Clennell 3, Morris 2
20		13	(h)	Manchester C	L 0-2	
21		20	(a)	Blackpool	D 1-1	Thompson
22		27	(a)	Rochdale	L 1-2	Thompson
23	Feb	3	(h)	Bolton W	W 1-0	Lovelady
24		10	(a)	Port Vale	D 1-1	Jefferis
25		17	(h)	Oldham A	W 2-0	Gouldson, Jefferis
26		24	(a)	Preston NE	D 2-2	Clennell, Cooper
27	Mar	3	(h)	Burnley	W 5-0	Clennell 2, Gault 2, Jefferis
28		10	(a)	Manchester U	W 2-0	Gault, Jefferis
29		17	(h)	Liverpool	D 2-2	Gault 2
30		24	(a)	Stockport C	L 1-5	Gault

FINAL LEAGUE POSITION: 5th in the Lancashire Section Principal Tournament

Appearances
Goals

31	Mar	31	(h)	Southport	W 4-2	Gault 3, Jefferis
32	Apr	7	(a)	Liverpool	W 4-0	Gault 2, Clennell, Donnachie
33		9	(h)	Stockport C	D 1-1	Clennell
34		14	(a)	Southport	W 1-0	Grenyer
35		21	(h)	Liverpool	W 5-0	Gault 3, Clennell 2
36		28	(a)	Stockport C	L 1-2	Gault

FINAL LEAGUE POSITION: 2nd in the Lancashire Section Subsidiary Tournament

Appearances
Goals

Blair J	Bradbury	Campney	Challinor	Chedgzoy S	Clennell J	Cooper	Donnachie J	Dunn	Elliott	Fern T	Fleetwood T	Gault W	Gouldson	Grenyer A	Harrison G	Hunter	Jefferis F	Kirsopp W	Lloyd	Lovelady	McNeal	Maconnachie J	Merritt	Mitchell F	Morris	Murray	Peet	Sheldon	Simpson R	Smith J	Stewart R	Thompson R	Twiss J	Wareing W	Williams A	
	9				10					1	4			6	11			8	7										3			2		5		1
	4	9			10					1	5			6	11			8	7										3			2				2
	4	9	5		10					1				6	11			8	7										3			2				3
	9				10					1	5				11		8		7		6							9	3			2				4
					8			2		1	6			4	7	5	10		11						9							3				5
					10						4			6	11			8	7					1	9					2		3		5		6
					10						4			6	11			8	7					1	9					2		3		5		7
					10						4			6	11			8	7					1	9					2		3		5		8
					10						4			6	11			8	7					1	9					2		3		5		9
					10						4			6	11			8	7					1	9					2		3		5		10
	6		4		10			3							11			8	7					1	9							2		5		11
					10			2			4			6	11		7	8						1	9							3		5		12
	4				10			2						6	11		7	8						1	9							3		5		13
	9				10						4			6	11		7	8						1						2		3		5		14
					10						4			6	11		7	8				2		1	9							3		5		15
9					10						4			6	11		8		7					1						3		2		5		16
9	6				10						4				11		8		7					1						2		3		5		17
9				7	10						4			6			8					3		1			11			2				5		18
	8				10		11				4			6					7					1	9						3	2		5		19
9					10		11				4			6					7					1	8					2		3		5		20
	10									1	4			6			8		7						9		11				3	2		5		21
			7				11		8	1	4			6			10								9					2		3		5		22
							11				4			6			10			8		3	7	1	9					2				5		23
						8	11							6			10						7	1	9					2	4	3		5		24
						8				1	4		11	6			10						7		9					2		3		5		25
					10	8				1	4	9	11	6									7							2		3		5		26
					10	7	11			1	4	9		6			8													2		3		5		27
					10	7	11				4	9		6			8							1						2		3		5		28
				7	10		11				4	9		6			8					3		1								2		5		29
10							11					9		6			8						7	1	4						3	2		5		30
5	10	2	3	2	24	5	9	4	1	10	25	5	2	27	17	1	18	13	16	1	1	4	5	20	18		2	1	4	17	4	28		26		
2					25	1						6	1		5		5	7	1						4							2		1		

Blair J	Bradbury	Campney	Challinor	Chedgzoy S	Clennell J	Cooper	Donnachie J	Dunn	Elliott	Fern T	Fleetwood T	Gault W	Gouldson	Grenyer A	Harrison G	Hunter	Jefferis F	Kirsopp W	Lloyd	Lovelady	McNeal	Maconnachie J	Merritt	Mitchell F	Morris	Murray	Peet	Sheldon	Simpson R	Smith J	Stewart R	Thompson R	Twiss J	Wareing W	Williams A	
							11			1	4	9					8					3				7				2			10	5	6	31
					10		11				4	9		6			8							1		7				2		3		5		32
					10						4	9		6		2	8							1	11	7						3		5		33
					10		11			1	4	9		6			8									7				2		3		5		34
					10		11			1	4	9		6			8									7				2		3		5		35
							11					9		6			8							1		7					2	3	10	5	4	36
					4		5			3	5	6		5		1	6					1		3	1	6				4	1	5	2	6	2	
					4		1					9		1			1																			

1917-18

1	Sep	1	(h)	Southport	W 6-1	Clennell 3, Donnachie, Gault, Jefferis
2		8	(a)	Southport	W 2-0	Clennell 2
3		15	(h)	Burnley	W 9-0	Gault 4, Clennell 2, Fleetwood 2, Jefferis
4		22	(a)	Burnley	W 5-0	Clennell 3, Fleetwood, Jefferis
5		29	(h)	Liverpool	D 2-2	Clennell, Gault
6	Oct	6	(a)	Liverpool	L 0-6	
7		13	(h)	Manchester U	W 3-0	Gault 2, Clennell
8		20	(a)	Manchester U	D 0-0	
9		27	(a)	Stockport C	D 0-0	
10	Nov	3	(h)	Stockport C	L 2-3	Clennell 2
11		10	(a)	Oldham A	W 3-1	Clennell 2, Jefferis
12		17	(h)	Oldham A	W 4-2	Clennell 3, Gault
13		24	(a)	Bury	W 5-2	Gault 4, Jefferis
14	Dec	1	(h)	Bury	W 7-1	Clennell 4, Wareing 2, Murray
15		8	(a)	Stoke C	L 0-3	
16		15	(h)	Stoke C	W 3-2	Clennell 2, Opp own-goal
17		22	(a)	Preston NE	W 1-0	Gault
18		29	(h)	Preston NE	W 6-0	Clennell 4, Wareing, Wright
19	Jan	5	(a)	Blackpool	L 0-1	
20		12	(h)	Blackpool	W 7-2	Gault 4, Wright 2, Bain
21		19	(a)	Manchester C	W 2-0	Gault, Wright
22		26	(h)	Manchester C	D 0-0	
23	Feb	2	(a)	Rochdale	D 2-2	Bain, Wright
24		9	(h)	Rochdale	D 2-2	Clennell, Wright
25		16	(a)	Blackburn R	W 6-0	Gault 3, Wareing 2, Clennell
26		23	(h)	Blackburn R	W 2-1	Gault, Wright
27	Mar	2	(a)	Port Vale	W 1-0	Gault
28		9	(h)	Port Vale	W 7-0	Clennell 4, Gault 2, Jefferis
29		16	(a)	Bolton W	W 3-2	Gault 2, Wareing
30		23	(h)	Bolton W	L 2-3	Gault 2

FINAL LEAGUE POSITION: 3rd in the Lancashire Section Principal Tournament

Appearances
Goals

31	Jan	1	(a)	Liverpool	L 1-4	Gault
32	Mar	29	(h)	Liverpool	W 3-2	Jefferis 2, Gault
33		30	(h)	Stockport C	W 4-0	Gault 2, Howarth, Wadsworth
34	Apr	6	(a)	Stockport C	W 1-0	Twiss
35		13	(h)	Southport	W 6-1	Gault 3, Clennell 2, Jefferis
36		20	(a)	Southport	W 4-0	Clennell, Gault, Jefferis, Wareing

FINAL LEAGUE POSITION: 2nd in Lancashire Section Subsidiary Tournament

Appearances
Goals

Bain G	Bull H	Burgess W	Challinor	Clennell J	Collins J	Cooper	Cordall S	Cotter F	Donnachie J	Fern T	Fleetwood T	Gault T	Grenyer A	Guttridge	Howarth H	Jefferis F	Kirsopp W	Lovelady	Maconnachie J	Mitchell F	Murphy J	Murray S	Newton	Redford C	Riley J	Robinson W	Scott	Smith J	South J	Stewart R	Thompson R	Twiss J	Wadsworth	Wareing W	Williams A	Wright W			
				10					11		4	9	6			8				1		7				2					3			5					1
				10					11			9	6			8				1		7				2					3			5	4				2
				10					11		4	9	6			8	7			1						3					2			5					3
				10					11		4	9	6			8				1		7				3					2			5					4
				10					11		4	9	6			8	7			1						3					2			5					5
				10					11		5	9	6			8				1		7				3					2				4				6
				10			5		11		4	9	6			8				1		7				3				2									7
				10			5		11		4	9	6			8				1		7				3								2					8
				10					11		4	9	6			8				1				7		3		2						5					9
				10							4	9	6			8				1	11			7		3					2			5					10
				10			5		11			9		2		8				1		7				4					3			6					11
				10			6		11		4	9		2		8				1		7									3			5					12
				10					11		4	9	6			8				1						3				7	2			5					13
				10					11		4	9	6			8				1		7				3					2			5					14
				10					11		4	9	6			8				1		7				3					2			5					15
				10					11		4	9	6			8			2	1		7							3					5					16
				10					11			9	6			4		8		1					2	3						7		5					17
	2			10					11			8	6			4				1		7				3								5		9			18
	2			10				4	11			8	6							1						3						7		5		9			19
7								4	11			9	6			8				1					2	3								5		10			20
				7				4	11			9	6			8				1						3		2						5		10			21
				7				4	11			9	6			8				1						3		2						5		10			22
7				10				4	11		5		6			8				1					2	3										9			23
7				10					11		4		6			8				1			2			3								5		9			24
7				10							4	9	6			8				1					2	3								5		11			25
		11			2						4	9	6			8				1		7				3								5		10			26
					2	7			11		4	9	6			8				1						3								5		10			27
				10	2			7	11		4	9	6			8				1						3								5					28
				10	2				11		4	9	6			8				1						3							7	5					29
								8	11		4	9	6			10				1						3		2					7	5					30
4	2	1		26	4	1	4	7	27		22	28	28	2		29	2	1	1	30	1	13	1	2	4	28		4	1	2	12	2	2	27	2	10			
2				35					1		3	30				6						1												6		7			

1 own-goal

Bain G	Bull H	Burgess W	Challinor	Clennell J	Collins J	Cooper	Cordall S	Cotter F	Donnachie J	Fern T	Fleetwood T	Gault T	Grenyer A	Guttridge	Howarth H	Jefferis F	Kirsopp W	Lovelady	Maconnachie J	Mitchell F	Murphy J	Murray S	Newton	Redford C	Riley J	Robinson W	Scott	Smith J	South J	Stewart R	Thompson R	Twiss J	Wadsworth	Wareing W	Williams A	Wright W			
	2		4	10					11	1		8	6								7					3								5		9			31
		11		10	2			4			5	9	6			8				1							3						7						32
		7			2						4	9	6		10					1						3						8	11	5					33
					2			4	11		5	9	6			8				1							3					10	7						34
		11		10	2			4			5	9	6			8				1							3						7						35
				10	2				11		4	9	6			8				1						3							7	5					36
	1	3	1	4	5			3	3	1	5	6	6		1	4				5	1					3	3					2	5	3		1			
				3								8				4																1	1	1					

1918-19

1	Sep	7	(a)	Burnley	W 6-0	Clennell 4, Donnachie, Gault
2		14	(h)	Burnley	W 6-1	Gault 2, Jefferis 2, Fleetwood, Miller
3		21	(a)	Southport	W 3-0	Gault 2, Donnachie
4		28	(h)	Southport	W 4-0	Clennell 3, Harrison
5	Oct	5	(a)	Liverpool	W 4-2	Grenyer 2, Gault, Miller
6		12	(h)	Liverpool	W 4-2	Clennell, Donnachie, Miller, Opp own-goal
7		19	(a)	Manchester U	D 1-1	Gault
8		26	(h)	Manchester U	W 6-2	Gault 3, Clennell, Jefferis, Miller
9	Nov	2	(h)	Stoke C	W 5-1	Gault 3, Donnachie, Miller
10		9	(a)	Stoke C	W 2-0	Gault, Wareing
11		16	(h)	Bury	W 5-1	Gault 3, Clennell, Miller
12		23	(a)	Bury	W 3-0	Clennell, Gault, Jefferis
13		30	(h)	Blackpool	W 6-0	Clennell 4, Fleetwood, Grenyer
14	Dec	7	(a)	Blackpool	W 3-1	Clennell 2, Gault
15		14	(h)	Stockport C	W 2-1	Clennell, Jefferis
16		21	(a)	Stockport C	D 0-0	
17		28	(a)	Blackburn R	W 4-1	Blair 2, Clennell, Grenyer
18	Jan	4	(h)	Blackburn R	W 9-0	Gault 5, Clennell 2, Miller, Wareing
19		11	(a)	Oldham A	W 3-0	Gault 2, Donnachie
20		18	(h)	Oldham A	W 3-1	Clennell 2, Gault
21		25	(a)	Manchester C	L 0-1	
22	Feb	1	(h)	Manchester C	W 3-0	Clennell, Gault, Grenyer
23		8	(a)	Port Vale	W 1-0	Gault
24		15	(h)	Port Vale	W 3-1	Clennell 2, Gault
25		22	(h)	Bolton W	W 4-1	Gault 3, Donnachie
26	Mar	1	(a)	Bolton W	W 6-3	Gault 3, Donnachie, Grenyer, Jefferis
27		8	(h)	Preston NE	W 3-2	Clennell, Gault, Jefferis
28		15	(a)	Preston NE	W 3-2	Clennell, Gault, Kirsopp
29		22	(h)	Rochdale	W 3-1	Rigsby 3
30		29	(a)	Rochdale	W 3-1	Clennell 2, Kirsopp
31	May	10	(a)	Nottingham F	D 0-0	
32		17	(h)	Nottingham F	L 0-1	

FINAL LEAGUE POSITION: 1st in the Lancashire Section Principal Tournament

Matches 31 and 32 were the Championship Decider against the winners of the Midland Section Principal Tournament.

Appearances

Goals

33	Jan	1	(h)	Liverpool	L 1-2	Jefferis
34	Apr	5	(a)	Stockport C	W 1-0	Gault
35		12	(h)	Stockport C	L 0-1	
36		18	(a)	Liverpool	D 1-1	Gault
37		19	(a)	Southport	L 1-4	Rigsby
38		23	(h)	Southport	L 1-2	Rigsby

FINAL LEAGUE POSITION: 4th in the Lancashire Section Subsidiary Tournament

Appearances

Goals

Baker	Blair J	Carlisle	Chedgzoy S	Clennell J	Cotter J	Dagnell	Donnachie J	Evans J	Fern T	Fleetwood T	Gault W	Grenyer A	Harrison G	Howarth H	Jefferis F	Kirsopp W	Maconnachie J	Miller J	Mitchell F	Page J	Peacock J	Pearson	Quinn	Rigsby H	Robinson W	Smith J	Sprace	Thompson R	Wareing W	Williams A	
			7	10			11			4	9	6			8				1						2			3	5		1
				10			11			4	9	6			8			7	1						2			3	5		2
				10	5		11			4	9	6			8			7	1						2			3			3
				10			7			4	9	6	11		8				1						2			3	5		4
				10			11			4	9	6			8			7	1						2			3	5		5
				10			11			4	9	6			8			7	1						3	2			5		6
				10	5		11			4	9	6			8			7	1						2				3		7
				10			11			4	9	6			8			7	1						2			3	5		8
				10	6		11			4	9				8			7	1						3	2			5		9
				10			11			4	9	6			8			7	1	3						2			5		10
				10			11			4	9	6			8			7	1						3	2			5		11
				10			11			4	9	6			8			7	1						3	2			5		12
				10	4		11			9		6			8			7	1						3	2			5		13
				10			11			4	9	6			8			7	1						3	2			5		14
				10			11			4	9	6			8			7	1						3	2			5		15
				10			11			4	9	6			8			7	1						3	2			5		16
	9			10			11			4		6				8		7	1						3	2			5		17
				10			11			4	9	6			8		3	7	1									2	5		18
				10			11			4	9	6			8			7	1						3	2			5		19
				10			11			4	9	6			8			7	1						3			2	5		20
							11			4	9	6			8				1	7					3	2			5	10	21
				10			11			4	9	6			8	7			1						3	2			5		22
				10			11			4	9	6			8	7			1						3	2			5		23
				10			11			4	9	6			8	7			1						3	2			5		24
							11				9				4	8		7	1					10	3	2			5	6	25
				10			11			4	9	6			8	7			1						3	2			5		26
				10				11		4	9	6			8	7			1						3	2			5		27
				10						4	9	6			8	11		7	1						3	2			5		28
				10						4		6			8	11		7	1					9	3	2			5		29
				10						4	9	6			8	11		7	1	2					3				5		30
				10						4	9	6	11		8			7	1						3	2			5		31
				10						4	9	6			8			7	1				11		3	2			5		32
	1		1	30	4		26	1		31	29	30	2		31	10	1	24	32	3			1	2	30	22		8	31	2	
	2			30			7			9	38	6	1		7	2		7						3					2		

1 own-goal

Baker	Blair J	Carlisle	Chedgzoy S	Clennell J	Cotter J	Dagnell	Donnachie J	Evans J	Fern T	Fleetwood T	Gault W	Grenyer A	Harrison G	Howarth H	Jefferis F	Kirsopp W	Maconnachie J	Miller J	Mitchell F	Page J	Peacock J	Pearson	Quinn	Rigsby H	Robinson W	Smith J	Sprace	Thompson R	Wareing W	Williams A	
				10			11			4	9				8	7			1						3	2			5	6	33
								11			9				8			7	1	2	4			10	3				5	6	34
			9	10								6	11		8			7	1		4				3			2	5		35
				10				11	1		9	6			8			7		2	4				3				5		36
10		5											11	8				7	1		4	3		9				2		6	37
			7	10		11						6			8				1	2		3		9			4		5		38
1		1	2	4		1	1	2	1	1	3	3	2	1	5	1		4	5	3	4	2		3	4	1	1	2	5	3	
											2				1									2							

1919-20

1	Aug	30	(h)	Chelsea	L 2-3	Grenyer, Mayson
2	Sep	3	(a)	Bradford	W 2-0	Gault, Rigsby
3		6	(a)	Chelsea	W 1-0	Gault
4		8	(h)	Bradford	W 2-0	Gault, Miller
5		13	(a)	West Brom A	L 3-4	Gault, Jefferis, Maconnachie
6		20	(h)	West Brom A	L 2-5	Gault, Kirsopp
7		27	(a)	Sunderland	W 3-2	Clennell, Grenyer, Kirsopp
8	Oct	4	(h)	Sunderland	L 1-3	Maconnachie
9		11	(h)	Arsenal	L 2-3	Chedgzoy, Gault
10		18	(a)	Arsenal	D 1-1	Gault
11		25	(h)	Blackburn R	W 3-0	Clennell, Gault, Kirsopp
12	Nov	1	(a)	Blackburn R	L 2-3	Clennell 2
13		8	(h)	Bradford C	W 4-1	Clennell 3, Kirsopp
14		15	(a)	Bradford C	D 3-3	Clennell 2, Jones
15		22	(h)	Bolton W	D 3-3	Kirsopp 2, Clennell
16		29	(a)	Bolton W	W 2-0	Clennell, Gault
17	Dec	6	(h)	Notts C	L 1-2	Gault
18		13	(a)	Notts C	D 1-1	Chedgzoy
19		20	(h)	Liverpool	D 0-0	
20		25	(a)	Manchester C	D 1-1	Clennell
21		26	(h)	Manchester C	W 2-0	Fleetwood, Gault
22		27	(a)	Liverpool	L 1-3	Parker
23	Jan	3	(h)	Sheffield W	D 1-1	Chedgzoy
24		17	(a)	Sheffield W	L 0-1	
25		24	(h)	Newcastle U	W 4-0	Parker 2, Grenyer, Rigsby
26	Feb	7	(h)	Aston Villa	D 1-1	Parker
27		11	(a)	Newcastle U	L 0-3	
28		14	(a)	Aston Villa	D 2-2	Gault, Rigsby
29		18	(h)	Oldham A	L 0-2	
30		28	(a)	Oldham A	L 1-4	Kearslake
31	Mar	6	(a)	Manchester U	L 0-1	
32		13	(h)	Manchester U	D 0-0	
33		20	(a)	Sheffield U	D 1-1	Kirsopp
34		27	(h)	Sheffield U	W 3-0	Howarth, Kirsopp, Peacock
35	Apr	2	(h)	Derby C	W 4-0	Blair 2, Howarth, Kirsopp
36		3	(a)	Middlesbrough	D 1-1	Kirsopp
37		5	(a)	Derby C	L 1-2	Grenyer
38		10	(h)	Middlesbrough	W 5-2	Rigsby 2, Grenyer, Kirsopp, Peacock
39		17	(a)	Burnley	L 0-5	
40		24	(h)	Burnley	D 2-2	Kirsopp 2
41		26	(a)	Preston NE	D 1-1	Kirsopp
42	May	1	(h)	Preston NE	L 0-1	

FINAL LEAGUE POSITION: 16th in Division One

Appearances
Goals

FA Cup

1	Jan	10	(a)	Birmingham	L 0-2	

Appearances
Goals

Berwick W	Blair J	Brewster G	Brown W	Chedgzoy S	Clennell J	Donnachie J	Downs R	Evans W	Fern T	Fleetwood T	Gault W	Greyner A	Harrison G	Howarth H	Jefferis F	Jones G	Kearslake J	Kirsopp W	Leivesley W	Maconnachie J	Mayson T	Miller J	Mitchell F	Page J	Parker R	Peacock J	Rigsby H	Robinson A	Robinson W	Thompson R	Wall A	Wareing W	Weller L	Williams O	
						11				4	9	6			8						10	7	1						3	2		5			1
						11				4	9	6			8							7	1				10		3	2		5			2
				7						4	9	6	11					8		3			1				10			2			5		3
						11				4	9	6			8					3		7	1				10			2		5			4
						11				4	9	6			8					3		7	1				10			2		5			5
					10	11				4	9	6						8				7	1						3	2		5			6
					10	11			1	4	9	6						8		3		7								2		5			7
					10					4	9	6			8			11		2		7	1									5	3		8
				7	10				1	4	9		11					8						2								5	3	6	9
				7	10				1	4	9	6	11					8		2												5	3		10
					10	11			1	4	9	6						8				7		2								5	3		11
				7	10				1	4	9	6	11					8						2								5	3		12
			4		10	11			1	5					8	7		9						2					6				3		13
			4		10	11			1	5					8	7		9						2					6				3		14
2			4		10	11				5					8	7		9					1						6				3		15
			4		10	11			1	5	9	6				7		8		2													3		16
					10	11			1	4	9	6				7		8		2												5	3		17
			4	8	10				1	5	9	6	11			7								2									3		18
			4	8	10				1	5		6	11			7		9						2									3		19
			4	7	10	11			1	5	9	6			8									2									3		20
			4		10				1	5	9		11		8	7														2		6	3		21
			4	7		11			1			6			8										9		10			2		5	3		22
		5	4	7		11			1		10				8										9				6	2			3		23
		5		7	10	11			1	2															9	4		8				6	3		24
		5	4	7				3	1	2		6	11					8							9		10								25
		5	4	7					1	2		6	11					8							9		10						3		26
		5	4	7					1	2		6	11					8							9		10						3		27
			4	7	8				1	5	9	6	11														10			2			3		28
			4	7					1	5	9	6	11														10			2	8		3		29
			4					3	1	5		6	11			7	9										10			2	8				30
			4	7			2		1	5		6	11					10		3					9						8				31
				7			2		1	5	8		11					10		3					9	4								6	32
							2		1	5		6	11	10		7		8		3						9							4		33
							2		1			6	11	10		7		8	5	3						9							4		34
	9						2		1			6	11	10		7		8	5	3													4		35
							2		1	5		6	11	10		7		8								9				3			4		36
	9						2		1			6	11	10		7		8	5	3													4		37
							2		1	4		6	11			7		8	5	3						9	10								38
							2		1	4		6	11			7		8	5	3						9	10								39
			4				2		1	5		6	11	10		7		8								9				3					40
	9		4				2		1	5		6	11	10		7		8												3					41
			4	7			2		1	5			11					8								9	10			3			6		42
1	3	5	20	18	18	16	12	2	34	37	21	33	25	7	12	18	1	29	5	16	1	8	8	8	8	9	14	1	7	17	3	15	28	2	
	2			3	12					1	12	5		2	1	1	1	14		2	1	1			4	2	5								

Berwick W	Blair J	Brewster G	Brown W	Chedgzoy S	Clennell J	Donnachie J	Downs R	Evans W	Fern T	Fleetwood T	Gault W	Greyner A	Harrison G	Howarth H	Jefferis F	Jones G	Kearslake J	Kirsopp W	Leivesley W	Maconnachie J	Mayson T	Miller J	Mitchell F	Page J	Parker R	Peacock J	Rigsby H	Robinson A	Robinson W	Thompson R	Wall A	Wareing W	Weller L	Williams O	
			4	7	10				1	5	9	6	11		8									2									3		1
			1	1	1				1	1	1	1	1		1									1									1		

1920-21

1	Aug	28	(a)	Bradford	D 3-3	Parker 2, Kirsopp
2	Sep	1	(h)	Newcastle U	W 3-1	Kirsopp 2, Crossley
3		4	(h)	Bradford	D 1-1	Harrison
4		8	(a)	Newcastle U	L 0-2	
5		11	(a)	Derby C	W 4-2	Peacock 3, Fleetwood
6		18	(h)	Derby C	W 3-1	Chedgzoy, Harrison, Kirsopp
7		22	(h)	Sheffield U	W 3-0	Crossley, Grenyer, Harrison
8		25	(a)	Blackburn R	D 0-0	
9	Oct	2	(h)	Blackburn R	W 2-1	Chedgzoy 2
10		4	(a)	Sheffield U	L 0-2	
11		9	(a)	Huddersfield T	W 1-0	Kirsopp
12		16	(h)	Huddersfield T	D 0-0	
13		23	(a)	Liverpool	L 0-1	
14		30	(h)	Liverpool	L 0-3	
15	Nov	6	(a)	Bradford C	D 2-2	Crossley 2
16		13	(h)	Bradford C	D 2-2	Crossley, Reid
17		20	(h)	Sunderland	D 1-1	Parker
18		27	(a)	Sunderland	W 2-0	Fazackerley, Harrison
19	Dec	4	(a)	Middlesbrough	L 1-3	Crossley
20		11	(h)	Middlesbrough	W 2-1	Parker 2
21		18	(a)	West Brom A	W 2-1	Fazackerley, Parker
22		25	(h)	Arsenal	L 2-4	Parker 2
23		27	(a)	Arsenal	D 1-1	Fazackerley
24	Jan	1	(h)	West Brom A	D 2-2	Fazackerley, Parker
25		15	(a)	Aston Villa	W 3-1	Harrison 2, Crossley
26		22	(h)	Aston Villa	D 1-1	Harrison
27	Feb	5	(h)	Manchester C	W 3-0	Crossley 2, Davies
28		12	(a)	Manchester U	W 2-1	Parker 2
29		23	(a)	Manchester C	L 0-2	
30		26	(a)	Chelsea	W 1-0	Crossley
31	Mar	9	(h)	Manchester U	W 2-0	Crossley, Davies
32		12	(a)	Tottenham H	L 0-2	
33		25	(a)	Bolton W	L 2-4	Crossley, Davies
34		26	(h)	Oldham A	W 5-2	Crossley 2, Chedgzoy, Davies, Reid
35		28	(h)	Bolton W	L 2-3	Crossley, Ried
36	Apr	2	(a)	Oldham A	W 1-0	Reid
37		6	(h)	Chelsea	W 5-1	Fazackerley 3, Harrison, Reid
38		9	(h)	Preston NE	L 0-1	
39		16	(a)	Preston NE	L 0-1	
40		23	(h)	Burnley	D 1-1	Fazackerley
41		27	(h)	Tottenham H	D 0-0	
42		30	(a)	Burnley	D 1-1	Chedgzoy

FINAL LEAGUE POSITION: 7th in Division One

Appearances
Goals

FA Cup

1	Jan	1	(h)	Stockport C	W 1-0	Opp own-goal
2		29	(h)	Sheffield W	D 1-1	Parker
R	Feb	3	(a)	Sheffield W	W 1-0	Crossley
3		19	(h)	Newcastle U	W 3-0	Crossley 2, Davies
4	Mar	5	(h)	Wolves	L 0-1	

Appearances
Goals

Baker B	Blair J	Brewster G	Brown W	Chedgzoy S	Clennell J	Crossley C	Davies S	Downs R	Fazackerley S	Fern T	Fleetwood T	Grenyer A	Harrison G	Jones G	Kirsopp W	Moffatt A	McDonald J	Parker R	Peacock J	Reid D	Thompson R	Wall A	Weller L	
		5		7		10		2		1		6			8		3	9		11			4	1
		5		7		10		2		1	4	6	11		8		3	9						2
		5		7		10		2		1	4	6	11		8		3	9						3
		5		7		10		2		1	4	6	11		8		3	9						4
		5		7		10		2		1	4	6	11		8		3		9					5
		5		7		10		2		1	4	6	11		8		3		9					6
		5		7		10		2		1	4	6	11		8		3		9					7
		5		7		10		2		1	4	6	11				3		9	8				8
		5		7		10		2		1	4	6	11		8		3		9					9
		5		7		10		2		1	4	6	11		8		3		9					10
		5		7				2		1	4	6	11		8		3		9	10				11
		5						2		1	4	6	11	7	8		3		9	10				12
		5								1	4	6	11	7	8		3		9	10	2			13
		5		7		8		2		1	4	6	11				3		9	10				14
				7		8		2		1	5	6	11				3	9	4	10				15
				7		8		2	9	1	5	6	11				3		4	10				16
				7		8		2		1	5	6	11				3	9	4	10				17
				7		10		2	8	1	5	6	11					9	4		3			18
				7		10		2	8	1	5	6	11				3	9	4					19
		5		7		10		2	8	1	4	6	11				3	9						20
		5		7		10		2	8	1	4	6	11				3	9						21
		5		7		10		2	8	1	4	6	11				3	9						22
		5		7		10		2	8	1	4		11				3	9	6					23
		5		7		10		2	8	1	4						3	9	6	11				24
		5		7		10		2	8	1	4		11				3	9	6					25
		5		7		10		2	8	1	4		11				3	9					6	26
			4	7		10	9	2		1	5		11				3					8	6	27
			4	7		10		2	8	1	5		11				3	9					6	28
		5				10	9	2		1	4			7	8					11	3		6	29
1		5		7		10	9	2	8		4						3			11			6	30
		5				10	9	2	8	1	4	6	11	7			3							31
1		5			8	10		2			4		11	7			3	9					6	32
			4	7		10	9	2	8	1	5		11				3		6					33
		5		7		10	9			1	4		11				2		6	8			3	34
		5		7		10	9	2		1	4		11				3		6	8				35
		5	4	7		10		2		1			11			9			6	8			3	36
			4			10		2	9	1	5		11	7			3		6	8				37
			4					2	9	1	5		11	7			3		6	8		10		38
			4	7			10	2	9	1	5		11				3		6	8				39
			4	7		10		2	9	1	5		11				3		6	8				40
			4	7			10	2	9	1	5		11				3		6	8				41
		5	4	7			10	2	9	1			11				3		6	8				42
2		29	10	35	1	35	10	40	20	40	39	23	38	7	13	1	39	17	28	21	3	2	9	
				5		15	4		8		1	1	8		5			11	3	5				

Baker B	Blair J	Brewster G	Brown W	Chedgzoy S	Clennell J	Crossley C	Davies S	Downs R	Fazackerley S	Fern T	Fleetwood T	Grenyer A	Harrison G	Jones G	Kirsopp W	Moffatt A	McDonald J	Parker R	Peacock J	Reid D	Thompson R	Wall A	Weller L	
		5		7		10		2	8	1			11				3	9	6				4	1
				7		10		2	8	1	5	6	11				3	9	4					2
	9	5		7		10		2	8	1	4		11				3						6	R
		5		7		10	9	2	8	1	4		11				3						6	3
		5		7		10	9	2	8	1	4		11				3						6	4
	1	4		5		5	2	5	5	5	4	1	5				5	2	2				4	
						3	1											1						

1 own-goal

1921-22

1	Aug	27	(h)	Manchester U	W 5-0	Davies 3, Brewster, Fazackerley
2		31	(a)	Newcastle U	L 0-3	
3	Sep	3	(a)	Manchester U	L 1-2	Harrison
4		7	(h)	Newcastle U	L 2-3	Blair, Davies
5		10	(h)	Birmingham	W 2-1	Fazackerley, Reid
6		17	(a)	Birmingham	D 1-1	Spencer
7		24	(h)	Arsenal	D 1-1	Fazackerley
8	Oct	1	(a)	Arsenal	L 0-1	
9		8	(h)	Blackburn R	W 2-0	Davies, Reid
10		15	(a)	Blackburn R	D 2-2	Fazackerley, Harrison
11		22	(h)	Oldham A	D 2-2	Fazackerley 2
12		29	(a)	Oldham A	D 0-0	
13	Nov	5	(h)	Liverpool	D 1-1	Brewster
14		12	(a)	Liverpool	D 1-1	Chedgzoy
15		19	(a)	Cardiff C	L 1-2	Fazackerley
16		26	(h)	Cardiff C	L 0-1	
17	Dec	3	(h)	West Brom A	L 1-2	Peacock
18		10	(a)	West Brom A	D 1-1	Crossley
19		17	(a)	Manchester C	L 1-2	Fazackerley
20		24	(h)	Manchester C	D 2-2	Fazackerley, Irvine
21		26	(a)	Sunderland	W 2-1	Chedgzoy, Wall
22		31	(h)	Bolton W	W 1-0	Fazackerley
23	Jan	2	(h)	Sunderland	W 3-0	Fazackerley, Irvine, Wall
24		14	(a)	Bolton W	L 0-1	
25		21	(h)	Aston Villa	W 3-2	Irvine 3
26	Feb	8	(a)	Aston Villa	L 1-2	Irvine
27		11	(a)	Middlesbrough	L 1-3	Crossley
28		25	(a)	Tottenham H	L 0-2	
29	Mar	1	(h)	Middlesbrough	W 4-1	Crossley, Fleetwood, Irvine, Spencer
30		4	(h)	Bradford C	W 2-0	Chadwick 2
31		11	(a)	Bradford C	L 1-3	Chadwick
32		15	(h)	Tottenham H	D 0-0	
33		18	(a)	Preston NE	L 0-1	
34	Apr	1	(a)	Chelsea	L 0-1	
35		8	(h)	Chelsea	L 2-3	Reid 2
36		10	(h)	Preston NE	D 0-0	
37		14	(h)	Huddersfield T	W 6-2	Chedgzoy 3, Irvine 3
38		15	(a)	Sheffield U	L 0-1	
39		18	(a)	Huddersfield T	W 2-1	Grenyer, Irvine
40		22	(h)	Sheffield U	D 1-1	Brewster
41		29	(a)	Burnley	L 0-2	
42	May	6	(h)	Burnley	W 2-0	Fazackerley, Wall

FINAL LEAGUE POSITION: 20th in Division One

Appearances
Goals

FA Cup

1	Jan	7	(h)	Crystal P	L 0-6	

Appearances
Goals

Alford F	Blair J	Brewster G	Brown W	Chadwick W	Chedgzoy S	Clennell J	Crossley C	Davies S	Downs R	Fazackerley S	Fern T	Fleetwood T	Grenyer A	Harrison G	Hart H	Irvine R	Jones G	Livingstone D	McDonald J	Peacock J	Reid D	Salt E	Spencer H	Wall A	Weller L	
		5	4		7		10	9	2	8	1			11					3	6						1
		5	4		7		10	9	2	8	1			11					3	6						2
			4		7	10		9		8	1	5		11				2	3	6						3
	9				7			10			1	5		11				2	3	6	8				4	4
					7					9	1	5	6	11				2	3	4	10		8			5
		5			7					9	1	4	6	11				2	3		10		8			6
		5			7				2	9	1	4	6	11					3		10		8			7
		5						9	2	8	1	4	6	11			7		3		10					8
		5			7			9	2	8	1	4		11					3	6	10					9
		5			7			9	2	8	1	4		11					3	6	10					10
11		5						9	2	8	1	4					7		3	6	10					11
		5			7		10	9	2	8	1	4	6	11					3							12
		5			7		10	9	2	8	1	4	6	11					3							13
		5			7		10		2	8	1	4		11		9			3	6						14
		5			7		10		2	8	1	4		11		9			3	6						15
		5			7				2	8	1	4	6	11					3		10			8		16
		5	4		9				2	8	1			11			7	3		6	10					17
		5	4		7		10		2	8	1			11		9		3		6						18
		5	4		7		10		2	8	1			11		9		3		6						19
		5	4		7					8	1			11		9		3	2	6				10		20
			4		7					8	1	5		11		9		3	2	6				10		21
			4		7					8	1	5		11		9		3	2	6				10		22
			4		7					8		5		11		9		3	2	6		1		10		23
					7					8		5		11	6	9		3	2	4		1		10		24
					7		10		2	8		5		11	6	9		3		4		1				25
					7		10		2	8	1	5		11	6	9		3		4						26
		5	4				10		2	8				11	6	9	7	3				1				27
					7		10		2	8	1	5		11	6	9		3		4						28
							10		2		1	5		11	6	9	7		3	4			8			29
				9			10		2		1	5		11	6		7		3	4			8			30
				9							1	5		11	6	10	7	2	3	4			8			31
				9	7		10				1	5		11	6				2	4			8		3	32
			4	9							1	5		11	6	10	7		2				8		3	33
	9		4		7				2		1	5		11		8				6				10	3	34
			4		7				2		1	5	6	11		9		3			10		8			35
		5	4		7						1	2	6	11	10	9		3			8					36
		5			7						1	2	6	11	4	9		3		8	10					37
		5	8		7				2		1		6	11	4	9		3			10					38
		5			7				2	8	1	4	10	11	6	9		3								39
		5			7				2		1		6	11	4	9		3		8	10					40
11		5			7				2		1	4			6	9				8	10				3	41
		5			7				2	8	1	4		11	6	9		3						10		42
2	2	25	16	4	35	1	15	10	28	29	38	33	13	40	17	25	8	24	26	29	16	4	9	8	5	
	1	3		3	5		3	5		12		1	1	2		11				1	4		2	3		

Alford F	Blair J	Brewster G	Brown W	Chadwick W	Chedgzoy S	Clennell J	Crossley C	Davies S	Downs R	Fazackerley S	Fern T	Fleetwood T	Grenyer A	Harrison G	Hart H	Irvine R	Jones G	Livingstone D	McDonald J	Peacock J	Reid D	Salt E	Spencer H	Wall A	Weller L	
			4		7					8	1	5		11		9		3	2	6				10		1
			1		1					1	1	1		1		1		1	1	1				1		

1922-23

1	Aug	26	(a)	Newcastle U	L 0-2	
2	Sep	2	(h)	Newcastle U	W 3-2	Brewster, Irvine, Williams
3		4	(a)	Tottenham H	L 0-2	
4		9	(h)	Blackburn R	W 2-0	Forbes, Irvine
5		16	(a)	Blackburn R	L 1-5	Harrison
6		23	(a)	Cardiff C	W 2-0	Williams 2
7		30	(h)	Cardiff C	W 3-1	Forbes, Hart, Irvine
8	Oct	7	(a)	Liverpool	L 1-5	Williams
9		14	(h)	Liverpool	L 0-1	
10		21	(a)	Nottingham F	L 1-2	Chadwick
11		28	(h)	Nottingham F	W 4-2	Chedgzoy 2, Fazackerley, Williams
12	Nov	4	(h)	Arsenal	W 1-0	Williams
13		11	(a)	Arsenal	W 2-1	Chadwick, Williams
14		18	(a)	West Brom A	D 0-0	
15		25	(h)	West Brom A	L 0-1	
16	Dec	2	(a)	Sunderland	L 1-3	Chadwick
17		9	(h)	Sunderland	D 1-1	Peacock
18		16	(a)	Birmingham	D 1-1	Chadwick
19		23	(h)	Birmingham	W 2-1	Chadwick, Jones
20		25	(h)	Manchester C	D 0-0	
21		26	(a)	Manchester C	L 1-2	Williams
22		30	(h)	Huddersfield T	L 0-3	
23	Jan	1	(h)	Tottenham H	W 3-1	Grenyer, Harrison, Peacock
24		6	(a)	Huddersfield T	L 0-1	
25		20	(h)	Stoke C	W 4-0	Williams 2, Cock, Peacock
26		27	(a)	Stoke C	L 1-4	Peacock
27	Feb	10	(h)	Chelsea	W 3-1	Chedgzoy, Cock, Williams
28		14	(a)	Chelsea	L 1-3	Williams
29		17	(a)	Middlesbrough	W 4-2	Chadwick 3, Irvine
30		28	(h)	Middlesbrough	W 5-3	Cock 3, Chadwick, Chedgzoy
31	Mar	3	(a)	Oldham A	L 0-1	
32		10	(h)	Oldham A	D 0-0	
33		17	(h)	Sheffield U	W 5-1	Irvine 2, Chadwick, Chedgzoy, Cock
34		30	(a)	Bolton W	W 2-0	Chadwick, Troup
35		31	(h)	Burnley	W 1-0	Forbes
36	Apr	2	(h)	Bolton W	D 1-1	Forbes
37		7	(a)	Burnley	W 1-0	Irvine
38		14	(h)	Aston Villa	W 2-1	Cock, Troup
39		16	(a)	Sheffield U	W 1-0	Irvine
40		21	(a)	Aston Villa	L 0-3	
41		28	(h)	Preston NE	W 1-0	Cock
42	May	5	(a)	Preston NE	D 2-2	Cock, Williams

FINAL LEAGUE POSITION: 5th in Division One

Appearances
Goals

FA Cup

1	Jan	13	(h)	Bradford	D 1-1	Chedgzoy
R		17	(a)	Bradford	L 0-1	

Appearances
Goals

Brewster G	Brown W	Chadwick W	Chedgzoy S	Cock J	Downs R	Fazackerley S	Fern T	Fleetwood T	Forbes F	Grenyer A	Harland A	Harrison G	Hart H	Irvine R	Jones G	Livingstone D	McBain N	McDonald J	Miller H	Parry F	Peacock J	Raitt D	Reid D	Troup A	Wall A	Williams W	
5					2	8	1					11	6	9	7			3			4					10	1
5			7		2		1		9			11	6	8				3			4					10	2
5			7				1		9			11	6	8				3			4	2				10	3
5			7				1		9			11	6	8				3			4	2				10	4
5			7				1		9			11	6	8				3			4	2				10	5
			7				1	5	9			11	6	8				3			4	2				10	6
			7				1	5	9			11	6	8				3			4	2				10	7
			7				1	5	9			11	6	8				3			4	2				10	8
		9	7				1	5				11	6	8				3			4	2				10	9
		9	7				1	5					6					3	8		4	2	11		10		10
		9	7			8	1	5					6					3			4	2	11			10	11
		9	7					5			1		6	8				3			4	2	11			10	12
		9	7					5			1		6	8				3			4	2	11			10	13
		9	7					5			1		6	8				3			4	2	11			10	14
		9	7					5			1		6	8				3			4	2	11			10	15
		9	7					5		6	1		4					3			8	2	11			10	16
	4	9	7					5			1		6					3			8	2	11			10	17
	4	9	7							6	1		5			3					8	2	11			10	18
	4	9						5			1		6		7	3					8	2	11			10	19
	4	9						5			1		6		7	3					8	2	11			10	20
	4	9						5			1		6	8				3		7		2	11			10	21
	4	9						5			1		6	8				3		7		2	11			10	22
	4		7							6	1	11	5	9		3					8	2				10	23
	4		7					5		6	1	11		9		3					8	2				10	24
			7	9	3			4		6	1	11	5								8	2				10	25
			7	9	3			4		6	1		5								8	2		11		10	26
			7	9	3			4		6	1			8			5					2		11		10	27
			7	9	3						1		6	8			5				4	2		11		10	28
		10	7	9	3		1						6	8			5				4	2		11			29
		10	7	9			1						6	8		3	5				4	2		11			30
		10	7	9			1	5					6	8		3					4	2		11			31
		10	7	9			1						6	8		3	5				4	2		11			32
		10	7	9	2		1						6	8			5	3			4			11			33
		10	7	9	2		1						6	8			5	3			4			11			34
		10	7				1	2	9				6	8			5	3			4			11			35
		10	7				1	2	9				6	8			5	3			4			11			36
		10	7				1		9				6	8			5	3			4	2		11			37
		10		9			1						6				5	3	8	7	4	2		11			38
		10	7	9			1						6	8			5	3			4	2		11			39
		10	7	9			1						6	8			5	3			4	2		11			40
		10	7	9			1						6	8			5	3			4	2		11			41
			7	9			1						6	8			5	3			4	2		11		10	42
5	8	27	36	15	9	2	25	23	10	7	17	12	40	32	3	8	15	29	2	3	39	36	13	17	1	28	
1		13	3	9		1			4	1		2	1	8	1						4			2		13	

Brewster G	Brown W	Chadwick W	Chedgzoy S	Cock J	Downs R	Fazackerley S	Fern T	Fleetwood T	Forbes F	Grenyer A	Harland A	Harrison G	Hart H	Irvine R	Jones G	Livingstone D	McBain N	McDonald J	Miller H	Parry F	Peacock J	Raitt D	Reid D	Troup A	Wall A	Williams W	
	4	9	7					5			1	11	6			2					8	3				10	1
	4		7					5			1		6	9		3					8	2	11			10	R
	2	1	2					2			2	1	2	1		2					2	2	1			2	
			1																								

1923-24

1	Aug	25	(h)	Nottingham F	W 2-1	Hart, Irvine
2		27	(a)	Burnley	D 2-2	Chadwick 2
3	Sep	1	(a)	Nottingham F	L 0-1	
4		3	(h)	Burnley	D 3-3	Chadwick 2, Chedgzoy
5		8	(h)	Blackburn R	D 0-0	
6		12	(a)	Aston Villa	D 1-1	Peacock
7		15	(a)	Blackburn R	L 0-2	
8		19	(h)	Aston Villa	W 2-0	Chadwick, Troup
9		22	(h)	Huddersfield T	D 1-1	Chadwick
10		29	(a)	Huddersfield T	L 0-2	
11	Oct	6	(h)	Liverpool	W 1-0	Chadwick
12		13	(a)	Liverpool	W 2-1	Chedgzoy, Cock
13		20	(a)	Notts C	D 1-1	Chadwick
14		27	(h)	Notts C	W 3-0	Chadwick, Chedgzoy, Irvine
15	Nov	3	(a)	Sheffield U	L 0-4	
16		10	(h)	Sheffield U	W 2-0	Chadwick 2
17		17	(h)	West Brom A	W 2-0	Chadwick, Cock
18		24	(a)	West Brom A	L 0-5	
19	Dec	1	(h)	Birmingham	W 2-0	Cock, Hart
20		8	(a)	Birmingham	W 1-0	Opp own-goal
21		15	(a)	Manchester C	L 1-2	Cock
22		22	(h)	Manchester C	W 6-1	Chadwick 4, Cock, Irvine
23		26	(h)	Sunderland	L 2-3	Cock, Irvine
24		29	(a)	Bolton W	L 0-2	
25	Jan	1	(a)	Sunderland	L 0-3	
26		5	(h)	Bolton W	D 2-2	Chadwick, Irvine
27		19	(h)	Middlesbrough	W 1-0	Cock
28		26	(a)	Middlesbrough	D 1-1	Cock
29	Feb	6	(h)	Preston NE	D 1-1	Cock
30		9	(a)	Preston NE	W 1-0	Cock
31		16	(h)	Chelsea	W 2-0	Chadwick, Irvine
32		23	(a)	Chelsea	D 1-1	Chadwick
33	Mar	1	(h)	Newcastle U	D 2-2	Chadwick, Cock
34		15	(a)	West Ham U	L 1-2	Irvine
35		22	(h)	West Ham U	W 2-1	Chadwick, Cock
36		29	(a)	Cardiff C	D 0-0	
37	Apr	2	(a)	Newcastle U	L 1-3	Chadwick
38		5	(h)	Cardiff C	D 0-0	
39		12	(a)	Tottenham H	W 5-2	Cock 2, Chadwick, Chedgzoy, Irvine
40		18	(h)	Arsenal	W 3-1	Chadwick 2, Cock
41		19	(h)	Tottenham H	W 4-2	Chadwick 3, Irvine
42		21	(a)	Arsenal	W 1-0	Chedgzoy

FINAL LEAGUE POSITION: 7th in Division One

Appearances
Goals

FA Cup

1	Jan	12	(h)	Preston NE	W 3-1	Chadwick, Chedgzoy, Cock
2	Feb	2	(a)	Brighton & HA	L 2-5	Chadwick, Cock

Appearances
Goals

Brown W	Chadwick W	Chedgzoy S	Cock J	Downs R	Fern T	Forbes F	Harland A	Harrison G	Hart H	Irvine R	Kendall J	Livingstone D	McBain N	McDonald J	Parry F	Peacock J	Raitt D	Reid D	Troup A	Williams W	
	10	7			1	9			6	8			5	3		4	2		11		1
4	10				1	9			6	8			5	3	7		2		11		2
4	9	7			1				6	8			5	3			2		11	10	3
4	9	7			1				6	8			5	3			2		11	10	4
	10	7		2	1	9			6	8		3	5			4			11		5
4	10	7		2	1				6	8		3	5			9			11		6
4	10	7		2	1				6	8		3	5			9			11		7
4	10	7	9		1				6	8		3	5	2					11		8
4	10	7	9		1				6	8		3	5	2					11		9
4	10		9		1			11	6	8		3	5	2	7						10
4	10	7	9		1				6	8		3	5	2					11		11
4	10	7	9		1				6	8		3	5	2					11		12
4	10	7	9		1				6			3	5	2		8			11		13
4	10	7	9		1				6	8		3	5	2					11		14
4	10	7	9		1				6	8		3	5	2					11		15
4	10	7	9		1				6	8		3	5	2					11		16
4	10	7	9		1				6	8		3	5	2					11		17
4	10	7	9		1				6	8		3	5	2					11		18
4	10	7	9		1				6	8		3	5				2		11		19
4	10	7	9		1				6	8		3	5				2		11		20
	10	7	9		1				6	8		3	5			4	2		11		21
	10	7	9		1				6	8		3	5			4	2		11		22
	10	7	9		1				6	8		3	5			4	2		11		23
4	10	7	9		1				6	8		3					2	5	11		24
4	10	7	9		1				6	8		3					2	5	11		25
4	10	7	9				1		6	8		3		2				5	11		26
4	10	7	9				1		6	8		3	5	2					11		27
4	10	7	9				1		6	8		3	5	2					11		28
4	10		9				1		6	8		3	5	2	7				11		29
4	10		9				1		6	8		3	5	2	7				11		30
4	10	7	9				1		6	8		3		2				5	11		31
4	10	7	9				1		6	8		3		2				5	11		32
4	10	7	9				1		6			3	5	2				8	11		33
4	10	7	9				1		6	8		3	5	2					11		34
4	10	7	9				1		6	8		3	5				2		11		35
4	10	7	9				1		6	8		3	5				2		11		36
4	10	7	9				1		6	8		3	5				2		11		37
4	10	7	9				1		6	8		3	5				2		11		38
4	10	7	9				1		6	8		3	5				2		11		39
4	10	7	9				1		6	8		3	5				2		11		40
4	10	7	9						6	8	1	3	5				2		11		41
4	10	7	9				1		6	8		3	5				2		11		42
37	42	38	35	3	25	3	16	1	42	40	1	38	37	24	4	8	19	6	41	2	
	28	5	15						2	9						1			1		

1 own-goal

Brown W	Chadwick W	Chedgzoy S	Cock J	Downs R	Fern T	Forbes F	Harland A	Harrison G	Hart H	Irvine R	Kendall J	Livingstone D	McBain N	McDonald J	Parry F	Peacock J	Raitt D	Reid D	Troup A	Williams W	
4	10	7	9				1		6	8		3	5	2					11		1
4	10	7	9				1			8		3	5	2		6			11		2
2	2	2	2				2		1	2		2	2	2		1			2		
	2	1	2																		

1924-25

1	Aug	30	(a)	Birmingham	D 2-2	Chadwick, Cock
2	Sep	6	(h)	West Brom A	W 1-0	Chadwick
3		8	(a)	Burnley	D 0-0	
4		13	(a)	Tottenham H	D 0-0	
5		17	(a)	Leeds U	L 0-1	
6		20	(h)	Bolton W	D 2-2	Chadwick, Chedgzoy
7		27	(a)	Notts C	L 1-3	Cock
8	Oct	4	(h)	Liverpool	L 0-1	
9		11	(h)	Sunderland	L 0-3	
10		18	(a)	Cardiff C	L 1-2	Chadwick
11		25	(a)	Nottingham F	W 1-0	Troup
12		29	(h)	Manchester C	W 3-1	Chedgzoy, Cock, Irvine
13	Nov	1	(h)	Bury	D 0-0	
14		8	(a)	Manchester C	D 2-2	Chadwick, Cock
15		15	(h)	Arsenal	L 2-3	Hargreaves, Irvine
16		22	(a)	Aston Villa	L 1-3	Hargreaves
17		29	(h)	Huddersfield T	L 0-2	
18	Dec	6	(a)	Blackburn R	L 0-3	
19		13	(h)	West Ham U	W 1-0	Cock
20		20	(a)	Sheffield U	D 1-1	Troup
21		25	(h)	Newcastle U	L 0-1	
22		26	(a)	Newcastle U	D 1-1	Broad
23		27	(h)	Birmingham	W 2-1	Broad, Williams
24	Jan	1	(h)	Burnley	W 3-2	Broad, Irvine, Weaver
25		3	(a)	West Brom A	L 0-3	
26		17	(h)	Tottenham H	W 1-0	Weaver
27		24	(a)	Bolton W	L 0-1	
28	Feb	7	(a)	Liverpool	L 1-3	Chadwick
29		14	(a)	Sunderland	L 1-4	Broad
30		25	(h)	Cardiff C	L 1-2	Broad
31		28	(h)	Nottingham F	W 3-1	Broad 2, Irvine
32	Mar	7	(a)	Bury	L 0-1	
33		18	(h)	Notts C	W 1-0	Broad
34		21	(a)	Arsenal	L 1-3	Kennedy
35		28	(h)	Aston Villa	W 2-0	Dean, Reid
36	Apr	4	(a)	Huddersfield T	L 0-2	
37		10	(a)	Preston NE	D 1-1	O'Donnell
38		11	(h)	Blackburn R	W 1-0	Kennedy
39		13	(h)	Preston NE	D 0-0	
40		18	(a)	West Ham U	L 1-4	Dean
41		27	(h)	Sheffield U	D 1-1	Reid
42	May	2	(h)	Leeds U	W 1-0	Kennedy

FINAL LEAGUE POSITION: 17th in Division One

Appearances
Goals

FA Cup

1	Jan	10	(h)	Burnley	W 2-1	Chadwick 2
2		31	(a)	Sunderland	D 0-0	
R	Feb	4	(h)	Sunderland	W 2-1	Chadwick, Irvine
3		21	(a)	Sheffield U	L 0-1	

Appearances
Goals

Bain D	Broad J	Brown W	Chadwick W	Chedgzoy S	Cock J	Dean W	Forbes F	Hargreaves F	Harland A	Hart H	Irvine R	Jones R	Kendall J	Kennedy F	Kerr J	Livingstone D	McBain N	McDonald J	O'Donnell J	Parry F	Peacock J	Raitt D	Reid D	Rooney W	Troup A	Virr A	Wall A	Weaver W	Williams W	
		4	10	7	9			8		6			1			3	5					2			11					1
		4	10	7	9			8		6			1			3	5					2			11					2
		4	10	7	9			8					1			3	5					2	6		11					3
		4	10	7	9			8		6			1			3	5					2			11					4
		4	10	7	9					6	8		1			3	5					2			11					5
		4	10	7	9			8		6			1			3	5					2			11					6
			10	7	9			8		6			1			3	5				4	2			11					7
		4	10	7	9				1	6	8					3	5					2			11					8
9		4		7					1	6	8					3	5					2			11				10	9
			10	7	9					6	8		1			3	5				4	2			11					10
			10	7	9					6	8		1			3	5				4	2			11					11
			10	7	9					6	8		1				5	3			4	2			11					12
			10	7	9					6	8		1				5	3			4	2			11					13
			10	7	9					6	8	1					5	3			4	2			11					14
			9	7				10		6	8	1					5	3			4	2			11					15
			10	7				8		6	8	1				3	5	2			4				11					16
			10	7	9				1	6	8					3	5	2			4				11					17
5	9			7	10		11		1	6	8				3	2					4									18
			10	7	9				1	6						3		2			4		5		11				8	19
			10	7	9				1	6	8					3		2			4		5		11					20
			10	7	9				1	6						3	5	2			4				11				8	21
	9			7					1	6	8					3		2			4		5					11	10	22
	9			7					1	6	8					3		2			4		5					11	10	23
	9			7					1	6	8					3		2			4		5					11	10	24
	9								1	6	8				3			2		7	4		5					11	10	25
	9	4	10						1								5	3		7		2				6	8	11		26
	9	4	10	7					1		8						5	3				2	6					11		27
		4	10	7	9				1		8						5	3				2	6		11					28
	9	4	10	7							8		1				5	3				2	6		11					29
5	9		10	7					1								4	2	3				6				8	11		30
	9			7					1		8						5	2	3				6	4				11	10	31
	9			7					1		8						5		3			2	6	4				11	10	32
	9			7					1		8			10			5	2	3				6	4	11					33
						9		8	1					10			5	2	3	7			6	4	11					34
		4		7		9			1		8			10			5	2	3				6		11					35
		4		7		9			1		8			10			5	2	3				6		11					36
		4		7		9			1		8			10			5	2	3				6		11					37
		4		7		9			1		8			10			5	2	3				6		11					38
		4		7		9			1		8			10			5	2	3				6		11					39
		4	8			9			1					10			5	2	3	7			6		11					40
	9	4	8	7					1					10			5	2	3				6		11					41
	9	4	8	7					1					10			5	2	3				6		11					42
3	14	20	27	38	19	7	1	9	27	24	28	3	12	10	2	20	35	29	13	4	17	20	23	4	32	1	2	9	9	
	8		6	2	5	2		2			4			3					1				2		2			2	1	

Bain D	Broad J	Brown W	Chadwick W	Chedgzoy S	Cock J	Dean W	Forbes F	Hargreaves F	Harland A	Hart H	Irvine R	Jones R	Kendall J	Kennedy F	Kerr J	Livingstone D	McBain N	McDonald J	O'Donnell J	Parry F	Peacock J	Raitt D	Reid D	Rooney W	Troup A	Virr A	Wall A	Weaver W	Williams W	
	9	4	10						1								5	3		7	8	2				6		11		1
	9	4	10	7					1		8						5	3				2	6					11		2
		4	10	7	9						8		1				5	3				2	6					11		R
5	9		10	7							8		1				4	3				2	6					11		3
1	3	3	4	3	1				2		3		2				4	4		1	1	4	3			1		4		
			3								1																			

1925-26

1	Aug	29	(h)	Sheffield U	D 2-2	Kennedy, Troup	36,243
2	Sep	2	(a)	West Brom A	D 1-1	Irvine	18,602
3		5	(a)	Cardiff C	L 1-2	Murray	13,914
4		9	(h)	Birmingham	D 2-2	Kennedy, Troup	15,811
5		12	(h)	Tottenham H	D 1-1	Peacock	37,506
6		16	(h)	West Brom A	W 4-0	Kennedy 2, Irvine, Troup	20,355
7		19	(a)	Manchester C	D 4-4	Kennedy 2, Dean, Irvine	11,393
8		21	(a)	Birmingham	L 1-3	Irvine	8,940
9		26	(a)	Liverpool	L 1-5	Kennedy	49,426
10	Oct	3	(h)	Huddersfield T	L 2-3	Chedgzoy, Troup	35,665
11		10	(a)	Sunderland	L 3-7	Troup 2, Dean	26,755
12		17	(a)	Burnley	W 3-1	Dean 3	10,343
13		24	(h)	Leeds U	W 4-2	Dean 3, Kennedy	28,660
14		31	(a)	Arsenal	L 1-4	McBain	24,926
15	Nov	7	(h)	Manchester U	L 1-3	Dean	12,387
16		14	(a)	Notts C	W 3-0	Dean 2, Irvine	14,962
17		21	(h)	Aston Villa	D 1-1	Dean	27,037
18		28	(a)	Leicester C	D 1-1	Dean	20,044
19	Dec	5	(h)	West Ham U	W 2-0	O'Donnell, Weaver	17,337
20		12	(a)	Newcastle U	D 3-3	Dean 3	36,274
21		19	(h)	Bolton W	W 2-1	Dean, O'Donnell	26,400
22		25	(a)	Blackburn R	D 2-2	Dean, O'Donnell	24,753
23		26	(h)	Blackburn R	W 3-0	O'Donnell 2, Irvine	47,356
24	Jan	1	(a)	Bury	L 0-1		19,999
25		2	(a)	Sheffield U	D 1-1	Dean	28,468
26		16	(h)	Cardiff C	D 1-1	Dean	26,553
27		23	(a)	Tottenham H	D 1-1	Dean	22,805
28		30	(h)	Leicester C	W 1-0	Opp own-goal	31,515
29	Feb	6	(h)	Liverpool	D 3-3	Chedgzoy, Dean, Irvine	45,793
30		10	(h)	Manchester C	D 1-1	Irvine	15,067
31		13	(a)	Huddersfield T	L 0-3		17,298
32		27	(h)	Burnley	D 1-1	Dean	22,691
33	Mar	6	(a)	Leeds U	D 1-1	Chedgzoy	18,613
34		13	(h)	Arsenal	L 2-3	Chedgzoy 2	30,515
35		17	(h)	Sunderland	W 2-1	Dean 2	16,313
36		20	(a)	Manchester U	D 0-0		30,058
37		27	(h)	Notts C	W 3-0	Batten, Chedgzoy, Dean	16,877
38	Apr	2	(h)	Bury	D 1-1	Dean	33,806
39		3	(a)	Aston Villa	L 1-3	Dean	20,555
40		17	(a)	West Ham U	L 0-1		15,866
41		24	(h)	Newcastle U	W 3-0	Dean 3	20,517
42	May	1	(a)	Bolton W	W 2-0	Chedgzoy, Dean	11,883
				FINAL LEAGUE POSITION: 11th in Division One			Appearances
							Goals

FA Cup

3	Jan	9	(h)	Fulham	D 1-1	Dean	
R		14	(a)	Fulham	L 0-1		
							Appearances
							Goals

Bain D	Batten H	Broad J	Brown W	Chadwick W	Chedgzoy S	Dean W	Hardy H	Harland A	Hart H	Irvine R	Kendall J	Kennedy F	Kerr J	Livingstone D	McBain N	McDonald J	Menham C	Murray D	O'Donnell J	Parry F	Peacock J	Raitt D	Reid D	Troup A	Virr A	Weaver W	
		9	4		7			1	6	8		10			5	2			3					11			1
		9	4		7			1	6	8		10			5	2			3					11			2
		9	4		7				6		1	10				2		8	3				5	11			3
		9	4		7				6		1	10				2		8	3				5	11			4
			4		7	9			6		1	10			5				3		8	2		11			5
			4		7	9			6	8	1	10			5				3			2		11			6
			4		7	9			6	8	1	10			5				3			2		11			7
					7	9			6	8	1	10			5				3		4	2		11			8
					7	9		1	6	8		10			5				3		4	2		11			9
			4		7	9		1	6	8		10			5	2			3					11			10
5			4	10		9			6	8						2	1		3		7			11			11
5			4	10		9			6	8				3		2	1				7			11			12
5			4		7	9			6			10		3		2	1				8			11			13
5			4		7	9	1		6			10		3	8	2								11			14
5			4		7	9	1		6			10		3	8	2								11			15
5			4		7	9	1			8						3			10			2		11	6		16
5			4		7	9	1			8						3			10			2		11	6		17
5			4		7	9	1			8						3			10			2			6	11	18
5			4		7	9	1			8						3			10			2			6	11	19
					7	9	1			8						3			10		4	2	5	11	6		20
5					7	9	1			8						3			10		4	2		11	6		21
5					7	9	1			8						3			10		4	2		11	6		22
5					7	9	1			8						3			10		4	2		11	6		23
5					7	9	1			8						3			10		4	2		11	6		24
5					7	9	1			8						3			10		4	2		11	6		25
5					7	9	1			8		11				3			10		4	2			6		26
5					7	9	1			8						3			10		4	2		11	6		27
5						9	1			8						3			10		4	2		11	6	7	28
5					7	9	1			8				2		3			10		4			11	6		29
5					7	9				8	1	10	3			2					4			11	6		30
5					7	9	1		6	8		10				3					4	2		11			31
5	10		4		7	9	1			8						3						2		11	6		32
5	8		4		7	9	1		6							3			10			2		11			33
5	8		4		7	9			6		1					3			10			2		11			34
	10		4		7	9	1		6	8						3						2	5	11			35
	10		4		7	9	1		6	8						3						2	5	11			36
	10		4		7	9	1		6	8						3						2	5	11			37
	10		4		7	9	1		6	8						3						2	5	11			38
	10		4			9	1		6	8						3				7		2	5	11			39
	8		4		7	9	1		6			10				3						2	5			11	40
	8		4		7	9	1		6			10				3						2	5	11			41
	8		4		7	9	1		6			10				3						2	5	11			42
23	11	4	28	2	38	38	27	4	26	31	8	19	1	5	10	37	3	2	27	1	18	30	11	38	16	4	
	1				7	32				8		8			1			1	5		1			6		1	

1 own-goal

Bain D	Batten H	Broad J	Brown W	Chadwick W	Chedgzoy S	Dean W	Hardy H	Harland A	Hart H	Irvine R	Kendall J	Kennedy F	Kerr J	Livingstone D	McBain N	McDonald J	Menham C	Murray D	O'Donnell J	Parry F	Peacock J	Raitt D	Reid D	Troup A	Virr A	Weaver W	
5					7	9	1			8						3			10		4	2		11	6		3
5					7	9	1			8						3			10		4	2		11	6		R
2					2	2	2			2						2			2		2	2		2	2		
						1																					

1926-27

1	Aug	28	(a)	Tottenham H	L 1-2	O'Connell	28,324
2	Sep	1	(a)	Bury	L 2-5	Dominy, Irvine	14,374
3		4	(h)	West Ham U	L 0-3		26,957
4		6	(a)	West Brom A	L 2-3	Dominy, O'Donnell	12,048
5		11	(a)	Sheffield W	L 0-4		22,889
6		15	(h)	West Brom A	D 0-0		15,310
7		18	(h)	Leicester C	L 3-4	Irvine 2, Bain	29,049
8		20	(a)	Birmingham	L 0-1		11,411
9		25	(h)	Liverpool	W 1-0	O'Donnell	43,973
10		29	(h)	Bury	D 2-2	Bain, Hart	17,186
11	Oct	2	(a)	Blackburn R	D 3-3	Dominy 2, Irvine	20,385
12		9	(h)	Huddersfield T	D 0-0		22,419
13		16	(h)	Newcastle U	L 1-3	Troup	41,746
14		23	(a)	Leeds U	W 3-1	Dean, Dominy, Irvine	24,867
15		30	(h)	Arsenal	W 3-1	Dean, Irvine, Troup	34,153
16	Nov	6	(a)	Sheffield U	D 3-3	Dominy 2, Dean	15,222
17		13	(h)	Derby C	W 3-2	Dean, Irvine, Virr	29,919
18		20	(a)	Manchester U	L 1-2	Dean	24,361
19		27	(h)	Bolton W	D 1-1	Opp own-goal	28,091
20	Dec	4	(a)	Aston Villa	L 3-5	Dean, Dominy, Irvine	25,182
21		11	(h)	Cardiff C	L 0-1		27,181
22		18	(a)	Burnley	L 1-5	Kerr	18,290
23		25	(h)	Sunderland	W 5-4	Dean 4, Irvine	37,500
24		27	(a)	Sunderland	L 2-3	Bain, Dean	32,574
25	Jan	1	(h)	Burnley	W 3-2	Dean 2, Irvine	44,586
26		15	(h)	Tottneham H	L 1-2	Dean	35,986
27		22	(a)	West Ham U	L 1-2	Irvine	11,235
28	Feb	5	(a)	Leicester C	L 2-6	Dean 2	21,369
29		12	(a)	Liverpool	L 0-1		52,840
30		19	(h)	Blackburn R	W 1-0	Dominy	39,093
31		26	(a)	Huddersfield T	D 0-0		20,660
32	Mar	2	(h)	Sheffield W	W 2-1	Dean, Dominy	19,455
33		5	(a)	Newcastle U	L 3-7	Dominy 2, Forshaw	40,202
34		12	(h)	Leeds U	W 2-1	Dean, Weldon	57,440
35		19	(a)	Arsenal	W 2-1	Troup, Weldon	33,788
36		26	(h)	Sheffield U	W 2-0	Forshaw, Weldon	20,861
37	Apr	2	(a)	Derby C	D 0-0		18,012
38		9	(h)	Manchester U	D 0-0		22,564
39		16	(a)	Bolton W	L 0-5		26,381
40		18	(h)	Birmingham C	W 3-1	Troup 2, Dean	32,880
41		23	(h)	Aston Villa	D 2-2	Dean 2	33,394
42		30	(a)	Cardiff C	L 0-1		18,341

FINAL LEAGUE POSITION: 20th in Division One

Appearances
Goals

FA Cup

3	Jan	8	(h)	Poole T	W 3-1	Dean, Irvine, Troup
4		22	(a)	Hull C	D 1-1	Virr
R	Feb	2	(h)	Hull C	D 2-2	Dean, Troup
2R		7	(n*)	Hull C	L 2-3	Dean, Dominy

* Played at Villa Park.

Appearances
Goals

Bain D	Baker B	Batten H	Brown W	Cresswell W	Critchley E	Davies A	Dean W	Dominy A	Forshaw R	Griffiths TP	Hamilton H	Hardy H	Hart H	Irvine R	Kelly J	Kennedy F	Kerr J	McDonald J	Millington T	Moffatt H	Murray D	O'Donnell J	Parker T	Peacock J	Raitt D	Reid D	Rooney W	Taylor E	Troup A	Virr A	Weaver W	Weldon A	Woodhouse R	
	1		4					8					6	7		10		3				9			2	5					11			1
	1	10	4					8					6	9				3					7		2	5					11			2
	1	10						8					6	9				3					7	4	2	5					11			3
	1	10	4					8					6					3				9	7		2	5					11			4
	1	10	4					8					6					3				9	7		2	5					11			5
5	1		4											8		10		3		7	9				2				11	6				6
9	1		4										5	8		10		3					7		2				11	6				7
9	1		4										5	8		10		2	7						3				11	6				8
9	1		4										5	8			3	2				10	7						11	6				9
9	1		4										5	8			3	2	7			10							11	6				10
	1		4					9					5	8			3	2	7										11	6			10	11
			4			1		10					5	8			3	2	7					9					11	6				12
			4			1		9					5	8		10	3	2	7										11	6				13
			4			1	9	10					5	8			3	2	7										11	6				14
			4			1	9	10					5	8			3	2		7									11	6				15
			4			1	9	10					5	8			3	2	7										11	6				16
			4			1	9	10					5	8			3	2	7										11	6				17
5			4			1	9	10						8			3	2	7										11	6				18
			4				9	10				1	5	8			3	2	7							6			11					19
			4				9	10				1	5	8				2	7			3							11	6				20
			4			1	9	10					5	8			3	2	7										11	6				21
			4			1	9	10					5	8			3	2											11	6			7	22
5			4		7	1	9	10					6	8								3			2				11					23
5			4		7		9	8				1	6				3					10			2				11					24
5			4		7		9	10				1	6	8								3			2				11					25
5					7		9	10			2	1	6	8								3							11	4				26
					7		9	10				1	5	8			3	2						4					11	6				27
			4	2	7		9	10		5		1		8				3								6			11					28
				2	7			8					5	9	4	10						3						1	11	6				29
				2	7		9	10					5	8	4							3						1	11	6				30
				2	7		9	10					5	8	4							3						1	11	6				31
				2	7		9	10					5	8	4							3						1	11	6				32
				2	7		9	10	8				5		4							3						1	11	6				33
				2			9		8				5		4				7			3						1	11	6		10		34
				2	7		9		8				5		4							3						1	11	6		10		35
				2	7		9		8				5		4							3						1	11	6		10		36
				2	7				9				5	8	4							3						1	11	6		10		37
				2	7		9		8				5		4							3						1	11	6		10		38
				2			9		8				5	7	4							3						1	11	6		10		39
				2			9		8				5	7	4							3						1	11	6		10		40
				2			9		8				5	7	4							3						1	11	6		10		41
				2			9		8				5	7	4							3						1	11	6		10		42
10	11	4	25	15	15	10	27	28	10	1	1	7	39	34	14	6	15	24	13	2	1	24	6	3	11	7		14	37	32	5	9	2	
3							21	12	2				1	11			1					3							5	1		3		

1 own-goal

Bain D	Baker B	Batten H	Brown W	Cresswell W	Critchley E	Davies A	Dean W	Dominy A	Forshaw R	Griffiths TP	Hamilton H	Hardy H	Hart H	Irvine R	Kelly J	Kennedy F	Kerr J	McDonald J	Millington T	Moffatt H	Murray D	O'Donnell J	Parker T	Peacock J	Raitt D	Reid D	Rooney W	Taylor E	Troup A	Virr A	Weaver W	Weldon A	Woodhouse R	
5							9	10				1		8								3	7		2		4		11	6				3
							9	10				1	5	8			3	2		7				4					11	6				4
8							9	10				1	5	7			3	2									4		11	6				R
						1	9	10					5	8			3		7			2					4		11	6				2R
2						1	4	4				3	3	4			3	2	1	1		2	1	1	1		3		4	4				
							3	1						1															2	1				

1927-28

1	Aug	27	(h)	Sheffield W	W 4-0	Dean, Forshaw, Troup, Weldon	39,485
2	Sep	3	(a)	Middlesbrough	L 2-4	Critchley, Dean	30,299
3		5	(a)	Bolton W	D 1-1	Dean	18,734
4		10	(h)	Birmingham	W 5-2	Dean 2, Troup 2, Forshaw	37,386
5		14	(h)	Bolton W	D 2-2	Dean, Forshaw	22,276
6		17	(a)	Newcastle U	D 2-2	Dean 2	50,539
7		24	(h)	Huddersfield T	D 2-2	Dean 2	37,269
8	Oct	1	(a)	Tottenham H	W 3-1	Dean 2, Troup	7,716
9		8	(h)	Manchester U	W 5-2	Dean 5	40,080
10		15	(h)	Liverpool	D 1-1	Troup	65,729
11		22	(h)	West Ham U	W 7-0	White 2, Critchley, Forshaw, O'Donnell, Weldon, Opp own-goal	20,151
12		29	(a)	Portsmouth	W 3-1	Dean 3	23,326
13	Nov	5	(h)	Leicester C	W 7-1	Dean 3, Weldon 2, Critchley, Troup	30,392
14		12	(a)	Derby C	W 3-0	Dean 2, Weldon	21,590
15		19	(h)	Sunderland	L 0-1		35,993
16		26	(a)	Bury	W 3-2	Dean 2, Critchley	24,727
17	Dec	3	(h)	Sheffield U	D 0-0		36,141
18		10	(a)	Aston Villa	W 3-2	Dean 3	40,353
19		17	(h)	Burnley	W 4-1	Critchley, Forshaw, Kelly, Troup	30,180
20		24	(a)	Arsenal	L 2-3	Dean, Troup	27,995
21		26	(h)	Cardiff C	W 2-1	Dean 2	56,305
22		27	(a)	Cardiff C	L 0-2		25,387
23		31	(a)	Sheffield W	W 2-1	Dean 2	18,354
24	Jan	2	(a)	Blackburn R	L 2-4	Dean 2	21,556
25		7	(h)	Middlesbrough	W 3-1	Dean 2, Irvine	46,432
26		21	(a)	Birmingham C	D 2-2	Irvine 2	33,675
27	Feb	4	(a)	Huddersfield T	L 1-4	Dean	50,012
28		11	(h)	Tottenham H	L 2-5	Troup 2	27,149
29		25	(a)	Liverpool	D 3-3	Dean 3	55,361
30	Mar	3	(a)	West Ham U	D 0-0		31,997
31		10	(h)	Portsmouth	D 0-0		29,803
32		14	(a)	Manchester U	L 0-1		25,667
33		17	(a)	Leicester C	L 0-1		26,625
34		24	(h)	Derby C	D 2-2	Dean 2	28,541
35		31	(a)	Sunderland	W 2-0	Easton, Virr	15,407
36	Apr	6	(h)	Blackburn R	W 4-1	Dean 2, Hart, Martin	48,521
37		7	(h)	Bury	D 1-1	Dean	37,597
38		14	(a)	Sheffield U	W 3-1	Dean 2, Martin	26,252
39		18	(h)	Newcastle U	W 3-0	Critchley, Dean, Weldon	28,266
40		21	(h)	Aston Villa	W 3-2	Dean 2, Weldon	39,825
41		28	(a)	Burnley	W 5-3	Dean 4, Martin	24,485
42	May	5	(h)	Arsenal	D 3-3	Dean 3	48,715

FINAL LEAGUE POSITION: 1st in Division One

Appearances

Goals

FA Cup

3	Jan	14	(a)	Preston NE	W 3-0	Dean, Irvine, Opp own-goal
4		28	(a)	Arsenal	L 3-4	Dean 2, Troup

Appearances

Goals

Bain D	Brown W	Cresswell W	Critchley E	Davies A	Dean W	Dominy A	Easton W	Forshaw R	Hardy H	Hart H	Houghton H	Irvine R	Kelly J	Martin G	Meston S	O'Donnell J	Raitt D	Rooney W	Taylor E	Troup A	Virr A	Weldon A	White T	
		2			9			8		5		7	4			3			1	11	6	10		1
		2	7		9			8		5			4			3			1	11	6	10		2
			7		9			8		5			4			3	2		1	11	6	10		3
			7		9			8		5			4			3	2		1	11	6	10		4
		2	7		9			8		5			4			3			1	11	6	10		5
		2	7		9			8		5			4			3			1	11	6	10		6
		2	7		9			8		5			4			3			1	11	6	10		7
		2	7		9			8		5			4			3			1	11	6	10		8
		2	7		9			8		5			4			3			1	11	6	10		9
		2	7		9			8		5			4			3			1	11	6	10		10
		2	7					8		5			4			3			1	11	6	10	9	11
		2	7		9			8		5			4			3			1	11	6	10		12
	4	2	7		9			8		5						3			1	11	6	10		13
		2	7	1	9			8		5			4			3				11	6	10		14
		2	7	1	9			8		5			4			3				11	6	10		15
		2	7		9			8		5		10	4			3			1	11	6			16
		2	7		9			8		5			4			3			1	11	6	10		17
		2	7		9			8		5			4			3		6	1	11		10		18
		2	7		9			8		5			4			3			1	11	6	10		19
		2	7		9			8		5			4			3			1	11	6	10		20
			7		9			8		5			4			3	2		1	11	6	10		21
			7		9							8	4			3	2	6	1	11	5	10		22
			7		9					5		8	4			3	2		1	11	6	10		23
			7		9					5		8	4			3	2		1	11	6	10		24
		2	7		9					5		8	4			3		6	1	11		10		25
		2	7		9	10				5		8	4			3		6	1	11				26
		2	7		9					5		8	4			3			1	11	6	10		27
	4	2	7		9					5		8				3			1	11	6	10		28
		2	7		9			8	1	5			4			3				11	6	10		29
		2	7		9			8	1	5			4			3				11	6	10		30
		2	7				8		1	5	10		4			3				11	6	9		31
		2	7		9		8		1	5			4			3				11	6	10		32
		2	7		9				1	5			4	8		3				11	6	10		33
8		2	7	1	9					5			4	10		3				11	6			34
9		2	7	1			8			5			4	10		3				11	6			35
		2	7	1	9					5			4	8		3				11	6	10		36
		2	7		9				1	5			4	8		3				11	6	10		37
		2		1	9					5			4	8	7	3				11	6	10		38
		2	7	1	9					5			4	8		3				11	6	10		39
		2	7	1	9					5			4	8		3				11	6	10		40
		2	7	1	9					5			4	8		3				11	6	10		41
		2	7	1	9					5			4	8		3				11	6	10		42
2	2	36	40	10	39	1	3	23	6	41	1	9	40	10	1	42	6	4	26	42	39	38	1	
			6		60		1	5		1		3	1	3		1				10	1	7	2	

1 own-goal

Bain D	Brown W	Cresswell W	Critchley E	Davies A	Dean W	Dominy A	Easton W	Forshaw R	Hardy H	Hart H	Houghton H	Irvine R	Kelly J	Martin G	Meston S	O'Donnell J	Raitt D	Rooney W	Taylor E	Troup A	Virr A	Weldon A	White T	
		2	7		9					5		8	4			3		6	1	11		10		3
		2	7		9					5		8	4			3			1	11	6	10		4
		2	2		2					2		2	2			2		1	2	2	1	2		
					3							1								1				

1 own-goal

1928-29

1	Aug	25	(a)	Bolton W	W 3-2	Dean 3	34,637
2		29	(h)	Sheffield W	D 0-0		39,011
3	Sep	1	(h)	Portsmouth	W 4-0	Dean 3, Ritchie	47,119
4		3	(a)	Sheffield W	L 0-1		24,322
5		8	(a)	Birmingham C	W 3-1	Critchley, Dean, Dunn	36,069
6		15	(h)	Manchester C	L 2-6	Dunn, Weldon	47,871
7		22	(a)	Huddersfield T	L 1-3	Troup	24,425
8		29	(h)	Liverpool	W 1-0	Troup	55,415
9	Oct	6	(h)	Arsenal	W 4-2	Dean 2, Ritchie 2	37,846
10		13	(a)	Blackburn R	L 1-2	Dean	33,966
11		20	(a)	West Ham U	W 4-2	Dean 2, Dunn, Weldon	33,221
12		27	(h)	Leeds U	L 0-1		41,504
13	Nov	3	(a)	Burnley	L 0-2		25,959
14		10	(h)	Cardiff C	W 1-0	Weldon	25,994
15		17	(a)	Sheffield U	L 1-2	Martin	17,839
16		24	(h)	Bury	W 1-0	Dean	18,115
17	Dec	1	(a)	Aston Villa	L 0-2		45,416
18		8	(h)	Leicester C	W 3-1	Dean, Martin, Troup	25,226
19		15	(a)	Manchester U	D 1-1	Troup	17,080
20		22	(h)	Newcastle U	W 5-2	Dean 3, Martin, Ritchie	23,295
21		25	(h)	Sunderland	D 0-0		37,583
22		29	(h)	Bolton W	W 3-0	Dean 3	34,443
23	Jan	1	(h)	Derby C	W 4-0	Dean 3, Dunn	17,200
24		5	(a)	Portsmouth	L 0-3		23,210
25		19	(h)	Birmingham	L 0-2		26,273
26		26	(a)	Manchester C	L 1-5	Forshaw	36,241
27	Feb	2	(h)	Huddersfield T	L 0-3		25,044
28		9	(a)	Liverpool	W 2-1	Griffiths, White	45,095
29		23	(h)	Blackburn R	W 5-2	Martin 2, White, Opp own-goals 2	29,006
30	Mar	9	(a)	Leeds U	L 1-3	Dean	22,459
31		16	(h)	Burnley	W 2-0	White 2	17,810
32		23	(a)	Cardiff C	W 2-0	Easton, White	14,681
33		29	(a)	Sunderland	D 2-2	Easton, Martin	33,066
34		30	(h)	Sheffield U	L 1-3	Troup	22,958
35	Apr	2	(a)	Derby C	L 0-3		15,833
36		6	(a)	Bury	W 2-1	Dean 2	14,407
37		10	(h)	West Ham U	L 0-4		7,996
38		13	(h)	Aston Villa	L 0-1		20,594
39		20	(a)	Leicester C	L 1-4	White	19,006
40		22	(a)	Arsenal	L 0-2		11,696
41		27	(h)	Manchester U	L 2-4	Cresswell, Griffiths	19,442
42	May	4	(a)	Newcastle U	L 0-2		19,743
FINAL LEAGUE POSITION: 18th in Division One							Appearances
							Goals

FA Cup

3	Jan	12	(a)	Chelsea	L 0-2		
							Appearances
							Goals

Attwood A	Common E	Cresswell W	Critchley E	Davies A	Dean W	Dunn J	Easton W	Forshaw R	Griffiths TP	Hart H	Kelly J	Kennedy A	Lewis T	Martin G	O'Donnell J	Ritchie H	Rooney W	Stein J	Troup A	Virr A	Weldon A	White T	
		2		1	9	8				5	4				3	7			11	6	10		1
		2		1	9	8				5	4				3	7			11	6	10		2
		2		1	9	8				5	4				3	7			11	6	10		3
		2	7	1	9					5	4			8	3				11	6	10		4
		2	7	1	9	8				5	4				3				11	6	10		5
		2	7	1	9	8				5	4				3				11	6	10		6
		2	7	1		8		9		5	4				3				11	6	10		7
		2		1	9	8				5	4				3	7			11	6	10		8
		2		1	9	8				5	4				3	7			11	6	10		9
		2		1	9	8				5	4				3	7			11	6	10		10
		2		1	9	8			4	5					3	7			11	6	10		11
		2		1	9				4	5				8	3	7			11	6	10		12
		2	7	1	9	8			4	5		3							11	6	10		13
		2	7	1	9	8			4	5					3				11	6	10		14
		2		1		8				5				9	3	7			11	6	10	4	15
		2		1	9	8			4	5					3	7			11	6	10		16
		2		1	9			8	4	5				10	3	7			11	6			17
		2	7	1	9			8		5				10	3				11	6		4	18
		2		1				8		5	4			10	3	7			11	6		9	19
		2		1	9	8				5				10	3	7			11	6		4	20
		2		1	9	8				5				10	3	7			11	6		4	21
		2	7	1	9	8				5				10	3			11		6		4	22
		2	7	1	9	8			4	5				10	3			11		6			23
		2	7	1	9	8			4	5					3			11		6	10		24
		2		1	9	8			4	5					3	7		11			10	6	25
		2	7	1	9		10	8	4	5					3		6		11				26
		2	7	1	9			8	4	5				10	3		6		11				27
	2			1		8	10		5	6	4				3	7			11			9	28
	2		7	1			8		5	6	4			10	3				11			9	29
	2		7	1	9		10		5	6	4				3				11			8	30
	2		7	1			8		5	6	4			10	3				11			9	31
	2		7	1			8		5	6	4			10	3				11			9	32
	2		7	1			8		5	6	4			10	3				11			9	33
	2		7	1		8	6		5		4			10	3				11			9	34
	2		7	1			8		5	6	4			10	3				11			9	35
	2		7	1	9		8		5	6	4				3				11			10	36
9	2		7	1			8		5	6	4				3				11			10	37
		2	7	1					5	6					3	8	4		11		10	9	38
		2		1		8			5	6					3	7	4		11		10	9	39
		2	7	1	9			5	4					10	3	8	6		11				40
		2	7	1	9		10	5	4	6					3				11			8	41
		2	7	1	9	8			4	5			6		3				11			10	42
1	10	32	25	42	29	24	12	8	26	40	21	1	1	18	41	19	5	4	38	24	20	21	
		1	1		26	4	2	1	2					6		4			5		3	6	

2 own-goals

Attwood A	Common E	Cresswell W	Critchley E	Davies A	Dean W	Dunn J	Easton W	Forshaw R	Griffiths TP	Hart H	Kelly J	Kennedy A	Lewis T	Martin G	O'Donnell J	Ritchie H	Rooney W	Stein J	Troup A	Virr A	Weldon A	White T	
		2		1	9	8			4	5					3	7		11		6	10		3
		1		1	1	1			1	1					1	1		1		1	1		

1929-30

1	Aug	31	(h)	Bolton W	D 3-3	Dean 2, Stein	40,808
2	Sep	2	(a)	Burnley	D 1-1	Stein	17,704
3		7	(a)	Liverpool	W 3-0	Dean 2, Martin	44,891
4		11	(h)	Leeds U	D 1-1	Dean	24,098
5		14	(a)	Derby C	L 1-2	Dean	22,257
6		16	(a)	Leeds U	L 1-2	Dean	16,677
7		21	(h)	Manchester C	L 2-3	Dean, Martin	32,711
8		28	(a)	Portsmouth	W 4-1	Dean 3, Stein	21,046
9	Oct	2	(a)	Sunderland	D 2-2	Dean, Martin	19,333
10		5	(h)	Arsenal	D 1-1	Ritchie	45,015
11		12	(a)	Aston Villa	L 2-5	Martin, Stein	35,243
12		19	(h)	Middlesbrough	W 3-2	Dean, Martin, White	30,657
13		26	(a)	Blackburn R	L 1-3	Dean	18,249
14	Nov	2	(h)	Newcastle U	W 5-2	Martin 2, Critchley, Dean, White	31,543
15		9	(a)	West Ham U	L 1-3	Dean	24,801
16		16	(h)	Huddersfield T	L 0-2		28,892
17		23	(a)	Birmingham	D 0-0		13,883
18		30	(h)	Leicester C	L 4-5	Rigby 2, Martin, White	18,836
19	Dec	7	(a)	Grimsby T	W 3-0	Griffiths, Rigby, Troup	9,503
20		14	(h)	Manchester U	D 0-0		18,182
21		21	(a)	Sheffield U	L 0-2		15,492
22		25	(h)	Sheffield W	L 1-4	White	30,835
23		26	(a)	Sheffield W	L 0-4		45,549
24		28	(a)	Bolton W	L 0-5		15,928
25	Jan	4	(h)	Liverpool	D 3-3	Dean 2, Critchley	52,600
26		18	(h)	Derby C	W 4-0	Dean 2, Critchley, Stein	35,436
27	Feb	1	(h)	Portsmouth	D 1-1	Dean	28,507
28		5	(a)	Manchester C	W 2-1	Griffiths, Rigby	24,063
29		8	(a)	Arsenal	L 0-4		27,302
30		22	(a)	Middlesbrough	W 2-1	Martin, Stein	17,730
31	Mar	1	(h)	Blackburn R	D 2-2	Dean, Martin	27,514
32		5	(h)	Aston Villa	L 3-4	Dean, Griffiths, Stein	15,946
33		8	(a)	Newcastle U	L 0-1		43,278
34		15	(h)	West Ham U	L 1-2	Stein	27,953
35		29	(h)	Birmingham	L 2-4	Johnson, Stein	28,547
36	Apr	5	(a)	Leicester C	L 4-5	Martin 2, Critchley, Johnson	13,897
37		12	(h)	Grimsby T	L 2-4	Johnson, Martin	47,407
38		18	(h)	Burnley	W 3-0	Griffiths, Rigby, White	47,897
39		19	(a)	Manchester U	D 3-3	Martin, Stein, White	13,320
40		26	(h)	Sheffield U	W 3-2	White 2, Martin	28,244
41		28	(a)	Huddersfield T	W 2-1	Rigby 2	11,180
42	May	3	(h)	Sunderland	W 4-1	White 3, Johnson	51,132

FINAL LEAGUE POSITION: 22nd in Division One

Appearances
Goals

FA Cup

3	Jan	11	(a)	Carlisle U	W 4-2	Critchley 2, Dean 2
4		25	(a)	Blackburn R	L 1-4	Martin

Appearances
Goals

Attwood A	Coggins W	Common E	Cresswell W	Critchley E	Davies A	Dean W	Dunn J	Griffiths TP	Hart H	Johnson T	Kelly J	McClure J	McPherson L	Martin G	O'Donnell J	Rigby A	Ritchie H	Robson T	Rooney W	Sagar E	Stein J	Thomson J	Troup A	Virr A	Weldon A	White T	Wilkinson J	Williams B	
			2		1	9	8		6		4			10	3		7				11					5			1
9			2		1		8		6					10	3		7		4		11					5			2
			2		1	9	8		6		4			10	3		7				11					5			3
			2	7	1	9	8		6		4			10	3						11					5			4
			2		1	9	8		6		4			10	3		7				11					5			5
			2		1	9	8		6		4			10	3		7				11					5			6
			2		1	9	8		6		4			10	3						11					5	7		7
			2		1	9	8		6					10	3		7	4			11					5			8
			2		1	9	8		6					10	3		7	4			11					5			9
			2		1				6					10	3		7	4			11				8	5	9		10
			2	7	1			5						10	3			4			11				8	6	9		11
		2		7	1	9		5	6					10	3			4			11					8			12
			2	7	1	9		5	6					10	3			4			11					8			13
		2		7	1	9		5	6					10	3			4			11					8			14
			2	7	1	9		5	6					10	3			4			11					8			15
			2	7	1	9		5	6					10	3			4			11					8			16
			2	7	1				5					8	3	10		4			11					6	9		17
			2	7	1				5					8	3	10		4			11			6		9			18
			2	7	1			5						8	3	10		4					11	6		9			19
			2	7	1			5						8	3	10		4					11	6		9			20
			2		1		8	5						7	3	10		4					11	6		9			21
		2		7	1	9		5						10	3	11		4						6		8			22
			2		1				6			5		8	3	11	7	4							10		9		23
			2	7	1							6		8	3	10		4					11			5	9		24
			2	7	1	9	8		5				6		3	10		4			11								25
				7		9			5				6	8	3	10		4		1	11							2	26
			2	7	1	9	8	5					6		3	10		4			11								27
				7	1	9		5						8	3	10		4			11					6		2	28
9				7	1			5						8	3	10		4			11					6		2	29
				7		9		5						8	3	10		4		1	11					6		2	30
				7		9		5						8	3	10		4		1	11					6		2	31
				7		9		5						8	3	10		4		1	11					6		2	32
				7		9		5		10				8	3	11		4		1						6		2	33
						9		5		10				8	3	11				1	7	6				4		2	34
		3		7				5		9				8		10		4		1	11	6						2	35
			2	7		9		4		10			6	8	3	11				1		5							36
	1		2	7		9		5		10			4	8	3	11						6							37
	1		2	7				5		10			4	8	3	11						6				9			38
	1		2	7				5		10			4	8	3						11	6				9			39
	1		2	7				5		10			4	8	3	11						6				9			40
	1		2	7				5		10			4	8	3	11						6				9			41
	1		2	7				5		10			4	8	3	11						6				9			42
2	6	4	30	30	28	25	12	26	20	10	6	2	10	40	41	25	9	27	1	8	29	9	4	5	3	35	6	9	
				4		23		4		4				15		7	1				10		1			11			

Attwood A	Coggins W	Common E	Cresswell W	Critchley E	Davies A	Dean W	Dunn J	Griffiths TP	Hart H	Johnson T	Kelly J	McClure J	McPherson L	Martin G	O'Donnell J	Rigby A	Ritchie H	Robson T	Rooney W	Sagar E	Stein J	Thomson J	Troup A	Virr A	Weldon A	White T	Wilkinson J	Williams B	
				7	1	9	8	5	6						3	10		4			11							2	3
				7		9			5				6	8	3	10		4		1	11							2	4
				2	1	2	1	1	2				1	1	2	2		2		1	2							2	
				2		2								1															

1930-31

1	Aug	30	(a)	Plymouth A	W 3-2	White 2, Martin	34,246
2	Sep	3	(h)	Preston NE	W 2-1	Griffiths, White	29,908
3		6	(h)	Swansea T	W 5-1	Dean 2, White 2, Martin	27,245
4		8	(a)	Cardiff C	W 2-1	White 2	11,463
5		13	(a)	West Brom A	W 2-1	Dean, White	23,556
6		17	(h)	Cardiff C	D 1-1	Dean	17,564
7		20	(h)	Port Vale	L 2-3	Rigby, White	27,142
8		27	(a)	Bradford C	W 3-0	Critchley, Griffiths, Rigby	20,361
9	Oct	4	(h)	Charlton A	W 7-1	Critchley 2, Dean 2, Dunn 2, Griffiths	29,440
10		11	(a)	Barnsley	D 1-1	Johnson	16,039
11		18	(a)	Nottingham F	D 2-2	Dean, Dunn	19,852
12		25	(h)	Tottenham H	W 4-2	Dean, Dunn, Johnson, Rigby	25,265
13	Nov	1	(a)	Reading	W 2-0	Critchley, Dunn	11,919
14		8	(h)	Wolves	W 4-0	Dean, Johnson, Rigby, Wilkinson	32,228
15		15	(a)	Millwall	W 3-1	Dunn, Stein, Wilkinson	18,290
16		22	(h)	Stoke C	W 5-0	Dean 3, Johnson 2	21,496
17		29	(a)	Bradford	L 1-4	Johnson	18,686
18	Dec	6	(h)	Oldham A	W 6-4	Dean 4, Critchley, Dunn	22,421
19		13	(a)	Burnley	L 2-5	Dean, Stein	17,849
20		20	(h)	Southampton	W 2-1	Dean 2	20,639
21		25	(a)	Bury	D 2-2	Dean, Dunn	23,247
22		27	(h)	Plymouth A	W 9-1	Dean 4, Stein 4, Johnson	37,018
23	Jan	1	(h)	Bury	W 3-2	Dean, Gee, McPherson	35,274
24		3	(a)	Swansea T	W 5-2	Dean 2, Critchley, Johnson, Stein	19,604
25		17	(h)	West Brom A	W 2-1	Dean, Martin	30,190
26		26	(a)	Port Vale	W 3-1	Critchley 2, Dean	10,455
27		31	(h)	Bradford C	W 4-2	Dean, Dunn, Gee, McClure	15,179
28	Feb	7	(a)	Charlton A	W 7-0	Dean 3, Critchley, Dunn, Johnson, Stein	16,859
29		18	(h)	Barnsley	W 5-2	Dean 2, Dunn 2, Critchley	19,042
30		21	(h)	Nottingham F	W 2-0	Dunn, Johnson	32,328
31	Mar	7	(h)	Reading	W 3-2	Critchley, Dunn, Johnson	23,873
32		16	(a)	Tottenham H	L 0-1		30,205
33		21	(h)	Millwall	W 2-0	Critchley, Johnson	26,162
34		25	(a)	Wolves	L 1-3	White	9,422
35		28	(a)	Stoke C	L 0-2		12,401
36	Apr	3	(a)	Bristol C	W 1-0	Stein	36,985
37		4	(h)	Bradford	W 4-2	Dean 2, Martin, Stein	32,213
38		6	(h)	Bristol C	L 1-3	Dean	23,058
39		11	(a)	Oldham A	D 3-3	Martin 2, Johnson	21,119
40		18	(h)	Burnley	W 3-2	Critchley, Johnson, Opp own-goal	19,144
41		25	(a)	Southampton	L 1-2	Dean	9,528
42	May	2	(a)	Preston NE	L 1-2	Martin	9,437

FINAL LEAGUE POSITION: 1st in Division Two

Appearances
Goals

FA Cup

3	Jan	10	(a)	Plymouth A	W 2-0	Dunn, Stein
4		24	(a)	Crystal P	W 6-0	Dean 4, Johnson, Opp own-goal
5	Feb	14	(h)	Grimsby T	W 5-3	Johnson 2, Stein 2, Dean
6		28	(h)	Southport	W 9-1	Dean 4, Critchley 2, Dunn 2, Johnson
SF	Mar	14	(n*)	West Brom A	L 0-1	

* Played at Old Trafford.

Appearances
Goals

Bocking W	Britton C	Coggins W	Cresswell W	Critchley E	Dean W	Dunn J	Gee C	Griffiths TP	Johnson T	Lowe H	McCambridge J	McClure J	McPherson L	Martin G	Rigby A	Stein J	Thomson J	White T	Wilkinson J	Williams B	
		1	3	7	9			5					4	10	11		6	8		2	1
		1	3	7	9			5					4	10	11		6	8		2	2
		1	3	7	9			5					4	10	11		6	8		2	3
		1	3	7	9			5					4	10	11		6	8		2	4
		1	3	7	9			5					4	10	11		6	8		2	5
		1	3	7	9			5					4	10	11		6	8		2	6
		1	3	7				5	10				4	8	11		6	9		2	7
		1	3	7		8		5	10		9		4		11		6			2	8
		1	3	7	9	8		5	10				4		11		6			2	9
		1	3	7	9	8		5	10				4		11		6			2	10
		1	3	7	9	8		5	10				4		11		6			2	11
	4	1	3	7	9	8		5	10						11		6			2	12
	4	1	3	7	9	8		5	10						11		6			2	13
	4	1	3		9	8		5	10						11		6		7	2	14
	4	1	3		9	8		5	10							11	6		7	2	15
	4	1	3		9	8		5	10							11	6		7	2	16
	4	1	3		9	8		5	10							11	6		7	2	17
		1	3	7	9	8		5	10	2			4			11	6				18
		1	3	7	9	8		5	10	2			4			11	6				19
	4	1	3	7	9	8		5	10	2						11	6				20
		1	3	7	9	8		5	10	2			4			11	6				21
		1	3	7	9	8		5	10				4			11	6			2	22
		1	3	7	9	8	5		10				4			11	6			2	23
		1	3	7	9	8	5		10				4			11	6			2	24
		1	3	7	9		5		10			4		8		11	6			2	25
		1	3	7	9	8	5		10			4				11	6			2	26
		1	3	7	9	8	5		10			4				11	6			2	27
		1	3	7	9	8	5		10			4				11	6			2	28
		1	3	7	9	8	5		10			4				11	6			2	29
		1	3	7	9	8	5		10			4				11	6			2	30
		1	3	7	9	8	5		10			4				11	6			2	31
		1	3		9	8	5		10			4				11	6		7	2	32
	4	1	3	7	9	8	5		10							11		6		2	33
	4	1	3	7		8	5		10							11	6	9		2	34
	4	1	3	7		8	5		10							11	6	9		2	35
		1	3	7	9		5		10			4		8		11	6			2	36
		1	3	7	9		5		10			4		8		11	6			2	37
		1	3	7	9		5		10			4		8		11	6			2	38
		1	3	7	9		5		10			4		8		11	6			2	39
		1	3	7	9		5		10			4		8		11	6			2	40
		1	3	7	9		5	2	10			4		8		11	6				41
2		1	3	7		8	5		10			4		9		11	6				42
1	10	42	42	37	37	28	20	23	36	4	1	15	17	15	14	28	41	10	5	36	
				13	39	14	2	3	14			1	1	7	4	10		10	2		

1 own-goal

Bocking W	Britton C	Coggins W	Cresswell W	Critchley E	Dean W	Dunn J	Gee C	Griffiths TP	Johnson T	Lowe H	McCambridge J	McClure J	McPherson L	Martin G	Rigby A	Stein J	Thomson J	White T	Wilkinson J	Williams B	
		1	3	7	9	8	5		10			4				11	6			2	3
		1	3	7	9	8	5		10			4				11	6			2	4
		1	3	7	9	8	5		10			4				11	6			2	5
		1	3	7	9	8	5		10			4				11	6			2	6
		1	3		9	8	5		10			4				11	6		7	2	SF
		5	5	4	5	5	5		5			5				5	5		1	5	
				2	9	3			4							3					

1 own-goal

1931-32

1	Aug	29	(h)	Birmingham	W 3-2	Dunn 3	39,146
2	Sep	2	(a)	Portsmouth	W 3-0	White 3	23,075
3		5	(a)	Sunderland	W 3-2	Griffiths, Johnson, Stein	28,474
4		12	(h)	Manchester C	L 0-1		32,570
5		16	(a)	Derby C	L 0-3		12,491
6		19	(a)	Liverpool	W 3-1	Dean 3	53,220
7		23	(h)	Derby C	W 2-1	Johnson 2	19,130
8		26	(a)	Arsenal	L 2-3	Critchley, Dean	47,637
9	Oct	3	(h)	Blackpool	W 3-2	Johnson 2, White	31,651
10		10	(a)	Sheffield U	W 5-1	Dean 3, Johnson, Stein	26,651
11		17	(h)	Sheffield W	W 9-3	Dean 5, Critchley, Johnson, Stein, White	38,186
12		24	(a)	Aston Villa	W 3-2	Critchley 2, White	61,663
13		31	(h)	Newcastle U	W 8-1	Dean 2, Johnson 2, White 2, Critchley, Stein	30,765
14	Nov	7	(a)	Huddersfield T	D 0-0		17,605
15		14	(h)	Chelsea	W 7-2	Dean 5, Johnson, Stein	32,758
16		21	(a)	Grimsby T	W 2-1	Stein, White	16,508
17		28	(h)	Leicester C	W 9-2	Dean 4, Johnson 2, White 2, Clark	33,513
18	Dec	5	(a)	West Ham U	L 2-4	Johnson, Stein	34,139
19		12	(h)	Middlesbrough	W 5-1	White 2, Critchley, Dean, Johnson	33,182
20		19	(a)	Bolton W	L 1-2	Dean	33,619
21		25	(a)	Blackburn R	L 3-5	White 2, Dean	40,059
22		26	(h)	Blackburn R	W 5-0	Dean 3, Johnson, White	52,991
23	Jan	2	(a)	Birmingham	L 0-4		26,256
24		16	(h)	Sunderland	W 4-2	Griffiths 2, Dean, White	29,491
25		27	(a)	Manchester C	L 0-1		26,363
26		30	(h)	Liverpool	W 2-1	Critchley, White	46,537
27	Feb	6	(h)	Arsenal	L 1-3	Johnson	56,698
28		13	(a)	Blackpool	L 0-2		16,346
29		20	(h)	Sheffield U	W 5-1	Dunn 2, Critchley, Dean, Johnson	38,190
30		27	(a)	Sheffield W	W 3-1	Dean 2, Dunn	24,279
31	Mar	5	(h)	Aston Villa	W 4-2	Dean 2, Dunn, Johnson	39,190
32		19	(h)	Huddersfield T	W 4-1	Dean 3, Johnson	30,748
33		25	(h)	West Brom A	W 2-1	Dean, Dunn	51,783
34		26	(a)	Chelsea	D 0-0		56,298
35		28	(a)	West Brom A	D 1-1	Stein	32,428
36	Apr	2	(h)	Grimsby T	W 4-2	Dunn 2, Dean, Johnson	28,456
37		9	(a)	Leicester C	W 1-0	Dean	23,229
38		16	(h)	West Ham U	W 6-1	Dean 3, Johnson 2, Stein	26,997
39		23	(a)	Middlesbrough	L 0-1		10,728
40		30	(h)	Bolton W	W 1-0	Dean	28,546
41	May	4	(a)	Newcastle U	D 0-0		30,898
42		7	(h)	Portsmouth	L 0-1		24,011

FINAL LEAGUE POSITION: 1st in Division One

Appearances
Goals

FA Cup

3	Jan	19	(h)	Liverpool	L 1-2	Dean

Appearances
Goals

Bocking W	Clark A	Coggins W	Cresswell W	Critchley E	Dean W	Dunn J	Gee C	Griffiths PH	Johnson T	Lowe H	McClure J	McPherson L	Martin G	Rigby A	Sagar E	Stein J	Thomson J	White T	Williams B	
2	4		3		9	8	5	7	10						1	11	6			1
2	4		3			8	5	7	10						1	11	6	9		2
2	4		3		9	8	5	7	10						1	11	6			3
2	4		3		9	8	5	7	10						1	11	6			4
2	4		3		9	8	5	7	10						1	11	6			5
2			3	7	9	8	5		10		4	6			1	11				6
2			3	7	9	8	5		10		4	6			1	11				7
2			3	7	9	8	5		10		4	6			1	11				8
	4		3	7	9		5		10						1	11	6	8	2	9
	4		3	7	9		5		10						1	11	6	8	2	10
	4		3	7	9		5		10						1	11	6	8	2	11
	4		3	7	9		5		10						1	11	6	8	2	12
	4		3	7	9		5		10						1	11	6	8	2	13
	4		3	7			5		10				9		1	11	6	8	2	14
	4		3	7	9		5		10						1	11	6	8	2	15
	4		3	7	9		5		10						1	11	6	8	2	16
	4		3	7	9		5		10						1	11	6	8	2	17
	4		3	7	9		5		10						1	11	6	8	2	18
	4		3	7	9		5		10						1	11	6	8	2	19
	4		3	7	9		5		10						1	11	6	8	2	20
	4		3	7	9		5		10						1	11	6	8	2	21
	4		3	7	9		5		10						1	11	6	8	2	22
	4		3	7			5		10				9		1	11	6	8	2	23
	4	1		7	9		5	11	10	3							6	8	2	24
	4		3	7	9		5	11	10						1		6	8	2	25
3	4			7	9				10		5			11	1		6	8	2	26
	4		3	7	9		5		10					11	1		6	8	2	27
	4		3	7	9				10		5			11	1		6	8	2	28
	4		3	7	9	8	5		10						1	11	6		2	29
	4		3	7	9	8	5		10						1	11	6		2	30
	4		3	7	9	8	5		10						1	11	6		2	31
	4		3	7	9	8	5		10						1	11	6		2	32
	4		3	7	9	8	5		10						1	11	6		2	33
	4		3	7	9	8	5		10						1	11	6		2	34
	4		3	7	9	8	5		10						1	11	6		2	35
	4		3	7	9	8	5		10						1	11	6		2	36
2	4		3	7	9	8	5								1	11	6	10		37
	4		3	7	9	8	5		10						1	11	6		2	38
	4		3	7	9	8	5		10						1	11	6		2	39
	4		3	7	9	8	5		10						1	11	6		2	40
	4		3	7		8			10		5				1	11	6	9	2	41
	4		3	7	9	8			10		5				1	11	6		2	42
10	39	1	40	37	38	22	38	7	41	1	7	3	2	3	41	37	39	23	33	
	1			8	45	10		3	22							9		18		

Bocking W	Clark A	Coggins W	Cresswell W	Critchley E	Dean W	Dunn J	Gee C	Griffiths PH	Johnson T	Lowe H	McClure J	McPherson L	Martin G	Rigby A	Sagar E	Stein J	Thomson J	White T	Williams B	
3	4			7	9		5		10						1	11	6	8	2	3
1	1			1	1		1		1						1	1	1	1	1	
					1															

1932-33

1	Aug	27	(a)	West Brom A	L 1-3	Dunn	31,922
2		31	(h)	Sheffield W	W 2-1	Johnson 2	28,007
3	Sep	3	(h)	Birmingham	W 4-1	Dean, Dunn, Johnson, Stein	27,559
4		5	(a)	Sheffield W	L 1-3	Dean	14,890
5		10	(a)	Sunderland	L 1-3	Stein	23,005
6		17	(h)	Manchester C	W 2-1	Dean 2	32,852
7		24	(a)	Arsenal	L 1-2	Critchley	51,182
8	Oct	1	(h)	Liverpool	W 3-1	Dean 2, Critchley	44,214
9		8	(h)	Blackpool	W 2-0	Dean, Johnson	18,359
10		15	(a)	Derby C	L 0-2		23,976
11		22	(a)	Leicester C	D 2-2	McGourty, Stein	17,770
12		29	(h)	Portsmouth	D 1-1	Dean	17,893
13	Nov	5	(a)	Newcastle U	W 2-1	Dean, Stein	30,877
14		12	(h)	Aston Villa	D 3-3	Dean, Johnson, Stein	38,769
15		19	(a)	Middlesbrough	W 2-0	Geldard, Johnson	9,662
16		26	(h)	Bolton W	D 2-2	Geldard, Johnson	27,529
17	Dec	3	(a)	Chelsea	L 0-1		33,962
18		10	(h)	Huddersfield T	W 2-0	Dunn, White	23,589
19		17	(a)	Sheffield U	L 2-3	Stein, Thomson	18,507
20		24	(h)	Wolves	W 5-1	Dean 2, Dunn, Johnson, Stein	21,795
21		26	(a)	Blackburn R	L 1-3	Geldard	35,987
22		27	(h)	Blackburn R	W 6-1	Johnson 3, Dunn, Stein, Opp own-goal	35,576
23		31	(h)	West Brom A	L 1-2	Dean	30,234
24	Jan	7	(a)	Birmingham C	L 0-4		17,365
25		21	(h)	Sunderland	W 6-1	Dean 2, Dunn, Johnson, Stein, Thomson	23,173
26	Feb	1	(a)	Manchester C	L 0-3		10,986
27		4	(h)	Arsenal	D 1-1	Stein	55,463
28		11	(a)	Liverpool	L 4-7	Dean 2, Johnson, Stein	41,469
29		22	(a)	Blackpool	L 1-2	Dunn	12,050
30		25	(h)	Derby C	W 4-2	Dean, Dunn, Geldard, Opp own-goal	14,125
31	Mar	8	(h)	Leicester C	W 6-3	Dean 3, Dunn 2, White	12,745
32		11	(a)	Portsmouth	D 2-2	Dean, Stein	19,501
33		25	(a)	Aston Villa	L 1-2	Cunliffe	27,463
34	Apr	1	(h)	Middlesbrough	D 0-0		21,068
35		5	(h)	Newcastle U	D 0-0		14,455
36		8	(a)	Bolton W	W 4-2	Dean 2, McGourty, Opp own-goal	12,112
37		15	(h)	Chelsea	W 3-2	Stein 2, Thomson	27,635
38		17	(h)	Leeds U	L 0-1		21,285
39		18	(a)	Leeds U	L 0-1		19,663
40		22	(a)	Huddersfield T	D 0-0		11,593
41	May	3	(h)	Sheffield U	W 1-0	Stein	18,363
42		6	(a)	Wolves	L 2-4	Geldard, Stein	34,546

FINAL LEAGUE POSITION: 11th in Division One

Appearances
Goals

FA Cup

3	Jan	14	(a)	Leicester C	W 3-2	Dean, Dunn, Stein
4		28	(h)	Bury	W 3-1	Johnson 2, Dean
5	Feb	18	(h)	Leeds U	W 2-0	Dean, Stein
6	Mar	3	(h)	Luton T	W 6-0	Johnson 2, Stein 2, Dean, Dunn
SF		18	(n*)	West Ham U	W 2-1	Critchley, Dunn
F	Apr	29	(n†)	Manchester C	W 3-0	Dean, Dunn, Stein

* Played at Molineux. † Played at Wembley.

Appearances
Goals

Archer J	Bocking W	Britton C	Cook W	Cresswell W	Critchley E	Cunliffe J	Dean W	Dunn J	Gee C	Geldard A	Griffiths PH	Johnson T	McClure J	McGourty J	Mercer J	Sagar E	Stein J	Stevens G	Thomson J	Turner G	Watson JG	White T	Williams B	
				3	7		9	8	5			10	4			1	11		6				2	1
				3	7		9	8				10	4			1	11		6			5	2	2
				3	7		9	8				10	4			1	11		6			5	2	3
				3	7		9	8				10	4			1	11		6			5	2	4
				3	7		9	8				10	4			1	11		6			5	2	5
		4		3	7		9	8				10				1	11		6			5	2	6
		4		3	7		9					10		8		1	11		6			5	2	7
		4		3	7		9					10		8		1	11		6			5	2	8
		4		3	7		9					10		8		1	11		6			5	2	9
		4		3	7		9					10		8		1	11		6			5	2	10
6		4		3	7		9					10		8		1	11		5				2	11
6		4		3	7		9					10		8		1	11		5				2	12
		4		3	7		9					10		8		1	11		6			5	2	13
		4		3	7		9					10		8		1	11		6			5	2	14
		4		3			9			7		10		8		1	11		6			5	2	15
		4		3			9			7		10		8		1	11		6			5	2	16
		4		3			9	8		7		10				1	11		6			5	2	17
		4		3			9	8		7		10				1	11		6			5	2	18
		4		3			9	8		7		10				1	11		6			5	2	19
		4		3			9	8		7		10				1	11		6			5	2	20
	2	4		3			9	8		7		10				1	11		6			5		21
	2	4		3			9	8		7		10				1	11		6			5		22
		4	2	3			9	8		7		10				1			6	11		5		23
		4	2	3			9		5	7		10				1			6	11		8		24
		4	2	3			9	8	5	7		10				1	11		6					25
		4	2	3				8	5	7		10				1	11	9	6					26
		4	2	3			9	8		7		10				1	11		6			5		27
		4	2	3			9	8		7		10				1	11		6			5		28
		4	2	3				8		7	9	10				1	11		6			5		29
		4	2	3			9	8		7		10				1	11		6			5		30
		4	2	3	7		9	8				10				1	11		6			5		31
		4	2	3	7		9	8	5			10				1	11		6					32
		4	2	3		8	9			7		10				1	11		6			5		33
		4	2	3		8	9			7						1	11		6		10	5		34
		4	2	3			9			7		10		8		1	11		6			5		35
		4	2	3			9			7		10		8		1	11		6			5		36
		4	2	3	8		9			7		10				1	11		6			5		37
		4	2	3			9		5	7		10		8		1	11		6					38
6	3		2					8	5	7				10	4	1	11	9						39
		4	2	3			9	8		7		10				1	11		6			5		40
		4	2	3			9	8		7		10				1	11		6			5		41
		4	2	3			9	8		7		10				1	11		6			5		42
3	3	36	20	41	17	2	39	25	7	26	1	40	5	14	1	42	40	2	41	2	1	34	20	
					2	1	24	10		5		13		2			16		3			2		

3 own-goals

Archer J	Bocking W	Britton C	Cook W	Cresswell W	Critchley E	Cunliffe J	Dean W	Dunn J	Gee C	Geldard A	Griffiths PH	Johnson T	McClure J	McGourty J	Mercer J	Sagar E	Stein J	Stevens G	Thomson J	Turner G	Watson JG	White T	Williams B	
		4	2	3			9	8		7		10				1	11		6			5		3
		4	2	3			9	8		7		10				1	11		6			5		4
		4	2	3			9	8		7		10				1	11		6			5		5
		4	2	3	7		9	8				10				1	11		6			5		6
		4	2	3	7		9	8				10				1	11		6			5		SF
		4	2	3			9	8		7		10				1	11		6			5		F
		6	6	6	2		6	6		4		6				6	6		6			6		
					1		5	4				4					5							

1933-34

No.	Month	Date	Venue	Opponents	Result	Score	Scorers	Attendance
1	Aug	26	(h)	West Brom A	W	1-0	Dean	32,212
2		30	(a)	Derby C	D	1-1	Dean	23,073
3	Sep	2	(a)	Birmingham	D	2-2	Dean 2	25,250
4		9	(h)	Sheffield W	L	2-3	Dean, White	33,340
5		16	(a)	Manchester C	D	2-2	Dean, Geldard	48,826
6		23	(h)	Arsenal	W	3-1	Dean, Dunn, White	53,792
7		30	(a)	Liverpool	L	2-3	Johnson, White	53,698
8	Oct	7	(a)	Middlesbrough	L	0-2		10,895
9		14	(h)	Blackburn R	W	7-1	White 3, Dunn, Geldard, Johnson, Stein	23,933
10		21	(h)	Tottenham H	D	1-1	White	35,082
11		28	(a)	Leicester C	L	1-3	White	15,538
12	Nov	4	(h)	Huddersfield T	L	0-1		31,708
13		11	(a)	Sheffield U	D	1-1	Dunn	13,816
14		18	(h)	Wolves	L	1-2	Dunn	20,543
15		25	(a)	Stoke C	W	2-1	Cunliffe, White	19,840
16	Dec	2	(h)	Chelsea	W	2-1	Cunliffe 2	15,584
17		9	(a)	Portsmouth	D	0-0		13,084
18		16	(h)	Sunderland	W	1-0	Critchley	21,728
19		23	(a)	Aston Villa	L	1-2	White	24,438
20		25	(a)	Newcastle U	W	2-1	White, Stein	34,211
21		26	(h)	Newcastle U	L	3-7	White 2, Critchley	39,109
22		30	(a)	West Brom A	D	3-3	Stein 2, Cunliffe	19,151
23	Jan	1	(h)	Derby C	L	0-3		24,534
24		6	(h)	Birmingham	W	2-0	Critchley, Cunliffe	20,582
25		20	(a)	Sheffield W	D	0-0		22,716
26	Feb	3	(a)	Arsenal	W	2-1	Cunliffe, White	24,025
27		7	(h)	Manchester C	W	2-0	Johnson, Stein	17,134
28		10	(h)	Liverpool	D	0-0		52,088
29		17	(h)	Middlesbrough	D	1-1	Stein	19,015
30		24	(a)	Blackburn R	D	1-1	Cunliffe	12,645
31	Mar	3	(a)	Tottenham H	L	0-3		26,121
32		10	(h)	Leicester C	D	1-1	Stein	21,959
33		24	(h)	Sheffield U	W	4-0	Higham 2, Geldard, Stein	18,682
34		30	(a)	Leeds U	D	2-2	Cunliffe, Higham	19,951
35		31	(a)	Wolves	L	0-2		25,396
36	Apr	2	(h)	Leeds U	W	2-0	Cunliffe, Geldard	25,624
37		7	(h)	Stoke C	D	2-2	Geldard, Higham	25,341
38		14	(a)	Chelsea	L	0-2		34,029
39		21	(h)	Portsmouth	D	1-1	Dean	25,766
40		25	(a)	Huddersfield T	L	0-1		4,842
41		28	(a)	Sunderland	L	2-3	Higham 2	5,976
42	May	5	(h)	Aston Villa	D	2-2	Dean, Stevenson	12,610

FINAL LEAGUE POSITION: 14th in Division One

Appearances
Goals

FA Cup

Round	Month	Date	Venue	Opponents	Result	Score
3	Jan	13	(a)	Tottenham H	L	0-3

Appearances
Goals

Archer J	Bocking W	Britton C	Coggins W	Cook W	Coulter J	Cresswell W	Critchley E	Cunliffe J	Dean W	Dunn J	Gee C	Geldard A	Higham N	Johnson T	Jones JE	McGourty J	Sagar E	Stein J	Stevenson A	Thomson J	Watson JG	White T	Williams B	
		4		2		3			9	8		7		10			1	11		6		5		1
		4		2		3			9	8		7		10			1	11		6		5		2
		4		2		3			9	8		7		10			1	11		6		5		3
		4	1	2		3			9	8		7		10				11		6		5		4
		4		2		3			9	8		7		10			1	11		6		5		5
		4		2		3			9	8		7		10			1	11		6		5		6
		4		2		3				8	5	7		10			1	11		6		9		7
		4		2		3				8	5	7		10			1	11		6		9		8
		4		2		3				8	5	7		10			1	11		6		9		9
	3	4		2						8	5	7		10			1	11		6		9		10
		4		2		3				8	5	7		10			1	11		6		9		11
		4		2		3			9	8		7		10			1	11		6		5		12
		4		2		3	7	9		8				10			1	11		6		5		13
		4		2		3	7	9		8							1	11		6	10	5		14
		4		2		3	7	8			5			10			1	11		6		9		15
		4				3	7	9		8	5			10			1	11		6			2	16
		4		2		3	7	9		8				10			1	11		6		5		17
6		4		2		3	7	10		8	5						1	11				9		18
6		4		2		3	7	10		8	5						1	11				9		19
6		4		2		3	7	10		8	5						1	11				9		20
6		4		2		3	7	10		8	5						1	11				9		21
6		4		2		3	7	10		8							1	11		5		9		22
6		4		2		3	7	10		8							1	11		5		9		23
		4		2		3	7	9		8				10			1	11		6		5		24
		4		3			7	10			5					8	1	11		6		9	2	25
		4		3			7	8			5						1	11	10	6		9	2	26
		4		3			7	8			5		10	9			1	11		6			2	27
		4	1	3			7	8			5			9				11	10	6			2	28
		4		3				9			5	7	10				1	11	8	6			2	29
		4		3				8	9		5	7	10				1	11		6			2	30
		4		3				8	9		5	7	10				1	11		6			2	31
		4		3				8			5	7	10				1	11		6		9	2	32
		4		3				8			5	7	9				1	11	10	6			2	33
		4		3				8			5	7	9				1	11	10	6			2	34
		4		3				8			5	7	9				1	11	10	6			2	35
		4						8			5	7	9		3		1	11	10	6			2	36
		4						8			5	7	9		3		1	11	10	6			2	37
		4				2		8			5	7			3		1	11	10	6		9		38
		4			10			8	9		5	7			3		1	11		6			2	39
		4			11						5		8		3		1	7	10	6		9	2	40
		4			11	3			9		5		8				1	7	10	6			2	41
		4		3					9		5	7	8				1	11	10	6			2	42
6	1	42	2	35	3	25	16	27	12	23	29	24	13	19	5	1	40	42	12	38	1	28	18	
							3	9	9	4		5	6	3				8	1			14		

Archer J	Bocking W	Britton C	Coggins W	Cook W	Coulter J	Cresswell W	Critchley E	Cunliffe J	Dean W	Dunn J	Gee C	Geldard A	Higham N	Johnson T	Jones JE	McGourty J	Sagar E	Stein J	Stevenson A	Thomson J	Watson JG	White T	Williams B	
		4		3		2	7	9		8				10			1	11		6		5		3
		1		1		1	1	1		1				1			1	1		1		1		

1934-35

1	Aug	25	(a)	Tottenham H	D 1-1	Dean	50,586
2		29	(h)	Leicester C	W 2-1	Dean, Leyfield	20,475
3	Sep	1	(h)	Preston NE	W 4-1	Leyfield 2, Dean, Stein	37,792
4		3	(a)	Leicester C	L 2-5	Dean, Leyfield	15,975
5		8	(a)	Grimsby T	D 0-0		16,343
6		15	(h)	Liverpool	W 1-0	Dean	43,001
7		22	(h)	Huddersfield T	W 4-2	Cunliffe 2, Dean, Stein	20,815
8		29	(a)	Wolves	L 2-4	Leyfield, Opp own-goal	15,169
9	Oct	6	(h)	Chelsea	W 3-2	Dean 2, Opp own-goal	17,827
10		13	(a)	Aston Villa	D 2-2	Cunliffe, Dean	37,707
11		20	(a)	Leeds U	L 0-2		16,731
12		27	(h)	West Brom A	W 4-0	Coulter, Cunliffe, Dean, Stevenson	27,005
13	Nov	3	(a)	Arsenal	L 0-2		50,350
14		10	(h)	Portsmouth	W 3-2	Dean 2, Cunliffe	25,365
15		17	(a)	Stoke C	L 2-3	Dean, Stevenson	29,140
16		24	(h)	Manchester C	L 1-2	Coulter	36,926
17	Dec	1	(a)	Middlesbrough	L 2-3	Opp own-goals 2	12,914
18		8	(h)	Blackburn R	W 5-2	Dean 2, Stevenson 2, Cunliffe	21,451
19		15	(a)	Sheffield W	D 0-0		19,266
20		22	(h)	Birmingham	W 2-0	Coulter, Stevenson	20,148
21		25	(h)	Sunderland	W 6-2	Cunliffe 2, Coulter, Dean, Geldard, Stevenson	37,931
22		26	(a)	Sunderland	L 0-7		35,271
23		29	(h)	Tottenham H	W 5-2	Dean 3, Coulter, Cunliffe	25,851
24	Jan	1	(h)	Derby C	D 2-2	Geldard 2	31,158
25		5	(a)	Preston NE	D 2-2	Cunliffe, Stevenson	22,675
26		19	(h)	Grimsby T	W 3-1	Cunliffe 2, Dean	24,493
27	Feb	7	(a)	Huddersfield T	D 1-1	Coulter	14,662
28		9	(h)	Wolves	W 5-2	Cunliffe 2, Stevenson 2, Coulter	28,992
29		20	(a)	Chelsea	L 0-3		11,701
30		23	(h)	Aston Villa	D 2-2	Dean, Stevenson	30,772
31	Mar	6	(h)	Leeds U	D 4-4	Coulter 2, Cunliffe, Dean	10,441
32		9	(a)	West Brom A	W 1-0	Coulter	16,706
33		16	(h)	Arsenal	L 0-2		50,389
34		20	(a)	Liverpool	L 1-2	Dean	31,965
35		23	(a)	Portsmouth	L 1-5	Coulter	14,262
36		30	(h)	Stoke C	W 5-0	Stein 2, Stevenson 2, Dean	17,016
37	Apr	6	(a)	Manchester C	D 2-2	Leyfield 2	26,138
38		13	(h)	Middlesbrough	D 1-1	Dean	15,214
39		20	(a)	Blackburn R	L 2-6	Geldard, Thomson	13,559
40		22	(a)	Derby C	L 1-4	Dean	17,718
41	May	1	(h)	Sheffield W	D 2-2	Geldard, Stevenson	7,802
42		4	(a)	Birmingham	W 3-2	Stevenson 2, Opp own-goal	16,634
				FINAL LEAGUE POSITION: 8th in Division One			Appearances
							Goals

FA Cup

3	Jan	12	(h)	Grimsby T	W 6-3	Geldard 3, Stevenson 2, Cunliffe
4		26	(a)	Sunderland	D 1-1	Cunliffe
R		30	(h)	Sunderland	W 6-4	Coulter 3, Geldard 2, Stevenson
5	Feb	16	(h)	Derby C	W 3-1	Coulter 2, Dean
6	Mar	2	(h)	Bolton W	L 1-2	Coulter

Appearances
Goals

	Bradshaw G	Britton C	Clark A	Cook W	Coulter J	Cresswell W	Cunliffe J	Dean W	Dickinson	Dunn J	Gee C	Geldard A	Higham N	Jackson G	Jones JE	King F	Leyfield C	Mercer J	Sagar E	Stein J	Stevenson A	Thomson J	White T	Williams B
1		4		3		2	8	9			5	7							1	11		6	10	
2		4		3		2	8	9			5						7		1	11		6	10	
3		4		3		2	8	9			5						7		1	11	10	6		
4		4		3		2	8	9			5						7		1	11	10	6		
5		4		3		2	8	9			5						7		1	11	10	6		
6		4		3		2	8	9			5						7		1	11	10	6		
7		4		3		2	8	9			5						7		1	11	10	6		
8				3		2		9		8	5						7	4	1	11	10	6		
9		4		3		2	8	9			5						7		1	11	10	6		
10		4		3		2	8	9			5						7		1	11	10	6		
11		4		3		2	8	9			5		10				7		1	11		6		
12		4		3	11	2	8	9			5	7							1		10	6		
13		4		3	11	2	8	9			5	7							1		10	6		
14		4		3	11	2	8	9			5	7							1		10	6		
15		4		3	11	2	8	9			5	7							1		10	6		
16		4		3	11	2	8	9			5	7							1		10	6		
17		4		3	11		8	9			5	7							1		10	6		2
18		4		3	11		8	9			5	7							1		10	6		2
19		4		3	11		10	9		8	5	7							1			6		2
20		4		3	11			9		8	5	7							1		10	6		2
21		4		3	11		8	9			5	7							1		10	6		2
22		4		3	11		8	9				7							1		10	6	5	2
23		4		3	11	2	8	9			5	7							1		10	6		
24		4		3	11	2	8	9			5	7							1		10	6		
25		4		3	11	2	8	9			5	7							1		10	6		
26		4			11	2	8	9			5	7			3				1		10	6		
27				2	11		8	9			5	7			3			4	1		10	6		
28		4		3	11		8	9			5	7		2					1		10	6		
29					11	3	8	9			5	7		2				4	1		10	6		
30	1	4		3	11			9		8	5	7		2							10	6		
31	1	4		2	11		8	9			5	7			3						10	6		
32		8			11		9				5	7		2	3			4	1		10	6		
33		4			11		9				5	7		2	3			8	1		10	6		
34		4			10		8	9			5	7		2	3				1	11		6		
35		4			11		8	10	9		5	7		2	3				1			6		
36		4				3	8	9				7							1	11	10	6	5	2
37						3	8	9									7	4	1	11	10	6	5	2
38		4				3	8	9			5	7				1				11	10	6		2
39		4					8	9			5	7			3	1				11	10	6		2
40		4				3	8	9			5	7		2		1				11	10	6		
41			5				9			8		7			3	1		4		11	10	6		2
42			5				9			8		7			3	1		4		11	10	6		2
	2	36	2	29	24	25	39	38	1	6	37	31	1	8	10	5	11	8	35	19	36	42	5	12
					11		15	26				5					7			4	15	1		

5 own-goals

	Bradshaw G	Britton C	Clark A	Cook W	Coulter J	Cresswell W	Cunliffe J	Dean W	Dickinson	Dunn J	Gee C	Geldard A	Higham N	Jackson G	Jones JE	King F	Leyfield C	Mercer J	Sagar E	Stein J	Stevenson A	Thomson J	White T	Williams B
3		4		3	11	2	8	9			5	7							1		10	6		
4		4		2	11		8	9			5	7			3				1		10	6		
R		4		2	11		8	9			5	7			3				1		10	6		
5		4		3	11		8	9			5	7		2					1		10	6		
6	1	4		2	11		8	9			5	7			3						10	6		
	1	5		5	5	1	5	5			5	5		1	3				4		5	5		
					6		2	1				5									3			

1935-36

1	Aug	31	(h)	Derby C	W 4-0	Dean, Geldard, Leyfield, Stevenson	43,680
2	Sep	4	(a)	Portsmouth	L 0-2		22,072
3		7	(a)	Liverpool	L 0-6		46,082
4		11	(h)	Portsmouth	W 3-0	Cunliffe, Geldard, Hartill	20,249
5		14	(a)	Bolton W	L 0-2		28,391
6		18	(a)	Preston NE	D 2-2	Stevenson 2	18,805
7		21	(h)	Huddersfield T	L 1-3	Cunliffe	31,043
8		28	(a)	Middlesbrough	L 1-6	Cunliffe	19,308
9	Oct	5	(h)	Aston Villa	D 2-2	Cunliffe, Stevenson	26,682
10		12	(a)	Wolves	L 0-4		30,627
11		19	(h)	Chelsea	W 5-1	Stevenson 2, Archer, Dean, Miller	18,934
12		26	(a)	Blackburn R	D 1-1	Archer	14,612
13	Nov	2	(h)	Stoke C	W 5-1	Cunliffe 4, Dean	27,638
14		9	(a)	Manchester C	L 0-1		39,883
15		16	(h)	Arsenal	L 0-2		46,990
16		23	(a)	Grimsby T	W 4-0	Bentham 2, Leyfield 2	10,247
17		30	(h)	Sunderland	L 0-3		39,366
18	Dec	7	(a)	West Brom A	L 1-6	Cunliffe	17,125
19		14	(h)	Leeds U	D 0-0		28,901
20		21	(a)	Birmingham	L 2-4	Cunliffe, Gillick	16,994
21		26	(h)	Sheffield W	W 4-3	Bentham, Britton, Cunliffe, Gillick	32,768
22		28	(a)	Derby C	D 3-3	Bentham, Cunliffe, Geldard	20,830
23	Jan	4	(h)	Liverpool	D 0-0		52,282
24		22	(h)	Bolton W	D 3-3	Dean 2, Stevenson	14,562
25		29	(a)	Huddersfield T	L 1-2	Gillick	3,404
26	Feb	1	(h)	Middlesbrough	W 5-2	Dean 2, Cunliffe, Geldard, Gillick	26,602
27		3	(a)	Sheffield W	D 3-3	Cunliffe 2, Dean	5,938
28		8	(a)	Aston Villa	D 1-1	Dean	53,837
29		15	(h)	Wolves	W 4-1	Geldard 2, Cunliffe, White	27,225
30		22	(a)	Chelsea	D 2-2	Dean 2	17,136
31		29	(h)	Manchester C	D 2-2	Gillick 2	14,418
32	Mar	7	(a)	Sunderland	D 3-3	Cunliffe, Dean, Stevenson	23,268
33		14	(h)	Blackburn R	W 4-0	Dean 2, Cunliffe, Mercer	25,694
34		25	(a)	Arsenal	D 1-1	Gillick	18,593
35		28	(h)	Grimsby T	W 4-0	Gillick, Stevenson, White, Opp own-goal	24,720
36	Apr	4	(a)	Stoke C	L 1-2	Stevenson	18,819
37		10	(h)	Brentford	L 1-2	Geldard	45,477
38		11	(h)	West Brom A	W 5-3	Cunliffe 4, White	24,793
39		13	(a)	Brentford	L 1-4	Gillick	29,790
40		18	(a)	Leeds U	L 1-3	Bell	13,738
41		25	(h)	Birmingham	W 4-3	Dean 3, Cunliffe	18,323
42	May	2	(h)	Preston NE	W 5-0	Bell 2, Leyfield 2, Britton	21,135

FINAL LEAGUE POSITION: 16th in Division One

Appearances
Goals

FA Cup

3	Jan	11	(h)	Preston NE	L 1-3	Geldard	

Appearances
Goals

Archer J	Bell J	Bentham S	Britton C	Cook W	Cresswell W	Cunliffe J	Dean W	Gee C	Geldard A	Gillick T	Hartill W	Jackson G	Jones JE	King F	Leyfield C	Mercer J	Miller W	Sagar E	Stevenson A	Thomson J	White T	Williams B	
			4	3			9		7						11		8	1	10	6	5	2	1
			4		3		9		7						11		8	1	10	6	5	2	2
			4		3		9		7						11		8	1	10	6	5	2	3
			4		3	10		5	7		9	2			11		8	1		6			4
			4		3	10		5	7		9	2			11		8	1		6			5
			4			10		5	7			2	3		11			1	8	6	9		6
			4			10		5	7			2	3		11			1	8	6	9		7
6						10		5	7		9	2	3		11	4		1	8				8
			4			10		5	7		9	2	3		11			1	8	6			9
			4			10		5	7		9	2	3		11			1	8	6			10
11			4				9		7			2	3	1		6	8		10		5		11
11			4	2			9		7				3			6	8	1	10		5		12
11			4	2		10	9		7				3			6	8	1			5		13
11			4	2		10	9		7				3			6	8	1			5		14
			4	2		10	9		7				3		11	6		1	8		5		15
		8	4	2		10	9		7				3		11	6		1			5		16
		8	4	2		10	9		7				3		11	6		1			5		17
		8	4	2		10	9		7				3		11	6		1			5		18
			4			10	9			7		2	3		11	6	8	1			5		19
		8	4			9			7	11		2	3			6	10	1			5		20
		8	4	2		9			7	11		3				6	10	1			5		21
		8	4	2		9			7	11			3	1		6	10				5		22
		8	4	2		9			7	11			3	1		6	10				5		23
			4	2		8	9		7	11			3	1		6			10		5		24
				2		8	9	5	7	11			3			4		1	10	6			25
				2		8	9		7	11			3			4		1	10	6	5		26
				3		8	9	5	7	11		2				4		1	10	6			27
				3		8	9		7	11		2				4		1	10	6	5		28
						8	9		7	11		2	3			4		1	10	6	5		29
				2		8	9		7	11			3			4		1	10	6	5		30
				2		8	9		7	11			3			4		1	10	6	5		31
				2		8	9		7	11			3			4		1	10	6	5		32
				2		8	9		7	11			3			4		1	10	6	5		33
				2		8	9		7	11			3			4		1	10	6	5		34
				2		8	9		7	11			3			4		1	10	6	5		35
				2		8	9		7	11			3	1		4			10	6	5		36
				2		8	9		7	11			3			4		1	10	6	5		37
				2		8	9		7	11			3			4		1	10	6	5		38
						8	9		7	11		2	3			4		1	10	6	5		39
11	9					8			7			2	3			4		1	10	6	5		40
			4			8	9			11		2	3		7	6	10	1			5		41
	9		4			8				11		2	3		7	6		1	10		5		42
6	2	7	25	25	4	37	29	9	39	23	5	18	34	5	17	33	15	37	29	25	35	3	
2	3	4	5			23	17		7	9	1				5	1	1		10		3		

1 own-goal

		8	4	2		9			7	11			3	1		6	10				5		3
		1	1	1		1			1	1			1	1		1	1				1		
									1														

1936-37

1	Aug	29	(a)	Arsenal	L 2-3	Dean, Stevenson	50,321
2	Sep	2	(h)	Sheffield W	W 3-1	Dean, Gillick, Stevenson	31,586
3		5	(h)	Brentford	W 3-0	Dean 2, Gillick	37,524
4		10	(a)	Sheffield W	L 4-6	Gillick 2, Miller, Stevenson	15,444
5		12	(a)	Bolton W	W 2-1	Gillick, Stevenson	18,029
6		19	(h)	Liverpool	W 2-0	Dean, Stevenson	55,835
7		26	(h)	Huddersfield T	W 2-1	Dean, Hurel	33,581
8	Oct	3	(a)	Sunderland	L 1-3	Stevenson	36,697
9		10	(h)	Wolves	W 1-0	Dean	33,153
10		17	(a)	Leeds U	L 0-3		16,861
11		24	(h)	Birmingham	D 3-3	Dean, Gillick, Stevenson	26,955
12		31	(a)	Middlesbrough	L 0-2		23,569
13	Nov	7	(h)	West Brom A	W 4-2	Dean 3, Cunliffe	20,901
14		14	(a)	Manchester C	L 1-4	Stevenson	27,818
15		21	(h)	Portsmouth	W 4-0	Coulter 2, Gillick, Stevenson	29,940
16		28	(a)	Chelsea	L 0-4		31,623
17	Dec	5	(h)	Stoke C	D 1-1	Dean	19,012
18		12	(a)	Charlton A	L 0-2		25,991
19		19	(h)	Grimsby T	W 3-0	Dean 2, Gillick	21,616
20		25	(h)	Derby C	W 7-0	Cunliffe 3, Dean 2, Stevenson 2	32,349
21		26	(h)	Arsenal	D 1-1	Gillick	59,440
22		28	(a)	Derby C	L 1-3	Dean	22,608
23	Jan	1	(h)	Preston NE	D 2-2	Gillick, Leyfield	28,824
24		2	(a)	Brentford	D 2-2	Coulter, Cunliffe	20,457
25		9	(h)	Bolton W	W 3-2	Dean 2, Stevenson	24,422
26		23	(a)	Liverpool	L 2-3	Stevenson 2	37,055
27	Feb	3	(a)	Huddersfield T	W 3-0	Bell, Coulter, Cunliffe	5,216
28		6	(h)	Sunderland	W 3-0	Dean 2, Coulter	41,147
29		13	(a)	Wolves	L 2-7	Cunliffe, Lawton	36,551
30		27	(a)	Birmingham	L 0-2		21,150
31	Mar	3	(h)	Leeds U	W 7-1	Dean 2, Stevenson 2, Geldard, Gillick, Lawton	17,064
32		6	(h)	Middlesbrough	L 2-3	Geldard, Stevenson	30,719
33		13	(a)	West Brom A	L 1-2	Gillick	26,284
34		20	(h)	Manchester C	D 1-1	Stevenson	31,921
35		26	(a)	Manchester U	L 1-2	Gillick	30,071
36		27	(a)	Portsmouth	D 2-2	Geldard, Gillick	24,411
37		29	(h)	Manchester U	L 2-3	Lawton, Stevenson	28,395
38	Apr	3	(h)	Chelsea	D 0-0		20,648
39		10	(a)	Stoke C	L 1-2	Cunliffe	17,749
40		14	(a)	Preston NE	L 0-1		8,675
41		17	(h)	Charlton A	D 2-2	Cunliffe, Dean	11,105
42		24	(a)	Grimsby T	L 0-1		9,773

FINAL LEAGUE POSITION: 17th in Division One

Appearances
Goals

FA Cup

3	Jan	16	(h)	Bournemouth	W 5-0	Gillick 2, Stevenson 2, Cunliffe
4		30	(h)	Sheffield W	W 3-0	Britton, Coulter, Dean
5	Feb	20	(h)	Tottenham H	D 1-1	Coulter
R		22	(a)	Tottenham H	L 3-4	Dean 2, Lawton

Appearances
Goals

Bell J	Bentham S	Britton C	Cook W	Coulter J	Cunliffe J	Dean W	Gee C	Geldard A	Gillick T	Hurel E	Jackson G	Jones JE	Jones TG	King F	Lawton T	Leyfield C	Mercer J	Miller W	Morton H	Sagar E	Stevenson A	Thomson J	Watson T	White T	Match
		4	3	11	8	9	5		7		2						6			1	10				1
		4	3	11	8	9	5		7		2						6			1	10				2
		4	3	11	8	9	5		7		2						6			1	10				3
		4	3	11		9	5		7		2						6	8		1	10				4
		4	3	11		9	5		7	8	2						6			1	10				5
		4	3	11	8	9	5		7		2						6			1	10				6
		4	3	11		9	5		7	8	2						6			1	10				7
		4	3	11		9	5		7	8	2						6			1	10				8
		4	3	11		9	5	7	8		2						6			1	10				9
		4	3			9		7	8		2		5			11	6			1	10				10
		4	3			9	5		7	8	2					11	6			1	10				11
		4				9	5		7	8	2	3				11	6			1	10				12
		4	3		8	9	5		7		2					11	6			1	10				13
		4	3		8	9	5		7		2					11	6			1	10				14
		4	2	11	8	9	5		7			3					6			1	10				15
		4	2		8	9	5	7	11			3					6			1	10				16
		4	2	11	8	9	5		7			3					6			1	10				17
9		4	2	11	8		5		7			3					6			1	10				18
		4	2		8	9	5		7			3				11	6			1	10				19
		4	2		8	9	5		7			3				11	6			1	10				20
		4	2		8	9	5		7			3				11	6			1	10				21
		4	2		8	9	5		7			3				11				1	10	6			22
		4	2		8	9	5		7			3				11	6			1	10				23
		4	2	11	8	9	5		7											1	10	3	6		24
		4	2	11	8	9	5		7			3		1			6				10				25
		4	2	11	8	9	5		7			3					6			1	10				26
9		4	2	11	8		5		7			3					6			1	10				27
		4	2	11	8	9	5		7			3		1			6				10				28
10		4	2	11	8				7			3			9		6			1				5	29
		4	2			9	5	7	11			3			8		6			1	10				30
		4	3			9	5	7	11		2				8		6			1	10				31
		4	3			9	5	7	11		2			1	8		6				10				32
		4	3		8		5	7	11		2				9		6		1		10				33
		4	3			9	5	7	11		2				8		6		1		10				34
		4	3		9		5	7	11		2				8		6		1		10				35
		4	3		8	9	5	7	11		2						6		1		10				36
		4	3			9	5	7	11		2				8		6		1		10				37
		4	3		8	9	5	7	11		2								1		10		6		38
		4	3		8		5	7	11		2				9		6		1		10				39
	4		3	11		9	5		7		2				8		6		1		10				40
	4		3	11	8	9	5		7		2						6		1		10				41
		4	3	11	8	9	5		7		2						6		1		10				42
3	2	40	41	21	28	36	40	13	42	5	26	16	1	3	10	10	39	1	10	29	41	2	2	1	
1				5	9	24		3	14	1					3	1		1			19				

Bell J	Bentham S	Britton C	Cook W	Coulter J	Cunliffe J	Dean W	Gee C	Geldard A	Gillick T	Hurel E	Jackson G	Jones JE	Jones TG	King F	Lawton T	Leyfield C	Mercer J	Miller W	Morton H	Sagar E	Stevenson A	Thomson J	Watson T	White T	Match
		4	2	11	8	9	5		7			3					6			1	10				3
		4	2	11	8	9	5		7			3					6			1	10				4
		4	2	11	8	9	5		7			3					6			1	10				5
		4	2		8	9	5	7	11			3			10		6			1					R
		4	4	3	4	4	4	1	4			4			1		4			4	3				
		1		2	1	3			2						1						2				

1937-38

1	Aug	28	(h)	Arsenal	L 1-4	Dean	53,856
2	Sep	1	(a)	Manchester C	L 0-2		27,603
3		4	(a)	Blackpool	L 0-1		27,423
4		8	(h)	Manchester C	W 4-1	Stevenson 2, Dougal, Lawton	27,290
5		11	(h)	Brentford	W 3-0	Cunliffe, Dougal, Stevenson	36,038
6		15	(a)	Derby C	L 1-2	Lawton	14,263
7		18	(a)	Bolton W	W 2-1	Lawton, Stevenson	35,691
8		25	(h)	Huddersfield T	L 1-2	Trentham	35,272
9	Oct	2	(a)	Liverpool	W 2-1	Lawton, Trentham	43,904
10		9	(a)	Wolves	L 0-2		30,863
11		16	(h)	Leeds U	D 1-1	Lawton	26,035
12		23	(a)	Grimsby T	L 1-2	Gillick	10,308
13		30	(h)	Preston NE	L 3-5	Lawton 2, Bell	26,250
14	Nov	6	(a)	Middlesbrough	W 2-1	Lawton 2	25,083
15		13	(h)	Chelsea	W 4-1	Lawton 2, Cunliffe, Trentham	29,930
16		20	(a)	West Brom A	L 1-3	Lawton	20,920
17		27	(h)	Stoke C	W 3-0	Lawton 2, Stevenson	27,661
18	Dec	4	(a)	Charlton A	L 1-3	Cunliffe	23,145
19		11	(h)	Birmingham	D 1-1	Geldard	17,018
20		18	(a)	Portsmouth	L 1-3	Trentham	19,103
21		25	(a)	Leicester C	L 1-3	Trentham	17,268
22		27	(h)	Leicester C	W 3-0	Lawton 2, Trentham	38,693
23	Jan	1	(a)	Arsenal	L 1-2	Cunliffe	36,953
24		15	(h)	Blackpool	W 3-1	Cunliffe, Lawton, Watson	22,219
25		26	(a)	Brentford	L 0-3		16,917
26		29	(h)	Bolton W	W 4-1	Geldard, Gillick, Lawton, Stevenson	25,848
27	Feb	5	(a)	Huddersfield T	W 3-1	Cunliffe, Gillick, Stevenson	15,394
28		16	(h)	Liverpool	L 1-3	Lawton	33,465
29		19	(h)	Wolves	L 0-1		39,863
30		26	(a)	Leeds U	D 4-4	Cunliffe 2, Lawton 2	23,497
31	Mar	5	(h)	Grimsby T	W 3-2	Lawton 2, Stevenson	35,637
32		12	(a)	Preston NE	L 1-2	Cunliffe	23,618
33		19	(h)	Middlesbrough	D 2-2	Bell, Boyes	28,808
34		26	(a)	Chelsea	L 0-2		27,043
35	Apr	2	(h)	West Brom A	W 5-3	Lawton 2, Cunliffe, Geldard, Stevenson	24,395
36		9	(a)	Stoke C	D 1-1	Lawton	16,187
37		15	(h)	Sunderland	D 3-3	Cunliffe 2, Thomson	40,010
38		16	(h)	Charlton A	W 3-0	Geldard 2, Lawton	31,518
39		18	(a)	Sunderland	L 0-2		22,332
40		23	(a)	Birmingham	W 3-0	Boyes, Cunliffe, Stevenson	22,224
41		30	(h)	Portsmouth	W 5-2	Stevenson 3, Boyes, Lawton	18,716
42	May	7	(h)	Derby C	D 1-1	Geldard	18,291

FINAL LEAGUE POSITION: 14th in Division One

Appearances
Goals

FA Cup

3	Jan	8	(a)	Chelsea	W 1-0	Stevenson	
4		22	(h)	Sunderland	L 0-1		

Appearances
Goals

Bell J	Boyes W	Britton C	Cook W	Coulter J	Cunliffe J	Dean W	Dougal P	Gee C	Geldard A	Gillick T	Greenhalgh N	Jackson G	Jones JE	Jones TG	Lawton T	Mercer J	Morton H	Sagar E	Stevenson A	Thomson J	Trentham D	Watson T	
		4	3	11	8	9		5	7			2				6		1	10				1
		4	3	11	8	9		5	7			2				6		1	10				2
		4	2			9	10	5	7				3		8	6		1			11		3
		4	2				10	5	7				3		9	6		1	8		11		4
		4	2		11		10	5	7				3		9	6		1	8				5
		4	2		11		10	5	7				3		9	6		1	8				6
			2		11		10	5	7				3		9	4		1	8			6	7
			2				10	5	7				3		9	4		1	8		11	6	8
			2				10	5	7				3		9	4		1	8		11	6	9
			2				10	5	7				3		9	4		1	8		11	6	10
		4	2				10	5	7	11			3		9	6		1	8				11
		4				9	10	5		7		2	3		8	6		1			11		12
10		4	2		8			5	7	11			3		9	6		1					13
		4	2		8				7				3	5	9	6	1		10		11		14
		4	2		8				7				3	5	9	6	1		10		11		15
		4	3		8				7			2		5	9	6	1		10		11		16
		4	2		8				7				3	5	9	6	1		10		11		17
		4	2		8				7	11			3	5	9	6	1		10				18
		4	2		8	9			7	11			3	5		6	1		10				19
		4	2		8		10		7				3	5	9	6	1				11		20
8		4	2		10				7				3	5	9	6		1			11		21
8		4	2		10					7			3	5	9	6		1			11		22
		4	2		8					7			3	5	9	6	1		10		11		23
		4	2		8					7			3	5	9	6	1		10			11	24
		4	2		8					7			3	5	9	6	1		10		11		25
		4	2		8				7	11	3			5	9	6	1		10				26
		4	2		8				7	11			3	5	9	6	1		10				27
		4	2		8				7	11			3	5	9	6	1		10				28
		4			8				7	11	2		3	5	9	6	1		10				29
	11	4			8			5	7		2		3		9		1		10			6	30
	11	4			8					7	2		3	5	9		1		10			6	31
	11	4			8					7	2		3	5	9			1	10			6	32
10	11	4			8					7	2		3	5	9			1				6	33
8	11	4							7		2		3	5	9			1	10	6			34
	11		2		8				7				3	5	9	4		1	10	6			35
	11		2		8				7				3	5	9	4		1	10	6			36
	11		2		8				7				3	5	9	4		1	10	6			37
	11	4	2		8				7		3			5	9			1	10	6			38
	11		2		8				7		3			5	9	4		1	10	6			39
	11		2		8				7		3			5	9	4		1	10	6			40
	11		2		8				7		3			5	9	4		1	10	6			41
	11		2		8				7		3			5	9	4		1	10	6			42
5	13	31	35	2	34	5	11	14	34	16	12	4	33	28	39	36	16	26	35	9	15	9	
2	3				13	1	2		6	3					28				13	1	6	1	

Bell J	Boyes W	Britton C	Cook W	Coulter J	Cunliffe J	Dean W	Dougal P	Gee C	Geldard A	Gillick T	Greenhalgh N	Jackson G	Jones JE	Jones TG	Lawton T	Mercer J	Morton H	Sagar E	Stevenson A	Thomson J	Trentham D	Watson T	
		4	2		8				7	11			3	5	9	6	1		10				3
		4	2		8					7			3	5	9	6	1		10		11		4
		2	2		2				1	2			2	2	2	2	2		2		1		
																			1				

1938-39

1	Aug	27	(a)	Blackpool	W 2-0	Lawton, Stevenson	29,647
2		31	(h)	Grimsby T	W 3-0	Lawton 2, Gillick	25,017
3	Sep	3	(h)	Brentford	W 2-1	Lawton 2	35,989
4		5	(a)	Aston Villa	W 3-0	Stevenson 2, Lawton	34,105
5		10	(a)	Arsenal	W 2-1	Lawton, Stevenson	64,555
6		17	(h)	Portsmouth	W 5-1	Bentham, Boyes, Gillick, Lawton, Opp own-goal	43,913
7		24	(a)	Huddersfield T	L 0-3		27,710
8	Oct	1	(h)	Liverpool	W 2-1	Bentham, Boyes	64,977
9		8	(h)	Wolves	W 1-0	Lawton	36,681
10		15	(a)	Bolton W	L 2-4	Lawton, Stevenson	57,989
11		22	(h)	Leeds U	W 4-0	Bell 3, Trentham	30,747
12		29	(a)	Leicester C	L 0-3		23,964
13	Nov	5	(h)	Middlesbrough	W 4-0	Lawton 3, Stevenson	35,683
14		12	(a)	Birmingham	L 0-1		27,548
15		19	(h)	Manchester U	W 3-0	Lawton 2, Gillick	31,809
16		26	(a)	Stoke C	D 0-0		26,725
17	Dec	3	(h)	Chelsea	W 4-1	Lawton 2, Gillick, Stevenson	27,959
18		10	(a)	Preston NE	W 1-0	Lawton	26,549
19		17	(h)	Charlton A	L 1-4	Gillick	22,053
20		24	(h)	Blackpool	W 4-0	Cunliffe 2, Cook, Gillick	24,040
21		26	(h)	Derby C	D 2-2	Cook, Gillick	55,401
22		27	(a)	Derby C	L 1-2	Cook	35,683
23		31	(a)	Brentford	L 0-2		27,861
24	Jan	14	(h)	Arsenal	W 2-0	Boyes, Lawton	47,178
25		28	(h)	Huddersfield T	W 3-2	Cook, Lawton, Stevenson	37,269
26	Feb	1	(a)	Portsmouth	W 1-0	Lawton	17,371
27		4	(a)	Liverpool	W 3-0	Lawton 2, Bentham	55,994
28		18	(h)	Bolton W	W 2-1	Gillick, Opp own-goal	38,961
29		22	(a)	Wolves	L 0-7		39,774
30		25	(a)	Leeds U	W 2-1	Bentham, Cunliffe	21,728
31	Mar	8	(h)	Leicester C	W 4-0	Boyes, Greenhalgh, Lawton, Stevenson	8,199
32		11	(a)	Middlesbrough	D 4-4	Lawton 4	20,014
33		18	(h)	Birmingham	W 4-2	Lawton 2, Bentham, Gillick	29,687
34		29	(a)	Manchester U	W 2-0	Gillick, Lawton	18,348
35	Apr	1	(h)	Stoke C	D 1-1	Lawton	38,601
36		7	(a)	Sunderland	W 2-1	Gillick, Lawton	40,521
37		8	(a)	Chelsea	W 2-0	Gillick, Stevenson	51,481
38		10	(h)	Sunderland	W 6-2	Betham 3, Caskie, Lawton, Stevenson	46,016
39		15	(h)	Preston NE	D 0-0		31,987
40		22	(a)	Charlton A	L 1-2	Gillick	26,338
41		29	(h)	Aston Villa	W 3-0	Bentham, Cook, Gillick	23,667
42	May	6	(a)	Grimsby T	L 0-3		11,016

FINAL LEAGUE POSITION: 1st in Division One

Appearances
Goals

FA Cup

3	Jan	7	(a)	Derby C	W 1-0	Boyes
4		21	(h)	Doncaster R	W 8-0	Lawton 4, Boyes 2, Gillick, Stevenson
5	Feb	11	(a)	Birmingham	D 2-2	Boyes, Stevenson
R		15	(h)	Birmingham	W 2-1	Cook, Gillick
6	Mar	4	(a)	Wolves	L 0-2	

Appearances
Goals

Barber E	Bell J	Bentham S	Boyes W	Britton C	Caskie J	Cook W	Cunliffe J	Gee C	Gillick T	Greenhalgh N	Jackson G	Jones TG	Lawton T	Mercer J	Milligan G	Morton H	Sagar E	Stevenson A	Thomson J	Trentham D	Watson T	
		8	11			2			7	3		5	9	4			1	10	6			1
		8	11			2			7	3		5	9	4			1	10	6			2
		8	11			2			7	3		5	9	4			1	10	6			3
		8	11			2			7	3		5	9	4			1	10	6			4
		8	11			2			7	3		5	9	4			1	10	6			5
		8	11			2			7	3		5	9	4			1	10	6			6
		8	11			2			7	3		5	9	4			1	10	6			7
		8	11			2			7	3		5	9	4			1	10	6			8
7		8	11				10			3	2	5	9	4			1		6			9
		8	11			2			7	3		5	9	4	6		1	10				10
	9	8				2		5	7	3				4			1	10		11	6	11
		8	11			2			7	3		5	9	4			1	10			6	12
		8	11			2			7	3		5	9	4			1	10	6			13
		8	11			2		5	7	3			9	4			1	10	6			14
		8	11			2			7	3		5	9	4			1	10	6			15
		8	11			2			7	3		5	9	4			1	10	6			16
		8	11			2			7	3		5	9	4			1	10	6			17
		8	11			2			7	3		5	9	4			1	10	6			18
		8	11			2			7	3		5	9	4			1	10	6			19
		8	11			2	10		7	3		5	9	4			1				6	20
	9	8	11			2	10		7	3		5		4			1		6			21
		8	11			2	10		7	3		5	9	4			1		6			22
		8	11			2	10		7	3		5	9	4			1		6			23
		8	11			2			7	3		5	9	4			1	10	6			24
		8	11			2			7	3		5	9	4			1	10	6			25
		8	11			2			7	3		5	9	4			1	10	6			26
		8	11			2			7	3		5	9	4			1	10	6			27
	9	8	11			2			7	3		5		4			1	10	6			28
	9		11			2			7	3		5	8	4		1		10	6			29
7		8	11				10			3	2	5	9	4			1				6	30
		8	11			2			7	3		5	9	4			1	10			6	31
		8	11			2			7	3		5	9	4			1	10			6	32
		8	11			2			7	3		5	9	4			1	10			6	33
		8	11			2			7	3		5	9	4			1	10			6	34
		8	11			2			7	3		5	9	4			1	10			6	35
		8	11			2			7	3		5	9	4			1	10			6	36
		8			11	2			7	3		5	9	4			1	10			6	37
		8			11	2			7	3			9	4			1	10	5		6	38
		8		4	11	2	9		7	3		5					1	10			6	39
		8			11	2			7	3		5	9	4			1	10			6	40
		8			11	2			7	3		5	9	4			1	10			6	41
		8	11			2			7	3		5	9	4			1	10			6	42
2	4	41	36	1	5	40	7	2	40	42	2	39	38	41	1	1	41	36	26	1	16	
	3	9	4		1	5	3		14	1			34					11		1		

2 own-goals

Barber E	Bell J	Bentham S	Boyes W	Britton C	Caskie J	Cook W	Cunliffe J	Gee C	Gillick T	Greenhalgh N	Jackson G	Jones TG	Lawton T	Mercer J	Milligan G	Morton H	Sagar E	Stevenson A	Thomson J	Trentham D	Watson T	
		8	11			2			7	3		5	9	4			1	10	6			3
		8	11			2			7	3		5	9	4			1	10	6			4
		8	11			2			7	3		5	9	4			1	10	6			5
		8	11			2			7	3		5	9	4			1	10	6			R
		8	11			2			7	3		5	9	4			1	10			6	6
		5	5			5			5	5		5	5	5			5	5	4		1	
			4			1			2				4					2				

1939-40

Manager: Theo Kelly

1	Aug	26	(h)	Brentford	D 1-1	Lawton
2		28	(a)	Aston Villa	W 2-1	Bentham, Lawton
3	Sep	2	(a)	Blackburn R	D 2-2	Lawton 2

Above games played in Division One before Football League closed down upon the outbreak of World War Two

FINAL LEAGUE POSITION: 5th in Division One

Appearances
Goals

War Regional League, Western Division

4	Oct	21	(h)	Stoke C	D 4-4	Boyes, T.G.Jones, Lawton, Stevenson
5		28	(a)	New Brighton	W 1-0	Gillick
6	Nov	11	(h)	Manchester C	W 3-1	Bentham, Gillick, Lawton
7		18	(a)	Chester	L 2-3	Bell, Stevenson
8		25	(h)	Crewe A	W 6-2	Bell 2, Simmons 2, Boyes, Johnson
9	Dec	2	(a)	Liverpool	D 2-2	Davies, Stevenson
10		9	(h)	Port Vale	W 3-1	Bentham, Mercer, Sweeney
11		23	(a)	Tranmere R	W 9-2	Lawton 4, Bentham 2, T.G.Jones, Mercer, Stevenson
12	Jan	6	(h)	Manchester U	W 3-2	Lawton, Stevenson, Sweeney
13		20	(a)	Wrexham	D 0-0	
14	Feb	10	(a)	Stoke C	L 0-1	
15		24	(h)	New Brighton	W 3-0	Bell, Stevenson, Wyles
16	Mar	9	(a)	Manchester C	D 2-2	Gillick, Greenhalgh
17		16	(h)	Chester	W 5-0	Boyes 3, Catterick, T.G.Jones
18		23	(a)	Crewe A	L 1-2	Stevenson
19		30	(h)	Liverpool	L 1-3	Lawton
20	Apr	3	(h)	Stockport C	W 7-0	Stevenson 4, Lawton 2, Wyles
21		6	(a)	Port Vale	L 1-2	Bentham
22		17	(h)	Tranmere R	W 5-3	Bentham, Boyes, Lawton, Mercer, Stevenson
23	May	22	(h)	Wrexham	L 1-2	Lawton
24		29	(a)	Stockport C	W 2-1	Bentham, Simmons
25	Jun	1	(a)	Manchester U	W 3-0	Stevenson 3

Appearances
Goals

War League Cup

26	Apr	20	(h)	Preston NE	W 3-1	Boyes, T.G.Jones, Stevenson
27		27	(a)	Preston NE	D 2-2	Bentham, Lawton
28	May	4	(h)	Rochdale	W 5-1	Lawton 3, T.G.Jones, Stevenson
29		11	(a)	Rochdale	L 2-4	Sumner, Wyles
30		18	(h)	Stoke C	W 1-0	Lawton
31		25	(a)	Fulham	L 2-5	Gillick, Lawton

Appearances
Goals

Matches 1 to 3 inclusive were played in the Football League which was abandoned when war broke out. The three games do not count in any record of League appearances and goals.
Matches 4 to 25 inclusive were played in the War Regional League, Western Division.
Matches 26 to 31 inclusive were played in the War League Cup. The first two rounds were played on a home and away two-legged basis. Thereafter, the competition was a sudden-death knockout.

Barber E	Bell R	Bentham S	Boyes W	Burnett G	Caskie J	Catterick H	Cook W	Davies J	Gee C	Gillick T	Greenhalgh N	Jackson G	Johnson A	Jones JE	Jones TG	Lawton T	Lindley W	Lyon J	Mercer J	Sagar E	Saunders G	Sharp N	Simmons S	Stevenson A	Sumner W	Sweeney F	Watson T	Wyles T	
		8	11				2			7	3				5	9			4	1				10			6		1
		8	11				2			7	3				5	9			4	1				10			6		2
		8	11				2			7	3				5	9			4	1				10			6		3
		3	3				3			3	3				3	3			3	3				3			3		
		1														4													
		8	11							7	3	2			5	9	4			1				10			6		4
		8	11							7	3	2			5	9	4			1				10			6		5
		8	11						5	7	3	2				9			4	1				10			6		6
	9	8	11	1					5		3	2					4					7		10			6		7
	9		11								3	2	7		5				4	1			8	10			6		8
	9	8	11					7				2			5		4			1	3			10			6		9
	9	8	11								3	2			5		6		4	1				10		7			10
		8	11								3	2			5	9			4	1				10		7	6		11
		8	11								3	2				9	5		4	1				10		7	6		12
		8	11								3	2			5	9	4			1				10			6	7	13
	9	8	11								3	2			5		4			1				10		7	6		14
	9	8	11								3	2			5				4	1				10			6	7	15
		8	11	1		9				7	3	2					5							10			6	4	16
		8	11			9					3	2			5				4	1				10			6	7	17
7		8	11								3	2			5	9			4	1				10			6		18
			11			8					3	2			5	9	4			1				10			6	7	19
			11								3	2			5	9	8		4	1				10			6	7	20
		8	11			7					3	2			5	9			4	1				10			6		21
		8	11								3	2				9	5		4	1				10	7		6		22
		8	11								3	2			5	9		10	4	1							6	7	23
		8	11								2			3		9	4		5	1			10		7		6		24
		8	11								3	2			5	9	7		4	1				10			6		25
1	6	19	22	2		4		1	2	4	21	21	1	1	16	14	14	1	14	20	1	1	2	20	2	4	21	7	
	4	7	6			1		1		3	1		1		3	12			3				3	15		2		2	
7		8	11								3	2			5	9			4	1				10			6		26
7		8	11								3	2			5	9			4	1				10			6		27
		8	11								3	2			5	9	7		4	1				10			6		28
		8	11								3	2				9	5			1				10	7		6	4	29
		8	11		7						3	2			5	9			4	1				10			6		30
		8	11						5	7	3	2				9			4	1				10			6		31
2		6	6		1				1	1	6	6			4	6	2		5	6				6	1		6	1	
		1	1							1					2	6								2	1			1	

1940-41

1	Aug	31	(a)	Manchester C	D 0-0	
2	Sep	7	(h)	Manchester C	W 1-0	Lawton
3		14	(a)	Preston NE	D 2-2	Bailey, Stevenson
4		21	(h)	Chester	W 4-3	Lawton 3, Stevenson
5		28	(h)	Leeds U	W 5-1	Bentham 2, Lawton, Mercer, Stevenson
6	Oct	5	(a)	Southport	W 1-0	Catterick
7		12	(h)	Stockport C	W 4-2	Catterick 2, Britton, Simmons
8		19	(a)	Chester	L 0-1	
9		26	(h)	Bury	W 3-1	Bentham, Lawton, Stevenson
10	Nov	2	(a)	Bury	L 1-2	Simmons
11		9	(h)	Manchester U	W 5-2	Lawton 4, Stevenson
12		16	(a)	Manchester U	D 0-0	
13		23	(a)	Tranmere R	W 9-0	Lawton 3, Stevenson 3, Simmons 2, Arthur
14		30	(h)	New Brighton	W 2-1	Boyes, Catterick
15	Dec	7	(h)	Southport	W 2-1	Catterick 2
16		14	(a)	Tranmere R	W 8-2	Bentham 3, Lawton 2, Boyes, Cook, Simmons
17		21	(h)	Preston NE	L 0-3	
18		25	(a)	Liverpool	L 1-3	Bentham
19	Jan	4	(a)	Liverpool*	W 2-1	Lawton, Lyon
20		11	(h)	Liverpool*	W 4-1	Jackson 4
21		25	(a)	Burnley*	W 3-2	Lawton 2, Lyon
22	Feb	1	(h)	Barnsley	W 3-1	Lawton 2, T.G.Jones
23		8	(a)	Liverpool	W 3-1	Catterick 3
24	Mar	29	(h)	Chesterfield	L 0-1	
25	Apr	5	(a)	Southport	W 5-3	Catterick 2, Bell, Lyon, Stevenson
26		12	(h)	Manchester U	L 1-2	Catterick
27		14	(h)	Blackpool	D 2-2	Catterick, Lawton
28		19	(a)	Chesterfield	L 1-4	Wyles
29		26	(a)	New Brighton	W 4-0	Catterick, Lyon, Mercer, Wyle
30	May	3	(h)	Burnley*	L 0-2	
31		17	(a)	Oldham A	D 1-1	Owen
32		24	(h)	Sheffield U	D 3-3	Lewis, Mercer, Stevenson
33		31	(a)	Liverpool	D 2-2	Mercer, Stevenson
34	Jun	2	(h)	Liverpool	W 3-1	Boyes 2, Jackson

FINAL LEAGUE POSITION: 5th in League North

Appearances
Goals

League War Cup

35	Feb	15	(a)	Manchester U	D 2-2	Lawton 2
36		22	(h)	Manchester U	W 2-1	Catterick, Mercer
37	Mar	1	(h)	Southport	W 5-0	Catterick 2, Lawton 2, T.G.Jones
38		8	(a)	Southport	W 5-0	Lawton 4, Bentham
39		15	(h)	Manchester C	D 1-1	Lyon
40		22	(a)	Manchester C	L 0-2	

Appearances
Goals

Matches 1 to 34 inclusive were played in the League North. Clubs did not all play the same number of matches and the positions were decided on goal average. Everton finished fifth with a goal average of 1.66.
Matches 19, 20 21 and 30 (marked thus*) were Lancashire Cup matches which also counted towards the League North.
Matches 35 to 40 inclusive were played in the League War Cup. The first two rounds were played on a home and away two-legged basis. Thereafter, the competition was a sudden-death knockout.

Arthur J	Bailey G	Barber E	Bell R	Bentham S	Boyes W	Britton C	Catterick H	Cook W	Finnis H	Greenhalgh N	Hankin N	Hill	Jackson G	Johnson A	Jones JE	Jones TG	Lawton T	Lewis C	Lindeman H	Lindley R	Lovett	Lyon J	Mercer J	Owen W	Penlington A	Powell J	Sagar E	Simmons S	Stevenson A	Sumner W	Thomson	Trentham D	Watson T	Wyles T	
				8				2		3						5	9						4		11		1		10	7			6		1
				8				2		3						5	9						4		11		1		10	7			6		2
	11			8		4		2		3							9						5				1		10				6	7	3
				8						3	4		2			5	9	11									1	7	10				6		4
				8		7				3			2			5	9	11					4				1		10				6		5
				8		4	9			3	7		2			5		11									1		10				6		6
				7		4	9			3			2			5		11									1	8	10				6		7
	11			7		4	9			3			2			5											1	8	10				6		8
				8		4		2		3						5	9						7		11		1		10				6		9
				4				2	6	3		7				5	9				1							8	10					11	10
7				4				2		3						5	9				1		6					8	10					11	11
7				8	11			2		3						5	9				1		4						10				6		12
7					11			2		3						5	9				1		4					8	10				6		13
7				4	11		9	2		3						5					1							8	10				6		14
7					11		9			3			2			5					1			8				4	10				6		15
7				8	11			2		3						5	9						4				1	10					6		16
				4	11		9			3			2	7		5											1	8	10				6		17
7				8				2		3			4			5	9	11									1	10					6		18
7				8	11			2		3						5	9					10	4				1						6		19
7				8				2		3			9		6	5							4		11		1		10						20
7				8	11			2		3			1			5	9					10	4										6		21
7				4	11		8	2		3						5	9					10	6				1								22
7				4	11		9	2		3					6	5											1	8	10						23
				4			8	2		3			9									11	5	7			1		10				6		24
			9	7			8		5	3			2		4						1	11							10				6		25
			9	7			8	2		3			11			5					1	10	4										6		26
			7	4			8	2		3			6				9				1	11	5										10		27
				8						3			2		11					4	1	10	5			9							6	7	28
				4			9	2		3						5			10		1	11	8										6	7	29
		8		4			9	2		3					11	5					1	10									6			7	30
				4			9	2		3		5									1	11		8					10				6	7	31
				4				2		3		5	6				9					11	8				1	7	10						32
				4	7		9	2		3						5					1	11	8						10				6		33
				4	7			2		3		6	9			5					1	11		10				8							34
12	2	1	3	32	12	6	16	25	2	34	2	4	17	1	5	27	17	5	1	1	15	14	20	4	4	1	18	14	23	2	1		26	7	
1	1		1	7	4	1	14	1					5			1	22					4	4	1				5	11					2	

Arthur J	Bailey G	Barber E	Bell R	Bentham S	Boyes W	Britton C	Catterick H	Cook W	Finnis H	Greenhalgh N	Hankin N	Hill	Jackson G	Johnson A	Jones JE	Jones TG	Lawton T	Lewis C	Lindeman H	Lindley R	Lovett	Lyon J	Mercer J	Owen W	Penlington A	Powell J	Sagar E	Simmons S	Stevenson A	Sumner W	Thomson	Trentham D	Watson T	Wyles T	
7				8	11			2		3						5	9						4				1		10				6		35
				8			7	2		3					6	5	9					10	4				1							11	36
				7			8	2		3					6	5	9						4				1		10						37
				7			8	2		3					6	5	9					11	4				1		10			11			38
				7			9	2		3						5						11	4				1	8	10				6		39
				8			9	2		3			7			5						11	4				1		10				6		40
1				6	1		5	6		6			1		3	6	4					4	6				6	1	5			1	3	1	
				1			3									1	8					1	1												

1941-42

Manager: Theo Kelly

1	Aug	30	(a)	Stoke C	L 3-8	Boyes, Catterick, Cook
2	Sep	6	(h)	Stoke C	W 3-1	Cook, Cunliffe, Mercer
3		13	(h)	Chester	D 1-1	H.Jones
4		20	(a)	Chester	L 0-2	
5		27	(a)	Manchester U	W 3-2	Owen 2, Stevenson
6	Oct	4	(h)	Manchester U	L 1-3	H.Jones
7		11	(h)	Tranmere R	W 3-2	Stevenson 2, Jackson
8		18	(a)	Tranmere R	W 4-0	Lyon 2, Owen, Stevenson
9		25	(a)	Liverpool	L 2-3	Cook, Lyon
10	Nov	1	(h)	Liverpool	W 5-3	Bentham 3, H.Jones, Lyon
11		8	(h)	Wrexham	W 3-1	Anderson, H.Jones, Owen
12		15	(a)	Wrexham	W 4-0	Boyes, H.Jones, Mercer, Stevenson
13		22	(a)	Manchester C	W 4-3	Lawton 3, Lyon
14		29	(h)	Manchester C	W 9-0	H.Jones 2, Stevenson 2, Bentham, Cook, Lyon, Mutch, Opp own-goal
15	Dec	6	(h)	New Brighton	W 4-0	H.Jones 2, T.G.Jones, Stevenson
16		13	(a)	New Brighton	W 5-1	Jackson 2, Owen 2, Stevenson
17		20	(a)	Stockport C	D 1-1	Mercer
18		25	(h)	Stockport C	W 6-0	Lawton 3, Cook, Kinnell, Stevenson

FINAL LEAGUE POSITION: 6th in League North (First Period) — Appearances / Goals

League North (Second Period)

19	Dec	27	(a)	Sheffield W	W 3-0	Lawton 3
20	Jan	3	(h)	Sheffield W	W 2-0	T.G.Jones 2
21		10	(h)	Blackburn R	D 0-0	
22		17	(a)	Blackburn R	D 0-0	
23		31	(h)	Wolves	W 2-1	Cook 2
24	Feb	7	(h)	Burnley	W 3-2	Anderson, Boyes, H.Jones
25		14	(a)	Burnley	L 0-1	
26		21	(a)	Oldham A	L 0-1	
27		28	(h)	Oldham A	W 4-0	Mercer 2, Jackson, Stevenson
28	Mar	7	(a)	Wolves	L 1-11	Anderson
29		14	(h)	Blackpool	D 2-2	Owen, Stevenson
30		21	(h)	Southport*	W 3-1	Mercer 2, Waring
31		28	(a)	Oldham	W 2-1	T.G.Jones, Wyles
32	Apr	4	(h)	Preston NE†	D 2-2	Cook, T.G.Jones
33		6	(a)	Preston NE†	W 2-1	T.G.Jones, Mercer
34		11	(a)	Liverpool†	W 2-0	Anderson, T.G.Jones
35		18	(h)	Liverpool†	L 0-1	
36		25	(a)	West Brom A†	L 1-3	Lawton
37		28	(a)	Southport*	L 1-2	Owen
38	May	2	(h)	West Brom A†	L 1-5	Bentham
39		9	(a)	Manchester C*	L 0-2	
40		16	(h)	Manchester C*	W 6-1	Lawton 3, Soo 2, Anderson
41		30	(a)	Liverpool*	L 1-4	Lawton

FINAL LEAGUE POSITION: 15th in League North (Second Period) — Appearances / Goals

Matches 19 to 41 inclusive were played in the League North (Second Period). The competition consisted of 38 teams and no team played all the others.

Matches marked thus* were in the Lancashire Cup and matches marked thus† were in the League War Cup, both of which were played on a two-legged home and away basis in the early rounds. The matches in these cups also counted towards the League North (second period).

Anderson A	Bailey G	Barber A	Bentham S	Boyes W	Burnett G	Caskie J	Catterick H	Cook W	Cunliffe J	Curwen G	Greenhalgh N	Higham N	Hill M	Ireland R	Jackson G	Jones H	Jones JE	Jones TG	Keen E	Kinnell R	Lawton T	Lovett P	Lyon J	Mercer J	Mutch G	Owen W	Sagar E	Seddon E	Sharp N	Soo F	Stevenson A	Thomson J	Waring	Watson T	Williams A	Wyles T				
		7	8	10			9	2			3		5				6					1	11	4																1
			4					2	8		3		7		9			5					11	6			1				10									2
7			4					2	10		3		5		6	9						1	11					8												3
7	11		4					2			3				9			5				1				8					10	6								4
7			4		1			2			3				9	5							11	6		8					10									5
7			4		1			2			3				9	8		5					11								10			6						6
7			4		1						3		6		9		2		5				11			8					10									7
7			4		1			2			3				9			5					11	6		8					10									8
7			4		1			2			3					5			6		9		11			8					10									9
			8		1			2			3					9		5					11	4		7					10			6						10
7			4		1			2			3					9			5				11			8					10			6						11
7			8	11	1			2			3					9		5	6					4							10									12
7			4		1			2			3					5					9		11			8					10			6						13
			7					2			3					9			5				11	4	8		1				10	6								14
7			4	11				2			3					9		5	6						8		1				10									15
7			4		1			2			3				9	5			6				11			8					10									16
7			8	11	1			2			3					9		5	6					4							10									17
11			7		1			2			3					5			6	9	8			4							10									18
14	1	1	18	4	12		1	17	2		18		4		8	13	2	8	9	1	3	3	13	9	2	9	3	1			16	2		4						
1			4	2			1	5	1						3	9		1		1	6		6	3	1	6					10									

1 own-goal

Anderson A	Bailey G	Barber A	Bentham S	Boyes W	Burnett G	Caskie J	Catterick H	Cook W	Cunliffe J	Curwen G	Greenhalgh N	Higham N	Hill M	Ireland R	Jackson G	Jones H	Jones JE	Jones TG	Keen E	Kinnell R	Lawton T	Lovett P	Lyon J	Mercer J	Mutch G	Owen W	Sagar E	Seddon E	Sharp N	Soo F	Stevenson A	Thomson J	Waring	Watson T	Williams A	Wyles T				
7			8	11	1			2			3					10		5	6		9			4																19
7			4	6	1			2			3				9			5					11			8					10									20
7			8		1			2			3					9		5	6				11	4							10									21
7			4	6				2			3	8			9	5							11				1				10									22
11			4					2			3					8		5	6		9					7	1				10									23
7			4	11				2			3					9		5	6					8			1				10									24
7			4	9				2			3					1		5	6					8		10								11						25
11			4								3				2	5					9			8			1				10			6	7					26
11			4					2			3				9	5			6					8			1				10				7					27
11			4		1			2			3							5	6		9			8		7					10									28
7			4		1			2		6	3								5				11			8					10		9							29
			4	11	1			2			3					5								8							10	6	9		7					30
11			4		1			2		6	3					5		7								8					10					9				31
7			4	11	1			2	8		3					5		9	6												10									32
7			4		1	11		2							3	5		9	6					8		10														33
11			4		1			2		6					3			9	5					8		7					10									34
7			4		1	11		2		6					3			9	5							8					10									35
7			4	11	1			2		6					3				5		9			8							10									36
11					1			2		4			7	3				5					10	8		9								6						37
			8	11	1			2							3			5	6		9			4					7		10									38
11			8		1			2		4			7				3		5							9					10			6						39
7			8		1			2									3	5	6		9			4						10	11									40
			4		1			2								5	3		6		9				8	7					10			11						41
20			22	9	17	2		22	1	7	14	1	2	1	9	13	3	15	17		8		5	14	1	12	5		1	1	19	1	2	5	3	1				
4			1	1				3							1	1		6			8			5		2				2	2		1			1				

1942-43

Manager: Theo Kelly

1	Aug	29	(h)	Manchester U	D 2-2	Anderson, Mutch
2	Sep	5	(a)	Manchester U	L 1-2	Jackson
3		12	(a)	Liverpool	L 0-1	
4		19	(h)	Liverpool	D 4-4	H.Jones 2, Jackson, Mutch
5		26	(h)	Burnley	W 2-1	Mutch, Urmston
6	Oct	3	(a)	Burnley	W 4-1	Cook, Higham, Jackson, Lawton
7		10	(h)	Wrexham	W 2-1	Jackson, Urmston
8		17	(a)	Wrexham	W 2-0	Bentham, Dellow
9		24	(h)	Bury	W 9-2	Curran 3, Bentham 2, Dellow 2, Fowler, Mutch
10		31	(a)	Bury	L 1-4	Fowler
11	Nov	7	(a)	Tranmere R	W 3-1	Curran 2, Stevenson
12		14	(h)	Tranmere R	L 3-5	Curran 2, Fowler
13		21	(h)	Crewe A	W 4-0	Fowler, H.Jones, Mutch, Stevenson
14		28	(a)	Crewe A	L 2-4	Curran, Jackson
15	Dec	5	(h)	Chester	W 3-1	Anderson, Bentham, H.Jones
16		12	(a)	Chester	W 3-2	Mutch 2, Curan
17		19	(a)	Manchester C	L 1-7	Mutch
18		25	(h)	Manchester C	W 6-3	Lawton 3, Grant, Stevenson, Wyles

FINAL LEAGUE POSITION: 15th in League North (First Period)

Appearances
Goals

League North (Second Period)

19		26	(a)	Tranmere R	L 1-2	Lawton
20	Jan	2	(h)	Tranmere R	W 4-0	Anderson, H.Jones, Mercer, Mutch
21		9	(h)	Liverpool	L 1-3	Mutch
22		16	(a)	Liverpool	L 1-2	Lawton
23		23	(a)	Manchester U	W 4-1	H.Jones 3, Bentham
24		30	(h)	Manchester U	L 0-5	
25	Feb	6	(h)	Chester	L 4-5	Dellow 2, Mercer, Stevenson
26		13	(a)	Chester	W 1-0	Fowler
27		20	(a)	Southport	W 8-3	Wyles 3, Mutch 2, Stevenson 2, Fowler
28		27	(h)	Southport	W 10-2	Lawton 4, Mutch 2, Cook, Fowler, Stevenson, Opp own-goal
29	Mar	6	(a)	Blackpool†	L 1-4	Wyles
30		13	(h)	Blackpool†	W 4-3	Lawton 2, Curwen, Stevenson
31		20	(a)	Southport*	L 1-4	Fowler
32		27	(h)	Southport*	W 2-1	Lawton, Mutch
33	Apr	3	(a)	Wrexham	L 1-4	Stevenson
34		10	(h)	Tranmere R‡	W 4-1	Lawton 2, Mutch, Stevenson
35		17	(a)	Tranmere R‡	W 2-1	Curran, Wyles
36		26	(a)	Liverpool‡	L 1-4	McIntosh
37	May	1	(a)	Tranmere R	D 1-1	McIntosh

FINAL LEAGUE POSITION: 25th in League North (Second Period)

Appearances
Goals

Matches 19 to 37 inclusive were played in the League North (Second Period).
Matches 19 to 28 inclusive were in the League War Cup Qualifying Competition.
Matches marked thus* were in the Lancashire Cup; matches marked thus† were in the League War Cup KO competition; matches marked thus‡ were in the Liverpool Cup. All three cup competitions were played on a home and away basis in the early rounds and all cup matches counted towards the League North (Second Period).
There were 48 and 54 teams respectively in the two competitions. No team played all the rest.

Anderson A	Ashcroft L	Beattie R	Bentham S	Birkett W	Boyes W	Burnett G	Carey J	Cook W	Curran F	Curwen G	Dellow	Dunkley R	Fairfoull T	Fowler	Grant J	Greenhalgh N	Higham N	Humphreys J	Jackson G	Jones H	Jones JE	Jones TG	Lawton T	Linaker J	Lowe W	Lyon J	McDonnell M	McIntosh J	Makin G	Mercer J	Mutch G	Owen W	Rosenthall	Stevenson A	Urmston T	Watson T	Williams E	Wyles T	
11			7			1										3					2	5	9							4	8			10		6			1
11			9			1												4	2	5	3					7					8			10		6			2
11			4			1		2							10				7	9	3	5									8					6			3
11			4			1		2											7	9	3	5									8			10		6			4
			4			1		2								3		5	7							11					8			10	9	6			5
					11	1		2								3	10		7	5			9							4	8					6			6
			4			1		2								3	11		7	5											8			10	9	6			7
			11			1		2			7					3			9	5										4	8			10		6			8
			4			1		2	9		7			11		3				5											8			10		6			9
			4			1		2	9		7			11		3											5				8			10		6			10
			7			1		2	9					11		3				5										4	8			10		6			11
			4		7	1		2	9					11		3				5											8			10		6			12
			4			1					7			11		3			2	9		5									8			10		6			13
						1			9		7		4	11		3			2	5											8			10		6			14
11			7			1		2					4			3				9		5								6	8			10					15
			4			1			9		7			11		3			2	5											8			10		6			16
11			4			1		2			7					3			9	5											8			10		6			17
			4			1		2						11	8	3		5					9											10		6		7	18
6			16		2	18		13	6		7		2	8	2	15	2	3	11	14	4	5	3			2	1			5	17			16	2	17		1	
2			4					1	9		3			4	1		1		5	4			4								8			3	2			1	

Anderson A	Ashcroft L	Beattie R	Bentham S	Birkett W	Boyes W	Burnett G	Carey J	Cook W	Curran F	Curwen G	Dellow	Dunkley R	Fairfoull T	Fowler	Grant J	Greenhalgh N	Higham N	Humphreys J	Jackson G	Jones H	Jones JE	Jones TG	Lawton T	Linaker J	Lowe W	Lyon J	McDonnell M	McIntosh J	Makin G	Mercer J	Mutch G	Owen W	Rosenthall	Stevenson A	Urmston T	Watson T	Williams E	Wyles T	
			4		6									11		3			2	5			9								8			10		1		7	19
11			7	1	6			2								3		5		9										4	8			10					20
			4			1		2						11		3		5	7	9										6	8			10					21
			7	1				2		6						3		5	11				9							4	8			10					22
			7	1				2		6						3		5	11	9										4	8			10					23
			7	1				2		6						3		5		9	11									4	8			10					24
			9	1				2		6	7					3				5	11									4	8			10					25
			4	1				2			7			11		3						5								6	8	9		10					26
			4	1			5	2			7			11		3		6													8			10				9	27
			4	1			5	2			7			11		3		6					9								8			10					28
			4	1				2		6						3		5	11				9								8			10				7	29
	7			1						6			4	11		3			2			5	9										8	10					30
				1	6						7			11		3		4	2			5	9								8			10					31
			4			1				6		7		11		3			2				9				5				8			10					32
			8								7			11		3			2		5		9											10		6	1	4	33
						1				4						3		5	2		11		9		7						8			10		6			34
						1			9	4						3			2							11	5				8			10		6		7	35
		10	4			1										3		5	2		11			7				9						8		6			36
			4			1										3		5	2		6				7			9	11		8			10					37
1	1	1	15	11	3	6	2	10	1	9	6	1	1	9		19		12	13	6	6	3	9	1	2	1	2	2	1	7	16	1	1	19		5	1	5	
1			1					1	1	1	2			4						4			11					2		2	8			7				5	

1 own-goal

1943-44

Manager: Theo Kelly

1	Aug	28	(a)	Blackburn R	W 3-1	Lawton 2, McIntosh
2	Sep	4	(h)	Blackburn R	D 0-0	
3		11	(a)	Manchester U	L 1-4	Mutch
4		18	(h)	Manchester U	W 6-1	McIntosh 2, Wyles 2, Stevenson, Wainwright
5		25	(a)	Burnley	D 0-0	
6	Oct	2	(h)	Burnley	D 0-0	
7		9	(h)	Liverpool	L 4-6	Lawton, McIntosh, Stevenson, Opp own-goal
8		16	(a)	Liverpool	L 2-5	McIntosh, Stevenson
9		23	(a)	Wrexham	W 3-1	Lawton 3
10		30	(h)	Wrexham	W 4-2	Wyles 3, Bentham
11	Nov	6	(h)	Tranmere R	W 9-2	Lawton 5, Bentham 2, McIntosh, Stevenson
12		13	(a)	Tranmere R	W 6-2	Bentham 3, Grant, Stevenson, Wyles
13		20	(a)	Crewe A	W 8-0	Lawton 3, McIntosh 2, Stevenson 2, T.G.Jones
14		27	(h)	Crewe A	D 5-5	McIntosh 5
15	Dec	4	(a)	Chester	L 0-1	
16		11	(h)	Chester	L 0-1	
17		18	(h)	Manchester C	W 4-0	T.G.Jones, Lawton, McIntosh, Stevenson
18		25	(a)	Manchester C	W 5-3	Lawton 3, McIntosh, Stevenson

FINAL LEAGUE POSITION: 11th in League North (First Period) — Appearances / Goals

League North (Second Period)

19		27	(a)	Chester	W 5-3	Lawton 2, McIntosh 2, Wainwright
20	Jan	1	(h)	Chester	W 7-0	Stevenson 4, Boothway, McIntosh, Wainwright
21		8	(h)	Crewe A	W 9-1	McIntosh 3, Lawton 2, Stevenson 2, Boothway, Wainwright
22		15	(a)	Crewe A	W 6-2	Lawton 5, Wainwright
23		22	(a)	Liverpool	W 4-1	Wainwright 2, Lawton, Wyles
24		29	(h)	Liverpool	L 2-3	Lawton, Wyles
25	Feb	5	(h)	Wrexham	L 2-3	Lawton 2
26		12	(a)	Wrexham	L 1-2	Catterick
27		19	(a)	Tranmere R	W 1-0	McIntosh
28		26	(h)	Tranmere R	W 5-1	Lawton 2, Grant, T.G.Jones, Stevenson
29	Mar	4	(a)	Blackpool†	L 1-7	Lawton
30		11	(h)	Blackpool†	L 1-3	Jackson
31		18	(h)	Chester*	W 5-2	Stevenson 3, Jackson, McIntosh
32		25	(a)	Chester*	W 9-2	Lawton 4, Stevenson 3, McIntosh 2
33	Apr	1	(a)	Tranmere R‡	W 5-0	McIntosh 2, Bentham, Jackson, Wainwright
34		8	(h)	Tranmere R‡	W 4-0	Lawton 2, Bentham, Wainwright
35		10	(h)	Liverpool*	W 3-0	Grant, T.G.Jones, McIntosh
36		15	(a)	Liverpool*	L 0-3	
37		22	(a)	Liverpool*	L 2-4	T.G.Jones, Wyles
38		29	(a)	Bury	L 0-1	
39	May	21	(a)	Southport‡	D 1-1	McIntosh
40		22	(h)	Southport‡	L 0-1	

FINAL LEAGUE POSITION: 12th in League North (Second Period) — Appearances / Goals

Matches 19 to 39 inclusive were in the League North (Second Period).
Matches 19 to 28 inclusive were in the League War Cup Qualifying Competition.
Matches marked thus* were in the Lancashire Cup; matches marked thus† were in the League War Cup KO Competition; matches marked thus‡ were in the Liverpool Cup. All the cup matches, with the exception of Match 40, counted towards the League North (Second Period). There were 50 and 56 clubs respectively in these competitions and no club played every other club.

Astbury T	Bentham S	Boothway J	Boyes W	Britton C	Burnett G	Caskie J	Catterick H	Doyle R	Gillick T	Glidden D	Grant J	Greenhalgh N	Hall J	Hallard W	Higgins A	Humphreys J	Jackson G	Jones F	Jones JE	Jones S	Jones TG	Law N	Lawton T	Linaker J	Lowe W	McDonnell M	McIntosh	Makin G	Mercer J	Mutch G	Scott	Steele E	Stevenson A	Tatters C	Turner P	Wainwright E	Watson T	Wyles T	
	8				1							3					2			6	5		9				11			7		4	10						1
	8				1												2		3	6	5		9				11		4				10						2
	8				1												2		3		5		9				11		6	7		4				10			3
	4				1						7	3					2		6		5						11						10			8		9	4
					1						7	3					2		6				9			5	11						10			8			5
	4				1						7	3					2				5						11				6					8		9	6
	4				1						7	3							2		5		9				11				6		10			8			7
	4				1	8						3		6					2		5						11						10						8
	8				1						4	3		6					2		5		9		7		11						10						9
	8				1						4	3		6					2		5				7		11						10					9	10
	8				1						4	3				5			2	6			9		7		11						10						11
	8				1						7	3				4			2	6	5						11						10					9	12
					1						8	3		6			2		4		5		9	7			11						10						13
					1						8	3					2		4	6				7		5	11						10					9	14
					1						8	3					2		4	6	5						11								7		10	9	15
					1						8	3		6			2				5		9				11						10		7		4		16
					1						6	3					2				5		9				11	7	4				10			8			17
					1						7	3					2				5		9				11		4				10			8	6		18
	11				18	1					14	16		5		2	12		13	6	15		11	2	3	2	18	1	4	2	2	2	15		2	7	3	6	
	6											1									2		18				15			1			9			1		6	

1 own-goal

Astbury T	Bentham S	Boothway J	Boyes W	Britton C	Burnett G	Caskie J	Catterick H	Doyle R	Gillick T	Glidden D	Grant J	Greenhalgh N	Hall J	Hallard W	Higgins A	Humphreys J	Jackson G	Jones F	Jones JE	Jones S	Jones TG	Law N	Lawton T	Linaker J	Lowe W	McDonnell M	McIntosh	Makin G	Mercer J	Mutch G	Scott	Steele E	Stevenson A	Tatters C	Turner P	Wainwright E	Watson T	Wyles T	
					1						7	3					2				5		9				11		4				10			8	6		19
		9			1						4	3					2				5						11						10	7		8	6		20
		7			1						4	3					2				5		9				11						10			8	6		21
		7			1						4	3					2				5		9				11						10			8	6		22
					1						4						2		3		5		9				11							10		8	6	7	23
					1						4						2		3		5		9				11		6				10			8		7	24
					1						4	3	7				2				5		9				11						10			8	6		25
	8				1		9				4	3			7		2				5						11									10	6		26
	9				1						4	3					7		2							5	11						10			8	6		27
					1						7	3					2				5		9				11		4				10				6		28
	7				1						4	3					2				5		9				11						10			8	6		29
	8				1		9				4	3					7		2		5						11						10				6		30
			10		1						4	3					7		2		5		9				11						8				6		31
			10		1						4	3					7		2		5		9				11						8				6		32
	8				1						4	3					7		2		5						11									10	6	9	33
	8				1						4	3					7		2		5		9				11									10	6		34
			10	4	1				8		7	3					2				5		9				11										6		35
	8				1						4	3					7		2		5		9				11									10	6		36
8	10				1						4	3							2		5						11										6	9	37
	4				1			6			8	3					2	7	5								11									10		9	38
	10				1						4	3					7		2			5					11									8	6	9	39
	8				1					10	4	3					7		2	5			9				11										6		40
1	11	3	3	1	22		2	1	1	1	22	20	1		1		21	1	13	1	18	1	14			1	22		3				12	2		15	20	6	
	2	2					1				2						3				3		22				14						13			8		3	

Morley played number 4 in Match 5; G.Murphy played number 9 in Match 8; A.Roberts played number 7 in Match 8; E.Rogers played number 7 in Match 37; N.Sharp played number 10 in Match 6; A.Smith played number 7 in Match 2; L.Wootton played number 8 in Match 28.

1944-45

Manager: Theo Kelly

No	Month	Day	Venue	Opponent	Res	Score	Scorers
1	Aug	26	(h)	Manchester U	L	1-2	Rawlings
2	Sep	2	(a)	Manchester U	W	3-1	Boyes, Peters, Rawlings
3		9	(a)	Bury	W	2-1	Wainwright, Wyles
4		16	(h)	Bury	W	4-1	Wyles 2, Rawlings, Stevenson
5		23	(h)	Chester	W	6-2	Lawton 2, Makin 2, Rawlings, Wainwright
6		30	(a)	Chester	W	6-2	Wyles 3, Wainwright 2, Stevenson
7	Oct	7	(a)	Tranmere R	W	4-1	Lawton 3, Wainwright
8		14	(h)	Tranmere R	W	2-1	Stevenson, Wainwright
9		21	(h)	Liverpool	L	0-2	
10		28	(a)	Liverpool	D	0-0	
11	Nov	4	(a)	Manchester C	W	3-1	Lawton, Stevenson, Opp own-goal
12		11	(h)	Manchester C	W	4-1	Catterick 3, Stevenson
13		18	(h)	Crewe A	L	3-5	T.G.Jones, Lawton, Stevenson
14		25	(a)	Crewe A	W	5-1	Lawton 5
15	Dec	2	(a)	Wrexham	L	0-1	
16		9	(h)	Wrexham	D	2-2	Catterick, Makin
17		16	(h)	Stockport C	W	6-1	Lawton 2, Stevenson 2, T.G.Jones, Makin
18		23	(a)	Stockport C	W	7-0	T.G.Jones 3, Lawton 2, Wainwright 2

FINAL LEAGUE POSITION: 5th in League North (First Period)

Appearances
Goals

No	Month	Day	Venue	Opponent	Res	Score	Scorers
19		25	(h)	Tranmere R	L	2-4	Lawton 2
20		26	(h)	Liverpool	D	2-2	Stevenson, Wainwright
21		30	(a)	Tranmere R	W	4-0	T.G.Jones 3, Wainwright
22	Jan	6	(h)	Bolton W	W	2-1	Lawton 2
23		13	(a)	Bolton W	W	3-1	Lawton, Rawlings, Stevenson
24		20	(a)	Stockport C	W	3-0	Bentham 2, Catterick
25		27	(h)	Stockport C	W	9-2	Lawton 4, Bentham 2, McIntosh, Rawlings, Stevenson
26	Feb	3	(h)	Liverpool	W	4-1	Bentham, McIntosh, Rawlings, Wyles
27		10	(a)	Liverpool	L	1-3	Lawton
28		17	(h)	Southport	W	6-0	Rawlings 2, Wyles 2, Bentham, Stevenson
29		24	(a)	Southport	W	5-3	Wyles 2, Benthamm, Mercer, Stevenson
30	Mar	3	(h)	Chester*	W	4-1	Lawton 2, Bentham, Stevenson
31		10	(a)	Chester*	L	4-6	Bentham 2, Wyles 2
32		17	(h)	Preston NE	W	3-0	Wyles 3
33		24	(a)	Liverpool†	L	0-1	
34		31	(h)	Liverpool†	L	0-1	
35	Apr	2	(a)	Liverpool‡	W	3-1	Grant, Jackson, Wyles
36		7	(a)	Wrexham	W	2-1	Wyles 2
37		14	(h)	Wrexham	W	5-3	Stevenson 2, Wyles 2, Bentham
38		21	(a)	Southport*	W	5-0	Catterick 3, Boyes, Stevenson
39		28	(h)	Southport*	D	1-1	Wyles
40	May	5	(a)	Accrington S*	D	1-1	Rawlings
41		9	(a)	Tranmere R‡	W	3-0	Bentham, Catterick, Rawlings
42		12	(h)	Accrington S*	L	0-2	
43		19	(a)	Stoke C	L	1-5	Catterick
44		21	(h)	Tranmere R‡	W	4-1	Wyles 2, Bentham, Boyes
45		26	(h)	Stoke C	W	3-2	Wyles 2, Bentham

FINAL LEAGUE POSITION: 2nd in League North (Second Period)

Appearances
Goals

Matches 19 to 45 inclusive were played in the League North (Second Period).
Matches 19 to 29 inclusive were in the League War Cup Qualifying Competition.
Matches marked thus* were in the Lancashire Cup; matches thus† were in the League War Cup KO Competition; matches marked thus‡ were in the Liverpool Cup. All cup matches counted towards the League North (Second Period).
There were 54 and 60 teams respectively in the competitions and no team played all the others.

Ashley A	Bentham S	Boyes W	Burnett G	Catterick H	Curwen G	Doyle R	Dugdale G	Gillick T	Grant J	Greenhalgh N	Heath C	Hedley J	Hill	Humphreys J	Jackson G	Jones F	Jones TG	King T	Lawton T	Lindley	Logan J	McDonnell M	McIntosh	Makin G	Mercer J	Morris J	Peters T	Rawlings	Sharp N	Stevenson A	Wainwright E	Watson T	Wootton L	Wyles T	
			1						4	3					2				9			5		11				7		10	8	6			1
		11	1						4	3					2				9	5							10	7			8	6			2
		11	1						4	3					2					5							10	7			8	6		9	3
		11	1						4	3					2					5								7		10	8	6		9	4
			1						4	3					2				9	5				11				7		10	8	6			5
			1						4	3					2					5				11				7		10	8	6		9	6
			1			6			4	3					2				9	5				11				7		10	8				7
			1			6			4	3					2					5				11				7		10	8			9	8
			1						4	3					2					5							11	7		10	8	6		9	9
			1	9					4	3					2		11			5								7		10	8	6			10
			1	11					4	3					2				9	5								7		10	8	6			11
			1	9					4	3					2		8			5								7		10		6	11		12
			1	7					4	3					2		8		9	5										10		6	11		13
			1	8					4	3					2				9	5				11				7		10		6			14
	8	11	1						4	3					2				9	5								7		10		6			15
			1	9					4	3					2	8				5				11				7		10		6			16
			1						4	3					2		8		9	5				11				7		10		6			17
			1						4	3					2		8		9	5				11	10						7	6			18
	1	4	18	6		2			18	18					18	1	5		10	17		1		9	1		3	16		15	12	16	2	5	
		1		4													5		16					4			1	4		8	8			6	

1 own-goal

Ashley A	Bentham S	Boyes W	Burnett G	Catterick H	Curwen G	Doyle R	Dugdale G	Gillick T	Grant J	Greenhalgh N	Heath C	Hedley J	Hill	Humphreys J	Jackson G	Jones F	Jones TG	King T	Lawton T	Lindley	Logan J	McDonnell M	McIntosh	Makin G	Mercer J	Morris J	Peters T	Rawlings	Sharp N	Stevenson A	Wainwright E	Watson T	Wootton L	Wyles T	
			1						4	3					2				9	5				11					7	10	8	6			19
			1						4	3				7	2		9			5			11							10	8	6			20
			1						4	3					2		9			5			11		8					10	7	6			21
	5		1						4	3					2		8		9				11					7		10		6			22
	5		1	8					4	3					2				9				11					7		10		6			23
	8		1	9					4	3					2		5						11					7		10		6			24
	8		1						4	3					2		5		9				11					7		10		6			25
	8		1						4	3					2		5						11					7		10		6		9	26
	8	7	1						4	3					2				9	5			11							10		6			27
	8		1						4	3					2					5								7	11	10		6		9	28
	8		1							3					2		5								4			7	11	10		6		9	29
	8	11	1						4	3			5		2				9									7		10		6			30
	8	11	1						4	3			5		2														7	10		6		9	31
	8	11	1		5				4	3					2														7	10		6		9	32
	8	11	1	7					4	3					2											5				10		6		9	33
			1					8	4	3					2				9				11		5					10	7	6			34
			1					8	4	3					2								11		5					10	7	6		9	35
	7		1						4	3				5	2			8						11						10		6		9	36
	8	11	1						4	3				5	2													7		10		6		9	37
	8	11	1	9			3		4					5	2															10		6		7	38
	8	11	1	9					4	3				5	2															10		6		7	39
	10	11	1	8					4	3				5	2													7				6		9	40
	8	10	1	9					4	3				5	2									11				7				6			41
	8	10	1	9					4	3				5	2													7				6		11	42
8	10	11	1	9					4	3				5	2									7								6			43
	8	11	1						4	3		2		5							10			7								6		9	44
8	10		1						4	3	7			5	2									11								6		9	45
2	22	13	27	9	1		1	2	26	26	1	1	2	11	26		7	1	7	5	1		10	6	4	1		12	5	21	5	27		15	
	14	2		6					1						1		3		12				2		1			7		9	2			20	

1945-46

Manager: Theo Kelly

1	Aug	25	(h)	Bolton W	W 3-2	Bentham, Catterick, Mercer	24,898
2	Sep	1	(a)	Bolton W	L 1-3	Boyes	16,683
3		8	(a)	Preston NE	W 2-0	Mercer, Wainwright	17,542
4		12	(a)	Liverpool	L 1-2	Wyles	25,446
5		15	(h)	Preston NE	D 1-1	Wyles	23,043
6		22	(h)	Leeds U	L 0-2		19,711
7		29	(a)	Leeds U	W 3-2	Boyes 2, Wainwright	13,541
8	Oct	6	(a)	Manchester U	D 0-0		30,820
9		13	(h)	Manchester U	W 3-0	Catterick, Fielding, Rawlings	32,087
10		20	(h)	Sunderland	W 4-0	Lawton 3, Jones	31,636
11		27	(a)	Sunderland	W 4-0	Catterick 2, Fielding, Wainwright	19,153
12	Nov	3	(a)	Sheffield U	L 0-4		24,921
13		10	(h)	Sheffield U	W 1-0	Catterick	29,510
14		17	(h)	Middlesbrough	D 1-1	Catterick	23,248
15		24	(a)	Middlesbrough	D 0-0		18,197
16	Dec	1	(a)	Stoke C	W 3-2	Catterick 2, Rawlings	20,723
17		8	(h)	Stoke C	W 6-1	Wainwright 3, Catterick 2, Rawlings	28,627
18		15	(h)	Grimsby T	W 2-1	Catterick, Wainwright	23,212
19		22	(a)	Grimsby T	W 2-1	Bentham 2	10,137
20		25	(a)	Blackpool	L 2-5	Boyes, Jones	20,772
21		26	(h)	Blackpool	W 7-1	Catterick 3, Wainwright 3, Boyes	53,991
22		29	(h)	Liverpool	D 2-2	Boyes, Catterick	60,296
23	Jan	1	(h)	Bury	W 3-1	Boyes, Catterick, Elliott	20,638
24		12	(a)	Blackburn R	L 1-2	Catterick	9,055
25		19	(h)	Blackburn R	W 4-1	Catterick 3, Fielding	23,538
26	Feb	2	(h)	Bradford	D 0-0		28,832
27		9	(h)	Manchester C	W 4-1	Bell 2, Bentham, Boyes	41,670
28		16	(a)	Manchester C	W 3-1	Catterick, Mercer, Wainwright	31,501
29		23	(a)	Newcastle U	W 3-1	Wainwright 2, Catterick	49,660
30	Mar	2	(h)	Newcastle U	W 4-1	Boyes, Catterick, Wainwright, Opp own-goal	54,186
31		9	(h)	Sheffield W	D 2-2	Catterick, Stevenson	48,440
32		16	(a)	Sheffield W	D 0-0		28,000
33		23	(a)	Huddersfield T	W 1-0	Higgins	15,664
34		30	(h)	Huddersfield T	W 5-2	Wainwright 3, Higgins, Watson	40,000
35	Apr	3	(a)	Bradford	W 2-1	Boyes, Grant	10,072
36		6	(h)	Chesterfield	W 4-0	Boyes 2, Jones 2	40,000
37		13	(a)	Chesterfield	D 1-1	Stevenson	20,000
38		19	(a)	Barnsley	L 0-2		26,000
39		20	(h)	Burnley	W 2-0	Catterick, Greenhalgh	40,000
40		22	(h)	Barnsley	L 0-4		45,000
41		27	(a)	Burnley	L 0-1		14,000
42	May	4	(a)	Bury	L 1-3	Bentham	9,000

FINAL LEAGUE POSITION: 2nd in Football League North

Appearances

Goals

FA Cup

3	Jan	5	(a)	Preston NE	L 1-2	Catterick
		9	(h)	Preston NE	D 2-2	Elliott, Mercer

Appearances

Goals

Matches 1 to 42 inclusive were in the Football League North which contained 22 teams.
The programme was a normal peacetime fixture list with each club playing each other club home and away.
The FA Cup was resumed with matches up to and including the sixth round being played on a two-legged home and away basis.

Bell R	Bentham S	Bond T	Boyes W	Burnett G	Catterick H	Cookson J	Elliott T	Fielding W	Grant J	Greenhalgh N	Higgins W	Humphreys J	Jackson G	Johnson A	Jones TG	Lawton T	Lowe W	McIlhatton J	Makin G	Mercer J	Rawlings J	Stevenson A	Wainwright E	Watson T	Wyles T	
	8		10	1	9				7	3		5	2							4				6	11	1
			10	1	8				7	3		5	2			9			11	4				6		2
	4		11	1				10		3			2	7		9				5			8	6		3
5	4	7	10	1						3			2						11				8	6	9	4
5	4		10	1						3			2				7		11				8	6	9	5
	8		10	1					11	3		5	2				7			4				6	9	6
	4		10	1	9					3			2						11	5	7		8	6		7
	8		10	1					4	3			2			9	7		11	5				6		8
	4		11	1	9			10	8	3			2		5						7			6		9
	4		11	1				10		3			2		5	9					7		8	6		10
	4		11	1	9			10		3			2		5						7		8	6		11
	8		11	1				10		3			2		5	9				4	7			6		12
			11	1	9		8	10	4	3			2							5	7			6		13
			11	1	9		8	10	4	3			2							5	7			6		14
	6		11	1	9			10	4	3			2							5	7		8			15
	6		11	1	9	4	8	10		3			2		5						7					16
	6		11	1	9			10		3		5	2							4	7		8			17
	4		11	1	9			10		3			2		5						7		8	6		18
	8		11	1	9			10		3			2		5					4	7			6		19
	6		11	1	9			10		3			2		5					4	7		8			20
	4		11	1	9			10		3			2		5						7		8	6		21
	4		11	1	9			10		3			2							5	7	8		6		22
8	4		11	1	9		7			3			2							5		10		6		23
	3		11	1	9			10	4				2							5	7	8		6		24
	4		11	1	9			10		3		5	2									7	8	6		25
	6		11	1	9			10		3		5	2							4	7		8			26
9	8		11	1				10		3		5	2							4		7		6		27
			11	1	9			10		3		5	2							4		7	8	6		28
			11	1	9			10		3		5	2							4		7	8	6		29
			11	1	9			10		3		5	2							4		7	8	6		30
			11	1	9			10		3		5	2							4		7	8	6		31
			11	1				10		3	9	5	2							4		7	8	6		32
			11	1				10		3	9	5	2							4		7	8	6		33
			11	1				10		3	9	5	2	7						4			8	6		34
	4		11	1				10	7	3	9	5	2									8		6		35
	4		11	1				10		3		5	2		9							7	8	6		36
9	4		11	1				10		3		5	2									7	8	6		37
	4		11	1	9			10		3		5	2									7	8	6		38
	4		11	1	9			10		3		5	2									7	8	6		39
	4		11	1	9			10		3		5	2									7	8	6		40
	4		11	1	9			10		3		5	2									7	8	6		41
	4		11	1	9			10		3		5	2					7					8	6		42
5	32	1	42	42	28	1	4	34	10	41	4	22	42	2	10	5	3	1	5	25	17	18	27	37	4	
2	5		12		25		1	3	1	1	2				4	3				3	3	2	17	1	2	

1 own-goal

Bell R	Bentham S	Bond T	Boyes W	Burnett G	Catterick H	Cookson J	Elliott T	Fielding W	Grant J	Greenhalgh N	Higgins W	Humphreys J	Jackson G	Johnson A	Jones TG	Lawton T	Lowe W	McIlhatton J	Makin G	Mercer J	Rawlings J	Stevenson A	Wainwright E	Watson T	Wyles T	
	4		11	1	9		8	10		3		5	2							6	7					3
	4		11	1	9		8	10		3		5	2							6	7					
	2		2	2	2		2	2		2		2	2							2	2					
					1		1													1						

1946-47

Manager: Theo Kelly

1	Aug	31	(h)	Brentford	L 0-2		55,338
2	Sep	2	(a)	Aston Villa	W 1-0	Boyes	35,618
3		7	(a)	Blackburn R	L 1-4	Boyes	25,678
4		11	(h)	Arsenal	W 3-2	Livingstone 2, Bentham	40,093
5		14	(h)	Portsmouth	W 1-0	Bentham	47,909
6		21	(a)	Liverpool	D 0-0		48,875
7		28	(a)	Huddersfield T	L 0-1		19,208
8	Oct	5	(h)	Wolves	L 0-2		44,792
9		12	(a)	Sunderland	L 1-4	Eglington	40,830
10		19	(h)	Bolton W	W 2-1	Higgins, Stevenson	45,105
11		26	(a)	Charlton A	L 1-4	Stevenson	25,211
12	Nov	2	(h)	Grimsby T	D 3-3	Dodds, Jones, Stevenson	48,817
13		9	(a)	Leeds U	L 1-2	Dodds	22,992
14		16	(h)	Manchester U	D 2-2	Dodds 2	45,932
15		23	(a)	Stoke C	L 1-2	Dodds	27,948
16		30	(h)	Middlesbrough	W 2-1	Eglington, Wainwright	48,997
17	Dec	7	(a)	Chelsea	D 1-1	Dodds	41,255
18		14	(h)	Sheffield U	L 2-3	Dodds, Jones	36,513
19		21	(a)	Preston NE	L 1-2	Jones	23,334
20		25	(h)	Derby C	W 4-1	Wainwright 2, Boyes, Dodds	32,925
21		26	(a)	Derby C	L 1-5	Fielding	29,978
22		28	(a)	Brentford	D 1-1	Wainwright	29,360
23	Jan	1	(h)	Aston Villa	W 2-0	Dodds, Stevenson	49,665
24		4	(h)	Blackburn R	W 1-0	Wainwright	39,775
25		18	(a)	Portsmouth	L 1-2	Opp own-goal	30,002
26		29	(h)	Liverpool	W 1-0	Wainwright	30,612
27	Feb	1	(h)	Huddersfield T	W 1-0	Bentham	37,205
28		15	(h)	Sunderland	W 4-2	Wainwright 3, Eglington	39,658
29		22	(a)	Bolton W	W 2-0	Stevenson, Wainwright	21,080
30	Mar	8	(a)	Grimsby T	D 2-2	Wainwright 2	11,277
31		22	(a)	Manchester U	L 0-3		44,297
32		29	(h)	Stoke C	D 2-2	Eglington, Fielding	40,092
33	Apr	4	(h)	Blackpool	D 1-1	Stevenson	63,617
34		5	(a)	Middlesbrough	L 0-4		27,106
35		7	(a)	Blackpool	W 3-0	Dodds 2, Stevenson	23,699
36		12	(h)	Chelsea	W 2-0	Dodds 2	30,970
37		19	(a)	Sheffield U	L 0-2		28,675
38		26	(h)	Preston NE	W 2-0	Dodds, Fielding	26,371
39	May	10	(a)	Wolves	W 3-2	Dodds, Fielding, McIlhatton	40,033
40		24	(h)	Charlton A	D 1-1	Wainwright	32,558
41		26	(h)	Leeds U	W 4-1	Dodds 2, Grant, Stevenson	21,001
42		31	(a)	Arsenal	L 1-2	Eglington	23,785

FINAL LEAGUE POSITION: 10th in Division One

Appearances
Goals

FA Cup

3	Jan	11	(h)	Southend U	W 4-2	Fielding, Jones, McIlhatton, Wainwright
4		25	(a)	Sheffield W	L 1-2	Wainwright

Appearances
Goals

Bentham S	Boyes W	Burnett G	Catterick H	Davis J	Dodds E	Eglington T	Farrell P	Fielding W	Finnis H	Grant J	Greenhalgh N	Higgins W	Humphreys J	Jackson G	Johnson A	Jones TG	Livingstone A	McIlhatton J	Mercer J	Sagar E	Saunders G	Stevenson A	Wainwright E	Watson T	
	11	1	9					10			3			2		5		7	4				8	6	1
	11	1	9					10			3			2		5	8	7	4					6	2
	11	1	9	2				10			3					5		7	4				8	6	3
8		1				11					3					5	9	7	4		2	10		6	4
8		1				11					3					5	9	7	4		2	10		6	5
6		1				11		8			3	9				5		7	4		2	10			6
6		1				11		8			3	9				5		7	4		2	10			7
9		1				11		8		6	3					5		7	4		2	10			8
6		1				11		8			3					5	9	7	4		2	10			9
6		1				11		8			3	9	5					7	4		2	10			10
6		1				11		8			3	9				5		7	4		2	10			11
		1			9	11		8		6	3			2		5			4			10	7		12
4					9	11			3				5	2				7		1		10	8	6	13
4					9	11					3		2			5		7		1		10	8	6	14
4					9	11	6							2		5		7		1		10	8	3	15
4					9	11	6	10						2		5		7		1			8	3	16
4					9	11	6				2					5		7		1		10	8	3	17
4					9	11	6				2					5		7		1		10	8	3	18
4	11				9		6	10			3					5				1	2	7	8		19
4	11				9		6	10			3				7	5				1	2		8		20
4	11				9		6	10			3		5		7					1	2		8		21
4	11				9		6	10			3		5		7					1	2		8		22
4	11				9		6	10			3					5		7		1	2	8			23
4						11	6	10				9	5					7		1	2		8	3	24
4		1				11	6	10			3	9				5		7			2		8		25
4						11	6	10			3		5	2				7		1		8	9		26
4						11	6	10			3	8	5	2				7		1			9		27
4						11	6	10			3		5	2				7		1		8	9		28
4						11	6	10			3		5	2				7		1		8	9		29
4	6					11		10			3		5	2				7		1		8	9		30
4						11	6	10			3		5	2				7		1		8	9		31
4						11	6	10			3			2		5		7		1		8	9		32
4						11	6	10			3			2		5		7		1		8	9		33
4					9	11	6	10			3		5					7		1	2		8		34
					9	11	6			4	3		5	2				7		1		10	8		35
4					9	11	6	10			3		5					7		1	2	8			36
4					9	11	6	10			3		5					7		1	2	8			37
4					9	11	6	10			3		5					7		1	2	8			38
4					9	11	6	10			3		5					7		1	2		8		39
4					9	11	6				3		5					7		1	2	10	8		40
4					9	11	6			8	3		5					7		1	2	10			41
4					9	11	6			8	3		5					7		1	2	10			42
37	9	13	3	1	21	34	27	31	1	5	38	7	21	15	3	22	4	37	12	29	23	30	27	12	
3	3				17	5		4		1		1				3	2	1				8	13		

1 own-goal

Bentham S	Boyes W	Burnett G	Catterick H	Davis J	Dodds E	Eglington T	Farrell P	Fielding W	Finnis H	Grant J	Greenhalgh N	Higgins W	Humphreys J	Jackson G	Johnson A	Jones TG	Livingstone A	McIlhatton J	Mercer J	Sagar E	Saunders G	Stevenson A	Wainwright E	Watson T	
4					9	11	6	10			3					5		7		1	2		8		3
4					9	11	6	10			3		5	2				7		1			8		4
2					2	2	2	2			2		1	1		1		2		2	1		2		
								1								1		1					2		

1947-48

Manager: Theo Kelly

No.	Month	Day	Venue	Opponents	Result	Score	Scorers	Attendance
1	Aug	23	(a)	Blackburn R	W	3-2	Dodds, Eglington, Wainwright	24,536
2		27	(h)	Manchester C	W	1-0	Fielding	53,622
3		30	(h)	Blackpool	L	1-2	Wainwright	59,665
4	Sep	3	(a)	Manchester C	W	1-0	Stevenson	46,462
5		6	(a)	Derby C	L	0-1		29,089
6		8	(a)	Aston Villa	L	0-3		28,764
7		13	(h)	Huddersfield T	D	1-1	Wainwright	40,622
8		17	(h)	Aston Villa	W	3-0	Fielding 2, Opp own-goal	32,537
9		20	(a)	Chelsea	L	1-3	Catterick	42,955
10		27	(h)	Liverpool	L	0-3		66,776
11	Oct	4	(h)	Wolves	D	1-1	Boyes	48,106
12		11	(a)	Middlesbrough	W	1-0	Wainwright	38,686
13		18	(h)	Charlton A	L	0-1		40,177
14		25	(a)	Arsenal	D	1-1	Wainwright	56,645
15	Nov	1	(h)	Sheffield U	W	2-0	Dodds, Fielding	43,615
16		8	(a)	Stoke C	D	1-1	Stevenson	32,232
17		15	(h)	Burnley	L	0-3		49,442
18		22	(a)	Manchester U	D	2-2	Dodds, Fielding	36,715
19		29	(h)	Preston NE	W	2-1	Fielding, Wainwright	44,884
20	Dec	6	(a)	Portsmouth	L	0-3		25,525
21		13	(h)	Bolton W	W	2-0	Catterick, Wainwright	33,458
22		20	(h)	Blackburn R	W	4-1	Fielding 2, Farrell, Grant	32,655
23		25	(a)	Sunderland	L	0-2		40,925
24		26	(h)	Sunderland	W	3-0	Grant 2, Wainwright	47,828
25	Jan	3	(a)	Blackpool	L	0-5		21,685
26		17	(h)	Derby C	L	1-3	Wainwright	51,776
27	Feb	21	(a)	Wolves	W	4-2	Dodds 3, Eglington	24,105
28		28	(h)	Middlesbrough	W	2-1	Lello 2	46,364
29	Mar	6	(a)	Charlton A	W	3-2	Dodds 2, Eglington	32,973
30		13	(h)	Arsenal	L	0-2		64,059
31		20	(a)	Sheffield U	L	1-2	Farrell	30,284
32		26	(a)	Grimsby T	L	0-3		18,279
33		27	(h)	Stoke C	L	0-1		44,241
34		29	(h)	Grimsby T	W	3-1	Grant, Higgins, Jones	37,926
35	Apr	3	(a)	Burnley	W	1-0	Dodds	23,933
36		10	(h)	Manchester U	W	2-0	Dodds, Stevenson	44,098
37		14	(h)	Chelsea	W	2-3	Higgins 2	28,366
38		17	(a)	Preston NE	L	0-3		25,035
39		21	(a)	Liverpool	L	0-4		55,305
40		24	(h)	Portsmouth	L	0-2		18,089
41		28	(a)	Huddersfield T	W	3-1	Dodds 3	13,905
42	May	1	(a)	Bolton W	D	0-0		17,391

FINAL LEAGUE POSITION: 14th in Division One

Appearances
Goals

FA Cup

Round	Month	Day	Venue	Opponents	Result	Score	Scorers
3	Jan	10	(a)	Grimsby T	W	4-1	Wainwright 2, Dodds, Farrell
4		24	(a)	Wolves	D	1-1	Catterick
R		31	(h)	Wolves	W	3-2	Fielding 2, Grant
5	Feb	7	(a)	Fulham	D	1-1	Eglington
R		14	(h)	Fulham	L	0-1	

Appearances
Goals

Bentham S	Boyes W	Catterick H	Dodds E	Dugdale G	Eglington T	Farrell P	Fielding W	Gardner T	Grant J	Greenhalgh N	Hedley J	Higgins W	Humphreys J	Jackson G	Johnson A	Jones TG	Lello C	Lindley W	McIlhatton J	Pinchbeck C	Sagar E	Saunders G	Stevenson A	Wainwright E	Watson T	
4			9		11	6	10			3			5						7		1	2		8		1
4			9		11	6	10			3			5						7		1	2	8			2
4			9		11	6	10			3			5						7		1	2		8		3
4			9		11	6				3			5						7		1	2	8	10		4
			9		11	6				3			5					4	7		1	2	10	8		5
4			9		11	6	10			3			5						7		1	2		8		6
4			9		11	6	10			3			5						7		1	2		8		7
4		9			11	6	10			3	2		5						7		1		8			8
4		9			11	6	10			3	2		5						7		1			8		9
		9			11	6	7			3						5					1	2	10	8	4	10
	11	9		3			10	7								5		4			1	2		8	6	11
	11	9		3		4							5						7		1	2	10	8	6	12
	11	9		3		4							5						7		1	2	10	8	6	13
4	11			3			10						5						7		1	2	8	9	6	14
			9	3	11	4	10						5						7		1	2	8		6	15
			9		11	4	10			3			5								1	2	8	7	6	16
			9		11	4	10			3			5		7						1	2		8	6	17
			9	3	11	4	10								7	5					1	2		8	6	18
		9		3	11	4	10								7	5					1	2		8	6	19
		9		3	11	4	10				2				7	5					1			8	6	20
		9		3	11	4	10								7	5					1	2		8	6	21
			9	3	11	4	10		7							5					1	2		8	6	22
			9	3		4	10		7			11				5					1	2		8	6	23
			9	3		4	10		7			11				5					1	2		8	6	24
			9	3		4	10		7			11				5					1	2		8	6	25
4					11	6	10		7				5							9	1	2		8	3	26
			9	3	11	6	8		7							5	10	4			1	2				27
			9	3	11	6	8		7							5	10	4			1	2				28
			9	3	11	6	8		7							5	10	4			1	2				29
				3	11	6	8		7				5				10	4		9	1	2				30
				3	11	6	8		7				5				10	4			1	2		9		31
			9	3	11	6	8									5	10	4			1	2		7		32
			9			6	8		7		3	11				5	10	4			1	2				33
			9			6			7		3	11		2		5		4			1		10	8		34
			9			6	8		7		3	11				5		4			1	2	10			35
			9			6	8		7		3	11				5		4			1	2	10			36
			9			6	8		7		3	11				5		4			1	2	10			37
						6	10		7		3	11				5		4		9	1	2		8		38
					11	6					3	7				5	9	4			1	2	10	8		39
			9		11				4		3	7		2		5	10				1			8	6	40
			9		11	6					3	7				5		4			1	2	10	8		41
			9		11				6		3	7			8	5		4			1	2	10			42
10	4	9	27	19	29	38	33	1	18	12	13	13	18	2	6	24	9	17	13	3	42	37	17	30	18	
	1	2	13		3	2	8		4			3				1	2						3	9		

1 own-goal

Bentham S	Boyes W	Catterick H	Dodds E	Dugdale G	Eglington T	Farrell P	Fielding W	Gardner T	Grant J	Greenhalgh N	Hedley J	Higgins W	Humphreys J	Jackson G	Johnson A	Jones TG	Lello C	Lindley W	McIlhatton J	Pinchbeck C	Sagar E	Saunders G	Stevenson A	Wainwright E	Watson T	
4			9		11	6	10		7				5								1	2		8	3	3
4		9		3	11		10		7				5								1	2		8	6	4
4		9		3	11		10		7				5								1	2		8	6	R
4		9		3	11	6	10		7				5								1	2		8		5
8		9		3	11	4	10		7				5								1	2			6	R
5		4	1	4	5	3	5		5				5								5	5		4	4	
		1	1		1	1	2		1															2		

1948-49

Manager: Cliff Britton

1	Aug	21	(h)	Newcastle U	D 3-3	Dodds 2, Powell	57,729
2		25	(a)	Portsmouth	L 0-4		31,433
3		28	(a)	Middlesbrough	L 0-1		35,960
4	Sep	1	(h)	Portsmouth	L 0-5		41,511
5		4	(h)	Birmingham C	L 0-5		49,199
6		8	(h)	Stoke C	W 2-1	Juliussen, Powell	42,818
7		11	(a)	Chelsea	L 0-6		42,736
8		13	(a)	Stoke C	L 0-1		24,454
9		18	(h)	Liverpool	D 1-1	Dodds	78,299
10		25	(h)	Preston NE	W 4-1	Dodds 3, Stevenson	48,674
11	Oct	2	(a)	Burnley	L 0-1		31,341
12		9	(a)	Blackpool	L 0-3		22,070
13		16	(h)	Derby C	L 0-1		53,087
14		23	(a)	Arsenal	L 0-5		49,048
15		30	(h)	Huddersfield T	W 2-0	Catterick 2	46,632
16	Nov	6	(a)	Manchester U	L 0-2		45,636
17		13	(h)	Sheffield U	W 2-1	Bentham, Corr	29,816
18		20	(a)	Aston Villa	W 1-0	Catterick	43,382
19		27	(h)	Sunderland	W 1-0	Opp own-goal	38,170
20	Dec	4	(a)	Wolves	L 0-1		37,800
21		11	(h)	Bolton W	W 1-0	Eglington	40,407
22		18	(a)	Newcastle U	L 0-1		43,515
23		25	(h)	Manchester C	D 0-0		37,444
24		27	(a)	Manchester C	D 0-0		40,471
25	Jan	1	(h)	Middlesbrough	W 3-1	Eglington 2, Stevenson	39,445
26		22	(h)	Chelsea	W 2-1	Wainwright 2	52,700
27	Feb	5	(a)	Liverpool	D 0-0		50,132
28		12	(a)	Birmingham C	D 0-0		35,098
29		19	(a)	Preston NE	L 1-3	Wainwright	35,496
30		26	(h)	Burnley	W 2-1	Eglington 2	34,568
31	Mar	5	(h)	Blackpool	W 5-0	Wainwright 4, McIntosh	25,548
32		12	(a)	Derby C	L 2-3	Fielding, McIntosh	33,120
33		19	(h)	Aston Villa	L 1-3	Wainwright	50,201
34		26	(a)	Sunderland	D 1-1	McIntosh	36,226
35	Apr	2	(a)	Charlton A	L 1-3	Wainwright	28,529
36		9	(a)	Sheffield U	D 1-1	McIntosh	29,473
37		16	(h)	Arsenal	D 0-0		56,987
38		18	(h)	Charlton A	D 1-1	Eglington	45,059
39		23	(a)	Huddersfield T	D 1-1	Powell	19,051
40		27	(h)	Manchester U	W 2-0	McIntosh, Wainwright	39,106
41	May	4	(h)	Wolves	W 1-0	Eglington	40,488
42		7	(a)	Bolton W	L 0-1		22,725

FINAL LEAGUE POSITION: 18th in Division One

Appearances
Goals

FA Cup

3	Jan	8	(h)	Manchester C	W 1-0	Higgins
4		29	(a)	Chelsea	L 0-2	

Appearances
Goals

Bentham S	Boyes W	Burnett G	Cameron D	Catterick H	Clinton T	Corr P	Dodds E	Dugdale G	Eglington T	Farrell P	Fielding W	Grant J	Greenhalgh N	Hedley J	Higgins W	Humphreys J	Jones TG	Juliussen A	Lello C	Lindley W	McCormick H	McIlhatton J	McIntosh J	Powell A	Sagar E	Saunders G	Stevenson A	Wainwright E	Watson T	
							9	3	11	6	10						5			4		7		8	1	2				1
							9	3	11	6	10						5			4		7		8	1	2				2
							9	3	11	6	10	4				5			8			7			1	2				3
			5				9	3		6		4							10		11	7			1	2		8		4
								3		6	10	4			7	5		9			11				1	2	8			5
										4		6	3	2	7		5	9			11			8	1		10			6
										4		6	3	2	7		5	9			11			8	1		10			7
						7			11	4	8			3	9		5		10						1	2			6	8
4	11						9				8			3			5							7	1	2	10		6	9
4	11						9				8			3		5								7	1	2	10		6	10
4	11						9				8	7		3			5								1	2	10		6	11
4	11										8	6		3			5	9						7	1	2	10			12
4		1							11	6	8			3			5	9						7		2	10			13
4				9					11	6	8			3	7	5									1	2	10			14
4				9					11	6				3			5	10						7	1	2	8			15
4				9					11	6				3	7		5	10							1	2	8			16
8				9		7			11	6	10			3			5			4					1	2				17
8				9		7			11	6	10			3			5			4					1	2				18
8						7			11	6	10			3			5	9		4					1	2				19
8				9		7			11	6	10			3			5			4					1	2				20
						7			11	6	10			3			5	9		4					1	2	8			21
						7			11	6	10			3			5	9		4					1	2	8			22
4						7			11	6	10			3			5		9						1	2	8			23
									11	6	10			3	9		5			4		7		8	1	2				24
						7			11	6	10			3	9		5			4					1	2	8			25
				9					11	6	10			3			5			4					1	2	7	8		26
				9					11	4	10			3			5		6					7	1	2		8		27
				9					11	4	10			3			5		6					7	1	2		8		28
				9		7		3	11	4	10						5		6						1	2		8		29
					2			3	11	4	10				9		5		6					7	1			8		30
					2			3	11	4	10				7		5		6				9		1			8		31
					2			3	11	4	10				7		5		6				9		1			8		32
								3	11	4	10				7		5		6				9		1	2		8		33
					2			3	11	4	10						5		6				9	7	1			8		34
		1						3	11	4	10						5		6				9	7		2		8		35
								3	11	4	10				7		5		6				9		1	2	8			36
								3	11	4	10				7		5		6				9		1	2		8		37
								3	11	4	10						5		6				9		1	2	7	8		38
								3	11	4	10						5		6				9	7	1	2		8		39
								3	11	4	10						5		6				9	7	1	2		8		40
								3	11	4	10						5		6				9	7	1	2		8		41
								3	11	4							5		6				9	7	1	2	10	8		42
13	4	2	1	10	4	10	7	19	34	38	36	7	2	23	14	4	37	10	20	11	4	5	12	19	40	36	19	17	4	
1				3		1	6		7		1							1					5	3			2	10		

1 own-goal

Bentham S	Boyes W	Burnett G	Cameron D	Catterick H	Clinton T	Corr P	Dodds E	Dugdale G	Eglington T	Farrell P	Fielding W	Grant J	Greenhalgh N	Hedley J	Higgins W	Humphreys J	Jones TG	Juliussen A	Lello C	Lindley W	McCormick H	McIlhatton J	McIntosh J	Powell A	Sagar E	Saunders G	Stevenson A	Wainwright E	Watson T	
								3	11	6	10	7		2	9		5			4					1		8			3
				9					11	4	10			3			5		6			7			1	2		8		4
				1				1	2	2	2	1		2	1		2		1	1		1			2	1	1	1		
															1															

1949-50

Manager: Cliff Britton

1	Aug	20	(a)	Middlesbrough	W 1-0	Wainwright	41,722
2		24	(h)	Newcastle U	W 2-1	McIntosh, Wainwright	49,504
3		27	(h)	Liverpool	D 0-0		70,812
4		31	(a)	Newcastle U	L 0-4		43,677
5	Sep	3	(h)	Huddersfield T	W 3-0	Wainwright 3	42,512
6		7	(a)	Manchester U	D 0-0		27,331
7		10	(a)	Portsmouth	L 0-7		36,012
8		17	(h)	Wolves	L 1-2	Corr	59,593
9		24	(a)	Aston Villa	D 2-2	Higgins, Powell	47,186
10	Oct	1	(h)	Charlton A	L 0-1		45,557
11		8	(a)	Arsenal	L 2-5	Higgins, McIntosh	53,224
12		15	(h)	Bolton W	D 0-0		38,421
13		22	(a)	Birmingham C	D 0-0		32,209
14		29	(h)	Derby C	L 1-2	Powell	38,020
15	Nov	5	(a)	West Brom A	L 0-4		29,309
16		12	(h)	Manchester U	D 0-0		46,672
17		19	(a)	Chelsea	L 2-3	Buckle, Higgins	34,190
18		26	(h)	Stoke C	W 2-1	Buckle, McIntosh	27,671
19	Dec	3	(a)	Burnley	L 1-5	Wainwright	19,961
20		10	(h)	Sunderland	L 0-2		33,329
21		17	(h)	Middlesbrough	W 3-1	Buckle 2, Grant	25,864
22		24	(a)	Liverpool	L 1-3	Farrell	50,485
23		26	(h)	Fulham	D 1-1	Farrell	54,726
24		27	(a)	Fulham	D 0-0		36,020
25		31	(a)	Huddersfield T	W 2-1	Catterick, Wainwright	24,277
26	Jan	14	(h)	Portsmouth	L 1-2	Grant	50,428
27		21	(a)	Wolves	D 1-1	Buckle	36,414
28	Feb	4	(h)	Aston Villa	D 1-1	Catterick	43,634
29		18	(a)	Charlton A	L 0-2		30,312
30		25	(h)	Arsenal	L 0-1		43,632
31	Mar	8	(a)	Bolton W	W 2-1	Catterick, Higgins	14,807
32		11	(h)	Chelsea	D 1-1	Catterick	50,328
33		18	(a)	Stoke C	L 0-1		22,187
34		29	(h)	West Brom A	L 1-2	Wainwright	18,630
35	Apr	1	(a)	Manchester U	D 1-1	Grant	37,166
36		7	(h)	Blackpool	W 3-0	Wainwright 2, Buckle	71,008
37		8	(h)	Birmingham C	D 0-0		46,828
38		10	(a)	Blackpool	W 1-0	Catterick	22,942
39		15	(a)	Derby C	L 0-2		15,801
40		22	(h)	Burnley	D 1-1	Catterick	35,784
41		29	(a)	Sunderland	L 2-4	Catterick, Wainwright	23,519
42	May	6	(h)	Manchester C	W 3-1	Catterick 2, Eglington	29,627

FINAL LEAGUE POSITION: 18th in Division One

Appearances

Goals

FA Cup

3	Jan	7	(a)	Queen's Park R	W 2-0	Buckle, Catterick
4		28	(a)	West Ham U	W 2-1	Catterick 2
5	Feb	11	(h)	Tottenham H	W 1-0	Wainwright
6	Mar	4	(a)	Derby C	W 2-1	Buckle, Wainwright
SF		25	(n*)	Liverpool	L 0-2	

* Played at Maine Road.

Appearances

Goals

Buckle E	Burnett G	Catterick H	Corr P	Dugdale G	Eglington T	Falder D	Farrell P	Fielding W	Grant J	Hedley J	Higgins W	Hold O	Humphreys J	Jones TG	Lello C	Lindley W	McIntosh J	Moore E	Powell A	Sagar E	Saudners G	Wainwright E	
			7	3	11		4	10						5	6		9			1	2	8	1
	1		7	3	11		4	10						5	6		9				2	8	2
	1		7	3	11		4	10						5	6		9				2	8	3
	1		7	3	11		4	10						5	6		9				2	8	4
			7	3	11		4	10						5	6		9			1	2	8	5
		9	7	3	11		4	10						5	6					1	2	8	6
		9	7	3	11		4	10						5	6					1	2	8	7
			7	3	11		4						5		6		9		10	1	2	8	8
			7	3			4				9			5	6		11		10	1	2	8	9
			7	3			4				9			5	6		11		10	1	2	8	10
			7	3					4		9		5		6		11		10	1	2	8	11
			7	3	11		4	8					5		6				10	1	2	9	12
			7	3			4	8			11		5		6		9		10	1	2		13
			7	3			4				11		5		6		9		10	1	2	8	14
				3	11		4				7			5	6		9		10	1	2	8	15
11				3			4				7		5		6		9		10	1	2	8	16
11				3			4				7		5		6		9		10	1	2	8	17
7				3	11		4						5		6		9		10	1	2	8	18
7				3	11		4						5		6		9		10	1	2	8	19
7				3	11		4							5	6		9		10	1	2	8	20
7	1				11		4		6		9			5	10			2	8		3		21
7	1				11		8		4					5	6			2	10		3	9	22
7	1	9			11		10		4					5	6			2			3	8	23
7	1	9			11	5	10		4	3					6			2				8	24
7	1	9			11	5	10		4	3					6			2				8	25
7	1	9			11	5	10		4	3					6			2				8	26
7	1	9			11	5	10		4	3					6			2				8	27
	1	9			11	5	10		4	3	7				6			2				8	28
7	1	9			11	5	6	10	4	3								2				8	29
7	1	9			11	5	6	10	4	3								2				8	30
7	1	9			11	5	6	10	4	3	8							2					31
7	1	9			11	5	6	10	4	3	8							2					32
7	1				11	5	6	10	4	3	8	9						2					33
7	1				11	5	10		4		9					6		2			3	8	34
11	1	9				5	10		4	3						6		2	7			8	35
7	1	9			11	5	10		4	3					6			2				8	36
7	1	9			11	5	10		4	3					6			2				8	37
7	1	9			11	5	10		4	3					6			2				8	38
7	1	9			11	5	10		4	3					6			2				8	39
7	1	9			11	5	10		4	3					6			2				8	40
7	1	9			11	5	10		4	3					6			2				8	41
7		9			11	5	10		4	3					6			2		1		8	42
26	24	20	14	20	34	19	41	14	23	18	14	1	9	14	35	2	17	22	16	18	24	37	
6		9	1		1		2		3		4						3		2			11	

Buckle E	Burnett G	Catterick H	Corr P	Dugdale G	Eglington T	Falder D	Farrell P	Fielding W	Grant J	Hedley J	Higgins W	Hold O	Humphreys J	Jones TG	Lello C	Lindley W	McIntosh J	Moore E	Powell A	Sagar E	Saudners G	Wainwright E	
7	1	9			11	5	10		4	3					6			2				8	3
7	1	9			11	5	10		4	3					6			2				8	4
7	1	9			11	5	6	10	4	3								2				8	5
7	1	9			11	5	6	10	4	3								2				8	6
7	1	9			11	5	6	10	4	3								2				8	SF
5	5	5			5	5	5	3	5	5					2			5				5	
2		3																				2	

1950-51

Manager: Cliff Britton

1	Aug	19	(h)	Huddersfield T	W 3-2	Buckle 2, Grant	51,768
2		23	(a)	Middlesbrough	L 0-4		41,478
3		26	(a)	Newcastle U	D 1-1	Catterick	48,720
4		30	(h)	Middlesbrough	W 3-2	Eglington 2, McIntosh	43,459
5	Sep	2	(h)	West Brom A	L 0-3		46,502
6		6	(a)	Arsenal	L 1-2	Farrell	36,576
7		9	(a)	Stoke C	L 0-2		29,383
8		13	(h)	Arsenal	D 1-1	Hold	47,518
9		16	(h)	Liverpool	L 1-3	Eglington	71,150
10		23	(h)	Portsmouth	L 1-5	Catterick	40,281
11		30	(a)	Chelsea	L 1-2	Eglington	34,970
12	Oct	7	(a)	Fulham	W 5-1	Catterick 3, Buckle, Fielding	29,442
13		14	(h)	Bolton W	D 1-1	Buckle	53,421
14		21	(a)	Charlton A	L 1-2	Eglington	27,965
15		28	(h)	Manchester U	L 1-4	McIntosh	51,142
16	Nov	4	(a)	Blackpool	L 0-4		20,902
17		11	(h)	Tottenham H	L 1-2	Buckle	47,125
18		18	(a)	Wolves	L 0-4		31,275
19		25	(h)	Sunderland	W 3-1	Eglington, Hold, Potts	46,060
20	Dec	2	(a)	Aston Villa	D 3-3	Fielding, McIntosh, Potts	27,177
21		9	(h)	Derby C	L 1-2	Wainwright	37,757
22		16	(a)	Huddersfield T	W 2-1	McIntosh 2	12,253
23		23	(h)	Newcastle U	W 3-1	Fielding, Hold, Potts	35,870
24		25	(h)	Burnley	W 1-0	McIntosh	40,864
25		26	(a)	Burnley	D 1-1	Eglington	38,444
26		30	(a)	West Brom A	W 1-0	Eglington	17,912
27	Jan	13	(h)	Stoke C	L 0-3		31,771
28		20	(a)	Liverpool	W 2-0	McIntosh 2	48,688
29	Feb	3	(a)	Portsmouth	L 3-6	Hold, McIntosh, Potts	26,277
30		17	(h)	Chelsea	W 3-0	Farrell, Grant, Hold	33,005
31		28	(h)	Fulham	W 1-0	McIntosh	19,904
32	Mar	3	(a)	Bolton W	L 0-2		36,752
33		10	(h)	Charlton A	D 0-0		31,066
34		17	(a)	Manchester U	L 0-3		31,108
35		24	(h)	Blackpool	L 0-2		61,387
36		26	(h)	Sheffield W	D 0-0		33,331
37		31	(a)	Tottenham H	L 0-3		46,651
38	Apr	7	(h)	Wolves	D 1-1	Farrell	32,786
39		14	(a)	Sunderland	L 0-4		27,283
40		21	(h)	Aston Villa	L 1-2	McIntosh	45,245
41		28	(a)	Derby C	W 1-0	Potts	9,129
42	May	5	(a)	Sheffield W	L 0-6		41,303

FINAL LEAGUE POSITION: 22nd in Division One

Appearances
Goals

FA Cup

3	Jan	6	(a)	Hull C	L 0-2	

Appearances
Goals

Buckle E	Burnett G	Catterick H	Clinton T	Eglington T	Falder D	Farrell P	Fielding W	Gibson D	Grant J	Hampson A	Harris JA	Hold O	Humphreys J	Jones TE	Lindley W	Lindsay J	McIntosh J	Moore E	O'Neill J	Parker J	Potts H	Rankin G	Sagar E	Saunders G	Wainwright E	
7	1	9		11	5	6	10		4									2						3	8	1
7		9		11	5	6	10		4									2	1					3	8	2
7		9		11	5	6	10		4									2	1					3	8	3
7				11	5	6	10		4			8					9	2	1					3		4
7		9		11	5	6	10		4									2	1					3	8	5
7		9	2	11		6	10		4					5					1					3	8	6
7		9	2	11		6	10		4						5				1					3	8	7
7			2	11		6	10		4			9		5					1					3	8	8
7			3	11		6	10		4			9	5					2	1						8	9
7		9	3	11	5	8			4						6		10	2	1							10
7		9	2	11		6	10		4						5			3	1						8	11
7		9	2	11		6	10		4						5			3					1		8	12
7	1		2	11		6	8		4	10					5		9	3								13
7	1		2	11		6	8		4						5		9	3			10					14
7	1		2	11		6	8		4					5			9	3			10					15
7	1		2	11		6	8		4					5			9	3			10					16
7	1		2	11		6	8		4					5			9	3			10					17
7	1		2	11		6	8		4					5			9	3			10					18
			2	11		6	7		4			8		5			9	3			10		1			19
			2	11		6	7		4			8		5			9	3			10		1			20
				11		6	7		4			10		5			9	2				3	1		8	21
				11		6	7		4			8		5			9	2			10	3	1			22
				11		6	7		4			8		5			9	2			10	3	1			23
				11		6	7		4			8		5			9	2			10	3	1			24
				11		6	7		4			8		5			9	2			10	3	1			25
				11		6	7		4			8		5			9	2			10	3	1			26
				11		6	7		4			8		5			9	2			10	3	1			27
				11		6	7		4			8		5			9	2			10	3	1			28
				11		6	7		4			8		5			9	2			10	3	1			29
				11		6	7		4			8		5			9	2			10	3	1			30
7				11		6			4			8		5			9	2			10	3	1			31
7				11		6			4			8		5			9	2			10	3	1			32
				11		6	7		4			8		5			9	2			10	3	1			33
7		9				6			4			8		5		3	11	2			10		1			34
						6	7		4			8		5		3	9	2		11	10		1			35
						10			4		7			5	6		9	2		11	8	3	1			36
		9		11		6	7		4					5				2		10	8	3	1			37
				11		6	7		4					5			9	2		10	8	3	1			38
				11		6			7					5	4		9	2		10	8	3	1			39
7				11		6			4			8		5			9	2			10	3	1			40
		9		11		6		7	4					5		3				10	8		1	2		41
	1	9		11		6	7		4					5		3				10	8			2		42
22	8	13	15	39	6	42	34	1	42	1	1	21	1	30	8	4	29	37	10	7	28	18	24	10	11	
5		5		8		3	3		2			5					11				5				1	

				11		6	7		4			8		5			9	2			10	3	1			3
				1		1	1		1			1		1			1	1			1	1	1			

1951-52

Manager: Cliff Britton

1	Aug	18	(a)	Southampton	L 0-1		25,919
2		22	(h)	Brentford	W 1-0	Buckle	32,722
3		25	(h)	Sheffield W	D 3-3	Buckle 2, Eglington	42,025
4		27	(a)	Brentford	L 0-1		19,525
5	Sep	1	(a)	Leeds U	W 2-1	Eglington 2	16,873
6		5	(h)	Nottingham F	W 1-0	Parker	33,613
7		8	(h)	Rotherham U	D 3-3	Hickson, McNamara, Potts	44,838
8		12	(a)	Nottingham F	L 0-2		24,253
9		15	(a)	Cardiff C	L 1-3	Buckle	23,923
10		22	(h)	Birmingham C	L 1-3	Buckle	37,138
11		29	(a)	Leicester C	W 2-1	Buckle, McNamara	28,114
12	Oct	6	(h)	Blackburn R	L 0-2		39,756
13		13	(a)	Queen's Park R	D 4-4	Buckle 2, Eglington, Parker	17,256
14		20	(h)	Notts C	L 1-5	Parker	49,604
15		27	(a)	Luton T	D 1-1	Parker	16,667
16	Nov	3	(h)	Bury	D 2-2	Buckle 2	25,699
17		10	(a)	Swansea T	W 2-0	Buckle, Fielding	20,271
18		17	(h)	Coventry C	W 4-1	Hickson 2, McNamara, Parker	29,945
19		24	(a)	West Ham U	D 3-3	Fielding, Hickson, Parker	22,141
20	Dec	1	(h)	Sheffield U	W 1-0	Parker	40,127
21		8	(a)	Barnsley	L 0-1		8,003
22		15	(h)	Southampton	W 3-0	Hickson 2, Parker	32,037
23		22	(a)	Sheffield W	L 0-4		38,882
24		25	(a)	Doncaster R	L 1-3	Buckle	23,526
25		26	(h)	Doncaster R	D 1-1	Hickson	47,234
26		29	(h)	Leeds U	W 2-0	Eglington 2	37,616
27	Jan	5	(a)	Rotherham U	D 1-1	Hickson	17,754
28		19	(h)	Cardiff C	W 3-0	Clinton, Hickson, McNamara	49,230
29		26	(a)	Birmingham C	W 2-1	Hickson 2	32,980
30	Feb	9	(h)	Leicester C	W 2-0	Hickson, McNamara	40,535
31		16	(a)	Blackburn R	L 0-1		30,434
32	Mar	1	(h)	Queen's Park R	W 3-0	Clinton, Fielding, Parker	38,172
33		8	(a)	Notts C	D 0-0		29,380
34		15	(h)	Luton T	L 1-3	Parker	37,889
35		22	(a)	Bury	L 0-1		15,325
36		29	(h)	Swansea T	W 2-1	Lello, Parker	20,985
37	Apr	5	(a)	Coventry C	L 1-2	Parker	13,489
38		11	(h)	Hull C	W 5-0	Parker 3, Fielding, Hickson	42,980
39		12	(h)	West Ham U	W 2-0	Clinton, Hickson	36,498
40		14	(a)	Hull C	L 0-1		30,240
41		19	(a)	Sheffield U	W 2-1	Clinton, Eglington	22,182
42		26	(h)	Barnsley	D 1-1	Eglington	26,566

FINAL LEAGUE POSITION: 7th in Division Two

Appearances
Goals

FA Cup

3	Jan	12	(a)	Leyton O	D 0-0	
R		16	(h)	Leyton O	L 1-3	Parker

Appearances
Goals

Buckle E	Catterick H	Clinton T	Cummins G	Donovan D	Eglington T	Farrell P	Fielding W	Gibson D	Grant J	Hickson D	Jones TE	Lello C	Lewis G	Leyland H	Lindley W	Lindsay J	McNamara A	Moore E	O'Neill J	Parker J	Potts H	Rankin G	Sagar E	Saunders G	
7	9				11	10			4		5	6				3		2			8		1		1
7	9				11	6	8		4		5					3		2			10		1		2
7	9			4	11	6	8				5					3		2		10			1		3
7	9			4	11	6	8				2				5	3				10			1		4
				4	11	6	8			9	2				5	3	7			10			1		5
				4	11	6	8			9	2				5	3	7			10			1		6
				4	11	6	8			9	2				5	3	7				10		1		7
				4	11	6	8			9	2				5	3	7			10			1		8
10				4	11	6	8				5					3	7	2		9			1		9
10				4	11	6	8				2				5	3	7			9			1		10
10				4	11		8				5	6		1		3	7	2		9					11
10				4	11		8				5	6		1		3	7			9				2	12
10					11	4	8				5	6		1		3	7			9				2	13
10					11	4	8				5	6		1		3	7			9				2	14
10				4		6	8			9	2			1	5	3	7			11					15
10				4		6	8			9	2			1	5	3	7			11					16
10		2		4	11	6	8			9	5			1			7					3			17
		2		4	11	6	8			9	5			1		3	7			10					18
		2		4	11	6	8			9	5			1		3	7			10					19
		2		4	11	6	8			9	5					3	7		1	10					20
		2		4	11	6		7		9	5					3			1	10	8				21
		2		4	11	6	8			9	5					3	7		1	10					22
		2		4	11	6	8	7		9	5					3			1	10					23
8		2	10	4		6				9	5					3	7		1	11					24
7		2				10	8		4	9	5	6		1		3				11					25
		2		4	11	6	8			9	5			1		3	7			10					26
		2		4	11	6	8			9				1	5	3	7			10					27
		2			11	4	8			9		6			5	3	7		1	10					28
		2			11	10	8		4	9		6			5	3	7		1						29
		2			11	4	8			9		6			5	3	7		1	10					30
		2			11	4	8			9		6			5	3	7		1	10					31
		2	10		11	4	7			9	5	6				3			1	8					32
		2	10		11	4	7			9	5	6				3			1	8					33
		2	10		11	4				9	5	6				3	7		1	8					34
		2	10		11	8			4		5	6	9				7		1			3			35
		2			11	4	8			9	5	6				3	7		1	10					36
		2			11	4	8			9	5	6				3	7		1	10					37
		2			11	4	8			9	5	6				3	7		1	10					38
		2			11	4	8			9	5	6				3	7		1	10					39
		2			11	4	8			9	5	6				3	7		1	10					40
		2			11	4	8			9	5	6				3	7		1	10					41
		2			11	4	8			9	5	6				3	7		1	10					42
15	4	26	5	22	38	40	37	2	5	31	37	21	1	12	13	40	33	5	20	36	4	2	10	3	
12		4			8		4			14		1					5			15	1				

Buckle E	Catterick H	Clinton T	Cummins G	Donovan D	Eglington T	Farrell P	Fielding W	Gibson D	Grant J	Hickson D	Jones TE	Lello C	Lewis G	Leyland H	Lindley W	Lindsay J	McNamara A	Moore E	O'Neill J	Parker J	Potts H	Rankin G	Sagar E	Saunders G	
		2		4	11	6	8			9				1	5	3	7			10					3
7		2		4	11	6	8			9				1	5	3				10					R
1		2		2	2	2	2			2				2	2	2	1			2					
																				1					

1952-53

Manager: Cliff Britton

No	Month	Day	Venue	Opponents	Result	Score	Scorers	Attendance
1	Aug	23	(h)	Hull C	L	0-2		43,035
2		25	(a)	Sheffield U	L	0-1		30,620
3		30	(a)	Blackburn R	L	1-3	Fielding	27,134
4	Sep	3	(h)	Sheffield U	D	0-0		31,554
5		6	(h)	Nottingham F	W	3-0	Parker 2, Fielding	34,254
6		10	(a)	Barnsley	W	3-2	Farrell, Harris, Hickson	10,835
7		13	(a)	Southampton	D	1-1	Harris	18,021
8		20	(a)	Brentford	W	4-2	Parker 2, Potts 2	21,042
9		27	(h)	Doncaster R	W	7-1	Eglington 5, Parker 2	34,344
10	Oct	4	(a)	Swansea T	D	2-2	Hickson 2	22,954
11		11	(h)	Notts C	W	1-0	Fielding	40,626
12		18	(a)	Leicester C	L	2-4	Harris, Parker	36,819
13		25	(h)	West Ham U	W	2-0	Eglington, Harris	38,323
14	Nov	1	(a)	Fulham	L	0-3		26,775
15		8	(h)	Rotherham U	L	0-1		38,808
16		15	(a)	Plymouth A	L	0-1		24,960
17		22	(h)	Leeds U	D	2-2	Eglington, Potts	28,664
18		29	(a)	Luton T	L	2-4	Parker 2	15,160
19	Dec	6	(h)	Birmingham C	D	1-1	Potts	23,858
20		13	(a)	Bury	W	5-0	Potts 3, Eglington, Wainwright	12,549
21		20	(a)	Hull C	L	0-1		15,708
22		26	(a)	Lincoln C	D	1-1	Potts	19,524
23	Jan	1	(h)	Barnsley	W	2-1	Parker, Wainwright	25,485
24		3	(h)	Blackburn R	L	0-3		37,137
25		17	(a)	Nottingham F	D	3-3	Eglington, Fielding, Wainwright	22,298
26		24	(h)	Southampton	D	2-2	Eglington, Wainwright	25,278
27	Feb	7	(h)	Brentford	W	5-0	Hickson 3, Buckle, Eglington	36,431
28		18	(a)	Doncaster R	L	0-3		8,951
29		21	(h)	Swansea T	D	0-0		39,618
30	Mar	5	(a)	Notts C	D	2-2	Lewis 2	7,529
31		7	(h)	Leicester C	D	2-2	Buckle, Hickson	41,005
32		14	(a)	West Ham U	L	1-3	Lewis	19,022
33		25	(h)	Fulham	D	3-3	Parker 2, Fielding	10,829
34		28	(a)	Rotherham U	D	2-2	Hickson, Parker	12,633
35	Apr	4	(h)	Plymouth A	W	2-0	Eglington 2	38,794
36		6	(h)	Huddersfield T	W	2-1	Buckle 2	48,221
37		7	(a)	Huddersfield T	L	2-8	Hickson 2	30,721
38		11	(a)	Leeds U	L	0-2		15,363
39		15	(h)	Bury	W	3-0	Mayers 2, Hickson	11,787
40		18	(h)	Luton T	D	1-1	Buckle	32,948
41		22	(h)	Lincoln C	L	0-3		24,217
42		25	(a)	Birmingham C	L	2-4	Eglington, Hickson	17,083

FINAL LEAGUE POSITION: 16th in Division Two

Appearances
Goals

FA Cup

Round	Month	Day	Venue	Opponents	Result	Score	Scorers
3	Jan	10	(h)	Ipswich T	W	3-2	Hickson 2, Fielding
4		31	(h)	Nottingham F	W	4-1	Parker 2, Clinton, Eglington
5	Feb	14	(h)	Manchester U	W	2-1	Eglington, Hickson
6		28	(a)	Aston Villa	W	1-0	Hickson
SF	Mar	21	(n*)	Bolton W	L	3-4	Parker 2, Farrell

* Played at Maine Road, Manchester

Appearances
Goals

Buckle E	Clinton T	Cummings G	Donovan D	Easthope J	Eglington T	Farrall A	Farrell P	Fielding W	Grant J	Harris JA	Hickson D	Jones TE	Lello C	Lewis G	Leyland H	Lindsay J	McNamara A	Mayers D	Moore E	O'Neill J	Parker J	Potts H	Rankin G	Sagar E	Tansey J	Wainwright E	Woods M	
	2				11		4	8			9	5	6			3	7			1	10							1
					11		4	8	6	7	9	5				3			2	1	10							2
					11		4	8	6	7	9	5				3			2	1	10							3
					11		4	8	6	7	9	5				3			2	1	10							4
					11		4	8	6	7	9	5				3			2	1	10							5
					11		4	8	6	7	9	5				3			2	1	10							6
					11		4	8	6	7	9	5				3			2	1	10							7
					11		4	10	6	7		5				3			2	1	9	8						8
					11		4	10	6	7		5							2	1	9	8	3					9
					11		4		6	7	9	5							2	1	10	8	3					10
					11		4	10	6	7		5				3			2	1	9	8						11
					11		4	10	6	7		5				3			2	1	9	8						12
					11		4	8	6	7	9	5				3			2	1	10							13
					11		4	8	6	7	9	5				3			2	1	10							14
7	2				11		4	10	6			5								1	9	8	3					15
11	2	10	4									5	6				7				9	8	3	1				16
	2	10	4		11							5	6				7			1	9	8	3					17
	2	10			11		4		6			5				3	7			1	9	8						18
	2	10			11		4		6			5				3	7			1	9	8						19
	2				11		4	10			9	5	6			3				1		8				7		20
	2	10			11		4				9	5	6			3				1		8				7		21
	2	10			11		4					5	6			3				1	9	8				7		22
	2	10			11		4					5	6			3				1	9	8				7		23
	2	10			11				4			5	6			3				1	9	8				7		24
	2	10			11		4	8			9	5	6			3				1						7		25
	2	10			11		4				9	5	6			3				1		8				7		26
7	2	8			11		4				9	5	6			3				1	10							27
	2	8			11		4	10				5	6			3	7			1	9							28
7	2	8			11		4				9	5	6							1		10	3					29
	2			11			4	10				5	6	9			7			1		8			3			30
7	2	8	4		11		6				9	5	3							1	10							31
7	2	8	3		11		4					5	6	9						1	10							32
7			4	11				8			9	2	6		1						10		3				5	33
7			2		11		4	8			9	5	6		1						10		3					34
7		10	2		11		4	8			9	5	6			3				1								35
7		10			11		4	8			9	5	6			3				1					2			36
7					11		4	8			9	5	6			3				1		10			2			37
7					11		4	8			9	5	6			2				1	10		3					38
	2	8			11		4				9	5	6		1	3		7			10							39
7	2				11		4	8			9	5	6		1	3					10							40
		8			11	10	4				9	5	6		1	3		7	2									41
7	2				11		4	8			9	5	6		1						10		3					42
14	22	19	7	2	39	1	38	26	17	13	27	42	26	2	6	30	7	2	14	35	32	19	10	1	3	7	1	
5					14		1	5		4	12			3				2			13	8				4		

Buckle E	Clinton T	Cummings G	Donovan D	Easthope J	Eglington T	Farrall A	Farrell P	Fielding W	Grant J	Harris JA	Hickson D	Jones TE	Lello C	Lewis G	Leyland H	Lindsay J	McNamara A	Mayers D	Moore E	O'Neill J	Parker J	Potts H	Rankin G	Sagar E	Tansey J	Wainwright E	Woods M	
	2	10			11		4	7			9	5	6			3				1		8						3
7	2	8			11		4				9	5	6			3				1	10							4
7	2	8			11		4				9	5	6			3				1	10							5
7	2	8			11		4				9	5	6			3				1	10							6
7	2	8			11		4				9	5	6			3				1	10							SF
4	5	5			5		5	1			5	5	5			5				5	4	1						
	1				2		1	1			4										4							

1953-54

Manager: Cliff Britton

1	Aug	19	(a)	Nottingham F	D 3-3	Parker 2, Eglington	21,669
2		22	(a)	Luton T	D 1-1	Buckle	20,217
3		24	(a)	Hull C	W 3-1	Fielding, Hickson, Parker	26,511
4		29	(h)	Oldham A	W 3-1	Parker 3	45,923
5	Sep	2	(h)	Hull C	W 2-0	Buckle, Fielding	35,126
6		5	(a)	Bury	D 2-2	Eglington, Parker	17,650
7		10	(a)	Notts C	W 2-0	McNamara, Parker	12,515
8		12	(h)	Doncaster R	W 4-1	Eglington 2, Parker 2	58,110
9		19	(a)	Blackburn R	D 0-0		32,177
10		23	(h)	Notts C	W 3-2	Hickson 2, Eglington	32,005
11		26	(h)	Derby C	W 3-2	Eglington, Lello, Parker	54,216
12	Oct	3	(a)	Brentford	L 0-1		17,367
13		10	(a)	Plymouth A	L 0-4		26,342
14		17	(h)	Swansea T	D 2-2	Parker 2	48,644
15		24	(a)	Rotherham U	W 2-1	Fielding, Hickson	18,860
16		31	(h)	Leicester C	L 1-2	Eglington	51,811
17	Nov	7	(a)	Stoke C	W 4-2	Hickson 3, Parker	18,653
18		14	(h)	Fulham	D 2-2	Hickson, Parker	36,092
19		21	(a)	West Ham U	D 1-1	Lewis	24,515
20		28	(h)	Leeds U	W 2-1	Buckle, Hickson	55,970
21	Dec	5	(a)	Birmingham C	L 1-5	Parker	23,557
22		12	(h)	Nottingham F	D 3-3	Hickson 2, Parker	33,192
23		19	(h)	Luton T	W 2-1	Eglington, Parker	33,544
24		25	(h)	Bristol R	W 4-0	Hickson 2, Eglington, Wainwright	27,484
25		28	(a)	Bristol R	D 0-0		34,013
26	Jan	16	(h)	Bury	D 0-0		33,705
27		23	(a)	Doncaster R	D 2-2	Hickson, Wainwright	21,203
28	Feb	6	(h)	Blackburn R	D 1-1	Hickson	56,434
29		13	(a)	Derby C	W 6-2	Wainwright 3, Hickson, Lindsay, Parker	16,444
30		24	(h)	Brentford	W 6-1	Hickson 2, Parker 2, Fielding, Wainwright	23,145
31		27	(h)	Plymouth A	W 8-4	Parker 4, Hickson 2, Lello, Lindsay	44,496
32	Mar	6	(a)	Swansea T	W 2-0	Hickson, Parker	20,902
33		13	(h)	Rotherham U	W 3-0	Parker 3	52,302
34		20	(a)	Leicester C	D 2-2	Hickson 2	39,046
35		27	(h)	West Ham U	L 1-2	Wainwright	41,653
36	Apr	3	(a)	Leeds U	L 1-3	Wainwright	22,581
37		10	(h)	Stoke C	D 1-1	Eglington	46,411
38		16	(h)	Lincoln C	W 3-1	Farrell, Fielding, Lewis	61,231
39		17	(a)	Fulham	D 0-0		33,517
40		19	(a)	Lincoln C	D 1-1	Eglington	17,593
41		24	(h)	Birmingham C	W 1-0	Hickson	62,865
42		29	(a)	Oldham A	W 4-0	Parker 2, Hickson, Jones	30,072

FINAL LEAGUE POSITION: 2nd in Division Two

Appearances
Goals

FA Cup

3	Jan	9	(h)	Notts C	W 2-1	Eglington, Hickson
4		30	(h)	Swansea T	W 3-0	Parker 2, Hickson
5	Feb	20	(a)	Sheffield W	L 1-3	Hickson

Appearances
Goals

Buckle E	Clinton T	Donovan D	Eglington T	Farrall A	Farrell P	Fielding W	Grant J	Hickson D	Jones TE	Lello C	Lewis G	Leyland H	Lindsay J	McNamara A	Mayers D	Moore E	O'Neill J	Parker J	Potts H	Rankin G	Wainwright E	
7	2	3	11		4	8		9	5	6							1	10				1
7	2	3	11		4	8		9	5	6		1						10				2
	2	3	11		4	8		9	5	6		1		7				10				3
7	2	5	11		4	8		9		6		1						10		3		4
7		3	11		4	8		9	5	6		1				2		10				5
7		3	11	10	4	8			5	6		1				2		9				6
		2	11		4	8		9	5	6		1	3	7				10				7
		2	11		4	8		9	5	6		1	3	7				10				8
		2	11			8	4	9	5	6		1	3	7				10				9
7		2	11		4	8		9	5	6		1	3					10				10
7		2	11		4	8		9	5	6		1	3					10				11
11		2				8	4	9	5	6		1	3		7			10				12
7		2	11		4	8		9	5	6		1	3					10				13
7		2	11		4	8		9	5	6			3				1	10				14
7		2	11		4	8		9	5	6		1	3					10				15
7		2	11		4	8		9	5	6		1	3					10				16
7		2	11		4			9	5	6			3				1	10			8	17
7		2	11		4			9	5	6			3				1	10			8	18
7		2	11		4				5	6	9		3				1	10			8	19
7	2	5	11			10	4	9		6			3				1				8	20
7	2	5	11		4	8		9		6			3				1	10				21
7		5	11		4	8		9		6			3			2	1	10				22
		5	11		4	8		9		6			3			2	1	10			7	23
		2	11		4	8		9	5	6			3				1	10			7	24
		2	11		4	8		9	5	6			3				1	10			7	25
		2	11		4	8		9	5	6			3				1	10			7	26
		2	11		4	8		9	5	6			3				1	10			7	27
		2	11		4	8		9	5	6			3				1	10			7	28
		2	11		4	8		9	5	6			3				1	10			7	29
		2	11		4	8		9	5	6			3				1	10			7	30
		2	11		4	8		9	5	6			3				1	10			7	31
		2	11		4	8		9	5	6			3				1	10			7	32
		2	11		4	8		9	5	6			3				1	10			7	33
		2	11		4	8		9	5	6			3				1	10			7	34
		2	11		4	8		9	5	6			3				1	10			7	35
		2	11		4	8		9	5	6			3				1	10			7	36
		2	11		4	8		9	5	6			3				1	10			7	37
		3	11		4	8		9	5	6	10					2	1				7	38
		3	11		4	8		9	5	6						2	1		10		7	39
7		3	11		4	8		9	5	6	10					2	1					40
		3	11		4	8		9	5	6						2	1	10			7	41
		3	11		4	8		9	5	6						2	1	10			7	42
19	6	42	41	1	39	39	3	40	37	42	3	14	31	4	1	9	28	38	1	1	23	
3			11		1	5		25	1	2	2		2	1				31			8	

Buckle E	Clinton T	Donovan D	Eglington T	Farrall A	Farrell P	Fielding W	Grant J	Hickson D	Jones TE	Lello C	Lewis G	Leyland H	Lindsay J	McNamara A	Mayers D	Moore E	O'Neill J	Parker J	Potts H	Rankin G	Wainwright E	
		2	11		4	8		9	5	6			3				1	10			7	3
			11		4	8		9	5	6			3			2	1	10			7	4
		2	11		4	8		9	5	6			3				1	10			7	5
		2	3		3	3		3	3	3			3			1	3	3			3	
			1					3										2				

1954-55

Manager: Cliff Britton

1	Aug	21	(a)	Sheffield U	W 5-2	Parker 2, Wainwright 2, Eglington	32,913
2		25	(h)	Arsenal	W 1-0	Eglington	69,034
3		28	(h)	Preston NE	W 1-0	Lello	76,839
4		31	(a)	Arsenal	L 0-2		65,334
5	Sep	4	(a)	Burnley	W 2-0	Eglington, Parker	31,963
6		8	(h)	West Brom A	L 1-2	Jones	55,147
7		11	(h)	Leicester C	D 2-2	Hickson, Lewis	49,684
8		15	(a)	West Brom A	D 3-3	Parker 2, Hickson	32,271
9		18	(a)	Chelsea	W 2-0	Eglington, Parker	59,199
10		25	(h)	Cardiff C	D 1-1	Parker	54,248
11	Oct	2	(a)	Manchester C	L 0-1		45,737
12		9	(a)	Aston Villa	W 2-0	Hickson, McNamara	30,702
13		16	(h)	Sunderland	W 1-0	McNamara	61,189
14		23	(a)	Huddersfield T	L 1-2	Hickson	27,390
15		30	(h)	Manchester U	W 4-2	Jones 2, Eglington, Hickson	63,021
16	Nov	6	(a)	Portsmouth	L 0-5		32,402
17		13	(h)	Blackpool	L 0-1		57,137
18		20	(a)	Charlton A	L 0-5		20,387
19		27	(h)	Bolton W	D 0-0		43,681
20	Dec	4	(a)	Tottenham H	W 3-1	Parker 2, Opp own-goal	31,554
21		11	(h)	Sheffield W	W 3-1	Parker 2, Hickson	36,849
22		18	(h)	Sheffield U	L 2-3	Eglington, Parker	35,088
23		25	(a)	Wolves	W 3-1	Hickson 2, Wainwright	28,494
24		27	(h)	Wolves	W 3-2	Fielding, Hickson, Potts	75,322
25	Jan	1	(a)	Preston NE	D 0-0		33,881
26		15	(h)	Burnley	D 1-1	Fielding	29,520
27	Feb	5	(h)	Chelsea	D 1-1	McNamara	50,658
28		12	(a)	Cardiff C	L 3-4	Parker 2, Lello	17,108
29		23	(h)	Manchester C	W 1-0	Hickson	20,457
30	Mar	5	(a)	Sheffield W	D 2-2	Eglington, Parker	21,716
31		19	(a)	Manchester U	W 2-1	Eglington, Parker	34,152
32		23	(h)	Huddersfield T	W 4-0	Hickson, McNamara, Parker, Opp own-goal	15,561
33		26	(h)	Portsmouth	L 2-3	Jones, Parker	30,087
34	Apr	2	(a)	Blackpool	L 0-4		19,269
35		8	(h)	Newcastle U	L 1-2	Fielding	60,068
36		9	(h)	Tottenham H	W 1-0	Fielding	42,219
37		11	(a)	Newcastle U	L 0-4		45,329
38		16	(a)	Bolton W	L 0-2		26,722
39		20	(a)	Leicester C	D 2-2	Eglington, Hickson	21,122
40		23	(h)	Charlton A	D 2-2	Parker, Wainwright	27,969
41		30	(a)	Sunderland	L 0-3		20,989
42	May	4	(h)	Aston Villa	L 0-1		20,503

FINAL LEAGUE POSITION: 11th in Division One

Appearances
Goals

FA Cup

3	Jan	8	(h)	Southend U	W 3-1	Fielding, Hickson, Potts
4		29	(h)	Liverpool	L 0-4	

Appearances
Goals

Buckle E	Donovan D	Eglington T	Farrall A	Farrell P	Fielding W	Grant J	Hickson D	Jones TE	Lello C	Lewis G	Leyland H	McNamara A	Moore E	O'Neill J	Parker J	Potts H	Rankin G	Saunders R	Tansey J	Wainwright E	Woods M	
	3	11		4	8		9	5	6				2	1	10					7		1
	3	11		4	8		9	5	6				2	1	10					7		2
	3	11		4	8		9	5	6				2	1	10					7		3
	3	11		4	8		9	5	6				2	1	10					7		4
	3	11		4	8		9	5	6				2	1	10					7		5
	3	11		4	8		9	5	6				2	1	10					7		6
	3	11		4	8		9	5	6	10		7	2	1								7
	3	11		4	8		9	5	6			7	2	1	10							8
	3	11		4	8		9	5	6			7	2	1	10							9
	3	11		4	8		9	5	6			7	2	1	10							10
	3	11	8	4			9	5	6	10		7	2	1								11
	3	11		4			9	5	6			7	2	1	10					8		12
	3	11		4			9	5	6			7	2	1	10					8		13
	3	11		4			9	5	6			7	2	1	10					8		14
	3	11		4			9	5	6			7	2	1	10					8		15
11						4	9	5	6		1	7	2		10		3			8		16
	3	11		4			9	5	6			7	2	1	10					8		17
	3	11		4	8		9	5	6				2	1	10					7		18
	3	11		4	8		9	5	6				2	1	10					7		19
	3	11		4	8		9	5	6				2	1	10					7		20
	3	11		4	8		9	5	6				2	1	10					7		21
	3	11		4	8		9	5	6				2	1	10					7		22
	3	11		4	8		9	5	6				2	1		10				7		23
	3	11		4	8		9	5	6				2	1		10				7		24
		11		4	8		9	5	6				2	1		10	3			7		25
		11		4	8		9	5	6				2	1		10	3			7		26
	3	11		4	8		9	5	6			7	2	1	10							27
	3	11		4	8			5	6			7	2	1	10			9				28
	3	11		4	8		9	5	6			7	2	1	10							29
	3	11		4	8		9	5	6			7	2	1	10							30
	3	11		4	8		9	5	6			7	2	1	10							31
	3	11		4	8		9	5	6			7	2	1	10							32
	3	11		4	8		9	5	6			7	2	1	10							33
	2	11		4	8		9		6			7		1	10				3		5	34
	3	11		4	8		9	5	6			7	2	1	10							35
		11		4	8			5	6			7	2	1	10			9	3			36
		11		4	8			5	6			7	2	1	10			9	3			37
		11		4	8		9	5	6			7	2	1	10				3			38
		11		4	8		9	5	6			7	2	1	10				3			39
	3	11		4			9	5	6			7	2	1	10					8		40
	3	11		4			9	5	6	10		7	2	1						8		41
	3	11		4	10		9	5	6			7	2	1						8		42
1	35	41	1	41	33	1	39	41	42	3	1	27	41	41	34	4	3	3	5	24	1	
		9			4		12	4	2	1		4			19	1				4		

2 own-goals

Buckle E	Donovan D	Eglington T	Farrall A	Farrell P	Fielding W	Grant J	Hickson D	Jones TE	Lello C	Lewis G	Leyland H	McNamara A	Moore E	O'Neill J	Parker J	Potts H	Rankin G	Saunders R	Tansey J	Wainwright E	Woods M	
		11		4	8		9	5	6				2	1		10	3			7		3
		11		4	8		9	5	6				2	1		10	3			7		4
		2		2	2		2	2	2				2	2		2	2			2		
					1		1									1						

1955-56

Manager: Cliff Britton

1	Aug	20	(h)	Preston NE	L 0-4		54,357
2		24	(a)	West Brom A	L 0-2		24,254
3		27	(a)	Burnley	W 1-0	Jones	22,482
4		31	(h)	West Brom A	W 2-0	Fielding, J.Harris	38,449
5	Sep	3	(h)	Luton T	L 0-1		44,237
6		7	(a)	Manchester U	L 1-2	Wainwright	28,062
7		10	(a)	Charlton A	W 2-0	J.Harris, Wainwright	22,626
8		14	(h)	Manchester U	W 4-2	Parker 2, Eglington, Wainwright	35,238
9		17	(h)	Tottenham H	W 2-1	Eglington, Parker	42,851
10		24	(a)	Portsmouth	L 0-1		29,901
11	Oct	1	(a)	Newcastle U	W 2-1	Eglington, J.Harris	40,493
12		8	(h)	Arsenal	D 1-1	Wainwright	47,794
13		15	(a)	Bolton W	D 1-1	J.Harris	32,999
14		22	(h)	Aston Villa	W 2-1	J.Harris 2	55,431
15		29	(a)	Sunderland	D 0-0		45,978
16	Nov	5	(h)	Huddersfield T	W 5-2	Mayers 2, Eglington, Lello, Woods	36,423
17		12	(a)	Cardiff C	L 1-3	J.Harris	22,439
18		19	(h)	Manchester C	D 1-1	J.Harris	34,612
19		26	(a)	Wolves	L 0-1		31,251
20	Dec	3	(h)	Chelsea	D 3-3	Eglington, J.Harris, Jones	33,473
21		10	(a)	Blackpool	L 0-4		16,796
22		17	(a)	Preston NE	W 1-0	J.Harris	21,917
23		24	(h)	Burnley	D 1-1	McNamara	35,406
24		26	(a)	Birmingham C	L 2-6	B.Harris, J.Harris	25,541
25		27	(h)	Birmingham C	W 5-1	J.Harris 2, Wainwright 2, Eglington	42,236
26		31	(a)	Luton T	D 2-2	J.Harris, Parker	23,226
27	Jan	14	(h)	Charlton A	W 3-2	Fielding, J.Harris, Lello	44,011
28		21	(a)	Tottenham H	D 1-1	Wainwright	37,119
29	Feb	4	(h)	Portsmouth	L 0-2		36,875
30		11	(h)	Newcastle U	D 0-0		45,670
31		21	(a)	Arsenal	L 2-3	Eglington, J.Harris	16,039
32		25	(h)	Bolton W	W 1-0	Eglington	47,293
33	Mar	7	(a)	Manchester C	L 0-3		15,227
34		10	(h)	Sunderland	L 1-2	J.Harris	49,183
35		17	(a)	Huddersfield T	L 0-1		18,807
36		24	(h)	Cardiff C	W 2-0	McNamara, Wainwright	29,959
37		30	(h)	Sheffield U	L 1-4	Donovan	49,608
38		31	(a)	Aston Villa	L 0-2		28,052
39	Apr	2	(a)	Sheffield U	D 1-1	J.Harris	26,206
40		7	(h)	Wolves	W 2-1	Fielding, B.Harris	37,191
41		14	(a)	Chelsea	L 1-6	J.Harris	13,825
42		21	(h)	Blackpool	W 1-0	Farrell	57,823

FINAL LEAGUE POSITION: 15th in Division One

Appearances
Goals

FA Cup

3	Jan	7	(h)	Bristol C	W 3-1	Eglington, J.Harris, Wainwright
4		28	(a)	Port Vale	W 3-2	Eglington, B.Harris, Wainwright
5	Feb	18	(h)	Chelsea	W 1-0	Farrell
6	Mar	3	(a)	Manchester C	L 1-2	J.Harris

Appearances
Goals

Birch K	Donovan D	Eglington T	Farrall A	Farrell P	Fielding W	Harris A	Harris B	Harris J	Hickson D	Jones TE	Kirby G	Lello C	Lewis G	Leyland H	McNamara A	Mayers D	Moore E	O'Neill J	Parker J	Payne J	Potts H	Rankin G	Tansey J	Wainwright E	Williams G	Woods M	
	3	11		4	8				9	5		6					2	1	10					7			1
		11		4	8				9	5		6	10				2	1					3	7			2
		11		4	10		7	9		5		6					2	1			8		3				3
		11		4	10		7	9		5		6					2	1			8		3				4
		11		4	10		7	9		5		6					2	1			8		3				5
		11		4	8			9		5		6					2	1	10				3	7			6
		11		4	8			9		5		6					2	1	10				3	7			7
		11		4	8			9		5		6					2	1	10				3	7			8
		11		4	8			9		5		6					2	1	10				3	7			9
		11		4	8		7	9		5		6					2	1	10				3				10
		11		4			7	9		5		6					2	1	10				3	8			11
		11		4			7	9		5		6					2	1	10				3	8			12
		11		4				9		5		6				7	2	1	10				3	8			13
		11		4				9				6				7	2	1	10				3	8		5	14
		11		4				9				6				7	2	1	10				3	8		5	15
		11		4				9				6				7	2	1	10				3	8		5	16
				4	7			9		5		6				11	2	1	10				3	8			17
		11		4				9		5		6				7	2	1	10				3	8			18
		11		4				9		5		6				7	2	1	10				3	8			19
		11		4				9		5		6			7		2	1	10				3	8			20
		11		4				9		5		6			7		2	1	10				3	8			21
		11		4	10			9		5		6			7		2	1					3	8			22
		11		4	10			9		5		6			7		2	1					3	8			23
				4	10		7	9		5		6					2	1	11				3	8			24
		11		4	10		7	9		5		6					2	1				3		8			25
		11		4			7	9		5		6					2	1	10			3		8			26
		11		4	10		7	9		5		6					2	1					3	8			27
		11		4	10		7	9		5		6					2	1					3	8			28
		11		4	10		7	9		5		6		1			2						3	8			29
				4	10		11	9		5		6		1	7		2						3	8			30
		11		4	10		7	9		5		6		1			2						3	8			31
		11		4	10		7	9		5		6					2	1					3	8			32
		11		4	10		7	9		5		6					2	1					3	8			33
			8	4	10		7	9		5		6					2	1					3		11		34
	4	11		6	8			9		5							2	1	10				3		7		35
	8	11		4				9		5		6			7		2	1					3	10			36
	8	11		4				9		5		6			7		2	1					3	10			37
	8	11		4	10	1	7	9		5		6					2						3				38
4	8	11		6	10	1		7		5	9						2						3				39
4	8	11		6	10	1	7	9		5							2						3				40
4	8	11		6	10	1	7	9		5							2						3				41
4		11		6	8	1		9		5	10						2			7			3				42
4	8	38	1	42	29	5	20	40	2	39	2	37	1	3	7	7	42	34	20	1	3	2	39	31	2	3	
	1	8		1	3		2	19		2		2			2	2			4					8		1	

Birch K	Donovan D	Eglington T	Farrall A	Farrell P	Fielding W	Harris A	Harris B	Harris J	Hickson D	Jones TE	Kirby G	Lello C	Lewis G	Leyland H	McNamara A	Mayers D	Moore E	O'Neill J	Parker J	Payne J	Potts H	Rankin G	Tansey J	Wainwright E	Williams G	Woods M	
		11		4	10		7	9		5		6					2	1					3	8			3
		11		4	10		7	9		5		6		1			2						3	8			4
		11		4	10		7	9		5		6		1			2						3	8			5
		11		4	10		7	9		5		6					2	1					3	8			6
		4		4	4		4	4		4		4		2			4	2					4	4			
		2		1			1	2																2			

1956-57

Manager: Ian Buchan

1	Aug	18	(a)	Leeds U	L 1-5	Farrell	31,379
2		22	(h)	Blackpool	L 2-3	Farrell, Llewellyn	55,442
3		25	(h)	Bolton W	D 2-2	Llewellyn, McNamara	40,816
4		27	(a)	Blackpool	L 2-5	McNamara 2	14,709
5	Sep	1	(a)	Wolves	L 1-2	Kirby	37,470
6		3	(a)	Burnley	L 1-2	McNamara	24,185
7		8	(h)	Aston Villa	L 0-4		43,726
8		12	(h)	Burnley	W 1-0	Jones	27,591
9		15	(a)	Luton T	L 0-2		18,076
10		22	(h)	Sunderland	W 2-1	Kirby, Mayers	41,595
11		29	(a)	Charlton A	W 2-1	Fielding, Mayers	18,894
12	Oct	6	(a)	Preston NE	D 0-0		21,778
13		13	(h)	Chelsea	L 0-3		34,887
14		20	(a)	Manchester U	W 5-2	Kirby 2, Donovan, Eglington, McNamara	43,677
15		27	(h)	Arsenal	W 4-0	Farrell, Fielding, Jones, Kirby	52,478
16	Nov	3	(a)	West Brom A	L 0-3		23,671
17		10	(h)	Portsmouth	D 2-2	Fielding, Gauld	37,406
18		17	(a)	Newcastle U	D 0-0		32,263
19		24	(h)	Sheffield W	W 1-0	Kirby	34,247
20	Dec	1	(a)	Cardiff C	L 0-1		15,600
21		8	(h)	Birmingham C	W 2-0	Jones, Kirby	29,579
22		15	(h)	Leeds U	W 2-1	Gauld 2	33,765
23		25	(a)	Tottenham H	L 0-6		27,761
24		26	(h)	Tottenham H	D 1-1	Eglington	20,172
25		29	(h)	Wolves	W 3-1	McNamara 2, J.Harris	43,871
26	Jan	12	(a)	Aston Villa	L 1-5	J.Harris	25,274
27		19	(h)	Luton T	W 2-1	Gauld, Mayers	29,017
28	Feb	2	(a)	Sunderland	D 1-1	Fielding	31,463
29		9	(h)	Charlton A	W 5-0	J.Harris 2, Fielding, Gauld, Payne	35,423
30		23	(a)	Arsenal	L 0-2		30,582
31		27	(h)	Preston NE	L 1-4	Payne	23,235
32	Mar	6	(h)	Manchester U	L 1-2	Fielding	34,029
33		9	(a)	Birmingham C	W 3-1	Thomas 2, Williams	23,881
34		16	(h)	West Brom A	L 0-1		36,116
35		23	(a)	Portsmouth	L 2-3	Kirby, McNamara	23,273
36		30	(h)	Newcastle U	W 2-1	Gauld, McNamara	29,775
37	Apr	6	(a)	Sheffield W	D 2-2	McNamara, Temple	22,487
38		13	(h)	Cardiff C	D 0-0		24,397
39		19	(a)	Manchester C	W 4-2	Birch, Gauld, Haughey, Williams	28,009
40		20	(a)	Chelsea	L 1-5	Williams	28,317
41		22	(h)	Manchester C	D 1-1	Temple	28,887
42		27	(a)	Bolton W	D 1-1	Temple	16,016

FINAL LEAGUE POSITION: 15th in Division One — Appearances / Goals

FA Cup

3	Jan	5	(h)	Blackburn R	W 1-0	J.Harris
4		26	(h)	West Ham U	W 2-1	Farrell, Gauld
5	Feb	16	(a)	Manchester U	L 0-1	

Appearances
Goals

Birch K	Donovan D	Dunlop A	Eglington T	Farrall A	Farrell P	Fielding W	Gauld J	Glazzard J	Harris B	Harris J	Haughey W	Jones TE	Kirby G	Lello C	Llewellyn H	McNamara A	Mayers D	Moore E	O'Neill J	Payne J	Rea K	Sutherland J	Tansey J	Temple D	Thomas E	Tomlinson J	Williams G	Woods M	
	8		11		4				7	9		5		6			10	2	1				3						1
			11		4	10				9		2		6	8	7			1				3					5	2
			11		4	10				9		2		6	8	7			1				3					5	3
			11		4	10				9		2		6	8	7			1				3					5	4
			11		4			10				5	9		8	7			1		6	2	3						5
			11		4			10		8		5	9			7			1		6	2	3						6
			11		4			9		8		5		10		7			1		6	2	3						7
	2				4	10			7			5	9		8		11		1		6		3						8
	2				4	10			11			5	9		8		7		1		6		3						9
4	2					10						5	9		8	7	11		1		6		3						10
4	2					10						5	9		8	7	11		1		6		3						11
4	2					10						5	9		8	7	11		1		6		3						12
4	2					10						5	9		8	7	11		1		6		3						13
4	2	1	11		6	10	8					5	9			7							3						14
4	2	1	11		6	10	8					5	9			7							3						15
4	2	1	11		6	10	8					5	9			7							3						16
4	2	1	11		6	10	8					5	9			7							3						17
4	2	1	11		6	10	8					5	9										3			7			18
4	2	1	11		6	10	8					5	9			7							3						19
4	2	1	11		6	10	8					5	9			7							3						20
4	2	1	11		6	10	8					5	9			7							3						21
4	2	1	11		6	10	8					5	9			7							3						22
4	2	1	11		6	10	8					5	9			7							3						23
4	2	1	11			10	8					5	9			7					6		3						24
4	5	1	11			10	8			9						7					6	2	3						25
4	2	1	11		6	10	8			9		5											3			7			26
	5	1	11		4	10	8									7	9				6	2	3						27
	5	1	11		4	10	8			9										7	6	2	3						28
	2	1	11		4	10	8			9		5								7	6		3						29
4	2	1	11		6	10	8			9		5								7			3						30
4	2	1	11		6	10	8			9		5								7			3						31
	2	1	11		4	10	9			7		5									6		3		8				32
4	2	1			6	10						5	9			7							3		8		11		33
4	2	1			6	10						5	9			7							3		8		11		34
4	2	1	11		6	10						5	9			7							3		8				35
4	2	1			6	10	8					5				7							3	9			11		36
4	2	1			6	10						5				7							3	9	8		11		37
4	2	1		10	6							5				7							3	9	8		11		38
4	2	1			6		8				10	5				7							3	9			11		39
4	2	1			6	10						5				7							3	9	8		11		40
4	2	1			6		8				10	5				7							3	9			11		41
4	2	1			6		8				10	5				7							3	9			11		42
29	36	29	27	1	36	34	23	3	3	13	3	39	22	5	10	32	8	1	13	4	15	6	42	7	7	2	9	3	
1	1		2		3	6	7			4	1	3	8		2	10	3			2				3	2		3		

Birch K	Donovan D	Dunlop A	Eglington T	Farrall A	Farrell P	Fielding W	Gauld J	Glazzard J	Harris B	Harris J	Haughey W	Jones TE	Kirby G	Lello C	Llewellyn H	McNamara A	Mayers D	Moore E	O'Neill J	Payne J	Rea K	Sutherland J	Tansey J	Temple D	Thomas E	Tomlinson J	Williams G	Woods M	
4	5	1	11			10	8			9						7					6	2	3						3
	5	1	11		4	10	8						9				7				6	2	3						4
	2	1	11		4	10	8			9		5								7	6		3						5
1	3	3	3		2	3	3			2		1	1			1	1			1	3	2	3						
					1		1			1																			

1957-58

Manager: Ian Buchan

1	Aug	24	(h)	Wolves	W 1-0	J.Harris	58,229
2		28	(a)	Manchester U	L 0-3		59,343
3		31	(a)	Aston Villa	W 1-0	Temple	37,759
4	Sep	4	(h)	Manchester U	D 3-3	Temple 2, J.Harris	71,868
5		7	(h)	Chelsea	W 3-0	Fielding, Hickson, Temple	45,066
6		10	(a)	Arsenal	W 3-2	Fielding, J.Harris, Hickson	42,013
7		14	(h)	Sunderland	W 3-1	Hickson 2, Megan	47,119
8		21	(a)	Luton T	W 1-0	Fielding	19,797
9	Oct	5	(a)	Leicester C	D 2-2	Fielding, Hickson	28,992
10		12	(a)	Newcastle U	W 3-2	B.Harris, Hickson, Opp own-goal	30,472
11		16	(h)	Arsenal	D 2-2	B.Harris, Thomas	54,345
12		19	(h)	Burnley	D 1-1	Temple	45,024
13		26	(a)	Preston NE	L 1-3	J.Harris	31,449
14	Nov	2	(h)	West Brom A	D 1-1	J.Harris	53,579
15		9	(a)	Tottenham H	L 1-3	Temple	39,999
16		16	(h)	Birmingham C	L 0-2		34,875
17		20	(h)	Blackpool	D 0-0		47,765
18		23	(a)	Portsmouth	L 2-3	Temple, Thomas	27,015
19		30	(h)	Sheffield W	D 1-1	Temple	31,011
20	Dec	7	(a)	Manchester C	L 2-6	J.Harris 2	20,912
21		14	(h)	Nottingham F	D 1-1	J.Harris	29,099
22		21	(a)	Wolves	L 0-2		29,447
23		25	(h)	Bolton W	D 1-1	Kirby	29,584
24		26	(a)	Bolton W	W 5-1	B.Harris 2, J.Harris, Hickson, Keeley	23,462
25		28	(h)	Aston Villa	L 1-2	J.Harris	41,195
26	Jan	11	(a)	Chelsea	L 1-3	J.Harris	29,490
27		18	(a)	Sunderland	D 1-1	Thomas	26,507
28	Feb	1	(h)	Luton T	L 0-2		26,908
29		15	(h)	Leicester C	D 2-2	J.Harris, Thomas	23,460
30		22	(h)	Newcastle U	L 1-2	Thomas	22,448
31	Mar	1	(a)	Burnley	W 2-0	Thomas 2	19,657
32		8	(h)	Preston NE	W 4-2	Thomas 4	43,291
33		15	(a)	West Brom A	L 0-4		28,771
34		22	(h)	Portsmouth	W 4-2	Thomas 2, Williams 2	23,179
35		29	(a)	Birmingham C	L 1-2	Thomas	21,628
36	Apr	4	(h)	Leeds U	L 0-1		32,679
37		5	(h)	Tottenham H	L 3-4	Hickson 2, Thomas	30,149
38		7	(a)	Leeds U	L 0-1		25,188
39		12	(a)	Sheffield W	L 1-2	J.Harris	17,514
40		19	(h)	Manchester C	L 2-5	Ashworth 2	31,433
41		23	(a)	Blackpool	W 1-0	Ashworth	12,981
42		26	(a)	Nottingham F	W 3-0	B.Harris 2, J.Harris	16,879

FINAL LEAGUE POSITION: 16th in Division One

Appearances
Goals

FA Cup

3	Jan	4	(a)	Sunderland	D 2-2	Hickson 2
R		8	(h)	Sunderland	W 3-1	Keeley 2, Hickson
4		29	(h)	Blackburn R	L 1-2	J.Harris

Appearances
Goals

Ashworth A	Birch K	Donovan D	Dunlop A	Fielding W	Harris B	Harris J	Haughey W	Hickson D	Jones TE	Keeley J	King J	Kirby G	Labone B	Leeder F	Llewellyn H	McNamara A	Meagan M	O'Neill J	Rea K	Sanders A	Tansey J	Temple D	Thomas E	Williams G	
	4	2	1	10		7		9	5								6				3	8		11	1
	4	2	1	10		7		9	5								6				3	8		11	2
	4	2	1	10	11	7		9	5								6				3	8			3
	4	2	1	10	11	7		9	5								6				3	8			4
	4	2	1	10	11	7		9	5								6				3	8			5
		2	1	10	11	7		9	5								6		4		3	8			6
		2	1	10	11	7		9	5								6		4		3	8			7
		2	1	10	11	7		9	5								6		4		3	8			8
		2	1	10	11	7		9	5								6		4		3	8			9
	4	2	1		11			9	5							7	6				3	8	10		10
	4	2	1		11	7		9	5								6				3	8	10		11
	4	2	1	10	11	7		9	5								6				3	8			12
		2	1	10	11	7		9	5		4						6				3	8			13
		2	1	10	11	7		9	5								6		4		3	8			14
		5	1	10	11	7		9									6		4	2	3	8			15
		5	1	10	11	7		9									6		4	2	3	8			16
		5	1		11	7		9			4								6	2	3	8	10		17
		5	1		11	7		9									6		4	2	3	8	10		18
			1		11	7		9	5								6		4	2	3	8	10		19
		4	1			7		9	5										6	2	3	8	10	11	20
		4	1	10	11	7			5						9				6	2	3	8			21
		4	1	10	11	7			5			9							6	2	3	8			22
		4	1		11	7		9	5			10					6			2	3		8		23
			1		11	7		9	5	10							6		4	2	3		8		24
			1		11	7		9	5	10							6		4	2	3		8		25
			1			7		9	5	10				3			6		4	2			8	11	26
	4	3	1			7			5	10							6			2		9	8	11	27
	4	3	1		7	9	10		5								6			2			8	11	28
		2	1		11	7		9	5								6		4		3	10	8		29
		2	1		11	7		9	5								6		4		3	10	8		30
				10	11	7		9	5								6	1	4	2	3		8		31
				10	11	7		9	5								6	1	4	2	3		8		32
				10	11	7		9	5								6	1	4	2	3		8		33
				10		7		9	5								6	1	4	2	3		8	11	34
			1	10		7		9					5				6		4	2	3		8	11	35
			1	10		7			5								6		4	2	3	9	8	11	36
			1			7		9					5				6		4	2	3	10	8	11	37
		5	1			7		9									6		4	2	3	10	8	11	38
10		5	1			7		9									6		4	2	3		8	11	39
10		5	1			7		9			4						6			2	3		8	11	40
10				8	11	7					4		5				6	1		2	3		9		41
10				8	11	7					4		5				6	1		2	3		9		42
4	10	29	36	24	30	41	1	35	31	4	5	2	4	1	1	1	38	6	27	26	39	28	26	13	
3				4	6	14		9		1		1					1					8	15	2	

1 own-goal

Ashworth A	Birch K	Donovan D	Dunlop A	Fielding W	Harris B	Harris J	Haughey W	Hickson D	Jones TE	Keeley J	King J	Kirby G	Labone B	Leeder F	Llewellyn H	McNamara A	Meagan M	O'Neill J	Rea K	Sanders A	Tansey J	Temple D	Thomas E	Williams G	
			1		11	7		9	5	10							6		4	2	3		8		3
			1		11	7		9	5	10							6		4	2	3		8		R
	4	3	1		11	7			5	10							6			2		9	8		4
	1	1	3		3	3		2	3	3							3		2	3	2	1	3		
						1		3		2															

1958-59

Manager: Johnny Carey

1	Aug	23	(a)	Leicester C	L 0-2		34,446
2		27	(h)	Preston NE	L 1-4	Harburn	52,306
3		30	(h)	Newcastle U	L 0-2		36,602
4	Sep	1	(a)	Preston NE	L 1-3	Hickson	28,339
5		6	(h)	Arsenal	L 1-6	Temple	40,557
6		9	(a)	Burnley	L 1-3	Hickson	23,050
7		13	(a)	Manchester C	W 3-1	Collins, Fielding, J.Harris	35,437
8		17	(h)	Burnley	L 1-2	J.Harris	50,457
9		20	(h)	Leeds U	W 3-2	Jones, King, Opp own-goal	31,105
10		27	(a)	West Brom A	W 3-2	Hickson 2, Fielding	30,598
11	Oct	4	(h)	Birmingham C	W 3-1	Hickson 2, J.Harris	39,408
12		11	(a)	Tottenham H	L 4-10	J.Harris 3, Collins	37,794
13		18	(h)	Manchester U	W 3-2	Thomas 2, J.Harris	64,079
14		25	(a)	Blackpool	D 1-1	O'Hara	19,426
15	Nov	1	(h)	Blackburn R	D 2-2	J.Harris, Hickson	52,733
16		8	(a)	Aston Villa	W 4-2	Jones 2, O'Hara, Thomas	27,649
17		15	(h)	West Ham U	D 2-2	J.Harris, Thomas	40,819
18		22	(a)	Nottingham F	L 1-2	Collins	26,440
19		29	(h)	Chelsea	W 3-1	Hickson 2, Collins	30,638
20	Dec	6	(a)	Wolves	L 0-1		27,074
21		13	(h)	Portsmouth	W 2-1	Thomas 2	23,875
22		20	(h)	Leicester C	L 0-1		27,703
23		26	(h)	Bolton W	W 1-0	Hickson	61,692
24		27	(a)	Bolton W	W 3-0	J.Harris, Hickson, Williams	37,263
25	Jan	1	(a)	Newcastle U	L 0-4		42,475
26		17	(a)	Arsenal	L 1-3	Collins	39,272
27		31	(h)	Manchester C	W 3-1	J.Harris, Hickson, Jones	43,409
28	Feb	7	(a)	Leeds U	L 0-1		18,200
29		18	(h)	West Brom A	D 3-3	Hickson, Laverick, Temple	32,629
30		21	(a)	Birmingham C	L 1-2	J.Harris	22,660
31		28	(h)	Tottenham H	W 2-1	Collins, Thomas	36,782
32	Mar	7	(a)	Manchester U	L 1-2	Opp own-goal	51,254
33		14	(h)	Blackpool	W 3-1	Hickson, Laverick, Thomas	34,562
34		21	(a)	Blackburn R	L 1-2	B.Harris	26,914
35		27	(a)	Luton T	W 1-0	Opp own-goal	22,954
36		28	(h)	Aston Villa	W 2-1	Hickson, Parker	34,986
37		30	(h)	Luton T	W 3-1	J.Harris 2, Thomas	32,620
38	Apr	4	(a)	West Ham U	L 2-3	Hickson, Laverick	28,266
39		11	(h)	Nottingham F	L 1-3	Hickson	26,208
40		15	(a)	Portsmouth	W 3-2	Collins, Laverick, Thomas	12,714
41		18	(a)	Chelsea	L 1-3	Laverick	24,366
42		25	(h)	Wolves	L 0-1		29,414

FINAL LEAGUE POSITION: 16th in Division One

Appearances
Goals

FA Cup

3	Jan	10	(h)	Sunderland	W 4-0	Hickson 2, J.Harris, Thomas
4		24	(a)	Charlton A	D 2-2	Collins, Thomas
R		28	(h)	Charlton A	W 4-1	Collins 2, Hickson 2
5	Feb	14	(h)	Aston Villa	L 1-4	Hickson

Appearances
Goals

Ashworth A	Bramwell J	Collins R	Dunlop A	Fielding W	Griffiths B	Harburn P	Harris B	Harris J	Hickson D	Jones TE	King J	Labone B	Laverick R	Meagan M	O'Hara E	O'Neill J	Parker A	Rea K	Sanders A	Tansey J	Temple D	Thomas E	Williams G	
10			1			9		7		5				6	11			4	2	3		8		1
10			1			9		7		5				6	11			4	2	3		8		2
				10		9		7		5	4			6		1			2	3		8	11	3
				10	3	9		7	8	5	4			6	11	1			2					4
				10	3		4	7	9	5				6	11	1			2		8			5
	3			10			6	7	9	5	4				11	1			2		8			6
	3	8		10			6	7	9	5	4				11	1			2					7
	3	8		10			6	7	9	5	4				11	1			2					8
10	3			7			6	8	9	5	4				11	1			2					9
	3			7			6	8	9	5	4				11	1			2			10		10
	3	10		7			6	8	9	5	4				11	1			2					11
	3	10	1	7			6	8	9	5	4				11				2					12
10	3		1				6	7	9	5	4				11				2			8		13
	3	10	1				6	7	9	5	4				11				2			8		14
	3	10	1				6	7	9	5	4				11				2			8		15
	3	10	1				6	7	9	5	4				11		2					8		16
	3	10	1				6	7	9	5	4				11		2					8		17
	3	10	1				6	7	9	5	4				11		2					8		18
	3	10	1				6	7	9	5	4				11		2					8		19
	3	10	1				6	7	9	5	4				11		2					8		20
	3	10	1				6	7	9	5				4					2			8	11	21
	3	10	1				6	7	9	5							4		2			8	11	22
	3	10	1				6	7	9	5							4		2			8	11	23
	3	10	1				6	7	9	5							4		2			8	11	24
	3	10	1				6	7	9	5							4		2			8	11	25
	3	10	1				6	7	9	5							4		2			8	11	26
	3	10	1				6	7	9	5					11		4		2			8		27
	3	10	1					7	9	5				6	11		4		2			8		28
	3	10	1					7	9	5			11	6			4		2		8			29
	3	10	1					7	9			5	11	6			4		2		8			30
	3	10	1				4	7	9	5			11	6			2					8		31
	3	10	1				4	7	9	5			11	6			2					8		32
	3	10	1				4	7	9	5			11	6			2					8		33
	3	10	1				11	7	9	5				6			2	4				8		34
	3	10	1				11	7	9	5				6			2	4				8		35
11	3	10	1				4	7	9			5		6			2					8		36
	3	10	1				4	7	9			5	11	6			2					8		37
	3	10	1				4	7	9			5	11	6			2					8		38
10	3		1				4	7	9	5			11	6	11		2					8		39
	3	10	1				4	7	9	5			11	6			2					8		40
	3	10	1				4	7	9	5			11	6			2					8		41
	3	10	1				4	7	9	5			11	6			2					8		42
6	37	32	33	10	2	4	35	42	39	38	17	4	11	21	21	9	26	4	25	3	4	32	7	
		7		2		1	1	14	17	4	1		5		2		1				2	10	1	

3 own-goals

Ashworth A	Bramwell J	Collins R	Dunlop A	Fielding W	Griffiths B	Harburn P	Harris B	Harris J	Hickson D	Jones TE	King J	Labone B	Laverick R	Meagan M	O'Hara E	O'Neill J	Parker A	Rea K	Sanders A	Tansey J	Temple D	Thomas E	Williams G	
	3	10	1				6	7	9	5							4		2			8	11	3
	3	10	1				6	7	9	5							4		2			8	11	4
	3	10	1				6	7	9	5					11		4		2			8		R
	3	10	1				6	7	9	5					11		4		2			8		5
	4	4	4				4	4	4	4					2		4		4			4	2	
		3						1	5													2		

1959-60

Manager: Johnny Carey

1	Aug	22	(h)	Luton T	D	2-2	J.Harris, Hickson	38,539
2		25	(a)	Burnley	L	2-5	Thomas, Opp own-goal	29,165
3		29	(a)	Bolton W	L	1-2	Hickson	26,792
4	Sep	2	(h)	Burnley	L	1-2	Wignall	39,416
5		5	(h)	Fulham	D	0-0		31,980
6		12	(a)	Nottingham F	D	1-1	Opp own-goal	26,668
7		16	(h)	Blackburn R	W	2-0	Hickson 2	41,813
8		19	(h)	Sheffield W	W	2-1	Shackleton 2	37,375
9		21	(a)	Blackburn R	L	1-3	Collins	27,012
10		26	(a)	Wolves	L	0-2		35,230
11	Oct	3	(h)	Arsenal	W	3-1	Collins, Laverick, Thomas	40,587
12		10	(a)	Leeds U	D	3-3	Hickson 2, Collins	19,122
13		17	(h)	West Ham U	L	0-1		30,563
14		24	(a)	Chelsea	L	0-1		37,114
15		31	(h)	Leicester C	W	6-1	Thomas 2, Collins, B.Harris, Parker, Shackleton	22,587
16	Nov	7	(a)	Newcastle U	L	2-8	Thomas 2	23,727
17		14	(h)	Birmingham C	W	4-0	Shackleton 3, J.Harris	19,172
18		21	(a)	Tottenham H	L	0-3		39,432
19		28	(h)	Manchester U	W	2-1	Collins, Thomas	46,095
20	Dec	5	(a)	Preston NE	D	0-0		24,463
21		12	(h)	West Brom A	D	2-2	Shackleton, Thomas	25,769
22		19	(a)	Luton T	L	1-2	J.Harris	9,799
23		26	(h)	Manchester C	W	2-1	Collins, Shackleton	43,351
24		28	(a)	Manchester C	L	0-4		30,580
25	Jan	2	(h)	Bolton W	L	0-1		37,513
26		16	(a)	Fulham	L	0-2		21,226
27		23	(h)	Nottingham F	W	6-1	Thomas 3, Collins, Parker, Shackleton	32,279
28	Feb	6	(a)	Sheffield W	D	2-2	Shackleton, Thomas	33,066
29		13	(h)	Wolves	L	0-2		51,135
30		20	(a)	Arsenal	L	1-2	Vernon	28,702
31		27	(h)	Preston NE	W	4-0	Vernon 2, J.Harris, Lill	50,990
32	Mar	5	(a)	West Ham U	D	2-2	Vernon 2	25,029
33		12	(h)	Chelsea	W	6-1	Ring 2, Collins, J.Harris, Lill, Vernon	50,963
34		19	(a)	West Brom A	L	2-6	Collins, J.Harris	24,774
35		25	(h)	Newcastle U	L	1-2	Collins	54,868
36	Apr	2	(a)	Birmingham C	D	2-2	J.Harris, Vernon	24,872
37		9	(h)	Tottenham H	W	2-1	Collins, J.Harris	57,959
38		15	(h)	Blackpool	W	4-0	Vernon 2, Collins, J.Harris	65,719
39		16	(a)	Leicester C	D	3-3	Collins 2, Lill	22,390
40		18	(a)	Blackpool	D	0-0		25,697
41		23	(h)	Leeds U	W	1-0	Tyrer	37,885
42		30	(a)	Manchester U	L	0-5		43,878

FINAL LEAGUE POSITION: 16th in Division One

Appearances
Goals

FA Cup

3	Jan	9	(a)	Bradford C	L	0-3	

Appearances
Goals

Ashworth A	Bramwell J	Collins R	Dunlop A	Gabriel J	Godfrey B	Harris B	Harris J	Hickson D	Jones TE	King J	Labone B	Laverick R	Lill M	Meagan M	O'Hara E	O'Neill J	Parker A	Ring T	Sanders A	Shackleton A	Tansey J	Thomas E	Tyrer A	Vernon R	Wignall F	
		10	1			4	7	9	5					6	11		2				3	8				1
	3	10	1			4	7	9	5					6	11		2					8				2
		10	1			4	7	9	5					6	11		2				3	8				3
		10	1			6	7	9	5	4					11		2		3						8	4
		10	1			6	7	9	3	4	5				11				2						8	5
		10	1			6	7		3	4	5				11				2	9					8	6
		10	1			6	7	9	3	4	5								2	11					8	7
		10	1			6	7	9	3	4	5								2	11					8	8
10		7	1			6		9	3	4	5						2			11					8	9
		10	1			6		9	3	4	5	11					2			7		8				10
		10	1			6	7		3	4	5	11					2			9		8				11
	3	10	1			6	7	9	5	4							2			11		8				12
	3	10	1			6	7	9	5	4							2			11		8				13
	3	10	1			6	7	9	5	4							2			11		8				14
	3	10	1			6	7		5	4		11					2			9		8				15
	3	10	1			6	7		5	4		11					2			9		8				16
		10	1			6	7		3	4	5	11					2			9		8				17
		10	1			6	7		3	4	5	11					2			9		8				18
		10	1			6	7		3	4	5	11					2			9		8				19
		10	1			6	7		3	4	5	11					2			9		8				20
		10	1			6	7		3	4	5	11					2			9		8				21
		10	1			6	7		3	4	5	11					2			9		8				22
	3	10	1			6	7		5	4		11					2			9		8				23
	3	10	1			6	7		5	4					11		2			9		8				24
8		10	1			6	7		3	4	5				11		2			9						25
		10			11				3	4	5			6		1	2			9		8	7			26
		10					7		3	4	5			6		1	2	11		9		8				27
		10				7			3	4	5			6		1	2	11		9		8				28
	3	8					7			4	5			6		1	2	11		9				10		29
	3	8				4					5		7	6		1	2	11		9				10		30
	3	8	1			4	9				5		7	6			2	11						10		31
	3	8	1	4			9				5		7	6			2	11						10		32
	3	8	1	4			9				5		7	6			2	11						10		33
	3	8	1	4			9				5		7	6			2	11						10		34
	3	8	1	4			9				5		7	6			2	11						10		35
		8	1			4	9		3		5		7	6			2	11						10		36
		8	1			4	9		3		5		7	6			2	11						10		37
		8	1			4	9		3		5		7	6			2	11						10		38
		10	1	4			9		3		5		7	6			2	11					8			39
		8	1	4			9		3		5		7	6			2	11						10		40
		10	1	4			9		3		5		7	6			2	11					8			41
		8	1	4		6			3		5						2	11		9			7	10		42
2	15	42	37	8	1	32	36	12	35	26	31	11	12	19	8	5	38	16	5	26	2	21	4	12	6	
		14				1	9	6				1	3				2	2		10		12	1	9	1	

2 own-goals

		10	1			6	7		3	4	5	11					2			9					8	3
		1	1			1	1		1	1	1	1					1			1					1	

1960-61

Manager: Johnny Carey

1	Aug	20	(a)	Tottenham H	L 0-2		50,393
2		24	(h)	Manchester U	W 4-0	Collins 2, Lill 2	51,602
3		27	(h)	Leicester C	W 3-1	Ring 2, Collins	45,215
4		31	(a)	Manchester U	L 0-4		51,915
5	Sep	3	(a)	Aston Villa	L 2-3	Temple, Vernon	32,864
6		5	(a)	Blackpool	W 4-1	Collins, J.Harris, Temple, Vernon	24,945
7		10	(h)	Wolves	W 3-1	Vernon 2, J.Harris	53,728
8		14	(h)	Blackpool	W 1-0	Lill	46,943
9		17	(a)	Bolton W	W 4-3	Lill 2, Collins, Vernon	30,405
10		24	(h)	West Ham U	W 4-1	Vernon 2, Lill, Ring	46,291
11	Oct	1	(a)	Chelsea	D 3-3	Collins, Lill, Ring	31,457
12		8	(h)	Preston NE	D 0-0		36,717
13		15	(a)	Fulham	W 3-2	J.Harris 2, Vernon	30,603
14		24	(h)	Manchester C	W 4-2	Vernon 2, Collins, Temple	53,781
15		29	(a)	Nottingham F	W 2-1	Bingham, B.Harris	20,720
16	Nov	5	(h)	West Brom A	D 1-1	Opp own-goal	40,705
17		12	(a)	Cardiff C	D 1-1	Bingham	19,234
18		19	(h)	Newcastle U	W 5-0	Collins 3, Vernon, Wignall	41,123
19		26	(a)	Arsenal	L 2-3	Collins, Vernon	36,588
20	Dec	3	(h)	Sheffield W	W 4-2	Vernon 2, J.Harris, Opp own-goal	50,702
21		10	(a)	Birmingham C	W 4-2	Wignall 2, Bingham, Tyrer	27,717
22		17	(h)	Tottenham H	L 1-3	Wignall	61,052
23		26	(a)	Burnley	W 3-1	Bingham, Collins, B.Harris	44,232
24		27	(h)	Burnley	L 0-3		74,867
25		31	(a)	Leicester C	L 1-4	B.Harris	23,495
26	Jan	21	(a)	Wolves	L 1-4	Bingham	31,119
27	Feb	4	(h)	Bolton W	L 1-2	Collins	35,654
28		11	(a)	West Ham U	L 0-4		22,322
29		18	(h)	Chelsea	D 1-1	Vernon	34,449
30		25	(a)	Preston NE	L 0-1		17,812
31	Mar	4	(h)	Fulham	W 1-0	Gabriel	35,840
32		11	(a)	Manchester C	L 1-2	Vernon	29,751
33		18	(h)	Nottingham F	W 1-0	Bingham	27,579
34		22	(h)	Aston Villa	L 1-2	Wignall	28,115
35		25	(a)	West Brom A	L 0-3		20,590
36		31	(a)	Blackburn R	W 3-1	Young 2, Vernon	24,982
37	Apr	1	(h)	Birmingham C	W 1-0	Temple	31,872
38		3	(h)	Blackburn R	D 2-2	Bingham, Young	41,991
39		8	(a)	Newcastle U	W 4-0	Bingham 2, Vernon, Wignall	30,342
40		15	(h)	Cardiff C	W 5-1	Collins 3, Young 2	34,382
41		22	(a)	Sheffield W	W 2-1	Wignall 2	26,601
42		29	(h)	Arsenal	W 4-1	Vernon 3, Young	39,810

FINAL LEAGUE POSITION: 5th in Division One

Appearances
Goals

FA Cup

3	Jan	7	(h)	Sheffield U	L 0-1	

Appearances
Goals

League Cup

1	Oct	12	(h)	Accrington S	W 3-1	Wignall 2, J.Harris
2		31	(h)	Walsall	W 3-1	Collins, Vernon, Webber
3	Nov	23	(h)	Bury	W 3-1	Wignall 2, J.Harris
4	Dec	21	(a)	Tranmere R	W 4-0	Wignall 3, Bingham
5	Feb	15	(a)	Shrewsbury T	L 1-2	Young

Appearances
Goals

Bentley J	Bingham W	Collins R	Dunlop A	Fell J	Gabriel J	Green C	Harris B	Harris J	Jones TE	Kavanagh P	Labone B	Lill M	Meagan M	Parker A	Parnell R	Ring T	Sharples G	Temple D	Thomson G	Tyrer A	Vernon R	Webber K	Wignall F	Young A	
		8	1		4			9	3		5	7	6	2		11					10				1
		8	1		4			9	3		5	7	6	2		11					10				2
		8	1		4			9	3		5		6	2		11		7			10				3
		8	1		4			9	3		5		6	2		11		7			10				4
		8	1		4		6	9	3		5			2		11		7			10				5
		8	1		4	3	6	9			5			2		11		7			10				6
		8	1		4	3	6	9			5			2		11		7			10				7
		8	1		4		6	9	3		5	7		2		11					10				8
		8	1		4		6	9	3		5	7		2		11					10				9
		8	1		4		6	9	3		5	7		2		11					10				10
		8	1		4		6	9	3		5	7		2		11					10				11
		8	1		4		6	9	3		5	7		2						11	10				12
	7	8	1		4	3	6	9			5	11		2							10				13
	7	8	1		4	3	6	9			5			2				11			10				14
	7	8	1		4	3	6	9			5			2				11			10				15
	7	8	1			3	6	9			5			2			4	11			10				16
	7	8	1		4	3	6	9			5			2				11			10				17
	7	8	1		4		6		3		5			2				11			10		9		18
	7	8	1		4		6	11			5			2					3		10		9		19
	7	8	1		4		6	11			5			2					3		10		9		20
	7	10	1		4		6				5			2				11	3	8			9		21
	7	10	1		4		6				5			2				11	3				9	9	22
	7	8	1		4		6				5			2				11	3		10		9		23
	7	8	1		4		6				5			2				11	3		10		9		24
	7	8	1		4		6				5			2				11	3		10		9		25
	7	8	1		4		11		3		5				2		6				10		9		26
7		8	1		4		6		3		5			2				11			10			9	27
	7		1		4		11				5			2			6		3		10		9	8	28
		8	1		4		6			11	5			2					3		10	9		7	29
			1		4		6			11	5			2				7	3		10		8	9	30
	7	8	1		4		6			11	5			2					3		10			9	31
	7	8	1		4		6			11	5			2					3		10			9	32
	7	8	1		4		6			11	5			2					3		10			9	33
	7	10	1	11	4						5			2			6		3	8			9		34
	7	8	1				4			11	5			2			6		3		10		9		35
	7	8	1	11	4						5		6	2					3		10			9	36
	7	8	1		4						5		6	2				11	3		10			9	37
	7	8	1	11	4						5		6	2					3		10			9	38
	7	8	1		4						5		6	2				11	3		10		9		39
	7	8	1	11	4						5		6	2					3		10			9	40
	7	8	1	11	4						5		6	2					3		10		9		41
		8	1	11	4						5		6	2				7	3		10			9	42
1	26	40	42	6	40	7	30	19	13	6	42	8	11	41	1	11	5	20	22	3	39	1	15	13	
	9	16			1		3	5				7				4		4		1	21		8	6	

2 own-goals

Bentley J	Bingham W	Collins R	Dunlop A	Fell J	Gabriel J	Green C	Harris B	Harris J	Jones TE	Kavanagh P	Labone B	Lill M	Meagan M	Parker A	Parnell R	Ring T	Sharples G	Temple D	Thomson G	Tyrer A	Vernon R	Webber K	Wignall F	Young A	
	11	8	1		4		6		3		5			2						7	10		9		3
	1	1	1		1		1		1		1			1						1	1		1		

Bentley J	Bingham W	Collins R	Dunlop A	Fell J	Gabriel J	Green C	Harris B	Harris J	Jones TE	Kavanagh P	Labone B	Lill M	Meagan M	Parker A	Parnell R	Ring T	Sharples G	Temple D	Thomson G	Tyrer A	Vernon R	Webber K	Wignall F	Young A	
		8	1		4		6	7	3		5	11		2							10		9		1
	7	8	1		4	3	6		5					2				11			10	9			2
	7	10	1		4		6	8	3		5			2				11					9		3
	7	8	1		4		6				5			2				11	3		10		9		4
		8	1		4		11				5			2			6		3		10	9		7	5
	3	5	5		5	1	5	2	3		4	1		5			1	3	2		4	2	3	1	
	1	1						2													1	1	7	1	

1961-62

Manager: Harry Catterick

1	Aug	19	(h)	Aston Villa	W 2-0	Bingham, Young	52,289
2		23	(a)	West Brom A	L 0-2		21,594
3		26	(a)	Fulham	L 1-2	Temple	23,137
4		30	(h)	West Brom A	W 3-1	Bingham, Lill, Vernon	36,559
5	Sep	2	(h)	Sheffield W	L 0-4		42,596
6		6	(h)	Manchester C	L 0-2		38,023
7		9	(a)	Leicester C	L 0-2		19,889
8		16	(h)	Ipswich T	W 5-2	Temple 3, Bingham, Young	35,259
9		20	(a)	Manchester C	W 3-1	Temple, Wignall, Young	35,102
10		23	(a)	Burnley	L 1-2	Thomson	35,776
11		30	(h)	Arsenal	W 4-1	Vernon 2, Bingham, Gabriel	43,310
12	Oct	7	(h)	Nottingham F	W 6-0	Fell 2, Vernon 2, Gabriel, Young	42,431
13		14	(a)	Wolves	W 3-0	Gabriel, Young, Opp own-goal	31,648
14		21	(h)	Sheffield U	W 1-0	Vernon	42,888
15		28	(a)	Chelsea	D 1-1	Vernon	25,535
16	Nov	4	(h)	Tottenham H	W 3-0	Wignall 2, Bingham	54,234
17		11	(a)	Blackpool	D 1-1	Fell	23,026
18		18	(h)	Blackburn R	W 1-0	Vernon	40,359
19		25	(a)	West Ham U	L 1-3	Vernon	27,100
20	Dec	2	(h)	Manchester U	W 5-1	Vernon 2, Collins, Fell, Young	48,099
21		9	(a)	Cardiff C	D 0-0		15,782
22		16	(a)	Aston Villa	D 1-1	Collins	34,939
23		23	(h)	Fulham	W 3-0	Collins 2, Vernon	30,391
24		26	(h)	Bolton W	W 1-0	Bingham	45,462
25	Jan	13	(a)	Sheffield W	L 1-3	Vernon	31,051
26		20	(h)	Leicester C	W 3-2	Collins, Green, Vernon	33,934
27	Feb	3	(a)	Ipswich T	L 2-4	Bingham, B.Harris	22,572
28		10	(h)	Burnley	D 2-2	Vernon 2	54,369
29		24	(a)	Nottingham F	L 1-2	Vernon	22,499
30	Mar	3	(h)	Wolves	W 4-0	Vernon 2, Wignall 2	40,548
31		14	(a)	Sheffield U	D 1-1	Bingham	21,073
32		17	(h)	Chelsea	W 4-0	Young 2, Temple, Vernon	37,215
33		24	(a)	Tottenham H	L 1-3	Temple	47,343
34		30	(h)	Blackpool	D 2-2	Young 2	38,302
35	Apr	4	(a)	Bolton W	D 1-1	Vernon	20,428
36		7	(a)	Blackburn R	D 1-1	Stevens	13,047
37		14	(h)	West Ham U	W 3-0	Stevens, Temple, Vernon	35,108
38		20	(h)	Birmingham C	W 4-1	Gabriel, Temple, Vernon, Young	47,506
39		21	(a)	Manchester U	D 1-1	Stevens	31,926
40		24	(a)	Birmingham C	D 0-0		21,910
41		28	(h)	Cardiff C	W 8-3	Vernon 3, Bingham, Gabriel, Stevens, Temple, Young	31,186
42	May	1	(a)	Arsenal	W 3-2	Young 2, Gabriel	20,030

FINAL LEAGUE POSITION: 4th in Division One

Appearances
Goals

FA Cup

3	Jan	6	(h)	King's Lynn	W 4-0	Bingham, Collins, Fell, Vernon
4		27	(h)	Manchester C	W 2-0	Lill, Vernon
5	Feb	17	(a)	Burnley	L 1-3	Collins

Appearances
Goals

Bingham W	Collins R	Dunlop A	Fell J	Gabriel J	Gannon M	Green C	Harris B	Jones TE	Labone B	Lill M	Meagan M	Parker A	Parnell R	Stevens D	Temple D	Thomson G	Tyrer A	Vernon R	Webber K	West G	Wignall F	Young A	
7	8	1	11	4					5		6	2				3		10				9	1
7	8	1	11	4					5		6	2				3		10				9	2
9		1	11	4					5	7	6		2		8	3		10					3
7		1		4					5	11	6	2				3	8	10	9				4
7		1		4					5	11	6	2				3	8	10				9	5
7		1		4				5		11	6	2				3		10	9			8	6
7		1		4					5	11	6	2			10	3					9	8	7
7		1	11	4			6		5			2			10	3					9	8	8
		1	11	4			6		5	7		2			10	3					9	8	9
7		1	11	4			6		5			2			10	3					9	8	10
7	8	1	11	4			6		5			2				3		10				9	11
7	8	1	11	4			6		5			2				3		10				9	12
7	8	1	11	4			6		5			2				3		10				9	13
	8	1	11	4			6		5	7		2				3		10				9	14
	8	1	11	4			6		5			2				3		10			7	9	15
7		1	11	4			6		5			2				3		10			9	8	16
7		1	11	4		2	6		5							3		10			9	8	17
7		1	11	4		2	6		5							3		10			9	8	18
7	8	1	11	4			6		5			2				3		10				9	19
7	8	1	11	4			6		5			2				3		10				9	20
7	8	1	11	4			6		5			2				3		10				9	21
7	8	1	11	4			6		5			2				3		10				9	22
7	8	1	11	4			6		5			2				3		10				9	23
7	8	1	11	4			6		5			2				3		10				9	24
7	11	1		4		3	6		5			2						10			8	9	25
7	8	1	11	4		3	6		5			2						10				9	26
7	8	1		4		3	6		5	11		2						10				9	27
7	8	1		4		3	6		5	11		2						10				9	28
	8	1		4		3	6		5	7		2						10			9	11	29
7	8			4		3	6		5			2						10		1	9	11	30
7				4	3				5		6	2		8	9			10		1		11	31
7				4	3				5		6	2		8	11			10		1		9	32
7				4			6		5		3	2		8	11			10		1		9	33
7				4			6		5			2		8	11	3		10		1		9	34
7				4			6		5		2			8	11	3		10		1		9	35
7				4	3		6		5		2			8	11				9	1		10	36
7		1		4			6		5		2			8	11	3		10				9	37
7				4			6		5		2			8	11	3		10		1		9	38
				4			6		5	7	2			8	11	3		10		1		9	39
7				4			6		5		2			8	11	3		10		1		9	40
7				4			6		5		2			8	11	3		10		1		9	41
7				4			6		5		2			8	11	3		10		1		9	42
37	19	30	21	42	3	8	33	1	41	11	18	31	1	12	17	32	2	37	3	12	11	40	
9	5		4	6		1	1			1				4	10	1		26			5	14	

1 own-goal

Bingham W	Collins R	Dunlop A	Fell J	Gabriel J	Gannon M	Green C	Harris B	Jones TE	Labone B	Lill M	Meagan M	Parker A	Parnell R	Stevens D	Temple D	Thomson G	Tyrer A	Vernon R	Webber K	West G	Wignall F	Young A	
7	8	1	11	4			6		5			2				3		10				9	3
7	8	1		4		3	6		5	11		2						10				9	4
7	8	1		4		3	6		5	11		2						10				9	5
3	3	3	1	3		2	3		3	2		3				1		3				3	
1	2		1							1								2					

1962-63

Manager: Harry Catterick

1	Aug	18	(a)	Burnley	W 3-1	Bingham, Vernon, Young	37,100
2		22	(h)	Manchester U	W 3-1	Young 2, Parker	69,500
3		25	(h)	Sheffield W	W 4-1	Vernon 2, Stevens, Young	51,504
4		29	(a)	Manchester U	W 1-0	Vernon	63,675
5	Sep	1	(a)	Fulham	L 0-1		30,582
6		5	(h)	Leyton O	W 3-0	Bingham, Gabriel, Vernon	51,542
7		8	(h)	Leicester C	W 3-2	Stevens, Vernon, Young	48,738
8		12	(a)	Leyton O	L 0-3		21,847
9		15	(a)	Bolton W	W 2-0	Bingham, Gabriel	27,404
10		22	(h)	Liverpool	D 2-2	Morrissey, Vernon	72,488
11		29	(h)	West Brom A	W 4-2	Morrissey 3, Young	45,471
12	Oct	6	(a)	Wolves	W 2-0	Bingham, Young	44,506
13		13	(h)	Aston Villa	D 1-1	Vernon	53,035
14		27	(h)	Ipswich T	W 3-1	Morrissey 2, Vernon	39,695
15	Nov	3	(a)	Manchester C	D 1-1	Wignall	40,336
16		10	(h)	Blackpool	W 5-0	Young 2, Bingham, Gabriel, Stevens	39,517
17		13	(a)	Nottingham F	W 4-3	Vernon 2, Gabriel, Veall	31,610
18		17	(a)	Blackburn R	L 2-3	Harris, Stevens	30,243
19		24	(h)	Sheffield U	W 3-0	Vernon 2, Stevens	42,017
20	Dec	1	(a)	Tottenham H	D 0-0		60,626
21		8	(h)	West Ham U	D 1-1	Stevens	38,701
22		15	(h)	Burnley	W 3-1	Stevens, Vernon, Young	48,443
23		22	(a)	Sheffield W	D 2-2	Young, Opp own-goal	26,280
24	Feb	12	(a)	Leicester C	L 1-3	Vernon	35,743
25		23	(h)	Wolves	D 0-0		62,616
26	Mar	9	(h)	Nottingham F	W 2-0	Parker, Young	45,068
27		19	(a)	Ipswich T	W 3-0	Young 2, Opp own-goal	19,712
28		23	(h)	Manchester C	W 2-1	Morrissey, Young	46,101
29		26	(a)	Arsenal	L 3-4	Kay, Vernon, Young	38,061
30		30	(a)	Sheffield U	L 1-2	Scott	21,839
31	Apr	1	(a)	Aston Villa	W 2-0	Gabriel, Young	31,377
32		6	(h)	Blackburn R	D 0-0		39,790
33		8	(a)	Liverpool	D 0-0		56,060
34		13	(a)	Blackpool	W 2-1	Scott, Young	27,842
35		15	(h)	Birmingham C	D 2-2	Scott, Young	50,122
36		16	(a)	Birmingham C	W 1-0	Vernon	29,719
37		20	(h)	Tottenham H	W 1-0	Young	67,650
38		24	(h)	Arsenal	D 1-1	Vernon	56,034
39		27	(a)	West Ham U	W 2-1	Temple, Vernon	28,391
40	May	4	(h)	Bolton W	W 1-0	Vernon	52,047
41		7	(a)	West Brom A	W 4-0	Young 2, Vernon, Opp own-goal	25,280
42		11	(h)	Fulham	W 4-1	Vernon 3, Scott	60,578

FINAL LEAGUE POSITION: 1st in Division One

Appearances
Goals

FA Cup

3	Jan	15	(a)	Barnsley	W 3-0	Harris, Stevens, Vernon
4		29	(a)	Swindon T	W 5-1	Vernon 2, Bingham, Gabriel, Morrissey
5	Mar	16	(a)	West Ham U	L 0-1	

Appearances
Goals

Everton played in the Inter-City Fairs Cup (see *Everton in Europe*).

Bingham W	Dunlop A	Gabriel J	Harris B	Heslop G	Kay A	Labone B	Meagan M	Morrissey J	Parker A	Scott A	Sharples G	Stevens D	Temple D	Thomson G	Veall R	Vernon R	West G	Wignall F	Young A	
7		4	6			5	2					8		3	11	10	1		9	1
7		4	6			5			2			8		3	11	10	1		9	2
7			6			5		11	2		4	8		3		10	1		9	3
7		4	6			5		11	2			8		3		10	1		9	4
7		4	6			5		11	2			8		3		10	1		9	5
7		4	6			5	2	11				8		3		10	1		9	6
7		4	6			5	2	11				8		3		10	1		9	7
7			6			5	2	11			4	8		3		10	1		9	8
7		4	6			5	2	11				8		3		10	1		9	9
7		4	6			5	2	11				8		3		10	1		9	10
7		4	6			5	2	11				8		3		10	1		9	11
7		4	6			5	2	11				8		3		10	1		9	12
7		4	6			5	2	11				8		3		10	1		9	13
7		4	6			5	3	11	2			8				10	1		9	14
		4	6			5	3	7	2			8			11		1	10	9	15
7		4	6			5	3		2			8			11	10	1		9	16
7		4	6			5	3		2			8			11	10	1		9	17
7		4	6			5	3		2			8			11	10	1		9	18
7		4	6			5	3		2			8			11	10	1		9	19
7		4	6			5	3		2			8			11	10	1		9	20
7		4	6			5	3		2			8			11	10	1		9	21
7		4	6			5	3		2			8			11	10	1		9	22
7		4	6			5	3		2			8			11	10	1		9	23
		4			6	5	3	11	2	7		8				10	1		9	24
		4			6	5	3	11	2			8	7			10	1		9	25
		4			6	5	3	11	2	7		8				10	1		9	26
		4			6	5		11	2	7		8		3		10	1		9	27
		4			6	5		11	2	7		8		3		10	1		9	28
7		4			6	5		11	2			8		3		10	1		9	29
		4			6	5		11	2	7		8		3		10	1		9	30
		4			6	5		11	2	7		8		3		10	1		9	31
		4			6	5		11	2	7		8		3		10	1		9	32
		4			6	5	3	11	2	7		8				10	1		9	33
		4			6	5	3	11	2	7		8				10	1		9	34
		5	4		6		3	11	2	7		8				10	1		9	35
		4		5	6		3	11	2	7		8				10	1		9	36
		4			6	5	3	11	2	7		8				10	1		9	37
		4			6	5	3	11	2	7		8				10	1		9	38
	1	4			6	5	3		2	7		8	11			10			9	39
	1	4			6	5	3		2	7		8	11			10			9	40
	1	4			6	5	3		2	7		8	11			10			9	41
	1	4			6	5	3		2	7		8	11			10			9	42
23	4	40	24	1	19	40	32	28	33	17	2	42	5	19	11	41	38	1	42	
5		5	1		1			7	2	4		7	1		1	24		1	22	

3 own-goals

Bingham W	Dunlop A	Gabriel J	Harris B	Heslop G	Kay A	Labone B	Meagan M	Morrissey J	Parker A	Scott A	Sharples G	Stevens D	Temple D	Thomson G	Veall R	Vernon R	West G	Wignall F	Young A	
7		4	6			5	3	11	2			8				10	1		9	3
7		4			6	5	3	11	2			8				10	1		9	4
7		4			6	5	3	11	2			8				10	1		9	5
3		3	1		2	3	3	3	3			3				3	3		3	
1		1	1					1				1				3				

1963-64

Manager: Harry Catterick

1	Aug	24	(h)	Fulham	W 3-0	Scott, Temple, Opp own-goal	49,520
2		31	(a)	Manchester U	L 1-5	Vernon	63,206
3	Sep	4	(a)	Bolton W	W 3-1	Young 2, Temple	34,093
4		7	(h)	Burnley	L 3-4	Gabriel, Hill, Scott	54,409
5		11	(h)	Bolton W	W 2-0	Stevens, Young	48,301
6		14	(a)	Ipswich T	D 0-0		20,099
7		21	(h)	Sheffield W	W 3-2	Stevens, Vernon, Young	48,884
8		28	(a)	Liverpool	L 1-2	Vernon	51,976
9	Oct	2	(h)	Arsenal	W 2-1	Temple, Young	51,829
10		5	(a)	Birmingham C	W 2-0	Kay, Temple	23,593
11		7	(a)	Aston Villa	W 1-0	Vernon	23,999
12		15	(h)	Sheffield U	W 4-1	Young 2, Stevens, Temple	51,291
13		19	(a)	West Ham U	L 2-4	Kay, Rees	25,163
14		26	(h)	Tottenham H	W 1-0	Temple	65,386
15	Nov	2	(a)	Blackpool	D 1-1	Vernon	24,834
16		9	(h)	Blackburn R	L 2-4	Temple, Young	49,349
17		16	(a)	Nottingham F	D 2-2	Harris, Vernon	27,027
18		23	(h)	Stoke C	W 2-0	Kay, Temple	47,957
19		30	(a)	Wolves	D 0-0		25,133
20	Dec	7	(h)	Chelsea	D 1-1	Vernon	39,320
21		10	(a)	Arsenal	L 0-6		33,644
22		14	(a)	Fulham	D 2-2	Harris, Young	17,860
23		21	(h)	Manchester U	W 4-0	Harris, Stevens, Temple, Vernon	48,027
24		26	(a)	Leicester C	L 0-2		30,004
25		28	(h)	Leicester C	L 0-3		54,808
26	Jan	11	(a)	Burnley	W 3-2	Gabriel, Morrissey, Scott	23,082
27		18	(h)	Ipswich T	D 1-1	Scott	38,242
28	Feb	1	(a)	Sheffield W	W 3-0	Gabriel, Scott, Vernon	29,950
29		8	(h)	Liverpool	W 3-1	Vernon 2, Gabriel	66,515
30		18	(h)	Birmingham C	W 3-0	Rees, Stevens, Vernon	36,252
31		22	(a)	Sheffield U	D 0-0		20,032
32		28	(h)	Aston Villa	W 4-2	Scott, Stevens, Vernon, Young	50,292
33	Mar	7	(a)	Tottenham H	W 4-2	Vernon 2, Temple, Young	41,926
34		14	(h)	Nottingham F	W 6-1	Pickering 3, Stevens 2, Vernon	50,085
35		21	(a)	Blackburn R	W 2-1	Scott, Temple	35,142
36		27	(h)	West Brom A	D 1-1	Opp own-goal	61,187
37		28	(h)	Blackpool	W 3-1	Pickering 2, Young	49,504
38		31	(a)	West Brom A	L 2-4	Vernon 2	27,194
39	Apr	4	(a)	Stoke C	L 2-3	Gabriel, Pickering	35,297
40		11	(h)	Wolves	D 3-3	Pickering, Stevens, Temple	43,165
41		18	(a)	Chelsea	L 0-1		37,963
42		25	(h)	West Ham U	W 2-0	Pickering 2	33,090

FINAL LEAGUE POSITION: 3rd in Division One

Appearances
Goals

FA Cup

3	Jan	4	(a)	Hull C	D 1-1	Scott
R		7	(h)	Hull C	W 2-1	Harris, Scott
4		25	(a)	Leeds U	D 1-1	Vernon
R		28	(h)	Leeds U	W 2-0	Gabriel, Vernon
5	Feb	15	(a)	Sunderland	L 1-3	Harris

Appearances
Goals

Everton played in the European Cup (see *Everton in Europe*).

Brown A	Gabriel J	Harris B	Harvey C	Heslop G	Hill J	Kay A	Labone B	Meagan M	Morrissey J	Parker A	Parnell R	Pickering F	Rankin A	Rees B	Scott A	Sharples G	Stevens D	Temple D	Vernon R	West G	Young A	
	4					6	5	3	11	2					7		8	10		1	9	1
	4					6	5	3		2					7		8	11	10	1	9	2
	4				10	6	5	3		2					7		8	11		1	9	3
3	4				10	6	5			2					7		8	11		1	9	4
3		6			10	4	5			2					7		8	11		1	9	5
		6					5			2	3				7	4	8	11	10	1	9	6
3	4					6	5			2					7		8	11	10	1	9	7
3		6				4	5		11	2					7		8	9	10	1		8
3	4					6	5			2					7		8	11	10	1	9	9
	4	3				6	5			2					7		8	11	10	1	9	10
	4	3				6	5			2					7		8	11	10	1	9	11
	4	3				6	5			2					7		8	11	10	1	9	12
	4	3				6	5			2				9	7		8	11	10	1		13
	4					6	5	3		2					7		8	11	10	1	9	14
	4					6	5	3		2					7		8	11	10	1	9	15
	4					6	5	3		2					7		8	11	10	1	9	16
		4				6	5	3		2			1		7		8	11	10		9	17
2		4		5		6		3					1		7		8	11	10		9	18
2		4		5		6		3					1		7		8	11	10		9	19
2		4		5				3					1		7	6	8	11	10		9	20
2		4		5				3					1		7	6	8	11	10		9	21
2		6		5	8			3					1		7		4	11	10		9	22
2	4	6		5				3					1		7		8	11	10		9	23
2	4	3		5		6							1		7		8	11	10		9	24
2	4	6		5				3					1		7		8	11	10		9	25
2	4	6			10		5	3	11				1		7		8	9				26
2	4	3			10	6	5		11				1		7		8	9				27
2	9	4				6	5	3							7		8	11	10	1		28
2	9	4				6	5	3							7		8	11	10	1		29
2	4					6	5	3						9	7		8	11	10	1		30
2	4				10	6	5	3	11					9	7		8			1		31
2	4					6	5	3							7		8	11	10	1	9	32
2	4					6	5	3							7		8	11	10	1	9	33
2	4	3				6	5					9	1		7		8	11	10			34
2	4	3	10			6	5					9	1		7		8	11				35
2	4	6	10				5	3				9	1		7		8	11				36
2	4	6					5	3	11			9	1				8	7			10	37
2	4					6	5	3				9	1				8	11	10		7	38
2	4	3				6	5					9	1		7		8	11	10			39
2	4	3				6	5		11			9	1		7		8	10				40
2	4	6					5	3				9	1		7		8	11	10			41
2	4	6					5	3				9	1		7		8	11	10			42
30	33	28	2	8	7	31	34	26	7	17	1	9	20	3	40	3	42	41	31	22	27	
	5	3			1	3			1			9		2	7		9	12	18		12	

2 own-goals

Brown A	Gabriel J	Harris B	Harvey C	Heslop G	Hill J	Kay A	Labone B	Meagan M	Morrissey J	Parker A	Parnell R	Pickering F	Rankin A	Rees B	Scott A	Sharples G	Stevens D	Temple D	Vernon R	West G	Young A	
2	4	6		5				3					1		7		8	11	10		9	3
2	4	6					5	3					1		7		8	11	10		9	R
2	4	3				6	5								7		8	11	10	1	9	4
2	9	4				6	5	3							7		8	11	10	1		R
2	9	4				6	5	3							7		8	11	10	1		5
5	5	5		1		3	4	4					2		5		5	5	5	3	3	
	1	2													2				2			

1964-65

Manager: Harry Catterick

1	Aug	22	(a)	Stoke C	W 2-0	Temple, Vernon	44,015
2		25	(h)	Nottingham F	W 1-0	Pickering	53,590
3		29	(h)	Tottenham H	W 4-1	Pickering 3, Young	55,148
4	Sep	1	(a)	Nottingham F	L 1-3	Brown	40,382
5		5	(a)	Burnley	D 1-1	Brown	23,703
6		8	(h)	Manchester U	D 3-3	Pickering 2, Young	63,465
7		12	(h)	Sheffield U	D 1-1	Brown	47,765
8		16	(a)	Manchester U	L 1-2	Pickering	50,286
9		19	(a)	Liverpool	W 4-0	Harvey, Morrissey, Pickering, Temple	52,619
10		26	(a)	Birmingham C	W 5-3	Pickering 2, Scott 2, Morrissey	21,240
11	Oct	3	(h)	West Ham U	D 1-1	Harris	45,430
12		5	(a)	Aston Villa	W 2-1	Gabriel, Scott	23,115
13		10	(h)	Sheffield W	D 1-1	Scott	41,911
14		17	(a)	Blackpool	D 1-1	Scott	31,855
15		24	(h)	Blackburn R	L 2-3	Pickering, Young	40,948
16		31	(a)	Arsenal	L 1-3	Pickering	33,561
17	Nov	7	(h)	Leeds U	L 0-1		43,605
18		14	(a)	Chelsea	L 1-5	Gabriel	30,716
19		21	(h)	Leicester C	D 2-2	Gabriel, Pickering	35,015
20		28	(a)	Sunderland	L 0-4		41,581
21	Dec	5	(h)	Wolves	W 5-0	Pickering 2, Temple 2, Brown	27,533
22		12	(h)	Stoke C	D 1-1	Pickering	31,713
23		19	(a)	Tottenham H	D 2-2	Pickering 2	41,994
24		26	(h)	West Brom A	W 3-2	Pickering, Scott, Temple	46,719
25	Jan	2	(h)	Burnley	W 2-1	Pickering, Temple	42,177
26		16	(a)	Sheffield U	D 0-0		21,625
27	Feb	6	(h)	Birmingham C	D 1-1	Harvey	34,033
28		13	(a)	West Ham U	W 1-0	Temple	25,163
29		20	(a)	Sheffield W	W 1-0	Pickering	16,687
30		27	(h)	Blackpool	D 0-0		35,267
31	Mar	6	(a)	Blackburn R	W 2-0	Harris, Pickering	15,960
32		13	(h)	Aston Villa	W 3-1	Vernon 2, Morrissey	32,565
33		20	(a)	Leeds U	L 1-4	Temple	29,701
34		23	(a)	West Brom A	L 0-4		12,244
35		31	(h)	Chelsea	D 1-1	Gabriel	40,385
36	Apr	3	(a)	Leicester C	L 1-2	Temple	14,377
37		10	(h)	Sunderland	D 1-1	Pickering	29,455
38		12	(h)	Liverpool	D 2-1	Morrissey, Temple	65,402
39		16	(h)	Fulham	W 2-0	Pickering, Temple	38,537
40		17	(a)	Wolves	W 4-2	Brown, Harris, Morrissey, Pickering	19,698
41		19	(a)	Fulham	D 1-1	Pickering	13,323
42		24	(h)	Arsenal	W 1-0	Pickering	32,643

FINAL LEAGUE POSITION: 4th in Division One

Appearances
Goals

FA Cup

3	Jan	9	(h)	Sheffield W	D 2-2	Pickering, Opp own-goal
R		13	(a)	Sheffield W	W 3-0	Harvey, Pickering, Temple
4		30	(a)	Leeds U	D 1-1	Pickering
R	Feb	2	(h)	Leeds U	L 1-2	Pickering

Appearances
Goals

Everton played in the Inter-Cities Fairs Cup (see *Everton in Europe*).

Brown A	Gabriel J	Glover G	Harris B	Harvey C	Husband J	Labone B	Morrissey J	Parker A	Pickering F	Rankin A	Rees B	Scott A	Shaw S	Stevens D	Temple D	Vernon R	West G	Wilson R	Wright T	Young A	
			6			5		2	9	1		7		4	11	10		3		8	1
			6			5		2	9	1		7		4	11	10		3		8	2
3			6			5		2	9	1		7		4	11	10				8	3
3	4		6			5		2	9	1		7			11	10				8	4
3	4		6			5		2	9	1		7			11	10				8	5
3	4		6			5		2	9	1		7			11	10				8	6
3	4		6			5		2	9	1		7			11	10				8	7
3	4		2	10		5			9	1		7		6	11					8	8
3	4		2	8		5	11		9	1		7		6	10						9
3	4		2	8		5	11		9	1		7		6	10						10
3	9		6	8		5	11	2		1		7		4	10						11
3	10		6	8		5		2	9	1		7		4	11						12
3			6	10		5		2	9	1		7		4	11					8	13
3	4			8		5			9	1		7		6	11				2	10	14
	4		3	10		5		2	9	1			7	6	11					8	15
3	4					5	11	2	9	1		7		6		10				8	16
3	4					5	11		9	1	2			6	7	10				8	17
3	4		6	10		5	11		9	1				2	7					8	18
3	4					5	11		9	1		7		6	10				2	8	19
3	4		6	10		5	11		9	1				2	7					8	20
3	4		6	8		5	11		9	1					7	10			2		21
2	4		6	8		5			9	1		7			11	10		3			22
	4			6		5	11		9			7			10		1	3	2	8	23
	4			6		5	11		9			7			10		1	3	2	8	24
2	4			6		5	11		9			7			10		1	3		8	25
	4		6	8		5	11		9			7			10		1	3	2		26
	4		6	8		5	11		9						7		1	3	2	10	27
	4			8		5			9			7		6	11	10	1	3	2		28
			4	8		5			9			7		6	11	10	1	3	2		29
	4		6	8		5			9			7			11	10	1	3	2		30
	4		6	8		5			9			7			11	10	1	3	2		31
	4		6	8		5	11		9			7				10	1	3	2		32
	4		6	8		5	11		9			7			10		1	3	2		33
	4		6	8		5	11		9			7			10		1	3	2		34
6	4			8		5	11		9			7			10		1	3	2		35
6	4			8		5	11		9			7			10		1	3	2		36
3	4	6		8		5	11		9			7			10		1		2		37
3	4		6	8		5	11		9			7			10		1		2		38
3	4		6	8		5	11		9			7			10		1		2		39
3	4		6	8		5	11		9			7			10		1		2		40
3	4		6	8	10	5	11		9			7					1		2		41
3	4		6	8		5	11		9			7			10		1		2		42
28	37	1	31	32	1	42	25	12	41	22	1	36	1	18	39	16	20	17	22	20	
5	4		3	2			5		27			6			11	3				3	

Brown A	Gabriel J	Glover G	Harris B	Harvey C	Husband J	Labone B	Morrissey J	Parker A	Pickering F	Rankin A	Rees B	Scott A	Shaw S	Stevens D	Temple D	Vernon R	West G	Wilson R	Wright T	Young A	
2	4			6		5	11		9			7			10		1	3		8	3
	4		6	8		5	11		9			7			10		1	3	2		R
	4			8		5	11		9			7		6	10		1	3	2		4
	4			8		5	11		9			7		6	10		1	3	2		R
1	4		1	4		4	4		4			4		2	4		4	4	3	1	
				1					4						1						

1 own-goal

1965-66

Manager: Harry Catterick

1	Aug	21	(h)	Northampton T	W 5-2	Pickering 2, Temple 2, Young	48,489
2		25	(a)	Sheffield W	L 1-3	Scott	26,063
3		28	(a)	Stoke C	D 1-1	Pickering	30,544
4		31	(h)	Sheffield W	W 5-1	Young 3, Pickering 2	39,640
5	Sep	4	(h)	Burnley	W 1-0	Temple	44,633
6		7	(h)	West Brom A	L 2-3	Harvey, Scott	43,468
7		11	(a)	Chelsea	L 1-3	Temple	29,816
8		15	(a)	West Brom A	D 1-1	Young	25,513
9		18	(h)	Arsenal	W 3-1	Harris, Pickering, Temple	38,935
10		25	(a)	Liverpool	L 0-5		53,557
11	Oct	5	(h)	Blackburn R	D 2-2	Gabriel, Labone	34,694
12		9	(h)	Tottenham H	W 3-1	Gabriel 2, Pickering	40,022
13		16	(a)	Fulham	L 2-3	Pickering 2	18,110
14		23	(h)	Blackpool	D 0-0		33,766
15		30	(a)	Blackburn R	W 2-1	Pickering, Scott	15,096
16	Nov	6	(h)	Leicester C	L 1-2	Morrissey	30,195
17		13	(a)	Sheffield U	L 0-2		16,579
18		20	(h)	Leeds U	D 0-0		36,291
19		27	(a)	West Ham U	L 0-3		21,971
20	Dec	4	(h)	Sunderland	W 2-0	Hurst, Pickering	25,393
21		11	(a)	Aston Villa	L 2-3	Hurst, Pickering	18,826
22		16	(a)	Manchester U	L 0-3		32,896
23		18	(h)	Fulham	W 2-0	Temple, Young	20,670
24		27	(a)	Nottingham F	L 0-1		34,750
25	Jan	1	(a)	Tottenham H	D 2-2	Pickering, Temple	34,953
26		8	(h)	Aston Villa	W 2-0	Pickering, Trebilcock	34,641
27		11	(h)	West Ham U	D 2-2	Pickering, Scott	29,915
28		15	(a)	Blackpool	L 0-2		14,588
29		29	(a)	Northampton T	W 2-0	Scott, Temple	16,309
30	Feb	5	(h)	Stoke C	W 2-1	Pickering, Young	38,999
31		19	(a)	Burnley	D 1-1	Labone	19,670
32		26	(h)	Chelsea	W 2-1	Harris, Temple	52,752
33	Mar	12	(a)	Arsenal	W 1-0	Pickering	24,821
34		15	(h)	Nottingham F	W 3-0	Gabriel, Morrissey, Pickering	37,455
35		19	(h)	Liverpool	D 0-0		62,337
36	Apr	8	(a)	Newcastle U	D 0-0		30,731
37		9	(h)	Sheffield U	L 1-3	Gabriel	32,720
38		11	(h)	Newcastle U	W 1-0	Gabriel	32,598
39		16	(a)	Leeds U	L 1-4	Trebilcock	25,200
40		25	(h)	Manchester U	D 0-0		50,843
41		30	(a)	Sunderland	L 0-2		31,147
42	May	4	(a)	Leicester C	L 0-3		14,504

FINAL LEAGUE POSITION: 11th in Division One

Appearances
Sub Appearances
Goals

FA Cup

3	Jan	22	(h)	Sunderland	W 3-0	Pickering, Temple, Young
4	Feb	12	(a)	Bedford T	W 3-0	Temple 2, Pickering
5	Mar	3	(h)	Coventry C	W 3-0	Pickering, Temple, Young
6		26	(a)	Manchester C	D 0-0	
R		29	(h)	Manchester C	D 0-0	
2R	Apr	5	(n*)	Manchester C	W 2-0	Pickering, Temple
SF		23	(n†)	Manchester U	W 1-0	Harvey
F	May	14	(n‡)	Sheffield W	W 3-2	Trebilcock 2, Temple

* Played at Molineux. † Played at Burnden Park. ‡ Played at Wembley Stadium

Appearances
Goals

Everton played in the Inter-Cities Fairs Cup (see *Everton in Europe*).

Barnett G	Brown A	Darcy F	Gabriel J	Glover G	Harris B	Harvey C	Heslop G	Humphreys G	Hurst J	Husband J	Labone B	Morrissey J	Pickering F	Rankin A	Royle J	Scott A	Shaw S	Smith D	Stevens D	Temple D	Trebilcock M	West G	Wilson R	Wright T	Young A	
			4		6	10					5		9			7				11		1	3	2	8	1
			4		6	10					5		9			7				11		1	3	2	8	2
					6	10			12		5		9*			7			4	11		1	3	2	8	3
					6	10			4		5		9			7				11		1	3	2	8	4
					6	10			4		5		9			7				11		1	3	2	8	5
					6	10			4		5		9			7				11		1	3	2	8	6
					6	10	5		4				9			7				11		1	3	2	8	7
			4		6	10					5		9				7			11		1	3	2	8	8
			4		6	10					5		9				7			11		1	3	2	8	9
			4	12	6	10					5*	11	9			7						1	3	2	8	10
	3		4		6*	8			12	10	5		9			7			2	11		1				11
	2		4			8			6	10	5		9			7				11		1	3			12
	5		4		6	8						11	9	1		7				10			3	2		13
	5		4		6	8						11	9	1		7				10			3	2		14
	12		4*		6	8					5	11	9	1		7				10			3	2		15
					6	8					5	11	9	1		7			4	10			3	2		16
	3				6	8					5	11	9	1		7			4	10				2		17
					6	4					5	11	9	1					10	7			3	2	8	18
					6	4					5	11	9	1					10	7			3	2	8	19
1					6	4			10		5		9			7				11			3	2	8	20
1					6	4			10		5		9			7				11			3	2	8	21
1			8		6	4			10		5		9			7				11			3	2		22
1					6	4			10		5		9			7				11			3	2	8	23
1					6	4			10		5		9			7				11			3	2	8	24
1					6	4			8		5		9			7				11	10		3	2		25
1					6	4			8		5		9			7				11	10		3	2		26
1					6	4			8		5		9			7				11			3	2	10	27
1	3				6	4			10		5	12	9		8	7				11				2*		28
			4		6	10					5		9			7				11		1	3	2	8	29
			4		6	10					5		9			7				11		1	3	2	8	30
			4		6	10					5		9			7				11		1	3	2	8	31
			4		6	10					5		9			7				11		1	3	2	8	32
	2		4		6	10					5		9			7				11		1	3		8	33
	3		4		6	10					5	11	9			7						1		2	8	34
	2		4		6	10					5		9*			7				11		1	3	12	8	35
	2		4		6	10			9	7	5									11	8	1	3			36
	12		4		6	10					5		9			7				11		1	3*	2	8	37
	3		4		6	10			9		5					7				11	8	1		2		38
	2	3		6				8	4	7		11		1	9			5			10					39
	2		4		6				8		5		9			7				11	10	1	3			40
			4		6	10							9					5		11	7	1	3	2	8	41
	3		4		6	10		11	8		5		9	1		7								2		42
9	14	1	24	1	40	40	1	2	19	4	37	10	39	9	2	35	2	2	6	38	7	24	35	35	26	
	2			1					2			1												1		
			6		2	1			2		2	2	18			5				9	2				7	

Barnett G	Brown A	Darcy F	Gabriel J	Glover G	Harris B	Harvey C	Heslop G	Humphreys G	Hurst J	Husband J	Labone B	Morrissey J	Pickering F	Rankin A	Royle J	Scott A	Shaw S	Smith D	Stevens D	Temple D	Trebilcock M	West G	Wilson R	Wright T	Young A	
			4		6	10					5		9			7				11		1	3	2	8	3
			4		6	10					5		9			7				11		1	3	2	8	4
	2		4		6	10					5		9			7				11		1	3		8	5
	4				6	10					5	11				7				9		1	3	2	8	6
	4				6	10					5		9			7				11		1	3	2	8	R
			4		6	10					5		9			7				11		1	3	2	8	2R
	2		4		6	10					5					7				11	8	1	3		9	SF
			4		6	10					5					7				11	8	1	3	2	9	F
	4		6		8	8					8	1	5			8				8	2	8	8	6	8	
						1							4							6	2				2	

1966-67

Manager: Harry Catterick

1	Aug	20	(a)	Fulham	W 1-0	Ball	21,634
2		23	(h)	Manchester U	L 1-2	Temple	60,657
3		27	(h)	Liverpool	W 3-1	Ball 2, Brown	64,318
4		31	(a)	Manchester U	L 0-3		61,114
5	Sep	3	(h)	Stoke C	L 0-1		44,005
6		6	(h)	Burnley	D 1-1	Young	44,063
7		10	(a)	Sheffield U	D 0-0		21,229
8		17	(h)	West Brom A	W 5-4	Ball 2, Morrissey, Temple, Young	45,165
9		24	(a)	Leeds U	D 1-1	Temple	38,486
10	Oct	1	(h)	Newcastle U	D 1-1	Gabriel	38,364
11		8	(a)	West Ham U	W 3-2	Temple 2, Young	32,789
12		15	(h)	Sheffield W	W 2-1	Gabriel, Temple	38,355
13		25	(a)	Southampton	W 3-1	Ball 2, Temple	27,179
14		29	(h)	Leicester C	W 2-0	Scott, Temple	47,267
15	Nov	5	(a)	Sheffield W	W 2-1	Ball, Temple	27,424
16		12	(h)	Arsenal	D 0-0		45,745
17		19	(a)	Manchester C	L 0-1		39,572
18		26	(h)	Blackpool	L 0-1		38,127
19	Dec	3	(a)	Chelsea	D 1-1	Young	35,495
20		17	(h)	Fulham	W 3-2	Temple 2, Ball	31,396
21		23	(h)	Nottingham F	L 0-1		34,084
22		26	(a)	Nottingham F	L 0-1		36,227
23		31	(a)	Liverpool	D 0-0		53,744
24	Jan	7	(a)	Stoke C	L 1-2	Young	27,171
25		14	(h)	Sheffield U	W 4-1	Ball 2, Gabriel, Husband	36,722
26		21	(a)	West Brom A	L 0-1		26,104
27	Feb	4	(h)	Leeds U	W 2-0	Gabriel, Husband	48,738
28		11	(a)	Newcastle U	W 3-0	Ball, Husband, Morrissey	31,214
29		25	(h)	West Ham U	W 4-0	Husband, Morrissey, Temple, Young	42,504
30	Mar	4	(a)	Leicester C	D 2-2	Hurst, Young	24,757
31		18	(h)	Southampton	L 0-1		44,997
32		22	(h)	Tottenham H	L 0-1		50,108
33		25	(a)	Sunderland	W 2-0	Husband, Opp own-goal	34,134
34		27	(a)	Tottenham H	L 0-2		47,917
35	Apr	1	(h)	Aston Villa	W 3-1	Ball, Young, Opp own-goal	36,619
36		19	(h)	Chelsea	W 3-1	Royle 2, Hurst	39,316
37		22	(a)	Blackpool	W 1-0	Royle	13,823
38		25	(a)	Arsenal	L 1-3	Gabriel	20,567
39		29	(h)	Manchester C	D 1-1	Ball	33,239
40	May	6	(a)	Aston Villa	W 4-2	Pickering 2, Gabriel, Husband	25,302
41		13	(a)	Burnley	D 1-1	Ball	11,634
42		16	(h)	Sunderland	W 4-1	Morrissey 3, Harvey	30,943

FINAL LEAGUE POSITION: 6th in Division One

Appearances
Sub Appearances
Goals

FA Cup

3	Jan	28	(a)	Burnley	D 0-0	
R		31	(h)	Burnley	W 2-1	Young 2
4	Feb	18	(a)	Wolves	D 1-1	Ball
R		21	(h)	Wolves	W 3-1	Husband 2, Temple
5	Mar	11	(h)	Liverpool	W 1-0	Ball
6	Apr	8	(a)	Nottingham F	L 2-3	Husband 2

Appearances
Sub Appearances
Goals

Everton played in European Cup-winners Cup (see *Everton in Europe*).

Ball A	Brown A	Gabriel J	Harris B	Harvey C	Hurst J	Husband J	Kendall H	Labone B	Morrissey J	Pickering F	Rankin A	Royle J	Scott A	Smith D	Temple D	Trebilcock M	West G	Wilson R	Wright T	Young A	
8		4		6				5		9			7		11		1	3	2	10	1
8		4		6				5		9			7		11		1	3	2	10	2
8	12	4		6				5	11	9*					7		1	3	2	10	3
8		4		6				5					7		11	10	1	3	2	9	4
8*	9		4	6	12			5					7		11		1	3	2	10	5
			4	6	8			5	11				7		10		1	3	2	9	6
8		4		6	9			5					7		11		1	3	2	10	7
8			4	6	12			5	11	9*					7		1	3	2	10	8
8		4		6				5	11						7	10	1	3	2	9	9
8		4	10	6				5	11						7		1	3	2	9	10
8		4		6				5	11				7		10		1	3	2	9	11
8	12	4		6				5	11*				7		10		1	3	2	9	12
8		4		6				5	11				7		10		1	3	2	9	13
8		4		6				5	11				7		10		1	3	2	9	14
8		4		6				5	11				7		10		1	3	2	9	15
8		4		6				5	11*				7	12	10		1	3	2	9	16
8		4		6		11		5					7		10		1	3	2	9	17
8	10	4		6				5					7		11		1	3	2	9	18
8	3	4		6				5	11				7		10		1		2	9	19
8	3	4		6				5	11				7		10		1		2	9	20
8	3	4		6				5	11				7		10		1		2	9	21
8	3	4		6	7			5	11						10		1		2	9	22
8	3	4		6	7			5	11						10		1		2	9	23
8	3	4		6	7	11		5							10		1		2	9	24
8	3	7		6	4	10		5	11						12		1		2*	9	25
8		7		6	4	10		5	11								1	3	2	9	26
8		9		6	4	10			11					5			1	3	2	7	27
8	5	9		6	4	10			11								1	3	2	7	28
8	12			6	4	10		5	11						9*		1	3	2	7	29
8				6	4	10		5	11	9							1	3	2	7	30
8				10	4	9	6	5	11								1	3	2	7	31
8				10	4		6	5	11						9		1	3	2	7	32
8				10	4	9	6	5							11		1	3	2	7	33
8	12			6	4	10		5	11	9			7				1	3*	2		34
8	3			6	4	9		5	11		1		7						2	10	35
7	3	12		10	4	9	6*	5	11		1	8							2		36
7	3	6		10	4	9		5	11		1	8							2		37
7	3	6		10	4	9		5			1	8	11						2		38
7	3	6		10	4	9		5			1	8	11						2		39
7		10		6	4	8		5	11	9	1							3	2		40
7		10		6	4	8		5	11	9							1	3	2		41
7	12	10		6	4	8*		5	11								1	3	2	9	42
41	15	31	4	42	23	19	4	40	31	8	6	4	21	1	27	2	36	30	42	35	
	5	1			2									1	1						
15	1	6		1	2	6			6	2		3	1		12					8	

2 own-goals

Ball A	Brown A	Gabriel J	Harris B	Harvey C	Hurst J	Husband J	Kendall H	Labone B	Morrissey J	Pickering F	Rankin A	Royle J	Scott A	Smith D	Temple D	Trebilcock M	West G	Wilson R	Wright T	Young A	
8	12	7		6	4	10		5	11						9*		1	3	2		3
8	12	9		6	4	10		5*	11								1	3	2	7	R
8		9		6	4	10		5	11								1	3	2	7	4
8	12			6	4	10		5	11						9*		1	3	2	7	R
8				6	4	10		5	11						9		1	3	2	7	5
8	9			6	4	10		5	11		1							3	2	7	6
6	1	3		6	6	6		6	6		1				3		5	6	6	5	
	3																				
2						4									1					2	

1967-68

Manager: Harry Catterick

1	Aug	19	(h)	Manchester U	W 3-1	Ball 2, Young	61,452
2		23	(a)	Tottenham H	D 1-1	Opp own-goal	53,809
3		26	(a)	Sunderland	L 0-1		37,628
4		29	(h)	Tottenham H	L 0-1		57,790
5	Sep	2	(h)	Wolves	W 4-2	Ball 2, Brown, Royle	51,498
6		5	(h)	West Ham U	W 2-0	Kendall, Young	46,762
7		9	(a)	Fulham	L 1-2	Young	25,366
8		16	(h)	Leeds U	L 0-1		53,179
9		23	(a)	Liverpool	L 0-1		54,189
10		30	(a)	Leicester C	W 2-0	Ball 2	22,768
11	Oct	7	(h)	Southampton	W 4-2	Ball, Hunt, Kendall, Opp own-goal	47,896
12		14	(a)	Chelsea	D 1-1	Ball	34,206
13		24	(h)	West Ham U	W 2-1	Hunt, Kendall	44,092
14		28	(a)	Newcastle U	L 0-1		34,030
15	Nov	4	(h)	Manchester C	D 1-1	Hunt	47,144
16		11	(a)	Arsenal	D 2-2	Hurst, Husband	36,371
17		18	(h)	Sheffield U	W 1-0	Young	37,994
18		25	(a)	Coventry C	W 2-0	Husband, Royle	32,330
19	Dec	2	(h)	Nottingham F	W 1-0	Royle	44,765
20		9	(a)	Stoke C	L 0-1		34,434
21		16	(a)	Manchester U	L 1-3	Young	57,078
22		23	(h)	Sunderland	W 3-0	Ball, Husband, Royle	38,216
23		26	(h)	Burnley	W 2-0	Ball, Royle	54,324
24		30	(a)	Burnley	L 1-2	Husband	22,592
25	Jan	6	(a)	Wolves	W 3-1	Royle 2, Trebilcock	37,802
26		20	(a)	Leeds U	L 0-2		44,119
27	Feb	3	(h)	Liverpool	W 1-0	Kendall	64,482
28		26	(a)	Southampton	L 2-3	Ball, Royle	25,860
29	Mar	2	(h)	Coventry C	W 3-1	Royle 2, Ball	38,804
30		16	(a)	West Brom A	W 6-2	Ball 4, Morrissey, Royle	26,285
31		23	(h)	Newcastle U	W 1-0	Kendall	45,519
32	Apr	6	(h)	Arsenal	W 2-0	Royle 2	40,029
33		9	(h)	Leicester C	W 2-1	Morrissey, Royle	39,156
34		13	(a)	Sheffield U	W 1-0	Ball	25,547
35		15	(h)	Sheffield W	W 1-0	Hurst	44,530
36		16	(a)	Sheffield W	D 0-0		24,976
37		20	(h)	Chelsea	W 2-1	Hurst, Kendall	47,370
38		22	(a)	Nottingham F	L 0-1		23,809
39		29	(a)	Manchester C	L 0-2		37,786
40	May	4	(h)	Stoke C	W 3-0	Ball 2, Royle	43,302
41		11	(a)	West Ham U	D 1-1	Husband	28,319
42		21	(h)	Fulham	W 5-1	Hurst 2, Ball, Morrissey, Royle	38,337

FINAL LEAGUE POSITION: 5th in Division One

Appearances
Sub Appearances
Goals

FA Cup

3	Jan	27	(a)	Southport	W 1-0	Royle
4	Feb	17	(a)	Carlisle U	W 2-0	Husband, Royle
5	Mar	9	(h)	Tranmere R	W 2-0	Morrissey, Royle
6		30	(a)	Leicester C	W 3-1	Husband 2, Kendall
SF	Apr	27	(n*)	Leeds U	W 1-0	Morrissey
F	May	18	(n†)	West Brom A	L 0-1	

* Played at Old Trafford. †Played at Wembley Stadium.

Appearances
Sub Appearances
Goals

League Cup

2	Sep	13	(a)	Bristol C	W 5-0	Kendall 2, Brown, Hurst, Royle
3	Oct	11	(h)	Sunderland	L 2-3	Young 2

Appearances
Sub Appearances
Goals

Ball A	Barnett G	Bennett H	Brindle W	Brown A	Darcy F	Darracott T	Harvey C	Humphreys G	Hunt E	Hurst J	Husband J	Jackson T	Kendall H	Kenyon R	Labone B	Maher A	Morrissey J	Owen L	Royle J	Temple D	Trebilcock M	Turner D	West G	Whittle A	Wilson R	Wright T	Young A	
8							6			10			4		5		11		9				1		3	2	7	1
8*				12			6			10			4		5		11		9				1		3	2	7	2
				12			6			10	8		4		5		11*		9				1		3	2	7	3
				12			6			10			4		5		11		9	8			1		3	2*	7	4
8				3			6			10	12		4		5				9*	11			1			2	7	5
8				3			6			10			4		5				9	11			1			2	7	6
8				3			6		9	10			4		5					11			1			2	7	7
7					3		6		8	10			4		5				9	11			1			2		8
7				3			6		8	10			4		5		11						1			2	9	9
7		12		3			6		8	10			4		5*		11						1			2	9	10
7				3			6		8	10			4		5		11						1			2	9	11
8				7			6		4	10					5		11						1		3	2	9	12
7				12			6*		8	10			4		5		11						1		3	2	9	13
7				12			6		8	10			4		5		11*						1		3	2	9	14
7				2			6		8*	10			4		5	11			12				1		3		9	15
				11			6			10	8		4*	12	5				7				1		3	2	9	16
7				2*			6			10	8		4	12	5				11				1		3		9	17
7							6			10	8		4		5				11				1		3	2	9	18
8							6			10	11		4		5				9				1		3	2	7	19
8							6			10	11		4		5				9				1		3	2	7	20
8							6			10			4		5		11		9				1		3	2	7	21
8							10			6	11		4		5				9				1		3	2	7	22
8							6		12	10			4*		5		11		9				1		3	2	7	23
8*				12			6		7	10	11			4	5				9				1		3	2		24
7				12			6		8	10				4	5				9		11		1		3	2*		25
8							6			10	7		4*	12	5				9		11		1		3	2		26
8*				12			6		10	7	11		4		5				9				1		3	2		27
8				12			6			10	7		4		5		11		9				1		3*	2		28
8				3			6*		12	10	7		4		5		11		9				1			2		29
8										6	7		4		5		11		9				1	10	3	2		30
8				12						6	7		4		5		11		9				1	10*	3	2		31
8						3				10			4	6	5		11		9				1	7		2		32
8					3					10			4	6	5		11		9				1	7		2		33
8							3			10			4	6	5		11		9				1	7		2		34
				12	3			7*		10	8		4	6	5		11		9				1			2		35
				12	3*					10			4	6	5		11	8	9				1			2	7	36
							6	10		8	7		4	12	5		11		9			2*	1		3			37
		2	4					11		10		8		6	5			7*	9				1		3		12	38
8							6				7*	12	4	10	5		11		9				1		3	2		39
8							6						4	10	5		11		9				1	7	3	2		40
	1			3			6	7		10	8		4	5			11									2	9	41
8		6		12						10	7		4	5			11		9				1		3*	2		42
34	1	2	1	12	4	1	34	4	12	40	19	1	38	12	40	1	26	2	33	5	2	1	41	6	28	38	24	
				13					2		1	1		4					1								1	
20				1					3	5	5		6				3		16		1						5	

2 own-goals

Ball A	Barnett G	Bennett H	Brindle W	Brown A	Darcy F	Darracott T	Harvey C	Humphreys G	Hunt E	Hurst J	Husband J	Jackson T	Kendall H	Kenyon R	Labone B	Maher A	Morrissey J	Owen L	Royle J	Temple D	Trebilcock M	Turner D	West G	Whittle A	Wilson R	Wright T	Young A	
7				12			6			10	11		4		5				9				1		3*	2	8	3
8							6			10	7		4		5		11		9				1		3	2		4
				12					10	6	7*		4		5		11		9				1		3	2	8	5
8										10	7*		4	6	5		11		9				1		3	2	12	6
							6				7*	4	10	8	5		11		9				1		3	2	12	SF
8							6			10	7		4		5		11		9				1		3	2		F
4							4		1	5	6	1	6	2	6		5		6				6		6	6	2	
				2																							2	
											3		1				2		3									

Ball A	Barnett G	Bennett H	Brindle W	Brown A	Darcy F	Darracott T	Harvey C	Humphreys G	Hunt E	Hurst J	Husband J	Jackson T	Kendall H	Kenyon R	Labone B	Maher A	Morrissey J	Owen L	Royle J	Temple D	Trebilcock M	Turner D	West G	Whittle A	Wilson R	Wright T	Young A	
8				3			6			10			4		5				9	11			1			2	7	2
7				3			6		8	10			4		5		11						1			2	9	3
2				2			2		1	2			2		2		1		1	1			2			2	2	
				1						1			2						1								2	

1968-69

Manager: Harry Catterick

1	Aug	10	(a)	Manchester U	L 1-2	Ball	61,311
2		13	(h)	Burnley	W 3-0	Ball, Husband, Royle	48,903
3		17	(h)	Tottenham H	L 0-2		56,570
4		19	(a)	West Ham U	W 4-1	Ball, Harvey, Husband, Royle	34,895
5		24	(a)	Newcastle U	D 0-0		38,851
6		27	(h)	Liverpool	D 0-0		63,938
7		31	(h)	Nottingham F	W 2-1	Hurst, Royle	45,951
8	Sep	7	(a)	Chelsea	D 1-1	Morrissey	42,017
9		14	(h)	Sheffield W	W 3-0	Humphreys, Husband, Morrissey	44,517
10		21	(a)	Coventry C	D 2-2	Hurst, Husband	37,846
11		28	(h)	West Brom A	W 4-0	Ball 3, Harvey	47,792
12	Oct	5	(h)	Manchester C	W 2-0	Ball, Royle	55,399
13		8	(a)	Liverpool	D 1-1	Ball	54,496
14		12	(a)	Southampton	W 5-2	Husband 2, Ball, Royle, Wright	21,688
15		19	(h)	Stoke C	W 2-1	Harvey, Hurst	42,887
16		26	(a)	Wolves	W 2-1	Ball, Royle	34,744
17	Nov	2	(h)	Sunderland	W 2-0	Ball, Morrissey	40,492
18		9	(a)	Ipswich T	D 2-2	Royle 2	23,049
19		16	(h)	Queen's Park R	W 4-0	Harvey, Husband, Morrissey, Royle	43,552
20		23	(a)	Leeds U	L 1-2	Royle	41,716
21		30	(h)	Leicester C	W 7-1	Royle 3, Ball, Humphreys, Hurst, Husband	42,492
22	Dec	7	(a)	Arsenal	L 1-3	Ball	40,108
23		14	(h)	Southampton	W 1-0	Hurst	36,299
24		21	(a)	Stoke C	D 0-0		20,507
25		26	(a)	Manchester C	W 3-1	Husband 2, Royle	53,549
26	Jan	11	(a)	Sunderland	W 3-1	Royle 2, Kendall	24,106
27		18	(h)	Ipswich T	D 2-2	Brown, Husband	40,925
28		28	(h)	Wolves	W 4-0	Royle 2, Husband, Morrissey	48,057
29	Feb	1	(a)	Queen's Park R	W 1-0	Husband	26,476
30		8	(a)	Tottenham H	D 1-1	Royle	44,882
31	Mar	10	(h)	Manchester U	D 0-0		57,514
32		29	(h)	Chelsea	L 1-2	Royle	42,190
33	Apr	1	(h)	West Ham U	W 1-0	Husband	36,738
34		5	(a)	West Brom A	D 1-1	Ball	23,156
35		8	(a)	Burnley	W 2-1	Ball, Husband	17,134
36		12	(h)	Coventry	W 3-0	Hurst, Husband, Royle	36,165
37		14	(h)	Newcastle U	D 1-1	Husband	36,035
38		19	(a)	Sheffield W	D 2-2	Hurst, Husband	23,060
39		22	(h)	Leeds U	D 0-0		59,022
40		25	(a)	Nottingham F	L 0-1		26,629
41		29	(h)	Arsenal	W 1-0	Husband	39,689
42	May	14	(a)	Leicester C	D 1-1	Ball	41,130

FINAL LEAGUE POSITION: 3rd in Division One

Appearances
Sub Appearances
Goals

FA Cup

3	Jan	4	(h)	Ipswich T	W 2-1	Hurst, Royle
4		25	(h)	Coventry C	W 2-0	Hurst, Royle
5	Feb	12	(h)	Bristol C	W 1-0	Royle
6	Mar	1	(a)	Manchester U	W 1-0	Royle
SF		22	(n*)	Manchester C	L 0-1	

* Played at Villa Park

Appearances
Sub Appearances
Goals

League Cup

2	Sep	3	(h)	Tranmere R	W 4-0	Whittle 2, Ball, Royle
3		24	(h)	Luton T	W 5-1	Royle 2, Ball, Husband, Morrissey
4	Oct	16	(h)	Derby C	D 0-0	
R		23	(a)	Derby C	L 0-1	

Appearances
Sub Appearances
Goals

Ball A	Brown A	Darcy F	Darracott T	Harvey C	Humphreys G	Hurst J	Husband J	Jackson T	Kendall H	Kenyon R	Labone B	Morrissey J	Royle J	West G	Whittle A	Wilson R	Wright T	
8	3			6		10	7		4		5	11	9	1			2	1
8	3			6		10	7		4		5	11	9	1			2	2
8	3			6		10	7		4		5	11	9	1			2	3
8	3			6		10	7		4		5	11	9	1			2	4
8	3			6		10	7		4		5	11	9	1			2	5
8	3			6		10	7		4		5	11	9	1			2	6
8	3			6		10		7	4		5	11	9	1			2	7
8	3			6		10			4		5	11	9	1	7		2	8
8		3		6	11	10	7		4		5		9	1			2	9
8	3			6		10	7		4		5	11	9	1			2	10
8	3			6		10	7		4		5	11	9	1			2	11
8	3			6		10	7		4		5	11	9	1			2	12
8	3			6		10	7		4		5	11	9	1			2	13
8	3			6		10	7		4		5	11	9	1			2	14
8	3			6		10			4		5	11	9	1	7		2	15
8	3	12		6	7	10			4		5	11*	9	1			2	16
8	3			6	7	10			4		5	11	9	1			2	17
8	2			6	7	10			4		5	11	9	1		3		18
8	3		4	6		10	7				5	11	9	1			2	19
8	3			6		10	7		4		5	11*	9	1		12	2	20
8	3			6	11	10	7		4		5		9	1			2	21
8	3			6		10	7		4		5	11	9	1			2	22
	3			6		10	7		4	8	5	11	9	1			2	23
8	3			6		10	7		4		5	11	9	1			2	24
8	3			6		10	7		4		5	11	9	1			2	25
8	3					10	7		4	6	5	11	9	1			2	26
8	3					10	7		4	6	5	11	9	1			2	27
8	6					10	7		4		5	11	9	1		3	2	28
8	6					10	7		4*	12	5	11	9	1		3	2	29
8	3					10	7	4		6	5	11	9	1			2	30
8	3					6	7	4			5	11	9	1	10		2	31
8	3			6		10	7	4		12	5	11	9	1			2*	32
8	3			6		10	7	4			5	11	9	1			2	33
8	3	12		6		10	7	4			5	11	9*	1			2	34
8	3			6*		10	7	4			5	11	9	1		12	2	35
	3			6		10	7	4	12		5	11	9	1	8*		2	36
8				6		10	7	4			5	11	9	1		3	2	37
8	3			6		10	7	4		12	5	11	9*	1			2	38
8	3			6		10	7	4			5	11	9	1			2	39
8	3			6		10	7	4			5	11	9	1			2	40
8	3			6		10	7	4			5	11	9	1			2	41
8	3			6		10	7	4			5	11	9	1			2	42
40	40	1	1	36	5	42	36	14	28	4	42	40	42	42	4	4	41	
		2							1	3						2		
16	1			4	2	7	19		1			4	22				1	

Ball A	Brown A	Darcy F	Darracott T	Harvey C	Humphreys G	Hurst J	Husband J	Jackson T	Kendall H	Kenyon R	Labone B	Morrissey J	Royle J	West G	Whittle A	Wilson R	Wright T	
8	3			6		10	7		4		5	11	9	1			2	3
8	6					10	7		4		5	11	9	1		3	2	4
8	4	12		6*		10	7				5	11	9	1		3	2	5
8	3			6*		10	7	4		12	5	11	9	1			2	6
8	3			6		10	7	12	4*		5	11	9	1			2	SF
5	5			4		5	5	1	3		5	5	5	5		2	5	
		1						1		1								
						2							4					

Ball A	Brown A	Darcy F	Darracott T	Harvey C	Humphreys G	Hurst J	Husband J	Jackson T	Kendall H	Kenyon R	Labone B	Morrissey J	Royle J	West G	Whittle A	Wilson R	Wright T	
8	3			6		10			4		5	11	9	1	7		2	2
8	3			6		10	7		4*	12	5	11	9	1			2	3
8	3			6		10	7*		4	12	5	11	9	1			2	4
8	3			6	7*	10			4		5	11	9	1		12	2	R
4	4			4	1	4	2		4		4	4	4	4	1		4	
										2						1		
2							1					1	3		2			

1969-70

Manager: Harry Catterick

1	Aug	9	(a)	Arsenal	W 1-0	Hurst	44,364
2		13	(a)	Manchester U	W 2-0	Ball, Hurst	57,752
3		16	(h)	Crystal P	W 2-1	Morrissey, Royle	51,241
4		19	(h)	Manchester U	W 3-0	Ball, Morrissey, Royle	53,185
5		23	(a)	Manchester C	D 1-1	Morrissey	43,366
6		26	(h)	Sheffield W	W 2-1	Ball, Royle	46,480
7		30	(h)	Leeds U	W 3-2	Royle 2, Husband	53,253
8	Sep	6	(a)	Derby C	L 1-2	Kendall	37,708
9		13	(h)	West Ham U	W 2-0	Ball, Husband	49,052
10		17	(a)	Newcastle U	W 2-1	Husband 2	37,094
11		20	(a)	Ipswich T	W 3-0	Ball, Harvey, Royle	23,258
12		27	(h)	Southampton	W 4-2	Royle 3, Hurst	46,942
13	Oct	4	(a)	Wolves	W 3-2	Harvey, Morrissey, Royle	40,838
14		8	(a)	Crystal P	D 0-0		33,967
15		11	(h)	Sunderland	W 3-1	Kendall, Morrissey, Royle	47,271
16		18	(h)	Stoke C	W 6-2	Morrissey 2, Royle 2, Ball, Husband	48,663
17		25	(a)	Coventry C	W 1-0	Royle	37,816
18	Nov	1	(h)	Nottingham F	W 1-0	Wright	49,610
19		8	(a)	West Brom A	L 0-2		34,298
20		15	(a)	Chelsea	D 1-1	Husband	49,895
21		22	(h)	Burnley	W 2-1	Hurst, Royle	46,380
22	Dec	6	(h)	Liverpool	L 0-3		57,370
23		13	(a)	West Ham U	W 1-0	Whittle	26,689
24		20	(h)	Derby C	W 1-0	Ball	44,914
25		23	(h)	Manchester C	W 1-0	Whittle	51,864
26		27	(a)	Leeds U	L 1-2	Whittle	46,770
27	Jan	10	(h)	Ipswich T	W 3-0	Royle 2, Kendall	42,510
28		17	(a)	Southampton	L 1-2	Morrissey	27,156
29		24	(h)	Newcastle U	D 0-0		42,845
30		31	(h)	Wolves	W 1-0	Royle	45,681
31	Feb	14	(h)	Arsenal	D 2-2	Whittle 2	48,564
32		21	(h)	Coventry C	D 0-0		45,934
33		28	(a)	Nottingham F	D 1-1	Royle	29,174
34	Mar	7	(a)	Burnley	W 2-1	Ball, Hurst	21,114
35		11	(a)	Tottenham H	W 1-0	Whittle	27,764
36		14	(h)	Tottenham H	W 3-2	Ball, Royle, Whittle	51,533
37		21	(a)	Liverpool	W 2-0	Royle, Whittle	54,496
38		28	(h)	Chelsea	W 5-2	Royle 2, Ball, Kendall, Whittle	58,337
39		30	(a)	Stoke C	W 1-0	Whittle	33,111
40	Apr	1	(h)	West Brom A	W 2-0	Harvey, Whittle	58,523
41		4	(a)	Sheffield W	W 1-0	Morrissey	30,690
42		8	(a)	Sunderland	D 0-0		28,774

FINAL LEAGUE POSITION: 1st in Division One

Appearances
Sub Appearances
Goals

FA Cup

3	Jan	3	(a)	Sheffield U	L 1-2	Ball

Appearances
Sub Appearances
Goals

League Cup

2	Sep	3	(a)	Darlington	W 1-0	Ball
3		24	(a)	Arsenal	D 0-0	
R	Oct	1	(h)	Arsenal	W 1-0	Kendall
4		15	(a)	Manchester C	L 0-2	

Appearances
Sub Appearances
Goals

Ball A	Bennett H	Brindle W	Brown A	Darcy F	Harvey C	Humphreys G	Hurst J	Husband J	Jackson T	Kendall H	Kenyon R	Labone B	Morrissey J	Newton K	Royle J	West G	Whittle A	Wright T	
			3		6		10	7	8	4*	12	5	11		9	1		2	1
8			3		6		10	7	4			5	11		9	1		2	2
8			3		6		10	7	4			5	11		9	1		2	3
8*			3	12	6		10	7	4			5	11		9	1		2	4
8			3		6		10	7	4			5	11		9	1		2	5
8			3		6		10	7	4			5	11		9	1		2	6
8			3		6		10	7	4			5	11		9	1		2	7
8			3		6		10	7		4		5	11		9	1		2	8
8			3		6		10	7		4		5	11		9	1		2	9
8			3		6		10	7		4		5	11		9	1		2	10
8			3		6		10	7		4		5	11		9	1		2	11
8			3		6		10	7		4		5	11		9	1		2	12
8			3		6		10	7		4		5	11		9	1		2	13
8			3		6		10	7		4		5	11		9	1		2	14
8			3		6		10	7		4		5	11		9	1		2	15
8			3		6		10	7		4		5	11		9	1		2	16
8			3		6		10	7		4		5	11		9	1		2	17
8			3		6		10	7		4		5	11		9	1		2	18
8			3		6		10	7		4		5	11		9	1		2	19
8			3		6		10	7		4		5	11		9	1		2	20
8			3	12			10	7*	6	4		5	11		9	1		2	21
8			3				10		6	4		5	11		9	1	7	2	22
8			3	12			10		6	4		5	11		9	1	7	2*	23
8			12				10	7*	6	4		5	11	3	9	1		2	24
8			12			11*	10		6	4		5		3	9	1	7	2	25
8							10		6	4		5	11	3	9	1	7	2	26
8							10	7	6	4		5	11	3	9	1		2	27
			10		6*		8	7	12	4		5	11	3	9	1		2	28
			12		6		10	7		4		5	11	3	9	1	8	2*	29
			12		6*		10	7		4		5	11	3	9	1	8	2	30
					6		10	7		4		5	11	3	9	1	8	2	31
8					6		10	7		4		5	11	3	9	1		2	32
8					6		10	7		4		5	11	3	9	1		2	33
8					6		10			4		5	11	3	9	1	7	2	34
8			12		6		10			4	5		11	3*	9	1	7	2	35
8			3		6		10			4	5		11		9	1	7	2	36
8			3		6		10			4	5		11		9	1	7	2	37
8			3		6		10			4	5		11		9	1	7	2	38
8			3		6		10			4	5		11		9	1	7	2	39
8			3		6		10			4	5		11		9	1	7	2	40
8			3	12	6		10			4*	5		11		9	1	7	2	41
8			3	12	6		10	7		4*	5		11		9	1		2	42
37			31		35	1	42	30	14	36	8	34	41	12	42	42	15	42	
			5	5					1		1								
10					3		5	6		4			9		23		11	1	

Ball A	Bennett H	Brindle W	Brown A	Darcy F	Harvey C	Humphreys G	Hurst J	Husband J	Jackson T	Kendall H	Kenyon R	Labone B	Morrissey J	Newton K	Royle J	West G	Whittle A	Wright T	
8			12				10		6	4		5	11	3	9	1	7	2*	3
1							1		1	1		1	1	1	1	1	1	1	
			1																
1																			

Ball A	Bennett H	Brindle W	Brown A	Darcy F	Harvey C	Humphreys G	Hurst J	Husband J	Jackson T	Kendall H	Kenyon R	Labone B	Morrissey J	Newton K	Royle J	West G	Whittle A	Wright T	
8			3		6		10	7		4		5	11		9	1		2	2
8			3		6		10			4	12	5	11		9	1	7	2*	3
8			3		6		10	7		4		5	11		9	1		2	R
	10	8	3			11			6	4		5			9	1	7	2	4
3	1	1	4		3	1	3	2	1	4		4	3		4	4	2	4	
											1								
1										1									

1970-71

Manager: Harry Catterick

1	Aug	15	(h)	Arsenal	D 2-2	Morrissey, Royle	50,248
2		18	(h)	Burnley	D 1-1	Morrissey	44,717
3		22	(a)	Leeds U	L 2-3	Brown, Husband	46,718
4		26	(a)	Chelsea	D 2-2	Husband, Royle	48,195
5		29	(h)	Manchester C	L 0-1		50,724
6	Sep	2	(a)	Manchester U	L 0-2		49,599
7		5	(a)	West Ham U	W 2-1	Husband, Royle	29,171
8		12	(h)	Ipswich T	W 2-0	Kendall, Whittle	41,596
9		19	(a)	Blackpool	W 2-0	Husband, Morrissey	30,705
10		26	(h)	Crystal P	W 3-1	Harvey, Morrissey, Royle	43,443
11	Oct	3	(a)	Coventry C	L 1-3	Hurst	29,212
12		10	(h)	Derby C	D 1-1	Morrissey	46,614
13		17	(a)	Arsenal	L 0-4		50,053
14		24	(h)	Newcastle U	W 3-1	Kendall, Royle, Whittle	43,135
15		31	(a)	West Brom A	L 0-3		29,628
16	Nov	7	(h)	Nottingham F	W 1-0	Whittle	39,255
17		14	(a)	Stoke C	D 1-1	Hurst	26,765
18		21	(a)	Liverpool	L 2-3	Royle, Whittle	53,777
19		28	(h)	Tottenham H	D 0-0		44,301
20	Dec	5	(a)	Huddersfield T	D 1-1	Ball	27,658
21		12	(h)	Southampton	W 4-1	Royle 2, Morrissey, Whittle	31,139
22		19	(h)	Leeds U	L 0-1		47,393
23		26	(a)	Wolves	L 0-2		30,178
24	Jan	9	(a)	Burnley	D 2-2	Johnson, H.Newton	17,512
25		16	(h)	Chelsea	W 3-0	Husband, H.Newton, Royle	43,628
26		30	(a)	Tottenham H	L 1-2	Royle	42,105
27	Feb	6	(h)	Huddersfield T	W 2-1	Royle 2	37,213
28		16	(a)	Southampton	D 2-2	Harvey, Wright	22,183
29		20	(h)	Liverpool	D 0-0		56,846
30		23	(h)	Manchester U	W 1-0	Wright	52,544
31		27	(h)	West Brom A	D 3-3	Husband, K.Newton, Royle	35,940
32	Mar	13	(h)	Stoke C	W 2-0	Royle, Whittle	38,924
33		17	(a)	Newcastle U	L 1-2	Royle	22,874
34		20	(a)	Nottingham F	L 2-3	Hurst, Lyons	21,643
35		30	(h)	West Ham U	L 0-1		29,094
36	Apr	3	(a)	Manchester C	L 0-3		26,885
37		6	(a)	Ipswich T	D 0-0		20,288
38		10	(h)	Wolves	L 1-2	H.Newton	35,484
39		12	(h)	Coventry C	W 3-0	Royle 2, Ball	24,371
40		17	(a)	Derby C	L 1-3	Whittle	28,793
41		24	(h)	Blackpool	D 0-0		26,286
42	May	1	(a)	Crystal P	L 0-2		21,590

FINAL LEAGUE POSITION: 14th in Division One

Appearances
Sub Appearances
Goals

FA Cup

3	Jan	2	(h)	Blackburn R	W 2-0	Husband 2
4		23	(h)	Middlesbrough	W 3-0	Harvey, H.Newton, Royle
5	Feb	13	(h)	Derby C	W 1-0	Johnson
6	Mar	6	(h)	Colchester U	W 5-0	Kendall 2, Ball, Husband, Royle
SF		27	(n*)	Liverpool	L 1-2	Ball

* Played at Old Trafford.

Appearances
Sub Appearances
Goals

Everton played in the European Cup (see *Everton in Europe*).

Ball A	Brown A	Darcy F	Darracott T	Davies D	Harvey C	Hurst J	Husband J	Jackson T	Johnson D	Jones G	Kendall H	Kenny W	Kenyon R	Labone B	Lyons M	Morrissey J	Newton H	Newton K	Rankin A	Royle J	West G	Whittle A	Wright T	
8					6	10					4			5		11		3		9	1	7	2	1
8	12				6*	10					4			5		11		3		9	1	7	2	2
8	6					10	7				4			5		11		3		9	1		2	3
8	6					10	7				4		5			11		3		9	1		2	4
8	12				6	10	7				4*		5					3		9	1	11	2	5
8					6	10	7				4		5			11		3		9	1		2	6
8	12				6	10	7				4		5			11*		3		9	1		2	7
8					6	10					4		5			11		3		9	1	7	2	8
8	12				6	10	7*				4		5			11		3	1	9			2	9
8*	12				6	10					4		5			11		3	1	9		7	2	10
8	12				6	10					4		5			11		3	1	9		7	2*	11
	2				6	10		8			4		5			11		3	1	9		7		12
8					6						4		5			11	10	3	1	9		7	2	13
8					6	10					4		5			11		3	1	9		7	2	14
8					6	10					4		5			11		3	1	9		7	2	15
8	12				6*	10					4			5		11	3		1	9		7	2	16
8	3					10					4			5		11	6		1	9		7	2	17
8					6	10					4*			5		11	3	12	1	9		7	2	18
8					6	10	11				4			5				3	1	9		7	2	19
8					6	10					4			5		11	3		1	9		7	2	20
8					6	10					4		5			11	3		1	9		7	2	21
8					6	10					4		5			11	3		1	9		7	2	22
8					6	10					4			5		11	3		1	9		7	2	23
8					6	10	7		9		4			5		11	3		1				2	24
8					6	10	7				4			5		11	3		1	9			2	25
8					6	10	7				4		12	5*		11	3		1	9			2	26
8					6	10	7				4		5			11	3		1	9			2	27
	9				6	10	7		11		4		5				8	3			1		2	28
8					6	10	7				4		5			11	3			9	1		2	29
8					6	10			11		4		5			7	3			9	1		2	30
8					6	10	7				4		5			11		3		9	1		2	31
8					6	10			11		4			5				3	1	9		7	2	32
8	4			1	6	10								5		7		3		9		11	2	33
	12			1		10					4	8*	7	5	6	11		3		9			2	34
8					6	10			11		4		5				3		1	9		7	2	35
8		6				10			12		4		5			11	3		1	9		7	2*	36
8		2	6			10			7		4		5			11	3		1	9				37
8		12			6	10	7				4*		5			11	3		1	9			2	38
8			4		6	10			7	11			5		12		3		1	9*			2	39
8					6	10			11		4		5				3		1	9		7	2	40
8					6	10			11		4		5				3		1	9		7	2	41
8					6				7		4		10	5		11	3		1	9			2	42
39	6	2	2	2	36	40	15	1	10	1	40	1	28	16	1	34	23	21	28	40	12	24	40	
	8	1							1				1		1			1						
2	1				2	3	6		1		2				1	6	3	1		17		7	2	

Ball A	Brown A	Darcy F	Darracott T	Davies D	Harvey C	Hurst J	Husband J	Jackson T	Johnson D	Jones G	Kendall H	Kenny W	Kenyon R	Labone B	Lyons M	Morrissey J	Newton H	Newton K	Rankin A	Royle J	West G	Whittle A	Wright T	
8					6	10	7				4			5		11	3		1	9			2	3
8					6	10	7				4			5		11	3		1	9			2	4
8					6	10	7		11		4		5				3			9	1		2	5
8	12				6	10	7				4		5			11	3		1	9			2*	6
8	12				6	10					4			5*		11		3	1	9		7	2	SF
5					5	5	4		1		5		2	3		4	4	1	4	5	1	1	5	
	2																							
2					1		3		1		2						1			2				

1971-72

Manager: Harry Catterick

1	Aug	14	(a)	Ipswich T	D 0-0		23,757
2		18	(a)	West Brom A	L 0-2		29,055
3		21	(h)	Sheffield U	L 0-1		41,727
4		24	(h)	Chelsea	W 2-0	Harvey 2	38,854
5		28	(a)	West Ham U	L 0-1		26,878
6		31	(h)	Manchester U	W 1-0	Johnson	52,151
7	Sep	4	(h)	Derby C	L 0-2		41,024
8		11	(a)	Wolves	D 1-1	Royle	26,833
9		18	(h)	Arsenal	W 2-1	Johnson, Royle	39,710
10		25	(a)	Crystal P	L 1-2	Opp own-goal	25,619
11	Oct	2	(h)	Coventry C	L 1-2	Lyons	36,882
12		9	(a)	Manchester C	L 0-1		33,538
13		16	(h)	Ipswich T	D 1-1	Royle	31,590
14		23	(a)	Leeds U	L 2-3	Ball, Royle	34,208
15		30	(h)	Newcastle U	W 1-0	Ball	38,811
16	Nov	6	(a)	Tottenham H	L 0-3		40,005
17		13	(h)	Liverpool	W 1-0	Johnson	56,293
18		20	(h)	Southampton	W 8-0	Royle 4, Johnson 3, Ball	28,718
19		27	(a)	Leicester C	D 0-0		29,662
20	Dec	4	(h)	Stoke C	D 0-0		35,463
21		11	(a)	Nottingham F	L 0-1		18,639
22		18	(a)	Derby C	L 0-2		27,895
23		27	(h)	Huddersfield T	D 2-2	Johnson, Scott	41,262
24	Jan	1	(a)	Arsenal	D 1-1	Kendall	47,031
25		8	(h)	West Ham U	W 2-1	Harvey, Johnson	38,482
26		22	(h)	West Brom A	W 2-1	Husband, Kendall	36,412
27		29	(a)	Chelsea	L 0-4		38,558
28	Feb	12	(h)	Leeds U	D 0-0		45,935
29		19	(a)	Newcastle U	D 0-0		29,584
30	Mar	1	(h)	Tottenham H	D 1-1	H.Newton	21,601
31		4	(a)	Liverpool	L 0-4		53,922
32		8	(a)	Manchester U	D 0-0		38,415
33		11	(h)	Manchester C	L 1-2	Lyons	44,649
34		18	(a)	Sheffield U	D 1-1	B.Wright	28,244
35		21	(h)	Crystal P	D 0-0		27,979
36		25	(h)	Wolves	D 2-2	Kendall, Lyons	29,675
37	Apr	1	(a)	Huddersfield T	D 0-0		17,265
38		4	(a)	Coventry C	L 1-4	Johnson	22,129
39		8	(a)	Southampton	W 1-0	Buckley	19,711
40		15	(h)	Leicester C	D 0-0		33,342
41		22	(a)	Stoke C	D 1-1	Kendall	16,808
42	May	2	(h)	Nottingham F	D 1-1	Royle	21,513

FINAL LEAGUE POSITION: 15th in Division One

Appearances
Sub Appearances
Goals

FA Cup

3	Jan	15	(a)	Crystal P	D 2-2	Harvey, Whittle
R		18	(h)	Crystal P	W 3-2	Hurst, Kenyon, Scott
4	Feb	5	(h)	Walsall	W 2-1	Johnson, Whittle
5		26	(h)	Tottenham H	L 0-2	

Appearances
Sub Appearances
Goals

League Cup

2	Sep	7	(a)	Southampton	L 1-2	Johnson

Appearances
Sub Appearances
Goals

Bali A	Buckley M	Connolly J	Darracott T	Harvey C	Hurst J	Husband J	Johnson D	Jones G	Kendall H	Kenny W	Kenyon R	Labone B	Lyons M	McLaughlin J	Morrissey J	Newton H	Newton K	Royle J	Scott P	Seargeant S	West G	Whittle A	Wilson A	Wright B	Wright T	
8					10	7			4		12	5			11		3	9	6		1				2*	1
8			6		10	7	11		4			5					3	9	2		1					2
8			6		10	7			4			5			11		3	9	2		1					3
8				6	10	7	9		4			5*	12		11		3		2		1					4
8				6*	10	7	9		4		12		5		11		3		2		1					5
8			6		10	7	9		4		5				11		3		2		1					6
8			6		10	7	9		4*		5				11		3	12	2		1					7
8			6		10		9			4	5						3	7	2		1	11				8
			6		10		9			8	5					4	3	7	2		1	11				9
				6	10		9		12	8*	5					4	3	7	2		1	11				10
				6	10		9				5		12		11	4	3		2		1	7	8*			11
			6		10		9			8*	5		12			4	3	7	2		1	11				12
					10	8	9		6		5				12	4	3	7	2		1	11*				13
8				6*	10	9					5			3	11	4	2	7	12		1					14
8				6	10	9					5			3	11	4		7			1				2	15
8				6	10	9					5			3	11	4		7			1				2	16
8				6	10	9	7	11	4		5			3		2					1					17
8					10		7		4		5			3				9	6		1	11			2	18
8					10		7		4		5			3				9	6		1	11			2	19
8				6*	10	12	7		4		5			3				9			1	11			2	20
8					10	7			4		5			3		6		9			1	11			2	21
8					10	7			4		5			3		6		9			1	11			2	22
			6		10	7	8	11	4		5		12	3				9*	2		1					23
			6				11	7	4		5		8	3				9	2		1	10				24
			6	8*			7		4	12	5		10	3				9	2		1	11				25
			6		8	7	9*		4				5	3				12	2	10	1	11				26
			12	6	8	7			4*		5		10				3	9	2		1	11				27
				8	10	7	9		4				5	3		6					1	11			2	28
					10	7	9	11	4				5	3		6					1	8			2	29
			6			12	7	11*	4		5		10	3		8		9	2		1					30
			8	6		7	9*		4		5		10	3							1	11		12	2	31
			8	6					4	7	5		9	3					2		1			11	10	32
			8	6					4	7	5		9			3			2		1	12		11	10*	33
				6					4		5		10	3	11	8		9	2		1			7		34
			6						4		5		10	3	11	8		9	2		1			7		35
	8								4		5		10	3	11	6		9	2		1			7		36
	8				10	7			4		5		9	3		6			2		1			11		37
	8						7		4		5		10	3	11	6			2		1			9		38
	8				12	7	9		4		5		10	3	11*	6					1				2	39
	8	9				7	11		4		5		10	3		6					1				2	40
	8					7	11		4		5		10	3		6		9			1				2	41
		11		8		7			4		5		10	3		6		9			1				2	42
17	6	2	16	17	28	25	27	5	34	6	34	4	20	27	15	24	15	26	28	1	42	18	1	7	17	
			1		1	2			1	1	2		4		1			2	1			1		1		
3	1			3		1	9		4				3			1		9	1					1		

1 own-goal

Bali A	Buckley M	Connolly J	Darracott T	Harvey C	Hurst J	Husband J	Johnson D	Jones G	Kendall H	Kenny W	Kenyon R	Labone B	Lyons M	McLaughlin J	Morrissey J	Newton H	Newton K	Royle J	Scott P	Seargeant S	West G	Whittle A	Wilson A	Wright B	Wright T	
			6	8			7		4		5		10	3				9	2		1	11				3
			6	8*	12	7	9		4		5		10	3					2		1	11				R
				8	10		7		4				5	3		6		9			1	11			2	4
					12		7	11	4		5		10	3		6		9	2		1	8*				5
			2	3	1	1	4	1	4		3		4	4		2		3	3		4	4			1	
					2																					
				1	1		1				1								1			2				

Bali A	Buckley M	Connolly J	Darracott T	Harvey C	Hurst J	Husband J	Johnson D	Jones G	Kendall H	Kenny W	Kenyon R	Labone B	Lyons M	McLaughlin J	Morrissey J	Newton H	Newton K	Royle J	Scott P	Seargeant S	West G	Whittle A	Wilson A	Wright B	Wright T	
8			6		10		9				5	4					3	7	2		1	11				2
1			1		1		1				1	1					1	1	1		1	1				
							1																			

1972-73

Manager: Harry Catterick

1	Aug	12	(a)	Norwich C	D 1-1	Royle	25,851
2		16	(a)	Manchester C	W 1-0	Connolly	38,676
3		19	(h)	Manchester U	W 2-0	Connolly, Royle	52,348
4		22	(h)	Crystal P	D 1-1	Royle	38,429
5		26	(a)	Stoke C	D 1-1	Royle	26,360
6		29	(h)	Derby C	W 1-0	Royle	39,780
7	Sep	2	(h)	West Brom A	W 1-0	Royle	36,269
8		9	(a)	Leicester C	W 2-1	Connolly, Opp own-goal	21,080
9		16	(h)	Southampton	L 0-1		37,739
10		23	(a)	Birmingham C	L 1-2	Newton	37,133
11		30	(h)	Newcastle U	W 3-1	Connolly, Johnson, Royle	33,028
12	Oct	7	(a)	Liverpool	L 0-1		55,975
13		14	(h)	Leeds U	L 1-2	Whittle	47,821
14		21	(a)	Sheffield U	W 1-0	Whittle	22,946
15		28	(h)	Ipswich T	D 2-2	Kenyon, Whittle	30,185
16	Nov	4	(a)	Crystal P	L 0-1		28,614
17		11	(h)	Manchester C	L 2-3	Belfitt, Kenyon	32,924
18		18	(a)	Arsenal	L 0-1		35,738
19		25	(h)	West Ham U	L 1-2	B.Wright	27,558
20	Dec	2	(a)	Coventry C	L 0-1		22,774
21		9	(h)	Wolves	L 0-1		24,170
22		16	(h)	Tottenham H	W 3-1	Kendall 2, Hurst	31,129
23		23	(a)	Chelsea	D 1-1	Harper	23,385
24		26	(h)	Birmingham C	D 1-1	Harper	39,363
25	Jan	6	(h)	Stoke C	W 2-0	Buckley, Connolly	26,818
26		24	(a)	Manchester U	D 0-0		58,970
27		27	(h)	Leicester C	L 0-1		31,531
28	Feb	10	(a)	Southampton	D 0-0		16,756
29		24	(a)	Tottenham H	L 0-3		27,427
30	Mar	3	(h)	Liverpool	L 0-2		54,856
31		10	(a)	Leeds U	L 1-2	Lyons	39,663
32		17	(h)	Sheffield U	W 2-1	Harper, Lyons	24,781
33		24	(a)	Ipswich T	W 1-0	Harper	20,580
34		31	(a)	West Ham U	L 0-2		24,531
35	Apr	3	(h)	Norwich C	D 2-2	Belfitt, Kendall	21,806
36		7	(h)	Coventry C	W 2-0	Harper 2	25,474
37		11	(a)	West Brom A	L 1-4	Bernard	21,281
38		14	(a)	Wolves	L 2-4	Connolly, Harper	21,775
39		17	(h)	Chelsea	W 1-0	Kendall	24,999
40		21	(h)	Arsenal	D 0-0		42,888
41		25	(a)	Newcastle U	D 0-0		22,390
42		28	(a)	Derby C	L 1-3	Connolly	24,094

FINAL LEAGUE POSITION: 17th in Division One

Appearances
Sub Appearances
Goals

FA Cup

3	Jan	13	(h)	Aston Villa	W 3-2	Belfitt, Buckley, Harper
4	Feb	3	(h)	Millwall	L 0-2	

Appearances
Sub Appearances
Goals

League Cup

2	Sep	5	(a)	Arsenal	L 0-1	

Appearances
Sub Appearances
Goals

Belfitt R	Bernard M	Buckley M	Connolly J	Darracott T	Harper J	Harvey C	Hurst J	Husband J	Johnson D	Jones G	Kendall H	Kenyon R	Lawson D	Lyons M	McLaughlin J	Newton H	Royle J	Scott P	Seargeant S	Styles A	West G	Whittle A	Wilson A	Wright B	Wright T	
	8		11			10		7			4	5	1	6	3	2	9									1
	8		11*			10		7	12		4	5	1	6		2	9								3	2
	8		11			10		7			4		1	6		2	9		5						3	3
	8		11			10		7			4		1	6		3	9		5						2	4
	8		11			10			7		4	5	1	6		3	9								2	5
	8		11			10			7		4	5	1			3	9					6			2	6
	8		11			10			7		4	5	1			3	9		6						2	7
	8		11			10*			7		4	5	1	12		3	9		6						2	8
	8		11			10			7		4	5	1	6		3	9								2	9
	8		11			10			7		4	5	1	6		3	9								2	10
	8		11			10			7	12	4*	5	1			3	9		6						2	11
	8		11			10	6		7		4*	5	1	12		3	9								2	12
	8		11			10*	6		7		4	5	1			3	9					12			2	13
	8		11			10	6				4	5	1			3	9	2				7				14
		8	11			10	6		9		4	5	1			3		2				7				15
9	8		11			10	6				4	5	1			3		2				7				16
9			11	8		10	6	12			4	5	1			3		2				7*				17
9			11	8		10	6	7			4	5	1			3		12							2*	18
9			11	8		10	6				4	5	1			3		2						7		19
9		8	11			12	10				4	5	1		6*	3		2						7		20
9	12	8	11			10	6				4*	5	1			2				3				7		21
9	8	10*	11		7	12	6				4	5	1							3					2	22
9	8		11		7	10*	6				4	5	1	12						3					2	23
9	8	10	11		7		6				4	5	1	12						3					2*	24
9	8	10	11		7		6				4	5	1							3					2	25
9	8	10	11		7		6				4	5	1							3					2	26
9	8	10	11		7		6				4*	5	1	12						3					2	27
			11		9	10	6			7		5	1	4		8				3					2	28
	12		11		9	10	4*			7	8	5	1	6						3					2	29
			11	6	9		4			7	8	5	1	10						3					2	30
9			11	12		6*	4			7	8	5	1	10						3					2	31
	6		11	12	10		4	7			8*	5	1	9						3					2	32
			11	7	10		4				8	5	1	9		6*		3		12					2	33
12		7	11	6	10		4				8	5	1	9*						3					2	34
9*	8		11	12	10		6	7			4	5	1		3										2	35
	6		11	7	10		4			9	8	5	1							3					2	36
	10			6	9		4	7		11	8	5	1*	12						3					2	37
	6		11	12	10		4			7	8	5		9				3			1				2*	38
	6		11	12	10		4			7	8	5		9	2					3*	1					39
	6		11	3	10					7	8	5		9	2				4		1					40
	6		11	3	10		12			7	8*	5		9	2				4		1					41
12	6		11	3*	10					7		5	1	`9	2				4				8			42
14	30	9	41	11	20	24	28	8	10	11	40	40	38	19	7	23	14	8	8	16	4	5	1	3	30	
2	2			5		2	1	1	1	1				6				1		1		1				
2	1	1	7		7		1		1		4	2		2		1	7					3		1		

1 own-goal

9	8	10	11		7		6				4	5	1							3					2	3
9	8	10	11		7		6				4	5	1							3					2	4
2	2	2	2		2		2				2	2	2							2					2	
1		1			1																					

	8		11			10			7		4	5	1	6		3	9								2	2
	1		1			1			1		1	1	1	1		1	1								1	

1973-74

Manager: Billy Bingham

1	Aug	25	(a)	Leeds U	L 1-3	Harper	39,425
2		28	(h)	Leicester C	D 1-1	Kenyon	33,139
3	Sep	1	(h)	Ipswich T	W 3-0	Connolly, Harper, Hurst	32,469
4		5	(a)	Stoke C	D 0-0		22,395
5		8	(a)	Derby C	L 1-2	Husband	27,638
6		11	(h)	Stoke C	D 1-1	Harper	30,242
7		15	(h)	Queen's Park R	W 1-0	Lyons	30,795
8		22	(a)	Wolves	D 1-1	Royle	21,484
9		29	(h)	Arsenal	W 1-0	McLaughlin	31,369
10	Oct	6	(a)	Coventry C	W 2-1	Connolly, Lyons	26,834
11		13	(h)	West Ham U	W 1-0	Harper	34,708
12		20	(h)	Burnley	W 1-0	Clements	41,018
13		27	(a)	Birmingham C	W 2-0	Connolly, Harper	31,181
14	Nov	3	(h)	Tottenham H	D 1-1	Connolly	37,827
15		10	(a)	Chelsea	L 1-3	Kenyon	26,398
16		17	(a)	Norwich C	W 3-1	Bernard, Clements, Opp own-goal	19,825
17		24	(h)	Newcastle U	D 1-1	Lyons	34,376
18	Dec	1	(a)	Southampton	L 0-2		16,992
19		8	(h)	Liverpool	L 0-1		56,098
20		15	(h)	Sheffield U	D 1-1	Clements	21,747
21		22	(a)	Arsenal	L 0-1		19,986
22		26	(h)	Manchester C	W 2-0	Buckley, Hurst	36,007
23		29	(h)	Derby C	W 2-1	Buckley, Royle	37,429
24	Jan	1	(a)	Ipswich T	L 0-3		23,444
25		12	(a)	Queen's Park R	L 0-1		20,051
26		19	(h)	Leeds U	D 0-0		55,740
27	Feb	2	(a)	Sheffield U	D 1-1	Bernard	19,492
28		9	(h)	Wolves	W 2-1	Bernard, Lyons	26,504
29		16	(a)	West Ham U	L 3-4	Telfer 2, Harvey	29,374
30		23	(h)	Coventry C	W 1-0	Hurst	34,762
31	Mar	2	(a)	Leicester C	L 1-2	Latchford	22,286
32		9	(h)	Birmingham C	W 4-1	Latchford 2, Lyons 2	33,944
33		16	(a)	Burnley	L 1-3	Latchford	19,365
34		23	(h)	Chelsea	D 1-1	Bernard	29,542
35		30	(a)	Tottenham H	W 2-0	Connolly, Latchford	19,839
36	Apr	2	(a)	Manchester C	D 1-1	Lyons	22,918
37		6	(a)	Newcastle U	L 1-2	Latchford	45,497
38		13	(h)	Norwich C	W 4-1	Buckley, Latchford, Lyons, Telfer	27,962
39		15	(a)	Manchester U	L 0-3		48,424
40		20	(a)	Liverpool	D 0-0		55,848
41		23	(h)	Manchester U	W 1-0	Lyons	46,183
42		27	(h)	Southampton	L 0-3		30,509

FINAL LEAGUE POSITION: 7th in Division One

Appearances
Sub Appearances
Goals

FA Cup

3	Jan	5	(h)	Blackburn R	W 3-0	Clements, Harper, Hurst
4		27	(h)	West Brom A	D 0-0	
R		30	(a)	West Brom A	L 0-1	

Appearances
Sub Appearances
Goals

League Cup

2	Oct	8	(h)	Reading	W 1-0	Buckley
3		30	(h)	Norwich C	L 0-1	

Appearances
Sub Appearances
Goals

Everton played in the Texaco Cup (see *Everton in Other Competitions*).

Bernard M	Buckley M	Clements D	Connolly J	Darracott T	Harper J	Harvey C	Hurst J	Husband J	Irving D	Jones G	Kendall H	Kenny W	Kenyon R	Latchford R	Lawson D	Lyons M	McLaughlin J	Newton H	Royle J	Seargeant S	Smith J	Styles A	Telfer G	
	10		11	3	8	7					6		5		1	4	2		9					1
			11	2	10	7	6				4		5		1	12	3*	8	9					2
12			11	2	10	7*	6				4		5		1	8		3	9					3
8			11	2	10	7	6				4		5		1	9		3						4
8			11	2	10	7	4	12			6*		5		1	9		3						5
4			11	2	10		6						5		1	8	3	7	9					6
4*			11	2	10		6	12					5		1	8	3	7	9					7
	7	4	11	2	10		6						5		1	8			9	3				8
	8	4	11	2	10	7*	6	12					5		1	9	3							9
12	7	4	11	2	10		6	8*					5		1	9	3							10
7	8	4	11	2	10		6		12				5		1	9*	3							11
7	8	4	11	2	10		6		12				5		1	9*	3							12
7	8	4	11	2	10		6						5		1	9	3							13
7	8	4	11	2	10		6						5		1	9	3							14
8	10	4	11	2	7		6						5		1	9	3							15
7	8	4	11	2	10		6						5		1	9	3							16
7	10	4	11	2	8		6								1	5	3		9					17
7	10	4	11	2	8*		6								1	5	3		9	12				18
7	10	4	11	2	8		6								1	5	3		9					19
7	8	4	11	2			6						5		1	10			9			3		20
7	8*	4		2	12		6						5		1	10			9			3	11	21
7	8	4		2			6						5		1	10			9			3	11	22
7	8	4		2			6						5		1	10			9			3	11	23
7	8	4		2	12		6						5		1	10			9			3	11*	24
	8	4		2	11		6			10			5*		1	12	3		9		7			25
7	8	4	11*	2	12		6			10					1	5	3		9					26
7	8	6*		2		12				10	4		5		1	9						3	11	27
6	8*			2		7				10	4	12	5		1	9	3						11	28
6	8			2		7	4			10			5	9	1		3						11	29
4	7*			2		8	6			10			5	9	1	12	3						11	30
4	8			2		7	6			10			5	9	1	12	3						11*	31
7	8	6	11	2			4						5	9	1	10				3				32
7	8	6	11	2			4						5	9	1	10				3				33
7	8	6	11	2			4			10			5		1	9				3				34
2	8	6	11			7	4			12			5	9*	1	10				3				35
2	8	6	11			7	4			12			5	9*	1	10				3				36
2	8	4				7	6						5	9	1	10				3			11	37
7	8	6		2			4						5	9	1	10				3			11	38
7	8*	6		2			4			12			5	9	1	10				3			11	39
2		4				7	6			8			5	9	1	10				3			11	40
2		4				7	6			8				9	1	5			10	3			11	41
2		8					3					6		10	1	4			9	5	7		11	42
35	33	31	26	36	20	15	39	1		10	7	1	36	13	42	37	21	6	18	12	2	6	15	
2					3	1		3	2	3		1				4				1				
4	3	3	5		5	1	3	1					2	7		9	1		2				3	

1 own-goal

Bernard M	Buckley M	Clements D	Connolly J	Darracott T	Harper J	Harvey C	Hurst J	Husband J	Irving D	Jones G	Kendall H	Kenny W	Kenyon R	Latchford R	Lawson D	Lyons M	McLaughlin J	Newton H	Royle J	Seargeant S	Smith J	Styles A	Telfer G	
7	8	4		2	11		6			12			5		1	10			9			3		3
7	8	4		2	11		6			10*					1	5	3		9				12	4
7	8			2			6			10	4				1	5			9			3	11	R
3	3	2		3	2		3			2	1		1		3	3	1		3			2	1	
										1													1	
		1			1		1																	

Bernard M	Buckley M	Clements D	Connolly J	Darracott T	Harper J	Harvey C	Hurst J	Husband J	Irving D	Jones G	Kendall H	Kenny W	Kenyon R	Latchford R	Lawson D	Lyons M	McLaughlin J	Newton H	Royle J	Seargeant S	Smith J	Styles A	Telfer G	
7	8	4	11	2	10		6						5		1	9	3							2
7	8	4		2	10	12	6	11*					5		1		3		9					3
2	2	2	1	2	2		2	1					2		2	1	2		1					
						1																		
	1																							

1974-75

Manager: Billy Bingham

1	Aug	17	(h)	Derby C	D 0-0		42,293
2		20	(h)	Stoke C	W 2-1	Royle 2	35,817
3		24	(a)	West Ham U	W 3-2	Harvey, Latchford, Royle	22,486
4		28	(a)	Stoke C	D 1-1	Latchford	27,954
5		31	(h)	Arsenal	W 2-1	Latchford 2	42,438
6	Sep	7	(a)	Ipswich T	L 0-1		23,393
7		14	(h)	Wolves	D 0-0		36,875
8		21	(a)	Coventry C	D 1-1	Latchford	15,217
9		24	(a)	Queen's Park R	D 2-2	Latchford, Pearson	16,638
10		28	(h)	Leeds U	W 3-2	Clements, Lyons, Seargeant	41,824
11	Oct	5	(h)	Newcastle U	D 1-1	Buckley	40,000
12		12	(a)	Sheffield U	D 2-2	Buckley, Lyons	23,655
13		15	(h)	West Ham U	D 1-1	Lyons	31,882
14		19	(h)	Chelsea	D 1-1	Jones	35,806
15		26	(a)	Burnley	D 1-1	Jones	22,599
16	Nov	2	(h)	Manchester C	W 2-0	Connolly, Jones	43,905
17		9	(a)	Tottenham H	D 1-1	Connolly	29,052
18		16	(h)	Liverpool	D 0-0		57,190
19		30	(h)	Birmingham C	W 4-1	Connolly, Dobson, Jones, Lyons	38,369
20	Dec	7	(a)	Leicester C	W 2-0	Hurst, Telfer	21,451
21		14	(a)	Derby C	W 1-0	Latchford	24,891
22		21	(h)	Carlisle U	L 2-3	Latchford 2	33,489
23		26	(a)	Wolves	L 0-2		33,120
24		28	(h)	Middlesbrough	D 1-1	Latchford	41,105
25	Jan	11	(h)	Leicester C	W 3-0	Jones, Lyons, Pearson	31,985
26		18	(a)	Birmingham C	W 3-0	Latchford 2, Opp own-goal	32,284
27	Feb	1	(h)	Tottenham H	W 1-0	Pearson	40,912
28		8	(a)	Manchester C	L 1-2	Opp own-goal	44,718
29		22	(a)	Liverpool	D 0-0		55,853
30		25	(h)	Luton T	W 3-1	Dobson, Latchford, Telfer	35,714
31	Mar	1	(a)	Arsenal	W 2-0	Dobson, Lyons	32,216
32		8	(h)	Queen's Park R	W 2-1	Latchford, Lyons	39,567
33		15	(a)	Leeds U	D 0-0		50,084
34		18	(a)	Middlesbrough	L 0-2		32,813
35		22	(h)	Ipswich T	D 1-1	Lyons	46,269
36		29	(a)	Carlisle U	L 0-3		16,049
37		31	(h)	Coventry C	W 1-0	Dobson	39,770
38	Apr	4	(h)	Burnley	D 1-1	Latchford	46,882
39		9	(a)	Luton T	L 1-2	Latchford	13,437
40		12	(a)	Newcastle U	W 1-0	Dobson	29,585
41		19	(h)	Sheffield U	L 2-3	Jones, Smallman	38,348
42		26	(a)	Chelsea	D 1-1	Latchford	28,432

FINAL LEAGUE POSITION: 4th in Division One

Appearances
Sub Appearances
Goals

FA Cup

3	Jan	4	(h)	Altrincham	D 1-1	Clements
R		7	(a*)	Altrincham	W 2-0	Latchford, Lyons
4		25	(a)	Plymouth A	W 3-1	Lyons 2, Pearson
5	Feb	15	(h)	Fulham	L 1-2	Kenyon

* Played at Old Trafford.

Appearances
Sub Appearances
Goals

League Cup

2	Sep	11	(a)	Aston Villa	D 1-1	Latchford
R		18	(h)	Aston Villa	L 0-3	

Appearances
Sub Appearances
Goals

Bernard M	Buckley M	Clements D	Connolly J	Darracott T	Davies D	Dobson M	Harvey C	Hurst J	Irving D	Jones G	Latchford R	Lawson D	Lyons M	Kenny W	Kenyon R	McLaughlin J	McNaught K	Marshall C	Pearson J	Royle J	Scott P	Seargeant S	Smallman D	Telfer G	
2	7	4	11				8	6			10	1			5					9		3			1
	7	4	11	2			8*	6			10	1	12		5					9		3			2
	7	4	11	2			8	6			10	1	5							9		3			3
	7	4	11	2			8	6			10	1	5							9		3			4
	7	4	11	2		8		6*			10	1	12		5					9		3			5
	7	4	11	2		8					10	1	6		5					9		3			6
2	7	4	11			8					10	1	6		5					9		3			7
2	6	11	12		1	8					10		4	7*	5				9			3			8
2	6	11	12		1	8					10		4	7*	5				9			3			9
2	7	6	11		1	8		12			10*		4		5				9			3			10
2	7	6	11		1	8					10		4		5				9			3			11
2	7	6	11		1	8		12			10*		4		5				9			3			12
2	7	6	11		1	8							4		5				9	10		3			13
2	7	6	11		1	8		4		12			10		5				9*			3			14
2	7*		11		1	8		6		4			9		5	12			10			3			15
2	7	4	11		1	8		6		10			9		5							3			16
2	7	4	11		1	8		6		10			9		5							3			17
2	7*	4	11		1	8		6		10			9		5				12			3			18
2		4	11		1	8		6		7	10		9		5							3			19
2		4	11		1	8*		6		7	10		9		5							3		12	20
2		4	11		1			6		7	10		9		5				12			3		8*	21
2	12	4	11		1			6		7	10		9		5							3		8*	22
2	8	4	11		1			6		7	10		9		5				12			3*			23
2	8	4	11		1				9	7	10		6		5*	3								12	24
		4			1					7*	10		8		5	3	6	12	9		2			11	25
12	8*	3			1						10		4		5		6	7	9		2			11	26
		4			1	8					10		9		5		6	7*	12		2	3		11	27
12		4			1	8					10		9		5		6		7		2*	3		11	28
2		4			1	8		6		7	9		10		5				12			3		11*	29
2	12	4			1	8		6		7	10		9		5							3		11*	30
2	7	4			1	8		6		11	10		9		5							3			31
2	7*	4			1	8		6		11	10		9		5				12			3			32
2		4			1	8		6		7	10		9		5							3		11	33
2		4*			1	8		6		7	10		9		5				12			3		11	34
	7	4			1			6		11	10		9		5				8		2	3			35
	7	4*			1	8		6		11	10		9		5				12		2	3			36
2	4				1	8		6		7	9		10		5				12			3		11*	37
2	4	12			1	8		6		7	9		10		5				11			3*			38
2	4	3			1	8		6		7	9				5				11				10		39
2	4	3			1	8		6		7	9				5				11				10*	12	40
2	4	3			1	8		6		7	9				5				11*				10	12	41
2	4	3			1			6		7	9		8		5				11				10		42
31	31	39	22	5	35	30	4	29	1	25	36	7	36	2	40	2	4	2	17	8	6	35	4	11	
2	2	1	2					2		1			2			1		1	9					4	
	2	1	3			5	1	1		6	17		8						3	3		1	1	2	

2 own-goals

Bernard M	Buckley M	Clements D	Connolly J	Darracott T	Davies D	Dobson M	Harvey C	Hurst J	Irving D	Jones G	Latchford R	Lawson D	Lyons M	Kenny W	Kenyon R	McLaughlin J	McNaught K	Marshall C	Pearson J	Royle J	Scott P	Seargeant S	Smallman D	Telfer G	
2		4	11*		1				9	7	10		6			3	5		8					12	3
		4			1	8				7	10		6			3	5		9		2			11	R
12		4			1	8							10		5		6	7*	9		2	3		11	4
2		4			1	8		6		7	10*		9		5				11			3		12	5
2		4	1		4	3		1	1	3	3		4		2	2	3	1	4		2	2		2	
1																								2	
		1									1		3		1				1						

Bernard M	Buckley M	Clements D	Connolly J	Darracott T	Davies D	Dobson M	Harvey C	Hurst J	Irving D	Jones G	Latchford R	Lawson D	Lyons M	Kenny W	Kenyon R	McLaughlin J	McNaught K	Marshall C	Pearson J	Royle J	Scott P	Seargeant S	Smallman D	Telfer G	
2	7	4	11			8					10	1	6		5					9		3			2
2	7	4*	11			8					10	1	6		5				12	9		3			R
2	2	2	2			2					2	2	2		2					2		2			
																			1						
											1														

1975-76

Manager: Billy Bingham

1	Aug	16	(h)	Coventry C	L	1-4	Kenyon	32,343
2		19	(a)	Burnley	D	1-1	Smallman	20,069
3		23	(a)	Birmingham C	W	1-0	Smallman	26,814
4		26	(h)	Sheffield U	W	3-0	Latchford, Lyons, Smallman	25,846
5		30	(h)	Derby C	W	2-0	Latchford, Lyons	32,483
6	Sep	6	(a)	Norwich C	L	2-4	Latchford, Pearson	19,672
7		13	(h)	Newcastle U	W	3-0	Clements, Latchford, Lyons	28,938
8		20	(a)	Arsenal	D	2-2	Buckley, Smallman	24,864
9		27	(h)	Liverpool	D	0-0		55,769
10	Oct	4	(a)	West Ham U	W	1-0	G.Jones	31,985
11		11	(a)	Queen's Park R	L	0-5		23,435
12		18	(h)	Aston Villa	W	2-1	G.Jones 2	30,376
13		25	(a)	Wolves	W	2-1	Dobson, G.Jones	20,063
14	Nov	1	(h)	Leicester C	D	1-1	Smallman	24,930
15		8	(a)	Stoke C	L	2-3	Pearson, Telfer	24,677
16		15	(h)	Manchester C	D	1-1	Telfer	32,077
17		22	(a)	Aston Villa	L	1-3	Telfer	33,949
18		29	(a)	Leeds U	L	2-5	Clements, Latchford	30,879
19	Dec	6	(h)	Ipswich T	D	3-3	Dobson 2, Latchford	24,601
20		10	(a)	Totenham H	D	2-2	Latchford, Telfer	18,638
21		13	(h)	Birmingham C	W	5-2	Dobson, Hamilton, G.Jones, Latchford, Telfer	20,188
22		19	(a)	Coventry C	W	2-1	G.Jones, Latchford	14,419
23		23	(h)	Manchester U	D	1-1	Latchford	41,732
24		27	(a)	Middlesbrough	D	1-1	Latchford	29,275
25	Jan	10	(a)	Newcastle U	L	0-5		31,726
26		17	(h)	Norwich C	D	1-1	Dobson	23,164
27		31	(h)	Burnley	L	2-3	Hamilton 2	21,389
28	Feb	7	(a)	Sheffield U	D	0-0		20,113
29		21	(a)	Manchester C	L	0-3		33,148
30		24	(h)	Tottenham H	W	1-0	Lyons	18,126
31		28	(h)	Wolves	W	3-0	Telfer 2, Hamilton	21,827
32	Mar	6	(a)	Leicester C	L	0-1		18,490
33		13	(h)	Queen's Park R	L	0-2		25,006
34		20	(h)	Leeds U	L	1-3	Lyons	28,566
35		27	(a)	Ipswich T	L	0-1		22,373
36	Apr	3	(a)	Liverpool	L	0-1		54,632
37		7	(h)	Stoke C	W	2-1	Bernard, Hamilton	16,974
38		10	(h)	Arsenal	D	0-0		20,774
39		17	(a)	Manchester U	L	1-2	Telfer	61,879
40		19	(h)	Middlesbrough	W	3-1	Connolly, Latchford, Pearson	18,204
41		21	(a)	Derby C	W	3-1	King 2, Pearson	22,488
42		24	(h)	West Ham U	W	2-0	Bernard, Pearson	26,101

FINAL LEAGUE POSITION: 11th in Division One

Appearances
Sub Appearances
Goals

FA Cup

3	Jan	3	(a)	Derby C	L	1-2	G.Jones

Appearances
Sub Appearances
Goals

League Cup

2	Sep	9	(h)	Arsenal	D	2-2	Lyons, Smallman
R		23	(a)	Arsenal	W	1-0	Kenyon
3	Oct	8	(h)	Carlisle U	W	2-0	Dobson, Latchford
4	Nov	11	(h)	Notts C	D	2-2	Irving, G.Jones
R		25	(a)	Notts C	L	0-2	

Appearances
Sub Appearances
Goals

Everton played in UEFA Cup (see *Everton in Europe*).

Bernard M	Brand D	Buckley M	Clements D	Connolly J	Darracott T	Davies D	Dobson M	Goodlass R	Hamilton B	Hurst J	Irving D	Jones D	Jones G	Kenyon R	King A	Latchford R	Lawson D	Lyons M	McLaughlin J	McNaught K	Marshall C	Pearson J	Robinson N	Seargeant S	Smallman D	Telfer G	
2			4				8			6				5		9	1	7				11		3	10		1
2			4				8							5		9	1	6			7	11		3	10		2
		7	3		2		8			12				5		9	1	6			11*	4			10		3
2		7	3				8							5		9	1	6			11*	4			10	12	4
2		7	3				8							5		9	1	6			11*	4			10	12	5
2		7	3				8						11	5		9	1	6				4			10		6
2		7	12				8						11	5		9	1	6				4*		3	10		7
2		7					8						11	5		9	1	6				4		3	10		8
		7				1	8						11	5		9		6	2			4		3	10		9
		7	3			1	8						11	5		9		6		12		4*		2		10	10
2		7	10			1	8						11	5		9		6				4		3			11
2		7*	10			1	8						11			9		6		5		4		3	12		12
2		7				1	8						11	5*		9		6		12		4		3	10		13
		7				1	8					12	11*			9		6	2	5		4		3	10		14
		7*			2	1	8			11	9							6		5		4		3	10	12	15
		7			2		8				9*		11				1	6		5		4		3	10	12	16
		7			2*		8						11	4		9	1	6		5		12		3		10	17
	1	7*	4		2		8		10					5		9		6				12		3		11	18
4			3		2		8		7*				11	5		9	1	6				12				10	19
4		12			2	1	8		7				11	5		9		6						3*		10	20
2		7			3	1	8		4				11	5		9		6								10	21
2		7			3	1	8		4	12			11	5		9		6								10*	22
2					3	1	8	11	7	4				5		9		6							10		23
2					3*	1	8		7	4			11	5		9		6	12			10					24
2				12	3	1	8		7	4			11*	5		9		6				10					25
2		6			3		8		7			12	11	5		9	1	4				10*					26
		6					8		7				11	5		9	1	4					2	3		10	27
		6		10	2		8		7								1	4		5		9		3		11	28
2				10	3		8		7	6	9		12	5*			1	4								11	29
2		6		10	3		8		7				11				1	4		5						9	30
2		6			3		8	10	7				11				1	4		5						9	31
2		6		10			8		7			3	11				1	4		5						9	32
2		6		10*			8	12	7			3	11				1	4		5						9	33
2		6		10			8		7			3	11*				1	4		5				12		9	34
2		6		10			8		7			3					1	4		5		11				9	35
2		6		10		1	8		7			3		12		9		4		5*						11	36
2				10		1	8		7			3		6				4		5		9				11	37
2				10		1	8		7*			3		12		9		4		5		6				11	38
		7*		10	2	1	8		12			3		6		9		4		5						11	39
				10	2	1	8		7*	12		3		5	6	9		4				11					40
12				10	2	1	8					3		5*	6	9		4		7		11					41
2		7		10			8					3			6	9	1	4		5		11					42
29	1	30	11	14	20	19	42	2	22	6	3	11	24	28	3	31	22	42	2	18	4	26	1	17	14	20	
1		1	1	1				1	1	3		2	1	2					1	2		3		1	1	4	
2		1	2	1			5		5				6	1	2	12		5				5			5	8	

Bernard M	Brand D	Buckley M	Clements D	Connolly J	Darracott T	Davies D	Dobson M	Goodlass R	Hamilton B	Hurst J	Irving D	Jones D	Jones G	Kenyon R	King A	Latchford R	Lawson D	Lyons M	McLaughlin J	McNaught K	Marshall C	Pearson J	Robinson N	Seargeant S	Smallman D	Telfer G	
2				12	3	1	8		7	4			11	5		9		6				10*					3
1					1	1	1		1	1			1	1		1		1				1					
				1																							
													1														

Bernard M	Brand D	Buckley M	Clements D	Connolly J	Darracott T	Davies D	Dobson M	Goodlass R	Hamilton B	Hurst J	Irving D	Jones D	Jones G	Kenyon R	King A	Latchford R	Lawson D	Lyons M	McLaughlin J	McNaught K	Marshall C	Pearson J	Robinson N	Seargeant S	Smallman D	Telfer G	
2		7	3				8						11	5		9	1	6				4			10		2
2		7				1	8						11	5		9		6				4		3	10		R
12		7	3			1	8						11	5		9		6				4		2		10*	3
		7	3*		2		8			4	9		11				1	6		5		10				12	4
		7	3				8						11	5		9	1	6				4*		2	12	10	R
2		5	4		1	2	5			1	1		5	4		4	3	5		1		5		3	2	2	
1																									1	1	
							1				1		1	1		1		1							1		

1976-77

Manager: Billy Bingham

1	Aug	21	(a)	Queen's Park R	W 4-0	Latchford 2, Bernard, Opp own-goal	24,449
2		24	(h)	Ipswich T	D 1-1	Telfer	33,070
3		28	(h)	Aston Villa	L 0-2		32,055
4	Sep	4	(a)	Leicester C	D 1-1	Latchford	18,083
5		11	(h)	Stoke C	W 3-0	Telfer 2, Latchford	22,277
6		18	(a)	Arsenal	L 1-3	Telfer	34,076
7		25	(h)	Bristol C	W 2-0	Dobson, Latchford	25,761
8	Oct	2	(a)	Sunderland	W 1-0	Goodlass	34,670
9		5	(h)	Manchester C	D 2-2	Dobson, King	31,370
10		16	(a)	Liverpool	L 1-3	Dobson	55,141
11		23	(h)	West Ham U	W 3-2	King, Latchford, Lyons	23,163
12		30	(a)	Tottenham H	D 3-3	King, Latchford, McNaught	26,047
13	Nov	6	(h)	Leeds U	L 0-2		32,618
14		20	(h)	Derby C	W 2-0	King, Latchford	23,020
15		24	(a)	Newcastle U	L 1-4	Lyons	31,203
16		27	(a)	West Brom A	L 0-3		21,078
17	Dec	11	(a)	Coventry C	L 2-4	Kenyon, King	18,977
18		18	(h)	Birmingham C	D 2-2	McKenzie 2	32,532
19		27	(a)	Manchester U	L 0-4		56,786
20		29	(h)	Middlesbrough	D 2-2	Latchford, McNaught	28,169
21	Jan	15	(a)	Ipswich T	L 0-2		25,570
22		22	(h)	Queen's Park R	L 1-3	McKenzie	26,875
23	Feb	5	(a)	Aston Villa	L 0-2		41,305
24		12	(h)	Leicester C	L 1-2	Latchford	28,024
25		19	(a)	Stoke C	W 1-0	Dobson	19,543
26	Mar	1	(h)	Arsenal	W 2-1	Jones, Latchford	29,902
27		5	(a)	Bristol C	W 2-1	Latchford, Opp own-goal	21,108
28		22	(h)	Liverpool	D 0-0		56,562
29		26	(h)	Tottenham H	W 4-0	Dobson, King, Latchford, Lyons	32,549
30	Apr	2	(a)	West Ham U	D 2-2	Goodlass, Pearson	22,518
31		5	(h)	Manchester U	L 1-2	Dobson	38,216
32		9	(a)	Middlesbrough	D 2-2	Latchford, Pearson	16,159
33		16	(a)	Derby C	W 3-2	Latchford, McKenzie, Pejic	23,443
34		19	(h)	Norwich C	W 3-1	King, McNaught, Pearson	28,856
35		30	(a)	Norwich C	L 1-2	Pearson	19,091
36	May	4	(a)	Leeds U	D 0-0		22,175
37		7	(h)	Coventry C	D 1-1	Rioch	24,569
38		10	(a)	Manchester C	D 1-1	Lyons	38,004
39		14	(a)	Birmingham C	D 1-1	Latchford	22,660
40		16	(h)	West Brom A	D 1-1	Dobson	20,102
41		19	(h)	Sunderland	W 2-0	Latchford, Rioch	36,075
42		24	(h)	Newcastle U	W 2-0	Dobson, McKenzie	25,208

FINAL LEAGUE POSITION: 9th in Division One

Appearances
Sub Appearances
Goals

FA Cup

3	Jan	8	(h)	Stoke C	W 2-0	Lyons, McKenzie
4		29	(a)	Swindon T	D 2-2	Latchford, McKenzie
R	Feb	1	(h)	Swindon T	W 2-1	Dobson, Jones
5		26	(a)	Cardiff C	W 2-1	Latchford, McKenzie
6	Mar	19	(h)	Derby C	W 2-0	Latchford, Pearson
SF	Apr	23	(n*)	Liverpool	D 2-2	McKenzie, Rioch
R		27	(n*)	Liverpool	L 0-3	

* Played at Maine Road.

Appearances
Sub Appearances
Goals

League Cup

2	Aug	30	(h)	Cambridge U	W 3-0	Dobson, King, Latchford
3	Sep	20	(a)	Stockport C	W 1-0	Latchford
4	Oct	26	(h)	Coventry C	W 3-0	King 2, Lyons
5	Dec	1	(a)	Manchester U	W 3-0	King 2, Dobson
SF	Jan	18	(h)	Bolton W	D 1-1	McKenzie
	Feb	15	(a)	Bolton W	W 1-0	Latchford
F	Mar	12	(n*)	Aston Villa	D 0-0	
R		16	(n†)	Aston Villa	D 1-1	Latchford
2R	Apr	13	(n‡)	Aston Villa	L 2-3	Latchford, Lyons

* Played at Wembley Stadium. † Played at Hillsborough. ‡ Played at Old Trafford.

Appearances
Sub Appearances
Goals

Bernard M	Brand D	Buckley M	Darracott T	Davies D	Dobson M	Goodlass R	Hamilton B	Higgins M	Jones D	Kenyon R	King A	Latchford R	Lawson D	Lyons M	McKenzie D	McNaught K	Pearson J	Pejic M	Rioch B	Robinson N	Seargeant S	Smallman D	Telfer G	
2				1	8				3	5	7	9		4		6	10						11	1
2				1	8					6	7	9		4		5	10				3		11	2
2				1	8				3	6	7	9		4		5	10*					12	11	3
2				1	8	10			3	6	7	9		4		5							11	4
2				1	8	10			3	6	7	9		4		5							11	5
2*			12	1	8	10			3	6	7	9		4		5							11	6
			2	1	8	10	6		3		7	9		4		5							11	7
			2	1	8	10	6		3		7	9		4		5							11	8
				1	8	10	6	3	2		7	9		4		5							11	9
6*			2	1	8	10			3		7	9		4		5	12						11	10
			2	1	8*	10	6		3		7	9		4		5	12						11	11
2			12	1	8	10	6		3		7	9		4		5							11*	12
2		12		1	8		10		3	6	7	9		4		5						11*		13
2				1	8	10			3	6	7	9		4		5							11	14
2			12	1	8	10			3	6	7*	9		4		5							11	15
			2	1	8	10	11		3	6	7	9		4*		5							12	16
			2	1	8	11			3	6	7	9			10	5			4					17
			2		8	11			3		7	9	1	4	10	5			6					18
			2		8	11			3		7	9	1	4	10	5			6					19
					8	11			2		7	9	1	4	10	5			6		3			20
					8		11		2		7	9	1	4	10	5			6		3			21
			2*		8	11	12		3		7	9	1	4	10	5			6					22
2					8		11		3		7	9	1	4	10	5			6					23
2					8	12	11		3		7*	9	1	4	10	5			6					24
					8	11	7		2			9	1	6	10	5		3	4					25
					8	11	7		2			9	1	4	10	5		3	6					26
					8	11	7		2		6	9	1	4	10	5		3						27
			2		8					7*	6	9	1	4		5	11	3	10				12	28
			2		8	11					6	9	1	4	7	5		3	10					29
			6		8	11	7		2			9	1	4		5	12	3					10*	30
		12	2		8	11			3*	7	6	9	1	4		5	10							31
			2		8	11				4*	6	9	1	12		5	10	3	7					32
		12		1	8	11	7					9*		4	10	5		3	6	2				33
		12		1	8	11					6*			4	9	5	10	3	7	2				34
		7	2	1		11*	12				8			4	10	5	9	3	6					35
		7	2	1			8				11			4	10	5	9	3	6					36
		7	2	1	8						11			4	10	5	9	3	6					37
		7	2	1	8						12			4	10	5	9	3	6		11*			38
12		7	2	1	8						11	9		4		5		3	6				10*	39
6		7	2	1	8	12					11			4		5	9	3					10*	40
		7		1	8	11						9		4	10	5		3	6	2				41
	1				8	11		4			7	9*			10	5	12	3	6	2				42
14	1	7	20	26	40	29	16	2	28	14	36	36	15	39	20	42	12	17	22	4	4	1	17	
1		4	3			2	2				1			1			4					1	2	
1					8	2			1	1	7	17		4	5	3	4	1	2				4	

2 own-goals

Bernard M	Brand D	Buckley M	Darracott T	Davies D	Dobson M	Goodlass R	Hamilton B	Higgins M	Jones D	Kenyon R	King A	Latchford R	Lawson D	Lyons M	McKenzie D	McNaught K	Pearson J	Pejic M	Rioch B	Robinson N	Seargeant S	Smallman D	Telfer G	
					8	11			3		7	9	1	4	10	5			6	2				3
			2*		8	11	12		3		7	9	1	4	10	5			6					4
2					8	11			3		7	9	1	4	10	5			6					R
					8	11	7		2			9	1	4	10	5		3	6					5
			2			11				8	6	9*	1	4		5	10	3	7				12	6
		7	2		8*	11	12						1	4	10	5	9	3	6					SF
		7	2		8*	11					12		1	4	10	5	9	3	6					R
1		2	4		6	7	1		4	1	4	5	7	7	6	7	3	4	7	1				
							2				1												1	
					1				1			3		1	4		1		1					

Bernard M	Brand D	Buckley M	Darracott T	Davies D	Dobson M	Goodlass R	Hamilton B	Higgins M	Jones D	Kenyon R	King A	Latchford R	Lawson D	Lyons M	McKenzie D	McNaught K	Pearson J	Pejic M	Rioch B	Robinson N	Seargeant S	Smallman D	Telfer G	
2				1	8	11	12		3	6	7	9		4		5						10*		2
			2	1	8	10	6		3		7	9		4		5							11	3
2				1	8	10	6		3		7	9		4		5							11	4
			2	1	8	10	12		3	6	7	9		4*		5							11	5
					8	11	6		3		7	9	1	4	10	5·				2				SF
2					8	11	6		3		7	9	1	4	10	5								
			3		8	11	7		2		6	9	1	4	10	5								F
2			3			11	7*			8	6	9	1	4	10	5	12							R
			3		8	11	7				6	9	1	4		5	10*			2	12			2R
4			5	4	8	9	7		7	3	9	9	5	9	4	9	1			2		1	3	
							2										1				1			
					2						5	5		2	1									

1977-78

Manager: Gordon Lee

1	Aug	20	(h)	Nottingham F	L 1-3	Pearson	38,001
2		23	(a)	Arsenal	L 0-1		32,954
3		27	(a)	Aston Villa	W 2-1	McKenzie 2	37,806
4	Sep	3	(h)	Wolves	D 0-0		36,636
5		10	(a)	Leicester C	W 5-1	King 2, Latchford, McKenzie, Thomas	16,425
6		17	(h)	Norwich C	W 3-0	Dobson, McKenzie, Rioch	34,405
7		24	(a)	West Ham U	D 1-1	McKenzie	25,296
8	Oct	1	(h)	Manchester C	D 1-1	Latchford	43,286
9		4	(h)	West Brom A	W 3-1	Higgins, King, Latchford	34,582
10		8	(a)	Queen's Park R	W 5-1	Latchford 4, McKenzie	20,495
11		15	(h)	Bristol C	W 1-0	King	39,230
12		22	(a)	Liverpool	D 0-0		51,668
13		29	(h)	Newcastle U	D 4-4	Latchford 2, Lyons, Pejic	37,647
14	Nov	5	(a)	Derby C	W 1-0	Lyons	29,335
15		12	(h)	Birmingham C	W 2-1	Latchford 2	37,743
16		19	(a)	Ipswich T	D 3-3	Buckley, Lyons, Pearson	22,790
17		26	(h)	Coventry C	W 6-0	Latchford 3, Dobson, King, Pearson	43,309
18	Dec	3	(a)	Chelsea	W 1-0	Latchford	33,890
19		10	(h)	Middlesbrough	W 3-0	Latchford 2, Buckley	38,647
20		17	(a)	Birmingham C	D 0-0		22,177
21		26	(h)	Manchester U	L 2-6	Dobson, Latchford	48,335
22		27	(a)	Leeds U	L 1-3	Dobson	46,727
23		31	(h)	Arsenal	W 2-0	King, Latchford	47,035
24	Jan	2	(a)	Nottingham F	D 1-1	Ross	44,030
25		14	(h)	Aston Villa	W 1-0	King	40,630
26		21	(a)	Wolves	L 1-3	Ross	23,777
27	Feb	4	(h)	Leicester C	W 2-0	Latchford 2	33,707
28		18	(h)	West Ham U	W 2-1	McKenzie, Thomas	33,826
29		25	(a)	Manchester C	L 0-1		46,817
30	Mar	4	(h)	Queen's Park R	D 3-3	Dobson, King, Ross	33,861
31		11	(a)	Bristol C	W 1-0	Ross	25,614
32		15	(a)	Norwich C	D 0-0		18,905
33		24	(a)	Newcastle U	W 2-0	Latchford, McKenzie	28,933
34		25	(h)	Leeds U	W 2-0	Latchford, McKenzie	45,020
35		27	(a)	Manchester U	W 2-1	Latchford 2	55,277
36	Apr	1	(h)	Derby C	W 2-1	Dobson, Latchford	38,213
37		5	(h)	Liverpool	L 0-1		52,759
38		8	(a)	Coventry C	L 2-3	Latchford, Lyons	26,008
39		15	(h)	Ipswich T	W 1-0	Latchford	33,402
40		22	(a)	Middlesbrough	D 0-0		15,969
41		25	(a)	West Brom A	L 1-3	Telfer	20,247
42		29	(h)	Chelsea	W 6-0	Latchford 2, Dobson, Lyons, Robinson, Wright	39,500

FINAL LEAGUE POSITION: 3rd in Division One

Appearances
Sub Appearances
Goals

FA Cup

3	Jan	7	(h)	Aston Villa	W 4-1	King, Latchford, McKenzie, Ross
4		28	(a)	Middlesbrough	L 2-3	Lyons, Telfer

Appearances
Sub Appearances
Goals

League Cup

2	Aug	30	(a)	Sheffield U	W 3-0	King, Latchford, McKenzie
3	Oct	25	(h)	Middlesbrough	D 2-2	King, Telfer
R		31	(a)	Middlesbrough	W 2-1	Lyons, Pearson
4	Nov	29	(a)	Sheffield W	W 3-1	Dobson, Lyons, Pearson
5	Jan	18	(a)	Leeds U	L 1-4	Thomas

Appearances
Sub Appearances
Goals

Buckley M	Darracott T	Dobson M	Goodlass R	Higgins M	Jones D	Kenyon R	King A	Latchford R	Lyons M	McKenzie D	Pearson J	Pejic M	Rioch B	Robinson N	Ross T	Seargeant S	Telfer G	Thomas D	Wood G	Wright W	
	8*		12	6	2	5	7		4	10	9	3						11	1		1
	2			12		5*	7	9	4	10	8	3	6					11	1		2
	2			5			7	9	4	10	8	3	6					11	1		3
	2	6		5			7	9	4	10	8	3						11	1		4
	2*	8		5	12		7	9	4	10		3	6					11	1		5
	2	8		5	12		7	9	4	10		3	6*					11	1		6
	2	8		5	12		7	9	4	10		3	6					11*	1		7
	2	8		5			7	9	4	10		3	6					11	1		8
		8		5	2		7	9	4	10	6	3						11	1		9
		8		5	2		7	9	4	10	6	3						11	1		10
6*	12	8		5	2		7	9	4		10	3					11		1		11
		8		5	2		7	9	4		10	3	6					11	1		12
		8		5	2		7	9*	4		10	3	6				12	11	1		13
6		8		5	2*		7	9	4		10				3	12		11	1		14
6		8		5	2		7	9	4		10	3						11	1		15
6		8		5	2		7	9	4		10	3*			12			11	1		16
6		8		5	2		7	9	4		10	3						11	1		17
6		8		5	2		7	9	4		10	3						11	1		18
6		8		5	2		7	9	4		10	3						11	1		19
6		8		5	2		7	9	4		10	3						11	1		20
6		8		5	2		7	9	4		10*	3			12			11	1		21
		8		5	2		7	9	4	10		3			6			11	1		22
	2	8				5	7	9	4	10		3			6			11	1		23
	2	8			12	5*	7	9	4	10		3			6			11	1		24
	2	8		5			7	9	4	10		3			6			11	1		25
	2*				12	5	7	9	4	10	8	3			6			11	1		26
		8		5	2		7	9	4	10		3			6		11*		1	12	27
		8		5	2		7	9*	4	10		3			6		12	11	1		28
		8		5	2		7		4	10	9	3			6		11		1		29
		8			2*	5	7		4	10	9	3			6		12	11	1		30
		8			2	5	7	9	4	10		3			6			11	1		31
	5	8			2		7	9	4	10		3			6			11	1		32
	2	8			2		7	9	4	10*	12	3			6		11		1		33
	5	8			2		7	9	4	10		3			6			11	1		34
	5	8			2		7	9	4	10		3			6			11	1		35
	5	8			2		7	9	4	10		3			6			11	1		36
	5	8			2		7	9	4	10		3			6			11	1		37
	5	8			2		7	9	4	10		3			6			11	1		38
6		8			2		7	9	4	10		3		5				11	1		39
		8			3		7	9	4		6			2			10	11	1	5	40
6		8					7	9	4			3		2			10	11	1	5	41
6		8					7	9	4			3		2			10	11	1	5	42
12	19	38		25	29	7	42	39	42	28	21	40	8	4	18		7	38	42	3	
	1		1	1	5						1				2	1	3			1	
2		7		1			8	30	5	9	3	1	1	1	4		1	2		1	

Buckley M	Darracott T	Dobson M	Goodlass R	Higgins M	Jones D	Kenyon R	King A	Latchford R	Lyons M	McKenzie D	Pearson J	Pejic M	Rioch B	Robinson N	Ross T	Seargeant S	Telfer G	Thomas D	Wood G	Wright W	
	2	8		5			7	9	4	10		3			6			11	1		3
		8			2	5*	7	9	4	12	11	3			6		10		1		4
	1	2		1	1	1	2	2	2	1	1	2			2		1	1	2		
										1											
							1	1	1	1					1		1				

Buckley M	Darracott T	Dobson M	Goodlass R	Higgins M	Jones D	Kenyon R	King A	Latchford R	Lyons M	McKenzie D	Pearson J	Pejic M	Rioch B	Robinson N	Ross T	Seargeant S	Telfer G	Thomas D	Wood G	Wright W	
	2			5	3		7	9	4	10	8		6	12				11*	1		2
		8		5	2		7	9*	4		10	3	6				12	11	1		3
6		8		5	2		7	9	4		10	3						11	1		R
6		8		5	2		7	9	4		10	3						11	1		4
6*	2	8		5	12		7	9	4	10		3						11	1		5
3	2	4		5	4		5	5	5	2	4	4	2					5	5		
					1									1			1				
		1					2	1	2	1	2						1	1			

1978-79

Manager: Gordon Lee

1	Aug	19	(a)	Chelsea	W 1-0	King	32,683
2		22	(h)	Derby C	W 2-1	King, Nulty	40,125
3		26	(h)	Arsenal	W 1-0	Thomas	41,161
4	Sep	2	(a)	Manchester U	D 1-1	King	53,982
5		9	(h)	Middlesbrough	W 2-0	Dobson, Lyons	36,191
6		16	(a)	Aston Villa	D 1-1	Walsh	38,636
7		23	(h)	Wolves	W 2-0	King, Latchford	38,895
8		30	(a)	Bristol C	D 2-2	Latchford 2	22,502
9	Oct	7	(h)	Southampton	D 0-0		38,769
10		14	(a)	Ipswich T	W 1-0	Latchford	22,830
11		21	(a)	Queen's Park R	D 1-1	Latchford	21,171
12		28	(h)	Liverpool	W 1-0	King	53,141
13	Nov	4	(a)	Nottingham F	D 0-0		35,515
14		11	(h)	Chelsea	W 3-2	Dobson 2, King	38,346
15		18	(a)	Arsenal	D 2-2	Dobson, Ross	39,711
16		21	(h)	Manchester U	W 3-0	King, Latchford, Ross	42,126
17		25	(a)	Norwich C	W 1-0	Lyons	18,930
18	Dec	9	(a)	Birmingham C	W 3-1	Latchford, Ross, Todd	23,391
19		16	(h)	Leeds U	D 1-1	Ross	37,997
20		23	(a)	Coventry C	L 2-3	Latchford, Lyons	22,778
21		26	(h)	Manchester C	W 1-0	Wright	46,996
22		30	(h)	Tottenham H	D 1-1	Lyons	44,572
23	Jan	31	(h)	Aston Villa	D 1-1	Thomas	29,079
24	Feb	3	(a)	Wolves	L 0-1		21,892
25		10	(h)	Bristol C	W 4-1	King 3, Wright	29,116
26		17	(a)	Southampton	L 0-3		20,681
27		24	(h)	Ipswich T	L 0-1		29,031
28	Mar	3	(h)	Queen's Park R	W 2-1	Latchford, Telfer	24,809
29		6	(a)	Middlesbrough	W 2-1	Jack, Latchford	16,084
30		10	(h)	Nottingham F	D 1-1	Telfer	37,745
31		13	(a)	Liverpool	D 1-1	King	52,352
32		24	(a)	Derby C	D 0-0		20,814
33		30	(h)	Norwich C	D 2-2	Lyons 2	26,825
34	Apr	3	(a)	Bolton W	L 1-3	Ross	27,263
35		7	(a)	West Brom A	L 0-1		29,593
36		10	(h)	Coventry C	D 3-3	Kidd, Latchford, Ross	25,302
37		14	(a)	Manchester C	D 0-0		39,711
38		16	(h)	Bolton W	W 1-0	Higgins	31,214
39		21	(a)	Leeds U	L 0-1		29,125
40		28	(h)	Birmingham C	W 1-0	King	23,048
41	May	1	(h)	West Brom A	L 0-2		30,083
42		5	(a)	Tottenham H	D 1-1	Kidd	26,077

FINAL LEAGUE POSITION: 4th in Division One

Appearances
Sub Appearances
Goals

FA Cup

3	Jan	10	(a)	Sunderland	L 1-2	Dobson

Appearances
Sub Appearances
Goals

League Cup

2	Aug	29	(h)	Wimbledon	W 8-0	Latchford 5, Dobson 3
3	Oct	3	(h)	Darlington	W 1-0	Dobson
4	Nov	7	(h)	Nottingham F	L 2-3	Latchford, Opp own-goal

Appearances
Sub Appearances
Goals

Everton played in the UEFA Cup (see *Everton in Europe*).

Barton J	Darracott T	Dobson M	Eastoe P	Heard T	Higgins M	Jack R	Jones D	Kenyon R	Kidd B	King A	Latchford R	Lyons M	Nulty G	Pejic M	Robinson N	Ross T	Telfer G	Thomas D	Todd C	Walsh M	Wood G	Wright W	
	2	8			5					7	9	4	6	3				11		10	1		1
	2	8								7	9	4	6	3				11		10	1	5	2
	2	8								7	9	4	6	3				11		10	1	5	3
	2	8								7	9	4	6	3				11		10	1	5	4
	2	8								7	9	4	6	3				11		10	1	5	5
	2	8								7	9	4	6	3				11		10	1	5	6
		8								7	9	4		3		6		11	2	10	1	5	7
		8								7	9	4		3		6		11	2	10	1	5	8
		8								7	9	4		3		6		11	2	10	1	5	9
		8								7	9	4		3		6		11	2	10	1	5	10
		8								7	9	4*	6	3	12			11	2	10	1	5	11
		8						4		7	9		6	3				11	2	10	1	5	12
	2	8								7	9			3		6		11	4	10	1	5	13
		8								7	9	4		3	12	6		11	2	10*	1	5	14
		8								7	9	4	12	3		6		11	2	10	1	5*	15
		8								7	9	4	12	3		6		11	2	10*	1	5	16
		8						10		7	9	4		3		6		11	2		1	5	17
		8			10					7	9	4		3		6		11	2		1	5	18
		8*			10					7	9	4	12	3		6		11	2		1	5	19
		8			10		3			7	9	4	6					11	2		1	5	20
		8			10		3*			7	9	4	6		12		11		2		1	5	21
		8						3		7	9	4	6		10		11		2		1	5	22
		8			3					7	9	4				6		11	2	10	1	5	23
		8		12	3					7	9	4				6		11	2	10*	1	5	24
		8			3					10	9	4			2	6		11	7		1	5	25
		8		6	3					10	9	4			2			11	7		1	5	26
		8		6	3					7	9	4					10	11*	2	12	1	5	27
		8*		3						7	9	4			2	6	10	11		12	1	5	28
		8		3	2	7					9	4				6	10	11			1	5	29
		8		3	2					7	9	4				6	10*	11		12	1	5	30
		8		3						7	9	4				6	10	11	2		1	5	31
		8		3	9					7		4				6	10	11	2		1	5	32
12		8		3	9*					7		4				6	10	11	2		1	5	33
5		8					3		7	9		4				6	10	11	2		1		34
2		8	12				3		10	7	9	4				6		11*	5		1		35
2		8	11				3		10	7	9*	4				6	12				1	5	36
2			11		4		3*		10	9			8			6	12		7		1	5	37
2		8	11		5		3		10			4	7			6					1	9	38
2			11	8	5		3		10	7		4				6					1	9	39
2		8	11*		5		3		10	7	9		12						4		1	6	40
2		8	11		5		3		10	7	9	4									1	6	41
2		8	11		5		3		10	7	9								4		1	6	42
9	7	40	7	9	20	1	11	3	9	40	36	37	13	19	4	26	10	33	29	18	42	39	
1			1	1									4		3		2			3			
		4			1	1			2	12	11	6	1			6	2	2	1	1		2	

Barton J	Darracott T	Dobson M	Eastoe P	Heard T	Higgins M	Jack R	Jones D	Kenyon R	Kidd B	King A	Latchford R	Lyons M	Nulty G	Pejic M	Robinson N	Ross T	Telfer G	Thomas D	Todd C	Walsh M	Wood G	Wright W	
	3	8								7	9	4				6		11	2	10	1	5	3
	1	1								1	1	1				1		1	1	1	1	1	
		1																					

Barton J	Darracott T	Dobson M	Eastoe P	Heard T	Higgins M	Jack R	Jones D	Kenyon R	Kidd B	King A	Latchford R	Lyons M	Nulty G	Pejic M	Robinson N	Ross T	Telfer G	Thomas D	Todd C	Walsh M	Wood G	Wright W	
		8								7	9	4	6	3	2	12		11		10*	1	5	2
		8								7	9	4	11	3		6			2	10	1	5	3
	2	8								7	9			3		6		11	4	10	1	5	4
	1	3								3	3	2	2	3	1	2		2	2	3	3	3	
																1							
		4									6												

1 own-goal

1979-80

Manager: Gordon Lee

1	Aug	18	(h)	Norwich C	L 2-4	Nulty, Ross	27,555
2		22	(a)	Leeds U	L 0-2		27,783
3		25	(a)	Derby C	W 1-0	King	17,820
4	Sep	1	(h)	Aston Villa	D 1-1	Bailey	29,271
5		8	(a)	Stoke C	W 3-2	Bailey, Kidd, King	23,460
6		15	(h)	Wolves	L 2-3	Kidd, Ross	31,807
7		22	(a)	Ipswich T	D 1-1	Kidd	19,279
8		29	(h)	Bristol C	D 0-0		24,733
9	Oct	6	(a)	Coventry C	L 1-2	King	17,205
10		13	(h)	Crystal P	W 3-1	Kidd, King, Latchford	30,645
11		20	(a)	Liverpool	D 2-2	Kidd, King	52,201
12		27	(h)	Manchester U	D 0-0		37,708
13	Nov	3	(a)	Norwich C	D 0-0		18,025
14		10	(h)	Middlesbrough	L 0-2		25,155
15		13	(h)	Leeds U	W 5-1	Latchford 3, Kidd, Opp own-goal	23,319
16		17	(a)	Arsenal	L 0-2		33,450
17		24	(h)	Tottenham H	D 1-1	Latchford	31,079
18	Dec	1	(a)	West Brom A	D 1-1	King	21,237
19		8	(h)	Brighton & HA	W 2-0	Kidd, King	23,595
20		15	(a)	Southampton	L 0-1		19,850
21		22	(h)	Manchester C	L 1-2	Kidd	26,314
22		26	(a)	Bolton W	D 1-1	McBride	18,220
23		29	(h)	Derby C	D 1-1	King	22,554
24	Jan	1	(h)	Nottingham F	W 1-0	Kidd	34,622
25		12	(a)	Aston Villa	L 1-2	Eastoe	22,635
26	Feb	2	(a)	Wolves	L 0-0		21,663
27		9	(h)	Ipswich T	L 0-4		31,603
28		19	(a)	Bristol C	L 1-2	Ross	16,317
29		23	(a)	Crystal P	D 1-1	Eastoe	23,400
30	Mar	1	(h)	Liverpool	L 1-2	Eastoe	53,018
31		12	(a)	Manchester U	D 0-0		45,515
32		15	(h)	Coventry C	D 1-1	Eastoe	25,970
33		18	(h)	Stoke C	W 2-0	Eastoe, Latchford	23,847
34		22	(a)	Middlesbrough	L 1-2	Hartford	17,587
35		28	(h)	Arsenal	L 0-1		28,184
36	Apr	2	(a)	Manchester C	D 1-1	King	33,437
37		5	(h)	Bolton W	W 3-1	Eastoe, Kidd, Megson	28,037
38		19	(a)	Tottenham H	L 0-3		25,245
39		26	(h)	Southampton	W 2-0	Gidman, Stanley	23,552
40		28	(h)	West Brom A	D 0-0		20,356
41	May	3	(a)	Brighton & HA	D 0-0		21,204
42		9	(a)	Nottingham F	L 0-1		22,122

FINAL LEAGUE POSITION: 19th in Division One

Appearances
Sub Appearances
Goals

FA Cup

3	Jan	5	(h)	Aldershot	W 4-1	Hartford, Kidd, King, Latchford
4		26	(h)	Wigan A	W 3-0	Kidd, Latchford, McBride
5	Feb	16	(h)	Wrexham	W 5-2	Eastoe 2, Latchford, Megson, Ross
6	Mar	8	(h)	Ipswich T	W 2-1	Kidd, Latchford
SF	Apr	12	(n*)	West Ham U	D 1-1	Kidd
R		16	(n†)	West Ham U	L 1-2	Latchford

* Played at Villa Park. †Played at Elland Road.

Appearances
Sub Appearances
Goals

League Cup

2	Aug	28	(h)	Cardiff C	W 2-0	Kidd 2
	Sep	5	(a)	Cardiff C	L 0-1	
3	Sep	25	(a)	Aston Villa	D 0-0	
R	Oct	9	(h)	Aston Villa	W 4-1	Latchford 2, Kidd, King
4		30	(a)	Grimsby T	L 1-2	Kidd

Appearances
Sub Appearances
Goals

Everton played in the UEFA Cup (see *Everton in Europe*).

Bailey J	Barton J	Eastoe P	Gidman J	Hartford A	Heard T	Higgins M	Hodge M	Kidd B	King A	Latchford R	Lyons M	McBridge J	Megson G	Nulty G	O'Keefe E	Ratcliffe K	Ross T	Sharp G	Stanley G	Todd C	Varadi I	Wood G	Wright W	
3	2	12			11*			10	9		4			7			6			8		1	5	1
3	2					5		10	9		4			7			6			8		1	11	2
3	2					5		10	9		4			7			6			8		1	11	3
3		11		7		5		10	9		4						6		8			1	2	4
3		11		7		5		10	9		4						6		8			1	2	5
3	12	11*		7		5		10	9		4						6		8			1	2	6
3	2	11		7		5		10			4			9			6					1	8	7
3	2*	11		7		5		10	9		4						6		8			1	12	8
3	2			7		5		10	11	9*	4			6					8		12	1		9
3				7*		5		10	11	9	4			12			6		8			1	2	10
3						5		10	11	9	4			7			6		8			1	2	11
3		11	2			5		10		9	4			7			6					1	8	12
3			2			5		10	11	9	4						6		7			1	8	13
3			2	7*		5		10	11	9	12						6		8			1	4	14
3			2	7		5	1	10	11	9*	12						6		8				4	15
3			2	7		5	1	10	11	9*	12						6		8				4	16
3			2	7		5	1	10	11	9							6		8				4	17
3			2	7		5	1	10	11	9							6		8				4	18
3			2	7		5	1	10	11	9							6		8				4	19
3		12	2	7		5	1		11	9*							6		8		10		4	20
3			2	7			1	10	11	9	5						6		8*		12		4	21
3			2	7			1	10			5	11			6				8		9		4	22
3			2	7			1	10	6	9	5	11							8				4	23
3			2	7			1	10	6	9	5	11							8				4	24
3		8	2	7			1	10		9	5	11			12		6*						4	25
3		8	2	10			1			9	5	11	7						6				4	26
3		8	2	10			1			9	5	11	7		6								4	27
3		8	2	9			1	10			5	11	7				6						4	28
3		8		9			1	10			5	11	7	4			6						2	29
3		12	2	7				10	9		5	11		4*			6					1	8	30
3		6					1	10	8	9	5	11	7			4							2	31
3		6	2	10			1		8	9	5	11	7										4	32
3		6	2	10			1		8	9	5	11	7										4	33
3		6	2	10			1		8	9	5	11	7										4	34
3		6	2	10			1		8	9	5	11	7*				12						4	35
3		6	2	10			1	9	8		5		7				11						4	36
3		6	2	10			1	9	8		5		7				11						4	37
3*		8	4	10			1	9			5	12	7			6	11						2	38
3		7	2	10						9	5	11					6		8			1	4	39
3		7	2	10						9	5	11					6		8			1	4	40
3		7	2	10						9*	5	11					6	12	8			1	4	41
3		7	2	10							5				11		6	9	8			1	4	42
42	6	23	29	35	1	19	23	31	29	26	35	17	12	9	3	2	31	1	24	3	2	19	40	
	1	3									3	1		1	1		1	1			2		1	
2		6	1	1				10	9	6		1	1	1			3		1					

1 own-goal

Bailey J	Barton J	Eastoe P	Gidman J	Hartford A	Heard T	Higgins M	Hodge M	Kidd B	King A	Latchford R	Lyons M	McBridge J	Megson G	Nulty G	O'Keefe E	Ratcliffe K	Ross T	Sharp G	Stanley G	Todd C	Varadi I	Wood G	Wright W	
3			2	7			1	10	6	9	5	11							8				4	3
3		8	2	7			1	10		9	5	11							6				4	4
3		8	2	10			1			9	5	11	7				6						4	5
3		6	2					10	8	9	5	11	7									1	4	6
3		6	2	10			1	9	8	12	5		7*				11						4	SF
3		7	2	10			1		8*	9	5					6	11				12		4	R
6		5	6	5			5	4	4	5	6	4	3			1	3		2			1	6	
										1											1			
		2		1				4	1	5		1	1				1							

Bailey J	Barton J	Eastoe P	Gidman J	Hartford A	Heard T	Higgins M	Hodge M	Kidd B	King A	Latchford R	Lyons M	McBridge J	Megson G	Nulty G	O'Keefe E	Ratcliffe K	Ross T	Sharp G	Stanley G	Todd C	Varadi I	Wood G	Wright W	
3	2					5		10	9		4			7			6		8			1	11	2
3	2	11		7		5		10	9		4						6		8			1		
3	2	11		8		5		10	9*		4			7			6		12			1		3
3				7		5		10	11	9	4			6					8			1	2	R
3		11				5		10		9	4			7*	12		6		8			1	2	4
5	3	3		3		5		5	4	2	5			4			4		4			5	3	
															1				1					
								4	1	2														

1980-81

Manager: Gordon Lee

No	Month	Day	Venue	Opponents	Result	Score	Scorers	Attendance
1	Aug	16	(a)	Sunderland	L	1-3	Eastoe	32,005
2		19	(h)	Leicester C	W	1-0	Eastoe	23,337
3		23	(h)	Nottingham F	D	0-0		25,981
4		30	(a)	Ipswich T	L	0-4		20,879
5	Sep	6	(h)	Wolves	W	2-0	Eastoe, Wright	21,820
6		13	(a)	Aston Villa	W	2-0	Eastoe, Lyons	25,673
7		20	(h)	Crystal P	W	5-0	Latchford 3, Eastoe, Gidman	26,950
8		27	(a)	Coventry C	W	5-0	Latchford 2, McBride 2, Eastoe	14,810
9	Oct	4	(h)	Southampton	W	2-1	McBride 2	36,544
10		7	(a)	Brighton & HA	W	3-1	Lyons, McBride, McMahon	16,523
11		11	(a)	Leeds U	L	0-1		25,601
12		18	(h)	Liverpool	D	2-2	Hartford, McBride	52,565
13		21	(h)	West Brom A	D	1-1	Eastoe	24,046
14		25	(a)	Manchester U	L	0-2		54,260
15	Nov	1	(h)	Tottenham H	D	2-2	Eastoe, McMahon	26,174
16		8	(a)	Norwich C	L	1-2	Latchford	14,557
17		12	(a)	Leicester C	W	1-0	Eastoe	15,511
18		15	(h)	Sunderland	W	2-1	Hartford, O'Keefe	24,099
19		22	(a)	Arsenal	L	1-2	Wright	30,911
20		29	(h)	Birmingham C	D	1-1	O'Keefe	22,258
21	Dec	6	(a)	Stoke C	D	2-2	McBride, Varadi	15,650
22		13	(h)	Brighton & HA	W	4-3	Eastoe 2, McMahon, Varadi	19,157
23		26	(h)	Manchester C	L	0-2		36,194
24		27	(a)	Middlesbrough	L	0-1		20,210
25	Jan	10	(h)	Arsenal	L	1-2	O'Keefe	29,360
26		17	(h)	Ipswich T	D	0-0		25,516
27		31	(a)	Nottingham F	L	0-1		25,611
28	Feb	7	(h)	Aston Villa	L	1-3	Ross	31,434
29		21	(h)	Coventry C	W	3-0	Eastoe, McMahon, Ross	26,731
30		28	(a)	Crystal P	W	3-2	Eastoe, McMahon, Varadi	14,594
31	Mar	14	(h)	Leeds U	L	1-2	Varadi	23,014
32		17	(a)	Southampton	L	0-3		20,829
33		21	(a)	Liverpool	L	0-1		49,743
34		28	(h)	Manchester U	L	0-1		25,854
35		31	(a)	West Brom A	L	0-2		14,833
36	Apr	4	(a)	Tottenham H	D	2-2	Hartford, Varadi	27,208
37		11	(h)	Norwich C	L	0-2		16,254
38		18	(h)	Middlesbrough	W	4-1	Hartford 2, Eastoe, Megson	15,706
39		20	(a)	Manchester C	L	1-3	Varadi	34,434
40		25	(h)	Stoke C	L	0-1		15,352
41	May	2	(a)	Birmingham C	D	1-1	Eastoe	12,863
42		4	(a)	Wolves	D	0-0		16,269

FINAL LEAGUE POSITION: 15th in Division One

Appearances
Sub Appearances
Goals

FA Cup

Round	Month	Day	Venue	Opponents	Result	Score	Scorers
3	Jan	3	(h)	Arsenal	W	2-0	Lyons, Opp own-goal
4		24	(h)	Liverpool	W	2-1	Eastoe, Varadi
5	Feb	14	(a)	Southampton	D	0-0	
R		17	(h)	Southampton	W	1-0	O'Keefe
6	Mar	7	(h)	Manchester C	D	2-2	Eastoe, Ross
R		11	(a)	Manchester C	L	1-3	Eastoe

Appearances
Sub Appearances
Goals

League Cup

Round	Month	Day	Venue	Opponents	Result	Score	Scorers
2	Aug	26	(h)	Blackpool	W	3-0	Eastoe, Latchford, McBride
	Sep	3	(a)	Blackpool	D	2-2	Latchford 2
3		24	(h)	West Brom A	L	1-2	Gidman

Appearances
Sub Appearances
Goals

Bailey J	Barton J	Eastoe P	Gidman J	Hartford A	Higgins M	Hodge M	Latchford R	Lodge P	Lyons M	McBride J	McDonagh J	McMahon S	Megson G	O'Keefe E	Ratcliffe K	Ross T	Sharp G	Stanley G	Telfer G	Varadi I	Wright W	
		12	2	10			9		5	11	1	7	6*		3		8				4	1
		8	2	10			9		5	11	1	7			3			6			4	2
		8	2	10			9		5	11	1	7			3			6			4	3
		10	2	8			9		5	11	1	7		12	3			6*			4	4
3		8	2	10			9*		5	11	1	7		12				6			4	5
3		8*	2	10			9		5	11	1	7		12				6			4	6
3		8	2	10			9		5	11	1	7						6			4	7
3		8	2	10*			9		5	11	1	7		12				6			4	8
3		8	2				9		5	11	1	7	10					6			4	9
3		8*	2	10			9		5	11	1	7		12				6			4	10
3		8	2	10			9		5	11	1	7		12				6*			4	11
3		8	2*	10			9		5	11	1	7		12				6			4	12
3		8		10			9		5	11	1	7				2		6			4	13
3		8	2	10			9		5	11	1	7		12				6*			4	14
3		8	2	10			9*		5	11	1	7		12				6			4	15
3		8	2	10			9		5*	11	1	7		12				6			4	16
3		8	2	10			9			11	1	7		6				5			4	17
3		8	2	10			9*			11	1	7	12	6				5			4	18
3		8	2	10						11	1	7	6	9				5			4	19
3		8	2	10						11	1	7	6	9				5			4	20
3		8		10	5					11	1	7		6				4		9	2	21
3		8		10	5				12	11	1	7		6*				4		9	2	22
3		8	2	10					12	11*	1	7		6	5					9	4	23
3		8	2	10					12	11	1	7			5	6				9*	4	24
3		8	2	10							1	7		11	5	6				9	4	25
3		8		10					5	12	1	7		11*	2	6				9	4	26
3		8		10		1			5	12		7		11*	2	6				9	4	27
3		8		10		1		12	5				7	11*	2	6				9	4	28
		8	2*	10				12	5		1	7		11	3	6				9	4	29
		8	2	10				12	5		1	7		11	3	6*				9	4	30
3		8	2	10					5	11	1	7				6				9	4	31
		8	2	10					5*	12	1	7			3	11		6		9	4	32
3		8	2					10		12	1	7		11		6		5		9*	4	33
3*		8	2					10			1	7		11	12	6		5		9	4	34
		8	2	10				11			1	7*			3	6		5	9	12	4	35
3		8	2	10				11	6		1					7		5	12	9*	4	36
		8*	2	10				11	5		1		12		3	7		6		9	4	37
		8	2	10				11	5		1		7		3		12	6*		9	4	38
		8*	2	10				6	5	11	1		7		3		12			9	4	39
3	2	8		10				6	5	11*	1		7		4		9			12		40
3	2	8	6	10					5		1				4	11				9	7	41
3	2	8*	6	10			12		5		1				4	11				9	7	42
31	3	41	35	39	2	2	18	8	30	27	40	34	8	15	20	17	2	28	1	20	41	
		1					1	3	3	4			2	10	1		2		1	2		
		15	1	5			6		2	7		5	1	3		2				6	2	

Bailey J	Barton J	Eastoe P	Gidman J	Hartford A	Higgins M	Hodge M	Latchford R	Lodge P	Lyons M	McBride J	McDonagh J	McMahon S	Megson G	O'Keefe E	Ratcliffe K	Ross T	Sharp G	Stanley G	Telfer G	Varadi I	Wright W	
3		8	2	10					12	11	1	7			5	6				9*	4	3
3		8		10		1		5				7		11	2	6				9	4	4
3		8	6	10				5			1			11	2	7				9	4	5
		8	2	10				5			1	7		11	3	6				9	4	R
		8	2	10				5			1	7		11*	3	6		12		9	4	6
3		8	2	10				5		11	1	7				6				9	4	R
4		6	5	6		1		5		2	5	5		4	5	6				6	6	
									1									1				
		3							1					1		1				1		

1 own-goal

Bailey J	Barton J	Eastoe P	Gidman J	Hartford A	Higgins M	Hodge M	Latchford R	Lodge P	Lyons M	McBride J	McDonagh J	McMahon S	Megson G	O'Keefe E	Ratcliffe K	Ross T	Sharp G	Stanley G	Telfer G	Varadi I	Wright W	
		8	2	10			9	5		11	1	7			3			6			4	2
12		8	2	10			9	5		11	1	7			3*			6			4	
3		8	2	10			9	5		11	1	7*		12				6			4	3
1		3	3	3			3	3		3	3	3			2			3			3	
1														1								
		1	1				3			1												

1981-82

Manager: Howard Kendall

1	Aug	29	(h)	Birmingham C	W 3-1	Ainscow, Biley, Eastoe	33,045
2	Sep	2	(a)	Leeds U	D 1-1	Biley	26,502
3		5	(a)	Southampton	L 0-1		21,624
4		12	(h)	Brighton & HA	D 1-1	Wright	27,352
5		19	(a)	Tottenham H	L 0-3		31,219
6		22	(h)	Notts C	W 3-1	Eastoe, O'Keefe, Ross	22,175
7		26	(h)	West Brom A	W 1-0	Lyons	23,871
8	Oct	3	(a)	Stoke C	L 1-3	McBride	16,007
9		10	(a)	West Ham U	D 1-1	McMahon	31,608
10		17	(h)	Ipswich T	W 2-1	Ferguson, Stevens	25,146
11		24	(a)	Middlesbrough	W 2-0	Ferguson 2	13,423
12		31	(h)	Manchester C	L 0-1		31,305
13	Nov	7	(a)	Liverpool	L 1-3	Ferguson	48,861
14		21	(h)	Sunderland	L 1-2	Eastoe	19,759
15		24	(a)	Notts C	D 2-2	Biley, Sharp	7,771
16		28	(a)	Arsenal	L 0-1		25,860
17	Dec	5	(h)	Swansea C	W 3-1	O'Keefe 2, Sharp	23,860
18		19	(h)	Aston Villa	W 2-0	Eastoe, Lyons	16,538
19		28	(h)	Coventry C	W 3-2	Higgins 2, Sharp	23,895
20	Jan	6	(a)	Manchester U	D 1-1	Sharp	40,451
21		19	(h)	Southampton	D 1-1	Richardson	22,355
22		23	(a)	Wolves	W 3-0	Irvine 2, Richardson	11,784
23		30	(h)	Tottenham H	D 1-1	Sharp	30,717
24	Feb	6	(a)	Brighton & HA	L 1-3	Heath	16,148
25		13	(h)	Stoke C	D 0-0		20,656
26		20	(a)	West Brom A	D 0-0		14,819
27		27	(h)	West Ham U	D 0-0		28,618
28	Mar	6	(a)	Ipswich T	L 0-3		19,360
29		13	(h)	Middlesbrough	W 2-0	Higgins, Sharp	15,807
30		20	(a)	Manchester C	D 1-1	Heath	33,002
31		27	(h)	Liverpool	L 1-3	Sharp	51,847
32	Apr	3	(a)	Nottingham F	W 1-0	McMahon	17,323
33		6	(a)	Birmingham C	W 2-0	Ainscow, Heath	12,273
34		10	(h)	Manchester U	D 3-3	Heath, Lyons, Sharp	29,317
35		13	(a)	Coventry C	L 0-1		11,858
36		17	(a)	Sunderland	L 1-3	Irvine	18,359
37		20	(h)	Nottingham F	W 2-1	Sharp 2	15,460
38		24	(h)	Arsenal	W 2-1	Heath, Wright	19,136
39	May	1	(a)	Swansea C	W 3-1	Sharp 2, Heath	16,243
40		4	(h)	Leeds U	W 1-0	Sharp	17,137
41		8	(h)	Wolves	D 1-1	Eastoe	20,124
42		15	(a)	Aston Villa	W 2-1	Sharp 2	20,446

FINAL LEAGUE POSITION: 8th in Division One

Appearances
Sub Appearances
Goals

FA Cup

3	Jan	2	(a)	West Ham U	L 1-2	Eastoe

Appearances
Sub Appearances
Goals

League Cup

2	Oct	6	(h)	Coventry C	D 1-1	Ferguson
		27	(a)	Coventry C	W 1-0	Ferguson
3	Nov	11	(h)	Oxford U	W 1-0	O'Keefe
4	Dec	15	(h)	Ipswich T	L 2-3	McMahon 2

Appearances
Sub Appearances
Goals

Ainscow A	Arnold J	Bailey J	Biley A	Borrows B	Eastoe P	Ferguson M	Hartford A	Heath A	Higgins M	Irvine A	Kendall H	Lodge P	Lyons M	McBride J	McMahon S	O'Keefe E	Ratcliffe K	Richardson K	Rimmer S	Ross T	Sharp G	Southall N	Stevens G	Thomas M	Walsh M	Wright W	
7	1	3	9		8		10						5							11				6	4	2	1
11	1		9		8		10						5		7		3							6	4	2	2
11	1		9		8	12	10						5		7*		3							6	4	2	3
11	1		9		8		10						5		7		3							6	4	2	4
11	1		9		8		10						5		7*	12	3							6	4	2	5
11	1		9*		8		10						5			12	3			7				6	4	2	6
	1		9				10						5	12	8*	11	3			7				6	4	2	7
	1	3*	9										5	11	7	8				10	12			6	4	2	8
	1	3	8*			9			4				5	11	7	12				10			2	6			9
		3	12			9							5	11	7	8				10		1	2	6*	4		10
10*	1	3	12			9			4			6	5	11	7	8							2				11
10*	1	3				9			4			6	5	11	7	8					12		2				12
10*	1	3	12			9			4			6	5	11	7	8							2				13
10	1	3	9		8*							6	5	11	7			12					2		4		14
11*	1		10								8	6	5		7		3	12			9		2		4		15
	1		10									6	5		7	11	3			8	9		2		4		16
	1		10								6		5		7	11	3			8	9		2		4		17
					10				4	7	6	11	5				3			8	9	1	2				18
					10				4	11	6		5		7		3			8	9	1	2				19
					10				4	6		11	5		7		3	8			9	1	2				20
					10			8	4	7		11	5				3	6			9	1	2				21
					10			8	4	7		11	5				3	6			9	1	2				22
					10			8	4	7		11	5				3	6			9	1	2				23
					10			8	4	7		11	5				3	6			9	1	2				24
				2		10		8	4	7							3	6		11	9	1				5	25
		3	10	2				8	4	7								6		11	9	1				5	26
		3	10	2				8	4	7								6		11	9	1				5	27
		3	10*	2				8	4	7					12			6		11	9	1				5	28
12		3		2				8	4	7					10*			6		11	9	1				5	29
				2				8	4	7					10		3	6		11	9	1				5	30
				2				8	4	7					10		3	6		11	9	1				5	31
12				2	10			8	4	7					6		3			11	9*	1				5	32
10				2	12			8	4	7					6		3			11	9	1				5*	33
10				2				8	4	7		12	5		6		3			11	9	1*					34
10				2				8	4	7			5		6		3			11	9	1					35
10				2		9		8	4	7*			12		6		3	11				1				5	36
				2				8	4	7					6		3	10		11	9	1				5	37
								8	4	7					6			10		11	9	1	2		3	5	38
								8	4	7					6			12	10*	11	9	1	2		3	5	39
					12			8	4	7					6				10*	11	9	1	2		3	5	40
				2	10			8	4	7					6					11	9	1			3	5	41
				2	10			8	4	7					6					11	9	1			3	5	42
15	16	12	16	15	17	7	7	22	29	25	4	12	26	7	31	8	25	15	2	27	27	26	19	10	18	24	
2			3		2	1						1	1	1	1	3		3			2						
2			3		5	4		6	3	3			3	1	2	3		2		1	15		1			2	

Ainscow A	Arnold J	Bailey J	Biley A	Borrows B	Eastoe P	Ferguson M	Hartford A	Heath A	Higgins M	Irvine A	Kendall H	Lodge P	Lyons M	McBride J	McMahon S	O'Keefe E	Ratcliffe K	Richardson K	Rimmer S	Ross T	Sharp G	Southall N	Stevens G	Thomas M	Walsh M	Wright W	
					10				4		6	11	5			12	3	7		8*	9	1	2				3
					1				1		1	1	1				1	1		1	1	1	1				
																1											
					1																						

Ainscow A	Arnold J	Bailey J	Biley A	Borrows B	Eastoe P	Ferguson M	Hartford A	Heath A	Higgins M	Irvine A	Kendall H	Lodge P	Lyons M	McBride J	McMahon S	O'Keefe E	Ratcliffe K	Richardson K	Rimmer S	Ross T	Sharp G	Southall N	Stevens G	Thomas M	Walsh M	Wright W	
	1	3				9							5	11	7	8				10			2	6	4		2
10	1	3				9			4			6	5	11	7	8							2				
12	1	3	10			9*			4			6	5	11	7	8							2				3
	1		10*			12					6		5		7	11	3			8	9		2		4		4
1	4	3	2			3			2		1	2	4	3	4	4	1			2	1		4	1	2		
1						1																					
						2									2	1											

1982-83

Manager: Howard Kendall

1	Aug	28	(a)	Watford	L 0-2		19,630
2		31	(h)	Aston Villa	W 5-0	Heath 2, Sharp 2, King	24,026
3	Sep	4	(h)	Tottenham H	W 3-1	McMahon, Sheedy, Wright	30,553
4		8	(a)	Manchester U	L 1-2	King	43,186
5		11	(a)	Notts C	L 0-1		9,197
6		18	(h)	Norwich C	D 1-1	Irvine	20,281
7		25	(a)	Coventry C	L 2-4	Heath, King	9,319
8	Oct	2	(h)	Brighton & HA	D 2-2	Heath, Wright	17,539
9		9	(h)	Manchester C	W 2-1	King, McMahon	25,158
10		16	(a)	Swansea C	W 3-0	McMahon, Richardson, Opp own-goal	11,183
11		23	(h)	Sunderland	W 3-1	Johnson, Richardson, Sharp	20,360
12		30	(a)	Southampton	L 2-3	King, Wright	18,141
13	Nov	6	(h)	Liverpool	L 0-5		52,741
14		13	(a)	Arsenal	D 1-1	King	23,067
15		20	(h)	West Brom A	D 0-0		16,001
16		27	(a)	West Ham U	L 0-2		21,424
17	Dec	4	(h)	Birmingham C	D 0-0		13,707
18		11	(a)	Ipswich T	W 2-0	Richardson, Sheedy	17,512
19		18	(h)	Luton T	W 5-0	Heath 2, Bailey, Curran, Sheedy	14,982
20		27	(a)	Stoke C	L 0-1		25,427
21		28	(h)	Nottingham F	W 3-1	Sharp 2, McMahon	25,147
22	Jan	1	(a)	West Brom A	D 2-2	Higgins, Sharp	15,194
23		3	(a)	Tottenham H	L 1-2	Sharp	28,455
24		15	(h)	Watford	W 1-0	Johnson	19,233
25		22	(a)	Norwich C	W 1-0	Ratcliffe	14,180
26	Feb	5	(h)	Notts C	W 3-0	Heath, King, Sheedy	14,541
27		12	(a)	Aston Villa	L 0-2		21,117
28		26	(h)	Swansea C	D 2-2	King 2	17,112
29	Mar	2	(a)	Manchester C	D 0-0		22,253
30		5	(a)	Sunderland	L 1-2	Sharp	16,051
31		15	(h)	Southampton	W 2-0	Heath, Sheedy	15,002
32		19	(a)	Liverpool	D 0-0		44,737
33		26	(h)	Arsenal	L 2-3	Ainscow, Heath	16,318
34	Apr	2	(a)	Nottingham F	L 0-2		14,815
35		4	(h)	Stoke C	W 3-1	Sheedy 2, Sharp	15,360
36		9	(a)	Brighton & HA	W 2-1	Sheedy 2	14,534
37		19	(h)	Manchester U	W 2-0	Heath, Sharp	21,707
38		23	(a)	Birmingham C	L 0-1		11,045
39		30	(h)	West Ham U	W 2-0	Sharp 2	16,355
40	May	2	(h)	Coventry C	W 1-0	Sharp	12,972
41		7	(a)	Luton T	W 5-1	Sharp 2, Sheedy 2, Johnson	12,447
42		14	(h)	Ipswich T	D 1-1	Opp own-goal	17,420

FINAL LEAGUE POSITION: 7th in Division One

Appearances
Sub Appearances
Goals

FA Cup

3	Jan	8	(a)	Newport C	D 1-1	Sheedy
R		11	(h)	Newport C	W 2-1	King, Sharp
4		30	(h)	Shrewsbury T	W 2-1	Heath, Sheedy
5	Feb	19	(h)	Tottenham H	W 2-0	King, Sharp
6	Mar	12	(a)	Manchester U	L 0-1	

Appearances
Sub Appearances
Goals

League Cup

2	Oct	5	(a)	Newport C	W 2-0	King, McMahon
		27	(h)	Newport C	D 2-2	Johnson, King
3	Nov	9	(h)	Arsenal	D 1-1	Stevens
R		23	(a)	Arsenal	L 0-3	

Appearances
Sub Appearances
Goals

Ainscow A	Arnold J	Bailey J	Borrows B	Curran T	Heath A	Higgins M	Irvine A	Johnson D	Keeley G	King A	McMahon S	Mountfield D	Ratcliffe K	Reid P	Richardson K	Ross T	Sharp G	Sheedy K	Southall N	Stevens G	Walsh M	Wright W	
		3	2		6	4		8		10	7*				12		9	11	1			5	1
		3	2		8	4	7*			10	6				12		9	11	1			5	2
7		3	2		8	4				10	6						9	11	1			5	3
7*		3	2		8	4				10	6				12		9	11	1			5	4
7		3	2		8	4				10	6						9	11	1			5	5
			2		8		7*			10	6		4			12	9	11	1		3	5	6
					8	4	12			10	6				2	7*	9	11	1		3	5	7
		3	2		7	4		8		10	6						9	11	1			5	8
		3	2		7	4		8		10	6						9	11	1			5	9
		3	2			4		8		10	6				7		9	11	1			5	10
		3	2		7*	4		8		10	6				12		9	11	1			5	11
		3	2			4	12	8*		10	6				7		9	11	1			5	12
		3	2		7			8*	4	10	6				12		9	11	1			5	13
	1				7	4	12	8		10	6		3		11*		9			2		5	14
	1				7	4	11	8		10	6		3				9			2		5	15
	1				8*	4	7	12		10	6		3				9	11		2		5	16
	1	3		7	8	4				10	6						9	11		2		5	17
	1	3		7	8	5		9			6		4		10			11		2			18
	1	3		7	8	5		9*			6		4		10		12	11		2			19
	1	3		7	8	5		9			6		4		10		12	11		2*			20
	1	3		7	12	5		9*			6		4	10			8	11		2			21
	1	3		7		5		9			6		4	10			8	11		2			22
	1	3		7		5		9			6		4	10			8	11		2			23
	1	3			7	5		12		9	6		4	10*			8	11		2			24
	1	3			8	5				7	6		4	10			9	11		2			25
	1	3			7*	5		12		9			4	10	6		8	11		2			26
	1	3			7	5		12		9			4	10*	6		8	11		2			27
	1	3			10	5	7*	12		8			4		6		9	11		2			28
	1	3			10	5		7		8			4		6		9	11		2			29
	1	3			10	5	12	7		8*			4		6		9	11		2			30
	1	3			10	5	7				8		4		6		9	11		2			31
12	1	3			10	5	7*				8		4		6		9	11		2			32
7	1	3			10	5	12				8		4		6		9	11		2*			33
7	1	3			10	5		12			8		4		6*		9	11		2			34
7	1	3			10	5		8			6		4		2		9	11					35
7	1	3			10	5		8					4		6		9	11		2			36
	1	3			10	5		8			7		4		6		9	11		2			37
12	1	3			10			8			7*	5	4		6		9	11		2			38
7		3			10	5		8					4		6		9	11	1	2			39
		3			10	5	12	8*			7		4		6		9	11	1	2			40
		3			10	5		8			7		4		6		9	11	1	2			41
7		3			10	5	12	8					4		6*		9	11	1	2			42
9	25	37	12	7	37	39	7	25	1	24	34	1	29	7	24	1	39	40	17	28	2	17	
2					1		7	6							5	1	2						
1		1		1	10	1	1	3		9	4		1		3		15	11				3	

2 own-goals

Ainscow A	Arnold J	Bailey J	Borrows B	Curran T	Heath A	Higgins M	Irvine A	Johnson D	Keeley G	King A	McMahon S	Mountfield D	Ratcliffe K	Reid P	Richardson K	Ross T	Sharp G	Sheedy K	Southall N	Stevens G	Walsh M	Wright W	
	1	3			7	5				9	6		4	10			8	11		2			3
	1	3			7	5				9	6		4	10			8	11		2			R
	1	3			7	5				9	6		4	10			8	11		2			4
	1	3			10	5	7			8			4		6		9	11		2			5
	1	3			10	5	7				8		4		6		9	11		2			6
	5	5			5	5	2			4	4		5	3	2		5	5		5			
					1					2							2	2					

Ainscow A	Arnold J	Bailey J	Borrows B	Curran T	Heath A	Higgins M	Irvine A	Johnson D	Keeley G	King A	McMahon S	Mountfield D	Ratcliffe K	Reid P	Richardson K	Ross T	Sharp G	Sheedy K	Southall N	Stevens G	Walsh M	Wright W	
		3	2		7*			8		10	6		4		12		9	11	1			5	2
		3	2		7*			8		10	6		4		12		9	11	1			5	
	1				7	4	12	8*		10	6		3		11		9			2		5	3
	1				7	4		8		10	6		3				9	11		2		5	R
	2	2	2		4	2		4		4	4		4		1		4	3	2	2		4	
							1								2								
								1		2	1									1			

1983-84

Manager: Howard Kendall

1	Aug	27	(h)	Stoke C	W 1-0	Sharp	22,658
2		29	(h)	West Ham U	L 0-1		20,375
3	Sep	3	(a)	Coventry C	D 1-1	Sheedy	12,532
4		6	(a)	Ipswich T	L 0-3		16,543
5		10	(h)	West Brom A	D 0-0		15,548
6		17	(a)	Tottenham H	W 2-1	Reid, Sheedy	29,125
7		24	(h)	Birmingham C	D 1-1	Sharp	15,253
8	Oct	1	(a)	Notts C	W 1-0	Reid	7,949
9		15	(h)	Luton T	L 0-1		14,325
10		22	(h)	Watford	W 1-0	Johnson	13,571
11		29	(a)	Leicester C	L 0-2		10,953
12	Nov	6	(a)	Liverpool	L 0-3		40,875
13		12	(h)	Nottingham F	W 1-0	Heath	17,546
14		19	(a)	Arsenal	L 1-2	King	24,330
15		26	(h)	Norwich C	L 0-2		14,106
16	Dec	3	(a)	Manchester U	W 1-0	Sheedy	43,664
17		10	(h)	Aston Villa	D 1-1	Gray	15,810
18		17	(a)	Queen's Park R	L 0-2		11,608
19		26	(h)	Sunderland	D 0-0		18,683
20		27	(a)	Wolves	L 0-3		12,761
21		31	(h)	Coventry C	D 0-0		13,659
22	Jan	2	(a)	Birmingham C	W 2-0	King, Stevens	10,004
23		14	(a)	Stoke C	D 1-1	Heath	7,945
24		21	(h)	Tottenham H	W 2-1	Heath 2	18,003
25	Feb	4	(h)	Notts C	W 4-1	Heath 3, Sheedy	13,016
26		11	(a)	West Brom A	D 1-1	Mountfield	10,313
27		25	(a)	Watford	D 4-4	Sharp 2, Gray, Heath	16,982
28	Mar	3	(h)	Liverpool	D 1-1	Harper	51,245
29		13	(a)	Nottingham F	L 0-1		13,647
30		17	(h)	Ipswich T	W 1-0	Mountfield	18,013
31		20	(h)	Leicester C	D 1-1	Richardson	15,142
32		31	(h)	Southampton	W 1-0	Gray	20,244
33	Apr	7	(a)	Luton T	W 3-0	Heath 2, Mountfield	9,224
34		9	(h)	Arsenal	D 0-0		21,174
35		17	(a)	Southampton	L 1-3	Richardson	16,978
36		21	(a)	Sunderland	L 1-2	Heath	15,876
37		23	(h)	Wolves	W 2-0	Gray, Steven	17,185
38		28	(a)	Norwich C	D 1-1	Gray	13,624
39	May	5	(h)	Manchester U	D 1-1	Wakenshaw	28,817
40		7	(a)	Aston Villa	W 2-0	Richardson, Sharp	16,792
41		12	(h)	Queen's Park R	W 3-1	Sharp 2, Heath	20,679
42		14	(a)	West Ham U	W 1-0	Richardson	25,452

FINAL LEAGUE POSITION: 7th in Division One

Appearances
Sub Appearances
Goals

FA Cup

3	Jan	6	(a)	Stoke C	W 2-0	Gray, Irvine
4		28	(h)	Gillingham	D 0-0	
R		31	(a)	Gillingham	D 0-0	
R	Feb	6	(a)	Gillingham	W 3-0	Sheedy 2, Heath
5		18	(h)	Shrewsbury T	W 3-0	Irvine, Reid, Opp own-goal
6	Mar	10	(a)	Notts C	W 2-1	Gray, Richardson
SF	Apr	14	(n*)	Southampton	W 1-0	Heath
F	May	19	(n†)	Watford	W 2-0	Gray, Sharp

* Played at Highbury. † Played at Wembley Stadium.

Appearances
Sub Appearances
Goals

League Cup

2	Oct	4	(a)	Chesterfield	W 1-0	Sharp
		26	(h)	Chesterfield	D 2-2	Heath, Steven
3	Nov	9	(h)	Coventry C	W 2-1	Heath, Sharp
4		30	(a)	West Ham U	D 2-2	Reid, Sheedy
R	Dec	6	(h)	West Ham U	W 2-0	King, Sheedy
5	Jan	18	(a)	Oxford U	D 1-1	Heath
R		24	(h)	Oxford U	W 4-1	Heath, Richardson, Sharp, Sheedy
SF	Feb	15	(h)	Aston Villa	W 2-0	Richardson, Sheedy
		22	(a)	Aston Villa	L 0-1	
F	Mar	25	(n*)	Liverpool	D 0-0	
R		28	(n†)	Liverpool	L 0-1	

* Played at Wembley Stadium. † Played at Maine Road.

Appearances
Sub Appearances
Goals

Arnold J	Bailey J	Bishop I	Curran T	Gray A	Harper A	Heath A	Higgins M	Hughes D	Irvine A	Johnson D	King A	Mountfield D	Ratcliffe K	Reid P	Richardson K	Rimmer S	Sharp G	Sheedy K	Southall N	Steven T	Stevens G	Wakenshaw R	
1	3				2	8	5				10	4			6		9	11		7			1
1	3				2	8	5			12	10	4			6*		9	11		7			2
1	3				2	8*	5			12	10		4		6		9	11		7			3
1	3*		7		2		5			10			4	12	6		9	11		8			4
1	3		7*		2	8	5			10			4		12		9	11		6			5
1	3				2	8	5			10			4	6*	12		9	11		7			6
1	3				2	8	5			10	12		4	6			9	11		7*			7
	3				2	8	5		10				4	6			9	11	1	7			8
	3				2	8	5				10		4	6			9	11	1	7			9
	3				2		5		12	8	10		4		6		9	11	1	7*			10
	3				2	8	5		12		10		4		6		9	11*	1	7			11
	3				2	8	5		7		10		4				9	11	1	6			12
	3			9	2	8	5		7		10		4	6				11	1				13
	3			9	2	8			7		10	5	4	6				11	1				14
	3			9	2	8*			7		10	5	4	6				11	1		12		15
				10			5		7		8	4	3	6			9	11	1		2		16
	3			9	12	8			7		10*	5	4	6				11	1		2		17
					3	8			7	9	10	5	4	6				11	1		2		18
				9	3	8			7	10		5	4	6				11	1		2		19
				9				3	7			5	4	6	8	10		11*	1	12	2		20
	3			9		8*			7		10	5	4	6	12			11	1		2		21
	3			9		8			7		10	5	4	6				11	1		2		22
	3			10		8			7			5	4	6	2		9	11	1				23
					3	8			7			5	4	6	10		9	11	1		2		24
	3			9		8			7			5	4	6	10			11	1		2		25
	3			9		8			7			5	4	6	10			11	1		2		26
	3			10		8			7			5	4	6			9	11	1		2		27
	3			10	12	8						5	4	6			9	11	1	7*	2		28
	3			10	11				7			5	4	6	8		9		1		2		29
				10	3	8			7			5	4	6	11		9*		1	12	2		30
	3			9		8					10	5	4	6	11				1	7	2		31
	3			10	7*	8						5	4	6	11		9		1	12	2		32
	3		7		4	8						5		6	11		9		1	10	2		33
	3		7	10		8						5	4	6	11		9*		1	12	2		34
			7	9	3	8						5	4	6	11				1	10	2		35
	3		7		12	8						5	4	6*	11		9		1	10	2		36
	3		7	9		8						5	4	6	11				1	10	2		37
	3		7*	9		8						5	4	6	11		12		1	10	2		38
	3	12			4						8	5		6	11		9		1	10	2	7*	39
	3					8					7	5	4	6	11		9		1	10	2		40
				10	3	8						5	4	6	11		9		1	7	2		41
					3	8					10	5	4	6	11		9		1	7	2		42
7	33		8	23	26	36	14	1	19	7	19	31	38	34	25	1	27	28	35	23	26	1	
		1			3				2	2	1			1	3		1			4	1		
				5	1	12				1	2	3		2	4		7	4		1	1	1	

Arnold J	Bailey J	Bishop I	Curran T	Gray A	Harper A	Heath A	Higgins M	Hughes D	Irvine A	Johnson D	King A	Mountfield D	Ratcliffe K	Reid P	Richardson K	Rimmer S	Sharp G	Sheedy K	Southall N	Steven T	Stevens G	Wakenshaw R	
	3			10		8			7			5	4	6			9	11	1		2		3
				10	3	8			7			5	4	6			9	11	1		2		4
	3			12		8			7			5	4	6	10		9*	11	1		2		R
	3			9		8			7			5	4	6	10			11	1		2		2R
	3			9		8*			7		10	5	4	6			12	11	1		2		5
	3			10	12				7			5	4	6	8		9	11*	1		2		6
	3			9		8			7			5	4	6	11		12		1	10*	2		SF
	3			10		8						5	4	6	11		9		1	7	2		F
	7			7	1	7			7		1	8	8	8	5		5	6	8	2	8		
				1	1												2						
				3		2			2					1	1		1	2					

1 own-goal

Arnold J	Bailey J	Bishop I	Curran T	Gray A	Harper A	Heath A	Higgins M	Hughes D	Irvine A	Johnson D	King A	Mountfield D	Ratcliffe K	Reid P	Richardson K	Rimmer S	Sharp G	Sheedy K	Southall N	Steven T	Stevens G	Wakenshaw R	
	3				2	8	5						4	6	10		9	11	1	7			2
	3				2	8	5		7				4		6		9	11	1	10			
	3				2	8	5		7		10		4	12			9	11	1	6*			3
						8	5		7		10	4	3	6			9	11	1		2		4
						8	5		7		10	4	3	6			9	11	1		2		R
					3	8			7	10*		5	4	6	12		9	11	1		2		5
					3	8			7			5	4	6	10		9	11	1		2		R
	3					8			7			5	4	6	10		9	11	1		2		SF
	3					8			7		10	5	4	6			9	11	1		2		
	3				12	8			7			5	4	6	10		9	11*	1		2		F
	3				11	8			7*		12	5	4	6	10		9		1		2		R
	7				6	11	5		10	1	4	8	11	9	6		11	10	11	3	8		
					1						1			1	1								
						4					1			1	2		3	4		1			

1984-85

Manager: Howard Kendall

No	Month	Day	Venue	Opponents	Res	Score	Scorers	Att
1	Aug	25	(h)	Tottenham H	L	1-4	Heath	35,630
2		27	(a)	West Brom A	L	1-2	Heath	13,464
3		31	(a)	Chelsea	W	1-0	Richardson	17,734
4	Sep	4	(h)	Ipswich T	D	1-1	Heath	22,314
5		8	(h)	Coventry C	W	2-1	Sharp, Steven	20,013
6		15	(a)	Newcastle U	W	3-2	Gray, Sheedy, Steven	26,944
7		22	(h)	Southampton	D	2-2	Mountfield, Sharp	22,354
8		29	(a)	Watford	W	5-4	Heath 2, Mountfield, Sharp, Steven	18,335
9	Oct	6	(a)	Arsenal	L	0-1		37,049
10		13	(h)	Aston Villa	W	2-1	Heath, Sharp	25,089
11		20	(a)	Liverpool	W	1-0	Sharp	45,545
12		27	(h)	Manchester U	W	5-0	Sheedy 2, Heath, Sharp, Stevens	40,769
13	Nov	3	(h)	Leicester C	W	3-0	Heath, Sheedy, Steven	27,784
14		10	(a)	West Ham U	W	1-0	Heath	24,089
15		17	(h)	Stoke C	W	4-0	Heath 2, Reid, Steven	6,705
16		24	(a)	Norwich C	L	2-4	Sharp, Sheedy	16,925
17	Dec	1	(h)	Sheffield W	D	1-1	Sharp	35,440
18		8	(a)	Queen's Park R	D	0-0		14,338
19		15	(h)	Nottingham F	W	5-0	Sharp 2, Reid, Sheedy, Steven	22,487
20		22	(h)	Chelsea	L	3-4	Sharp 2, Bracewell	29,887
21		26	(a)	Sunderland	W	2-1	Mountfield 2	19,714
22		29	(a)	Ipswich T	W	2-0	Sharp 2	16,045
23	Jan	1	(h)	Luton T	W	2-1	Steven 2	31,682
24		12	(h)	Newcastle U	W	4-0	Sheedy 2, Mountfield, Sharp	32,156
25	Feb	2	(h)	Watford	W	4-0	Stevens 2, Sheedy, Steven	7,026
26		23	(a)	Leicester C	W	2-1	Gray 2	17,345
27	Mar	2	(a)	Manchester U	D	1-1	Mountfield	51,150
28		16	(a)	Aston Villa	D	1-1	Richardson	22,625
29		23	(h)	Arsenal	W	2-0	Gray, Sharp	7,389
30		30	(a)	Southampton	W	2-1	Richardson 2	18,754
31	Apr	3	(a)	Tottenham H	W	2-1	Gray, Steven	48,108
32		6	(h)	Sunderland	W	4-1	Gray 2, Sharp, Steven	35,978
33		16	(h)	West Brom A	W	4-1	Sharp 2, Atkin, Sheedy	29,750
34		20	(a)	Stoke C	W	2-0	Sharp, Sheedy	9,285
35		27	(h)	Norwich C	W	3-0	Bracewell, Mountfield, Steven	32,085
36	May	4	(a)	Sheffield W	W	1-0	Gray	37,381
37		6	(h)	Queen's Park R	W	2-0	Mountfield, Sharp	50,514
38		8	(h)	West Ham U	W	3-0	Mountfield 2, Gray	32,657
39		11	(a)	Nottingham F	L	0-1		18,784
40		23	(h)	Liverpool	W	1-0	Wilkinson	15,045
41		26	(a)	Coventry C	L	1-4	Wilkinson	21,224
42		28	(a)	Luton T	L	0-2		11,509

FINAL LEAGUE POSITION: 1st in Division One

Appearances
Sub Appearances
Goals

FA Cup

Rd	Month	Day	Venue	Opponents	Res	Score	Scorers
3	Jan	5	(a)	Leeds U	W	2-0	Sharp, Sheedy
4		26	(h)	Doncaster R	W	2-0	Steven, Stevens
5	Feb	16	(h)	Telford U	W	3-0	Reid, Sheedy, Steven
6	Mar	9	(h)	Ipswich T	D	2-2	Mountfield, Sheedy
R		13	(a)	Ipswich T	W	1-0	Sharp
SF	Apr	13	(n*)	Luton T	W	2-1	Mountford, Sheedy
F	May	18	(n†)	Manchester U	L	0-1	

* Played at Villa Park. † Played at Wembley Stadium.

Appearances
Sub Appearances
Goals

League Cup

Rd	Month	Day	Venue	Opponents	Res	Score	Scorers
2	Sep	26	(a)	Sheffield U	D	2-2	Mountfield, Sharp
	Oct	10	(h)	Sheffield U	W	4-0	Bracewell, Heath, Mountfield, Sharp
3		30	(a)	Manchester U	W	2-1	Sharp, Opp own-goal
4	Nov	20	(h)	Grimsby T	L	0-1	

Appearances
Sub Appearances
Goals

Everton won the European Cup-winners' Cup (see *Everton in Europe*).

Atkin I	Bailey J	Bracewell P	Curran T	Danskin J	Gray A	Harper A	Heath A	Hughes D	Morrissey J	Mountfield D	Oldroyd D	Ratcliffe K	Reid P	Richardson K	Rimmer N	Sharp G	Sheedy K	Southall N	Steven T	Stevens G	Van den Hauwe P	Wakenshaw R	Walsh D	Wilkinson P	
	3	10			12		8			5		4	6	11*		9		1	7	2					1
	3		7				8			5		4	6	11		9		1	10	2					2
	3	10					8			5		4	6	11		9		1	7	2					3
	3	10	12				8			5		4	6	11*		9		1	7	2					4
	3	10	12				8			5		4	6	11*		9		1	7	2					5
	3	10			9		8			5		4	6				11	1	7	2					6
	3	10					8			5		4	6			9	11	1	7	2					7
	3	10	12				8			5		4	6			9	11*	1	7	2					8
		10					8			5		4	6	11		9		1	7	2	3				9
		10				11	8			5		4	6			9		1	7	2	3				10
		10				11	8			5		4	6			9		1	7	2	3				11
		10			12		8			5		4	6			9	11*	1	7	2	3				12
		10			12		8			5		4	6			9*	11	1	7	2	3				13
		10					8			5		4	6			9	11	1	7	2	3				14
		10					8			5		4	6			9	11	1	7	2	3				15
		10			12		8			5		4	6			9	11	1	7	2	3*				16
		10			12		8*			5		4	6			9	11	1	7	2	3				17
		10			8					5		4	6			9	11	1	7	2	3				18
		10	12		8*					5		4	6			9	11	1	7	2	3				19
	3	10			8					5		4	6			9	11	1	7	2					20
2	3	10			8					5		4	6			9	11	1	7						21
	3	10	8							5		4	6			9	11	1	7		2				22
	3	10	8							5		4	6			9	11	1	7		2				23
		10			8					5		4	6			9	11	1	7	2	3				24
		10			8					5		4	6			9	11	1	7	2	3				25
		10			9	8				5		4	6				11	1	7	2	3				26
		10	8		9					5		4	6				11	1	7	2	3				27
		10			9	11				5		4		6		8		1	7	2	3				28
					9	10				5		4	6	11		8		1	7	2	3				29
		10			9					5		4	6	11		8*		1	7	2	3			12	30
		10			9*	12				5		4	6			8	11	1	7	2	3				31
	3	10			9	12				5		4	6			8	11*	1	7	2					32
5		10			9							4	6			8	11	1	7	2	3				33
5		10			9							4	6			8	11	1	7	2	3				34
		10			9	11				5		4		6		8		1	7	2	3				35
		10			9					5		4	6			8	11	1	7	2	3				36
		10			9					5		4	6			8	11	1	7	2	3				37
4		10			9*					5			6	12		8	11	1	7	2	3				38
10						8*				5	12	4		6			11	1	7	2	3			9	39
10*	3				9	7						4		6			11	1		2	5	12		8	40
		10				2		5				4		6		9	11	1	7		3			8	41
	3			10		4		2	7					6	12			1			5	8	11	9*	42
6	15	37	4	1	21	10	17	2	1	37		40	36	14		36	29	42	40	37	31	1	1	4	
			4		5	2					1			1	1							1		1	
1		2			9		11			10			2	4		21	11		12	3				2	

Atkin I	Bailey J	Bracewell P	Curran T	Danskin J	Gray A	Harper A	Heath A	Hughes D	Morrissey J	Mountfield D	Oldroyd D	Ratcliffe K	Reid P	Richardson K	Rimmer N	Sharp G	Sheedy K	Southall N	Steven T	Stevens G	Van den Hauwe P	Wakenshaw R	Walsh D	Wilkinson P	
12		10			8					5		4	6			9	11	1	7	2*	3				3
		10			8					5		4	6			9	11	1	7	2	3				4
		10			8	12				5		4	6			9*	11	1	7	2	3				5
		10	8		9					5		4	6				11	1	7	2	3				6
		10			9	11				5		4	6			8		1	7	2	3				R
		10			9					5		4	6			8	11	1	7	2	3				SF
		10			9					5		4	6			8	11	1	7	2	3				F
		7	1		7	1				7		7	7			6	6	7	7	7	7				
1						1																			
										2			1			2	4		2	1					

Atkin I	Bailey J	Bracewell P	Curran T	Danskin J	Gray A	Harper A	Heath A	Hughes D	Morrissey J	Mountfield D	Oldroyd D	Ratcliffe K	Reid P	Richardson K	Rimmer N	Sharp G	Sheedy K	Southall N	Steven T	Stevens G	Van den Hauwe P	Wakenshaw R	Walsh D	Wilkinson P	
	3	10					8			5		4	6			9	11	1	7	2					2
		10					8			5		4	6	11		9		1	7	2	3				
		10				11	8			5		4	6			9		1	7	2	3				3
		10*			12		8			5		4	6			9	11	1	7	2	3				4
	1	4				1	4			4		4	4	1		4	2	4	4	4	3				
					1																				
		1					1			2						3									

1 own-goal

1985-86

Manager: Howard Kendall

1	Aug	17	(a)	Leicester C	L 1-3	Mountfield	16,932
2		20	(h)	West Brom A	W 2-0	Heath 2	26,788
3		24	(h)	Coventry C	D 1-1	Sharp	27,691
4		26	(a)	Tottenham H	W 1-0	Lineker	29,720
5		31	(h)	Birmingham C	W 4-1	Lineker 3, Stevens	28,066
6	Sep	3	(a)	Sheffield W	W 5-1	Lineker 2, Mountfield, Steven, Heath	30,065
7		7	(a)	Queen's Park R	L 0-3		16,544
8		14	(h)	Luton T	W 2-0	Sheedy, Sharp	26,419
9		21	(h)	Liverpool	L 2-3	Sharp, Lineker	51,509
10		28	(a)	Aston Villa	D 0-0		22,048
11	Oct	5	(h)	Oxford U	W 2-0	Sharp, Bracewell	24,553
12		12	(a)	Chelsea	L 1-2	Sheedy	27,634
13		19	(h)	Watford	W 4-1	Sharp 2, Heath, Bracewell	26,425
14		26	(a)	Manchester C	D 1-1	Heath	28,807
15	Nov	2	(a)	West Ham U	L 1-2	Steven	23,844
16		9	(h)	Arsenal	W 6-1	Lineker 2, Heath 2, Steven, Sharp	28,620
17		16	(a)	Ipswich T	W 4-3	Heath, Sharp, Sheedy, Steven	13,910
18		23	(h)	Nottingham F	D 1-1	Bracewell	27,860
19		30	(a)	Southampton	W 3-2	Lineker, Heath, Steven	16,917
20	Dec	7	(a)	West Brom A	W 3-0	Sheedy, Van den Hauwe, Lineker	12,206
21		14	(h)	Leicester C	L 1-2	Richardson	23,347
22		21	(a)	Coventry C	W 3-1	Lineker 2, Sharp	11,059
23		26	(h)	Manchester U	W 3-1	Sharp 2, Lineker	42,551
24		28	(h)	Sheffield W	W 3-1	Lineker 2, Steven	41,536
25	Jan	1	(a)	Newcastle U	D 2-2	Steven, Sharp	27,820
26		11	(h)	Queen's Park R	W 4-3	Sharp 2, Lineker, Wilkinson	26,015
27		18	(a)	Birmingham C	W 2-0	Lineker 2	10,502
28	Feb	1	(h)	Tottenham H	W 1-0	Reid	33,178
29		11	(h)	Manchester C	W 4-0	Lineker 3, Sharp	30,006
30		22	(a)	Liverpool	W 2-0	Ratcliffe, Lineker	45,445
31	Mar	1	(h)	Aston Villa	W 2-0	Sharp, Lineker	32,133
32		16	(h)	Chelsea	D 1-1	Sheedy	30,145
33		22	(a)	Luton T	L 1-2	Richardson	10,949
34		29	(h)	Newcastle U	W 1-0	Richardson	41,116
35		31	(a)	Manchester U	D 0-0		51,189
36	Apr	12	(a)	Arsenal	W 1-0	Heath	28,251
37		15	(a)	Watford	W 2-0	Lineker, Sharp	18,960
38		19	(h)	Ipswich T	W 1-0	Sharp	39,055
39		26	(a)	Nottingham F	D 0-0		30,171
40		30	(a)	Oxford U	L 0-1		13,939
41	May	3	(h)	Southampton	W 6-1	Lineker 3, Mountfield, Steven, Sharp	33,057
42		5	(h)	West Ham U	W 3-1	Lineker 2, Steven	40,073

FINAL LEAGUE POSITION: 2nd in Division One

Appearances
Sub Appearances
Goals

FA Cup

3	Jan	5	(h)	Exeter C	W 1-0	Stevens
4		25	(h)	Blackburn R	W 3-1	Lineker 2, Van den Hauwe
5	Mar	4	(a)	Tottenham H	W 2-1	Heath, Lineker
6		8	(a)	Luton T	D 2-2	Heath, Opp own-goal
R		12	(h)	Luton T	W 1-0	Lineker
SF	Apr	5	(n*)	Sheffield W	W 2-1	Harper, Sharp
F	May	10	(n†)	Liverpool	L 1-3	Lineker

* Played at Villa Park. † Played at Wembley Stadium.

Appearances
Sub Appearances
Goals

League Cup

2	Sep	25	(h)	Bournemouth	W 3-2	Lineker, Marshall, Opp own-goal
	Oct	8	(a)	Bournemouth	W 2-0	Lineker, Richardson
3		29	(a)	Shrewsbury T	W 4-1	Heath, Sharp, Opp own-goal, Sheedy
4	Nov	26	(a)	Chelsea	D 2-2	Bracewell, Sheedy
R	Dec	10	(h)	Chelsea	L 1-2	Lineker

Appearances
Sub Appearances
Goals

Aspinall W	Atkins I	Bailey J	Billinge P	Bracewell P	Harper A	Heath A	Lineker G	Marshall I	Mimms R	Mountfield D	Pointon N	Ratcliffe K	Reid P	Richardson K	Sharp G	Sheedy K	Southall N	Steven T	Stevens G	Van den Hauwe P	Wilkinson P	
				10		12	8			5		4	6		9	11*	1	7	2	3		1
				10	6	9	8	5				4				11	1	7	2	3		2
	12			10	4	6	8	5							9	11*	1	7	2	3		3
				10	6	9*	8	5				4			12	11	1	7	2	3		4
				10		9	8			5		4	6			11	1	7	2	3		5
				10		12	8			5		4	6*		9	11	1	7	2	3		6
				10		11	8			5		4	6		9		1	7	2	3		7
				10	6	9*	8			5		4			12	11	1	7	2	3		8
				10	6	12	8	5*				4			9	11	1	7	2	3		9
				10	6		8	5				4			9	11	1	7	2	3		10
				10	6		8	5				4		12	9	11*	1	7	2	3		11
		3		10		12	8					4		6*	9	11	1	7	2	5		12
				10	12	6	8	5*				4			9	11	1	7	2	3		13
				10	3	6	8		1			4		12	9	11*		7	2	5		14
				10	3	6	8					4			9	11	1	7	2	5		15
				10	2	6	8				3	4			9	11	1	7	5			16
				10	2	6	8					4			9	11	1	7	5	3		17
				10	2	6	8					4			9	11	1	7	5	3		18
				10	2	6	8					4				11	1	7	5	3	9	19
				10	2	6	8				12	4				11	1	7	5	3	9	20
				10		6	8	5			3	4		11	9		1	7	2			21
				10		6	8				3	4			9	11	1	7	2	5		22
				10		6	8				3	4			9	11	1	7	2	5		23
				10	12	6*	8				3	4			9	11	1	7	2	5		24
				10*	12	6	8				3	4			9	11	1	7	2	5		25
					7	6	8				3	4		10	9	11*	1		2	5	12	26
					6	11	8				3	4		10	9		1	7	2	5		27
				10			8				3	4	6	11	9		1	7	2	5		28
				10			8				3	4	6	12	9	11*	1	7	2	5		29
				10*	12		8				3	4	6	11	9		1	7	2	5		30
						10	8				3	4	6	11	9		1	7	2	5		31
				10		12	8			5	3			6*	9	11	1	7	2	4		32
				10	2		8	12		5	3			6	9	11*	1	7		4		33
				10		12	8		1	5		4	6	11	9			7	2	3*		34
				10		12	8*		1	5		4	6	11	9			7	2	3		35
				10		12	8*		1	5		4	6	11	9			7	2	3		36
				10		12	8*		1	5		4	6	11	9			7	2	3		37
				10		8			1	5		4	6	11	9			7	2	3		38
				10		12	8		1	5		4	6		9	11*		7	2	3		39
				10		12	8		1	5		4		6*	9	11		7	2	3		40
				10*		12	8		1	5		4	6		9	11		7	2	3		41
12			5			10	8*		1			4		6		11		7	2	3	9	42
		1	1	38	17	24	41	8	10	15	14	39	15	16	35	31	32	41	41	40	3	
1	1				4	12					1			3	2						1	
				3		10	30			3		1	1	3	19	5		9	1	1	1	

Aspinall W	Atkins I	Bailey J	Billinge P	Bracewell P	Harper A	Heath A	Lineker G	Marshall I	Mimms R	Mountfield D	Pointon N	Ratcliffe K	Reid P	Richardson K	Sharp G	Sheedy K	Southall N	Steven T	Stevens G	Van den Hauwe P	Wilkinson P	
					7	6	8				3	4		10	9		1		2	5	11	3
				10	12		8				3	4		6	9	11*	1	7	2	5		4
				10	2	12	8				3	4*	6	11	9		1	7		5		5
				10	4	12	8				3*		6	11	9		1	7	2	5		6
				10	4	12	8				3		6		9	11*	1	7	2	5		R
				10	12	8			1	5		4	6*	11	9			7	2	3		SF
				10		12	8		1	5		4	6		9	11		7	2*	3		F
				6	4	2	6		2	2	5	5	5	5	7	3	5	6	6	7	1	
					2	4																
					1	2	5								1				1	1		

1 own-goal

Aspinall W	Atkins I	Bailey J	Billinge P	Bracewell P	Harper A	Heath A	Lineker G	Marshall I	Mimms R	Mountfield D	Pointon N	Ratcliffe K	Reid P	Richardson K	Sharp G	Sheedy K	Southall N	Steven T	Stevens G	Van den Hauwe P	Wilkinson P	
				10	6		8	5				4			9	11	1	7	2	3		2
		3		10			8					4		6	9	11	1	7	2	5		
				10	3	6	8					4			9	11	1	7	2	5		3
				10	2	6	8					4			9	11	1	7	5	3		4
				10	2	6	8	12				4		11	9		1	7	5	3*		R
		1		5	4	3	5	1				5		2	5	4	5	5	5	5		
								1														
				1		1	3	1						1	1	2						

2 own-goals

1986-87

Manager: Howard Kendall

1	Aug	23	(h)	Nottingham F	W 2-0	Sheedy 2	35,198
2		25	(a)	Sheffield W	D 2-2	Langley, Sharp	33,007
3		30	(a)	Coventry C	D 1-1	Marshall	13,504
4	Sep	2	(h)	Oxford U	W 3-1	Harper, Langley, Steven	26,018
5		6	(h)	Queen's Park R	D 0-0		30,173
6		13	(a)	Wimbledon	W 2-1	Sheedy, Sharp	11,708
7		21	(h)	Manchester U	W 3-1	Heath, Sharp, Sheedy	25,843
8		27	(a)	Tottenham H	L 0-2		28,007
9	Oct	4	(h)	Arsenal	L 0-1		30,007
10		11	(a)	Charlton A	L 2-3	Sheedy 2	10,564
11		18	(a)	Southampton	W 2-0	Steven, Wilkinson	18,009
12		25	(h)	Watford	W 3-2	Mountfield 2, Steven	28,577
13	Nov	2	(a)	West Ham U	L 0-1		19,094
14		8	(h)	Chelsea	D 2-2	Steven, Sheedy	29,727
15		15	(a)	Leicester C	W 2-0	Heath, Sheedy	13,450
16		23	(h)	Liverpool	D 0-0		48,247
17		29	(a)	Manchester C	W 3-1	Heath 2, Power	27,097
18	Dec	6	(h)	Norwich C	W 4-0	Heath, Power, Pointon, Steven	26,746
19		13	(a)	Luton T	L 0-1		11,151
20		20	(h)	Wimbledon	W 3-0	Heath, Sheedy, Steven	25,553
21		26	(a)	Newcastle U	W 4-0	Heath, Steven 2, Power	35,079
22		28	(h)	Leicester C	W 5-1	Heath 2, Sheedy, Wilkinson, Opp own-goal	39,730
23	Jan	1	(h)	Aston Villa	W 3-0	Harper, Steven, Sheedy	40,203
24		3	(a)	Queen's Park R	W 1-0	Sharp	19,287
25		17	(h)	Sheffield W	W 2-0	Steven, Watson	33,011
26		25	(a)	Nottingham F	L 0-1		17,009
27	Feb	7	(h)	Coventry C	W 3-1	Heath, Steven, Stevens	30,402
28		14	(a)	Oxford U	D 1-1	Wilkinson	11,878
29		28	(a)	Manchester U	D 0-0		47,421
30	Mar	8	(a)	Watford	L 1-2	Heath	14,014
31		14	(h)	Southampton	W 3-0	Opp own-goal, Power, Watson	26,564
32		21	(h)	Charlton A	W 2-1	Steven, Stevens	27,291
33		28	(a)	Arsenal	W 1-0	Clarke	36,218
34	Apr	4	(a)	Chelsea	W 2-1	Harper, Opp own-goal	21,914
35		11	(h)	West Ham U	W 4-0	Clarke, Reid, Stevens, Watson	35,731
36		18	(a)	Aston Villa	W 1-0	Sheedy	31,218
37		20	(h)	Newcastle U	W 3-0	Clarke 3	43,576
38		25	(a)	Liverpool	L 1-3	Sheedy	44,827
39	May	2	(h)	Manchester C	D 0-0		37,541
40		4	(a)	Norwich C	W 1-0	Van den Hauwe	23,489
41		9	(h)	Luton T	W 3-1	Sharp, Steven 2	44,092
42		11	(h)	Tottenham H	W 1-0	Mountfield	28,287

FINAL LEAGUE POSITION: 1st in Division One

Appearances
Sub Appearances
Goals

FA Cup

3	Jan	10	(h)	Southampton	W 2-1	Sharp 2
4		31	(a)	Bradford C	W 1-0	Snodin
5	Feb	22	(a)	Wimbledon	L 1-3	Wilkinson

Appearances
Sub Appearances
Goals

League Cup

2	Sep	24	(h)	Newport C	W 4-0	Langley, Heath, Wilkinson 2
	Oct	7	(a)	Newport C	W 5-1	Sharp, Wilkinson 3, Opp own-goal
3		28	(h)	Sheffield W	W 4-0	Wilkinson 2, Heath, Mountfield
4	Nov	19	(a)	Norwich C	W 4-1	Heath, Sheedy, Sharp, Steven
5	Jan	21	(h)	Liverpool	L 0-1	

Appearances
Sub Appearances
Goals

Adams N	Aspinall W	Clarke W	Harper A	Heath A	Langley K	Marshall I	Mimms R	Mountfield D	Pointon N	Power P	Ratcliffe K	Reid P	Richardson K	Sharp G	Sheedy K	Snodin I	Southall N	Steven T	Stevens G	Van den Hauwe P	Watson D	Wilkinson P	
			2	8	6		1			3	4		10*	9	11			7			5	12	1
			2	8	6		1			3	4			9	11			7			5	10	2
10			2	8	6*	12	1			3	4			9	11			7			5		3
10			2	8	6		1			3	4			9	11			7			5		4
10*			2	8	6	12	1			3	4			9	11			7			5		5
			2	8*	6		1	10		3	4			9	11			7			5	12	6
12				8	6		1	2		3	4			9	11*			7			5	10	7
12				8	6		1	2		3	4			9	11*			7			5	10	8
8	12				6		1	2*		3	4			9	11			7			5	10	9
7			2	10	6*		1			3	4			9	11			8			5	12	10
	12		2	8	11		1	6		3	4			9				7			5*	10	11
7			2	8	6			5		3	4			9			1	10				11	12
	12		2	8	6*			5		3	4			9	11		1	7				10	13
			2	8	6			5		3	4			9	11		1	7				10	14
10	12		2	8	6			5		3	4			9	11		1	7*					15
10			2	8	6*			5		3	4			9	11		1	7				12	16
10			2	8				5	3	6*	4			9	11		1	7				12	17
			10	8					3	6	4			9*	11		1	7	2		5	12	18
			10	8					3*	6	4			9	11		1	7	2		5	12	19
			10	8					3*	6	4	12		9	11		1	7	2		5		20
			10	8					3	6	4			9*	11		1	7	2		5	12	21
	12		10	8					3	6*	4				11		1	7	2		5	9	22
	12		10	8					3	6*	4				11		1	7	2		5	9	23
			10	8					3	6	4			9	11		1	7	2		5		24
			10	8					3	6	4			9	11	12	1	7	2		5*		25
			10	8				5	12	3*	4				11	6	1	7	2			9	26
			12	8						11	4	6		9*		10	1	7	2	3	5		27
			12	8						11	4	6				10	1	7	2	3*	5	9	28
			8	9						11	4	6*				10	1	7	2	3	5	12	29
		9		8						11	4	6				10	1	7	2	3*	5	12	30
		9	12	8						11	4	6*				10	1	7	2	3	5		31
		9	12	8						11	4	6				10	1	7	2	3*	5		32
		9*	12	8						11	4	6				10	1	7	2	3	5		33
		9	10	8					12	3	4	6			11*		1	7	2		5		34
		9	10	8						3	4	6			11		1	7	2		5		35
		9	12	8						3	4	6			11*	10	1	7	2		5		36
		9	6	8					3	11	4					10	1	7	2		5		37
		9		8						3	4	6			11	10	1	7	2		5		38
		9	12	8						11	4	6*				10	1	7	2	3	5		39
				8						11	4	6		9		10	1	7	2	3	5		40
			11	8							4	6		9		10	1	7	2	3	5		41
11			7	8*				12			4	6		9		10	1		2	3	5		42
10		10	29	41	16		11	12	10	40	42	15	1	27	28	15	31	41	25	11	35	12	
2	6		7			2		1	2			1				1						10	
		5	3	11	2	1		3	1	4		1		5	13			14	2	1	4	3	

3 own-goals

Adams N	Aspinall W	Clarke W	Harper A	Heath A	Langley K	Marshall I	Mimms R	Mountfield D	Pointon N	Power P	Ratcliffe K	Reid P	Richardson K	Sharp G	Sheedy K	Snodin I	Southall N	Steven T	Stevens G	Van den Hauwe P	Watson D	Wilkinson P	
			10	8					3	6	4			9	11		1	7	2		5		3
				8						11	4	6				10	1	7	2	3	5	9	4
			14	8					12	11	4	6*				10	1	7	2	3*	5	9	5
			1	3					1	3	3	2		1	1	2	3	3	3	2	3	2	
			1						1														
														2		1						1	

Adams N	Aspinall W	Clarke W	Harper A	Heath A	Langley K	Marshall I	Mimms R	Mountfield D	Pointon N	Power P	Ratcliffe K	Reid P	Richardson K	Sharp G	Sheedy K	Snodin I	Southall N	Steven T	Stevens G	Van den Hauwe P	Watson D	Wilkinson P	
11				8	6		1	2		3	4			9				7			5	10	2
7†	14		2		6		1		12	3*	4			9	11			8			5	10	
			2	8	6			5		3	4			9	11		1	7				10	3
10			2	8	6			5		3	4			9	11		1	7					4
			10	8				5	3*	6†	4			9	11	14	1	7	2			12	5
3			4	4	4		2	4	2	5	5			5	4		3	5	1		2	3	
	1								1							1						1	
				3	1			1						2	1			1				7	

1 own-goal

1987-88

Manager: Howard Kendall

1	Aug	15	(h)	Norwich C	W 1-0	Power	31,728
2		18	(a)	Wimbledon	D 1-1	Sharp	7,763
3		22	(a)	Nottingham F	D 0-0		20,445
4		29	(h)	Sheffield W	W 4-0	Clarke 2, Steven 2	29,649
5	Sep	2	(a)	Queen's Park R	L 0-1		15,380
6		5	(h)	Tottenham H	D 0-0		32,389
7		12	(a)	Luton T	L 1-2	Pointon	8,124
8		19	(h)	Manchester U	W 2-1	Clarke 2	38,439
9		26	(h)	Coventry C	L 1-2	Clarke	28,153
10	Oct	3	(a)	Southampton	W 4-0	Sharp 4	15,719
11		10	(h)	Chelsea	W 4-1	Heath 2, Sharp 2	32,004
12		17	(a)	Newcastle U	D 1-1	Snodin	20,266
13		24	(h)	Watford	W 2-0	Heath, Sharp	28,501
14	Nov	1	(a)	Liverpool	L 0-2		44,760
15		14	(h)	West Ham U	W 3-1	Reid, Sharp, Watson	29,405
16		21	(a)	Portsmouth	W 1-0	Sharp	17,724
17		28	(h)	Oxford U	D 0-0		25,443
18	Dec	5	(a)	Charlton A	D 0-0		7,208
19		12	(h)	Derby C	W 3-0	Heath, Snodin, Steven	26,224
20		19	(a)	Arsenal	D 1-1	Watson	34,857
21		26	(h)	Luton T	W 2-0	Heath 2	32,242
22		28	(a)	Manchester U	L 1-2	Watson	47,024
23	Jan	1	(a)	Sheffield W	L 0-1		26,443
24		3	(h)	Nottingham F	W 1-0	Clarke	21,680
25		16	(a)	Norwich C	W 3-0	Heath, Sharp 2	15,750
26	Feb	13	(h)	Queen's Park R	W 2-0	Opp own-goal, Pointon	24,724
27		27	(h)	Southampton	W 1-0	Power	20,764
28	Mar	5	(h)	Newcastle U	W 1-0	Clarke	25,674
29		9	(a)	Tottenham H	L 1-2	Opp own-goal	18,662
30		12	(a)	Chelsea	D 0-0		17,390
31		20	(h)	Liverpool	W 1-0	Clarke	44,162
32		26	(a)	Watford	W 2-1	Clarke, Sheedy	13,503
33		29	(h)	Wimbledon	D 2-2	Pointon, Steven	20,351
34	Apr	4	(a)	West Ham U	D 0-0		21,195
35		9	(h)	Portsmouth	W 2-1	Heath, Steven	21,292
36		19	(a)	Coventry C	W 2-1	Heath, Sharp	15,641
37		23	(a)	Oxford U	D 1-1	Clarke	7,619
38		30	(h)	Charlton A	D 1-1	Steven	20,372
39	May	2	(a)	Derby C	D 0-0		17,974
40		7	(h)	Arsenal	L 1-2	Watson	22,445

FINAL LEAGUE POSITION: 4th in Division One

Appearances
Sub Appearances
Goals

FA Cup

3	Jan	9	(a)	Sheffield W	D 1-1	Reid
R		13	(h)	Sheffield W	D 1-1	Sharp
2R		25	(h)	Sheffield W	D 1-1	Steven
3R		27	(a)	Sheffield W	W 5-0	Sharp 3, Heath, Snodin
4		30	(h)	Middlesbrough	D 1-1	Sharp
R	Feb	3	(a)	Middlesbrough	D 2-2	Steven, Watson
2R		9	(h)	Middlesbrough	W 2-1	Sharp, Opp own-goal
5		21	(h)	Liverpool	L 0-1	

Appearances
Sub Appearances
Goals

League Cup

2	Sep	22	(h)	Rotherham U	W 3-2	Clarke, Snodin, Wilson
	Oct	6	(a)	Rotherham U	D 0-0	
3		28	(a)	Liverpool	W 1-0	Stevens
4	Nov	17	(h)	Oldham A	W 2-1	Adams, Watson
5	Jan	20	(h)	Manchester C	W 2-0	Heath, Sharp
SF	Feb	7	(h)	Arsenal	L 0-1	
		24	(a)	Arsenal	L 1-3	Heath

Appearances
Sub Appearances
Goals

Adams N	Bracewell P	Clarke W	Harper A	Heath A	Jones P	Marshall I	Mimms R	Mountfield D	Pointon N	Power P	Ratcliffe K	Reid P	Sharp G	Sheedy K	Snodin I	Southall N	Steven T	Stevens G	Van den Hauwe P	Watson D	Wilson I	
10		8	6				1		3	11	4		9				7		2	5		1
7		8	6			10*	1	12	3	11	4		9						2	5		2
		8	7			12	1		3	11	4	6	9*		10				2	5		3
		8	2				1		3	11*	4	6	9	12	10		7			5		4
		8*	2				1	12	3	11†	4	6	9	14	10		7			5		5
		8*	2	12			1		11		4	6	9		10		7		3	5		6
9*			2	8		12		14	11†		4	6			10	1	7		3	5		7
		9	2	8					11		4	6			10	1	7		3	5		8
		8	6*	12				14	3		4		9		10	1	7		2†	5	11	9
		8*	12	14							4	6	9		10	1	7	2	3	5	11†	10
				8			1				4	6	9		10		7	2	3	5	11	11
			12	8			1				4	6	9		10		7	2*	3	5	11	12
				8					3		4	6	9		10	1	7	2		5	11	14
		8*						12			4	6	9		10	1	7	2	3	5	11	14
			12	8							4	6	9	11*	10	1	7†	2	3	5	14	15
		12	7	8*					14		4	6	9	11†	10	1		2	3	5		16
				8							4	6	9	11	10*	1	7	2	3	5	12	17
12				8*					3		4	6	9	11	10	1	7	2		5		18
				8					3		4	6	9	11	10	1	7	2		5		19
				8					3		4	6	9	11*	10	1	7	2		5	12	20
				8					3		4	6	9		10	1	7	2		5	11	21
		12		8					3		4	6	9		10	1	7	2		5	11*	22
		12		8*					3		4	6	9		10	1	7	2		5	11	23
		9		8							4	6			10	1	7	2	3	5	11	24
			12	8					3			6*	9		10	1	7	2	4	5	11	25
			12	8		14			3	11		6	9		10*	1	7†	2	4	5		26
7*		8	4	6	12				3	11			9		10	1		2		5		27
10		8	6						3				9	11		1	7	2	4	5		28
10*		8	6	12					3	14			9	11		1	7	2†	4	5		29
		8	6						3	10			9	11		1	7	2	4	5		30
		8*	10	12					3	14		6	9	11†		1	7	2	4	5		31
		8	6					5	3	10			9	11		1	7	2	4			32
		8	4	9				5	3	10		6		11		1	7	2				33
		8*	10	9				5	3			6		11	12	1	7	2	4			34
			10	9					3			6		11	8	1	7	2	4	5		35
		8		12					3			6	9		10*	1	7	2	4	5	11	36
		8	12	10*					3			6	9		14	1	7	2	4	5	11†	37
11		9	10	8					3			6				1	7	2	4	5		38
		9	8					4	3	11		6			10	1	7	2		5		39
		8*	12						3	11		6	9	14	10†	1	7	2	4	5		40
7		24	21	23		1	8	4	32	12	24	32	32	14	29	32	36	31	28	37	13	
1		3	7	6	1	3								3	2						3	
		10		9					3	2		1	13	1	2		6			4		

2 own-goals

Adams N	Bracewell P	Clarke W	Harper A	Heath A	Jones P	Marshall I	Mimms R	Mountfield D	Pointon N	Power P	Ratcliffe K	Reid P	Sharp G	Sheedy K	Snodin I	Southall N	Steven T	Stevens G	Van den Hauwe P	Watson D	Wilson I	
		8	12	14							4*	6	9		10	1	7	2	3	5	11†	3
		12		8					3			6	9		10	1	7	2	4	5	11*	R
		12	14	8*					3			6	9		10	1	7	2	4	5	11†	2R
	12	14	11	8					3			6	9†		10*	1	7	2	4	5		3R
		12	11*	8					3			6	9		10	1	7	2	4	5		4
		12	11*	8					3			6	9		10	1	7	2	4	5		R
		12		8					3	11*		6	9		10	1	7	2	4	5		2R
	12		14	8					3	11*		6†	9		10	1	7	2	4	5		5
		1	3	7					7	2	1	8	8		8	8	8	8	8	8	3	
	2	6	3	1																		
				1								1	6		1		2			1		

1 own-goal

Adams N	Bracewell P	Clarke W	Harper A	Heath A	Jones P	Marshall I	Mimms R	Mountfield D	Pointon N	Power P	Ratcliffe K	Reid P	Sharp G	Sheedy K	Snodin I	Southall N	Steven T	Stevens G	Van den Hauwe P	Watson D	Wilson I	
		9	2	8*							4	6	12		10	1	7		3	5	11	2
		8*		12							4	6	9		10	1	7	2	3	5	11	
				8							4	6	9		10	1	7	2	3	5	11	3
7				8							4	6	9	11	10	1		2	3	5		4
		12		8					3			6	9*		10	1	7	2	4	5	11	5
		12	11*	8					3			6	9		10	1	7	2	4	5		SF
	6	8	12	14					3	11			9		10*	1	7	2	4†	5		
1	1	3	2	5					3	1	4	6	6	1	7	7	6	6	7	7	4	
		2	1	2									1									
1		1		2									1		1			1		1	1	

1988-89

Manager: Colin Harvey

No	Month	Day	Venue	Opponents	Result	Scorers	Att
1	Aug	27	(h)	Newcastle U	W 4-0	Cottee 3, Sharp	41,560
2	Sep	3	(a)	Coventry C	W 1-0	Cottee	18,625
3		10	(h)	Nottingham F	D 1-1	Heath	34,003
4		17	(a)	Millwall	L 1-2	Opp own-goal	17,507
5		24	(h)	Luton T	L 0-2		26,017
6	Oct	1	(a)	Wimbledon	L 1-2	Heath	6,367
7		8	(h)	Southampton	W 4-1	Cottee 2, Steven, Watson	25,356
8		22	(a)	Aston Villa	L 0-2		26,636
9		30	(h)	Manchester U	D 1-1	Cottee	27,005
10	Nov	5	(a)	Sheffield W	D 1-1	Steven	21,761
11		12	(a)	Charlton A	W 2-1	Reid, Sharp	8,627
12		19	(h)	Norwich C	D 1-1	Steven	28,118
13		26	(a)	West Ham U	W 1-0	Steven	22,176
14	Dec	3	(h)	Tottenham H	W 1-0	Cottee	29,657
15		11	(a)	Liverpool	D 1-1	Clarke	42,372
16		17	(a)	Queen's Park R	D 0-0		10,067
17		26	(h)	Middlesbrough	W 2-1	Cottee, Steven	32,651
18		31	(h)	Coventry C	W 3-1	Sheedy 2, Bracewell	30,790
19	Jan	2	(a)	Nottingham F	L 0-2		26,008
20		14	(h)	Arsenal	L 1-3	Watson	34,825
21		21	(a)	Luton T	L 0-1		9,013
22	Feb	4	(h)	Wimbledon	D 1-1	Sharp	23,365
23		11	(a)	Southampton	D 1-1	Sheedy	15,845
24		14	(h)	Aston Villa	D 1-1	Cottee	20,142
25		25	(a)	Derby C	L 2-3	Clarke, Sharp	17,103
26	Mar	11	(h)	Sheffield W	W 1-0	Cottee	22,542
27		22	(a)	Newcastle U	L 0-2		20,933
28		25	(h)	Millwall	D 1-1	Sheedy	27,062
29		27	(a)	Middlesbrough	D 3-3	Cottee, Nevin, Sheedy	21,351
30	Apr	1	(h)	Queen's Park R	W 4-1	Clarke, Cottee, Sheedy, Steven	23,028
31		8	(a)	Arsenal	L 0-2		37,608
32		10	(h)	Charlton A	W 3-2	Nevin, Sharp, Sheedy	16,316
33		22	(a)	Tottenham H	L 1-2	McDonald	28,568
34	May	3	(h)	Liverpool	D 0-0		45,994
35		6	(a)	Norwich C	L 0-1		13,239
36		10	(a)	Manchester U	W 2-1	Sharp 2	26,722
37		13	(h)	West Ham U	W 3-1	Bracewell, Sheedy, Watson	21,694
38		15	(h)	Derby C	W 1-0	Wilson	17,826

FINAL LEAGUE POSITION: 8th in Division One

Appearances
Sub Appearances
Goals

FA Cup

Rd	Month	Day	Venue	Opponents	Result	Scorers	Att
3	Jan	7	(a)	West Brom A	D 1-1	Sheedy (pen)	31,186
R		11	(h)	West Brom A	W 1-0	Sheedy	31,697
4		28	(a)	Plymouth A	D 1-1	Sheedy (pen)	27,566
R		31	(h)	Plymouth A	W 4-0	Sharp 2, Nevin, Sheedy	28,542
5	Feb	18	(a)	Barnsley	W 1-0	Sharp	32,551
6	Mar	19	(h)	Wimbledon	W 1-0	McCall	24,562
SF	Apr	15	(n*)	Norwich C	W 1-0	Nevin	46,553
F	May	20	(n†)	Liverpool	L 2-3	McCall 2	82,800

*Played at Villa Park, Birmingham. †Played at Wembley Stadium.

Appearances
Sub Appearances
Goals

League Cup

Rd	Month	Day	Venue	Opponents	Result	Scorers	Att
2	Sep	27	(h)	Bury	W 3-0	Sharp, McDonald (pen), McCall	11,071
	Oct	11	(a)	Bury	D 2-2	Steven (pen), Sharp	4,592
3	Nov	8	(h)	Oldham A	D 1-1	Steven (pen)	17,230
R		29	(a)	Oldham	W 2-0	Cottee 2	14,573
4	Dec	14	(a)	Bradford C	W 1-3	Watson	15,055

Appearances
Sub Appearances
Goals
Sub Appearances
Goals

Adams N	Bracewell P	Clarke W	Cottee A	Ebbrell J	Heath A	McCall S	McDonald N	Nevin P	Pointon N	Ratcliffe K	Reid P	Sharp G	Sheedy K	Snodin I	Southall N	Steven T	Stowell M	Van den Hauwe P	Watson D	Wilson I	
			10	5		8	2	11	3		6	9	12	4	1	7*			5		1
			10			8	2	7	3		6	9	11	4	1				5		2
			10		12	8	2	7*	3		6	9	11†	4	1				5	14	3
		12	10		7	8*	2		3		6	9	11†	4	1			14	5		4
		12	10		7	8	2*				6	9	11	4	1				5	3	5
			10		7	8	2		3		6	9	11	4	1			5			6
			10		7	8				4	6	9		2	1	11		3	5		7
			10		7	8			12	4	6	9		2	1	11†		3*	5	14	8
			10		7*	8				4	6	9		2	1	11		3	5	12	9
			10			8				4	6	9		2	1	7		3	5	11	10
			10			8				4	6	9		2	1	7		3	5	11	11
			10			8				4	6	9		2	1	7		3	5	11	12
			10			8				4	6	9		2	1	7		3	5	11	13
	6	12	10			8				4		9*		2	1	7		3	5	11	14
	6*	9	10			8				4	12			2	1	7		3	5	11	15
	6	9	10			8		11*		4			12	2	1	7		3	5		16
	6	12	10*			8		9	3		14		11†	2	1	7		4	5		17
	6		10					9	12	4	8		11	2	1	7		3*	5		18
	6		10					9*	3	4	8		11	2	1	7			5	12	19
	6	9	10			12	14	7	3	4	8*		11†	2	1				5		20
	6	9	10			8*	14	7*	3	4			11	2	1				5	12	21
			10	12		8	2	7		4		9			1	6		3	5	11*	22
		12	10†			8	2	14		4		9	11		1	7		3	5	6*	23
	6		10			8	2	12		4		9	11		1	7		3*	5		24
		10				8	2	12	3	4		9*	11	6	1	7			5		25
	6	9	10			8	14	12	3	4			11*	2†	1	7			5		26
	6	12	10†			8*	2	14	3	4		9	11		1	7		5			27
	6	10*	12			14	2	8	3	4		9	11†		1	7		5			28
	6	9	10*				2	8	3	4			11		1	7		5		12	29
	6	9	10				2	8	3	4			11		1	7			5		30
	6	9	10	12		5	2	8	3				11		1	7*		4			31
	6	10		12		8	2	7*	3	4		9	11		1			5			32
	6*	12	10			14	2	7		4		9	11†		1	8		3	5		33
	6		10			12	2	7		4		9	11*		1	8		3	5		34
	6	9	10			7	2		3	4			11		1	8			5		35
			10			6	2	7	12	4		9			1	8		3*	5	11	36
	6		10				2	7	3	4		9	11*		1	8			5	12	37
		12	10	8		6	2	7	3	4		9*			1				5	11	38
	20	12	35	1	6	29	22	20	20	30	16	26	24	23	38	29		24	32	11	
		8	1	3	1	4	3	5	3		2		2					1		7	
	2	3	13		2		1	2			1	7	8			6			3	1	

1 own-goal

Adams N	Bracewell P	Clarke W	Cottee A	Ebbrell J	Heath A	McCall S	McDonald N	Nevin P	Pointon N	Ratcliffe K	Reid P	Sharp G	Sheedy K	Snodin I	Southall N	Steven T	Stowell M	Van den Hauwe P	Watson D	Wilson I	
	6	12	10					9	3	4	8		11*	2	1	7		5			3
	6	9	10					7	12	4	8		11	2	1			3*	5		R
	6		10			8				4		9	11	2	1	7		3	5		4
		14	10			8		7†		4		9	11	2*	1	6		3	5	12	R
			10			8	2	12	3	4		9	11	6*	1	7			5		5
	6		10			8	2		3	4		9	11		1	7			5		6
	6		10				2	7		4		9	11		1	8		3	5		SF
	6*		10			12	2	7		4		9	11†		1	8		3	5	14	F
	6	1	8			4	4	5	3	8	2	6	8	5	8	7		6	7		
		2				1		1	1											2	
						3		2				3	4								

Adams N	Bracewell P	Clarke W	Cottee A	Ebbrell J	Heath A	McCall S	McDonald N	Nevin P	Pointon N	Ratcliffe K	Reid P	Sharp G	Sheedy K	Snodin I	Southall N	Steven T	Stowell M	Van den Hauwe P	Watson D	Wilson I	
		12	10		7	8	2				6*	9	11	4	1			5		3	2
			10		7				12	4	6	9		2	1	11		3*	5	8	
12			10			8				4	6	9		2	1	7		3	5	11*	3
			10			8				4	6	9		2	1	7		3	5	11	R
	6		10			8		9		4	14		12	2	1	7		3	5	11*	4
	1		5		2	4	1	1		4	4	4	1	5	5	4		5	4	5	
1		1							1		1		1								
			2			1	1					2				2			1		

1989-90

Manager: Colin Harvey

1	Aug	19	(a)	Coventry C	L 0-2		17,981
2		22	(h)	Tottenham H	W 2-1	Newell, Sheedy	34,402
3		26	(h)	Southampton	W 3-0	McCall, Newell, Whiteside	27,807
4		30	(a)	Sheffield W	D 1-1	Sheedy	19,657
5	Sep	9	(h)	Manchester U	W 3-2	Nevin, Newell, Sharp	37,916
6		16	(a)	Charlton A	W 1-0	Newell	11,491
7		23	(h)	Liverpool	L 1-3	Newell	42,453
8		30	(a)	Crystal P	L 1-2	Newell	15,943
9	Oct	14	(h)	Millwall	W 2-1	Sheedy, Whiteside	26,125
10		21	(h)	Arsenal	W 3-0	Nevin 2, McDonald	32,917
11		28	(a)	Norwich C	D 1-1	Cottee	18,627
12	Nov	5	(a)	Aston Villa	L 2-6	Cottee, Opp own-goal	17,637
13		11	(h)	Chelsea	L 0-1		33,737
14		18	(h)	Wimbledon	D 1-1	Sheedy	21,561
15		25	(a)	Nottingham F	L 0-1		20,709
16	Dec	2	(h)	Coventry C	W 2-0	McCall, Watson	21,171
17		9	(a)	Tottenham H	L 1-2	Cottee	29,374
18		17	(h)	Manchester C	D 0-0		21,737
19		26	(a)	Derby C	W 1-0	McCall	21,314
20		30	(a)	Queen's Park R	L 0-1		11,683
21	Jan	1	(h)	Luton T	W 2-1	Sharp, Whiteside	21,743
22		13	(a)	Southampton	D 2-2	Whiteside 2	19,381
23		20	(h)	Sheffield W	W 2-0	Sheedy 2	25,545
24	Feb	3	(a)	Liverpool	L 1-2	Sharp	38,370
25		10	(h)	Charlton A	W 2-1	Cottee, Whiteside	21,442
26	Mar	3	(a)	Wimbledon	L 1-3	Sheedy	6,512
27		14	(a)	Manchester U	D 0-0		37,398
28		17	(h)	Crystal P	W 4-0	Cottee 2, Sharp, Whiteside	19,274
29		21	(a)	Millwall	W 2-1	Cottee, Pointon	11,495
30		24	(h)	Norwich C	W 3-1	Cottee 2, Sharp	21,707
31		31	(a)	Arsenal	L 0-1		35,223
32	Apr	4	(h)	Nottingham F	W 4-0	Cottee 2, Whiteside 2	17,795
33		7	(h)	Queen's Park R	W 1-0	Cottee	19,887
34		14	(a)	Luton T	D 2-2	Cottee, Sharp	9,538
35		16	(h)	Derby C	W 2-1	Atteveld, Sheedy	23,933
36		21	(a)	Manchester C	L 0-1		32,144
37		28	(a)	Chelsea	L 1-2	Nevin	18,879
38	May	5	(h)	Aston Villa	D 3-3	Newell, Sheedy, Opp own-goal	29,551

FINAL LEAGUE POSITION: 6th in Division One

Appearances
Sub Appearances
Goals

FA Cup

3	Jan	6	(a)	Middlesbrough	D 0-0		20,075
R		10	(h)	Middlesbrough	D 1-1*	Sheedy	24,352
2R		17	(h)	Middlesbrough	W 1-0	Whiteside	23,866
4		28	(a)	Sheffield W	W 2-1	Whiteside 2	31,754
5	Feb	17	(a)	Oldham A	D 2-2	Sharp, Cottee	19,320
R		21	(h)	Oldham A	D 1-1*	Sheedy (pen)	36,663
2R	Mar	10	(a)	Oldham A	L 1-2*	Cottee	19,346

*After extra-time

Appearances
Sub Appearances
Goals

League Cup

2	Sep	19	(a)	Leyton O	W 2-0	Newell, Sheedy	8,214
	Oct	3	(h)	Leyton O	D 2-2	Whiteside, Sheedy	10,128
3		24	(h)	Luton T	W 3-0	Newell 2, Nevin	18,428
4	Nov	22	(a)	Nottingham F	L 0-1		21,324

Appearances
Sub Appearances
Goals

Atteveld R	Beagrie P	Cottee A	Ebbrell J	Keown M	McCall S	McDonald N	Nevin P	Newell M	Pointon N	Ratcliffe K	Rehn S	Sharp G	Sheedy K	Snodin I	Southall N	Watson D	Whiteside N	Wright M	
		12			8		7	10*	3	4		9	11	2	1	5	6		1
					8		7	10	3	4		9	11	2	1	5	6		2
			12		8		7	10	3	4		9*	11	2	1	5	6		3
		10†		12	8	14	7	9	3	4			11	2	1	5*	6		4
					8	12	7	10	3	4		9	11	2	1	5	6*		5
					8	12	7*	10	3	4	6	9	11	2	1	5			6
					8	12	7	10	3*	4	14	9	11	2	1	5	6†		7
					8	3	7	10		4	12	9	11	2	1	5	6*		8
		10	8	4		3	7	9			12*	14	11	2†	1	5	6		9
		10	2	4	8	3	7	9					11		1	5	6		10
		10	2	4	8	3	7	9					11		1	5	6		11
	14	10	2	4	8	3	7	9				12	11		1	5†	6*		12
	6	10*	2	4	8	5	7	9	3			12	11		1				13
	6		2	4	8	5		10	3			9	11	7	1				14
	7*	12	14	4	8	2		10	3†			9	11	6	1	5			15
2	7	10	6		8	3				4		9	11		1	5			16
2	7	10	6*		8	3		12		4		9	11		1	5			17
2	7	10	6*		8	3		12		4		9	11		1	5			18
6†	7	10*			8	3	14	12		4		9	11	2	1	5			19
6†	7	10*			8	3	14	12		4		9	11	2	1	5			20
12	11*				8	3	7	10		4		9		2	1	5	6		21
	7*			5	8	3	12	10		4		9	11	2	1		6		22
				5	8	3	7	10		4		9	11	2	1		6		23
				10	8	3	7*	12		4		9	11	2	1	5	6		24
		10		5	8	3*	7			4		9	11	2	1	12	6		25
6		10†		7	8	3*		14		4		9	11	2	1	5	12		26
7	12	10		5	8				3	4		9	11*	2	1		6		27
7*		10		5	8		12		3	4		9	11	2	1		6		28
7*	12	10		5	8				3	4		9	11	2	1		6		29
7	12	10		5	8		14		3	4†		9	11*	2	1		6		30
	12	10		4†	8	14	7		3			9	11*	2	1	5	6		31
7	11	10			8	4	14		3*			9	12	2†	1	5	6		32
2	11	10	3		8	4	7*					9	12		1		6	5	33
2	11	10	3		8	4	7					9	6		1	5			34
2	11*	10	3		8	4	7					9	12		1	5	6		35
2		10	12		8	4	7		3			9*	11		1	5	6		36
7*		10	12	4	8	2	14	9	3				11		1	5	6†		37
14		10	11*	2	8	6	7	9	3	4			12		1	5†			38
16	14	25	13	19	37	26	23	20	19	24	1	30	33	25	38	28	26	1	
2	5	2	4	1		5	7	6			3	3	4			1	1		
1		13			3	1	4	7	1			6	9			1	9		

2 own-goals

Atteveld R	Beagrie P	Cottee A	Ebbrell J	Keown M	McCall S	McDonald N	Nevin P	Newell M	Pointon N	Ratcliffe K	Rehn S	Sharp G	Sheedy K	Snodin I	Southall N	Watson D	Whiteside N	Wright M	
7	11				8	3		10		4		9		2	1	5	6		3
	7†	12		5	8	3	14	10		4		9	11	2	1		6*		R
14		12		5	8	3	7	10*		4		9	11†	2	1		6		2R
				7	8	3	12	10*		4		9	11	2	1	5	6		4
		10	7		8	3				4		9	11	2	1	5	6		5
7†		10			8	3*	12	14		4		9	11	2	1	5	6		R
7†	14	10	6	5	8	3*		12		4		9	11	2	1				2R
3	2	3	2	4	7	7	1	4		7		7	6	7	7	4	6		
1	1	2					3	2											
		2										1	2				3		

Atteveld R	Beagrie P	Cottee A	Ebbrell J	Keown M	McCall S	McDonald N	Nevin P	Newell M	Pointon N	Ratcliffe K	Rehn S	Sharp G	Sheedy K	Snodin I	Southall N	Watson D	Whiteside N	Wright M	
					8		7	10	3	4	6	9	11	2	1	5			2
		14			8	3	7	10		4*	12	9*	11	2	1	5	6		
		10*	2	4	8	3	7	9				12	11		1	5	6		3
		12	6	4	8	2	7*	10	3			9	11	5	1				4
		1	2	2	4	3	4	4	2	2	1	3	4	3	4	3	2		
		2									1	1							
							1	3					2				1		

1990-91

Manager: Howard Kendall

1	Aug	25	(h)	Leeds U	L 2-3	Ebbrell, Nevin	34,412
2		29	(a)	Coventry C	L 1-3	Nevin	12,902
3	Sep	1	(a)	Manchester C	L 0-1		31,456
4		8	(h)	Arsenal	D 1-1	Newell	29,919
5		15	(a)	Sunderland	D 2-2	Newell, Sharp	25,004
6		22	(h)	Liverpool	L 2-3	Hinchcliffe, McCall	39,847
7		29	(h)	Southampton	W 3-0	Cottee 2, Ebbrell	23,093
8	Oct	7	(a)	Nottingham F	L 1-3	McDonald	25,790
9		20	(h)	Crystal P	D 0-0		24,504
10		27	(a)	Luton T	D 1-1	Nevin	10,047
11	Nov	3	(h)	Queen's Park R	W 3-0	McDonald, Nevin, Newell	22,352
12		10	(a)	Sheffield U	D 0-0		21,447
13		18	(h)	Tottenham H	D 1-1	McCall	28,716
14		24	(a)	Wimbledon	L 1-2	Sheedy	6,411
15	Dec	1	(h)	Manchester U	L 0-1		32,400
16		8	(h)	Coventry C	W 1-0	McCall	17,472
17		16	(a)	Leeds U	L 0-2		27,775
18		22	(a)	Norwich C	L 0-1		14,294
19		26	(h)	Aston Villa	W 1-0	Sharp	27,804
20		29	(h)	Derby	W 2-0	Nevin, Newell	25,361
21	Jan	1	(a)	Chelsea	W 2-1	Sharp, Opp own-goal	18,351
22		13	(h)	Manchester C	W 2-0	Beagrie, Sheedy	22,774
23		19	(a)	Arsenal	L 0-1		35,349
24	Feb	2	(h)	Sunderland	W 2-0	Beagrie, Sheedy	23,124
25		9	(a)	Liverpool	L 1-3	Nevin	25,116
26		23	(h)	Sheffield U	L 1-2	Cottee	28,148
27	Mar	2	(a)	Manchester U	W 2-0	Newell, Watson	45,656
28		16	(a)	Southampton	W 4-3	Cottee, Milligan, Newell, Watson	15,410
29		23	(h)	Nottingham F	D 0-0		23,078
30		30	(a)	Aston Villa	D 2-2	Warzycha 2	27,660
31	Apr	1	(h)	Norwich C	W 1-0	Newell	20,485
32		10	(h)	Wimbledon	L 1-2	Cottee	14,590
33		13	(h)	Chelsea	D 2-2	Cottee, Ebbrell	19,526
34		20	(a)	Crystal P	D 0-0		16,439
35		24	(a)	Tottenham H	D 3-3	Cottee, Nevin, Opp own-goal	21,675
36	May	4	(h)	Luton T	W 1-0	Cottee	19,809
37		8	(a)	Derby C	W 3-2	Cottee 2, Sheedy	12,403
38		11	(a)	Queen's Park R	D 1-1	Nevin	12,508

FINAL LEAGUE POSITION: 9th in Division One

Appearances
Sub Appearances
Goals

FA Cup

3	Jan	5	(a)	Charlton A	W 2-1	Ebbrell 2	12,234
4		27	(h)	Woking	W 1-0	Sheedy	34,724
5	Feb	17	(a)	Liverpool	D 0-0		38,323
R		20	(h)	Liverpool	D 4-4	Cottee 2, Sharp 2	37,766
2R		27	(h)	Liverpool	W 1-0	Watson	40,201
6	Mar	11	(a)	West Ham U	L 1-2	Watson	28,162

Appearances
Sub Appearances
Goals

League Cup

2	Sep	25	(a)	Wrexham	W 5-0	Cottee 3, McDonald, Nevin	9,072
	Oct	9	(h)	Wrexham	W 6-0	Sharp 3, Cottee, Ebbrell, McDonald	7,415
3		30	(a)	Sheffield U	L 1-2	Opp own-goal	15,045

Appearances
Sub Appearances
Goals

Atteveld R	Barlow S	Beagrie P	Cottee A	Ebbrell J	Hinchcliffe A	Jenkins I	Keown M	McCall S	McDonald N	Milligan M	Nevin P	Newell M	Ratcliffe K	Sharp G	Sheedy K	Snodin I	Southall N	Warzycha R	Watson D	Whiteside N	Youds E	
				11	3		4	8*	2	6	7	10		9	12		1		5			1
11†				6	3		4		2*	8	7	10	12	9			1		5	14		2
12				8	3		2			6	7	10	4	9	11*		1		5			3
2			12	11	3			8*		6	7	10	4	9			1		5			4
2				11	3			8		6	7	10	4	9			1		5			5
2			12	11	3			8	14	6*	7	10*	4	9			1		5			6
2			10	11	3			8	6		7	12	4	9*			1		5			7
2			10	11	3			8	6		7*	12	4	9			1		5			8
2			10	11	3*		14	8	6		7	12	4*	9			1		5			9
2			10	11			3	8	6		7		4	9			1		5			10
2		11		10			3	8	6		7	9	4				1		5			11
2		12		11			3	8	6		7	9	4		10*		1		5			12
2			10	3			5	8	6*		14	12	4	9	11	7*	1					13
7			12	3			5	8	2		14	10	4	9*	11		1			6†		14
6			10	3*			5	8	2		7	9	4	12	11		1					15
			10*	14			3	8	2	6	7	9	4	12	11†		1		5			16
7		11	12	6*			3	8	2		14	10	4	9†			1		5			17
8			10*	6	11		3†		2		7	9	4	12			1		5		14	18
		11†		6	3		14		8		7*	12	4	9	10		1		5		2	19
		11*		6	3			8	2		7	12	4	9	10		1		5			20
		11		6	3			8	2		7		4	9	10		1		5			21
		11*	12	6	3			8	2		7		4	9	10		1		5			22
		11	12	3			14	8	2	6*	7		4	9	10		1		5†			23
		11	12	3				8	2	6*	7		4	9	10		1		5			24
		11*	12	3				8	2	6	7		4	9	10		1		5			25
			10	11	3		6	8	2	7	14	12	4†	9*			1		5			26
14			12	11	3		6	8	2		7*	10	4	9*			1		5			27
14		12	10†	3			6	8	2	11	7*	9	4				1		5			28
			10	3			2		14	6	11*	12	4	9	8		1	7	5†			29
			10		3		5	8	2	6	12		4	9	11*		1	7				30
			10	14	3		5	8	2	6	12	9			11†		1	7*			4	31
	12	11	10		3			8	2*	6*	9		4				1	7	5		14	32
	12		10	6			4	8			7	9*	3		11		1		5		2	33
		14	10*	6			4	8			7	9	3		11		1	12	5†		2	34
		11	10	6	3		5	8			9		4		12		1	7			2*	35
6		11	10	2	3			8				9	4				1	7	5			36
2		11	10	3				8			9	12	4		6		1	7*	5			37
		11	10*	2		3		8		12	7	9	4		6		1		5†		14	38
17		14	20	34	21	1	21	33	27	16	31	20	35	24	20	1	38	7	32	1	5	
3	2	3	9	2			3		2	1	6	9	1	3	2			1		1	3	
		2	10	3	1			3	2	1	8	7		3	4			2	2			

2 own-goals

Atteveld R	Barlow S	Beagrie P	Cottee A	Ebbrell J	Hinchcliffe A	Jenkins I	Keown M	McCall S	McDonald N	Milligan M	Nevin P	Newell M	Ratcliffe K	Sharp G	Sheedy K	Snodin I	Southall N	Warzycha R	Watson D	Whiteside N	Youds E	
		11*		6	3			8	2		7	12	4	9	10		1		5			3
		12	8*	11	3		14	6	2		7		4	9†	10		1		5			4
7			12	3			6	8	2		11		4	9	10*		1		5			5
2*			14	11	3		6	12	8		7†	10	4	9			1		5			R
7*				11	3		6	8	2		12	10	4	9			1		5			2R
			12	11	3		6	8	2*	10†	7	14	4	9			1		5			6
3		1	1	6	5		4	5	6	1	5	2	6	6	3		6		6			
		1	3				1	1			1	2										
			2	2										2	1				2			

Atteveld R	Barlow S	Beagrie P	Cottee A	Ebbrell J	Hinchcliffe A	Jenkins I	Keown M	McCall S	McDonald N	Milligan M	Nevin P	Newell M	Ratcliffe K	Sharp G	Sheedy K	Snodin I	Southall N	Warzycha R	Watson D	Whiteside N	Youds E	
2			10	11	3			8	6		7*	12	4	9			1		5			2
2			10†	11	3			8*	6	12	7	14	4	9			1		5			
2			10*	11			3	8	6		12	7	4	9			1		5			3
3			3	3	2		1	3	3		2	1	3	3			3		3			
										1	1	2										
			4	1					2		1			3								

1 own-goal

1991-92

Manager: Howard Kendall

1	Aug	17	(a)	Nottingham F	L 1-2	Pearce (og)	24,422
2		20	(h)	Arsenal	W 3-1	Ward 2, Cottee	31,200
3		24	(h)	Manchester U	D 0-0		36,085
4		28	(a)	Sheffield W	L 1-2	Watson	28,690
5		31	(a)	Liverpool	L 1-3	Newell	39,072
6	Sep	3	(h)	Norwich C	D 1-1	Ward	19,197
7		7	(h)	Crystal P	D 2-2	Warzycha, Beardsley	21,065
8		14	(a)	Sheffield U	L 1-2	Beardsley	19,817
9		17	(a)	Manchester C	W 1-0	Beardsley	27,509
10		21	(h)	Coventry C	W 3-0	Beardsley 3 (1 pen)	20,542
11		28	(a)	Chelsea	D 2-2	Ebbrell, Beardsley	19,038
12	Oct	5	(h)	Tottenham H	W 3-1	Cottee 3 (1 pen)	29,505
13		19	(h)	Aston Villa	L 0-2		27,688
14		26	(a)	Queen's Park R	L 1-3	Cottee	10,002
15	Nov	2	(a)	Luton T	W 1-0	Warzycha	8,022
16		16	(h)	Wimbledon	W 2-0	Cottee (pen), Watson	18,762
17		23	(h)	Notts C	W 1-0	Cottee	24,230
18		30	(a)	Leeds U	L 0-1		30,043
19	Dec	7	(h)	West Ham U	W 4-0	Cottee, Beagrie, Beardsley, Johnston	21,563
20		14	(a)	Oldham A	D 2-2	Sheedy, Nevin	14,955
21		21	(a)	Arsenal	L 2-4	Warzycha, Johnston	29,684
22		26	(h)	Sheffield W	L 0-1		30,788
23		28	(h)	Liverpool	D 1-1	Johnston	37,681
24	Jan	1	(a)	Southampton	W 2-1	Ward, Beardsley	16,546
25		11	(a)	Manchester U	L 0-1		46,619
26		19	(h)	Nottingham F	D 1-1	Watson	17,717
27	Feb	2	(a)	Aston Villa	D 0-0		17,451
28		8	(h)	Queen's Park R	D 0-0		18,212
29		23	(h)	Leeds U	D 1-1	Jackson	19,248
30		29	(a)	West Ham U	W 2-0	Johnston, Ablett	20,976
31	Mar	7	(h)	Oldham A	W 2-1	Beardsley 2	21,014
32		10	(a)	Wimbledon	D 0-0		3,569
33		14	(h)	Luton T	D 1-1	Johnston	16,707
34		17	(a)	Notts C	D 0-0		7,480
35		21	(a)	Norwich C	L 3-4	Johnston 2, Beardsley	11,900
36	Apr	1	(h)	Southampton	L 0-1		15,201
37		4	(a)	Crystal P	L 0-2		14,338
38		11	(h)	Sheffield U	L 0-2		18,285
39		18	(a)	Coventry C	W 1-0	Beagrie	14,669
40		20	(h)	Manchester C	L 1-2	Nevin	21,101
41		25	(a)	Tottenham H	D 3-3	Beardsley 2, Unsworth	34,630
42	May	2	(h)	Chelsea	W 2-1	Beardsley (pen), Beagrie	20,163

FINAL LEAGUE POSITION: 12th in Division One

Appearances
Sub Appearances
Goals

FA Cup

3	Jan	4	(h)	Southend U	W 1-0	Beardsley	22,606
4		26	(a)	Chelsea	L 0-1		21,152

Appearances
Sub Appearances
Goals

League Cup

2	Sep	24	(h)	Watford	W 1-0	Beardsley	8,264
	Oct	8	(a)	Watford	W 2-1	Newell, Beardsley	11,561
3		30	(h)	Wolves	W 4-1	Beagrie 2, Cottee, Beardsley	19,065
4	Dec	4	(h)	Leeds U	L 1-4	Atteveld	25,467

Appearances
Sub Appearances
Goals

Ablett G	Atteveld R	Barlow S	Beagrie P	Beardsley P	Cottee A	Ebbrell J	Harper A	Hinchcliffe A	Jackson M	Jenkins I	Johnston M	Keown M	McDonald N	Nevin P	Newell M	Ratcliffe K	Sheedy K	Southall N	Unsworth D	Ward M	Warzycha R	Watson D	Youds E		
				9	10	3	2					6	12	14		4	8	1		11*	7†	5			1
				9	10	3	2					6		12		4	8	1		11*	7	5			2
				9	10†	3	2					6		12	14	4	8	1		11	7*	5			3
				9	10†	3	2					6	12		14	4	8	1		11	7*	5			4
				8	10*	3	2					6*	4		9	12	11	1		7	14	5			5
				8		6	2	3							9	4	10	1		11	7	5			6
				8		3	2†	14				6		12	9	4	10	1		11	7*	5			7
	2			8	12	4		3				6			9		10	1		11*	7	5			8
	2			8		4		3				6	12		9		10	1		11	7*	5			9
	2			8		4		3				6	12		9		10*	1		11	7	5			10
	2			8	12	4		3				6		11	9		10	1			7*	5			11
	14			8	9	4	2					6			12	3	10†	1		11*	7	5			12
	14			8	9	4	10		2			6			12	3*	11†	1			7	5			13
	14			8	9	4		3	2			6			12		10	1		11†	7*	5			14
	10		11	8	12	4		3	2†			6		7*	9			1			14	5			15
			11	8	9	4	10	3	2			6						1		7		5			16
			11*	8	10	4	14	3	2		9†	6						1		7	12	5			17
	9		11	8	10	4	3		2			6						1		7*	12	5			18
			11	8	10	4		3	2		9	6						1		7*	12	5			19
			11	8		4	12	3	2		9	6		14			10*	1			7†	5			20
	2		11†	8	12	4	3		6		9			14			10*	1			7	5			21
			12	8	10	4	3		2		9	6						1		11	7*	5			22
			11	8		4	3		2		9	6		12				1		10	7*	5			23
	14		11†	8		4	3		2		9	6		12				1		10	7*	5			24
	14		11*	8	12	4	3		2		9	6						1		10	7†	5			25
3			14	8	12	4	10		2†		9	6						1		11	7*	5			26
3			9	8*	10	4			2			6		7				1		11	12	5			27
3			11	8		4	10*		2		9†	6		14				1		7	12	5			28
3			12	8	10*	4		14	2		9	6						1		11	7†	5			29
3			12	8	10†	4	14	11	2*		9	6						1		7		5			30
3			12	8		4	10	11	2		9	6*						1		7		5			31
3			12	8		4	14	11	2		9*	6						1		7	10†	5			32
3			11	8		4	10	14	2†		9*	6						1		7	12	5			33
3			14	8		4	10	11*	2		9	6						1		7	12	5†			34
3*	5	12		8		4	10		2		9	6						1		11	7				35
5			11	8	12	4	3		2		9	6						1		10	7*				36
5		12	11	8		4	3		2		9	6						1		10	7*				37
3		12	11	8	10†	4	2		5		9	6*		14				1		7					38
3		12	11	8			10		2		9*	6		7				1		4		5			39
5		9	11	8		4	3		2†	14		6		7*				1		10	12				40
5		9	11	8			4		6	3*				7				1	12	10	2				41
5		9*	11	8			4†		2	14		6		7				1	3	10	12				42
17	8	3	20	42	17	39	29	15	30	1	21	39	1	7	8	8	16	42	1	37	26	35			
	5	4	7		7		4	3		2			4	10	5	1			1		11				
			3	15	8	1			1		7			2	1		1		1	4	3	3			

1 own-goal

Ablett G	Atteveld R	Barlow S	Beagrie P	Beardsley P	Cottee A	Ebbrell J	Harper A	Hinchcliffe A	Jackson M	Jenkins I	Johnston M	Keown M	McDonald N	Nevin P	Newell M	Ratcliffe K	Sheedy K	Southall N	Unsworth D	Ward M	Warzycha R	Watson D	Youds E		
3			11	8	12	4	3*		2		9	6		14				1		10	7†	5			3
			11	8	9	4			2			6		7*				1		10	12	5			4
1			2	2	1	2	1		2		1	2		1				2		2	1	2			
					1									1							1				
				1																					

Ablett G	Atteveld R	Barlow S	Beagrie P	Beardsley P	Cottee A	Ebbrell J	Harper A	Hinchcliffe A	Jackson M	Jenkins I	Johnston M	Keown M	McDonald N	Nevin P	Newell M	Ratcliffe K	Sheedy K	Southall N	Unsworth D	Ward M	Warzycha R	Watson D	Youds E	
	2			8	12	6		3				4		7	9		10	1		11*		5		2
	12			8	9	4	2					6*		11	14	3	10	1			7†	5	14	
	2		11	8	9†	4		3				6		7*	10			1			12	5		3
	11		14	8	10†	2	12	3			9	6				4*		1		7		5	6	4
	3		1	4	3	4	1	3			1	4		3	2	2	2	4		2	1	4	1	
	1		1		1		1								1						1		1	
	1		2	3	1										1									

1992-93

Manager: Howard Kendall

1	Aug	15	(h)	Sheffield W	D 1-1	Horne	27,687
2		19	(a)	Manchester U	W 3-0	Beardsley, Johnston, Warzycha	31,901
3		22	(a)	Norwich C	D 1-1	Beardsley	14,150
4		25	(h)	Aston Villa	W 1-0	Johnston	22,372
5		29	(h)	Wimbledon	D 0-0		18,118
6	Sep	5	(a)	Tottenham H	L 1-2	Beardsley	26,503
7		12	(h)	Manchester U	L 0-2		30,002
8		15	(a)	Blackburn R	W 3-2	Cottee 2, Ebbrell	19,583
9		19	(h)	Crystal P	L 0-2		18,080
10		26	(a)	Leeds U	L 0-2		27,915
11	Oct	4	(a)	Oldham A	L 0-1		13,013
12		17	(h)	Coventry C	D 1-1	Beagrie	17,587
13		24	(a)	Arsenal	L 0-2		28,052
14		31	(h)	Manchester C	L 1-3	Opp own-goal	20,242
15	Nov	7	(a)	Nottingham F	W 1-0	Rideout	20,941
16		21	(h)	Chelsea	L 0-1		17,418
17		28	(a)	Ipswich T	L 0-1		18,034
18	Dec	7	(h)	Liverpool	W 2-1	Beardsley, Johnston	35,826
19		12	(a)	Sheffield U	L 0-1		16,266
20		19	(h)	Southampton	W 2-1	Beardsley, Rideout	14,051
21		26	(h)	Middlesbrough	D 2-2	Beardsley, Rideout	24,391
22		28	(a)	Queen's Park R	L 2-4	Barlow 2	14,802
23	Jan	9	(a)	Crystal P	W 2-0	Beardsley, Jackson	13,227
24		16	(h)	Leeds U	W 2-0	Cottee 2	21,031
25		26	(a)	Wimbledon	W 3-1	Cottee 2, Snodin	3,039
26		30	(h)	Norwich C	L 0-1		20,301
27	Feb	6	(a)	Sheffield W	L 1-3	Cottee	24,979
28		10	(h)	Tottenham H	L 1-2	Sansom	16,164
29		20	(a)	Aston Villa	L 1-2	Beardsley	32,913
30		27	(h)	Oldham A	D 2-2	Barlow, Beardsley	18,025
31	Mar	3	(h)	Blackburn R	W 2-1	Cottee, Opp own-goal	18,086
32		7	(a)	Coventry C	W 1-0	Ward	11,285
33		10	(a)	Chelsea	L 1-2	Kenny	12,739
34		13	(h)	Nottingham F	W 3-0	Cottee 2, Hinchcliffe	21,271
35		20	(a)	Liverpool	L 0-1		44,619
36		24	(h)	Ipswich T	W 3-0	Barlow, Cottee, Jackson	15,638
37	Apr	10	(a)	Middlesbrough	W 2-1	Radosavijevic, Watson	16,627
38		12	(h)	Queen's Park R	L 3-5	Barlow, Cottee, Radosavijevic	19,057
39		17	(a)	Southampton	D 0-0		16,911
40	May	1	(h)	Arsenal	D 0-0		19,044
41		4	(h)	Sheffield U	L 0-2		15,197
42		8	(a)	Manchester C	W 5-2	Jackson, Beagrie 2, Beardsley, Radosavijevic	25,180

FINAL LEAGUE POSITION: 13th in FA Premier Division

Appearances
Sub Appearances
Goals

FA Cup

3	Jan	2	(h)	Wimbledon	D 0-0		7,818
R		12	(a)	Wimbledon	L 1-2	Watson	15,293

Appearances
Sub Appearances
Goals

League Cup

2	Sep	23	(a)	Rotherham U	L 0-1		7,736
	Oct	7	(h)	Rotherham U	W 3-0	Rideout 2, Cottee	10,302
3		28	(h)	Wimbledon	D 0-0		9,541
R	Nov	10	(a)	Wimbledon	W 1-0	Beardsley	3,686
4	Dec	2	(h)	Chelsea	D 2-2	Barlow, Beardsley	14,457
R		16	(a)	Chelsea	L 0-1		19,496

Appearances
Sub Appearances
Goals

Ablett G	Barlow S	Beagrie P	Beardsley P	Cottee A	Ebbrell J	Harper A	Hinchcliffe A	Holmes P	Horne B	Jackson M	Jenkins I	Johnston M	Kearton J	Keown M	Kenny W	Moore N	Radosavijevic P	Rideout P	Sansom K	Snodin I	Southall N	Unsworth D	Ward M	Warzycha R	Watson D	
6		11	8		4		3		10*	2								9			1		7	12	5	1
6		12	8		4	2	3		10			13						9*			1		11	7†	5	2
6		12	8		4†	2	3		10			13						9			1		11	7*	5	3
6		12	8		4	2	3		10			11						9*			1		7		5	4
6		12	8		4	2	3		10			13						9†			1		11*	7	5	5
6	12	13	8		4	2	3		10			9*									1		11	7†	5	6
6		12	8		4*	2	3		10			9									1		11	7	5	7
6			8	10	11	2	3		4	13								9†			1		7*	12	5	8
6		7	8†	10	4	2	3		11	13		12						9*			1				5	9
6		13		10	4	2	3		8			12					11				1	9*		7†	5	10
6		12		13	4	2	3		8			10†					11*	9			1			7	5	11
6		11	8	9			3		10†					4	7		12			13	1			2*	5	12
6		11	8	9		13	3*		10					4				12		2†	1			7	5	13
3	8	11							10*	2				6	4		12	9			1			7	5	14
3			8		11	7*			10	2				6				9		4	1			12	5	15
3	12		8			7†	11		10*	2				6				9		4	1			13	5	16
3	9		8	10*		2	11							6	7			13		4†	1			12	5	17
3	9	12	8						2			10		6	7			13		4†	1	11*			5	18
3	9	13	8						7	2*		10		6			11†	12		4	1				5	19
3		11	8						4					6	10			9		2	1			7	5	20
6	13	11	8						4						10		12	9		2*	1	3		7†	5	21
3	12	11*	8						4		2		13	6	10			9			1			7†	5	22
3	12		8		11					2				6	10		7	9*		4	1				5	23
3	12	11†	8	9*	4	13			10	2				6			7				1				5	24
3	12		8	9		7			10	2				6			11*			4	1				5	25
6	13		8	9		3			10	2					11		7†	12		4*	1				5	26
6	12		8	9						2			13		10		11†		3	4	1			7*	5	27
6			8	9		2†			11	4		13			7*		12	10	3		1				5	28
6	12		8	9					11	2		10†	1				13		3	4				7*	5	29
6	11*		8	9					10	2			1		7			12	3	4					5	30
6	12		8	9	11				10	2					4*				3		1		7		5	31
6			8	9	11				10	2							12		3	4*	1		7		5	32
6	11		8	9			3		10	2					4*		12				1		7		5	33
6	12		8	9			3			2					10		11†		13	4*	1		7		5	34
6	13		8	9	11		3			2					10†		12			4	1		7*		5	35
	11	12	8	9	10		3	2		6								13		4*	1		7†		5	36
6	12*		8	9	11		3		4	2							13	10†			1		7		5	37
6	12		8	9	11		3		4	2*							13			10	1		7†		5	38
	10*		8	9	4		3	2		6					12		7				1		11		5	39
6	12		8	9	10		3		4	2							7				1		11*		5	40
6	12	11	8	9	4		3	2	10†	5						13	7*				1					41
6	12	11	8	9	4		3	2		5			13				10†				1*		7			42
40	8	11	39	25	24	16	25	4	34	25	1	7	2	13	16		13	17	6	19	40	3	19	15	40	
	18	11		1		2				2		6	2		1	1	10	7	1	1				5		
	5	3	10	12	1		1		1	3		3			1		3	3	1	1			1	1	1	

2 own-goals

Ablett G	Barlow S	Beagrie P	Beardsley P	Cottee A	Ebbrell J	Harper A	Hinchcliffe A	Holmes P	Horne B	Jackson M	Jenkins I	Johnston M	Kearton J	Keown M	Kenny W	Moore N	Radosavijevic P	Rideout P	Sansom K	Snodin I	Southall N	Unsworth D	Ward M	Warzycha R	Watson D	
3	12		8		11	7*			13	2				6	10			9		4†	1				5	3
3	9		8		11	13				2			1	6	10†		7			4*				12	5	R
2	1		2		2	1				2			1	2	2		1	1		2	1				2	
	1					1			1															1		
																									1	

Ablett G	Barlow S	Beagrie P	Beardsley P	Cottee A	Ebbrell J	Harper A	Hinchcliffe A	Holmes P	Horne B	Jackson M	Jenkins I	Johnston M	Kearton J	Keown M	Kenny W	Moore N	Radosavijevic P	Rideout P	Sansom K	Snodin I	Southall N	Unsworth D	Ward M	Warzycha R	Watson D	
6	9†	12		10	4	2	3		8	7*							11				1	13			5	2
6		11		10			2		8†			12			4	13		9*			1	3		7	5	
3	12	11	8*				13		10	2				6	4			9			1			7†	5	3
3			8		11†	7	12		10	2*				6				9		4	1			13	5	R
3	9		8	13		2	11*		12			10†		6	7					4	1				5	4
3	12	11	8			2†			4		13			6	10			9			1			7*	5	R
6	2	3	4	2	2	4	3		5	3		1		4	4		1	4		2	6	1		3	6	
	2	1		1			2		1		1	1				1						1		1		
	1		2	1														2								

Everton Against Other League Clubs

Everton have played 67 clubs in the Football League since 1888-89. Below is their record against each club. Some clubs have changed their names (eg Small Heath became Birmingham then Birmingham City) and some clubs modified their titles (eg Leicester Fosse became Leicester City). In all cases the last name used by each club covers all games under previous names. Since 1981-82 three points have been awarded for a win. A percentage success-rate is therefore shown instead of a points-won total.

	P	W	D	L	F	A	%
ACCRINGTON	10	5	3	2	21	16	65
ARSENAL	144	49	30	65	189	222	44
ASTON VILLA	156	64	36	56	259	244	53
BARNSLEY	6	3	2	1	12	8	66
BIRMINGHAM CITY	104	54	27	23	200	134	65
BLACKBURN ROVERS	114	46	25	43	207	195	51
BLACKPOOL	46	20	11	15	66	55	55
BOLTON WANDERERS	112	57	25	30	190	151	62
BRADFORD	8	5	2	1	19	12	75
BRADFORD CITY	22	8	8	6	32	29	54
BRENTFORD	16	7	2	7	29	22	50
BRIGHTON & HOVE A	8	4	3	1	15	11	60
BRISTOL CITY	20	12	3	5	34	22	67
BRISTOL ROVERS	2	1	1	0	4	0	75
BURNLEY	98	41	28	29	161	147	56
BURY	52	21	16	15	87	72	56
CARDIFF CITY	30	10	8	12	43	35	47
CARLISLE UNITED	2	0	0	2	2	6	0
CHARLTON ATHLETIC	32	13	7	12	57	50	52
CHELSEA	108	41	31	36	181	168	52
COVENTRY CITY	54	27	11	16	93	67	60
CRYSTAL PALACE	20	7	7	6	28	20	53
DARWEN	4	2	1	1	17	10	62
DERBY COUNTY	112	56	19	37	223	158	58
DONCASTER ROVERS	6	2	2	2	15	11	50
FULHAM	26	12	8	6	46	29	61
GLOSSOP	2	1	1	0	5	2	75
GRIMSBY TOWN	22	12	4	6	46	28	64
HUDDERSFIELD TOWN	56	22	13	21	80	81	51
HULL CITY	6	3	0	3	10	5	50
IPSWICH TOWN	44	17	16	11	61	53	57
LEEDS UNITED	82	22	19	41	105	128	38
LEICESTER CITY	80	32	19	29	159	133	52
LEYTON ORIENT	2	1	0	1	3	3	50
LINCOLN CITY	4	1	2	1	5	6	50
LIVERPOOL	148	49	44	55	183	205	48
LUTON TOWN	38	16	8	14	56	46	53
MANCHESTER CITY	130	45	35	50	183	186	48
MANCHESTER UNITED	128	50	33	45	208	180	52
MIDDLESBROUGH	86	42	21	23	151	118	61
MILLWALL	6	4	1	1	11	6	75
NEWCASTLE UNITED	118	47	25	46	181	179	50
NORTHAMPTON TOWN	2	2	0	0	7	2	100

	P	W	D	L	F	A	%
NORWICH CITY	36	13	12	11	54	43	53
NOTTINGHAM FOREST	112	48	26	38	186	139	54
NOTTS COUNTY	66	37	13	16	126	68	66
OLDHAM ATHLETIC	26	7	8	11	39	45	42
OXFORD UNITED	6	2	3	1	7	4	50
PLYMOUTH ARGYLE	6	4	0	2	22	12	66
PORTSMOUTH	44	16	8	20	71	89	47
PORT VALE	2	1	0	1	5	4	50
PRESTON NORTH END	88	33	25	30	120	120	52
QUEEN'S PARK RANGERS	36	16	9	11	60	49	57
READING	2	2	0	0	5	2	100
ROTHERHAM UNITED	6	2	3	1	11	8	58
SHEFFIELD UNITED	116	46	28	42	177	151	52
SHEFFIELD WEDNESDAY	114	52	33	29	209	167	60
SOUTHAMPTON	52	27	10	15	99	61	62
STOKE CITY	104	50	27	27	183	112	61
SUNDERLAND	132	56	20	56	219	225	50
SWANSEA CITY	12	8	4	0	31	12	82
TOTTENHAM HOTSPUR	112	41	33	38	161	174	51
WATFORD	12	9	1	2	29	16	78
WEST BROMWICH ALBION	132	52	31	49	224	221	51
WEST HAM UNITED	80	39	15	26	135	101	58
WIMBLEDON	14	4	6	4	19	16	50
WOLVERHAMPTON W	114	54	20	40	195	162	56
TOTAL	3690	1552	892	1246	6071	5256	57

CONSOLIDATED COMPETITIVE RECORD 1884-1993

	P	W	D	L	F	A
Premier	42	15	8	19	53	55
First Division	3480	1460	839	1181	5670	4944
Second Division	168	77	45	46	348	257
FA Cup	346	187	68	91	639	386
League Cup	113	57	26	30	206	111
Zenith Data	8	5	1	2	20	14
European Cup	8	2	5	1	12	6
European CW Cup	13	9	3	1	19	5
UEFA Cup	8	3	1	4	12	5
Fairs Cup	12	7	2	3	22	15
Texaco Cup	2	0	1	1	0	1
FA Charity Shield	10	7	1	2	18	10
Super Cup	8	4	1	3	11	11
Simod Cup	5	3	0	2	9	7
Full Members' Cup	2	1	1	-	7	4
British Championship	2	1	1	0	4	2
TOTAL	4227	1838	1003	1386	7050	5833

Everton in Europe

European Cup

1963-64
Round 1 (1st leg)
Sep 18 v Internazionale (h) 0-0
West; Parker, Harris, Gabriel, Labone, Kay, Scott, Stevens, Young, Vernon, Temple.
Round 1 (2nd leg)
Sep 25 v Internazionale (a) 0-1 (agg 0-1)
West; Parker, Harris, Stevens, Labone, Kay, Scott, Harvey, Young, Vernon, Temple.

1970-71
Round 1 (1st leg)
Sep 16 v IB Keflavik (h) 6-2
Ball 3, Royle 2, Kendall
West; Wright, K.Newton, Kendall, Kenyon, Harvey, Husband (Whittle), Ball, Royle, Hurst, Morrissey.
Round 1 (2nd leg)
Sep 30 v IB Keflavik (a) 3-0 (agg 9-2)
Royle 2, Whittle
Rankin; Wright, K.Newton, Kendall, Labone, Harvey(Brown), Whittle, Ball(Jackson), Royle, Hurst, Morrissey.
Round 2 (1st leg)
Oct 21 v Borussia Mönchengladbach (a) 1-1
Kendall
Rankin; Wright, K.Newton, Kendall, Kenyon, Harvey, Whittle, Ball, Royle, Hurst, Morrissey.
Round 2 (2nd leg)
Nov 4 v Borussia Mönchengladbach (h) 1-1 (agg 1-1; Everton won 4-3 on penalties)
Morrissey
Rankin; Wright, K.Newton(Brown), Kendall, Kenyon, Harvey, Whittle(Husband), Ball, Royle, Hurst, Morrissey.
Round 3 (1st leg)
Mar 9 v Panathinaikos (h) 1-1
Johnson
Rankin; Wright, K.Newton, Kendall, Kenyon, Harvey, Husband(Johnson), Ball, Royle, Hurst, Morrissey.
Round 3 (2nd leg)
Mar 24 v Panathinaikos (a) 0-0 (agg 1-1; Panathinaikos won on away goals rule).
Rankin; Wright, K.Newton, Kendall, Labone, Harvey, Whittle, Ball, Royle, Hurst, Morrissey(Johnson).

European Cup-winners' Cup

1966-67
Round 1 (1st leg)
Sep 28 v AaB Aalborg (a) 0-0
West; Wright, Wilson, Gabriel, Labone, Harvey, Temple, Ball, Young, Trebilcock, Morrissey.
Round 1 (2nd leg)
Oct 11 v AaB Aalborg (h) 2-1 (agg 2-1)
Morrissey, Ball
West; Wright, Wilson, Gabriel, Labone, Harvey, Temple, Ball, Young, Husband, Morrissey.
Round 2 (1st leg)
Nov 9 v Real Zaragoza (a) 0-2
West; Wright, Wilson, Gabriel, Labone, Harvey, Scott, Ball, Young, Temple, Morrissey.
Round 2 (2nd leg)
Nov 23 v Real Zaragoza (h) 1-0 (agg 1-2)
Brown
West; Wright, Wilson, Gabriel, Labone, Harvey, Scott, Ball, Young, Brown, Temple.

1984-85
Round 1 (1st leg)
Sep 19 v UC Dublin (a) 0-0
Southall; Stevens, Bailey, Ratcliffe, Mountfield, Reid, Steven(Curran), Heath, Sharp, Bracewell, Sheedy.
Round 1 (2nd leg)
Oct 2 v UC Dublin (h) 1-0 (agg 1-0)
Sharp
Southall; Stevens, Bailey, Ratcliffe, Mountfield, Reid, Steven, Heath(Wakenshaw), Sharp, Bracewell, Cruran.
Round 2 (1st leg)
Oct 24 v Slovan Bratislava (a) 1-0
Bracewell
Southall;;Stevens, Bailey, Ratcliffe, Mountfield, Reid, Steven, Heath, Sharp, Bracewell, Harper.
Round 2 (2nd leg)
Nov 7 v Slovan Bratislava (h) 3-0 (agg 4-0)
Heath, Sharp, Sheedy
Southall; Stevens, Bailey, Ratcliffe, Mountfield, Reid(Harper), Steven, Heath, Sharp, Bracewell, Sheedy(Morrissey).
Round 3 (1st leg)
Mar 6 v Fortuna Sittard (h) 3-0
Gray 3
Southall; Stevens, Van den Hauwe, Ratcliffe, Mountfield, Reid(Richardson), Steven, Curran, Gray, Bracewell, Sheedy.
Round 3 (2nd leg)
Mar 20 v Fortuna Sittard (a) 2-0 (agg 5-0)
Reid, Sharp
Southall; Stevens, Van den Hauwe, Ratcliffe(Atkins), Mountfield, Reid, Steven, Curran, Sharp (Wakenshaw), Harper, Richardson.
Semi-final (1st leg)
Apr 10 v Bayern Munich (a) 0-0
Southall; Stevens, Van den Hauwe, Ratcliffe, Mountfield, Reid, Steven, Harper, Sharp, Bracewell, Richardson.
Semi-final (2nd leg)
Apr 24 v Bayern Munich (h) 3-1 (agg 3-1)
Gray, Sharp, Steven
Southall; Stevens, Van den Hauwe, Ratcliffe, Mountfield, Reid, Steven, Sharp, Gray, Bracewell, Sheedy.

Final
May 15 v Rapid Vienna (at Rotterdam) 3-1
Gray, Sheedy, Steven
Southall; Stevens, Van den Hauwe, Ratcliffe, Mountfield, Reid, Steven, Sharp, Gray, Bracewell, Sheedy.

Inter-Cities Fairs' Cup

1962-63
Round 1 (1st leg)
Oct 24 v Dunfermline Athletic (h) 1-0
Stevens
West; Parker, Thomson, Gabriel, Labone, Harris, Bingham, Stevens, Young, Vernon, Morrissey.
Round 1 (2nd leg)
Oct 31 v Dunfermline Athletic (a) 0-2 (agg 1-2)
West; Parker, Meagan, Gabriel, Labone, Harris, Bingham, Stevens, Young, Vernon, Morrissey.

1964-65
Round 1 (1st leg)
Sep 23 v Vålerengens IF (a) 5-2
Pickering 2, Harvey, Scott, Temple
Rankin; Harris, Brown, Gabriel, Labone, Stevens, Scott, Harvey, Pickering, Temple, Morrissey.
Round 1 (2nd leg)
Oct 14 v Vålerengens IF (h) 4-2 (agg 9-4)
Young 2, Vernon, Opp own-goal
Rankin; Wright, Brown, Stevens, Labone, Harris, Scott, Young, Pickering, Vernon, Temple.
Round 2 (1st leg)
Nov 11 v Kilmarnock (a) 2-0
Temple, Morrissey
Rankin; Stevens, Brown, Gabriel, Labone, Harris, Temple, Young, Pickering, Vernon, Morrissey.
Round 2 (2nd leg)
Nov 23 v Kilmarnock (h) 4-1 (agg 6-1)
Pickering 2, Harvey, Young
Rankin; Harris, Brown, Gabriel, Labone, Stevens, Temple, Young, Pickering, Harvey, Morrissey.
Round 3 (1st leg)
Jan 20 v Manchester United (a) 1-1
Pickering
West; Wright, Wilson, Gabriel, Labone, Stevens, Scott, Harvey, Pickering, Vernon, Temple.
Round 3 (2nd leg)
Feb 4 v Manchester United (h) 1-2 (agg 2-3)
Pickering
West; Wright, Wilson, Gabriel, Labone, Stevens, Scott, Harvey, Pickering, Pickering, Vernon, Temple.

1965-66
Round 1 (1st leg)
Sep 28 v 1.FC Nuremberg (a) 1-1
Harris
West; Wright, Wilson, Gabriel, Brown, Harris, Temple, Stevens, Pickering, Harvey, Morrissey.
Round 1 (2nd leg)
Oct 12 v 1.FC Nuremberg (h) 1-0 (agg 2-1)
Gabriel
West(Rankin); Wright, Wilson, Gabriel, Labone, Harris, Scott, Harvey, Pickering, Young, Temple.
Round 2 (1st leg)
Nov 3 v Újpesti Dózsa (a) 0-3
Rankin; Wright, Wilson, Stevens, Labone, Harris, Scott, Harvey, Pickering, Temple, Morrissey.
Round 2 (2nd leg)
Nov 16 v Újpesti Dózsa (h) 2-1 (agg 2-4)
Harris, Opp own-goal
Rankin; Wright, Wilson, Harvey, Labone, Harris, Temple, Gabriel, Young, Husband, Morrissey.

UEFA Cup

1975-76
Round 1 (1st leg)
Sep 17 v Milan AC (h) 0-0
Lawson; Bernard, Seargeant, Pearson, Kenyon, Lyons, Buckley(Clements), Dobson, Latchford, Smallman (Hurst), G.Jones.
Round 1 (2nd leg)
Oct 1 v Milan AC (a) 0-1 (agg 0-1)
Davies; Bernard, Seargeant, Pearson, Kenyon, Lyons, Buckley, Dobson, Latchford, Smallman, G.Jones.

1978-79
Round 1 (1st leg)
Sep 12 v Finn Harps (a) 5-0
King 2, Latchford, Thomas, Walsh
Wood; Darracott, Pejic, Lyons(Higgins), Wright, Nulty, King, Ross, Latchford, Walsh, Thomas.
Round 1 (2nd leg)
Sep 26 v Finn Harps (h) 5-0 (agg 10-0)
Dobson, King, Latchford, Ross, Walsh
Wood; Darracott, Pejic, Lyons(Higgins), Wright, Ross, King, Dobson, Latchford, Walsh, Thomas (Nulty).
Round 2 (1st leg)
Oct 18 v Dukla Prague (h) 2-1
King, Latchford
Wood; Darracott(Robinson), Pejic, Lyons, Wright, Ross, King, Dobson, Latchford, Thomas, Walsh.
Round 2 (2nd leg)
Nov 1 v Dukla Prague (a) 0-1 (agg 2-2; Dukla Prague won on away goals).
Wood; Darracott, Pejic, Kenyon, Wright, Nulty, Ross, Dobson, Latchford, Walsh, Thomas.

1979-80
Round 1 (1st leg)
Sep 19 v Feyenoord (a) 0-1
Wood; Barton, Bailey, Lyons, Higgins, Ross, Nulty, Wright, King, Kidd, Eastoe.
Round 1 (2nd leg)
Oct 3 v Feyenoord (h) 0-1 (agg 0-2)
Wood; Barton, Bailey, Lyons, Higgins, Nulty, McBride(Varadi), Wright, King, Kidd, Eastoe (Latchford).

Everton in Other Competitions

Texaco Cup

1973-74
Round 1 (1st leg)
Sep 18 v Heart of Midlothian (h) 0-1
Lawson; Darracott, McLaughlin, Buckley, Kenyon, Hurst, H.Newton, Lyons, Belfitt(Bernard), Harper, Connolly.
Round 1 (2nd leg)
Oct 3 v Heart of Midlothian (a) 0-0 (agg 0-1)
Lawson; Darracott, McLaughlin, Clements, Kenyon, Hurst, Buckley, Husband, Lyons, Harper, Connolly.

FA Charity Shield

1928
Oct 24 v Blackburn Rovers (at Old Trafford) 2-1
Dean 2
Davies; Cresswell, O'Donnell, Griffiths, Hart, Virr, Ritchie, Forshaw, Dean, Weldon, Troup.

1932
Oct 12 v Newcastle United (a) 5-3
Dean 4, Johnson
Sagar; Williams, Cresswell, Britton, White, Thomson, Critchley, McGourty, Dean, Johnson, Stein.

1933
Oct 18 v Arsenal (h) 0-3
Sagar; Cook, Bocking, Britton, Gee, Thomson, Geldard, Dunn, White, Johnson, Stein.

1963
Aug 17 v Manchester United (h) 4-0
Gabriel, Stevens, Temple, Vernon
West; Parker, Meagan, Gabriel, Labone, Kay, Scott, Stevens, Young, Vernon, Temple.

1966
Aug 13 v Liverpool (h) 0-1
West; Wright, Wilson, Gabriel, Labone, Glover, Scott, Young, Trebilcock, Harvey, Temple.

1970
Aug 8 v Chelsea (a) 2-1
Kendall, Whittle
West; Wright, K.Newton, Kendall, Labone, Harvey, Husband, Ball, Royle, Hurst, Whittle.

1984
Aug 18 v Liverpool (Wembley) 1-0
Opp own goal
Southall; Stevens, Bailey, Ratcliffe, Mountfield, Reid, Steven, Heath, Sharp, Bracewell, Richardson.

1985
Aug 10 v Manchester United (Wembley) 2-0
Steven, Heath
Southall; Stevens, Ratcliffe, Mountfield, Van den Hauwe(Bailey), Steven, Bracewell, Reid, Sheedy, Sharp, Lineker(Heath).

1986
Aug 16 v Liverpool (Wembley) 1-1
Heath
Mimms; Harper, Power, Ratcliffe, Marshall, Langley, Steven, Heath, Sharp, Richardson, Sheedy (Adams[Wilkinson]).

1987
Aug 1 v Coventry City (Wembley) 1-0
Clarke
Mimms; Harper, Power, Ratcliffe, Watson, Reid, Steven, Clarke, Sharp, Heath, Sheedy(Pointon).

Full Members' Cup

1986-87
Round 1
3 Dec v Newcastle United (h) 5-2
Sharp 3, Heath, Sheedy
Southall; Harper, Pointon, Ratcliffe, Watson, Power(Mountfield), Steven, Heath, Sharp, Adams, Sheedy.
Round 2
Mar 3 v Charlton Athletic (h) 2-2 (Everton lost 4-6 on penalties)
Stevens, Wilkinson
Southall; Van den Hauwe, Pointon, Mountfield, Watson, Harper(Ebbrell), Stevens(Langley), Heath, Wilkinson, Snodin, Adams.

Simod Cup

1987-88
Feb 16 v Luton Town (h) 1-2
Power
Southall; Jones, Pointon, Van den Hauwe, Harper, Sheedy, Adams, Heath, Marshall, Bracewell, Power.

1988-89
Round 3
Dec 20 v Millwall (h) 2-0
Hurlock og, Cottee
Stowell; McDonald, Pointon, Ratcliffe(Ebbrell), Watson, Bracewell, Steven, Reid, Nevin, Cottee, Sheedy.
Att: 3,703
Quarter-Final
Jan 18 v Wimbledon (a) 2-1
Clarke 2
Southall; McDonald, Pointon, Ratcliffe, Watson, Steven(Wilson), Nevin, McCall, Clarke, Cottee, Sheedy.
Att: 2,477
Semi-Final
Feb 28 v Queen's Park Rangers (h) 1-0
Nevin
Southall; McDonald(Bracewell), Pointon, Ratcliffe, Watson, Snodin, Nevin, McCall, Clarke, Cottee, Sheedy.
Att: 7,072
Final (at Wembley)
Apr 30 v Nottingham Forest (n) 3-4 (aet: 90 minutes 2-2)

Cottee 2, Sharp
Southall; McDonald, Vanden Hauwe, Ratcliffe, Watson, Bracewell(McCall), Steven, Nevin, Sharp, Cottee, Sheedy.
Att: 46,606

Zenith Data Systems Cup

1990-91
Round 2
18 Dec v Blackburn Rovers (a) 4-1
Watson 2, Newell, Cottee
Southall; McDonald, Hinchcliffe, Ratcliffe, Watson, Ebbrell, Nevin, McCall, Newell, Cottee, Begree.
Att: 5,410
Northern Quarter-final
Jan 22 v Sunderland (h) 4-1
Cottee 4
Southall; McDonald, Ebbrell, Ratcliffe, Keown, McCall, Nevin, Cottee, Sharp(Atteveld), Sheedy(Milligan), Beagrie.
Att: 4,609
Northern Semi-final
Mar 13 v Barnsley (a) 1-0
Cottee
Southall; Keown, Ebbrell, Ratcliffe, Watson, Milligan, Nevin, McCall, Newell, Cottee, Beagrie(McDonald).
Att: 10,287
Northern Final (1st leg)
Mar 19 v Leeds United (a) 3-3
Beagrie, Warzycha, Milligan
Southall; McDonald, Ebbrell, Ratcliffe, Watson, Keown, Warzycha(Nevin), McCall, Newell(Cottee), Milligan, Beagrie
Att: 13,387
Northern Final (2nd leg)
Mar 21 v Leeds United (h) 3-1 (aet)
Cottee 2, Ebbrell
Southall; McDonald(Cottee), Ebbrell, Ratcliffe, Watson, Keown, Warzycha, McCall, Newell, Milligan, Beagrie(Nevin).
Att: 12,603
Final
Apr 7 v Crystal Palace (at Wembley) 1-4 (aet)
Warzycha
Southall; McDonald, Hincliffe, Keown(Ratcliffe), Watson, Milligan, Warzycha, McCall, Newell(Nevin), Cottee, Sheedy.
Att: 52,460

1991-92
Round 2
Oct 1 v Oldham Athletic (h) 3-2
Newell, Watson, Cottee
Southall; Harper, Hinchliffe, Ebbrell, Watson, Youds, Nevin, Beardsley, Newell(Atteveld), Cottee, Sheedy.
Att: 4,588
Quarter-finals
Nov 27 v Leicester City (a) 1-2
Beardsley
Southall; Jackson(Atteveld), Hinchcliffe, Harper, Watson, Keown, Warzycha(Beagrie), Beardley, Johnston, Cottee, Ward.
Att: 13,242

Screen Sport Super Cup

1985-86
Sep 18 v Manchester United (a) 4-2
Sheedy 2, Lineker, Sharp
Southall; Stevens, Van den Hauwe, Ratcliffe, Marshall, Harper, Steven, Lineker(Heath), Sharp, Bracewell, Sheedy.
Oct 2 v Norwich City (h) 1-0
Lineker
Southall; Stevens, Van den Hauwe, Ratcliffe, Marshall, Harper, Steven, Lineker, Sharp, Bracewell, Sheedy.
Oct 23 v Norwich City (a) 0-1
Southall; Stevens, Van den Hauwe, Ratcliffe, Harper, Heath, Steven, Lineker(Richardson), Sharp (Wilkinson), Bracewell, Sheedy.
Dec 4 v Manchester United (h) 1-0
Stapleton (og)
Southall; Harper(Pointon), Van den Hauwe, Ratcliffe, Stevens, Heath, Steven, Lineker, Wilkinson, Bracewell, Richardson.
Semi-final (1st leg)
Feb 5 v Tottenham Hotspur (a) 0-0
Southall; Stevens, Pointon, Marshall, Van den Hauwe, Reid, Steven, Coyle, Wilkinson, Billinge, Richardson.
Semi-final (2nd leg)
Mar 19 v Tottenham Hotspur (h) 3-1
Heath, Mountfield, Sharp
Southall; Billinge(Van den Hauwe), Pointon, Marshall, Mountfield, Richardson, Harper, Heath, Wilkinson (Sharp), Coyle, Sheedy.
Final (1st leg)
Sep 16 v Liverpool (a) 1-3
Sheedy
Mimms; Billinge, Power, Ratcliffe, Marshall, Langley, Adams, Wilkinson, Sharp, Steven, Sheedy(Aspinall).
Final (2nd leg)
Sep 30 v Liverpool (h) 1-4
Sharp
Mimms; Billinge, Power, Ratcliffe, Mountfield, Steven, Adams, Heath(Aspinall), Sharp, Wilkinson, Sheedy(Pointon).

British Championship

1963
Nov 27 v Glasgow Rangers (a) 3-1
Scott, Temple, Young
Rankin; Brown, Meagan, Harris, Heslop, Kay, Scott, Stevens, Young, Vernon, Temple
Dec 2 v Glasgow Rangers (h) 1-1 (agg 4-2)
Young
Rankin; Brown, Meagan, Gabriel, Heslop, Harris, Scott, Stevens, Young, Vernon, Temple.

Football League Centenary Match

1987
Nov 25 v Bayern Munich (h) 3-1
Sharp 2, Heath
Southall; Stevens, Van den Hauwe, Ratcliffe, Watson, Reid(Wilson), Harper, Heath, Sharp, Snodin, Sheedy(Adams).

International Blues

Many players won additional caps with other clubs, but the totals given here are solely for appearances made while Everton players. Before 1924 there was only one Ireland team, then the Republic of Ireland began separate international matches, that position is reflected here. For some time, Northern Ireland could select, for the Home International Championship, players born in the Republic. Tommy Eglington and Peter Farrell were two such players who won caps with two countries. The date given for each match is the actual year in which that match was played.

England

Abbott W. 1902 v Wales (1).

Baker B.H. 1921 v Belgium; 1925 v Northern Ireland (2).

Ball A.J. 1966 v Northern Ireland, Czechoslovakia, Wales; 1967 v Scotland, Spain, Austria, Wales, USSR; 1968 v Scotland, Spain (twice), West Germany, Yugoslavia, Romania; 1969 v Romania, Northern Ireland, Wales, Scotland, Mexico, Uruguay, Brazil, Portugal; 1970 v Belgium, Wales, Scotland, Colombia, Ecuador, Romania, Brazil, Czechoslovakia (sub), West Germany, East Germany; 1971 v Malta, Greece, Malta (sub), Northern Ireland, Scotland, Switzerland, Greece (39).

Balmer W. 1905 v Ireland (1).

Booth T. 1903 v Scotland (1).

Boyes W. 1938 v Wales, Rest of Europe (2).

Bracewell P. 1985 v West Germany (sub), USA, Northern Ireland (3).

Britton C.S. 1934 v Wales, Italy; 1935 v Northern Ireland, Scotland; 1936 v Northern Ireland, Hungary, Scotland, Norway, Sweden (9).

Chadwick E. 1891 v Wales, Scotland; 1892 v Scotland; 1893 v Scotland; 1894 v Scotland; 1896 v Ireland; 1897 v Scotland (7).

Chedgzoy S. 1920 v Wales, Ireland; 1921 v Wales, Scotland, Ireland; 1923 v Scotland; 1924 v Wales, Northern Ireland (8).

Cottee A.R. 1989 v Denmark, Sweden; 1990 v Czechoslovakia.

Cresswell W. 1929 v Northern Ireland (1).

Cunliffe J.N. 1936 v Belgium (1).

Dean W.R. 1927 v Wales, Scotland, Belgium, France, Luxembourg, Northern Ireland, Wales; 1928 v Scotland, France, Belgium, Northern Ireland, Wales; 1929 v Scotland; 1931 v Scotland, Spain; 1932 v Northern Ireland (16).

Dobson M. 1974 v Czechoslovakia (1).

Downs R.W. 1920 v Ireland (1).

Freeman B.C. 1909 v Wales, Scotland (2).

Geary F. 1890 v Ireland; 1891 v Scotland (2).

Gee C.W. 1931 v Wales, Spain; 1936 v Northern Ireland (3).

Geldard A. 1933 v Italy, Switzerland; 1935 v Scotland; 1937 v Northern Ireland (4).

Hardman H.P. 1905 v Wales; 1907 v Ireland, Scotland; 1908 v Wales (4).

Harrison G. 1921 v Belgium, Ireland (2).

Harvey J.C. 1971 v Malta (1).

Holt J. 1890 v Wales; 1891 v Wales, Scotland; 1892 v Ireland, Scotland; 1893 v Scotland; 1894 v Ireland, Scotland; 1895 v Scotland (9).

Howarth R.H. 1894 v Ireland (1).

Jefferis F. 1912 v Wales, Scotland (2).

Johnson T.C.F. 1931 v Spain; 1932 v Scotland, Northern Ireland (3).

Kay A.H. 1963 v Switzerland (1).

Labone B.L. 1963 v France, Northern Ireland, Wales; 1967 v Spain, Austria; 1968 v Scotland, Spain, Sweden, West Germany, Yugoslavia, USSR, Romania, Bulgaria; 1969 v Northern Ireland, Scotland, Mexico, Uruguay, Brazil; 1970 v Belgium, Wales, Scotland, Colombia, Ecuador, Romania, Brazil, West Germany (26).

Latchford R.D. 1977 v Italy; 1978 v Brazil, Wales, Denmark, Republic of Ireland, Czechoslovakia (sub); 1979 v Republic of Ireland, Northern Ireland, Wales, Scotland, Bulgaria, Austria (12).

Lawton T. 1938 v Wales, Rest of Europe, Norway, Northern Ireland; 1939 v Scotland, Italy, Yugoslavia, Romania (8).

Lineker G. 1985 v Romania, Turkey, Northern Ireland; 1986 v Egypt, USSR, Canada, Portugal, Morocco, Poland, Paraguay, Argentina (11).

Makepeace H. 1906 v Scotland; 1910 v Scotland; 1912 v Wales, Scotland (4).

Mercer J. 1938 v Northern Ireland; 1939 v Scotland, Italy, Yugoslavia, Romania (5).

Milward A. 1891 v Wales, Scotland; 1897 v Wales, Scotland (4).

Newton K.R. 1970 v Holland, Northern Ireland, Scotland, Colombia, Ecuador, Romania, Czechoslovakia, West Germany (8).

Pickering F. 1964 v USA, Northern Ireland, Belgium (3).

Reid P. 1985 v Mexico (sub), West Germany, USA (sub), Romania; 1986 v Scotland (sub), Canada (sub), Poland, Paraguay, Argentina; 1987 v Brazil, West Germany, Yugoslavia (sub); 1988 v Switzerland (13).

Royle J. 1971 v Malta; 1972 v Yugoslavia (2).

Sagar E. 1935 v Northern Ireland; 1936 v Scotland, Austria, Belgium (4).

Settle J. 1902 v Ireland, Scotland; 1903 v Ireland(3).

Sharp J. 1903 v Ireland; 1905 v Scotland (2).

Steven T. 1984 v Northern Ireland; 1985 v Republic of Ireland, Romania, Finland, Italy, USA (sub), Turkey (sub); 1986 v Egypt, USSR (sub), Mexico (sub), Poland, Paraguay, Argentina, Sweden, Yugoslavia (sub); 1987 v Spain (sub), Turkey, Yugoslavia; 1988 v Holland, Hungary, Scotland, Switzerland, Holland, USSR; 1989 v Scotland (25).

Stevens G. 1985 v Italy, West Germany, Romania, Turkey, Northern Ireland; 1986 v Egypt, Israel, Scotland, Canada, Portugal, Morocco, Poland, Paraguay, Argentina; 1987 v Brazil, Scotland, Turkey, Yugoslavia; 1988 v Israel, Holland, Hungary (sub), Scotland, Switzerland, Republiic of Ireland, Holland, USSR (26).

Temple D.W. 1965 v West Germany (1).

Watson D. 1986 v Northern Ireland; 1988 v Israel, Holland, Scotland, Switzerland (sub), USSR (6).

West G. 1968 v Bulgaria; 1969 v Wales, Mexico (3).

White T.A. 1933 v Italy (1).

Wilson R. 1965 v Scotland, Hungary, Yugoslavia, West Germany, Sweden, Wales, Austria, Northern Ireland, Spain; 1966 v Poland, West Germany (sub); Yugoslavia, Finland, Denmark, Poland, Uruguay, Mexico, France, Argentina, Portugal, West Germany, Northern Ireland, Czechoslovakia, Wales; 1967 v Scotland, Austria, Northern Ireland, USSR; 1968 v Scotland, Spain (twice), Yugoslavia, USSR (33).

Wolstenholme S. 1904 v Scotland (1).

Wright T.J. 1968 v USSR, Romania; 1969 v Romania, Mexico (sub), Uruguay, Brazil, Holland; 1970 v Belgium, Wales, Romania (sub), Brazil (11).

England 'B'

Lyons M. 1979 v Czechoslovakia (1).

Wright W. 1979 v Austria; 1981 v Australia (2).

Scotland

Bell J. 1896 v England; 1897 v England; 1898 v England; 1899 v Wales, Ireland, England; 1900 v Wales, England (8).

Brewster G. 1921 v England (1).

Collins R.Y. 1958 v Wales, Northern Ireland; 1959 v England, West Germany, Holland, Portugal (6).

Connolly J. 1973 v Switzerland (1).

Dunn J. 1928 v Wales (1).

Gabriel J. 1960 v Wales; 1963 v Norway(sub) (2).

Gillick T. 1937 v Austria, Czechoslovakia; 1938 v Northern Ireland, Wales, Hungary (5).

Gray A. 1985 v Iceland (1).

Hartford A. 1979 v Peru, Belgium; 1981 v Northern Ireland (sub), Israel, Wales, Northern Ireland, England (7).

McBain N. 1923 v Ireland; 1924 v Wales (2).

McCall S.M. 1990 v Argentina, East Germany, Egypt, Poland, Malta, Costa Rica, Sweden, Brazil; 1991 v Switzerland, USSR, San Marino (11).

Parker A. 1958 v Paraguay (1).

Rioch B.D. 1977 v Wales, Northern Ireland, England, Chile, Brazil, Czechoslovakia (6).

Robertson J.T. 1898 v England (1).

Scott A.S. 1963 v Wales, Norway; 1964 v Finland; 1966 v Portugal, Brazil (5).

Sharp G. 1985 v Iceland, Wales, Australia (twice, both sub); 1986 v Israel, Romania, Uruguay, Republic of Ireland; 1987 v Belgium (sub), Bulgaria, Luxembourg; 1988 v Malta (12).

Thomson J.R. 1932 v Wales (1).

Troup A. 1926 v England (1).

Wilson G.W. 1907 v England (1).

Wood G. 1979 v Northern Ireland, England, Argentina (sub) (3).

Young A. 1961 v Republic of Ireland; 1966 v Portugal (2).

Young A. 1905 v England; 1907 v Wales (2).

Wales

Arridge S. 1894 v Ireland; 1895 v Ireland; 1896 v England (3).

Davies J. 1899 v Scotland, Ireland (2).

Davies S. 1921 v Scotand, England, Ireland (3).

Davies W.D. 1975 v Hungary, Luxembourg, Scotland, England, Northern Ireland; 1976 v Yugoslavia, England, Northern Ireland, Yugoslavia, West Germany, Scotland; 1977 v Czechoslovakia, Scotland, England, Northern Ireland, Kuwait (16).

Griffiths T.P. 1927 v England, Northern Ireland; 1928 v England; 1929 v England; 1931 v Northern Ireland, Scotland, England, Northern Ireland (8).

Hughes E. 1899 v Ireland, Scotland (2).

Humphreys J.V. 1947 v Northern Ireland (1).

Jones R.S. 1894 v Ireland (1).

Jones T.G. 1938 v Northern Ireland, England, Scotland; 1939 v Northern Ireland; 1946 v Scotland, England; 1947 v England, Scotland; 1948 v Northern Ireland, England; 1949 v Northern Ireland, Portugal, Belgium, Switzerland, England, Scotland, Belgium (17).

Parry C.F. 1891 v England, Scotland; 1893 v England; 1894 v England; 1895 v England, Scotland (6).

Powell A. 1948 v England; 1949 v Belgium (2).

Ratcliffe K. 1981 v Czechoslovakia, Republic of Ireland, Turkey, Scotland, England, USSR; 1982 v Czechoslovakia, Iceland, USSR, Spain, England, Yugoslavia; 1983 v England, Bulgaria, Scotland, Northern Ireland, Brazil, Norway, Romania, Bulgaria, Yugoslavia; 1984 v Scotland, England, Northern Ireland, Norway, Israel, Iceland, Spain, Iceland; 1985 v Norway, Scotland, Spain, Scotland, Hungary; 1986 v Saudi Arabia, Uruguay, Finland; 1987 v USSR, Finland, Czechoslovakia, Denmark (twice), Czechoslovakia; 1988 v Finland; 1989 v Israel, Sweden, West Germany, Finland; 1990 v Denmark, Belgium, Luxembourg; 1991 v Belgium, Republic of Ireland, Iceland, Poland, West Germany, Brazil, Germany (58).

Roose L.R. 1905 v Scotland, England (2).

Smallman D.P. 1975 v Hungary (sub), England, Northern Ireland (sub), Austria (4).

Southall N. 1982 v Northern Ireland, Norway; 1983 v England, Bulgaria, Scotland, Northern Ireland, Brazil, Norway, Romania, Bulgaria, Yugoslavia; 1984 v Scotland, England, Northern Ireland, Norway, Israel, Iceland, Spain, Iceland; 1985 v Norway, Scotland, Spain, Norway, Scotland, Hungary; 1986 v Saudi Arabia, Republic of Ireland; 1987 v USSR, Finland, Czechoslovakia, Denmark, Czechoslovakia; 1988 v Yugoslavia, Sweden, Holland, Finland; 1989 v Sweden, West Germany, Finland, Holland (twice), West Germany (twice), England; 1990 v Sweden, Costa Rica, Denmark, Belgium (twice), Luxembourg; 1991 v Republic of Ireland, Iceland, Poland, Brazil, Germany, Luxembourg; 1992 v Republic of Ireland, Austria, Romania, Holland, Argentina, Japan (62).

Thomas M. 1981 v Czechoslovakia (1).

Van den Hauwe P.W.R. 1984 v Spain; 1985 v Scotland, Hungary; 1987 v USSR, Finland, Czechoslovakia, Denmark (twice), Czechoslovakia; 1988 v Yugoslavia, Italy, Finland; 1989 v Sweden (13).

Vernon T.R. 1960 v Northern Ireland, Republic of Ireland, Scotland, England; 1962 v Northern Ireland, Brazil (twice), Mexico, Scotland, Hungary, England; 1963 v England, Scotland (13).

Williams B.D. 1931 v Northern Ireland, England; 1932 v Scotland, England, Northern Ireland; 1935 v Northern Ireland (6).

Northern Ireland

(and Ireland before 1924)

Bingham W.P. 1960 v West Germany, Scotland; 1961 v Italy, Greece, West Germany, Greece, England; 1962 v Poland, England, Scotland, Poland; 1963 v Spain (12).

Clements D. 1973 v Bulgaria, Portugal; 1974 v Scotland, England, Wales, Norway; 1975 v Yugoslavia, England, Scotland, Wales, Sweden, Yugoslavia (12).

Cook W. 1935 v England, Scotland; 1936 v Wales, Scotland, England; 1937 v Wales, England, Scotland; 1938 v Wales, Scotland, England; 1939 v Wales (12).

Coulter J. 1934 v Scotland; 1935 v England, Wales; 1936 v Scotland; 1937 v Wales (5).

Eglington T.J. 1946 v Scotland; 1947 v Wales, Scotland, England; 1948 v Wales, Scotland (6).

Farrell P.D. 1946 v Scotland; 1947 v Wales, Scotland, England; 1948 v Wales, England; 1949 v Wales (7).

Hamilton B. 1976 v Israel, Scotland, England, Wales, Holland, Belgium; 1977 v West Germany, England, Scotland, Wales, Iceland (11).

Harris V. 1909 v England, Scotland, Wales; 1910 v England, Scotland, Wales; 1911 v Wales, England, Scotland; 1912 v England; 1913 v England, Scotland; 1914 v Wales, Scotland (14).

Hill M.J. 1963 v Scotland, Spain, England (3).

Houston J. 1913 v England, Scotland; 1914 v Scotland (3).

Irvine R.W. 1922 v Scotland, England; 1923 v Wales, England; 1924 v Scotland, England; 1925 v England; 1926 v England; 1927 v Wales, England; 1928 v Scotland (11).

Jackson T. 1968 v Israel; 1969 v England, Scotland, Wales, USSR (twice, once as sub) (6).

Lacey W. 1909 v England, Scotland, Wales; 1910 v England, Scotland, Wales; 1911 v Wales, England, Scotland; 1912 v England (10).

Scott P.W. 1975 v Wales, Yugoslavia (2).

Scott W. 1905 v England, Scotland; 1907 v England, Scotland; 1908 v England, Scotland, Wales; 1909 v England, Scotland, Wales; 1910 v England, Scotland; 1911 v Wales, England, Scotland; 1912 v England (16).

Sheridan J. 1903 v England, Scotland, Wales; 1904 v England, Scotland (5).

Stevenson A.E. 1934 v Scotland; 1935 v England, Scotland; 1936 v Wales, England; 1937 v Wales, England; 1938 v Wales, Scotland, England; 1939 v Wales; 1946 v Scotland; 1947 v Wales, Scotland (14).

Republic of Ireland

Clinton T.J. 1951 v Norway; 1953 v France, Luxembourg (3).

Corr P.J. 1949 v Portugal, Spain, England, Sweden (4).

Donovan D. 1954 v Norway; 1955 v Holland, Norway, West Germany; 1957 v England (5).

Eglington T.J. 1946 v England; 1947 v Spain, Portugal; 1948 v Portugal, Switzerland; 1949 v Portugal, Sweden; 1950 v Norway; 1951 v Argentina, West Germany; 1952 v West Germany, Austria, Spain, France; 1953 v Austria, France, Luxembourg, France; 1954 v Norway; 1955 v Holland, West Germany, Spain (22).

Farrell P.D. 1947 v Spain, Portugal; 1948 v Portugal, Spain, Switzerland; 1949 v Portugal (sub), Spain, England, Finland, Sweden; 1951 v Argentina, Norway, West Germany; 1952 v West Germany, Austria, Spain, France; 1953 v Austria, France (twice); 1954 v Norway; 1955 v Holland, West Germany, Yugoslavia, Spain; 1957 v England (26).

McDonagh J. 1981 v Wales, Belgium, Czechoslovakia (3).

Meagan M.K. 1961 v Scotland; 1962 v Austria, Iceland; 1964 v Spain (4).

O'Keefe E. 1981 v Wales (1).

O'Neill J.A. 1952 v Spain, France; 1953 v Austria, France, Luxembourg, France; 1954 v Norway; 1955 v Holland, Norway, West Germany, Yugoslavia, Spain; 1956 v Denmark; 1958 v Mexico, Poland; 1959 v Czechoslovakia (twice) (17).

Sheedy K. 1983 v Holland (sub), Malta; 1984 v Denmark; 1985 v Italy, Israel, Switzerland (twice), Denmark; 1986 v Scotland, Poland; 1987 v Northern Ireland; 1988 v Romania, Poland, England (sub), USSR, Holland (sub), Northern Ireland, Tunisia; 1989 v Hungary, Spain, Malta, Hungary, Northern Ireland, Malta; 1990 v Wales (sub), USSR, Finland (sub), Turkey, England, Egypt, Holland, Romania, Italy; 1991 v Wales, England, Poland, Chile, USA (38).

Walsh M.A. 1978 v Northern Ireland (sub) (1).

Walsh M. 1982 v Chile, Brazil, Trinidad & Tobago, Spain (4).

Victory & Wartime Internationals

1919 and 1946 Victory Internationals. 1939-45 Wartime Internationals. No caps were awarded for these matches.

England

Britton C.S. 1941 v Wales (twice); 1942 v Scotland, Wales (twice); 1943 v Scotland (twice), Wales (three times); 1944 v Scotland, Wales (12).

Fleetwood T. 1919 v Scotland (twice) (2).

Greenhalgh N.H. 1939 v Scotland (1).

Grenyer A. 1919 v Wales (1).

Lawton T. 1939 v Scotland; 1941 v Scotland; 1942 v Scotland (three times), Wales (twice); 1943 v Scotland; 1944 v Scotland (three times), Wales (twice); 1945 v France, Scotland (twice), Wales, Northern Ireland (18).

Mercer J. 1939 v Scotland; 1940 v Scotland; 1941 v Scotland (three times), Wales; 1942 v Scotland (twice), Wales; 1943 v Scotland (twice), Wales (twice); 1944 v Scotland (three times), Wales (twice); 1945 v Scotland (twice), Wales (twice), France, Northern Ireland; 1946 v Belgium, Scotland (26).

Scotland

Caskie J. 1939 v England; 1941 v England (three times); 1942 v England; 1944 v England (three times) (8).

Gillick T. 1941 v England; 1942 v England; 1943 v England (3).

Note: Although Jimmy Caskie is listed as an Everton player for wartime internationals, it should be noted that he made only four wartime appearances for the club.

Wales

Jones T.G. 1939 v England; 1940 v England (twice); 1941 v England (twice); 1942 v England (twice); 1943 v England (three times); 1946 v Northern Ireland (11).

Northern Ireland

Stevenson A.E. 1946 v Scotland (1).

Everton Career Records

Where known, the date of signing and leaving (eg Apr 1925) is given; where this is not known, the first and last seasons in which the player appeared are shown (eg 1925 means 1925-26). An asterisk signifies that the player was still on Everton's books at the end of 1992-93; ‡signifies the player joined Everton from local junior football; †signifies that the player's contract was cancelled. A section mark after a player's name (eg GRAY A. §) shows that additional appearances are to be found in the Everton in Europe section.

PLAYER	BIRTHPLACE	FROM	TO	LEAGUE App	LEAGUE Gls	FA CUP App	FA CUP Gls	FL CUP App	FL CUP Gls	TOTAL App	TOTAL Gls
ABBOTT W.	Birmingham	Small Heath 1899	Burnley 1907	257	32	34	5	0	0	291	37
ABLETT G.I.	Liverpool	Liverpool Jan 92	*	57	1	3	0	6	0	66	1
ADAMS J.	Edinburgh	Hearts 1894	Hearts 1895	40	1	3	0	0	0	43	1
ADAMS N.J.	Stoke	Stoke C Jul 1986	Oldham A Aug 1989	17/3	0	0	0	4/1	0	21/4	0
ADAMSON H.		Lochgelly 1907	Bolton W Dec 1909	25	0	0	0	0	0	25	0
AINSCOW A.	Bolton	Birmingham C Aug 1981	† May 1983	24/4	3	0	0	1/1	0	25/5	3
ALFORD F.J.	Swindon	Swindon T 1921	Barrow 1921	2	0	0	0	0	0	2	0
ALLAN J.	Carlisle	Carlisle U 1909	Manchester C Jun 1912	19	0	0	0	0	0	19	0
ANGUS J.A.		Sunderland A 1888	retired 1890	16	0	1	0	0	0	17	0
ARCHER J.W.	Wednesbury	Walsall 1932	Coventry C 1935	15	2	0	0	0	0	15	2
ARNOLD J.	Stafford	Blackburn R Aug 1981	Port Vale June 1985	48	0	5	0	6	0	59	0
ARRIDGE S.	Sunderland	Bootle 1893	New Brighton 1896	51	0	5	0	0	0	56	0
ASHWORTH A.	Southport	‡May 1957	Luton T Oct 1960	12	3	0	0	0	0	12	3
ASHWORTH S.B.	Stoke	Manchester C Sep 1904	Port Vale 1904	11	0	0	0	0	0	11	0
ASPINALL W.	Wigan	Wigan A Feb 1986	Aston Villa Feb 1987	0/7	0	0	0	0/1	0	0/8	0
ATKIN I. §	Birmingham	Sunderland Nov 1984	Ipswich Oct 1987	6/1	1	0/1	0	0	0	6/2	1
ATTEVELD R.	Amsterdam	RJC Haarlem Aug 1989	Bristol C Mar 1992	41/10	1	6	0	6	1	53/10	2
ATTWOOD A.A.	Walsall	Walsall 1928	Bristol R 1929	3	0	0	0	0	0	3	0
BAILEY J. §	Liverpool	Blackburn R Jul 1979	Newcastle U Oct 1985	171	3	22	0	20/1	0	213/1	3
BAIN D.	Rotherglen	Manchester U 1924	Bristol C Nov 1928	38	3	5	0	0	0	43	3
BAKER B.H.	Liverpool	Blackburn R 1920	Chelsea 1926	13	0	0	0	0	0	13	0
BALL A.J. §	Farnworth	Blackpool Aug 1966	Arsenal Dec 1971	208	66	21	5	10	3	239	74
BALMER R.	Liverpool	‡1902	1911	165	0	23	0	0	0	188	0
BALMER W.	Liverpool	South Shore 1897	Croydon 1907	293	1	38	0	0	0	331	1
BANKS H.		Army 1896	Third Lanark 1896	2	0	0	0	0	0	2	0
BARBER E.		‡1938	1938	2	0	0	0	0	0	2	0
BARDSLEY J.C.	Southport	N.Nomads 1909	Manchester C Nov 1911	1	0	0	0	0	0	1	0
BARKER G.		‡1896	Bristol C 1897	10	0	0	0	0	0	10	0
BARLOW G.H.		Preston NE 1908	Preston NE 1910	34	5	8	1	0	0	42	6
BARLOW J.	Prescot	‡1897	Reading 1898	4	0	0	0	0	0	4	0
BARLOW S.	Liverpool		*	11/24	5	1/1	0	2/2	1	14/27	6
BARNETT G.C.	Northwich	‡May 1964	Arsenal Oct 1969	10	0	0	0	0	0	10	0
BARTON J.S. §	Birmingham	Worcester C Dec 1978	Derby C Mar 1982	18/2	0	0	0	3	0	21/2	0
BATTEN H.G.	Bristol	Plymouth A Feb 1926	Bradford C Nov 1926	15	1	0	0	0	0	15	1
BEAGRIE P.S.	Middlesbrough	Stoke Nov 1989	*	59/26	8	5/2	0	4/1	2	68/29	10
BEARDSLEY P.A.	Newcastle upon Tyne	Liverpool Aug 1991	*	81	25	4	1	8	5	93	31
BEARE G.	Southampton	Blackpool 1910	Cardiff C Jun 1914	104	18	14	1	0	0	118	19
BELFITT R.M.	Doncaster	Ipswich T Nov 1972	Sunderland Oct 1973	14/2	2	2	1	0	0	16/2	3
BELL J.	Dumbarton	Dumbarton 1892 New Brighton T 1901	Tottenham H 1898 Preston NE 1903	177	62	22	8	0	0	199	70
BELL L.	Dumbarton	Sheffield W Jul 1897	Bolton W 1898	41	17	7	3	0	0	48	0
BELL R.C.	Birkenhead	Tranmere R Mar 1936	1938	14	9	0	0	0	0	14	9
BENNETT H.	Liverpool	‡Mar 1967	Aldershot Jan 1971	2	0	0	0	1	0	3	0
BENTHAM S.J.	Lawton St Mary's	Wigan A Jan 1934	retired 1948	110	17	15	0	0	0	125	17
BENTLEY J.	Liverpool	‡Nov 1959	Stockport C May 1961	1	0	0	0	0	0	1	0
BERNARD M.P.	Shrewsbury	Stoke C May 1972	Oldham A Jul 1977	139/8	8	9/1	0	11/1	0	159/10	8
BERRY A.	Liverpool	Fulham 1909	Liverpool 1910	27	7	2	0	0	0	29	7
BERRY C.H.	Warrington	‡1908	1911	3	0	0	0	0	0	3	0
BERWICK W.	Northampton	Glossop NE 1919	1919	1	0	0	0	0	0	1	0
BEVERIDGE R.	Polmudi	Nottingham F 1900	Died Oct 1901	4	0	0	0	0	0	4	0
BILEY A.	Leighton Buzzard	Derby C July 1981	Portsmouth Aug 1982	16/3	3	0	0	2	0	18/3	3
BILLINGE P.			Crewe A Feb 1987	1	0	0	0	0	0	1	0
BINGHAM W.P. §	Belfast	Luton T Oct 1960	Port Vale Aug 1963	86	23	7	2	3	1	96	26
BIRCH K.J.	Birkenhead	‡Aug 1951	Southampton Mar 1958	43	1	2	0	0	0	45	1
BIRNIE A.		‡1905	Norwich C 1905	3	0	0	0	0	0	3	0
BISHOP I.	Liverpool	‡Jun 1981	Carlisle U Oct 1984	0/1	0	0	0	0/1	0	0/2	0

PLAYER	BIRTHPLACE	FROM	TO	LEAGUE App	Gls	FA CUP App	Gls	FL CUP App	Gls	TOTAL App	Gls
BLACK W.	Isle of Mull	Celtic 1905	1906	20	0	0	0	0	0	20	0
BLAIR J.E.	Liverpool	1919	Oldham A 1921	5	3	1	0	0	0	6	3
BLYTHE J.		Jarrow 1898	West Ham U 1901	34	1	1	0	0	0	35	1
BOCKING W.	Stockport	Stockport C Apr 1931	Stockport C Aug 1934	15	0	1	0	0	0	16	0
BOLTON H.	Port Glasgow	Newcastle U Jan 1906	Bradford Dec 1908	75	27	12	7	0	0	87	34
BONE J.		‡1901	1901	2	0	0	0	0	0	2	0
BOOTH T.	Manchester	Blackburn R May 1900	Preston NE 1907	175	9	10	2	0	0	185	11
BORROWS B.	Liverpool	‡July 1977	Bolton W Mar 1983	27	0	0	0	2	0	29	0
BORTHWICK J.		Hibernian 1907	Millwall 1910	25	0	0	0	0	0	25	0
BOWMAN A.		East Stirling 1901	Blackburn R 1902	9	3	2	0	0	0	11	3
BOYES W.E.	Sheffield	West Brom A Feb 1938	Notts C Jul 1949	66	11	7	4	0	0	73	15
BOYLE D.		New Brighton T 1901	Dundee 1901	7	0	0	0	0	0	7	0
BOYLE R.H.	Dumbarton	Dumbarton 1890	Dundee Jun 1902	222	7	21	1	0	0	243	8
BRACEWELL P.W. §	Heswall	Sunderland May 1984	Sunderland Sep 1989	95	7	19/2	0	10	2	124/2	9
BRADSHAW F.	Sheffield	Northampton T Nov 1911	Arsenal Aug 1914	66	19	8	2	0	0	74	21
BRADSHAW G.F.	Southport	New Brighton 1934	Arsenal 1934	2	0	1	0	0	0	3	0
BRADY A.		Sunderland Nov 1889	Celtic 1890	34	17	2	3	0	0	36	20
BRAMWELL J.	Ashton-in-Makerfield	‡Apr 1958	Luton T Oct 1960	52	0	4	0	0	0	56	0
BRAND D.S.	Edinburgh	‡Nov 1975	Crewe A Feb 1977	2	0	0	0	0	0	2	0
BRANNICK J.		1912	St Mirren Apr 1914	3	2	0	0	0	0	3	2
BREARLEY J.	Liverpool	Middlesbrough 1902	Tottenham H 1902	22	7	2	1	0	0	24	8
BREWSTER G.	Culsalmond	Aberdeen Jan 1920	Wolves Nov 1922	64	4	4	0	0	0	68	4
BRIGGS H.F.		Darwen 1895	1896	11	0	0	0	0	0	11	0
BRINDLE W.	Liverpool	‡Aug 1967	Barnsley May 1970	1	0	0	0	1	0	2	0
BRISCOE W.		1888	1888	3	0	0	0	0	0	3	0
BRITTON C.S.	Bristol	Bristol R June 1930	Burnley May 1945	221	2	19	1	0	0	240	3
BROAD J.	Stalybridge	Sittingbourne Nov 1924	New Brighton Dec 1925	18	8	3	0	0	0	21	8
BROMLOW W.	Liverpool	1912	1912	1	0	0	0	0	0	1	0
BROWELL A.	Walbottle	Hull C 1912	West Stanley 1912	1	0	0	0	0	0	1	0
BROWELL T.	Walbottle	Hull C Dec 1911	Manchester C Oct 1913	50	26	10	11	0	0	60	37
BROWN A.D. §	Grangemouth	Partick T Sep 1963	Shrewsbury T May 1971	176/33	9	16/8	0	10	1	202/41	10
BROWN W.		Stanley 1888	1888	6	2	0	0	0	0	6	2
BROWN W.	Cambuslang	Partick T 1914	Nottingham F May 1928	170	0	9	0	0	0	179	0
BUCK H.		Tranmere R 1908	1908	1	0	0	0	0	0	1	0
BUCKLE E.W.	Southwark	Manchester U Nov 1949	Exeter C Jul 1955	97	31	10	2	0	0	107	33
BUCKLEY M.J. §	Manchester	‡June 1971	Sunderland Aug 1978	128/7	10	7	1	12	1	147/7	12
BURNETT G.G.	Liverpool	‡1946	Oldham A Oct 1951	47	0	7	0	0	0	54	0
BURTON A.D.	Lochgelly	Bristol C 1911	Reading 1911	12	4	0	0	0	0	12	4
CAIN R.		Airdrie 1889	Bootle 1889	10	0	0	0	0	0	10	0
CAIN T.		Stoke C 1894	Southampton 1894	11	0	1	0	0	0	12	0
CALDWELL J.H.	Carronshore	Reading 1912	Arsenal Jun 1913	31	0	5	0	0	0	36	0
CAMERON D.P.	Dublin	Shelbourne U Jul 1948	Sligo R Sep 1949	1	0	0	0	0	0	1	0
CAMERON J.	Ayr	Queen's Park Sep 1895	Tottenham H 1897	42	12	6	2	0	0	48	14
CAMPBELL W.C.		Bootle 1890	Clyde 1896	20	2	0	0	0	0	20	2
CASKIE J.		St Johnstone 1938	Rangers 1938	5	1	0	0	0	0	5	1
CATTERICK H.	Darlington	Stockport C 1946	Crewe A Dec 1951	59	19	12	5	0	0	71	24
CHADWICK A.	Church	‡1888	Accrington 1892	5	0	0	0	0	0	5	0
CHADWICK E.W.	Blackburn	Blackburn R 1888	Burnley May 1899	270	97	30	13	0	0	300	110
CHADWICK T.		Blackburn R 1901	1907	21	0	1	0	0	0	22	0
CHADWICK W.	Bury	‡Feb 1922	Leeds U Nov 1925	102	50	7	5	0	0	109	55
CHEDGZOY S.	Ellesmere Port	‡Dec 1910	USA May 1926	279	33	21	3	0	0	300	36
CLARK A.W.	Shoreham	Luton T May 1931	Tranmere R Mar 1936	41	1	1	0	0	0	42	1
CLARK C.		1901	Plymouth A 1902	6	1	1	0	0	0	7	1
CLARKE H.	Walsall	‡1898	Portsmouth 1898	12	2	0	0	0	0	12	2
CLARKE W.	Wolverhampton	Birmingham C Mar 1987	Leicester C Jul 1989	46/11	18	1/7	0	3/3	1	50/21	19
CLEMENTS D. §	Larne	Sheffield W Sep 1973	† Feb 1976	81/2	6	6	2	8	0	95/2	8
CLENNELL J.	Sunderland	Blackburn R Jan 1914	Cardiff C Oct 1921	68	30	6	3	0	0	74	33
CLIFFORD R.		Bolton W Nov 1908	Fulham 1910	37	0	8	0	0	0	45	0
CLINTON T.J.	Dublin	Dundalk Mar 1948	Blackburn R Apr 1955	73	4	7	1	0	0	80	5
COCK J.G.	Hayle	Chelsea Jan 1923	Plymouth A Mar 1925	69	29	3	2	0	0	72	31
COGGINS W.H.	Bristol	Bristol C Mar 1930	Queen's Park R 1933	51	0	5	0	0	0	56	0
COLEMAN J.G.	Kettering	Arsenal 1907	Sunderland 1909	69	29	2	1	0	0	71	30
COLLINS H.		1905	1905	3	0	0	0	0	0	3	0

PLAYER	BIRTHPLACE	FROM	TO	LEAGUE App	LEAGUE Gls	FA CUP App	FA CUP Gls	FL CUP App	FL CUP Gls	TOTAL App	TOTAL Gls
COLLINS J.		Cambuslang 1891	1892	15	0	0	0	0	0	15	0
COLLINS R.Y.	Glasgow	Celtic Sep 1958	Leeds U Mar 1962	133	42	9	5	5	1	147	48
COMMON E.W.	Seaton Delaval	Blyth Spartans Jan 1928	Preston NE Nov 1933	14	0	0	0	0	0	14	0
CONNOLLY J.	Glasgow	St Johnstone Mar 1972	Birmingham C Sep 1976	105/3	16	3/1	0	4	0	112/4	16
COOK H.E.		1905	1905	7	3	2	0	0	0	9	3
COOK W.		Celtic Dec 1932	Wrexham 1945	225	5	24	1	0	0	249	6
CORR P.J.	Dundalk	Preston NE Aug 1948	Bangor 1949	24	2	0	0	0	0	24	2
CORRIN T.		1900	Southampton 1903	11	1	1	0	0	0	12	1
COSTLEY J.T.		Blackburn R 1888	1888	6	3	0	0	0	0	6	3
COTTEE A.R.	West Ham	West Ham Aug 1988	*	122/20	56	13/6	4	14/4	8	149/29	68
COULTER J.	Co Antrim	Belfast Celtic Feb 1934	Grimsby T Oct 1937	50	16	8	8	0	0	58	24
COUPER G.		Hearts 1906	1907	4	1	0	0	0	0	4	1
COX W.		Burnley 1889	Nottingham F 1889	4	0	0	0	0	0	4	0
COYNE		Gainsborough T 1888	1888	2	1	0	0	0	0	2	1
CRELLEY J.	Liverpool	Millwall A 1899	Exeter C 1907	116	0	11	0	0	0	127	0
CRESSWELL W.	South Shields	Sunderland Feb 1927	Port Vale May 1936	290	1	16	0	0	0	306	1
CRITCHLEY E.	Ashton	Stockport C Dec 1926	Preston NE Jun 1934	217	37	12	5	0	0	229	42
CROMPTON T.		1898	1898	3	1	1	0	0	0	4	1
CROSSLEY C.A.	Walsall	Sunderland 1920	West Ham U Jun 1922	50	18	5	3	0	0	55	21
CUMMINS G.R.	Dublin	‡Nov 1950	Luton T Aug 1953	24	0	5	0	0	0	29	0
CUNLIFFE J.N.	Blackrod	Adlington May 1930	Rochdale Sep 1946	174	73	13	3	0	0	187	76
CURRAN T. §	Kingsley	Sheffield U. Sep 1983	† Apr 1985	19/4	1	1	0	0	0	20/4	1
DANSKIN J.	Winsford	‡Jul 1984	Mansfield T Apr 1987	1	0	0	0	0	0	1	0
DARCY F.J.	Liverpool	‡Aug 1964	Tranmere R Jul 1972	8/8	0	0/1	0	0	0	8/9	0
DARRACOTT T. §	Liverpool	‡Jul 1968	† Feb 1979	138/10	0	12	0	12	0	162/10	0
DAVIDSON W.	Glasgow	Middlesbrough 1911	St Mirren Jun 1913	38	3	7	1	0	0	45	4
DAVIE	Renton	1888	1888	2	0	0	0	0	0	2	0
DAVIES A.L.	Wallasey	Flint Aug 1926	Exeter C Aug 1930	90	0	3	0	0	0	93	0
DAVIES J.		1888	Chirk 1888	8	2	0	0	0	0	8	2
DAVIES J.W.	Denbigh	Cardiff C 1946	Plymouth A Feb 1947	1	0	0	0	0	0	1	0
DAVIES S.	Chirk	Preston NE Jan 1921	West Brom A Nov 1921	20	9	2	1	0	0	22	10
DAVIES W.D. §	Ammanford	Swansea C Dec 1970	Wrexham Sep 1977	82	0	5	0	6	0	93	0
DAWSON H.		Rossendale 1908	Blackpool Mar 1909	4	0	1	0	0	0	5	0
DEAN W.R.	Birkenhead	Tranmere R Mar 1925	Notts C Mar 1938	399	349	32	28	0	0	431	377
DEPLEDGE R.P.	Wallasey	‡1906	1906	1	0	0	0	0	0	1	0
DEWAR J.		1892	1892	1	0	0	0	0	0	1	0
DICK A.		Kilmarnock 1888	1888	9	0	0	0	0	0	9	0
DICKINSON	Saltney	‡1934	Port Vale 1934	1	0	0	0	0	0	1	0
DILLY T.	Arbroath	Hearts 1902	West Brom A Mar 1906	9	2	0	0	0	0	9	2
DIVER J.		Celtic Apr 1897	Celtic 1898	30	11	2	0	0	0	32	11
DOBSON G.		Bolton W 1888	1888	18	0	0	0	0	0	18	0
DOBSON M. §	Blackburn	Burnley Aug 1974	Burnley Aug 1979	190	29	13	2	22	8	225	39
DODDS E.	Grangemouth	Blackpool Nov 1946	Lincoln C Oct 1948	55	36	3	1	0	0	58	37
DOMINY A.A.	Southampton	Southampton May 1926	Gillingham Mar 1928	29	12	4	1	0	0	33	13
DONALDSON J.		‡1905	Preston NE 1905	2	0	0	0	0	0	2	0
DONNACHIE J.	Kilmarnock	Newcastle U Feb 1906 Rangers 1919	Oldham A Oct 1908 Blackpool Jun 1920	56	0	2	0	0	0	58	0
DONOVAN D.	Cork	‡May 1949	Grimsby T Aug 1958	179	2	8	0	0	0	187	2
DOUGAL P.G.		Arsenal Aug 1937	Bury Jun 1938	11	2	0	0	0	0	11	2
DOWNS R.W.	Midridge	Barnsley Mar 1920	Brighton & HA Aug 1923	92	0	5	0	0	0	97	0
DOYLE D.	Paisley	Bolton W 1889	Celtic 1890	42	0	3	1	0	0	45	1
DUGDALE G.	Liverpool	‡Jun 1947	Retired 1949	58	0	5	0	0	0	63	0
DUNLOP A.	Liverpool	‡Aug 1949	Wrexham Nov 1963	211	0	15	0	5	0	231	0
DUNN J.	Glasgow	Hibernian Apr 1928	Exeter C May 1935	140	42	14	7	0	0	154	49
EARP M.J.	Nottingham	Nottingham F 1891	Nottingham F 1891	9	0	1	0	0	0	10	0
EASTHOPE J.	Liverpool	‡Apr 1950	Stockport C Jun 1954	2	0	0	0	0	0	2	0
EASTOE P.R. §	Tamworth	Queen's Park R Mar 1979	West Brom A Aug 1982	88/7	26	12	6	6	1	106/7	33
EASTON W.C.	Blyth	Blyth Spartans Mar 1927	Swansea T Jan 1930	15	3	0	0	0	0	15	3
EBBRELL J.K.	Bromborough	‡ 1988	*	111/9	5	12	2	12	1	135/9	8
ECCLES G.S.	Newcastle	Wolves Apr 1898	West Ham U May 1902	56	0	4	0	0	0	60	0
EGLINGTON T.	Dublin	Shamrock R Jul 1946	Tranmere R Jun 1957	394	76	34	6	0	0	428	82
ELLIOTT J.		1890	1895	14	1	1	0	0	0	15	1
ELLIOTT T.		1945	1945	0	0	2	1	0	0	2	1

PLAYER	BIRTHPLACE	FROM	TO	LEAGUE App	LEAGUE Gls	FA CUP App	FA CUP Gls	FL CUP App	FL CUP Gls	TOTAL App	TOTAL Gls
EVANS W.B.	Llandiloes	1919	Swansea T 1919	2	0	0	0	0	0	2	0
FALDER D.E.J.	Liverpool	Wigan A 1949	Ellesmere Port 1950	25	0	5	0	0	0	30	0
FARMER G.		Oswestry 1888	1889	31	1	0	0	0	0	31	1
FARRALL A.	Hoylake	‡Mar 1953	Preston NE May 1957	5	0	0	0	0	0	5	0
FARRELL P.D.	Dublin	Shamrock R Aug 1946	Tranmere R Oct 1957	422	13	31	4	0	0	453	17
FAZACKERLEY S.	Preston	Sheffield U Nov 1920	Wolves Nov 1922	51	21	6	0	0	0	57	21
FELL J.I.	Grimsby	Grimsby T Mar 1961	Newcastle U Mar 1962	27	4	1	1	0	0	28	5
FERGUSON M.	Newcastle	Coventry C Aug 1981	Birmingham C Jun 1983	7/1	4	0	0	3/1	2	10/2	6
FERN T.E.	Measham	Lincoln C 1913	Port Vale Jun 1924	219	0	12	0	0	0	231	0
FIELDING W.A.	Edmonton	Charlton A 1946	Southport Jan 1959	380	49	30	5	0	0	410	54
FINNIS H.A.	Liverpool	‡Jun 1946	Retired 1946	1	0	0	0	0	0	1	0
FLEETWOOD T.	Liverpool	Rochdale Mar 1911	Oldham A Aug 1923	264	9	21	1	0	0	285	10
FLEMING G.		1888	1888	4	2	0	0	0	0	4	2
FLEWITT A.	Beeston	Lincoln C 1895	West Brom A 1895	3	1	0	0	0	0	3	1
FORBES F.J.	Edinburgh	Hearts 1922	Plymouth A Mar 1925	14	4	0	0	0	0	14	4
FORSHAW R.	Widnes	Liverpool Mar 1927	Wolves Aug 1929	41	8	0	0	0	0	41	8
FREEMAN B.C.	Birmingham	Arsenal 1907	Burnley Apr 1911	86	63	8	4	0	0	94	67
GABRIEL J. §	Dundee	Dundee Mar 1960	Southampton Jul 1967	255/1	33	25	2	5	0	285/1	35
GALT J.	Saltcoats	Rangers May 1914	Third Lanark Oct 1920	32	2	4	2	0	0	36	4
GANNON M.J.	Liverpool	‡Feb 1960	Scunthorpe U May 1962	3	0	0	0	0	0	3	0
GARDNER T.		Jun 1947	1947	1	0	0	0	0	0	1	0
GAULD J.	Aberdeen	Charlton A Oct 1956	Plymouth A Oct 1957	23	7	3	1	0	0	26	8
GAULT W.E.	Wallsend	1912	Cardiff C May 1920	29	13	1	0	0	0	30	13
GEARY F.	Hyson Green	Notts C 1889	Liverpool 1894	91	78	7	8	0	0	98	86
GEE C.W.	Stockport	Stockport C Jul 1930	Retired May 1940	196	2	15	0	0	0	211	2
GEE E.	Grassmoor	Chesterfield 1897	Notts C 1899	31	0	1	0	0	0	32	0
GELDARD A.	Bradford	Bradford Nov 1932	Bolton W Jul 1938	167	31	12	6	0	0	179	37
GIBSON D.J.	Runcorn	‡Aug 1950	Swindon T Nov 1954	3	0	0	0	0	0	3	0
GIDMAN J.	Liverpool	Aston Villa Oct 1979	Manchester U Jul 1981	64	2	11	0	3	1	78	3
GILLICK T.	Airdrie	Rangers Dec 1935	Rangers Nov 1945	121	40	12	4	0	0	133	44
GLAZZARD J.	Normanton	Huddersfield T Aug 1956	Mansfield T Dec 1956	3	0	0	0	0	0	3	0
GLOVER G.J.	Liverpool	‡Aug 1964	Mansfield T Sep 1967	2/1	0	0	0	0	0	2/1	0
GODFREY B.C.	Flint	‡May 1958	Scunthorpe U Jun 1960	1	0	0	0	0	0	1	0
GOLDIE H.		St Mirren 1895	Celtic 1896	18	1	1	0	0	0	19	1
GOODLASS R.	Liverpool	‡Jul 1971	† Oct 1977	31/4	2	7	0	9	0	47/4	2
GORDON P.		Renton 1890	Liverpool 1892	18	3	5	2	0	0	23	5
GOURLAY J.	Annbank	Port Glasgow 1909	Morton May 1913	54	8	4	1	0	0	58	9
GRACIE T.	Glasgow	Morton 1910	Liverpool Feb 1912	13	1	0	0	0	0	13	1
GRAHAM R.		Third Lanark 1906	Bolton W 1906	2	0	1	0	0	0	3	0
GRANT J.A.	Gateshead	High Spon A Aug 1942	Rochdale Jun 1956	121	10	12	1	0	0	133	11
GRAY A. §	Glasgow	Wolves Nov 1983	Aston Villa Jul 1985	44/5	14	14/1	3	0/1	0	58/7	17
GRAY R.		Partick Thistle 1899	Southampton 1900	20	1	1	0	0	0	21	1
GREEN C.R.	Wrexham	‡Feb 1959	Birmingham C Dec 1962	15	1	2	0	1	0	18	1
GREENHALGH N.	Bolton	New Brighton Jan 1938	Bangor C 1948	106	1	9	0	0	0	115	1
GRENYER A.	North Shields	North Shields 1910	South Shields Nov 1924	142	9	6	0	0	0	148	9
GRIFFITHS B.	Liverpool	‡Mar 1956	Southport Jun 1960	2	0	0	0	0	0	2	0
GRIFFITHS P.	Tylorstown	Port Vale 1931	West Brom A 1932	8	3	0	0	0	0	8	3
GRIFFITHS T.	Wrexham	Wrexham Dec 1926	Bolton W Dec 1931	76	9	2	0	0	0	78	9
GRUNDY H.		1905	Reading 1905	2	0	0	0	0	0	2	0
HAMILTON B.	Belfast	Ipswich T Nov 1975	Millwall Jul 1977	38/3	5	2/2	0	7/2	0	47/7	5
HAMILTON H.	Wallasey	‡1926	Preston NE May 1927	1	0	0	0	0	0	1	0
HAMMOND H.		1889	1889	1	0	0	0	0	0	1	0
HAMPSON A.	Prescot	‡Aug 1949	Halifax T Nov 1952	1	0	0	0	0	0	1	0
HANNAH A.B.	Renton	Renton 1889	Renton 1890	42	0	2	0	0	0	44	0
HANNAH J.		Celtic 1905	1905	1	0	0	0	0	0	1	0
HARBURN P.	Finsbury	Brighton & HA Aug 1958	Scunthorpe U Jan 1959	4	1	0	0	0	0	4	1
HARDMAN H.P.	Manchester	Blackpool 1903	Manchester U Aug 1908	130	25	26	4	0	0	156	29
HARDY H.J.	Stockport	Stockport C Oct 1925	Bury Jul 1928	40	0	5	0	0	0	45	0
HARGREAVES F.	Ashton	Oldham A 1924	Oldham A May 1925	9	2	0	0	0	0	9	2
HARLAND A.I.	Crookstown	Linfield Oct 1922	Runcorn 1925	64	0	6	0	0	0	70	0
HARPER A. §	Liverpool	Liverpool June 1983 Manchester C Aug 1991	Sheffield W Jul 1988	148/29	4	12/9	1	22/3	0	182/41	5
HARPER J.	Greenock	Aberdeen Dec 1972	Hibernian Feb 1974	40/3	12	4	2	2	0	46/3	14

PLAYER	BIRTHPLACE	FROM	TO	LEAGUE App	LEAGUE Gls	FA CUP App	FA CUP Gls	FL CUP App	FL CUP Gls	TOTAL App	TOTAL Gls
HARRIS A.E.	Liverpool	‡Jan 1955	Tranmere R May 1957	5	0	0	0	0	0	5	0
HARRIS B. §	Bebington	‡Jan 1954	Cardiff C Oct 1966	310	23	31	4	5	0	346	27
HARRIS J.	Birkenhead	‡Sep 1951	Birmingham C Dec 1960	191	65	14	5	2	2	207	72
HARRIS J.A.	Liverpool	‡Jul 1950	Bangor C 1952	14	4	0	0	0	0	14	4
HARRIS V.	Dublin	Shelbourne 1907	Shelbourne 1913	190	1	24	1	0	0	214	2
HARRISON G.	Church Gresley	Leicester F Apr 1913	Preston NE Dec 1923	177	17	13	0	0	0	190	17
HART H.	Glasgow	Airdrie Jan 1922	Retired 1929	289	5	11	0	0	0	300	5
HARTFORD A.	Clydebank	Nottingham F Aug 1979	Manchester C Oct 1981	81	6	11	1	6	0	98	7
HARTILL W.J.	Wolverhampton	Wolves 1935	Liverpool 1935	5	1	0	0	0	0	5	1
HARTLEY A.		Dumbarton 1892	Liverpool Dec 1897	50	24	11	4	0	0	61	28
HARVEY J.C. §	Liverpool	‡Oct 1962	Sheffield W Sep 1974	317/3	18	34	4	10/1	0	361/4	22
HAUGHEY W.	Glasgow	‡June 1956	Falkirk Jun 1958	4	1	0	0	0	0	4	1
HEARD P.	Hull	‡Sep 1978	Aston Villa Oct 1979	10/1	0	0	0	0	0	10/1	0
HEATH A.P. §	Stoke	Stoke C Jan 1982	Aston V Aug 1989	206/19	71	24/5	6	33/2	11	263/26	88
HEDLEY J.R.	Wellington Quay	‡1947	Sunderland Jul 1950	54	0	7	0	0	0	61	0
HENDERSON W.	Linlithgow	Southampton 1902	Reading 1903	15	0	2	0	0	0	17	0
HESLOP G.W.	Wallsend	Newcastle U Mar 1962	Manchester C Sep 1965	10	0	1	0	0	0	11	0
HICKSON D.	Ellesmere Port	‡May 1948 Huddersfield T Jul 1957	Aston Villa Sep 1955 Liverpool Nov 1959	225	95	18	16	0	0	243	111
HIGGINS M.		1888	1888	1	0	0	0	0	0	1	0
HIGGINS M.N. §	Buxton	‡Aug 1976	Retired 1984	150/1	6	7	0	19	0	176/1	6
HIGGINS W.C.	Tranmere	Tranmere R 1946	Bogota (Colombia) 1949	48	8	1	1	0	0	49	9
HIGHAM N.	Chorley	‡1933	Middlesbrough 1934	14	6	0	0	0	0	14	6
HILL M.J.	Carrickfergus	Norwich C Aug 1963	Port Vale Oct 1965	7	1	0	0	0	0	7	1
HILL P.		Southampton 1905	Manchester C Nov 1906	14	0	2	0	0	0	16	0
HILLMAN J.	Tavistock	Burnley Feb 1895	Dundee 1895	35	0	3	0	0	0	38	0
HINCHCLIFFE A.G.	Manchester	Manchester C Jul 1990	*	61/3	2	5	0	8/2	0	74/5	2
HODGE M.	Southport	Plymouth A July 1979	Sheffield W Sep 1983	25	0	6	0	0	0	31	0
HODGE W.	Kilwinning	1912	1913	10	0	0	0	0	0	10	0
HOLBEM W.	Sheffield	Sheffield W 1911	St Mirren 1913	18	0	0	0	0	0	18	0
HOLD O.	Barnsley	Notts C Feb 1950	Queen's Park R Feb 1952	22	5	1	0	0	0	23	5
HOLMES P.	Sheffield		*	4	0	0	0	0	0	4	0
HOLT J.	Blackburn	Bootle 1888	Reading Oct 1898	225	3	27	1	0	0	252	4
HORNE B.	St Asaph		*	34	1	0/1	0	5/1	0	39/2	1
HOUGHTON H.	Liverpool	‡1927	Exeter C Jun 1928	1	0	0	0	0	0	1	0
HOUSTON J.	Belfast	Linfield Feb 1913	Linfield 1914	26	2	2	0	0	0	28	2
HOWARTH H.B.	Liverpool	1914	1919	8	2	0	0	0	0	8	2
HOWARTH R.H.	Preston	Preston NE Nov 1891	Preston NE 1893	59	0	9	0	0	0	68	0
HUGHES D.	Prescott	‡Jul 1982	Shrewsbury T Jun 1985	3	0	0	0	0	0	3	0
HUGHES D.	Ruabon	1898	Tottenham H 1898	8	0	0	0	0	0	8	0
HUMPHREYS G.	Llandudno	‡Sep 1963	Crystal P Jun 1970	12	2	0	0	2	0	14	2
HUMPHREYS J.	Llandudno	1946	Llandudno T 1950	53	0	8	0	0	0	61	0
HUNT E.	Swindon	Wolves Sep 1967	Coventry C Mar 1968	12/2	3	1	0	1	0	14	3
HUREL E.	Jersey	St Helier 1936	Northampton T 1936	5	1	0	0	0	0	5	1
HURST J.W. §	Blackpool	‡Oct 1964	Oldham A Jun 1976	336/11	29	30/2	4	13	1	379/13	34
HUSBAND J. §	Newcastle	‡Oct 1964	Luton T Nov 1973	158/7	44	22	10	5	1	185/7	55
IRVINE A.	Glasgow	Queen's Park May 1981	Crystal P Nov 1984	51/9	4	9	2	10/1	0	70/10	6
IRVINE R.W.	Belfast	Dunmurry Sep 1921	Portsmouth Mar 1928	199	54	15	3	0	0	214	57
IRVINE D.	Workington	Workington T Jan 1973	Oldham A Jun 1976	4/2	0	1	0	1	1	6/2	1
JACK R.	Avoch	‡Feb 1977	Norwich C Dec 1979	1	1	0	0	0	0	1	1
JACKSON G.	Liverpool	‡1934	Retired 1947	75	0	4	0	0	0	79	0
JACKSON M.A.	Leeds	Luton T Oct 1991	*	55/2	4	4	0	3	0	62/2	4
JACKSON T. §	Belfast	Glentoran Feb 1968	Nottingham F Oct 1970	30/2	0	3/1	0	1	0	34/3	0
JAMIESON J.		1889	Sheffield W 1892	15	0	0	0	0	0	15	0
JARDINE D.		Bootle Nov 1890	Nelson 1893	37	0	0	0	0	0	37	0
JEFFERIS F.	Fordingbridge	Southampton Mar 1911	Preston NE Jan 1920	125	22	12	3	0	0	137	25
JENKINS I.	Prescot	‡ Jun 1991	*	3/2	0	0	0	0/1	0	3/3	0
JOHNSON A.	Weaverham	‡1946	Chesterfield Sep 1948	9	0	0	0	0	0	9	0
JOHNSON D.E. §	Liverpool	‡Apr 1969 Liverpool Aug 1982	Ipswich T Nov 1972 Manchester C Mar 1984	79/10	15	5	2	7	2	91/10	19
JOHNSON T.C.	Dalton-in-Furness	Manchester C Mar 1930	Liverpool Mar 1934	146	56	13	8	0	0	159	64
JOHNSTON L.		1913	1913	8	1	0	0	0	0	8	1
JOHNSTON M.T.	Glasgow	Rangers Nov 1991	*	28/6	10	1	0	2/1	0	31/7	10
JOLIFFE C.		1888	1888	5	0	0	0	0	0	5	0

PLAYER	BIRTHPLACE	FROM	TO	LEAGUE App	Gls	FA CUP App	Gls	FL CUP App	Gls	TOTAL App	Gls
JONES D.R.	Liverpool	‡May 1974	Coventry C Jun 1979	79/7	1	5	1	11/1	0	95/8	2
JONES G.K. §	Liverpool	‡Oct 1968	Birmingham C Jul 1976	76/6	12	7/1	1	5	1	88/7	14
JONES G.W.	Crook	Gwersylt 1919	Wigan B Jan 1923	36	2	0	0	0	0	36	2
JONES J.E.	Bromborough	Ellesmere Port 1933	Sunderland Dec 1945	98	0	10	0	0	0	108	0
JONES P.	Liverpool	‡1987	Wigan A Mar 1991	0/1	0	0	0	0	0	0/1	0
JONES R.		1888	Manchester C 1892	7	1	0	0	0	0	7	1
JONES R.H.	Liverpool	‡1924	Southport 1924	3	0	0	0	0	0	3	0
JONES T.		1905	Birmingham Sep 1910	15	5	0	0	0	0	15	5
JONES T.E.	Liverpool	‡Jan 1948	Retired 1961	383	14	25	0	3	0	411	14
JONES T.G.	Queensferry	Wrexham Mar 1936	Pwllheli Apr 1950	165	4	10	1	0	0	175	5
JORDAN W.C.	Langley	West Brom A 1911	Wolves Jul 1912	2	0	0	0	0	0	2	0
JULIUSSEN A.	Blyth	Portsmouth Sep 1948	Berwick R Aug 1951	10	1	0	0	0	0	10	1
KAVANAGH P.J.	Romford	‡Feb 1961	† Jun 1961	6	0	0	0	0	0	6	0
KAY A.H. §	Sheffield	Sheffield W Dec 1962	Suspended *sine die* 1963	50	4	5	0	0	0	55	4
KEARTON J.B.	Ipswich (Aust)	Brisbane Lions Oct 1988	*	2/3	0	1	0	0	0	3/3	0
KEELEY J.	Liverpool	‡May 1954	Accrington S Jul 1959	4	1	3	2	0	0	7	3
KEELEY G.M.	Basildon	Blackburn R Oct 1982	Blackburn R Dec 1982	1	0	0	0	0	0	1	0
KEELEY S.		1897	Dundee 1897	1	0	0	0	0	0	1	0
KEELEY J.	Hamilton	Ayr U Feb 1927	Carlisle U Aug 1929	81	1	2	0	0	0	83	1
KELSO R.	Renton	Newcastle U 1888 Preston NE 1891	Preston NE 1888 Dundee 1895	89	5	14	0	0	0	103	5
KENDALL H. §	Durham	Preston NE Mar 1967	Birmingham C Feb 1974	231/2	21	23	3	12	3	266/2	27
KENDALL J.	Broughton	Lincoln C Apr 1924	Preston NE May 1927	21	0	2	0	0	0	23	0
KENNEDY A.L.	Belfast	Arsenal 1928	Tranmere R Jun 1930	1	0	0	0	0	0	1	0
KENNEDY F.	Bury	Manchester U 1924	Middlesbrough May 1927	35	11	0	0	0	0	35	11
KENNEY W.A.	Liverpool	‡Jul 1969	Tranmere R Mar 1975	10/2	0	0	0	0	0	10/2	0
KENNY W.	Liverpool	‡ Jun 1992	*	16/1	1	2	0	4	0	22/1	1
KENT J.		1891	1891	1	0	0	0	0	0	1	0
KENYON R.N. §	Blackpool	‡Sep 1966	† Feb 1979	254/13	6	15/1	2	13/3	1	282/17	9
KEOWN M.R.	Oxford	Aston Villa Aug 1989	Arsenal	92/4	0	12/1	0	11	0	115/5	0
KERR J.	Burnbank	Bathgate Dec 1923	Preston NE Mar 1927	18	1	3	0	0	0	21	1
KERSLAKE J.G.	Southampton	1919	Wigan B 1919	1	1	0	0	0	0	1	1
KEYS		1888	1888	1	0	0	0	0	0	1	0
KIDD B. §	Manchester	Manchester C Mar 1979	Bolton W May 1980	40	12	4	4	5	4	49	20
KING A.	Luton	Luton T Apr 1976 West Brom A Jul 1982	Queen's Park R Sep 1980 † Jun 1984	193/2	49	16/1	4	29/1	11	238/4	64
KING F.O.	Radcliffe	Blyth Spartans Oct 1933	Derby C 1936	13	0	1	0	0	0	14	0
KING J.A.	Marylebone	‡Mar 1956	Bournemouth&BA Jul 1960	48	1	1	0	0	0	49	1
KIRBY G.	Liverpool	‡Jun 1952	Sheffield W Mar 1959	26	9	1	0	0	0	27	9
KIRKWOOD D.		1889	Broxburn 1891	35	1	3	1	0	0	38	2
KIRSOPP W.	Liverpool	‡Apr 1914	Bury May 1921	58	28	5	1	0	0	63	29
KIRWAN J.	Wicklow	Southport Jul 1898	Tottenham H 1898	24	5	2	0	0	0	26	5
KITCHEN G.W.	Fairfield	Stockport C 1898	1903	87	0	3	0	0	0	90	0
LABONE B.L. §	Liverpool	‡Jul 1957	Retired 1971	451	2	45	0	15	0	511	2
LACEY W.	Wexford	Shelbourne 1908	Liverpool Feb 1912	37	11	3	0	0	0	40	11
LANGLEY K.	St Helens	Wigan 1986	Manchester C Jun 1987	16	2	0	0	4	1	20	3
LATCHFORD R.D. §	Birmingham	Birmingham C Feb 1974	Swansea C Jul 1981	235/1	106	17/1	10	28	19	280/2	135
LATTA A.	Dumbarton	Dumbarton 1889	Liverpool 1895	136	69	12	1	0	0	148	70
LAVERICK R.	Castle Eden	Chelsea Feb 1959	Brighton & HA Jun 1960	22	6	1	0	0	0	23	6
LAWSON D. §	Newcastle	Huddersfield T Jun 1972	Luton T Oct 1978	124	0	12	0	13	0	149	0
LAWTON T.	Bolton	Burnley Jan 1937	Chelsea Nov 1945	87	65	8	5	0	0	95	70
LEE J.		1902	1902	2	0	0	0	0	0	2	0
LEEDER F.	Seaton Delaval	‡Mar 1955	Darlington Jul 1958	1	0	0	0	0	0	1	0
LEIVESLEY W.		1919	Reading 1919	5	0	0	0	0	0	5	0
LELLO C.F.	Ludlow	Shrewsbury T Sep 1947	Rochdale Nov 1956	237	9	17	0	0	0	254	9
LEWIS G.	Bangor	‡May 1948	Rochdale Jun 1956	10	6	0	0	0	0	10	6
LEWIS T.H.	Wolverhampton	‡1928	Wrexham Jun 1930	1	0	0	0	0	0	1	0
LEWIS W.		1888	1888	3	1	0	0	0	0	3	1
LEYFIELD C.	Chester	1934	Sheffield U 1936	38	13	0	0	0	0	38	13
LEYLAND H.K.	Liverpool	‡Aug 1950	Blackburn R Aug 1956	36	0	4	0	0	0	40	0
LILL M.J.	Barking	Wolves Feb 1960	Plymouth A Jun 1962	31	11	2	1	1	0	34	12
LINDLEY M.W.	Keighley	‡Feb 1946	Swindon T 1951	51	0	3	0	0	0	54	0
LINDSAY J.S.	Glasgow	Rangers Mar 1951	Bury May 1956	105	2	10	0	0	0	115	2
LINDSAY W.	Stockton	‡1893	Grimsby T 1893	9	0	0	0	0	0	9	0

PLAYER	BIRTHPLACE	FROM	TO	LEAGUE App	Gls	FA CUP App	Gls	FL CUP App	Gls	TOTAL App	Gls
LINEKER G.	Leicester	Leicester Jul 1985	Barcelona Jun 1986	41	30	6	5	5	3	52	38
LIVINGSTONE A.	Pencaithland	Bury May 1946	Southport Jun 1947	4	2	0	0	0	0	4	2
LIVINGSTONE D.	Dumbarton	Celtic Apr 1921	Plymouth A Feb 1926	95	0	5	0	0	0	100	0
LLEWELLYN H.	Golborne	‡May 1956	Crewe A Jul 1958	11	2	0	0	0	0	11	2
LOCHHEAD A.	St Johnstone	Third Lanark 1890	Third Lanark 1891	6	0	0	0	0	0	6	0
LODGE P.	Liverpool	‡June 1977	Preston NE Feb 1983	20/4	0	6	0	5	0	31/4	0
LOWE H.	Skelmersdale	Southport 1930	Preston NE 1931	5	0	0	0	0	0	5	0
LYONS M. §	Liverpool	‡Jul 1969	Sheffield W Jul 1982	364/25	48	29/1	6	34	5	427/26	59
McBAIN N.	Campbeltown	Manchester U Jan 1923	St Johnstone 1925	97	1	6	0	0	0	103	1
McBRIDE J. §	Glasgow	‡Aug 1978	Rotherham U Aug 1982	51/6	9	6	1	6	1	63/6	11
McCALL S.M.	Leeds	Bradford C Jun 1988	Rangers Aug 1991	99/4	6	16/2	3	11	1	126/6	10
McCAMBRIDGE J.	Larne	Ballymena U 1930	Cardiff C 1930	1	0	0	0	0	0	1	0
McCLURE J.H.	Workington	‡1929	Brentford Jun 1933	29	1	5	0	0	0	34	1
McCORMICK H.	Coleraine	Derby C Jul 1948	Coleraine Sep 1949	4	0	0	0	0	0	4	0
McDERMOTT T.	Glasgow	Celtic 1903	Chelsea Oct 1905	64	15	7	4	0	0	71	19
McDONALD A.		Jarrow 1899	Southampton 1900	23	6	0	0	0	0	23	6
McDONALD J.	Dykehead	Airdrie 1920	New Brighton Aug 1927	208	0	16	0	0	0	224	0
McDONALD J.	Rotherham	Bolton W Jul 1980	Bolton W Aug 1981	40	0	5	0	3	0	48	0
McDONALD N.R.	Newcastle upon Tyne	Newcastle U Aug 1988	Oldham A Oct 1991	76/14	5	17	0	7	0	100/14	8
McFARLANE R.	Greenock	Third Lanark 1897	East Stirling 1897	9	0	0	0	0	0	9	0
McGOURTY J.	Fauldhouse	Partick T May 1932	Hamilton A Aug 1934	15	2	0	0	0	0	15	2
McILHATTON J.	Ardeer	Albion R Apr 1946	Dundee 1948	55	1	3	1	0	0	58	2
McINNESS T.		Third Lanark 1894	Luton T 1895	42	18	5	0	0	0	47	18
McINTOSH J.M.	Dunfries	Blackpool Mar 1949	Distillery May 1952	58	19	1	0	0	0	59	19
McKENZIE D.	Grimsby	Anderlecht Dec 1976	Chelsea Sep 1978	48	14	7/1	5	6	2	61/1	21
McKINNON A.		Hibernian 1888	1888	6	4	0	0	0	0	6	4
McLAUGHLIN J.	Stirling	Falkirk Oct 1971	† Apr 1976	59/2	1	7	0	2	0	68/2	1
McLAUGHLIN W.		Hamilton 1904	Plymouth A 1905	15	5	0	0	0	0	15	5
McLEAN D.	Dumbarton	Renton Nov 1890	Liverpool 1891	25	0	1	0	0	0	26	0
McMAHON S.	Liverpool	‡Dec 1977	Aston Villa May 1983	99/1	11	9	0	11	3	119/1	14
McMILLAN J.		1892	1892	7	5	0	0	0	0	7	5
McNAMARA A.	Birkenhead	‡May 1950	Liverpool Dec 1957	111	22	2	0	0	0	113	22
McNAUGHT K.	Kirkcaldy	‡May 1972	Aston Villa Aug 1977	64/2	3	10	0	10	0	84/2	3
MACONACHIE J.	Aberdeen	Hibernian Apr 1907	Swindon T Aug 1920	245	6	25	1	0	0	270	7
McPHERSON L.	Glasgow	Swansea T Jan 1930	New Brighton Aug 1932	30	1	1	0	0	0	31	1
MAGNER E.	Newcastle	Gainsborough T 1910	St Mirren Jan 1912	6	2	3	1	0	0	9	3
MAHER A.	Liverpool	‡Dec 1964	Plymouth A Oct 1968	1	0	0	0	0	0	1	0
MAKEPEACE H.	Middlesbrough	‡1902	Retired 1914	284	16	52	7	0	0	336	23
MALEY W.		1896	1896	2	0	0	0	0	0	2	0
MARSDEN J.	Darwen	Darwen 1891	Retired 1891	1	0	0	0	0	0	1	0
MARSHALL C.	Liverpool	‡Nov 1973	Southport Sep 1976	6	0	1	0	0	0	7	0
MARSHALL I	Liverpool		Oldham A	9/6	1	0	0	1/1	1	10/7	2
MARTIN G.S.	Bathgate	Hull C Mar 1928	Middlesbrough May 1932	85	31	1	1	0	0	86	32
MAXWELL A.		Cambuslang Oct 1891	Darwen Nov 1893	43	13	7	3	0	0	50	16
MAYERS D.	Liverpool	‡Aug 1952	Preston NE May 1957	18	7	1	0	0	0	19	7
MAYSON T.	Whitehaven	Grimsby T 1919	Wolves May 1921	1	1	0	0	0	0	1	1
MEAGAN M.K. §	Dublin	‡Sep 1952	Huddersfield T Jul 1964	165	1	10	0	0	0	175	1
MEECHAM P.		Celtic 1896	Southampton 1897	24	0	4	0	0	0	28	0
MEGSON G.J.	Manchester	Plymouth A Feb 1980	Sheffield W Aug 1981	20/2	2	3	1	0	0	23/2	3
MEIKLEJOHN G.		1896	1896	1	0	0	0	0	0	1	0
MENHAM C.		1925	1925	3	0	0	0	0	0	3	0
MENHAM R.C.	North Shields	‡Jan 1897	Wigan B 1896	18	0	5	0	0	0	23	0
MERCER J.	Ellesmere Port	Ellesmere Port Sep 1932	Arsenal Dec 1946	170	1	14	1	0	0	184	2
MESTON S.W.	Southampton	Gillingham 1927	Tranmere R Jul 1928	1	0	0	0	0	0	1	0
MEUNIER J.B.	Birmingham	Southport 1910	Lincoln C Jun 1912	5	0	0	0	0	0	5	0
MICHAELS W.		1909	1909	3	0	0	0	0	0	3	0
MILLER H.J.	Preston	Leyland 1922	Preston NE 1922	2	0	0	0	0	0	2	0
MILLER J.	Tynemouth	Grimsby T 1919	Coventry C Dec 1920	8	1	0	0	0	0	8	1
MILLER W.R.	Bainsford	Partick T Jul 1935	Burnley Oct 1936	16	2	1	0	0	0	17	2
MILLIGAN G.H.	Failsworth	Oldham A May 1938	1938	1	0	0	0	0	0	1	0
MILLIGAN M.J.	Manchester	Oldham A Aug 1990	Oldham A Jul 1991	16/1	1	1	0	/1	0	17/2	1
MILLINGTON T.	Wrexham	Oswestry Mar 1925	Gillingham Mar 1928	13	0	1	0	0	0	14	0
MILWARD A.	Great Marlow	Great Marlow 1888	New Brighton 1896	201	85	23	11	0	0	224	96

PLAYER	BIRTHPLACE	FROM	TO	LEAGUE App	LEAGUE Gls	FA CUP App	FA CUP Gls	FL CUP App	FL CUP Gls	TOTAL App	TOTAL Gls
MIMMS R.	York	Rotherham May 1985	Tottenham Jan 1988	29	0	2	0	2	0	33	0
MITCHELL F.W.	Elgin	Motherwell 1913	Liverpool 1919	23	0	1	0	0	0	24	0
MOFFATT A.		East Fife 1920	Wrexham 1920	1	0	0	0	0	0	1	0
MOFFATT H.		Luton T 1926	Oldham A 1926	2	0	1	0	0	0	3	0
MOLYNEUX G.	Liverpool	Wigan B 1896	Southampton 1899	43	0	2	0	0	0	45	0
MOORE E.	St Helens	‡Feb 1949	Chesterfield Jan 1957	171	0	13	0	0	0	184	0
MOORE N.	Liverpool	‡ Jun 1991	*	0/1	0	0	0	0/1	0	0/2	0
MORRIS		1888	1888	1	0	0	0	0	0	1	0
MORRISSEY J. §	Liverpool	Liverpool Sep 1962	Oldham A May 1972	257/2	43	29	3	8	1	294/2	47
MORRISSEY J.	Liverpool	‡Mar 1983	Wolves Jul 1985	1/1	0	0	0	0	0	1/1	0
MORTON H.	Chadderton	Aston Villa Mar 1937	Burnley May 1939	27	0	2	0	0	0	29	0
MOUNTFIELD D. §	Liverpool	Tranmere R Jun 1982	Aston Villa May 1988	100/6	19	17	2	16	3	133/6	24
MOUNTFORD H.	Hanley	Burslem Port Vale 1907	Burnley Apr 1911	25	5	0	0	0	0	25	5
MUIR W.	Ayr	Kilmarnock Apr 1897	Dundee May 1902	127	0	10	0	0	0	137	0
MURRAY D.B.		Rangers 1903	Liverpool 1903	2	0	0	0	0	0	2	0
MURRAY D.J.	South Africa	1925	Bristol C Oct 1926	3	1	0	0	0	0	3	1
MURRAY J.J.		Rangers 1891	Swindon T 1892	8	0	0	0	0	0	8	0
NEVIN P.K.	Glasgow	Chelsea Jul 1988	Tranmere R(loan) Mar 1992	81/28	16	12/6	2	10/1	2	103/35	20
NEWELL M.C.	Liverpool	Leicester C Jul 1989	Blackburn R Nov 1991	48/20	15	6/4	0	7/3	4	61/27	19
NEWTON H.A.	Nottingham	Nottingham F Oct 1970	Derby C Sep 1973	76	5	6	1	1	0	83	6
NEWTON K.R. §	Manchester	Blackburn R Dec 1969	Burnley Jun 1972	48/1	1	2	0	1	0	51/1	1
NULTY G. §	Prescott	Newcastle U Jul 1978	Retired 1979	22/5	2	0	0	6	0	28/5	2
NUTTALL T.A.	Manchester	Manchester U 1913	St Mirren 1914	19	7	0	0	0	0	19	7
O'DONNELL J.	Gateshead	Darlington Jan 1925	Blackpool Dec 1930	188	10	9	0	0	0	197	10
O'HARA A.E.	Glasgow	Falkirk Jun 1958	Rotherham U Feb 1960	29	2	2	0	0	0	31	2
O'KEEFE E.	Manchester	Mossley Jul 1979	Wigan A Jan 1982	26/14	6	4/1	1	4/2	1	34/17	8
O'NEILL J.A.	Dublin	‡May 1949	Stoke C Jul 1960	201	0	12	0	0	0	213	0
OLDHAM W.		1898	Blackburn R 1899	22	11	0	0	0	0	22	11
OLDROYD D.	Omskirk	‡Nov 1984	Free transfer Jul 1986	0/1	0	0	0	0	0	0/1	0
OLIVER F.	Southampton	Brentford 1905	Clapton O 1905	4	4	1	0	0	0	5	4
ORR		1889	1889	1	1	0	0	0	0	1	1
OWEN L.T.	Liverpool	‡Dec 1966	Bradford C Jun 1970	2	0	0	0	0	0	2	0
OWEN W.		Wolves 1898	1898	13	3	0	0	0	0	13	3
PAGE J.	Liverpool	‡1913	Cardiff C May 1920	9	0	1	0	0	0	10	0
PAGE T.		Rochdale 1913	St Mirren May 1914	7	2	0	0	0	0	7	2
PALMER J.		1896	1896	1	0	0	0	0	0	1	0
PALMER W.		Bristol R May 1913	Bristol R 1914	22	2	1	0	0	0	23	2
PARKER A.H. §	Irvine	Falkirk Jun 1958	Southport Sep 1965	198	5	12	0	5	0	215	5
PARKER J.W.	Birkenhead	‡Dec 1948	Bury May 1956	167	82	9	7	0	0	176	89
PARKER R.N.	Possil Park	Rangers Nov 1913	Nottingham F May 1921	84	68	8	3	0	0	92	71
PARKER T.	Blackrod	‡1926	1926	6	0	1	0	0	0	7	0
PARKINSON H.		1888	1888	1	0	0	0	0	0	1	0
PARNELL R.	Birkenhead	‡Oct 1960	Tranmere R Aug 1964	3	0	0	0	0	0	3	0
PARRY C.F.		1889	Ardwick 1895	86	5	8	0	0	0	94	5
PARRY F.T.	Liverpool	‡1922	Grimsby T Jun 1926	12	0	1	0	0	0	13	0
PATRICK	Kilsyth	St Mirren 1896	St Mirren 1896	1	0	0	0	0	0	1	0
PATERSON		R Albert 1901	1901	5	1	0	0	0	0	5	1
PAYNE J.B.	Liverpool	Liverpool Apr 1956	Retired 1956	5	2	1	0	0	0	6	2
PEACOCK J.	Wigan	Atherton 1919	Middlesbrough May 1927	151	12	10	0	0	0	161	12
PEARSON J.F. §	Falkirk	St Johnstone Jul 1974	Newcastle U Aug 1978	76/17	15	9	2	10/2	2	95/19	19
PEJIC M. §	Chesterton	Stoke C Feb 1977	Aston Villa Sep 1979	76	2	6	0	7	0	89	2
PICKERING F. §	Blackburn	Blackburn R Mar 1964	Birmingham C Aug 1967	97	56	9	8	0	0	106	64
PINCHBECK C.B.	Grimsby T	‡Dec 1947	New Brighton Aug 1949	3	0	0	0	0	0	3	0
PINKNEY E.	Glasgow	W Hartlepool 1909	Gillingham Jul 1913	8	1	0	0	0	0	8	1
PINNELL A.		1892	1892	3	0	0	0	0	0	3	0
POINTON N.G.	Warsop Vale	Scunthorpe U Nov 1985	Manchester C Jul 1990	95/6	6	16/2	0	6/2	0	117/10	6
POLLOCK		1888	1888	1	0	0	0	0	0	1	0
POTTS H.	Wetton-le-Hole	Burnley Oct 1950	Wolves Jul 1956	59	15	4	1	0	0	63	16
POWELL A.	Swansea	Leeds U Jul 1948	Birmingham C Aug 1950	35	5	0	0	0	0	35	5
POWER P.	Manchester	Manchester C Jun 1986	*	52	6	5	0	6	0	63	6
PRATT C.		Barrow 1909	Exeter C 1909	2	0	0	0	0	0	2	0
PROUDFOOT J.		Blackburn R 1898	Watford 1901	84	30	5	1	0	0	89	31
RADOSAVIJEVIC P.	Belgrade		*	13/10	3	1	0	1	0	15/10	3

PLAYER	BIRTHPLACE	FROM	TO	LEAGUE App	Gls	FA CUP App	Gls	FL CUP App	Gls	TOTAL App	Gls
RAFFERTY D.		1907	1909	7	0	0	0	0	0	7	0
RAITT D	Buckhaven	Dundee May 1922	Blackburn R Aug 1928	122	0	9	0	0	0	131	0
RANKIN A.G. §	Liverpool	‡Oct 1961	Watford Nov 1971	85	0	7	0	0	0	92	0
RANKIN B.	Glasgow	‡1901	West Brom A 1905	37	7	1	0	0	0	38	7
RANKIN G.	Liverpool	‡Aug 1948	Southport Jul 1956	36	0	3	0	0	0	39	0
RATCLIFFE K.	Mancot	‡Jul 1977	Cardiff	356/3	2	57/	0	47	0	460/3	2
RAWLINGS J.	Wombwell	Millwall 1945	Plymouth A May 1945	0	0	2	0	0	0	2	0
REA K.W.	Liverpool	‡Jun 1952	Runcorn 1958	46	0	5	0	0	0	51	0
REAY H.		Newcastle U 1893	Southampton 1893	1	1	1	0	0	0	2	1
REES B.G.	Rhyl	‡Sep 1961	Brighton & HA Jan 1965	4	2	0	0	0	0	4	2
REHN S.	Stockholm	Djurgårdens IF Jun 1989	Gothenberg Jan 90	1/3	0	0	0	1/1	0	2/4	0
REID D.	Glasgow	Distillery May 1920	Distillery Feb 1927	97	11	4	0	0	0	101	11
REID P. §	Liverpool	Bolton W Dec 1982	Queen's Park R Feb 1889	159/4	8	35	3	23/2	1	213/6	12
RENNIE A.		1892	1892	4	0	0	0	0	0	4	0
RICHARDSON K. §	Newcastle	‡May 1979	Watford Sep 1986	95/15	16	13	1	10/3	3	118/18	20
RIDEOUT P.D.	Bournemouth	Notts Co Aug 1992	*	17/7	3	1	0	4	2	22/7	5
RIGBY A.	Manchester	Blackburn R Nov 1929	Middlesbrough May 1932	42	11	2	0	0	0	44	11
RIGSBY H.	Aintree	Southport 1919	Swansea T 1919	14	5	0	0	0	0	14	5
RIMMER N.	Liverpool	‡Apr 1984	† Jun 1985	0/1	0	0	0	0	0	0/1	0
RIMMER S.	Southport	‡May 1981	Chester C Mar 1985	3	0	0	0	0	0	3	0
RING T.	Glasgow	Clyde Jan 1960	Barnsley Nov 1961	27	6	0	0	0	0	27	6
RIOCH B.D.	Aldershot	Derby C Dec 1976	Derby C Nov 1977	30	3	7	1	2	0	39	4
RITCHIE H.M.	Perth	Hibernian Aug 1928	Dundee Feb 1930	28	5	1	0	0	0	29	5
ROBERTS		1888	1888	1	0	0	0	0	0	1	0
ROBERTS J.		1914	1914	1	0	0	0	0	0	1	0
ROBERTSON H.		Partick T 1890	Bootle 1892	29	1	2	1	0	0	31	2
ROBERTSON J.T.	Dumbarton	Morton 1895	Southampton 1897	30	1	6	0	0	0	36	1
ROBINSON A.J.	Birkenhead	1919	Tranmere R 1919	1	0	0	0	0	0	1	0
ROBINSON N. §	Liverpool	‡May 1974	Swansea C Oct 1979	13/3	1	1	0	3/1	0	17/4	1
ROBINSON W.	Birkenhead	1919	Chester 1919	7	0	0	0	0	0	7	0
ROBSON T.	Morpeth	Blyth Spartans Apr 1929	Sheffield W Oct 1930	27	0	2	0	0	0	29	0
ROCHE W.		1901	1901	1	0	0	0	0	0	1	0
ROONEY W.F.	Liverpool	1924	Wrexham 1929	14	0	4	0	0	0	18	0
ROSS N.J.		Preston NE Jul 1888	Preston NE Feb 1889	19	5	0	0	0	0	19	5
ROSS T. §	Ashton-under-Lyne	Arsenal Nov 1977	† 1982	120/4	16	13	3	8/1	0	141/5	19
ROUSE F.W.	Bracknell	Stoke C 1906	Chelsea Oct 1907	9	2	1	0	0	0	10	2
ROYLE J. §	Liverpool	‡Aug 1966	Manchester C Dec 1974	229/3	102	23	9	14	4	266/3	115
RUSSELL J.		1902	West Ham U 1902	3	0	0	0	0	0	3	0
SAGAR E.	Moorends	‡Mar 1929	Retired May 1953	463	0	32	0	0	0	495	0
SALT E.	Walsall	1921	Accrington S 1921	4	0	0	0	0	0	4	0
SANSOM K.G.	Camberwell	Coventry C(loan) Feb 1993	Brentford	6/1	1	0	0	0	0	6/1	1
SAUNDERS A.	Salford	‡Jul 1956	Swansea T Nov 1959	56	0	7	0	0	0	63	0
SAUNDERS G.E.	Birkenhead	‡Feb 1939	1951	133	0	7	0	0	0	140	0
SAUNDERS R.	Birkenhead	Feb 1951	Tonbridge May 1957	3	0	0	0	0	0	3	0
SCHOFIELD A.	Liverpool	1895	Manchester U 1899	13	2	0	0	0	0	13	2
SCOTT A.S. §	Falkirk	Rangers Feb 1963	Hibernian Sep 1967	149	23	17	2	0	0	166	25
SCOTT P.W.	Liverpool	‡Jul 1970	York C Dec 1975	42/2	1	5	1	1	0	48/2	2
SCOTT Walter	Worksop	Grimsby T 1909	Sunderland Jul 1911	18	0	0	0	0	0	18	0
SCOTT William	Belfast	Linfield 1904	Leeds C Aug 1912	251	0	38	0	0	0	289	0
SEARGEANT S. §	Liverpool	‡Jul 1968	† Feb 1978	77/3	1	2	0	5/1	0	84/4	1
SETTLE J.	Millom	Bury Apr 1899	Stockport C May 1908	237	84	32	13	0	0	269	97
SHACKLETON A.	Padiham	Leeds U Sep 1959	Oldham A Aug 1961	26	10	1	0	0	0	27	10
SHARP B.	Hereford	Aston Villa 1899	Southampton 1901	9	0	1	0	0	0	10	0
SHARP G.M. §	Glasgow	Dumbarton Apr 1980	Oldham A Jul 1991	306/16	111	52/2	20	46/2	15	404/20	146
SHARP J.	Hereford	Aston Villa 1899	Retired 1909	300	68	42	12	0	0	342	80
SHARPLES G.	Ellesmere Port	‡Sep 1960	Blackburn R Mar 1965	10	0	0	0	1	0	11	0
SHAW S.	Liverpool	‡Dec 1961	Crystal P Dec 1966	3	0	0	0	0	0	3	0
SHEEDY K.M. §	Builth Wells	Liverpool Aug 1982	Newcastle U Mar 1992	263/11	67	38	15	31/1	9	332/12	91
SHERIDAN J.		Cambuslang 1902	Stoke C 1903	20	4	0	0	0	0	20	4
SIMMS S.		1912	Swindon T Jun 1913	2	1	0	0	0	0	2	1
SIMPSON R.H.	Redcar	1912	1914	21	0	2	0	0	0	23	0

PLAYER	BIRTHPLACE	FROM	TO	LEAGUE App	LEAGUE Gls	FA CUP App	FA CUP Gls	FL CUP App	FL CUP Gls	TOTAL App	TOTAL Gls
SIMPSON T.	Keyworth	Leicester F 1903	Leicester F 1903	1	0	0	0	0	0	1	0
SINGLETON		Bury 1901	Grimsby T 1901	3	0	0	0	0	0	3	0
SLOAN D.		Linfield 1906	Liverpool 1907	6	0	0	0	0	0	6	0
SMALLEY R.E.		Preston NE 1888	1890	36	0	2	0	0	0	38	0
SMALLMAN D.P. §	Connah's Quay	Wrexham Mar 1975	Wrexham Jul 1980	19/2	6	0	0	3/1	1	22/3	7
SMITH D.L.	Liverpool	‡Nov 1963	Tranmere R Mar 1968	3/1	0	0	0	0	0	3/1	0
SMITH Joseph	West Stanley	Hull C 1911	Bury Dec 1913	10	0	0	0	0	0	10	0
SMITH John	Liverpool	‡Sep 1970	Carlisle U Jun 1976	2	0	0	0	0	0	2	0
SNODIN I.	Thrybergh	Leeds Jan 1987	*	112/4	3	24	2	17/1	1	153/5	6
SOUTHALL N. §	Llandudno	Bury Jul 1981	*	411	0	56	0	54	0	521	0
SOUTHWORTH J.	Blackburn	Blackburn R Aug 1893	Retired 1894	31	36	1	0	0	0	32	36
SPENCER H.G.		‡1921	Wigan B 1921	9	2	0	0	0	0	9	2
STANLEY G.E.	Burton upon Trent	Chelsea Aug 1979	Swansea C Oct 1981	52	1	2/1	0	7/1	0	61/2	1
STEIN J.	Coatbridge	Dunfermline A 1928	Burnley Oct 1936	199	57	16	8	0	0	215	65
STEPHENSON G.		1888	1888	1	0	0	0	0	0	1	0
STEVEN T.M. §	Berwick	Burnley Jul 1983	Rangers Jul 1989	210/4	48	33	4	27	4	270/4	56
STEVENS D. §	Dudley	Bolton W Mar 1962	Oldham A Dec 1965	120	20	10	1	0	0	130	21
STEVENS G. §	Barrow	‡Jun 1979	Rangers Jul 1988	207/1	8	38	2	30	2	275/1	12
STEVENS G.L.	New Brighton	New Brighton 1932	Southend U 1932	2	0	0	0	0	0	2	0
STEVENS T.		Clyde 1912	1912	5	0	0	0	0	0	5	0
STEVENSON A.	Dublin	Rangers Jan 1934	Bootle 1948	255	82	16	8	0	0	271	90
STEVENSON W.	Accrington	Accrington S 1907	1913	111	0	14	0	0	0	125	0
STEWART A.		Burnley Dec 1892	Nottingham F 1892	12	1	7	0	0	0	19	1
STEWART W.S.	Arbroath	Preston NE 1893	Bristol C 1893	122	6	15	0	0	0	137	6
STORRIER D.	Arbroath	Arbroath 1893	Celtic 1897	55	0	10	0	0	0	65	0
STRETTLE S.		1906	Exeter C Aug 1913	4	0	0	0	0	0	4	0
STYLES A.	Liverpool	‡Aug 1967	Birmingham C Feb 1974	22/1	0	4	0	0	0	26/1	0
SUGG F.H.	Ilkeston	Derby C 1888	Burnley 1889	10	0	0	0	0	0	10	0
SUTHERLAND J.	Cork	‡May 1950	Chesterfield Jun 1957	6	0	2	0	0	0	8	0
SUTTON		1894	1894	1	0	0	0	0	0	1	0
TANSEY J.	Liverpool	‡May 1948	Crewe A Jun 1960	133	0	9	0	0	0	142	0
TAYLOR E.H.	Liverpool	Huddersfield T Feb 1927	Wrexham Nov 1928	40	0	2	0	0	0	42	0
TAYLOR J.D.	Dumbarton	St Mirren 1896	South Liverpool 1909	400	66	56	14	0	0	456	80
TEFLER G.A. §	Liverpool	‡Aug 1972	Scunthorpe U Jun 1981	81/16	20	4/4	1	5/2	1	90/22	22
TEMPLE D. §	Liverpool	‡Aug 1956	Preston NE Sep 1967	231/1	72	21	8	4	0	256/1	80
THOMAS		1892	1892	1	0	0	0	0	0	1	0
THOMAS D. §	Liverpool	Queen's Park R Aug 1977	Wolves Oct 1979	71	4	2	0	7	1	80	5
THOMAS E.	Newton-le-Willows	‡Oct 1951	Blackburn R Feb 1960	86	39	7	2	0	0	93	41
THOMAS M.	Mochdre	Manchester U Jul 1981	Brighton & HA Nov 1981	10	0	0	0	1	0	11	0
THOMPSON R.		1892	1892	1	0	0	0	0	0	1	0
THOMPSON R.	Newcastle	Leicester F Apr 1913	Millwall 1920	83	0	6	0	0	0	89	0
THOMSON G.M. §	Edinburgh	Hearts Nov 1960	Brentford Nov 1963	73	1	1	0	2	0	76	1
THOMSON J.R.	Thornton	Dundee Mar 1930	Retired Dec 1939	272	5	22	0	0	0	294	5
THOMSON S.		Wolves 1891	Accrington Oct 1891	3	1	0	0	0	0	3	1
TODD C.	Chester-le-Street	Derby C Sep 1978	Birmingham C Sep 1979	32	1	1	0	2	0	35	1
TOMAN W.	Bishop Auckland	Burnley Apr 1899	Southampton 1901	29	10	0	0	0	0	29	10
TOMLINSON J.	Birkenhead	‡Jun 1952	Chesterfield Jun 1957	2	0	0	0	0	0	2	0
TREBILCOCK M. §	Gunnislake	Plymouth A Dec 1965	Portsmouth Jan 1968	11	3	2	2	0	0	13	5
TRENTHAM D.	Chirbury	‡Dec 1936	Ellesmere Port Aug 1949	16	7	1	0	0	0	17	7
TROUP A.	Forfar	Dundee Jan 1923	Dundee Feb 1930	249	32	10	3	0	0	259	35
TURNER D.	Derby	‡Oct 1966	Southport May 1970	1	0	0	0	0	0	1	0
TURNER G.	Mansfield	Luton T 1932	Bradford C 1932	2	0	0	0	0	0	2	0
TURNER J.H.	Burslem	Stoke 1898	Southampton Apr 1900	34	8	2	1	0	0	36	9
TURNER R.F.	Leicester	Leicester F 1908	Preston NE 1910	34	1	0	0	0	0	34	1
TYRER A.	Liverpool	‡Dec 1959	Mansfield T Jul 1963	9	2	1	0	0	0	10	2
UNSWORTH D.	Preston	‡ May 1992	*	4/1	1	0	0	1/1	0	5/2	1
UREN H.J.	Bristol	Liverpool 1911	Wrexham 1912	24	3	0	0	0	0	24	3
VAN den HAUWE P.W.R.§	Dendermonde	Birmingham C Sep 1984	Tottenham H Aug 1989	134/1	2	30	1	20	0	184/1	3
VARADI I. §	Paddington	Sheffield U Mar 1979	Newcastle U Aug 1981	22/4	6	6/1	1	0	0	28/5	7
VAUGHAN A.		1898	1898	1	0	0	0	0	0	1	0
VEALL R.J.	Skegness	Doncaster R Sep 1961	Preston NE May 1965	11	1	0	0	0	0	11	1
VERNON T.R. §	Ffynnongroew	Blackburn R Feb 1960	Stoke C Mar 1965	176	101	12	7	4	1	192	109
VIRR A.E.	Liverpool	‡1924	Retired 1929	117	2	9	1	0	0	126	3

PLAYER	BIRTHPLACE	FROM	TO	LEAGUE App	Gls	FA CUP App	Gls	FL CUP App	Gls	TOTAL App	Gls
WAINWRIGHT E.	Southport	Southport Mar 1944	Rochdale Jun 1956	207	68	21	8	0	0	228	76
WAKENSHAW R. §	Ashington	‡Jun 1982	Carlisle U	2/1	1	0	0	0	0	2/1	1
WALKER J.		Gainsborough 1893	Leicester F 1893	3	1	0	0	0	0	3	1
WALL A.	Liverpool	1919	Swindon T Jun 1925	16	3	1	0	0	0	17	3
WALSH D.	Hamilton	‡Oct 1984	Charlton A Mar 1987	1	0	0	0	0	0	1	0
WALSH M.A. §	Chorley	Blackpool Aug 1978	Queen's Park R Mar 1979	18/3	1	1	0	3	0	22/3	1
WALSH M.T.	Manchester	Bolton Aug 1981	Fort Lauderdale May 1983	20	0	0	0	2	0	22	0
WARD M.W.	Huyton	Manchester C Aug 1991	*	56	5	2	0	2	0	60	5
WAREING W.	Southport	Preston NE 1912	Swindon T 1919	64	4	5	2	0	0	69	6
WARMBEY		1888	1888	1	0	0	0	0	0	1	0
WARZYCHA R.	Wielun, Poland	Górnik Zabrze Mar 1991	*	48/17	6	1/1	0	4/2	0	53/20	6
WATSON D.	Liverpool	Norwich Aug 1986	*	239/1	17	32	4	29	2	300/1	23
WATSON J.		Dundee 1899	Tottenham H 1901	44	0	0	0	0	0	44	0
WATSON J.G.	Wolsingham	Blyth Spartans 1932	Coventry C 1933	2	0	0	0	0	0	2	0
WATSON R.		1888	Gorton Villa 1888	18	4	0	0	0	0	18	4
WATSON T.G.	Wolsingham	‡Jan 1933	Retired 1948	61	1	5	0	0	0	66	1
WAUGH D.		Burnley 1888	Retired 1888	7	2	0	0	0	0	7	2
WEAVER W.	Birkenhead	Burnley 1924	Wolves Oct 1926	18	3	4	0	0	0	22	3
WEBBER K.J.	Cardiff	Feb 1960	Brighton & HA Apr 1963	4	0	0	0	2	1	6	1
WEIR J.		Hibernian 1888	1889	19	0	0	0	0	0	19	0
WELDON A.	Croy	Airdrie Mar 1927	Hull C Jun 1930	70	13	3	0	0	0	73	13
WELLER L.C.	Stoke	Chesterfield 1909	1921	65	2	5	0	0	0	70	2
WEST G. §	Barnsley	Blackpool Mar 1962	Tranmere R Oct 1975	335	0	40	0	11	0	386	0
WHITE T.A.	Manchester	Southport Feb 1927	Northampton T Oct 1937	193	66	9	0	0	0	202	66
WHITE W.	Hurlford	Bolton W Nov 1908	Fulham Oct 1910	43	10	9	3	0	0	52	13
WHITEHEAD		1893	1893	2	0	0	0	0	0	2	0
WHITESIDE N.	Belfast	Manchester U Aug 1989		27/2	9	6	3	2	1	35/2	13
WHITLEY J.	Seacombe	Aston Villa 1920	Leeds C 1903	11	0	3	0	0	0	14	0
WHITTLE A. §	Liverpool	‡ Aug 1967	Crystal P Dec 1972	72/2	21	6	2	4	2	82/2	25
WIGNALL F.	Blackrod	Horwich RMI May 1958	Nottingham F Jun 1958	33	15	2	0	3	7	38	22
WILDMAN W.	Liverpool	1904	West Ham U 1905	2	0	0	0	0	0	2	0
WILKINSON J.	Esh Winning	Newcastle U 1929	Blackpool May 1931	11	2	1	0	0	0	12	2
WILKINSON P.	Louth	Grimsby T Mar 1985	Nottingham F Mar 1987	19/11	6	3	1	3/1	7	25/12	14
WILLIAMS B.D.	Penrhiwceiber	Swansea T Dec 1929	Newport C 1935	131	0	8	0	0	0	139	0
WILLIAMS G.G.	Wrexham	Bradford C Mar 1956	Swansea T Feb 1959	31	6	2	0	0	0	33	6
WILLIAMS O.	Holyhead	South Liverpool 1919	Wigan B 1919	2	0	0	0	0	0	2	0
WILLIAMS R.		‡1891	Luton T 1894	58	0	12	0	0	0	70	0
WILLIAMS W.		1894	Blackburn R 1897	23	4	1	1	0	0	24	5
WILLIAMS W.D.	Manchester	Darwen 1922	Blackpool Mar 1925	39	14	2	0	0	0	41	14
WILSON A.	Liverpool	‡Jul 1970	Southport Jul 1975	2	0	0	0	0	0	2	0
WILSON D.	Lochgelly	Hearts 1906	Portsmouth Jun 1907	5	0	0	0	0	0	5	0
WILSON G.W.	Lochgelly	Hearts May 1906	Newcastle U Nov 1907	28	3	6	1	0	0	34	14
WILSON I.W.	Aberdeen	Leicester C	Kocaelispor Aug 1989	24/10	1	3/2	0	9	1	36/12	2
WILSON R. §	Shirebrook	Huddersfield T July 1964	Oldham A. Jul 1969	114/2	0	26	0	0/1	0	140/3	0
WILSON W.		1888	1888	1	0	0	0	0	0	1	0
WINTERHALDER		West Ham U 1907	Preston NE 1907	4	0	0	0	0	0	4	0
WOLSTENHOLME S.	Little Lever	Horwich 1897	Blackburn R 1903	160	8	10	0	0	0	170	8
WOOD G. §	Douglas	Blackpool Aug 1977	Arsenal Aug 1980	103	0	4	0	13	0	120	0
WOODHOUSE R.	Leyland	Preston NE 1926	Wrexham May 1927	2	0	0	0	0	0	2	0
WOODS L.G.		‡1907	1907	4	0	0	0	0	0	4	0
WOODS M.	Skelmersdale	‡Nov 1949	Blackburn R Nov 1956	8	1	0	0	0	0	8	1
WRIGHT B.P.	Birmingham	Walsall Feb 1972	Walsall Jan 1973	10/1	2	0	0	0	0	10/1	2
WRIGHT M.	Manchester		*	1	0	0	0	0	0	1	0
WRIGHT R.		‡1905	Burnley 1905	1	0	0	0	0	0	1	0
WRIGHT T.J. §	Liverpool	‡Mar 1963	Retired 1972	307/1	4	35	0	11	0	353/1	4
WRIGHT W. §	Liverpool	‡Aug 1974	Birmingham C Jun 1983	164/2	10	13	0	13	0	190/2	10
WRIGHT W.P.		St Mirren 1914	Tranmere R 1914	2	0	0	0	0	0	2	0
WYLE T.G.	Maybole	Rangers Dec 1890	Liverpool 1891	20	5	1	0	0	0	21	5
YOUDS E.P.	Liverpool	‡ Jun 1988	Ipswich T Nov 1991	5/3	0	0	0	0/1	0	5/4	0
YOUNG A.	Slamannan	Falkirk 1901	Tottenham H 1910	275	110	39	15	0	0	314	125
YOUNG A. §	Loanhead	Hearts Nov 1960	Glentoran Aug 1968	227/1	77	25/2	4	3	3	255/3	84
YOUNG R.	Swinhill	Middlesbrough 1910	Wolves Nov 1911	38	7	3	1	0	0	41	8